COMPANY
ADMINISTRATION
HANDBOOK

COMPANY ADMINISTRATION HANDBOOK

Third Edition

A Gower Press Handbook

First published in Great Britain by Gower Press Limited 1970

Second edition 1972

Third edition published in 1977 by Gower Press,
Teakfield Limited, Westmead, Farnborough, Hampshire, England.

Reprinted 1978 (twice)
Reprinted 1979

ISBN 0 566 02011 4

Printed in Great Britain by Unwin Brothers, Gresham Press, Old Woking,
Surrey. (A member of the Staples Printing Group).

Contents

PART THREE COMMERCIAL FUNCTIONS

trade practices–The Secretary of State–Sale of Goods–Trade Descriptions–
Misrepresentation–Unsolicited Goods and Services–Voluntary codes of practice

PART FOUR OFFICE ADMINISTRATION

PART SIX MANAGEMENT OF PHYSICAL ASSETS

Illustrations

Figure

Notes on Contributors

John Ashton (Managing Office Equipment) is Senior Lecturer in O & M and Systems Analysis at Leicester Polytechnic where he has set up the Centre for Office Efficiency Studies. He trained as an accountant and spent several years in commerce before going to Dar es Salaam as Treasury Accountant for the Government of Tanganyika. His practical knowledge of office machinery was gained as a sales executive with Remington Rand Ltd. Mr. Ashton is an Associate of the Institute of Chartered Secretaries and Administrators. He runs his own management consultancy practice in Leicester and in 1973 was the United Kingdom nominee for appointment as an international expert in office administration to the International Labour Office in Geneva.

Stephen Badger (Procedures for Raising Capital) is a Senior Assistant Director of Morgan Grenfell & Co. Limited, where he advises companies on mergers, raising long-term capital and general financial problems. He joined Morgan Grenfell after leaving Oxford where he read Greats. Mr. Badger is an Associate of the Institute of Bankers and of the Institute of Chartered Secretaries and Administrators.

Frank Bex (Building Management and Maintenance) is Services Manager of Unilever Limited, where he is responsible for building services and communications media management. He is Chairman of the British Standards Institution's Office Furniture Technical Committee.

Michael Blee (Electronic Data Processing) is a freelance journalist, formerly working as Editor of *Data Systems*. After obtaining a BSc degree, he became a computer programmer before moving into journalism, specializing in the computer field.

G A Bloxam (Patents and Trade-Marks) is Head of the Patent Department of Albright & Wilson Limited, the chemical manufacturing group. His degree in chemistry and physics is from Cambridge and before joining Albright & Wilson he was Patents Manager of the National Research Development Corporation. Mr. Bloxam is a fellow of the Chartered Institute of Patent Agents and a member of the Institute's Council.

T Cartledge (Issue and Transfer of Shares) has had 20 years experience of Company Secretarial, New Issues and Share Registration procedures and is now employed by a professional firm of Registrars. A Yorkshireman, he was educated at Barnsley Grammar School and gained his LL.B from Leeds University.

T F Cox (Conduct of Meetings) is a Company Secretary within the Royal Doulton group of companies. Until 1974 he was a manager in the secretary's department of Unilever Limited. From 1966 to 1971 he was visiting lecturer in secretarial practice at the City of London Polytechnic School of Business Studies. Before joining Unilever, he worked with the London Electricity Board, Sagit Trust Limited and the United Africa Company Limited. Mr. Cox is a fellow of the Institute of Chartered Secretaries and Administrators.

J C Craig (Taxation) is a taxation partner at Thomson McLintock and Company where he deals with both personal and company taxation. He is a member of the Institute of Chartered Accountants of Scotland and a former convener of its taxation committee.

Lindsay Duncan (Administering Value Added Tax) commenced his life in the Inland Revenue and later became Head of the Taxation Department of a major industrial company. He is now Principal of one of the main tax consultancies in the City of London, specializing in international corporate taxation and the problems of U.K. companies operating outside this country. In addition he has taxation practices in Amsterdam and Zurich.

He is retained by many major industrial and commercial concerns to advise on taxation and also advises many trade and professional organizations. Also he lectures both in the U.K. and on the Continent to universities, business schools and other bodies.

Lindsay Duncan is a member of various committees which include the Taxation Committee of the Confederation of British Industry. He also serves on the British Taxation Committees of the International Fiscal Association and the International Chamber of Commerce.

He was closely involved with Customs and Excise during the setting up of Value Added Tax in the United Kingdom.

Pat George (Working Conditions) was Senior Adviser of the Industrial Society's Information and Personnel Advisory Services Department. Miss George is an Associate Member of the Institute of Personnel Management, and is now a District Personnel Officer with the Kensington, Chelsea and Westminster Area Health Authority.

V J Gersten (Company Law) is a solicitor in general practice in central London. He was born in Liverpool and, on graduating with an LIB from Liverpool University, lectured for some years in law at Hendon College of Technology.

A C L Grear (Occupation, Ownership and Administration of Property and Property Dealings) is a partner in a London firm of surveyors, valuers, estate agents and property consultants. He is an experienced valuer of land, property and related business assets and has a detailed knowledge of the many functions of property ownership and the use of land and buildings. He and John Oxborough wrote *Commercial Property Management* (Gower Press, 1970). Mr. Grear is a Fellow of the Incorporated Society of Valuers and Auctioneers.

Alan Hobkirk (Law of Contract) is Principal Lecturer in Law at Slough College of Higher Education where he teaches company, mercantile and industrial law. He was born in Edinburgh and gained MA and LL.B degrees from the University there. Before becoming a full-time lecturer he worked for eight years in the legal civil service. Mr. Hobkirk is Chief Examiner in Mercantile Law for the Scottish Council for Business Education.

Ivor Hussey (Fair Trading) is a Barrister and Senior Legal Adviser at the Confederation of British Industry where he is responsible for legislation and proposals in both the United Kingdom and the Common Market. He gained his degree in Administrative law at Cambridge, after which he qualified as a Barrister at the Inner Temple.

Irene Innes (Salary and Wage Management) is Personnel Manager with the Sanderson Wallcoverings Division of The Wall Paper Manufacturers Ltd. She was formerly the Industrial Society's pay specialist for some five years. Born in Aberdeen, she qualified as a teacher at Jordanhill College of Education and after teaching commercial subjects for three years, moved into personnel management with Wiggins Teape Limited.

Peter Lebus (Setting up a New Office) is Managing Director of C E Planning Limited, which provides a planning and design service for office users. He has been responsible for the development of several new office planning techniques, and also lectures and writes on many aspects of office planning. Before specializing in this field, Mr. Lebus spent ten years in British and US industry working in production, O & M and computer studies.

P D V Marsh (Negotiation) is Commercial Director at M.T.S.O. Ltd. He was formerly Manager, Projects and Operations Coordination with the Submarine Systems Division of Standard Telephones and Cables Limited. He started his career as Chief Contracts Officer for the National Coal Board, moving to Central Contracts Manager of AEI Limited, followed by Contracts Administration Manager, STC Limited. Mr. Marsh qualified as a Solicitor in 1951 and is a Fellow of the Institute of Purchasing and Supply.

G Metliss (Debt Collection) is a manager dealing with insolvency matters with a firm of London solicitors. He was born in London and educated at the City of London School. Mr. Metliss is a frequent lecturer on the special problems of debt collection and insolvency.

Peter A Mumford (Administering Redundancy) is responsible for organizing and running residential and in-company training courses for managers and supervisors at Brighton Polytechnic. He has wide experience in industry in purchasing, general administration, O & M and personnel (where he first worked on redundancy schemes).

Eric Oliver (Security Policy and Administration) from 1959 to 1973 was Security Adviser to Unilever Ltd. and is a director of Consolidated Safeguards Ltd., a company supplying security services. He served in the Metropolitan Police until 1959 gaining extensive experience of commercial and industrial security whilst serving in the Criminal Investigation Department at New Scotland Yard and latterly as Detective Superintendent in the Company Fraud Department. Mr. Oliver is a Founder Fellow of the Institution of Industrial Security. He lectures frequently on security practices. With John Wilson, Mr. Oliver wrote *Practical Security in Commerce and Industry*, Second Revised Edition, (Gower Press, 1975).

J Oxborough (Occupation, Ownership and Administration of Property and Property Dealings) is a partner in a London firm of surveyors, estate agents and property consultants. He is a chartered surveyor with a wide experience in private practice in London and provincial firms and in local government with the Greater London Council. He is a co-author (with Arthur Grear) of *Commercial Property Management* (Gower Press, 1970). Mr. Oxborough is a BSc (Estate Management) and a Fellow of the Royal Institution of Chartered Surveyors.

Betty Ream (Pensions and Employee Benefits) is a Research Officer with the Work Research Unit of the Department of Employment, having previously been Head of the Industrial Society's Information and Personnel Advisory

Services Department. Miss Ream's extensive experience in personnel management was gained with Hoover, Simms Motor Units, the George Cohen 600 group, the Automobile Association and Westfield College London. She saw the employees' side of management problems when working for four and a half months at the factory bench as an assembler. Miss Ream's degree is in modern history: she is a member of the Institute of Personnel Management.

R H Reed (Role of O & M) is Administrative Manager of GKN Screws and Fasteners Limited, Health Street Division. He trained as a telecommunications engineer in the Royal Corps of Signals and taught the subject, was a departmental manager with Marks & Spencer and then supervised oil process plants in the Persian Gulf. Mr Reed is a Fellow of the Institute of Administrative Management and an honorary member of the Federation of Productivity Services Associations. He was a founder member and Fellow of the O & M Society, and is a Fellow of the recently merged Institute of Work Study, Organization and Methods.

W P Ridley (The Annual Accounts) is a Partner and Head of Research of Wood Mackenzie and Company, a firm of stockbrokers he joined in 1973 after five years as a financial consultant with Merrett Cyriax Associates. He read law at Oxford and became an Associate of the Institute of Chartered Accountants in 1961. He taught in Uganda and at Hendon Technical College before joining the Economic and Investment Research Department of the Bank of London and South America. Between 1965 and 1968, Mr Ridley worked for the Commonwealth Development Corporation.

R W Rooke (Insurance of Company Assets) is Insurance Manager of British Gas Corporation. After graduating from Nottingham University, he taught mathematics before joining Atlas Assurance. He then became Insurance Manager of Berk Limited and Thomas De La Rue International Limited. Mr Rooke is an Associate of the Chartered Insurance Institute and a member of the Association of Insurance and Risk Managers in Industry and Commerce. He was chairman of the Association's research group which in 1968 investigated the status and techniques of insurance managers.

F W Rose (Employment Law and Labour Relations) is Principal Lecturer in Law at Birmingham Polytechnic where he is tutor for the BA (Law) course. Mr Rose was born in Birmingham and gained his LIB from its University: his LIM is from King's College London. He is an Associate of the Institute of Chartered Secretaries and Administrators and has contributed to the Institute's journal and to *Secretaries Chronicle* and *Legal Executive.* Mr Rose was called to the bar at Gray's Inn in 1958. His book, *Personnel Management Law,* was published by Gower Press in 1972.

Richard Sleight (Role of the Company Secretary) is a Fellow of the Institute of Chartered Secretaries and a member of council. He has been assistant to the chief executive of Legal and General Assurance Society, the second largest insurance company in the U.K., the secretary to the company, and is now the head of the investment planning department. He has contributed articles on pensions, employee benefits and other financial subjects to leading newspapers and journals, has broadcast from time to time and writes regularly for the *Guardian* newspaper on these topics.

P M Smith (Design and Control of Documentation) is a senior O & M Analyst with International Combustion Division, Clarke Chapman Limited. Most of his business experience has been gained in the engineering industry, first in sales and then, after formal training with the Organization and Methods Training Council, in O & M. Mr Smith is a member of the Institute of Practitioners in Work Study, Organization and Methods.

L G Titman (Reducing Office Costs) is Senior Consultant in the Strategic and Financial Services Group of PA Management Consultants where he specializes in organization structure, company finance, administration and O & M. He is a Fellow of the Institute of Work Study Practitioners, a Member of the Council of the Institute of Administrative Management and a member of the Institute of Management Consultants. Mr Titman's practical management experience was gained with National Westminster Bank, Unilever, Sainsbury and Trust House Fortes. He is co-author of *Company Organization – Theory and Practice* (Allen and Unwin).

Derek Torrington (Management–Union Relations and Industrial Training Requirements) is Lecturer in Personnel Management at the University of Manchester Institute of Science and Technology, following five years as Principal Lecturer in Industrial Relations at Manchester Polytechnic. Previously he held senior management responsibility for personnel affairs in an engineering company. He is a magistrate and a member of both the IPM and BIM. His previous publications include *Successful Personnel Management* (Staples Press 1969), *Face to Face* (Gower Press 1972), *Handbook of Industrial Relations* (Gower Press 1972), *Handbook of Management Development*, with D F Sutton (Gower Press 1973), *Administration of Personnel Policies*, with Rachel Naylor (Gower Press 1974), and *Encyclopaedia of Personnel Management* (Gower Press 1974).

Leonard H Verreck (Managing Mergers and Acquisitions) trained as an accountant, read economics and industrial psychology. He spent many years as a consultant, and advisory member of a number of company boards particularly concerned with corporate planning and growth. He has written and lectured extensively on his own subjects. He is a freelance industrial sociologist but has recently taken up an academic post with a government department.

John Wilson (Security Policy and Administration) is the Company Security Officer for Yorkshire Imperial Metals Limited, the largest manufacturer of non-ferrous plate, tube and fittings in Europe and possibly in the world. His role is primarily advisory to the Board and to the numerous factories in the group on all matters of security policy and practice, but with an operational responsibility for investigation of distribution losses and any others of magnitude.

A former Detective Chief Inspector in Leeds City Police, Mr Wilson is a Fellow of the Institution of Industrial Security, past National Chairman of the Industrial Police and Security Association, co-author with Mr Oliver of the two standard textbooks for Institution examinations and a lecturer to senior managerial seminars on security matters in the U.K. and abroad.

Frank H Woodward (Managing Transport Services) is Transport Services Executive with the Plessey Company Limited. He has been involved in industrial distribution management for the past twenty years. Before that he served in the Royal Air Force on a permanent commission. Mr Woodward controls a division of the Plessey Company responsible for the distribution of all its goods within a budget of over £5 million p.a. He is author of *Managing the Transport Services Function*, published by Gower Press in 1972.

ACKNOWLEDGEMENTS

The publishers wish to thank the following for permission to quote their work:

The Controller of Her Majesty's Stationery Office: Figure 19.6
The Council of the Stock Exchange: Listing agreement (companies) in Chapter 6

The publishers would like to thank Mr. David M. Martin, ACIS, AIPM, ACommA, AMBIM, for his advice in the preparation of this edition

REFERENCES TO LAW

The law in this book is stated as at 31st August 1976

PART ONE

Constitution and Conduct of Companies

1

The Role of the Company Secretary

Richard Sleight

THE SECRETARY'S LEGAL STATUS

In 1885, every employee was expected to know his place, not least the company secretary. The classic legal view of the secretary's role was given in that year by Lord Brett, Master of the Rolls, in the case of Newlands *v* National Employers' Accident Association Limited:

> A secretary is a mere servant; his position is that he is to do what he is told, and no person can assume that he has any authority to represent anything at all; nor can anyone assume that statements made by him are necessarily to be accepted as trustworthy without further inquiry...

Not only a servant but likely enough a rogue as well!

Yet in spite of the gradual change in the social fabric since then, this view of the secretary's function continued to persist in law, partly perhaps because it provided a convenient excuse for anyone who wished to avoid a contract. In 1900 it was held that a company secretary could not issue notices for a company meeting unless he had the authority of the directors contained in a board resolution. Similarly, five years later, judgment was given that a company secretary had no power to register a transfer of shares if the directors could reject transfers and had not given their consent to this particular transfer. Again, in 1916 (Daimler Company Limited *v* Continental Tyre & Rubber Company (Great Britain) Limited), it was held that a company secretary could not begin legal proceedings in the company's name unless he had the authority of the directors contained in a board resolution.

Surprisingly enough, a similar view of the company secretary's role was expressed in cases coming before the courts as late as 1966. Surprising, because this traditional legal view ran directly counter to commonly accepted business practice and to the very different picture of the secretary's function which emerged from the Companies Acts. In the 1948 Act for example, the secretary is defined as an 'officer' of the company equated in this respect with directors and managers (s455). And any 'officer' may be personally liable if certain provisions of the Act have not been complied with (ss5, 7, 24, 25 or 30). On a winding-up, it is the secretary, together with other 'officers' of the company who can be proceeded against for misapplication or misappropriation of the company's assets, for misfeasance or breach of trust.

Moreover, the authority and responsibility of the secretary as an officer whose actions can bind the company does not only arise in relation to certain defined events. The responsibility also emerges with regard to the day-to-day functions he carries out. Examples are: issuing share and debenture certificates (s80), signing the annual return and certifying the documents attached to it (ss126(1) and 127(1)), delivering particulars of mortgages and charges for registration (ss96 and 97), issuing notices for company meetings (ss130, 131 and 132), notifying the Registrar of alterations to the share capital (ss62 and 63), and preparing agenda and keeping the minutes for meetings (s145).

But in spite of these indications in the Companies Acts, defendants continued to argue successfully that a company contract authorized by a company secretary was not binding on the company. Case law was at last brought into line with modern practice in the case of Panorama Development (Guildford) Limited v Fidelis Furnishing Fabrics Limited in May 1971.

The only unfortunate feature of this case from the point of view of the secretarial profession was that it required a fraudulent action by a company secretary to establish that a company secretary had authority to act on behalf of his company. Here the company, Fidelis Furnishing Fabrics, known to be a company of good repute and credit, entered into a contract with the plaintiff company to hire executive cars to meet important customers and potential buyers at Heathrow Airport. The actual hiring and insurance agreements were signed by the Fidelis company secretary and it later emerged that the cars had not been employed to meet customers but had been used by the company secretary for his own private use.

As in similar cases in the past, the defendant company Fidelis disputed the payment of any hire charges for the cars on the grounds that even if it were agreed that the contract had been concluded with Fidelis and not just with the company secretary of Fidelis acting in his personal capacity, a contract entered into by the company secretary was not binding on the company. Both the judge of first instance and the Court of Appeal answered that the company secretary's action must be regarded as binding on the company. It was especially (and at last!) remarked that the much earlier cases allocating a humbler role to a secretary had arisen in relation to the Companies Acts as they had stood at the time these earlier cases came to court and that since then the secretary's position and status had greatly increased, an increase that was recognized in the current Companies Acts. Since the case itself was concerned with the administrative operations of the company's affairs, the judgment did not go further than to pronounce the secretary as capable of acting on behalf of the company in these affairs, such as employing staff, ordering cars and 'so forth'. A clear-cut pronouncement on the secretary's authority with regard to other contracts which a company may enter into awaits another case bearing on this aspect.

BASIC DUTIES OF THE COMPANY SECRETARY

Having discussed the secretary's legal status as an officer of the company, it is interesting to consider the actual responsibilities he normally undertakes in the modern company. In order to obtain an objective description of the tasks he might actually perform, I quote below from an independent source. It is the job description for the position of company secretary prepared by a leading firm of management consultants. The description is based on an examination of the jobs carried out by the company secretary in 173 UK companies having annual sales varying in size from £600 000 to £500 million and covering the wide field of commerce, industry and financial services. The description was published in *Executive Remuneration, the United Kingdom* by Management Centre Europe's executive compensation service, Brussels.

The job description falls into two parts:

Basic function

1 The company secretary serves as secretary of the corporation in accordance with the corporation's charter, by-laws and other legal requirements
2 He arranges for meetings of the board of directors and keeps the minutes of such meetings
3 He signs corporate documents and affixes the corporate seal thereto where proper
4 He attends to corporate notices and correspondence, and conducts relations with shareholders on matters concerning the meetings of the shareholders and general corporate policy

Responsibilities

1 He makes arrangements for and gives notice of all board of directors' and shareholders' meetings
2 He directs the preparation of all minutes, agenda, notices, proxies, waivers of notice and subsequent correspondence in connection with meetings of the directors and shareholders
3 He attends all meetings of the board of directors and shareholders and keeps a record of the proceedings

4   He prepares written minutes of each board meeting and is responsible for providing departments with copies of resolutions or extracts from the minutes, where appropriate

5   He acts as custodian of the seal of the corporation; affixes the corporate seal and attests, signs or countersigns corporate documents when authorized

6   He acts as custodian of corporate documents, contracts, leases, deeds to corporate-owned property, minute books and all general records other than those required to be kept by the treasurer and the controller

7   He attends to corporate correspondence including inquiries from shareholders and the public concerning matters of general corporate policy

8   He keeps a current register of the names and addresses of each shareholder; signs, with the president, certificates for shares of the corporation

9   He maintains general charge of the stock transfer books of the corporation; files all corporate reports as prescribed by federal, state or other governmental authorities

10   He performs special assignments as requested by the president

SIGNIFICANCE OF THE SECRETARIAL DUTIES

The bare list of these secretarial duties needs further examination in order to convey some idea of the significance of the various activities and the purpose of the secretarial role in the modern company or organization. The tasks themselves, as listed in the job description, are covered in detail in other chapters of this book. So also are the governing conditions which control the exercise of these duties. These conditions are contained in statutes and their attaching regulations, in case law, in stock exchange requirements and in the organization's own rules and regulations set out in the memorandum and articles or similar document. What this chapter is concerned to do is to take a wider view and specify the key roles of the secretary in the modern business organization, in the public sector or in the very varied activities which can be loosely grouped together as connected with non-profit-making organizations. In what follows, the word 'company' should be read as far as the text allows, to include all of these three areas.

Company's legality

The secretary has a broad general responsibility to ensure that the company's actions and the company's existence remain within the law—he is the custodian of the company's legality.

The degree to which he exercises this responsibility will depend on the type of company and its organizational structure. At one end of the scale, a small company operating in a limited sector of the home market whose shares were not publicly held would afford the secretary comparatively restricted tasks under many of the items listed in the job description. On the other hand, simply because of the company's small size, the secretary would probably be very much more involved in the company's business operations.

At the other end of the scale, the large multinational company with operating subsidiaries in overseas countries would almost inevitably generate a large number of problems relating to its various corporate legal existences. Because of the volume of this legal work, it would not be unusual to find the secretarial function supplying centralized legal services to the company with the secretary in charge of the company's legal department.

But whatever the range of secretarial duties under this heading, the exercise of this responsibility is always essential and may sometimes be crucial to the continued existence of the company.

Legal disputes

Board disputes do happen—perhaps more frequently than some suppose. An important implication of the secretary's duty to ensure that the actions of the board are in compliance with the provisions of the law, is that if an occasion did arise when some or all of the directors wished to support a course of action which was not within the law, or the company's own powers, then the secretary would be obliged to make clear the legal implications of the proposed act and if necessary to take a stand against it being carried out. Similar professional and statutory obligations do of course govern the conduct of a company's accountant or the actuary of a life insurance company.

It is interesting to see that this issue is very much a live one in the secretarial profession in India today. In that country, in order to strengthen the ability of the secretary to take such a stand against the board on a point of law, the Ministry of Industrial Development and Company Affairs has considered the practicability of introducing a statutory requirement that a secretary with more than five years' service should not be removable without either a special resolution being passed or the approval of the central government. Clearly, the business life of an Indian company secretary is a good deal more hazardous than that of his UK counterpart!

Responsibility to whom?

In view of what has been said about the secretary's legal responsibilities, it is clear that he owes part of his duties to the board as a whole. And in so far as the board's powers are exercised by and through the president or chairman, then in practice the secretary's responsibility will be to him. An equally common company structure would place the managing director, chief executive officer, or whatever title he may be known by, as the central person through whom the power of the board is exercised and by whom it is interpreted to the management. In these circumstances, therefore, the secretary would, again in practice, be responsible to him.

But in whatever way the role of president and managing director may vary from company to company or are combined in one individual, the central point to emerge is that the secretary, unlike any other purely executive officer of the company, derives a substantial part of his responsibilities and authority from the board and is in turn responsible to them, through either the chairman or the managing director. Conversely, if the secretary does not derive his responsibilities and authority in this way, although he may be secretary in name, in fact he cannot fully exercise a secretarial function and should more exactly be named as a chief administrative officer of the company.

Independence of the secretarial function

It follows that if the company secretary is to fulfil the complete secretarial role, it is of fundamental importance that in this respect he should be independent of any particular function, department or division within the company. It is worth repeating that the reason for this important principle of independence lies in the fact that the secretarial function relates to the activities of the company as a whole and this is why he is responsible to the effective representative of the board, be he president or managing director.

As corroboration of this view from outside the profession itself, not only is the secretary's independence commonly recognized in business practice but it is widely accepted by management consultants both in the UK and the USA and is implicit in the detailed job description set out earlier.

It is no contradiction of this argument to say that it is not unusual to find the generalist role of the company secretary combined, in one and the same person, with a specialized function at *board level*. But because it is at board level, the separation of the secretarial function is preserved in, for example, the common combination of financial director and company secretary in one person.

Given this background, the secretary's contribution to his organization's success should stem from his uniquely privileged position—that he is afforded an overall view of the organization's activities. Exactly how this contribution is made will depend on the particular structure of the organization he works for. It may centre on a coordinating role aimed at producing the optimum conditions for board and management cooperation in the running of the company. That contribution may extend into any number of diverse fields including personnel work, public relations, legal work, corporate finance, investment, forward planning and so on. But however extended the secretarial role, one of its characteristic and essential features remains that of a separate function concerned with the affairs of the company as a whole.

THE INSTITUTE OF CHARTERED SECRETARIES AND ADMINISTRATORS

In 1970, a merger was successfully completed between the two main professional bodies representing secretaries. These were the Institute of Chartered Secretaries with 30 000 members and the Corporation of Secretaries with 12 000 members. An overwhelming vote from both organizations in favour of the amalgamation ensured not only that the merger proposals obtained the requisite two-thirds majority on both sides but that, once passed, the combined body really was an integrated organization in which the somewhat different interests of the two earlier bodies were successfully united. Total current membership is now approaching 45 000, and there are 30 000 students.

Thus the Institute is now the one and only body representing the interests of the secretary, whether he is concerned in company work, either as an employee or as a consultant or whether he is employed in non-company work in, for example, the very wide field of local government administration.

The widening and developing role of the secretary in every type of administration has been recognized in a change of title and a change of function by the institute which represents him. The name is now The Institute of Chartered Secretaries and Administrators.

The inclusion of 'administrators' in the Institute's title implicitly recognizes the cross-fertilization of disciplines which has been taking place for some time between the traditional subjects of secretarial knowledge—such as company law or taxation—and the growing multiplicity of management knowledge. The change of title accepts in the fullest sense that it is the management and administrative skills which translate the technical expertise of a specialized field like company law or taxation into usable concepts with a practical application in modern business.

Of all the professional qualifications, it is perhaps that of the Institute which gives the widest conspectus of the business world whether this relates to a corporate or a non-corporate organization. And the evidence for this statement lies in the number of the Institute's members who take the examinations, not because they were intending to undertake a specifically secretarial job, but because they wanted a business qualification which would give them some general acquaintance with the problems facing senior management and boards of directors in today's world.

QUALIFICATIONS AND EXAMINATIONS

What then are the qualifications? Before itemizing the various areas of knowledge covered by the examinations, it is worth re-emphasizing that the subjects are treated from the point of view of top management or the board. This is just as much the case, whether the subject relates directly to a board activity or whether it is concerned, for example, in evaluating the role of white collar unions as a preliminary to framing a personnel policy.

It follows that fundamental to the exercise of the secretarial function should be an ability to see the wood for the trees. In sorting through a very wide range of knowledge, it is essential to see beyond the minutiae of the subject which in company law for example can be very involved. The end-purpose is always the effective and practical administration of the business or organization.

Analysing a situation, putting together recommendations and summarizing both clearly and concisely, then seeing that action is taken accordingly and monitoring the results are requirements in the exercise of any management position and the Institute's examinations point the way in this direction. It is alas only too common to find, even at the highest managerial levels, those executives who believe their colleagues or the board of directors prefer to read a fifteen-page report or suffer its equivalent in meeting time when, in ninety-nine cases out of a hundred, one or two pages could succinctly sum up the essence of the situation. So the qualifications themselves require a considerable knowledge in a wide variety of subjects, and are equivalent to a degree of a British university.

Sweeping changes have been made in the examination structure and educational programme. These changes go hand in hand with the evolving nature of the Institute's functions and have gradually been extended to include more aspects of business administration, as well as the specific secretarial function. There are now three main career streams: company secretarial, general and financial administration and public service administration. The new examination arrangements came fully into force in 1975.

The main subjects are financial accounting (on which particular stress is laid), business law, office administration, economic policies and problems, company law, company secretarial practice, taxation, business finance, and principles and policy of personnel and management. There are appropriate alternative papers depending on the country in which the examinee may be working and the sort of business in which he is employed. For example, in the general and financial administration stream, a management techniques and services paper would replace that on company secretarial practice. Similarly, those in public service would take papers dealing with local government administration and finance. Throughout, the emphasis is on producing an examination suitable to cover the full background of knowledge necessary for a top administrator.

Passing the examinations normally takes a minimum five years' part-time study and provided the Council of the Institute elect him, the examinee becomes an associate of the Institute (ACIS). Again, with the emphasis on practical experience, fellowship is granted only after the associate has had appropriate experience in the office of an organization, usually for at least six years. If he has not been employed in a secretarial capacity, he must have been employed in a job equivalent to that of a secretary or assistant secretary for a minimum of three years. Equivalence here is intended to cover the multiplicity of jobs, other than those of specifically secretarial nature, which might be performed by a chartered secretary or administrator.

Professional Administration, the journal of the Institute, carries on where the examinations and the necessarily circumscribed activities of a particular job leave off. The journal is recognized as one of the leading monthly business periodicals.

The subjects covered by the journal make it clear that today's chartered secretary may be working in a corporate business, in a part of today's very large public sector or in a non-profit-making organization such as a trade association, charity, research, educational or social organization, or a public relations service, parliamentary lobby, etc.,—a pretty formidable range of activities!

FUTURE DEVELOPMENTS

Today, probably more intensely than at any time in the past, there are pressures on companies to change and to change rapidly if they are to survive. And the symptom of these pressures is a general uncertainty about the main direction in which the concept of the company should evolve. The company secretary and the secretarial profession in general are uniquely placed to see the results of such pressures in action, and play an active role in making clear what the issues are and where the way forward lies.

The waves and ripples spreading out from the bankruptcy of Rolls-Royce, the disaster of Vehicle and General and the crises of British Leyland and Burmah Oil still have far to travel. It is a truism to say that the death or contraction of a large company is not confined in its effect to the employees who lose their jobs or the shareholders who lose their capital. Customers and consumers may be vitally affected and large sums of public money may be at stake. There is nothing new about these effects. What is different today is the degree of public concern and involvement—and the growing degree of government intervention in part reflecting that concern.

Yet the passivity of shareholders when confronted by managerial ineffectiveness has long been an object for easy derision. Sooner or later, the immense power which is becoming more and more concentrated in the hands of institutional shareholders must find expression in ways and means of monitoring and influencing the financial results of management to a greater degree than at present. Whatever the feelings of individual company boards against more disclosure of information which has hitherto been reserved for management, the pressure of institutional shareholders seeking to protect and improve the value of their shareholdings must force more disclosure, as they themselves come under greater pressure to produce investment performance superior to that of their competitors, for the benefit of their policy holders.

The UK's entry into the Common Market puts this question in a still wider context. The USA has set a pattern for disclosure and we are still far behind America in what we reveal. But by comparison with ourselves, European companies are positively Victorian in the prudery with which they conceal their vital statistics.

Moreover, the question of disclosure leads beyond the financial re-sults of a company, to consideration of its corporate goals. Is the function of the modern company simply to maximize profits for its shareholders within the legal limits of the country where it operates? Or should the company have other corporate goals like the welfare of its employees, the long-term satisfaction of its customers or the public interest, however imprecisely this may be defined? Most companies by their actions implicitly pay some attention to these other goals, and a larger and larger number of companies, among them some of the biggest and most successful in the UK, explicitly adopt these other than profit-making concepts as part of their corporate philosophy.

Whether or not such thinking is simply realistic self-interest is beside the point. What matters is that this thinking recognizes and seeks to come to terms with new forces in society like the powerful consumer pressure groups typified by the Nader groups in America and the consumer movements in the UK, or with the public interest as represented by the use to which taxpayers' subsidies are put or the public's refusal to accept present levels of urban pollution.

Given these modifications of what still remains the basic corporate goal—profit—what now becomes of the role of the board, hitherto simply and straightforwardly defined as the supervision of management's performance in maximizing the return on the shareholders' capital? Do these wider responsibilities fall squarely on their shoulders as well?

These are not theoretical questions but practical issues whose resolution will have a profound effect on UK companies because European thinking on these matters is crystallizing round a very different type of philosophy from that in the UK. For example, in the UK the non-executive director is considered the most effective guardian of the shareholders' interests. But in West Germany, the two-tier structure of a supervisory board over and above an executive board is common, although it is not entirely clear who, ideally, should appoint the members of the supervisory board nor how, once appointed, they should retain their independence.

In European thinking, two-tier boards are closely connected with the vexed subject of worker participation in management and, again using the West German example, with appointment of worker or trade union representatives to the board. In this country, management and trade unions initially shrank from the idea of workers' representatives on a board but support for the idea has since gathered strength. Perhaps it is time that the whole tradition of management staying on one side of the bargaining table and workers on the other should be rethought and replaced by the idea of a joint enterprise where both sides can agree to pursue certain common goals. Whichever way we want to develop in this country, time is short if we wish to have a decisive influence on European thinking and legislation.

And beyond this horizon, though not so very far beyond, lies the promise, given by the present government, as by the last, and the one before that, that new company legislation will be placed on the statute book. Just because our own disclosure practice is ahead of European practice and because our company legislation is also ahead of European requirements, it seems important that although the government's thinking on a new Companies Act is unlikely to be implemented in the near future, a decisive initiative in the planning and realization of a European company or of a European cooperative grouping should come from this country. If the UK concept of a company can be justified in terms of practical results—and it certainly looks as if flexibility in company formation and the absence of overrigid controls are great advantages—this concept ought to have a powerful influence in shaping European company legislation.

All that has been said implies as a necessary preliminary to moving forward, the careful definition and analysis of the aims and methods of our present company structure, and the relative responsibilities of employees, management, directors and shareholders. The work to be done requires the skills of lawyers, of accountants, of management consultants and many others. The company secretary needs to be fully aware of these developments if he is to adapt to the changing role of the company. At the same time he has a wide practical experience to contribute, covering many aspects of the problem often from the vantage point of a non-technical view which should enable him to see the broad significances involved. In all this the secretarial profession, acting among other ways through the collective voice of the Institute of Chartered Secretaries and Administrators can be expected to play an increasingly important role. It was because of the Institute's initiative that, among other points, provision for a company secretary on the UK model was specifically written into the EEC draft company law statute. No mean achievement, when it is remembered that on the continent the job of company secretary is usually shared between two or three executives and there is no exact equivalent to this post which is so well established in the UK and the ex-commonwealth countries.

2

Company Law

V J Gersten

The law deals with relations between persons—human beings who own property, make contracts and sue one another. The economic life of the country depends on the law's extension of the concept of person to include non-human persons called corporations.

When people associate for a common purpose, the law makes it possible for them to create a separate 'person', a corporation of which they are the members, to carry out that purpose. A corporation can perform many of the economic functions that humans can. It can, for example:

1   Own property
2   Employ people
3   Make contracts
4   Sue and be sued

It can do these things only through the agency of human beings, its members or people appointed by them. The advantage of the corporation is that its existence (and hence its ownership of property or its capacity to carry out contracts or be sued on them) is independent of its members and continues even when its membership changes.

LIMITED COMPANIES

The most common type of corporation is the limited company. Parliament has passed a series of Acts, starting with the Joint Stock Companies Act 1856 and ending with the Companies Act 1948 that have given a simple method for forming a corporation. The minimum requirements are:

1   Delivery of a printed document—the memorandum of association—with two witnessed signatures
2   Delivery of a statutory declaration that the requirements of the Act have been complied with
3   Delivery of a statement of nominal capital (on which duty is assessed)
4   Payment of a fee

—to the Registrar of Companies. The Registrar then issues a certificate of incorporation which is conclusive evidence of the existence of a separate legal person, a registered company. Its existence continues until either its members or a court terminates it by 'winding up'.

Types of registered company

The Companies Act 1948 distinguishes three main types of company:

1   Company limited by shares
2   Company limited by guarantee
3   Unlimited company

Most companies are of the first type and throughout this chapter, 'company' will be used to mean 'company limited by shares'.

Advantages of the company structure

The limited company format has been developed to facilitate the aggregation of money to be used for production and trading. The people who supply the money exchange it for shares in the company's capital and thereby become members of the company. The members appoint directors to manage the company's affairs, retaining the right to dismiss a director. The profits that the company makes are available for distribution as dividends to the members.

    The aspect of company structure that makes it attractive to investors is that the members are separated, not only from the management of the enterprise but, by the concept of limited liability, from the disasters of mismanagement also.

Shares and limited liability

Each share that a company issues when collecting money from its members has a nominal value which is fixed by the company's memorandum of association.

    It is not necessary for a member to pay the company the whole nominal value of a share when purchasing it from the company. If the company accepts less then it can, by making a *call*, require the shareholder to pay the difference between the initial payment and the nominal value.

The amount of money that has actually been paid to the company for its shares is called the paid-up capital.

At the time a company is wound up, a member is entitled to receive an amount, proportionate to his shareholding, of any of the company's money left over after its debts have been paid. This money is known as the equity: it could, of course be zero; the holder of a share that was not fully paid up might have a call made on him at the winding-up to help pay the company's debts, but he cannot be asked to pay more than the amount unpaid on his shares. That is the limit of his liability for the company's debts.

The company is distinct from its members

The principle that the company is separate from its members who own its shares cannot be too powerfully imprinted upon the mind of anyone in commerce. The idea is abstract but its practical consequences are only too apparent.

An unfortunate small trader may have to walk to a meeting of company creditors because, having failed to recover his debts from the company, he has had to sell his mini van. He then may be knocked down by the Rolls-Royce belonging to one of the company's directors on his way to the same meeting to explain that the company cannot pay its debts because the harsh economic climate caused it such losses that it had to cease trading. The director may keep his Rolls-Royce but the victim of the accident has no claim against the company. (Any claim for damages for the accident is of course another matter.) The director is not personally liable for the debts of the company even though those debts have been incurred because of recklessness or misjudgment on his part.

The armour plate of limited liability may be pierced only if the director concerned can be proved to have behaved fraudulently, but in practice fraud is extremely hard to prove. The expense and difficulty of proving it makes it virtually impossible for the individual creditor to use it as a method of getting his money back.

Moreover, most business failures are not the result of fraud but of recklessness, incompetence or misfortune. This is of little comfort to the small businessman, and anyone running a small company or a small business of any kind should never give extended credit to a small limited company without taking personal guarantees from the directors of that company. If this is done the individual directors will be liable for the company's debts like any other guarantor of a debt.

Conversely, the officers or other persons dealing with the affairs of a small limited company should make sure that they always deal in the company's name so that it can never be suggested that they were acting in their personal capacities or in some way guaranteeing the credit of the company.

The most famous cautionary student's case dealing with these principles is Salomon *v* Salomon and Company Ltd (1897), usually known as Salomon's Case. Salomon had a boot-manufacturing business. He created a company called Salomon and Company Ltd in which he was the principal shareholder, and sold his boot and shoe business to it partly for shares and partly for debentures; in other words he transferred his business to the company partly in consideration of a promise by the company (in which he was principal shareholder) to pay money to him secured in such a way as to give him priority over its future creditors. The company went into liquidation, its assets being sufficient to repay his loan but not to repay subsequent creditors to whom the company owed £7000. These creditors received nothing. The company was of course almost wholly owned by Salomon himself, and as he was trading for profit it might be thought unfair that the money which he ought to have had at risk was repaid to him in priority to the money risked by the suppliers who had given the company credit. The case was not as unfair as this suggests, because particulars of the notional loan made by Salomon to the company and the fact that this debt had priority over the claims of subsequent creditors could have been ascertained by checking the register of the company at the Companies Registry. If it is proposed to advance substantial sums of money to a company or to give it extended credit such a check should be made. It is clearly impracticable to do this every time a company is given credit, but the risk of the Salomon situation arising must be borne in mind by any creditor of a company.

Publicity

Because of the limitation on a company's liability to pay its debts, the Companies Acts requires it to send a great deal of information about itself to the Registrar.

Time-limits are laid down for filing the information, and severe penalties are provided for in the event of default. It may be of some comfort to company secretaries to know that these time-limits are not enforced with great stringency, and the maximum penalties for default are not normally exacted.

This information may be inspected by anyone and one of the purposes of the publicity is to enable people to judge the company's creditworthiness.

Another purpose is to help people to judge whether a company's shares are worth buying. This leads to a distinction between 'public' and 'private' companies. The basic difference is that a member of a public company can transfer his shares to anyone he likes, but a private company restricts this right of its members. The 1948 Act defined a class of 'exempt private companies' that were not required to file their annual accounts. This class was abolished by the Companies Act 1967, but the private company structure still retains some advantages.

Advantages of the private company

*S*28(1) of the 1948 Act defines a private company as one which, by its articles (as discussed later in the chapter):

1   Restricts the right to transfer its shares
2   Limits the number of its members to fifty, not including persons who are in the employment of the company and persons who, having been formerly in the employment of the company, were while in that employment, and have continued after the determination of that employment, to be members of the company (*s*28(1)(*b*))
3   Prohibits any invitation to the public to subscribe for any shares or debentures of the company

Joint holders of a share are counted as one person for the purposes of condition 2. Two differences between public and private companies are:

1   The minimum number of members of a private company is two—of a public company seven
2   The minimum number of directors of a private company is one—of a public company two

Prospectuses. Because a public company can invite the public to subscribe for its shares, the Act lays down strict conditions on what it may say in its invitation (called a 'prospectus'). Further, a public company must either issue a prospectus and send a copy to the Registrar, or send him a 'statement in lieu of prospectus' in the form given in the Fifth Schedule to the Act.

Commencing business. A company that registers as a public company cannot do any business until the Registrar has granted it a trading certificate. The conditions for issue of this are given in *s*109 of the Act. A prospectus or statement   in lieu must have been registered, the directors must have paid for their shares and, if a prospectus was issued to the public, there must have been an adequate response. Because of this hiatus in the public company's life, almost all new companies are registered as private companies, which can commence business immediately the certificate of incorporation is granted. A private company can convert itself to a public one by deleting the relevant provisions from its articles and registering a prospectus or statement in lieu.

Practical company formation

The first step to be taken when it is desired to form a new company is to write to the Companies Registration Office, Companies House, 55-71 City Road, London, EC1, asking whether the Registrar will approve the proposed name of the company. The company's name is dealt with in the next section. A reply will usually be obtained within fourteen days and the letter approving the name must be lodged with the other necessary documents.

Company formation firms. There are many firms who make a business of forming companies and the easiest way to make sure that all the statutory formalities are dealt with is to send the letter approving the name to one of them, telling them for what purpose the company is being formed and asking them to form it. They will then prepare the documents for lodging with the Registrar of Companies and either produce them for signature or form the company taking up the subscriber shares themselves, and then send the documents on with signed blank share transfers. Their fees for doing this vary in relation to their expertise (and the quality of their printing since the law requires that most of the documents be printed) but will not normally exceed £50.

Unless one has had previous experience of the formation of companies it is not wise to use these organizations direct. It is best to have the company formed through an accountant or solicitor who may use one of the company formation firms for printing and sometimes lodging the documents, but will take into consideration any special requirements of the particular company being formed.

For example, the vast majority of private limited companies are in fact small family businesses. In partnership agreements covering the same type of business, it is usual to provide that in the event of one of the partners retiring or dying the remaining partners shall have an option to purchase the partnership share of the retired or dead partner at a fair valuation, which may be fixed by the partnership accountant or in the event of dispute by some outside arbitrator. If one uses a company formation agency to form a company, they will provide a standard form of articles of association which normally, either by reference to Table *A* (see later) or specifically, includes a provision that the directors have the right to refuse to register transfers. It will not normally include a provision that a shareholder wishing to sell his shares must first offer them to the remaining shareholders at a fair valuation. In the family business type of company this provision is desirable.

There are many other provisions which it might be desirable to insert in the standard form of articles of association and which are not normally inserted by company formation agencies, and their existence makes the cost of professional advice well worth while.

Purchase of a company. A cheaper method of company acquisition is to buy one ready made, usually obtainable from the firms that form companies. It is generally possible to purchase an existing company designed to carry on the type of business required at a price considerably less than the fees for forming a new company. It is then merely necessary to change the name of the company, which, once the name has been approved by the Department of Trade, can be done by passing a special resolution. If it is necessary to change the articles of the company this too can be done by special resolution. It would nonetheless be unwise to buy a ready-made company without having its memorandum and articles checked by a professional adviser, and if this is done the ultimate saving will not be very great.

The remainder of this chapter will discuss in more detail the structure of registered companies limited by shares. All companies are now regulated by the Companies Act 1948 as amended by the Companies Act 1967. References to Acts of Parliament in the rest of this chapter are, unless otherwise stated, to the Companies Act 1948.

The court. The phrase 'the court' in the rest of this chapter means the court that has jurisdiction over the company as defined in *s*218. The High Court has jurisdiction over all companies. County courts also have jurisdiction over companies whose paid-up capital is less than £10 000.

Printed documents. The Companies Acts frequently require documents sent to the Registrar to be 'printed'. The Registrar has indicated that this requirement will be fulfilled if a document is produced by letterpress, gravure or lithography; by offset lithography, by electrostatic or photographic copying; or by stencil duplicating using wax stencils and black ink. However, thermographic, hectographic or dye-line copies will not be accepted.

MEMORANDUM OF ASSOCIATION

Every company must have a memorandum of association which must state (*s*2):

1   The name of the company
2   Whether the registered office will be in England or Scotland
3   The objects of the company
4   A statement that the liability of members is limited
5   The amount of the nominal capital and how it is divided into shares
6   A *declaration of association* signed by at least seven persons (for a public company—two for a private company), called the *subscribers,* in the presence of a witness. Each subscriber must take at least one share.

The form of the memorandum must follow that set out in Table *B* of the First Schedule to the 1948 Act.

The memorandum defines the company's legal personality and controls its relations with the rest of the world. It is filed by the Registrar, after incorporation, at Companies House where any person may inspect it for a fee of 5p. Any member of the company is entitled to be supplied by the company with a copy of its memorandum for a fee not exceeding 5p. Where an alteration is made in the memorandum every copy subsequently issued by the company must incorporate the alteration.

The Name

The Registrar may refuse to register a company with a name that he considers undesirable (s17). The usual reason for refusal is that the name is too like that of an existing company.

Another common ground is that the name misleadingly implies royal patronage or connection with a government or local authority. Names must not include the word 'cooperative' or 'building society'. The words 'bank' 'investment' or 'trust' will be allowed only when they accurately reflect the nature of the company.

Limited. The last word of the name must be 'limited' so that all who have dealings with the company are aware of its structure. The Department of Trade will issue a licence to allow a company's name to be registered without the word limited, if it is satisfied that the company's object is to promote 'commerce, art, science, religion, charity or any other useful object', and it intends to apply its profits or other income to promoting those objects and prohibits paying any dividend to its members (s19).

Change of name. If the Department of Trade discovers within six months of incorporation that a company has inadvertently been registered with a name that is too like that of an existing company, it may require the new company to change its name within six weeks (s18(2)),

A company may change its name by passing a special resolution (see p.74) in general meeting. It is prudent to ask the Registrar first whether he will object to the new name.

Publication of the name. The full name of the company must appear, in a conspicuous position, in letters easily legible outside every place at which it conducts business, and outside its registered office (s108(1)(a)). Limited may be abbreviated to Ltd (Stacey and Company Limited *v* Wallis (1912)).

The full name must also appear on all business letters, notices, official publications, bills of exchange, promissory notes, endorsements, cheques, orders for money or goods, invoices, receipts and letters of credit.

Section 9(7) of the European Communities Act 1972 which came into effect on the 1st January 1975 provides that the place of registration, registration number and address of the registered office shall appear on all business letters and order forms. Under the same section, a company exempted from using the word limited in its name must state that it is a limited company on all business letters and order forms.

If an officer of the company issues a cheque, bill of exchange, promissory note or order for goods or money, without using the company's name, he is personally liable on it unless the company honours it.

Trading under another name. If a company uses a business name that is not the name registered in its memorandum, then it must register that name with the Registrar of Business Names (who happens to be also the Registrar of Companies). The Registrar may refuse to register a business name he thinks undesirable (Companies Act 1947 s116). The only exception to this rule is the use of words in addition to the corporate name to indicate that the company is carrying on a previous owner's business.

Registered office

Notice of the address of the registered office must be sent to the Registrar within fourteen days of incorporation. Any change must also be notified within fourteen days (s107).

The memorandum has only to state whether the registered office will be in England (which includes Wales) or Scotland. This determines whether the company will be subject to English or Scottish law and it is not possible to move from one country to the other.

If the registered office is to be in England then the company must be registered at Companies House, 55 City Road, London EC1. If in Scotland it must be registered at Exchequer Chambers, 102 George Street, Edinburgh 2.

Writs and other documents may be served on a company by leaving them at, or posting them to, its registered office (s437).

Checklist of documents to be kept

The following documents must be kept at the registered office and must (except for the minute book) be available for inspection by anyone for at least two hours a day during normal business hours:

1   Register of directors and secretaries—see p.33 (s200(1))
2   Register of charges (s104(1)) and copies of the instruments
     creating the charges—see p.40
3   Minute books of general meetings—see p.84 (s146(1))

Inspection of the minutes may be refused to non-members.

In addition the following documents must be kept at the registered office, unless the work of making them up is done elsewhere when they can be kept where the work is done:

1   Register of members—see p.28 (s110(2))
2   Register of debenture holders—see p.40 (s86)

The following two documents must be kept together, either at the registered office or at the place where the register of members is kept:

1   Register of directors interests—see p.34 (Companies Act 1967 s29(7))
2   Register of substantial individual interests—see p.29. This register is not required if the company is not quoted on a stock exchange (Companies Act 1967 s34(5))

The last four documents must be available for inspection to anyone for at least two hours every business day during normal business hours.

OBJECTS OF THE COMPANY

The memorandum of association must set out the objects of the company, the purpose for which the company has been incorporated. The objects clause in fact takes up the bulk of the memorandum of association. It normally consists of a very lengthy main objects clause setting out the basic purpose of incorporation, then a large number of subsidiary clauses which are usually standardized and give the company power to buy land, borrow money, acquire other businesses and do anything which is necessary to carry out its main object. The standard form used by company formation agencies usually has a standard form of objects clause, leaving the main objects clause only to be specifically designed for the individual company.

Many of the subclauses in the objects clause would be taken by the courts to be subsidiary to the main objects clause, there merely to ensure that the company has power to do everything necessary to carry on the business described in the main objects clause. However, a declaration frequently appears at the end of the main objects clause to the effect that all the objects specified in any of the subclauses of the objects clause should, except where otherwise expressed, not be limited by reference or inference from the terms of any other paragraph or the name of the company and that all of them should be construed as main objects; and this declaration has been allowed by the courts to be effective. Most standard forms of objects clause drawn up in recent years contain such a declaration.

If a company does anything which is outside the scope of its objects, such action is *ultra vires* (beyond the powers) and void, and the company and its members can take no action to render it valid. The purpose of this part of the law is to protect investors in the company. Investors normally invest in a business which they expect to do well and they are entitled to expect that their money will be used for that business and not for some different business. However, the law proved totally ineffective in achieving this end and merely operated arbitrarily to deprive some classes of creditors, and occasionally employees, of just claims against companies. As a result, in 1962 the Company

Law Committee under the chairmanship of Lord Jenkins recommended changes in the *ultra vires* doctrine which have effectively been achieved by the European Communities Act 1972. *S*9(1) provided that in favour of a person dealing with a company in good faith any transaction decided on by the directors is deemed to be one which it is within the capacity of the company to enter into and the power of the directors to bind the company is deemed to be free of any limitation under the memorandum or articles of association. A party to a transaction so decided on is not bound to inquire as to the capacity of the company to enter into it or as to any such limitation on the power of the directors and is presumed to have acted in good faith unless the contrary is proved.

However, the danger that any transaction entered into by a company is *ultra vires* cannot be ignored. The changes in the law reduce the ability of a company to escape improperly from claims made by third parties but do not enable it to enforce an *ultra vires* contract against a third party. Whenever a company proposes to confer benefits such as pensions or bonuses on directors or make donations to charities, company secretaries should check the objects clause to make sure that the transaction is not *ultra vires*.

Changing the objects clause

Under *s*5, the objects clause may be altered for certain limited purposes by passing a special resolution (see p.74) in general meeting. For a period of twenty-one days after the resolution is passed there is an opportunity to apply to the court for the alteration to be cancelled. The application may be made by:

1 The holders of not less than 15 per cent of the company's issued share capital, or of fifteen per cent of any one class of that capital
2 The holders of at least 15 per cent of any debentures secured by a floating charge that were issued (or are part of a series whose issue commenced) before 1 December 1947. Such debenture holders are entitled to the same notice of a resolution to alter the objects clause as are members of the company

The second class is included because before 1 December 1947 all alterations of objects clauses had to be sanctioned by the court. Debenture holders are not normally entitled to notice of resolutions.

An objection cannot be made by someone who voted for the resolution. The main ground of objection is that the alteration does not fall within the categories permitted by *s*5(1). The court may confirm the resolution either wholly or in part and on such terms and conditions as it thinks fit. It may also adjourn the proceedings to enable a satisfactory arrangement for the purchase of the dissentient shareholders' interests to be made.

LIABILITY

This clause is a statement of the essential point that 'the liability of the members is limited'. The clause may not be altered unless the company is re-registered as an unlimited company following the procedure laid down in the Companies Act 1967 s43.

The liability of the members may however become unlimited by the operation of s31. This happens after a company has traded for more than six months with fewer than the minimum number of members (two for a private company, seven for a public company). If it then continues to trade with too few members the liability of those members who know it is doing so is unlimited.

The memorandum may, by s202, provide that the liability of directors is unlimited (assuming that directors have to be members). By s203, a company may, if it is authorized by its articles, pass a special resolution to render unlimited the liability of its directors or of a managing director.

CAPITAL CLAUSE

This states the amount of the nominal capital and how it is divided into shares. The shares may be divided into classes with different rights—see Shares, below.

Alteration of the capital clause

By s61(1)(a), a company may, if it is authorized by its articles, 'increase its share capital by new shares of such amount as it thinks expedient'.

The alteration must be made by a resolution at a general meeting (s61(2)) and a printed copy of the resolution together with a notice of the increase must be sent to the Registrar within fifteen days (s63). The copy resolution must either be printed or in some other form approved by the Registrar (s61(1) of the 1967 Act).

A company may (again if authorized by its articles and by a resolution passed at a general meeting):

1   Consolidate and divide any of its share capital into shares of a larger amount—for example consolidate twenty shares of 5p each into one £1 share—(s61(1)(b))
2   Convert any paid-up shares into stock or reconvert stock into shares of any denomination (s61(1)(c))
3   Subdivide shares into shares of a smaller amount (s61(1)(d))
4   Cancel shares that have not been taken or agreed to be taken

Notice of any of these four actions must be sent to the Registrar within one month (s62).

Stock

Until the Companies Act 1948, shares had to be numbered. In large companies, this meant that registering transfers of shares was a lengthy process, since the numbers must be given in the shareholder's entry in the register of members. Stock is not numbered because in principle it can be bought and sold in any quantity. Thus if £10 shares are converted into stock, the holder of £100 of stock may sell £57 of it. However, articles usually allow the directors to fix a minimum amount of transferable stock (a *stock unit*) as in article 41 of Table A. S74 now allows that, if all the issued shares of a particular class are fully paid up and rank *pari passu* for all purposes then they need not have numbers. This section has removed one of the reasons for converting shares into stock.

Reduction of capital

A reduction of the issued capital of a company may be made only with the consent of the court after passing a special resolution (s66).

S66 A company's creditors are entitled to assume that the capital represented by issued shares is available to meet the company's debts: they are prepared to take the risk that the capital will be lost because of bad management but not that the company will actually give it back to the shareholders. Before agreeing to a reduction, the court will, therefore, ensure that the creditors are happy about it and that different classes of shareholder are being treated equitably.

S66 prevents a company from buying shares in itself, because that would reduce the share capital. One exception to this rule is that s58 allows a company to issue fully paid redeemable preference shares. If redemption is made by a payment from profits (and not by issuing new shares) then this would reduce the company's issued share capital. Creditors are protected, however, by s58(1)(d) which provides that a sum equal to the nominal value of the redeemed shares must be transferred from profits to a 'capital redemption reserve fund' which is then treated as paid-up capital of the company.

ARTICLES OF ASSOCIATION

A company limited by shares must have a set of articles of association, which govern the management of the internal affairs of the company.

Unless it registers with its memorandum a different set of articles, a company will automatically be governed by the set of articles given in Table *A* in the First Schedule to the 1948 Act (s8(2)).

If the company does register special articles then the regulations in Table *A* will still apply in so far as the registered articles do not exclude or modify them (s8(2)).

Normally they are specifically adopted with modifications. It is usual for it to be stated at the commencement of the articles of association that Table *A* Part I or II (see Private companies, overleaf) is adopted save as specifically excluded, and then to continue with details of the provisions of Table *A* that are excluded. The company secretary should carefully collate with Table *A* the articles of the company for which he works, so that he knows exactly what has been excluded and can check whether new provisions have been inserted where necessary to replace the excluded provisions of Table *A*. Common cases where additions to Table *A* are advisable are in connection with the powers and duties of directors, the dismissal of directors and the voting rights attached to the shares. The prudent company secretary having found out exactly what the articles of his company are by checking them through with Table *A* will try to envisage the problems that may arise in his company. Articles of association may be changed by special resolution with few restrictions (see below). It is too late to alter the articles when a conflict between directors or shareholders has already arisen and the articles do not cover the situation.

Companies registered before 1 July 1948

The Companies Acts 1862, 1908 and 1929 each had a Table *A* containing a model set of articles. The Joint Stock Companies Act 1856 had a Table *B*. Companies registered under these Acts automatically took the relevant table as their articles in so far as they did not register modifying articles. These earlier tables continue to be the articles of the companies that adopted them.

Alteration of the articles

A company may alter or add to its articles by passing a special resolution (see p.74) in any way subject to its memorandum and the provisions of the Act (s10(1)).

The articles constitute a contract between the company and its members but s10(1) allows the company to alter articles against a member's will and even to his detriment, if the alteration is made *bona fide* for the benefit of the company as a whole.

This point was demonstrated in Sidebottom *v* Kershaw, Leese and Company Limited (1920). Sidebottom held a small number of shares in the company which was controlled by its directors. Sidebottom therefore received copies of the accounts of the company, which annoyed the directors because Sidebottom was also in business in competition with them. At that time, companies did not have to send their accounts to the Registrar and they were not publicly available. The directors altered the articles of association to enable them to require a shareholder who was also a competitor to sell his shares to a nominee of the directors. The Court of Appeal held that the alteration was valid. The articles may not be altered so as to:

1   Exceed the powers conferred by the memorandum, or conflict with it
2   Be inconsistent with the Companies Acts or any other statute
3   Increase the liability of existing members unless they give their consent in writing (*s*22)

Private companies

Table *A* is divided into two parts. Part I is the set of articles for a non-private company. Part II repeats all except two of these, which are replaced by:

1   The key regulation that 'the directors may, in their absolute discretion and without assigning any reason therefor, decline to register any transfer of any share, whether or not it is a fully paid share'
2   A provision that two members (instead of three) form a quorum at a general meeting

Part II also adds a regulation that repeats the definition in *s*28(1)—see Publicity—and a regulation that allows resolutions to be passed without a meeting taking place (see p.17).

MEMBERSHIP

The members of a company are persons who have both:

1   Agreed to be members, and
2   Had their names entered in the company's register of members

The usual way of signifying agreement to be a member is by paying for shares in the company, and the words 'member' and 'shareholder' are synonymous.

Register of members

By *s*110, every company must have a register of members, showing:

1   Name and address of each member
2   The number of shares held, and their numbers if they are numbered
3   The amount paid or agreed to be considered as paid on the shares
4   The date when each member was entered on the register
5   The date that a person ceased to be a member

If the company has more than fifty members then its register must either be in the form of an index or there must be a separate index which must contain sufficient information to enable any member's account to be found in the register (s111).

The register must be open for inspection for at least two hours every business day. Members have a right of free inspection. Non-members have a right of inspection but may be charged not more than 5p. Anyone may require a copy of the register and may be charged not more than 10p per 100 words for it.

Who may be a member?

Any person having the capacity to make a contract may be a member. This includes:

1   *Aliens*—a company registered in England will be English even if none of its members are. The Exchange Control Act 1947 restricts the sale of shares in a company to persons resident outside the Scheduled Territories

2   *Bankrupts*—although a bankrupt must exercise his vote according to the direction of his trustee and may not be a director without the permission of the court that adjudicated him bankrupt

3   *A registered company*—if authorized by its memorandum. However, a company may not own any of its own shares (see Reduction of capital, p.26) or (s27) shares in its holding company. (Company A is *subsidiary* of company B and B is A's *holding company* if B is a member of A and controls membership of A's board of directors, or if B holds more than half of A's equity share capital—see next section—or if A is a subsidiary of another company that is a subsidiary of B—s154(1))

4   *Infants*. Because a contract cannot always be enforced against an infant (see p.209), a company may, by its articles forbid infant membership

Register of substantial interests

A company is under no obligation to recognize the interest of any other person in the shares of one of its members. Thus, if shares are held by A who is the registered member on behalf of B then the company does not have to ensure that A deals with the shares in B's best interest. S117 provides that no notice of a trust may be entered on the register of shareholders. This makes it possible for a person to control shares in a company through nominee shareholders without his name appearing on the publicly available register.

To prevent an abuse of this provision, s34 of the 1967 Act requires a company whose shares are quoted on a recognized stock exchange to maintain a *register of substantial individual interests* at its registered office or at the place where the register of members is kept. The rules about its availability for inspection are the same as those for the register of members. S33 of the 1967 Act requires that anyone who acquires an interest in one-tenth or more of the issued shares that carry a right to vote in all circumstances at a general meeting, must notify the company within fourteen days of his acquisition. The company must enter in the register his name, address, the way he acquired the interest, the number and class of shares. The entry must be made within three days of receipt of the notice. Notification and a record in the register is then required of any changes in the interest, up to and including the time when it falls below the one-tenth mark. Failure to notify a substantial interest is a criminal offence. The maximum penalty is two years' imprisonment and a fine.

In addition all companies must maintain a register of directors' interests; this is discussed on p.36.

Termination of membership

Membership ceases when the name of the member is validly removed from the register of members. This is done when the member *transfers* (usually by sale) all his shares to someone else, or when his shares are *transmitted* to his executors (if he dies) or his trustee (if he is adjudicated bankrupt). The details of transfer and transmission are considered in Chapter 3.

SHARES

Shares may be issued in different classes with different rights of control of the company's affairs, participation in its profits, and repayment of their value and share in surplus assets on winding-up. A simple distinction is often made on the basis of the way annual profits are to be shared.

Ordinary shares entitle their holders to a share of the profits only if the directors think fit and to the extent they think fit. The ordinary shareholders are usually entitled to control the company's activities by voting at a general meeting (see Chapter 4).

Preference shares carry the right to a payment of a fixed percentage of their nominal value in every year that the company makes a sufficient profit. Because the risk of not getting a dividend is less than for ordinary shares, preference shareholders are usually denied the right to vote at a general meeting.

Preferential rights may be extended to the division of the company's assets on winding up. Preference shareholders may have the right to repayment of their capital first. To balance this they are not usually entitled to a share of any surplus assets the company has.

Any mixture of rights is possible: 'non-voting ordinary shares', 'participating preference shares' (eligible for a discretionary dividend in addition to the fixed one) and 'deferred shares' (where all other classes of shareholder must be paid dividends or repaid capital first) have been issued. Precise definition of the rights of any class will be given either in the memorandum or (more conveniently) in the articles .

Redeemable preference shares are discussed under Reduction of capital (p.26).

Equity shares are those whose rights, either to a dividend or to a share in surplus assets on winding up, are not limited to a specified amount.

Modification of class rights

The rights of each class of share will be defined either in the memorandum or in the articles. If the rights are specified in the memorandum there may also be specification of the way in which the rights can be modified. If this is not included then the rights can be altered only by a scheme of arrangement under s206, which must be sanctioned by the court.

When rights of a class are modified in accordance with procedures stated in the memorandum of articles then s72 prcvides that the holders of not less than 15 per cent of the issued shares of that class may apply to the court for the alteration to be cancelled. The application must be made within twenty-one days of completion of the procedure for changing the rights.

DIRECTORS

Members invest money in their company but do not usually run its day-to-day affairs, which are controlled by the directors. Every public company registered after 1 November 1929 must have at least two directors. Public companies registered before then and private companies must have at least one director (s178).

A director is not, as such, an employee or servant of the company, although he may hold office in addition to his directorship (such as sales director). A director has no right to be paid for his directorial services unless payment is authorized by the articles—which it normally is, as in Table *A* article 76.

Directors are, in law, agents of the company. Hence if directors make a contract in the name of the company, it is the company—the principal—which is liable on it, not the directors, provided they do not exceed the powers conferred on them by the memorandum and articles. If a director made an *ultra vires* contract (see p.23) then he would be personally liable on it.

Directors occupy a fiduciary position. A director may not deal with himself on behalf of the company. If a director makes a contract on his own behalf with the company of which he is a director, then the company may rescind the contract or call upon the director to surrender his profit. Directors are, therefore, required by s199 to declare their interests in any matter under discussion (see also p.78). Material interests of directors in significant contracts must be described in the directors' report (Chapter 5) by s16(1)(c) of the 1967 Act.

Who may be a director?

Anyone, including a company, except:

1   Beneficed clergymen of the Church of England (Pluralities Act 1838)
2   An undischarged bankrupt without the permission of the court that adjudicated him bankrupt
3   Persons disqualified by the court under s188 after conviction of certain offences connected with company management

Age limits. S185 provides that a person may not be a director of a public company or of a private subsidiary of a public company if he is over seventy. In such companies, a director must retire at the end of the annual general meeting that follows his seventieth birthday.

A company may include a clause in its articles abrogating these provisions (s185(7)). Alternatively, a person over seventy may be appointed a director at a general meeting by a resolution of which special notice has been given—the notice must state his age (s185(5)).

Appointment of directors

The articles state the procedure for the appointment of directors. The only statutory provisions are:

1   S180—a director's acts are valid even if it is subsequently discovered that his appointment was invalid
2   S181—the first directors of a company that is to be registered as a public company must sign and deliver to the Registrar a consent in writing so to act
3   S182 interprets articles that require share qualifications of directors
4   S183 ensures that when a meeting is voting on the appointment of directors it votes for each name separately

Removal of directors

S184(1) states one of the most important principles of company law:

> A company may by ordinary resolution remove a director before the expiration of his period of office, notwithstanding anything in its articles or in any agreement between it and him

Although no provision in a director's contract of service could prevent his dismissal under this section, he might well be able to sue for damages for breach of his contract if he were dismissed. Special notice (see p.76) is required of the resolution. Special notice is also required of a motion to appoint a director to replace one removed under s184(1), if it is to be moved at the same general meeting.

Publicity about directors

The following information about its directors must be made available by every company:

1   A register of directors and secretaries must be kept at the company's registered office
2   A register of directors' interests in shares and debentures must be kept, either at the registered office or at the place where the register of members is kept
3   Particulars of directors' service contracts must be available for inspection by members
4   The names of the directors must appear on certain documents issued by the company

Register of directors and secretaries (S200)

This register must show, in the case of directors who are individuals:

1   Present forename and surname, and any former forenames and surnames
2   Usual residential address
3   Present nationality
4   Business occupation
5   Any other directorships held by him. Directorships of wholly owned subsidiaries of the company need not be shown, neither does a directorship of the company's holding company if the company is a wholly owned subsidiary
6   If the company is public, or a private subsidiary of a public company, his age

In the case of directors who are corporations, the register must show the corporate name and registered or principal office.

The register must be kept at the registered office and the requirements for inspection are the same as those for the register of members. The particulars entered in the register must also be sent to the Registrar as must any change in them.

Register of directors' interests

Ss27–9 of the 1967 Act require every company to keep a register of directors' interests in the company's shares or debentures. The Act requires a director to notify his interests to the company:

1   Within fourteen days beginning the day after he was appointed a director
2   Within fourteen days beginning the day after he acquires an interest

Saturdays, Sundays and a day that is a bank holiday in any part of Great Britain are disregarded when counting the period of fourteen days. Persons who were directors on 27 October 1967 should have registered the interests they held on 26 October before 15 November 1967. Because the definition of 'interest' is so wide (it includes the interests of a director's spouse and infant children), the Act anticipates that there will be occasions on which a director does not know that he has acquired an interest within the meaning of the Act. If a director discovers that he does have a previously unknown interest then he must notify it within fourteen days beginning the day after his discovery.

Within three days beginning the day after the company was notified (but excluding Saturdays, Sundays and bank holidays) it must enter in the register the following information:

1   Name of the director giving the information
2   The information given
3   Date of entry in the register

Entries for each name must be in chronological order. If the register is not in the form of an index then there must be a separate index to the names in the register. Rights of inspection are the same as for the register of members (see Register of members, p.28.

In addition to recording information supplied by directors, the company must itself record the following information in the register:

1   The grant to a director of a right to subscribe for shares or debentures of a company (s29(2)(a))
2   The exercise of such a right (s29(2)(b))

Inspection of service contracts

S26 of the 1967 Act requires a company to allow its members, without charge during reasonable business hours, to inspect a copy of the service contract of every director. (If the contract is oral then a memorandum of its terms must be available for inspection.) There are two exceptions:

1   Contracts requiring a director to work wholly or mainly outside the United Kingdom
2   Contracts that have less than twelve months to run or that can be terminated by the company within the next twelve months without payment of compensation

The copies must be kept (all together) at one of the following places:

1   The registered office
2   The place where the register of members is kept
3   The company's principal place of business, provided it is in the same part of the United Kingdom that the company is registered in

If the documents are not kept at the registered office, then notice of their location must be sent to the Registrar.

Publication of directors' names

S201 requires companies registered after 23 November 1916 to show on all 'trade catalogues, trade circulars, showcards and business letters on or in which the company's name appears and which are issued or sent by the company to any person in any part of Her Majesty's dominions' the names of the company's directors.

In addition to the present forename (or its initials) and surname, there must be given any former forenames and surnames and the nationality, if not British. For corporate directors, the corporate name must be given.

The Department of Trade is given the power to exempt companies from the requirements of s201. Application should be made to Insurance and Companies Department, Sanctuary Buildings, 20 Great Smith Street, London W1.

SECRETARY

Every company is required to have a secretary (s177(1)). There is only one 'secretary' but the office may be performed by more than one person (for example, by a firm of solicitors). The secretary may be any individual, firm or company; however the Act forbids a company that has a sole director having that director as secretary also (*s*177(1)). *S*178 imposes two further rules to ensure that there is a secretary who is not also the sole director:

1   No company shall have as secretary a corporation whose sole director is the sole director of the company
2   No company shall have as sole director, a corporation whose sole director is secretary to the company

Apart from certain duties at the beginning and end of a company's life, the Act imposes only one statutory duty on the secretary. That is (*ss*126(1), 127(1)(*a*), 128 and 129(1)(*b*)) to sign the annual return and documents that accompany it. These are required to be signed both by a director and the secretary and *s*179 provides that this requirement is not satisfied if the document is signed by one person who is both a director and the secretary.

The duties of secretary have been defined by custom rather than statute. In general the secretary is responsible for the administration of the company, including some or all of the many topics discussed in this book. The responsible nature of their work is emphasized by the existence of a professional institution, the Institute of Chartered Secretaries and Administrators, with high standards of membership.

The nature of the secretary's work implies that he is responsible for performing many of the jobs that the Act requires of companies and for which fines are possible for default. These include the maintenance of registers and allowing people to inspect them, keeping minutes of general meetings, sending copies of balance sheets, directors' reports and auditors' reports and following the rules about publishing the company's name and those of its directors.

Register of directors and secretaries

This is described on p.33. The details about secretaries that must be included are (if the secretary is an individual):

1   Present forename and surname
2   Any former forename and surname
3   Usual residential address

If the secretary is a corporation, the register must show the corporate name and the registered or principal office. If all the partners in a firm are joint secretaries, only the name and principal office of the firm need be entered.

AUDITORS

Every company must keep proper books of account with respect to:

1   All sums of money received and expended by the company and
    the matters in respect of which the transactions take place
2   All sales and purchases of goods by the company
3   The assets and liabilities of the company

Book are not 'proper' if they do not give a true and fair view of the state of the
company's affairs and explain its transactions (s147).

Every company must appoint an auditor or auditors (s159(1)) whose duties
are to examine the company's accounts and make a report on them and on every
balance sheet, profit and loss account and set of group accounts that is presented
to members (s14(1) of the 1967 Act). This report must be read to the company
in general meeting and must be available for inspection by any member (s14(2) of
the 1967 Act), it must also be sent to the Registrar with the annual return—see
next section (s127(1)(b)).

The auditors have a right of access to all books and may require the company's
officers to give them any information they think necessary for the performance
of their duties (s14(7) of the 1967 Act). They also have the right to attend any
general meeting and receive any notices or communications about it that
members are entitled to.

Who may be an auditor?

In general only the following individuals may act as auditors:

1   Members of:
    (a) Institute of Chartered Accountants in England and Wales
    (b) Association of Certified Accountants
    (c) Institute of Chartered Accountants in Scotland
    (d) Institute of Chartered Accountants in Ireland
2   Individuals whom the Department of Trade has certified as having
    qualifications similar to the people in category 1 or as having
    adequate knowledge and experience

Certain other people may be authorized by the Department to act as auditors of
a restricted set of companies, by s13(1) of the 1967 Act. The following may not
act as auditor of a company:

1   An officer or servant of the company
2   A person who is a partner or in the employment of an officer or
    servant of the company
3   A body corporate
4   A person who is disqualified from acting as auditor of the
    company's holding company or any of its subsidiaries (s161)

Removal of auditors

The term of office of an auditor is from the end of the general meeting at which he is appointed until the end of the next annual general meeting. He is then automatically reappointed unless:

1   He signifies in writing that he does not wish to be reappointed
2   He is disqualified from acting as auditor
3   The company passes a resolution (which requires special notice—see p.76) appointing someone else or providing that he shall not be reappointed (ss159 and 160)

If an annual general meeting fails to appoint or reappoint an auditor then the company must, within one week, notify the Department of Trade which has the power to appoint an auditor to fill the vacancy (s159(3) and (4)).

If there is a casual vacancy in the office of auditor, the directors may fill it (s159(6)).

Remuneration of auditors

Auditors' remuneration (which includes expenses) is fixed by those who appoint them—the directors, the company in general meeting or the Department of Trade, as the case may be.

ANNUAL RETURN

By requiring that every company sends once a year details of its affairs to the Registrar, the Companies Acts ensure that the general public has access to a great deal of information about the activities and management of companies.

The return must be made every calendar year within forty-two days of the annual general meeting (ss124 and 126(1)). A company does not have to make a return in the first year of its incorporation. If the second year of incorporation ends before the company has been incorporated for eighteen months, then it does not have to make a return in the second year.

Contents

The matters to be included in the annual return are set out in the Sixth Schedule to the Act. The form of the return must be as near as possible to that given in Part II of the Schedule,. The contents include:

1   A list of the company's membership on the fourteenth day after the annual general meeting. The list must give the names and

addresses of the members, the number of shares held (divided into classes) and the number of shares transferred by the member since the date of the last annual return with the date that the transfer was registered. A complete list is required only every third year. In the intervening two years only changes need be shown

2   A list of all persons who have ceased to be members since the date of the last annual return, giving the same details as in list 1
3   The address of the place where the register of members is kept
4   Details of the share capital of the company
5   Details of the company's indebtedness in the form of mortgages and charges
6   For all persons who, at the date of the return, are directors or secretaries of the company, the information that is required to be in the register of directors and secretaries

The annual return gives information about the membership, management and capitalization of the company. The documents that (by *s*127(1)) have to be attached to the report give details of the company's activities during the year. They are:

1   Certified copies of every balance sheet and profit and loss account (in the form prescribed by Schedule 2 to the 1967 Act) that has been laid before the company in general meeting since the last return
2   Certified copies of the auditors' reports on the balance sheets
3   Certified copies of the directors' reports that accompanied the balance sheets

The certification is done by a director and the secretary. Preparation of these documents is described in Chapter 5.

Private companies (*s*128)

In addition to the documents mentioned above, a private company must file with its annual return:

1   A certificate that it has not issued an invitation to the public to subscribe for its shares or debentures
2   If the number of its members exceeds fifty, a certificate that the excess consists wholly of persons who can be ignored by *s*28(1)(*b*)–see p.18

BORROWING BY COMPANIES

Every trading company, unless prohibited by its memorandum or articles, has implied power to borrow for the purpose of its business and to give security for the loan. The power is normally exercised by the directors. When lending to a company it is extremely important to check that the purpose for which the loan is made is not *ultra vires* the borrowing company because, with certain exceptions, such borrowing and any security given for it is void.

Securities for borrowing by companies

A company may give a fixed charge over its assets, usually its land.This means that the company cannot deal with the asset charged without the consent of the lender. This is the normal way by which a small private company would secure loans made to it. A company may also give a floating charge that is a general charge over the assets of the company or part of the assets of the company (for example, its stock-in-trade) present and future which does not attach to any particular asset until it crystallizes. This occurs when the company ceases to carry on business, when the company is wound up or when the security is enforceable and the debenture holders or trustees enforce it (see below). A floating charge has the great advantage from the company's point of view of enabling the company to continue to deal with its assets quite freely without the consent of the lender until crystallization.

Registration of charges

S104 provides that every limited company shall keep at its registered office a register of all charges specifically affecting the property of the company and all floating charges on the undertaking or property of the company. The register must give:

1   A short description of the property charged
2   The amount of the charge
3   The names of the persons entitled thereto except in the case of
      bearer securities

A fine of £50 can be imposed on any officer of the company knowingly and wilfully failing to comply.

 S103 provides that every company must keep a copy of all instruments creating a charge required to be registered at its registered office. The copies and the company's register are open to inspection of any creditor or member of the company without fee, and to other persons for a fee not exceeding 5p, for at least two hours a day during business hours.Penalties are provided for failing to comply (s105).

 S95 provides that particulars of charges created by companies together with the instrument if any, creating them, must be delivered to the Registrar within twenty-one days after their creation. The charges requiring registration are:

1   A charge to secure an issue of debentures
2   A charge on uncalled share capital
3   A charge created by an instrument which if executed by an individual would require registration as a bill of sale (these would cover charges over physical movable assets of the company)
4   A charge on any land or any interest therein
5   A charge on the book debts of the company
6   A floating charge on the undertaking or property of the company
7   A charge on calls made but not paid
8   A charge on a ship or any share in a ship
9   A charge on goodwill on a patent or a licence under a patent or a trade mark or on a copyright or a licence under a copyright

The company is primarily responsible for registration under s95 but registration may be effected by the lender and the registration fees recovered from the company. It is of *vital importance* that charges be registered as required by the Act. In addition to penalties provided by the Act for non-registration, s95 provides that the unregistered charge is void against the liquidator and any creditor of the company, thus reducing the secured creditor to the level of an ordinary creditor. The court has power to extend the time-limit for registration with certain limitations, principally if the omission to register was accidental and will not prejudice the creditors or shareholders of the company. If a company acquires any property on which a charge already exists, it must register that charge as if it had created the charge itself within twenty-one days after completing the acquisition.

Debentures

Strictly speaking, any document containing an acknowledgement of indebtedness by the company is a debenture. It is defined by s455 as including debenture stock bonds and any other securities of a company whether constituting a charge on the assets of the company or not. However, the word is usually used to describe a form of loan to a company giving the investor a security comparable with a share in the company in that it is for a specified sum and is freely transferable like a share. Debentures of this type are normally issued in a series and give a fixed charge over the company's fixed assets and a floating charge on the companies stock in trade and other assets. The security is given by means of a trust deed. The trust deed provides that the company will pay debenture holders the principal money and interest secured by the debenture and gives the trustees a legal mortgage over the company's land and a floating charge over the rest of the company's property. If the company breaks any of the covenants contained in the trust deed, the trustees are given power to take possession of the properties charged to them, appoint a receiver and take all steps which are necessary to protect the interests of the debenture holders.

A debenture holder is a person who has lent money to the company and he is accordingly not, like a shareholder, a member of the company. Moreover, a company can purchase its own debentures. Interest on debentures may be paid out of capital. A debenture is normally a safer form of investment than an equity share but does not of course carry the same prospect of capital gain because the debenture holder owns no portion of the equity capital of the company. Debentures may be payable either to the registered holder or to bearer. The registered holder is normally issued with a document under the seal of the company promising the debenture holder to pay the principal sum on a specified day and to pay interest in the meantime on specified dates. Registered debentures are normally transferable in a similar manner to shares.

UNLIMITED AND GUARANTEE COMPANIES

The two other forms of company mentioned at the beginning of the chapter are available for special purposes. Both types of company are subject to all the rules of the Companies Acts unless specifically exempted.

Unlimited companies

$S434(1)$ forbids the formation of unincorporated associations of more than twenty people to carry on business for gain. This ensures that large associations are subject to the rules about publication of information that apply to companies and forces them to establish an independent, fixed 'person' responsible for carrying out contracts, rather than a fluctuating and possible untraceable collection of people.

In some professions, it is considered necessary that practitioners should be liable to the full extent of their means if they make a mistake. The 1967 Act and statutory instruments therefore allow associations of any number of solicitors, accountants, patent agents, and estate agents and related professionals.

If other people wish to demonstrate their confidence in their abilities, they can do so by forming an unlimited company in which, as its name suggests, the liability of members is without limit. This liability, however, does not come into effect until the company is wound up, and it is the company that is initially attacked by creditors.

Because one can be slightly less wary about giving credit to unlimited companies, and because they rarely offer their shares to the public (stock exchanges will not grant quotations to shares in unlimited companies) they are exempted from the requirements of $s127$: that is, no details of their accounts are made public. The 1967 Act abolished the category of exempt private company (which the 1948 Act exempted from filing accounts) and expected that some companies in this category, wishing to retain privacy would want to convert themselves into unlimited companies: *s*43 of the 1967 Act therefore gives a procedure for re-registration as unlimited.

Name. Unlimited companies must not have the word 'limited' in their names.

Share capital. An unlimited company's members are the people it agrees to enter in its register. It can, if it wants working capital, issue shares—even (unlike any other type of company) shares of no par value (*s*2(4)(*a*)). Because the basis of an unlimited company's credit-worthiness is the wealth of its members rather than the size of its issued share capital, they are exempted from the provision of *s*66 (see p.26) and may reduce their share capital at will.

Guarantee companies

The guarantee company format is useful for charitable organizations where goodwill rather than working capital is required from members. The members of a company limited by guarantee agree to pay up to a fixed amount to satisfy the debts of the company when it is wound up. They are rather like the holders of totally unpaid shares, except that the company cannot make calls on them until it is being wound up.

Guarantee companies are usually formed for charitable objects and therefore apply not to include 'limited' in their names (see p.21).

A guarantee company may, if it needs to, have a share capital (with limited liability) but this is rare.

Guarantee companies are not exempt from any of the requirements for filing information.

3

Issue and Transfer of Shares

T Cartledge

This chapter will outline the work involved in maintaining the register of members of a company limited by shares.

This work includes:

1 Recording the required information about each member's shareholding
2 Issuing each member with a certificate of his holding
3 Amending the register when a member *transfers* some or all of his shares to someone else
4 Amending the register when a member's shares are *transmitted* by operation of law to someone else

As in Chapter 2, unless otherwise stated, all references to statutes are to the Companies Act 1948 and to Table *A* of that Act.

ISSUING SHARES

The memorandum of a company states the number of shares and their nominal value that the company can sell or *issue*. The first issue is to the subscribers of the memorandum who must each take at least one share: they become the company's first members—indeed they are members before their names are entered on the register.

At various stages in the company's life it will make further issues of shares so as to acquire capital for its operations.

Issue of shares at a premium or a discount

S56 provides that shares may be issued at a premium, that is, at a price which exceeds their nominal value, but a sum equal to the amount or value of the premiums must be transferred to the share premium account.

S57 provides that shares may be issued at a discount, that is, at a price below their nominal value, only if (1) the shares are of a class already issued (2) the issue is authorized by a resolution passed in general meeting and specifying the maximum rate (3) the company has been entitled to commence business for one year (4) the court's permission is obtained (5) the issue is made within one month after the court's permission is obtained unless the time is extended (6) any prospectus relating to the issue contains particulars of the discount.

Payment of commission for subscribing

A company can pay a commission to persons subscribing or procuring subscriptions for shares only within the terms of s53, that is if (a) the commission is authorized by the articles, (b) the commission does not exceed either (1) 10 percent of the price at which the shares were issued or (2) the rate authorized by the articles, whichever is less, (c) the rate is (1) disclosed in the prospectus or (2) disclosed in the statement in lieu of prospectus, and (d) the number of shares for which persons have agreed to subscribe for a commission is disclosed.

This commission is not a discount.

Provision of finance for purchase of shares

By s54, a company cannot provide the finance for a person to purchase or subscribe for shares in the company except in certain circumstances, the main one being where they are purchased in accordance with the terms of a pension fund.

Numbering of shares

By s74, each share must be numbered unless a resolution is passed to unnumber the issued shares of a class when they have all become fully paid and rank *pari passu*. Such a resolution can be passed by the directors unless the articles of association provide for the shares to be numbered; if so, the articles should be amended to allow the directors to pass a resolution to unnumber the shares. It is usual for the issued shares of a public company to be unnumbered and, if they have been admitted to the Official List, it is usual to apply to The Stock Exchange for the shares to be admitted as unnumbered.

SHARE CERTIFICATES AND SHARE WARRANTS

A member of a company is entitled to be issued with a share certificate which shows that he is the registered holder of the shares. A specimen share certificate is shown in Figure 3.1. S81 provides that a share certificate issued under the common seal of a company which specifies the shares held by a member shall be *prima facie* evidence of the member's title. The practice of signing share certificates in the case of public companies is now dying out as many companies have amended their articles of association in such a way as to permit signatures to be dispensed with and for the certificates to bear only the seal.

A company is estopped from denying that a certificate issued under seal is valid in respect of the holder's title and in respect of the amount paid on the shares. The remedy of the holder of a certificate is to sue the company for the value of the shares. He cannot compel the company to register him as a member if he is not entitled to the shares nor can the true owner be deprived of them. The right of estoppel does not apply in the following circumstances:

1   Where it is proved that the holder knows that the amount shown on the certificate as having been paid has not been paid
2   When the certificate itself is a forgery
3   Where the certificate has been issued fraudulently and without the authority of the company

Stock Exchange requirements

In the case of companies whose shares have been admitted to the Official List by The Stock Exchange, the following requirements must be complied with:

1 The maximum size of the certificate must not exceed 9 inches by 8 inches (22.5cm by 20cm)
2 The front of the certificate must show the following items:
   (*a*)The act or other document under whose authority the company is constituted.
   (*b*) The number of shares or the amount of stock (including the units) in the top right-hand corner.
   (*c*)A statement that no transfer of the shares or stock can be registered without production of the certificate.
   (*d*)Where appropriate, the minimum amount and multiples in which transfers may be made.
3 Loan stock. When the certificate is in respect of loan stock, it must state on the front the dates of the interest payments and also the conditions as to redemption and conversion.
4 Preference shares. The certificates relating to any preference shares, where there is more than one class of share issued, must contain the conditions in

relation to capital and dividends.

5 Transfer. The company must undertake to issue certificates without charge, within fourteen days of the lodgment of a transfer or one month of the expiration of any renunciation period.

Lost share certificate and request for duplicate certificate

When a shareholder loses his share certificate, it is usual for the company to insist on his signing a letter of indemnity indemnifying the company and this should be guaranteed by a bank or insurance company. In some cases, the company can accept the indemnity of an agent if it can be shown that the certificate was lost before it reached the shareholder but this should also be guaranteed. The duplicate certificate should be clearly marked 'Duplicate' and a note made on the share account of the loss of the original and the issue of the duplicate. Care should also be taken that no notice in lieu of distringas (see p.65) has been received in respect of the shares.

Share warrants

Share warrants may be issued by a public company limited by shares under its common seal only if it is authorized to do so by its articles and in respect of fully paid shares only. A specimen share warrant is shown in Figures 3.2 and 3.3. It states that the bearer of the warrant is entitled to the shares mentioned in it ($s83$). In the case of a share warrant, the shares may be transferred simply by delivery of the warrant to the transferee. The consent of the Treasury to the issue of share warrants is necessary under the Exchange Control regulations except when the warrants are to be issued to a resident of the Scheduled Territories. The stamp duty on a share warrant is 6 per cent on the market value of the shares at the date of issue of the warrant. When the articles authorize the issue of share warrants, they usually provide for the deposit of the share warrant with the company within a certain number of days before any right is exercised and for advertising notices of meetings.

When a company issues a share warrant, the name of the holder of the shares is struck out of the register in the same way as if he had ceased to be a member and the following entries are made in the register:

1 A note that the warrant has been issued
2 The number of shares in the warrant with the distinguishing number of the shares if the shares have numbers
3 The date the warrant is issued ($s112(1)$)

The articles may provide that the bearer of a share warrant may be deemed to be a member of the company either fully or to such an extent as is defined in the articles ($s112(5)$). If the articles so provide, a share warrant can be cancelled and the holder

Certificate number	Transfer/ allotment number	Date of certificate	Account number	Number of shares

Pangloss Limited

(Incorporated under the Companies Acts 1948 to 1967)

Ordinary Shares of Ten Pence each

THIS IS TO CERTIFY THAT the undermentioned is/are the registered holder(s) of

Millions	Hundred Thousands	Ten Thousands	Thousands	Hundreds	Tens	Units

Ordinary Shares of ten pence each fully paid in the above Company, subject to the memorandum and articles of association.

Name and address of first holder

Name(s) of joint holder(s)

GIVEN under the Common Seal of the Company

Exd. ....

No transfer of any of the above Shares will be registered without production of this Certificate.

Date	Transfer number	Number of shares	Transferee(s)

Figure 3.1(b)   Share certificate (Back)

PANGLOSS LIMITED

(Incorporated under the Companies Acts 1948 to 1967)

Warrant number   Share numbers

0001   001-10

SHARE WARRANT TO BEARER

for 10 shares of £1 each

THIS IS TO CERTIFY that the bearer of this warrant is the proprietor of

TEN

fully paid shares (numbered as above) in the capital of PANGLOSS LIMITED subject to the memorandum and articles of association of the Company and to the conditions endorsed hereon

Given under the common seal of the company this

day of   19

Director

Secretary

PANGLOSS LIMITED

Share warrant number 0001

| Talon for fresh supply of coupons for share warrant to bearer representing 10 shares | The bearer of the above warrant will receive in exchange for this talon a fresh supply of coupons when those below have all fallen due |

Secretary

No 12 10 shares	No 9 10 shares	No 6 10 shares	No 3 10 shares
No 11 10 shares	No 8 10 shares	No 5 10 shares	No 2 10 shares
No 10 10 shares	No 7 10 shares	No 4 10 shares	No 1 10 shares

Figure 3.2 Share warrant

The form of a coupon is given in Figure 3.3

is entitled to be entered on the register ($s112(2)$). The same provisions apply to stock warrants to bearer.

In the case of the issue of share warrants, it is necessary to show on the Annual Return filed by the company each year at the Companies Registry the following:

1   The total amount of shares for which share warrants are

outstanding at the date of the Return
2   The total amount of share warrants issued and surrendered since the
     last Return
3   The number of shares comprised in each warrant

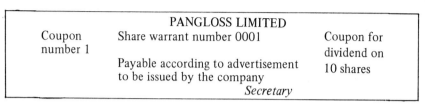

> **PANGLOSS LIMITED**
> Coupon   Share warrant number 0001   Coupon for
> number 1   dividend on
>   Payable according to advertisement 10 shares
>   to be issued by the company
>   *Secretary*

Figure 3.3 Dividend coupon from a share warrant

The following are the differences between a share warrant and a share certificate.

1   A warrant is a negotiable instrument
2   The shares are transferable by delivery of the warrants
3   The warrant bearer is not entered in the register
4   The warrant bearer is entitled to the shares specified in the warrant
5   Dividend coupons are attached to a warrant. Dividends are paid on
     production of the appropriate coupon after the dividend has been
     advertised. The company does not know to whom dividends are to
     be sent
6   The holding of a share warrant does not count as a director's share
     qualification when one is required

APPLICATION AND ALLOTMENT

Shares in a private company can be allotted by the directors as soon as the company
has been incorporated. Usually, persons wishing to subscribe for shares in a private
company apply to the directors for the allotment and enclose remittances for the
subscription monies. The directors then allot the shares formally, send the share
certificates to the applicants and file the return of allotments (form PUC2) at the
Companies Registry. Capital duty at the rate of £1 per £100 or part of £100 on the
actual value of issued share capital is payable except in the case of a capitalization
issue (see next section). Note that, in the case of many private companies, the
directors are the members and, therefore, the allotment of shares is completed
without the formality of application forms.

Public companies

Where shares in a public company are to be allotted, the procedure is more complicated and much more formal. In the majority of cases, the public are invited by means of an offer for sale to apply for the allotment of shares in a public company. The procedure is as follows:

1 Application form. The applicant completes the form of application and sends it with a cheque for the amount payable to the address specified in the form. This may be the company itself, or in the majority of cases, the bank that is undertaking the issue on behalf of the company. The form should arrive before the date and time specified. Care should be taken to sign the form and to complete every detail in full. If the applicant cannot make the declaration about residence in the Scheduled Territories required by the current Exchange Control regulations, the form should be lodged by an Authorized Depositary. The Scheduled Territories and Authorized Depositaries are defined in the Notices issued by the Bank of England and it is important that these Notices be complied with.

2 Allotment. When the subscription lists are closed, the company proceeds to allot the shares. In many issues, the subscription lists are closed very shortly after the time fixed for the opening and the offer is oversubscribed, that is applications are received in respect of more shares than have been offered for sale. In such cases, the company and its advisers decide on the basis of allotment. It should be noted that the cheques received with the application forms are banked immediately.

3 Informing applicants. When the basis of allotment has been decided, the allotment list is prepared from the details inserted on the application forms, and the allotment letters are prepared and posted to the successful applicants. At the same time, letters of regret are sent to the unsuccessful applicants and to successful applicants who have received a smaller allotment than they had applied for. The letters of regret are accompanied by cheques in respect of the return of all or part of the subscription monies.

4 Transfer. Shares offered for sale to the public can be bought and sold and the allotment letters will contain instructions for renunciation and registration in names other than the original allottee. These procedures are available for six weeks after the date of the allotment letter and no *ad valorem* stamp duty on the transfer of the shares is payable during that time.

5 Registration. When the period of six weeks has expired, the company will register the shares allotted in the names of the original allottees or, in the case of renunciation by the original allottees, in the names of the persons applying to be registered in respect of these shares. Share certificates are prepared, sealed and dispatched to the persons entitled to them. The return of allotments (form PUC2) is also prepared, signed and filed at the Companies Registry. This return consists of a list of original allottees and, in the case of renunciation by the original allottees, the persons applying to be registered in respect of these shares.

6 Revocation. An allotment of shares which have been paid up in full cannot be revoked unless the allotment has been induced by fraud. Where shares have been allotted subject to payment in instalments, the allotment can be revoked when

any instalment is in arrear.

CAPITALIZATION ISSUES

Article 128 of Table *A* provides that the members of a company can, by resolution passed at a general meeting, resolve to capitalize the whole or any part of its reserves and to apply the amount capitalized in paying up in full shares in the company and issuing them to the existing members in the proportion specified in the resolution. The articles of a company usually contain a specific clause authorizing the capitalization of reserves. This is known as a capitalization issue. The term 'bonus' issue is loosely used to describe the issue but this is a misnomer. In the case of a public company, it is usual for a formal agreement to be entered into between the company and one of the directors or secretary (on behalf of the members) for the formal allotment of the shares in the terms of the resolution. Where the issue involves fractions of a share, the agreement usually contains a provision for the sale of the new shares representing the aggregate of the fractions and the distribution of the net proceeds of sale to the members whose original holdings gave rise to fractions of a new share.

The procedure involved in the capitalization issue is as follows:

1 A list of members with their holdings is prepared as at the date specified (the record date)

2 Renounceable share certificates addressed to members are then prepared and dispatched to them. It is important to ensure that the shares comprised in the certificates are in the correct proportion as specified in the resolution for capitalization and that the number of shares does not exceed the total authorized by the resolution to be issued. The modern practice is to issue renounceable share certificates rather than allotment letters. After the last date for renunciation, the certificates become definitive and the members who have not renounced their shares are registered in respect of their shares

3 It is also usual to send out with the share certificate, the warrants for the payment of the net proceeds of sale of the new shares arising from fractions

4 Members may renounce their allotment of new shares during a period of six weeks from the date of allotment. At the expiration of the period of renunciation, the new shares are registered in the names of those members who have not renounced their shares and those persons who have applied to be registered in respect of the shares renounced (renouncees). Definitive share certificates are prepared for the renouncees and are sent to them or their agents

5 A return of allotments (form PUC7) comprising a list of the

original allottees who did not renounce and the renouncees, with details of the shares allotted, is prepared and filed at the Companies Registry

RIGHTS ISSUES

When a company wishes to raise capital for the purposes of its business, it may make what is known as a 'rights' issue. This involves the issue of shares to existing members at an advantageous price; usually below the current price at which the shares are dealt in on The Stock Exchange. Unless the issue involves an increase in the nominal capital of the company (in which case an extraordinary general meeting must be convened), a resolution of the directors will suffice to make the issue. The resolution should specify the following:

1   The class and number of shares to be issued
2   The proportion in which the shares are to be issued to existing members and the price at which they are to be issued
3   The qualifying or record date for the allotment
4   A formal provisional allotment of the shares
5   The time and date by which payment for the shares must be made in order that the provisional allotment may become definitive
6   The method of disposal of any shares not paid for. One method is for existing members to be given the right to apply for an allotment of shares not paid up and, for this purpose, a form of application for excess shares is sent to each member with the provisional allotment letter for their own entitlement of shares. A second method, which is beoming more common, is to sell the shares on which the 'calls' have not been paid and to distribute the net proceeds of sale, less the subscription monies, to the members who have not taken up their 'rights' in proportion to the shares provisionally allotted to them

If the company making the 'rights' issue is a public company, it is necessary to send a circular letter to members at the same time as the provisional allotment letter which will set out the terms of the issue, explain its purpose and the procedures to be followed in connection with renunciation, 'splitting' and registration of the shares comprised in the provisional allotment letter.

Provisional allotment

On the date fixed for members to qualify for the allotment of shares, the list of provisional allotments of shares is prepared and the total agreed.

A record sheet is prepared for each member on which are completed details of the existing holding, the number of shares provisionally allotted, and the amount to be paid on them. Further spaces are provided for recording the number of shares paid up and the amount paid thereon.

The provisional allotment letters are prepared, checked, the totals agreed and, on the date fixed, are posted to members. In 'rights' issues, it is usual to issue provisional allotment letters rather than renounceable share certificates.

Receipt of applications

When the cheques are received from members, they should be accompanied by the entire allotment letter. Details of the payment are recorded on the allotment sheets and the individual record sheets. If the cheques are in order, the payment slip is completed, detached from the allotment letter, filed, the allotment letter marked as fully paid and returned to the member or his agent who lodged the same for payment. Care should be taken to see that the payment slip is endorsed with the details of the source of payment, that is either the member or the agent, and that the number of the allotment letter is endorsed on the back of the cheque.

The remittances received should be totalled each day, agreed with the amounts shown on the payment slips for the day and paid into the bank daily.

The terms of the issue will specify whether payment should be made in instalments or in a single payment.

Renunciation and 'splitting nil paid'

The shares provisionally allotted can be sold on the market before payment is made. The provisional allotment can be renounced and application can be made to the company for 'split' allotment letters in the amounts specified which can then be delivered to the buyers. The original allotment letter duly renounced will still have the payment slip attached to it showing that the shares are 'nil paid'. Care should, therefore, be taken to ensure that the payment counterfoils are *not* detached from the 'split' allotment letters as eventually these will be sent in for payment and the counterfoils detached at that stage. Care should also be taken to see that the correct details are inserted on the individual record sheets as to the 'splitting nil paid'.

Final payment

When the date for final payment has passed, the total number of shares paid up is agreed with the total cash received and the number of shares not paid up established. These latter shares are allotted to those members who have applied for them, if the terms of the issue so provide, or they are sold on the market. The net proceeds of the sale, less the subscription money, are distributed to the members who did not take up their 'rights' in proportion to their provisional allotment. The provisional allotment to them is cancelled.

Renunciation and 'splitting' of fully paid shares

Shares which have been paid up can be renounced and 'split' allotment letters issued. Care should be taken to remove the payment counterfoils from the 'split' allotment letters issued in respect of shares which have been paid up.

The shares paid up can be renounced and transferred without a transfer deed and free of stamp duty for six weeks from the date of the allotment of the shares and the person to whom the shares are transferred will apply for registration of the shares into his or her name by completing the application form on the allotment letter. This is usually carried out by the stockbroker or bank involved and the declaration as to residence within the Scheduled Territories required by the Exchange Control Act 1947 should be signed. If the declaration cannot be completed, then the form must be lodged for registration by an Authorized Depositary, the main ones being defined in the Exchange Control regulations as stockbrokers, banks and solicitors.

When a renounced allotment letter is received with a request for 'split' allotment letters, the record sheet in the name of the allottee should be cancelled and removed from the files. A separate record sheet should be raised for each 'split' allotment letter and filed. Care should be taken to ensure that the 'split' allotment letters and record sheets are issued in the name of the original allottee and that the totals of the letters and sheets do not exceed the number of shares comprised in the cancelled allotment letter and record sheet.

When an application form is received for registration of the shares in a name other than the original allottee, then the appropriate record sheet should be removed from the file of original allottees' record sheets or the file of 'split' record sheets and endorsed with the name of the applicant for registration and placed in a separate file. It will thus be apparent that the total of the record sheets remaining in (*a*) the original allottees' file (*b*) the 'split' file (shares remaining in the original allottees' names being part of the original allotment) and (*c*) the registration application form file will equal the total number of shares originally allotted in respect of the 'rights' issue.

When the total number of shares has been reconciled as detailed in the paragraph above, the share accounts in the register of members are posted from the information contained in the record sheets in (*a*) the original allottees' file and (*b*) the 'splits' file and (*c*) on the registration application forms. The definitive share certificates are prepared at the same time and, when they have been sealed, they are dispatched to the members entitled thereto or to their agents.

The return of allotments (form PUC2) is then prepared from the above-mentioned information and is filed at the Companies Registry.

TRANSFER AND TRANSMISSION OF SHARES

Shares in a company are transferable in accordance with the provisions of the articles of association of the company and are personal estate—s73. A transfer is initiated by the act of the member; the death or the bankruptcy of a member gives rise to a transmission. When the probate or letters of administration (in the case of death) or the appointment of the trustee (in the case of bankruptcy) have been registered with the company, the company recognizes the authority of the executors, administrators or trustees to transfer the shares.

S75 forbids a company to register a transfer of shares or debentures unless a duly executed transfer is delivered to the company or the right to the shares is transmitted by operation of law.

Table *A* states that a transfer of shares shall be executed by, or on behalf of the transferor and the transferee. The transfer must be in writing in common form. The transferor remains the holder of the share until the name of the transferee is entered on the register in respect of the share.

Stock Transfer Act 1963

The Stock Transfer Act 1963 amended the provisions of Table *A*. By this Act, the necessity for the signature of the transferee was abolished together with the witnessing of the signature of the transferor. In the case of a transferor which is a corporate body, the transfer must be executed under the common seal.

The Stock Transfer Act introduced two new forms of transfer, namely, the stock transfer form and the broker's transfer form. The stock transfer form can be used for both Stock Exchange transactions and non-Stock Exchange transactions. In the case of the latter, a separate stock transfer form is required where the transferor is transferring his holding into separate amounts and to different transferees. The broker's transfer form can only be used for Stock Exchange transactions where more than one buyer is involved. The seller signs only one stock transfer form covering the total number of shares involved in the sale and it is not necessary to wait for this to be signed until the buyer's name is known. The stock transfer form can be sent to the seller with the contract note for the sale. The present transfer system has the following main advantages over the previous system:

1   Only one transfer has to be signed for the entire sale and separate broker's transfer forms (which do not require signature) are prepared for each buyer
2   The names of transferees are not completed on the transfers when they are presented for certification (see overleaf)
3   The transfer forms show the names and addresses of the brokers or other agents
4   Stamp duty is impressed on either the stock transfer form (when

that form is used on its own) or on the brokers transfer forms where these are used with a stock transfer form

CERTIFICATION

*S*79 defines the effect of certification in law. When a company certifies a transfer, it shall be taken as a representation to any person acting on the faith of the certification that such documents have been produced to the company as show, on the face of them, that the transferor has a title to the shares but it gives no representation that the transferor has a title. When a company is negligent and makes a false certification, the company is under the same liability to any person who acts on the faith of it as if the certification had been made fraudulently. A transfer is deemed to be certified if it contains the words 'certificate lodged' or similar words and these are signed or initialled by the person authorized by the company to certify transfers.

Certification of a transfer arises in the following circumstances:

1. Where delivery of the shares to several buyers is required
2. Where the document of title in respect of the shares is a temporary one such as a transfer receipt or balance ticket. A balance ticket is a temporary document of title issued where the seller is retaining part of the holding, and it has no legal validity
3. When part of the holding is being transferred thus involving the issue of a balance ticket or balance certificate
4. When it is necessary to verify the title of the seller, this not being shown by the share certificate, for example, when the transfer has been executed by an attorney on behalf of the seller or when the transfer has been signed by executors or administrators and the certificate does not bear the details of the death and probate

It is usual for brokers to have transfers certified by the Stock Exchange (acting as agents for the company) in the cases of numbers (1) and (3) above; in the cases of numbers (2) and (4) above, it is necessary for the company to certify transfers.

The types of certification and the procedures to be followed are as follows:

Stock transfer form certified by The Stock Exchange

The front of the transfer is stamped by The Stock Exchange and the certificate and the certification advice form are sent to the company. The advice gives details of the amounts of shares and number of stock transfer forms certified and shows the total amount of shares comprised in the certificates against which the forms are certified. It also gives details of any balance certificate required and to whom it is to be sent.

Stock transfer form certified by a company

The stock transfer form must be checked carefully and compared with the certificate. The appropriate box must be stamped with the selling broker's stamp. The company should note the number of shares in each form certified, record any balance, prepare a balance ticket or balance certificate and stamp the transfer form with its certifications stamp.

Stock transfer form certified with accompanying broker's transfer forms by The Stock Exchange

The back of the stock transfer form is stamped by The Stock Exchange and the boxes on the front of the broker's transfer forms are also stamped. The stock transfer form with the certificates are sent to the company and the broker's transfer forms are returned to the selling brokers. The number of shares specified in each broker's transfer form is shown on the back of the stock transfer form together with the details of any balance. When the stock transfer form is received by the company, it is checked for execution in the correct name and number of shares against the certificate and that the selling broker's stamp and date appears in the relevant box. The lower part of the form should also be marked as cancelled. The back of the stock transfer form is also checked to ensure that the total number of shares does not exceed the number of shares specified in the certificate. In this case, the stock transfer form does not show any consideration nor is it stamped.

Stock transfer form certified with accompanying broker's transfer forms by a company

The procedure for this is the same as in the preceding case but the company must also check the broker's transfer forms against the stock transfer form for correct transferor and execution details and correct broker's stamping and dating. If appropriate, a balance ticket is prepared and the broker's transfer forms stamped with the certification stamp.

REGISTRATION OF TRANSFERS

The following points should be considered when a transfer is received for registration by a company. It should be borne in mind that some points will not apply to transfers received for registration by a company that is not a public company:

Share certificate. The share certificate in the name of the transferor should accompany the transfer or the transfer should be a certified form.

Correct details.   The name of the company, the description of the shares and the number of shares in words and figures should all be correctly completed. The details of the transferor on the transfer and on the share certificate should agree.

Execution by transferor.   The transfer should be executed by the transferor. If the transfer has been executed by an attorney, the registration of the power of attorney should be verified. If the transferor is a corporation, the transfer should be executed under the common seal.

Selling broker's stamp.   The date and the stamp of the selling broker should appear on the transfer.

Consideration.   The consideration should be in line with the market price of the shares.

Stamp duty.   The transfer should be stamped with the appropriate stamp duty. By the Stamp Act 1891, all transfers must be correctly stamped and there are penalties for registering transfers which are not correctly stamped. The present *ad valorem* stamp duty is £1 per £50. If the transfer bears the fixed duty of £0.50 this denotes that the transaction falls within the categories set out on the reverse of the deed. Where this is so, the appropriate certificate is completed and signed and the Stamp Duty Office will mark the transfer 'Passed for £0.50'. In the case of any doubt whether a transfer is correctly stamped, the company can insist that the transfer be adjudicated by the Inland Revenue.

Under the provisions of the Finance Act 1976, Stamp duty has been abolished on transfers on and after 17th May 1976 of certain loan capital subject to the following conditions:

The loan capital must not, at the time when it is transferred,

1   carry a right (whether exercisable then or later) of conversion into shares of other securities or to the acquisition of shares or other securities, including loan capital of the same description;

or

2   If at the time is transferred or earlier it carries or has carried
    (a)   a right to interest the amount of which exceeds a reasonable commercial return on the nominal amount of the capital, or
    (b)   a right on repayment to an amount which exceeds the nominal amount of the capital and is not reasonably comparable with what is generally repayable under the terms of issue of loan capital listed in the Official List of The Stock Exchange.

In case of doubt about the eligibility of exemption of any transfer, adjudication should be requested.

Transferee's details.   The details of the transferee must be correctly completed.

Buying broker's stamp.   The stamp of the buying broker and the lodging agent (if this is not the same as the buying broker) must appear on the deed.

Amendments.   Any amendments appearing on the transfer must be initialled. If the details of the transferee's name have been amended, the lodging agent should be asked for an explanation and to certify that there has been no sub-sale.

Exchange Control. The Exchange Control regulations should be complied with. A transfer must be lodged for registration by an Authorized Depositary unless it is a transfer by an executor or administrator to a person entitled under a will or intestacy in the course of distribution of a deceased's estate when lodgment by an Authorized Depositary is not necessary. The main Authorized Depositaries are stockbrokers, banks and solicitors practising in the United Kingdom. If the transfer is not lodged by an Authorized Depositary, declarations of residence of both the transferor and transferee signed by an Authorized Depositary must accompany the transfer.

A non-returnable transfer receipt is sent to the lodging agent when the transfer has been checked. If, however, the share certificate is to be issued within a few days, it is not necessary to issue a transfer receipt.

The register of members must be checked against the certificates before registration or certification of transfers in order to ascertain that there is no restraint on transfer or that no duplicate certificate has been issued.

A further point to bear in mind when checking a broker's transfer form is that the appropriate stock transfer form has been received.

Change of address

It may be found that the shareholder has additional forenames to those shown in the register of members or on the share certificate. Such a situation often arises when a change of address is received. In such a case, confirmation should be requested that the person is one and the same. The additional names should then be entered on the register and the share certificate duly endorsed.

When a shareholder advises the company of his change of address, the appropriate amendment should be made on the share account. Such notification should be in writing and should be signed by the member. If it is signed by an attorney and the power of attorney has not been registered with the company, the power should be requested. Where the change of address is lodged by a bank, stockbroker, solicitor or other agent, it can be accepted without being signed by the shareholder.

DEATH OF A SHAREHOLDER

In the case of death of a shareholder, the executor or administrator becomes the person who is entitled to deal with the shares but it is essential that the probate or letters of administration should be registered with the company before the shares can be dealt with by the executor or administrator. It is usual for the articles of association of a company either to set out in full or incorporate the provisions of Table *A* and to allow the executors or administrators to be registered in their own names without reference to their capacity as executors or administrators. Such request is in writing, signed by the executors or administrators, is not required to be stamped, is regarded for all purposes as a transfer and can be lodged for registration by the executor or administrator even though he may not be an Authorized Depositary. The shares are posted out of the deceased's account and into a new account in the names of the executors or administrators. It is not necessary for executors or administrators to be registered in their own names; they can transfer the shares by signing in their representative capacity or the shares can remain in the deceased's name with the share account and certificates being endorsed with their names.

Where shares are registered in the joint names of two or more persons, on the death of one of the joint holders, the title to the shares is vested in the remaining holders. The death certificate of a deceased joint holder should be produced and registered in such a case.

Probates

When a member dies leaving a will and having appointed an executor or executors, the Probate Registry issues a grant of probate to the executors (or the surviving executors). The grant of probate constitutes the right of the executors to act under the will appointing them.

In Scotland the equivalent grant is called a Grant of Confirmation and is issued under the seal of the sheriff court and is signed by the sheriff clerk or the deputy sheriff clerk. The term 'Executors Nominate' is used to describe the persons named in the will who are to administer the estate.

It is no longer necessary to reseal Scottish and Northern Ireland grants in England.

A separate English grant must be taken out in the case of Eire, Channel Islands, Isle of Man and any foreign grant.

An important point to consider here is the situation which arises when a sole or surviving executor dies without having completed the administration of the estate leaving his estate to be administered by *his* executor. In such a case, the grant of probate to the deceased executor's executor authorizes him to continue the administration of the estate of the original deceased. The company will register the grant of probate to the executor's executor and by this will recognize his right to deal with the shares of the original deceased. This is called the Chain of Representation and passes only from executor to executor; it does not pass from an executor to an administrator appointed under letters of administration nor from an administrator to an executor.

The grant is stamped by the company as having been registered, the share certificates are endorsed with details of the executors and these documents are returned to the person lodging them for registration. The deceased's share account is endorsed with details of the grant and of the executors and the same details are recorded in the appropriate section of the documents register. If the name of the deceased on the grant differs from that on the register, confirmation should be obtained that they are one and the same person.

Letters of administration

Where a shareholder dies and leaves no will or does not appoint executors in his will, the Probate Registry issues a document called Letters of Administration which appoints a person to administer the estate. The Scottish grant is called a Grant of Confirmation but the administrators are called executors dative.

If a sole surviving executor dies without naming an executor in his will and has not completed the administration of the estate or if a sole surviving administrator dies without completing his administration, the grant is called Letters of Administration *de bonis non,* and this will enable the administration of the original estate to be completed.

The following grants are made in special circumstances and the grant will specify any limitation to the authority:

1   Administration *pendente lite* which is granted when there is any litigation relating to the deceased's estate or will
2   Administration *durante absentia* which is granted when the person who is entitled to the grant is absent abroad
3   Administration *cum testamento annexo* which is granted where the deceased has left a will but no executor has been appointed or the executor appointed is unable or unwilling to act
4   Administration *durante minor aetate* which is granted where the person who is entitled to the grant is a minor
5   Administration *ad litem* which is granted for the purpose of litigation only

The same procedure for registration of letters of administration is followed as for registration of probates. The letters of administration are endorsed with the details of the registration, the names of the administrators and the details of the grant are entered on the share account and the share certificates are endorsed.

Death certificate

When a company has agreed to register a death certificate as proof of death in cases where the estate of a deceased person is small (less than £500) and no grant has been obtained, the following items should also be obtained:

1   An indemnity from the legal representatives indemnifying the company against liability
2   A statutory declaration that the person swearing it is eligible to deal with the estate
3   A letter from the Inland Revenue that no Capital Transfer Tax is payable. This can be dispensed with where hardship would be caused in obtaining the latter, but at the Company's discretion.

The details of the death certificate should be recorded on the share account, the share certificate endorsed and the certificate marked as registered.

A death certificate is usually recorded on the death of one of a group of joint holders and is satisfactory evidence of the death.

REGISTRATION OF MISCELLANEOUS DOCUMENTS

It is usual to record all documents received for registration in a register in which the details are posted. Registration of the documents connected with the death of a shareholder was described in the previous section.

Appointment of liquidator

In the case of the liquidation of a company which has a shareholding in another company, the resolution for the appointment of the liquidator or the notice in the *London Gazette* should be requested and a note made on the share account. The liquidator executes a transfer under the seal of the company.

Powers of attorney

By this document, a person appoints another person or persons (jointly or alone) or a corporate body to act in his or her affairs. The following points should be borne in mind before registering:

1   The attorney must be acting within the powers granted to him
2   The document should be stamped with the duty of £0.50
3   The document should be signed and witnessed. If signed by a 'mark' this should be attested by a solicitor or doctor with an explanation of the circumstances

4   Where the power of attorney has been signed and sealed by the direction of, and in the presence of, the person granting the power two other persons must be present as witnesses, and must attest the document (s1(1) and 1(2) of the Powers of Attorney Act 1971)

5   A photocopy of a power of attorney, certified by the donor or by a solicitor or stockbroker, is sufficient proof of the existence and contents of the power (s3 of the Powers of Attorney Act 1971)

6   s5(2) of the Powers of Attorney Act 1971 provides that where a power has been revoked and a person, without knowledge of the revocation, deals with the donee, the transaction between them shall, in favour of that person, be as valid as if the power had been in existence. Accordingly, where an officer of a company registering the document accepts the same and allows the attorney to deal with the shareholding he is protected, even though the power has been revoked, provided he has no knowledge of the revocation

7   The document should be stamped with the usual registration details, a copy should be kept in order that the extent of the powers may be referred to and a note should be made on the share account

The filing of powers of attorney and copies of powers of attorney in the Central Office of the Supreme Court and the Land Registry is abolished (s2(1) of the Powers of Attorney Act 1971).

Marriage certificate and deed poll

These two items are dealt with together as they are both evidence of a change of name of a shareholder. In the case of a marriage certificate, this is evidence of a change of name of a woman on marriage. In the case of a deed poll, this shows the old and the new name by which a shareholder wishes to be known. The relevant details should be entered on the share account, the share certificate endorsed and the document marked with the registration details.

If the shareholder objects (as some often do) to her marriage certificate being endorsed with the company's registration stamp, it is suggested that a photocopy be taken which can then be endorsed with the stamp and returned to the shareholder with the certificate and this will provide evidence for the future that it has been registered. A photocopy of a marriage certificate may be accepted for registration if lodged by an Authorized Depositary or some other reputable person or firm and certified to be a true copy.

Notice in lieu of distringas

This is a notice served on a company restraining it from transferring any shares in a holding to which the notice refers. The notice is issued by the High Court when the necessary documents have been filed by a third party showing he has an interest in the particular shareholding. When the office copy of the notice has been registered on the particular share account, any transfer of the whole or any part of the holding must not be registered. The company sends a 'warning off' letter to the person who lodged the notice and to the person on whose behalf it was lodged informing them of the transfer. These persons are then allowed eight days in which to obtain an injunction. If an injunction is not issued and received by the company within the time limit, the transfer can proceed.

Injunction or restraining order

This order (which Scottish companies will not accept) is made by the Chancery Division of the High Court and is issued when a 'warning off' letter has been issued. The order prohibits the transfer of the shareholding until the trial of an action to decide the ownership of the holding. No transfer of the shares can be permitted until the order is cancelled or a subsequent order is made, such as a Vesting Order.

Vesting order

The Chancery Division of the High Court makes a vesting order to remove a person from the Register of Members. It is generally made after an injunction or where it is desired to remove the names of untraceable or unwilling trustees. The order should specify the details of the holding and it authorizes the company to register the transfer.

Bankruptcy order

This order is made by the Bankruptcy Court and appoints a receiver to deal with the affairs of a member who has been declared bankrupt. Sufficient evidence is supplied by the notice in the *London Gazette*. The order should be endorsed with details of the registration, the share certificate endorsed and the details entered on the share account.

Protection order

The Court of Protection makes a protection order which appoints a trustee or receiver to administer the affairs of a shareholder who is senile or whose mental capacity is impaired. A point to bear in mind is that the receiver cannot perform any act unless the order gives him authority to do so. A further protection order must be issued if the receiver wishes to deal with the shareholding in any way not authorized by the original order. A copy of any protection order must be retained to enable the company to know the exact powers granted to the receiver. The details are entered on the share account and the order is endorsed with the registration details. However, no details should be entered on the share certificate.

FURTHER READING

T E Cain (ed) *Charlesworth's Company Law,* Stevens, London, tenth edition, 1972

Share Registration Practice, London and Birmingham Registrars Groups of the Institute of Chartered Secretaries and Administrators, Editype, Brighton, tenth edition, 1968.

The Chartered Secretaries Manual of Company Secretarial Practice, Jordans, London, seventh edition revised, 1975.

4

Conduct of Meetings

T F Cox

In small private companies, it is often possible and usually quite sensible to minimize the formality connected with company meetings, but in larger companies—especially those under the constant surveillance of the financial press, the Stock Exchange or a shareholders' 'ginger' group—it is important that the procedures are carried out absolutely correctly, if only from the public relations point of view. More important, however, is the fact that under the Companies Acts precise provisions regarding meetings have been made for the protection of individual rights and for the benefit of all concerned, and it is obviously the duty of the officers or servants of a company responsible for meetings to see that the rules are carefully observed in the interest of the company, its directors and its shareholders. Meetings have often been set aside by the courts merely because of failure to comply with a particular provision of the Companies Acts or with a regulation contained in the articles of association of a company. Such an invalidation would without doubt cause considerable embarrassment to the employee or executive concerned and, of course, much preparatory work carried out prior to the abortive meeting may have to be repeated.

This chapter will refer mainly to companies limited by shares; it is designed to guide readers through the provisions of the Companies Act 1948, the Companies Act 1967 and Table *A* in the First Schedule to the Companies Act 1948 (these three items are hereinafter respectively referred to as the Act, the 1967 Act and Table *A*). Table *A* sets out regulations (articles of association) for companies limited by shares if incorporated after 1 July 1948. (Articles of association for companies incorporated before 1 July 1948 are set out in the Table *A* of the

Companies Act in force when the company was incorporated.) Part I of Table *A* relates to non-private companies (referred to in this chapter as public companies) and Part II of Table *A* to private companies although it will be seen from the first clause of Table *A* Part II that all the provisions of Part I with two exceptions apply also to private companies. Unless otherwise mentioned, references to Table *A* refer to Part I of Table *A*. Table *A* Part I or II may be modified or excluded altogether by any other articles of association which a company may have adopted and registered with the Registrar of Companies and consequently a company's own articles of association should always be consulted in the first instance. The Act also makes provisions for companies limited by guarantee and unlimited companies but such companies will be ignored for the main purpose of this chapter except in meetings of unlimited and guarantee companies, below. The chapter will not concern itself with chartered or statutory companies since such companies are rare and the regulations governing the meetings will in the main be found or referred to in the charter or statute concerned.

For ease of reading, the numerous decided cases upon which so much of the law of meetings is based and the many references to the Companies Acts are not quoted in the body of this chapter. Decided cases are covered in each of the first three books listed for further reading at the end of the chapter; references to the Acts are placed together under headings. As the material under each heading is a summary of the law the actual references in the Acts should be consulted for the precise requirements.

SHAREHOLDERS' MEETINGS

Statutory meeting (ss42(1), 130, 222(b), 224(1)(b) and 225(3)(a) and (b) of the Act)

The purpose of the statutory meeting is to give shareholders an early opportunity to satisfy themselves that the company has been properly established and that their funds have been correctly utilized. Only companies incorporated as public companies are required to hold statutory meetings within a period of not less than one month nor more than three months from the date at which the company concerned was entitled to commence business. Even if it is the intention that a new company should be a public company, it is usual for it to be incorporated as a private company in the first instance and later, or even immediately, it is converted to a public company, thereby avoiding the need for a statutory meeting. The holding of a statutory meeting is in fact a comparatively unusual occurrence and no more than about ten are held in the whole of the United Kingdom in any one year, as the annual report of the Registrar of Companies will verify.

Annual general meeting (ss126, 131, 140, 148, 153(2), 159 and 185(2) of the Act, s29(11) of 1967 Act and clause 52 of Table A)

A shareholders' meeting specifically described as the annual general meeting in the notice calling the meeting must be held by every company to give its shareholders the opportunity to review the progress and the management of the company and to deal with any other matters for which proper notice has been given. An annual general meeting must be held in each calendar year (except in the year of incorporation and the subsequent year provided the first annual general meeting is held within eighteen months of incorporation) and not more than fifteen months must elapse between one annual general meeting and the next. In practice it is always advisable for the annual general meeting to be held about the same time in each year and for a twelve-monthly pattern of procedure to be established quickly, rather than to take advantage of the permitted period of fifteen months between meetings. It only requires three or four annual general meetings, with fourteen or fifteen-month intervals between them, before it will be found that the flexibility offered by the fifteen-month provision in the Act has been whittled away and in the event of any unavoidable delay—in, for example, the production of the accounts—there will be no spare time available to rearrange the programme, with the result that it may be very difficult to comply with all the provisions of the Act. In planning the date for an annual general meeting the provisions regarding time-limits for making up and presenting the accounts (usually at the annual general meeting) should be borne in mind.

If an annual general meeting is not held within the required period, any one member can apply to the Department of Trade which may call or direct the calling of the meeting, giving such instructions as may be necessary, including a direction that one member present in person or by proxy shall be a quorum. If such an annual general meeting convened by the Department is not held in the year of default it shall not be deemed to be the annual general meeting of the year in which it is held, unless the members by ordinary resolution so agree. If a resolution to this effect is passed, a copy of it must be sent to the Registrar of Companies within fifteen days of its being passed. There is a default fine not exceeding £50 for the company and every officer of the company who does not comply with the provisions of the Act or with any instructions from the Department of Trade.

Subject to any special provisions in a company's articles of association, any business may be transacted at the annual general meeting, provided appropriate notice has been given. If, for example, it is desired to take the opportunity to make a change in the articles of association or change a company's name, such business is quite acceptable at the annual general meeting, provided the necessary additional formalities have been observed for passing a special resolution. It is however more usual for ordinary business only to be transacted at the annual general meeting. Table *A* for example, limits ordinary business to declaring a dividend, consideration of the report and accounts, election of directors and auditors and fixing the auditors' remuneration. By custom, these matters are normally dealt with at the annual general meeting, although under the Act the presentation of the accounts could take place at an extraordinary general meeting and the articles, as in the case of Table *A*, could provide for dividends to be declared at directors' meetings.

The directors usually hold the initiative in deciding the exact business to be transacted at the annual general meeting, but the Act does make provision whereby members representing not less than one-twentieth of the total voting rights of all members having the right to vote, or not less than 100 members holding shares in the company on which there has been paid up an average sum per member of not less than £100, may, with certain restrictions, requisition the directors in writing to give notice of any resolution which may be properly moved at the annual general meeting and to circulate to members a statement of not more than 1000 words with respect to the proposed resolution. The right to have a statement circulated also relates to a resolution being proposed at any other meeting of shareholders.

The organization and procedure for an annual general meeting will, of course, vary immensely from company to company, but the checklist given below, under Organization and Procedure, will serve for most annual general meetings; it also includes other matters of detail not referred to in this part of the chapter. The special requirements of the Stock Exchange regarding meetings are set out in the Appendix to Chapter 6.

Extraordinary general meeting (ss132, 134 and 135 of the Act and clause 49 of Table A)

When it is remembered that the annual general meeting was once known as the ordinary general meeting—that is, the general meeting at which the ordinary business was transacted—it will be easily understood that an extraordinary general meeting is any extra shareholders' meeting held during the year in addition to the annual general meeting. It is quite possible for all business which it may be necessary for shareholders to transact to be carried out at the annual general meeting so that it never becomes necessary for a company to hold an extraordinary general meeting. Calling and holding an extraordinary general meeting obviously involves extra work and therefore, unless the matter is really pressing, it is always preferable to delay any special business (all business other than the four items of ordinary business already mentioned) until the next annual general meeting if at all possible. The alteration of the articles of association, the increase of authorized share capital or a resolution to wind up a company are all items of special business requiring the sanction of shareholders in general meeting and they can just as easily be dealt with at an annual general meeting as at a specially convened extraordinary general meeting.

According to Table *A*, the initiative in calling an extraordinary general meeting, as with the annual general meeting, normally rests with the directors acting as a board. They may convene such a meeting whenever they think it necessary to do so. If there are not enough directors in the United Kingom to convene an extraordinary general meeting, Table *A* provides that any one director, or any two members, may convene an extraordinary general meeting. If the articles are silent on calling extraordinary general meetings, two or more members holding not less than one-tenth of the issued share capital—or, if the company has no share capital, not less than 5 per cent in number of the members of the company—may convene a meeting. If it becomes impracticable for a meeting to be held in accordance with the articles of association, the court on its own initiative, or at the request of any director or member entitled to vote at the meeting, may order the holding of a meeting with such regulations as it may care to lay down.

Where there are enough directors in the United Kingdom to constitute a board meeting for the purpose of convening an extraordinary general meeting but they do not wish to do so, the Act makes it mandatory upon them to convene such a meeting if so requisitioned by the holders of not less than one-tenth of the paid-up capital which has voting rights—or if there is no share capital by holders representing not less than one-tenth of the total voting rights. Such power to requisition by the shareholders only applies to extraordinary general meetings, as the shareholders' remedy for convening the annual general meeting is through the Department of Trade.

Any requisition must be in writing, be signed by all the requisitionists, state the object of the meeting and be left at the registered office of the company. The directors must then convene the meeting within twenty-one days of the deposit of the requisition, and in default the requisitionists, or any of them representing more than half the total voting rights of the requisitionists, may convene the meeting providing they do so within three months after the deposit of the requisition. The expenses of the requisitionists in convening the meeting are to be paid by the company and retained from the fees of the directors who were in default.

Class meeting (ss72, 143(4)(b) and (d), and 206 of the Act, clause 4 of Table A)

A class meeting is simply a meeting of members whose interests are common. Under Table *A*, for example, the rights attached to a class of shares where there is more than one class cannot be altered by the company in general meeting (usually the ordinary shareholders) unless the members of the particular class concerned have first been given an opportunity of meeting together at a class meeting to sanction the proposed modification by an extraordinary resolution passed at the separate class meeting. Actually, an alternative action is provided by Table A whereby the rights attached to a particular class of shares may be varied by a general meeting of the shareholders with the consent in writing of the holders of three-fourths of the issued shares of the class without recourse to a class meeting. In either case the Registrar requires a copy of the extraordinary resolution of the class meeting or of the consent in writing within fifteen days. Where holders of not less in the aggregate than 15 per cent of the issued shares of a class object to a modification of their rights they may, if they did not consent to or vote in favour of the resolution, apply to the court to have the variation cancelled. Any such application must be made within twenty-one days after the date on which the resolution was passed at the class meeting or on which the consent was given. Many schemes of capital reconstruction have passed through the courts in recent years and invariably such schemes require class meetings, which are convened and regulated by the court.

A suggested notice for a class meeting is given later in the chapter.

KINDS OF RESOLUTIONS

Basically there are three kinds of resolution known respectively as ordinary, extraordinary and special resolutions.

Ordinary resolutions

An ordinary resolution is one passed by the method ordinarily adopted by a body of voters under common law when no special rules exist. Such a resolution is passed by a simple majority of those who vote. The removal of a director under the Act is the one occasion in the Act where an ordinary resolution is specifically required . Where on other occasions the Act requires a decision to be made by the company in general meeting but does not call for a particular kind of resolution an ordinary resolution is quite sufficient unless the articles of association call for a particular majority. Fourteen days' notice is sufficient for an ordinary resolution although if the resolution is to be moved at an annual general meeting it would invariably be included in the necessary twenty-one days given in respect of the annual general meeting. The notice for an ordinary resolution need set out only the general nature of the business concerned although in some instances it is obviously more helpful to members if the exact resolution is given.

Extraordinary resolutions

An extraordinary resolution is called for in four places in the Act—ss278, 303, 306 and 341—all in connection with winding-up. Such a resolution is passed by a majority of not less than three-fourths of those who vote. The notice covering the resolution must set out the exact wording of the resolution and must also specify the intention to pass the resolution as an extraordinary resolution. As in the case of an ordinary resolution, fourteen days' notice will be sufficient unless it is to be proposed at an annual general meeting.

Special resolutions

On fourteen occasions in the Act and once in the 1967 Act a special resolution is called for. The notice for a special resolution must set out the exact wording of the resolution and must also mention the intention to pass the resolution as a special resolution. Twenty-one days' notice is required for any general meeting at which a special resolution is to be considered.

Checklist of events requiring a special resolution
1   Alteration of the memorandum:
    (*a*) To change the name (*ss*18(1) and 19(2))—see p.21
    (*b*) To change the objects (*s*5)(1))—see p.24
    (*c*) To make the liability of a director unlimited (*s*203(1))—see
       p.25
    (*d*) To change a condition that could lawfully have been inclu-
       ded in the articles (*s*23(1))
    (*e*) To change an unlimited to a limited company (1967 Act *s*44)
2   Alteration of the articles (*s*10(1))—see p.27
3   Approval of a director's assignment of his office (*s*204)
4   Creation of a reserve liability by providing that a portion of
    unpaid capital cannot be called for until the company is wound
    up (*s*60)
5   Payment of interest out of capital (*s*65(1))
6   Reduction of capital (*s*66(1))—see p.26
7   Declaration that the company's affairs should be investigated by
    the Department of Trade (*s*165(*a*))
8   Resolution to wind up (*ss*222(*a*) and 278(1)(*b*))
9   Sanctioning the liquidator's acceptance of shares as consideration
    for the sale of the company's assets (*s*287(1))

A copy of all extraordinary and special resolutions whether passed in general meeting or at class meetings must be filed with the appropriate Registrar of Companies within fifteen days of the meeting at which they are passed. Copies of ordinary resolutions are not required by the Registrar except on the three occasions mentioned in *s*63 (increase of capital), *s*131 and *s*143 of the Act.

In addition to the particular majorities required for the three basic types of resolution already mentioned the articles of association may provide for resolutions to be passed by special majorities.

NOTICE

The following elements should be included in the notice for any shareholders' meeting:

1   Name of company
2   The type of meeting
3   Date, time and place of meeting
4   The nature of any special business—according to Table *A* all
      business is special business with the exception of declaring a
      dividend, consideration of the report and accounts, the election
      of directors in place of those retiring and appointment of and
      fixing the remuneration of the auditors
5   Exact wording of any special or extraordinary resolution together
      with a statement specifying the intention to propose the
      resolution as a special or extraordinary resolution
6   The authority by which the notice is issued
7   The name of the person issuing the notice
8   If the company has a share capital, prominent note to the effect
      that members may appoint a proxy or proxies who need not also
      themselves be members
9   Date of notice

These points are illustrated in the specimen notices on p.100.

Length of notice

The articles of association will invariably set out the length of notice which must
be given to shareholders but in any event it must never be less than that laid
down in the Act which requires twenty-one days' notice for an annual general
meeting, or any general meeting at which a special resolution is to be considered,
and fourteen days for any other meeting in the case of a limited company and
seven days for an unlimited company. The Act does, however, provide for
shorter notice in the event of:

1   An annual general meeting, if agreement is given by all those
      entitled to attend and vote
2   An extraordinary general meeting, if agreement is given by a
      majority of members who between them *also* hold not less than
      95 per cent in nominal value of the shares giving the right to
      attend and vote or if there is no share capital not less than 95 per
      cent of the total voting rights at that meeting

It would appear that in either of the above cases the consent need not
necessarily be in writing.

Means of serving notice

The articles of association should always be carefully studied to ascertain the exact meaning of so many days' notice. Table A states that notice shall be exclusive of the day that the notice is served and also of the day of the meeting. It goes on to say that a notice is deemed served twenty-four hours after it is posted. It must be assumed in this case that the twenty-four hour period applies whether a letter is sent by first or second-class post. The articles may well state that a notice is deemed served at the time it would have been received in the normal course of post and in this case the class of postal service chosen would be taken into account. Yet again, some articles state that the day of posting is the day of service, so it is important that the calculation of the days of notice is worked out most carefully, in accordance with the articles of the particular company, to avoid the possibility of the meeting being set aside through lack of proper notice. If, as in the case of Table A, service is to be by means of post, it has been held that no other manner of service will be valid.

Entitlement to receive notice

Notice must be sent to all entitled to receive it or again a meeting may be invalidated. Table A does provide for accidental omission but it really must be a result of an accident and not of an error. Articles may well provide that preference shareholders (unless their dividends are in arrears) and debenture stockholders (who after all are not members) are not entitled to receive notice. It has been held that if a share carries no rights to vote, by implication it carries no right to attend meetings.

According to Table A it is not necessary to send notice outside the United Kingdom, although most companies with such a clause in their articles do so. In the case of joint holders it is sufficient to send notice to the first named. A copy of all notices to shareholders must be sent to the auditors.

Where a company has bearer shares, it is not possible to dispatch notice by post and meetings would be convened by notice in the press in accordance with the regulations in the company's articles.

Adjourned meetings

No notice need be given for an adjourned meeting unless the adjournment takes place after a period of thirty days from the original meeting.

Special notice

In three places the Act requires special notice to be given. This is not notice given by the company to the members but by the members to the company. To appoint an auditor other than the one retiring or to provide that the retiring auditor is not reappointed, or to remove a director before he is due to retire by rotation or to appoint a director who is over seventy, requires an ordinary resolution with a simple majority and fourteen days' notice. These three matters are, however, considered to be important enough to warrant shareholders giving them special thought, and under the Act it is necessary for a shareholder who will move the resolution to give the company twenty-eight days' notice of his intention to do so. The directors are then bound to inform the other shareholders of the proposed resolution and also to give the auditors or directors concerned, in the first two of the three occasions requiring special notice, the opportunity to have representation circulated to the shareholders.

Authority to give notice

It is important that a notice is always sent out with the authority of the board or whoever is convening the meeting. Authority to dispatch a notice is usually given to the secretary at a board meeting before notice is dispatched, but it would be sufficient for the dispatch by the secretary without prior authority to be ratified by the board, provided it takes place before the meeting is held.

A notice sometimes includes the expression 'any other business'. This is really meaningless except for the purpose of a general discussion or perhaps moving a vote of thanks. Certainly no resolution can be passed under this heading if proper notice has not been given to shareholders although if all those entitled to attend and vote are present and agree no prior notice of the resolution need be given.

Notice of meetings is dealt with in $ss108(1)(c)$, 133, 134(a), 136(2), 141(2), 142, 160(1), 184(2) and (3), 185(5) of the Act and $s14(7)$ of the 1967 Act and clauses 50, 51, 52, 57 and 131 to 134 of Table A.

QUORUM

The quorum for a meeting is the minimum number of members which must be present before any business can be validly transacted. The quorum for a meeting of shareholders is invariably set out in the articles of association of the company, but, in the unlikely event of such a provision not being made, the Act provides that in the case of any general meeting of a public company three members, and in the case of a private company two members, personally present, shall be a quorum. Table A makes the same provision for a public company, in that three members must be personally present, but for a private company the two members can be present in person or by proxy. It has been held that only those entitled to vote at a general meeting are qualified to help constitute a quorum.

Table A requires the quorum to be present only at the time when the meeting begins, so that if the number of members present in person (or by proxy) falls below the quorum at any time during the meeting it would seem that the business can be continued by those who remain.

If a meeting has been requisitioned by members in accordance with the Act and a quorum is not present within half an hour after the scheduled time for the meeting, it is dissolved. If the meeting has been convened by the directors and a quorum is not present within half an hour, the meeting stands adjourned for seven days or till some other time if the directors so decide. At that adjournment the members present shall be a quorum (s134 of the Act and clauses 53 and 54 of Table *A* Part I and clause 4 of Table *A* Part II).

CHAIRMAN

If the articles are silent on the question of who takes the chair at meetings of shareholders, the Act provides that the members present may elect a chairman from among themselves.

Who takes the chair?

The articles of association will normally give guidance on who shall take the chair at shareholders' meetings. Table *A* states that the chairman, if any, of the board shall take the chair. If there is no chairman of the board or he is not present within fifteen minutes after the scheduled time for the meeting, or he is not willing to act as chairman of the meeting, the other directors present shall elect a chairman from among themselves. If no director is willing to act as chairman or no director is present within fifteen minutes, the members present may elect a chairman from among their own ranks.

Casting vote

Under Table *A* the chairman has a right to demand a poll, and on a show of hands or a poll he has a second or casting vote in the case of an equality of votes.

Chairman's duties

It is at general meetings and particularly at the annual general meeting that the chairman will probably come into closest association with his company's shareholders. In spite of his efficient leadership and management capability as perhaps chief executive throughout the year the members and the press will often judge his effectiveness by the way in which he handles the annual general meeting. It is consequently of the utmost importance that the chairman and his staff should always ensure that he has been adequately prepared to deal with any situation which may arise at the meeting. The following list will serve to remind the chairman of some of his functions and duties in connection with general meetings although he may well delegate some of them to others:

1   To be familiar with the Act and the articles of association especially as regards the right of himself and others to demand a

poll and his right to adjourn the meeting

2 To ensure that when the meeting begins it has been properly constituted as regards notice, quorum and his appointment to the chair

3 To ensure that any agenda is followed unless the meeting agrees otherwise, to see that the business remains within the scope of the notice and to decide points of order

4 To maintain order and if necessary to initiate a pre-arranged procedure to have offenders removed from the meeting. The risk of an unruly element entering the meeting is reduced if those attending are screened as they arrive and are asked to sign an attendance sheet. If the number of meetings disturbed by demonstrators increases, the use of admission tickets may soon become a general necessity for shareholders' meetings

5 To answer shareholders' questions but to use care that he does not give information not available to all members which could affect the value of their shares

6 To ensure that all who wish to speak have an equal opportunity to do so

7 To be familiar with the mechanics for taking a poll and to be ready to instruct the shareholders in the completion of poll cards

8 To use his casting vote if he is so empowered

9 To demand a poll if he knows of the existence of proxy forms which, if counted on a poll would alter the result of a vote taken on a show of hands

10 To ensure that minutes are properly drawn up and signed

The chairman's appointment and duties are dealt with in *ss* 134 and 145(2) of the Act and clauses 55 and 61 of Table *A*.

AGENDA

The task of compiling the agenda for a general meeting is usually left to the company secretary who works very closely with his chairman. The agenda will set out the business already referred to in the notice but in greater detail, showing perhaps the wording of the actual resolutions to be moved and the names of the movers and seconders. The agenda is distributed to those taking part in the meeting and acts as a script so that the chairman, and others concerned, can readily see where they have to speak. If only a few members are expected at the meeting it may be helpful to give a copy to all those present and also to the press.

Items 14 to 25 in Organization and Procedure, below, will serve as a basis for an agenda for any annual general meeting and only a little adaptation will be needed for an extraordinary general meeting.

VOTING

If the articles of association exclude Table A and make no other provision in connection with voting, the Act states that each member shall have one vote for each share of £10 of stock held. This amounts to a poll but does not prevent a vote first being taken on a show of hands under common law when each member present would have one vote.

Right to vote

Table A provides that, subject to any rights or restrictions attached to particular shares, each member personally present shall have one vote on a show of hands and one vote for each share held in the case of a poll. In order to qualify a member for voting, any calls which may be due must have been paid. Preference shareholders are usually deprived of the right to vote unless their dividends are in arrears.

Joint accounts

In the case of a joint account, the vote of the senior (by order of the names in the register of members) who tenders a vote in person or by proxy will be accepted to the exclusion of the votes of any other person named in the joint account.

Members of unsound mind

The vote of a member of unsound mind may be exercised by his committee, receiver, curator bonis or other person appointed by the court.

Deceased and bankrupt members

Under Table A the personal representative of a deceased member or a bankrupt who has not taken steps to have his name placed in the register of members is entitled to receive dividends and other advantages but cannot exercise rights of membership at meetings. He is entitled to receive notice of meetings but he cannot vote until he is himself the registered holder of the shares concerned.

Bearer shareholders

The right to vote by a holder of bearer shares must be set out specifically in the articles of the company since Table A makes no provision for bearer shares. The articles will probably describe a procedure whereby the owner of a bearer share obtains a certificate of deposit from the bank holding the shares which he in turn lodges with the company. This procedure will give the owner of the bearer share the right to vote.

Show of hands

Most matters at general meetings are uncontroversial and the vote is usually taken on a show of hands. Although this entitles a member to only one vote, regardless of the number of shares he holds, at most meetings this sytem of voting is acceptable.

Polls

It could happen that the result of a vote on a show of hands (when each member receives only one vote and when votes of proxies are excluded) would have been different if a one vote for one share system, including votes of proxies, was adopted. Such an alternative system of voting is known as a poll and according to Table *A* the following persons may demand a poll before, or on the declaration of the results of, a show of hands:

1 The chairman
2 At least three members present in person or by proxy
3 Any member or members in person or by proxy representing not less than one-tenth of the total voting rights of all those having the right to vote at the meeting
4 A member or members holding shares having the right to vote on which the aggregate sum has been paid up equal to not less than one-tenth of the total sum paid up on all the shares with the right to vote

If no provision is made in the articles for demanding a poll, it may be demanded by any one member in accordance with common law principles. On the other hand, if the articles do make provision the requirements must be no more onerous than those set out in the Act, and which are similar to the provisions of Table A, except that the chairman is not included among those who can demand a poll and any article is void if it has the effect of making ineffective a demand for a poll by not less than five members who have the right to vote at the meeting.

It has been held that it is the duty of the chairman to demand a poll if he knows of the existence of proxies which, if used on a poll, would have an effect on the result of the vote. The Act provides that on a poll a member need not use all his votes in the same way. This provision enables a shareholder to vote for and against a resolution if, for example, he is holding the shares on behalf of more than one person. Bank nominee companies are more likely to make use of this provision than are individual shareholders. If a poll is demanded it is usually taken at once, although Table *A* provides that it may be taken at such time as the chairman of the meeting directs, unless it is on the election of the chairman or on the quesion of an adjournment, in which case it must be taken forthwith.

The important thing, from the point of view of the secretary or other executive supervising shareholders' meetings, is that he should never allow himself to be taken by surprise if a poll is demanded. A good secretary will always prepare himself for a poll, so that when it is actually demanded he knows immediately what he has to do. The following will serve as a procedure for taking or conducting a poll:

1   Be prepared! This means being familiar with the provisions of the articles of the company. It also means that the necessary staff and materials are always available in case of need
2   Check that the demand for the poll has been properly made
3   Chairman to rule when the poll will be taken—probably forthwith
4   (*a*) If the poll was expected (perhaps a requirement for a court meeting) voting cards can be issued to shareholders as they enter the meeting place showing their holdings which have been extracted from the register of members, or
     (*b*) If the poll was not anticipated, preprinted voting cards without holdings can be issued to those present by internal auditors, or
     (*c*) Voting lists can be strategically placed round the meeting place for signature
5   Chairman to give clear instructions to the voters. He will, for example, tell the members that they need not fill in the voting card or sign a voting list if they have already given a proxy. He may give simple instructions for filling in the card or finding the way to the voting lists
6   Internal auditors or scrutineers will collect the voting cards or lists and calculate the result by adding the votes cast during the poll to those previously cast by proxy
7   In the case of 4 (*a*), the chairman may be able to declare the result at once. In the case of 4 (*b*) or (*c*), the voting cards or lists should be checked against the register of members and it may only be possible to give a provisional result at the meeting which would be confirmed at a later date in the press

Proxies

The word proxy embraces both the piece of paper authorizing another to act as proxy and also the person who has been so appointed.

Under the Act every shareholder (unless the company has no share capital) has a right to appoint a proxy, regardless of any provision to the contrary in the articles. A proxy need not be a member of the company.

In the case of a private company, the Act provides that a proxy can speak at the meeting but, unless the articles otherwise provide, a proxy can vote only on a poll. A member of a private company can appoint only one proxy. At the shareholders' meeting of a private company a proxy can help form the quorum.

A proxy can join in demanding a poll. According to Table A a proxy must be in writing (a form of proxy is given) and lodged at the registered office not less than forty-eight hours before the meeting. Articles could provide for less than forty-eight hours but, according to the Act, cannot require proxies to be lodged with the company more than forty-eight hours before the meeting. A note regarding the time-limit for the deposit of proxies is usually printed on the proxy forms.

Proxies duly deposited with a company prior to a meeting are also valid for an adjournment of the meeting unless the articles of association provide otherwise. Under Table A a proxy may be deposited with the company between an original meeting and its adjournment provided it is lodged not less than forty-eight hours before the adjournment. It has been held that a break in a meeting to allow a poll to be taken does not amount to an adjournment allowing further proxies to be lodged but Table A does provide that proxies may be lodged in such circumstances not less than twenty-four hours before the poll is taken.

A very important provision of the Act regarding proxies states that proxy forms must not be sent out by a company to some only of its members (unless they request them in writing) suggesting a name for nomination as a proxy, unless such forms are sent to all members.

Proxies once lodged with the company are revoked in the following circumstances:

1   Notification of the death or insanity of the appointer is received by the company prior to the meeting covered by the proxy
2   The company becomes aware prior to the meeting of a transfer of the shares giving the holder the right to appoint a proxy
3   The company receives a notice of revocation or a further form of proxy within the necessary time-limit before the meeting
4   The appointer of the proxy attends the meeting and votes in person

The Act makes a special provision for a company which is a shareholder in another company. A corporate shareholder may appoint a proxy in the normal way (executed under seal according to Table A) but such proxy is in the same position as a proxy appointed by an individual and can only vote on a poll and speak at a meeting of a private company. The Act provides for a company shareholder, by resolution of its board of directors or other governing body, to authorize such person as it thinks fit to represent the corporation at the company meeting. The representative would prove his right to be present by producing a certified extract from the minutes of the board meeting appointing him. Such a representative is entitled to exercise the same powers as an individual member, in that he can vote on a show of hands and speak at a meeting of a private or public company.

Voting is dealt with in *ss*134(*e*), 136 to 138 and 139 of the Act, and clauses 32, 58 to 74 and 134 of Table *A*.

MINUTES

It is of course a businesslike procedure to keep minutes of general meetings but in fact the Act states that every company must do so. There is no set form, except that Table *A* requires them to include resolutions and proceedings of general meetings and there is no objection to loose-leaf minute books being used, so long as proper security arrangements are made to safeguard minutes of past meetings and the unused sheets for the minutes of future meetings. Minutes signed by the chairman of the meeting or by the chairman of the next succeeding meeting are *prima facie* evidence of the proceedings of the meeting. In the case of general meetings it is not usual to leave the minutes of one meeting to be signed by the chairman of the next, as this may involve minutes being left unsigned for twelve months or so. Such minutes are usually signed at the next board meeting.

The minute book of general meetings must be kept at the registered office of the company and must be open to inspection by members, free of charge, for not less than two hours in each working day. There is a provision in the Act entitling members to be furnished with copies of general meeting minutes within seven days of their request at a charge not exceeding 2½p for every 100 words. Because of these inspection provisions it is usual to keep minutes of shareholders' meetings separate from those of board meetings, which are not open to inspection by members. See *ss*145, 146 and 436 of the Act and clause 86 of Table *A* for provisions concerning minutes.

ADJOURNMENT AND POSTPONEMENT

In dealing with the quorum for general meetings convened by the board it was mentioned that if no quorum is present within half an hour of the scheduled time for the meeting it stands adjourned for a week. Table *A* also provides for adjournment on other occasions and states that the chairman with the consent of the meeting may, and shall if directed by the meeting, adjourn the meeting from time to time and from place to place. There is no power for the chairman to adjourn without the consent of the meeting unless it is to deal with disorder. Only unfinished business can be dealt with at an adjourned general meeting. No notice of the adjournment is necessary unless it is to a date more than thirty days after the date of the original meeting.

For most practical purposes the original meeting and the adjourned meeting are considered to be one meeting, but the Act provides that if a resolution is passed at an adjourned meeting the date of the resolution is the date of the adjourned meeting.

It has been held that once a meeting has been convened it cannot be postponed validly without the consent of all the members concerned. In one case, an annual general meeting was postponed but, nevertheless, sufficient members to form a quorum met on the appointed day and transacted the business; it was held that their action was valid. The correct action is to hold the meeting as originally planned and then adjourn it, if the majority of those present so agree. See s144 of the Act and clause 57 of Table A.

RESOLUTIONS IN WRITING

In the case of a company with only a few members, Table A Part II has a useful clause which avoids the need to hold a general meeting physically. The resolution or resolutions to be passed are set out on paper, then signed by each of those entitled to attend and vote. The resolution may be set out in several documents of like form, in which case one or more of those who would have been entitled to be present at a meeting will sign each sheet. The resolutions are effective when all the signatures have been appended and the signed resolution is then placed in the minute book as a permanent record. If the resolution passed is one which the Registrar would normally require to have filed with him, a copy of the resolution should be submitted to him within the usual time-limit. Although it is only Table A Part II which provides specifically for resolutions in writing, it would seem that a resolution similarly signed by all the members of a public company would be quite valid, since, as it must be signed by all the members entitled to attend and vote at meetings, they in effect unanimously alter the articles to provide for a resolution in writing to cover the particular piece of business being transacted. It is doubtful if a court would invalidate such an action even in the case where a meeting is actually called for by the Act or the articles. See s143(4)(c) of the Act and clause 5 of Table A Part II.

DIRECTORS' MEETINGS

There are a number of items of business in the Act or in Table A which must be carried out by the directors. For example: 'The directors may make calls....'or 'The directors may convene an extraordinary general meeting....' For the directors to do either of these things they must do so as a board at a meeting. Meetings of directors, like other meetings, must be properly constituted and should comply with any specific regulations laid down in the articles. The company secretary would probably be responsible for seeing that the preparations for a board meeting and the procedure at the meeting itself is properly carried out. A suggested procedure for a secretary in this connection is set out on p.91.

Notice (clause 98 of Table A)

Under Table *A* board meetings may be summoned by any one director, and the secretary must do so if requested by a director. There are no particular requirements regarding the length of notice for a board meeting, and such notice need not be in writing. The important point is that all directors entitled to attend are given a reasonable opportunity to do so, except that directors outside the United Kingdom are not entitled to a notice. As in the case of general meetings, the mere physical presence of directors does not constitute a quorum unless all entitled to a notice are present and agree. It has been held that there is no need for a notice of a forthcoming board meeting to set out the nature of the business since directors have the power to carry out a very wide range of business and should attend prepared for anything.

Agenda

Although there is no need to give formal notice of a board meeting, or indeed any notice at all if meetings are held on predetermined dates, most companies find it helpful to send out a reminder a day or two before the day of the meeting, in the form of an agenda accompanied by papers or reports that are to be considered at the meetings. As in the case of a general meeting, the secretary would consult the chairman about what business is to be carried out and he would compile the agenda accordingly. In some cases a preprinted agenda is used for all board meetings with provision for items to be added to the agenda if necessary. The following would serve as an agenda for board meetings:

Agenda for a meeting of directors to be held on Friday 29 May 1975 at 09 30 at the registered office.

1   Confirmation of minutes of previous meeting (copy herewith)
2   Matters arising:
     (*a*)
     (*b*)
3   Managing director's report
4   Cash position
5   Monthly results

6   Share transfers
7   Personnel
8
9
10 Any other business
11 Date of next meeting

The inclusion of the exact wording of the resolutions to be passed will save time, and a wide margin can be left down the right side to enable directors to take notes. The secretary of the meeting could use his copy of the agenda as a basis for the minutes. An agenda suitable for the first board meeting after incorporation can be found on p.91.

Quorum (s199 of the Act and clauses 84 and 99 of Table A)

The quorum for a board is usually set out in the articles of association. In the case of Table *A* the directors are given power to fix their own quorum, and in the event of their failing to do so specifically the quorum is two directors. Where the directors have the power to fix the quorum but do not do so and no figure is given for that eventuality, as in the case of Table *A*, it has been held that the quorum will be the number of directors who usually act. In the rare event of the articles making no provision for the quorum a majority of directors must be present before any business can be transacted.

Mere physical presence of a quorum does not constitute a meeting as there must have been an intention to meet which was known to those entitled to attend. Even if a board meeting has been properly called and the appropriate number of directors to constitute a quorum is present, there still may not be a quorum competent to transact business. If the articles are silent on the matter, or if Table *A* is excluded, a quorum for a board meeting must be a disinterested quorum—which means that none of the directors constituting the quorum may have any interest in the business to be transacted. However, with the advent of the professional director with wide business interests, very little would be done at board meetings if such a restriction were always applicable. In fact articles usually modify this common law rule as does Table *A*. Table *A* still acknowledges the principle, but the prohibition does not apply in connection with any arrangement to give a director, or a third party, security or indemnity in respect of money lent by the director to, or obligations undertaken by him for the benefit of, the company in connection with a contract by the director to subscribe for or underwrite shares or debentures of the company, or in connection with any contract or arrangement with any other company in which he is interested only as an officer or shareholder of the other company.

Under the Act every director is obliged to declare at an appropriate meeting of directors the nature of any direct or indirect interests in a contract or proposed contract with the company and consequently the board should always be in a position to know whether or not a disinterested quorum is present for a particular transaction.

Chairman (clause 101 of Table A)

For a board meeting to be properly constituted the proper person must be in the chair, and Table *A* provides that the board may elect one of their members to take the chair. One director is usually appointed chairman indefinitely or until he retires, but there is no objection to each meeting electing its own chairman. If there is a regular chairman and he is not present within five minutes, the directors present may choose one of their number to take the chair. Sometimes a deputy chairman is elected to take the chair automatically in the chairman's absence. Although, in practice, a deputy chairman would step down if the chairman later arrives he is not bound to do so. The chairman of the board usually presides at meetings of shareholders.

Voting (clause 98 of Table A)

Table *A* provides that questions arising at board meetings shall be decided by a majority of votes, and that in the event of an equality of votes the chairman shall have a second or casting vote. Such voting would be on a show of hands, there being no provision for polls and proxies in the case of directors' meetings.

In practice, voting at board meetings is unusual. A board usually works as a well-integrated team pulling in one direction and matters are usually settled without recourse to voting. If there is a constant disharmony among the directors there will probably very soon be a resignation or two followed by suitable payments in compensation for loss of office.

Minutes (ss145 and 436 of the Act and clause 86 of Table A)

As in the case of general meeting minutes, the Act makes it obligatory that minutes of board meetings must be maintained, but there is no provision for inspection—except by the directors and auditors. There is no need for the minute book to be kept at the registered office. Table *A* is rather more detailed than the Act, and requires minutes of board meetings to cover all appointments of officers made by the directors and to include the names of the directors present at each meeting and minutes of all resolutions and proceedings of the directors. Table *A* also requires each director present at any meeting to sign his name in an attendance book kept for that purpose.

Board minutes are usually approved at the subsequent board meeting and signed by the chairman of that meeting.

A selection of specimen board resolutions is given on p.92.

Resolution in writing (clause 106 of Table A)

Most articles, as in the case of Table *A*, make provision for directors to transact business without a physical meeting by the means of all those entitled to receive notice of the meeting signing their name on a written copy of the resolution. This is a useful provision enabling formal business to be done without need to call the directors to a meeting.

Committees (clauses 102 to 105 of Table A)

Directors often appoint committees to expedite their work, but before such committees can be appointed the articles should be consulted, as it has been held that a board cannot delegate to a committee unless the articles give them specific power to do so. Such power is contained in Table *A* and any one director can be constituted into a committee. The committee must conform to any regulations laid down by the board and, in the event of no particular regulations being given, it may regulate itself as it thinks proper.

The provisions of Table *A* regarding the chairman of a committee are the same as those for the chairman of a board meeting. A committee may be formed for any business which does not require the attention of the whole board. The most common committees are transfer committees for dealing with the approval and registration of share transfers and the sealing of new share certificates and sealing committees authorizing the use of the seal on documents other than share certificates. A resolution appointing a committee is given on p.93.

Alternate directors. There is no provision in the Act or Table *A* for a director to appoint an alternate or substitute to act in his absence but specific provision is often made in the articles of association of a company. The extent of the power of an alternate will be set out in the articles of the company concerned. It is usual for articles which provide for alternates to give the alternate the right to receive notice of board meetings and in the absence of the director to whom he is an alternate, to attend and vote at the meetings. It is not usually necessary for an alternate also to be a director in his own right but where he is he may be entitled to vote as an alternate in addition to his own right to vote as a director.

MEETINGS OF UNLIMITED AND GUARANTEE COMPANIES

Unlimited companies (ss11 and 136(1)(b) of the Act, ss43 and 47 of the 1967 Act and clause 4 of Table E)

Under the Companies Act 1967 provision has been made for the conversion of limited companies to unlimited companies. This provision is of use to smaller private companies that wish to avoid the requirement for all companies to publish their accounts. Companies which re-register as unlimited are not required to annex the usual documents to the annual return. Unlimited companies are obliged to adopt articles as near in form as possible to the articles set out in Table E in the First Schedule to the 1948 Companies Act; Table E embraces all the regulations of Table A Part I that relate to meetings. Consequently, most of what has been said in this chapter about companies limited by shares applies to meetings of unlimited companies.

Guarantee companies (ss11 and 130 of the Act, Table C and clause 2 of Table D)

A guarantee company limited by shares is obliged to adopt articles as near in form as possible to Table D which embraces all the regulations of Table A Part I. It follows that meetings of guarantee companies limited by shares are regulated in the same way as meetings of companies limited by shares.

In the case of a guarantee company without a share capital, Table C (or as near as circumstances permit) must be adopted. Table C is very similar to Table A, Part I, as far as meetings are concerned except:

1   There is specific provision for a members' resolution in writing (this provision is only found in Part II of Table A)
2   Every member has one vote under Table C
3   There is no provision for a director to help form the quorum and vote in connection with business in which he has an interest, as there is in certain cases in Table A. The quorum must always be disinterested

Inasmuch as some guarantee companies have no share capital, a few of the provisions of the Act, which relate to companies limited by shares, do not apply or are modified:

1   A guarantee company without a share capital need not hold a statutory meeting
2   Members of a company without a share capital have no right to appoint proxies
3   Some of the provisions of the Act (ss132, 133 and 137, for example), which require action by certain proportions of the share capital, provide for the qualifications to act being related to a proportion of the voting rights

Apart from these points, the regulations regarding meetings of a guarantee company without a share capital are very similar to those governing companies that have a share capital.

MEETINGS OF DEBENTURE HOLDERS

Debenture holders are not, of course, members of the company but a special class of secured creditors. There are occasions when the debenture holders may wish to meet and such meetings will be covered by the regulations set out in the debenture trust deed, which usually contains provisions regarding meetings, similar in nature to those in the articles of association of the company.

SECRETARY'S DUTIES IN CONNECTION WITH A BOARD MEETING

1 Accumulate papers and items for submission to the next board meeting–bank statements, transfers for approval, reports
2 Consult the chairman and others for any special items to be included in the agenda
3 Draft ånd reproduce the agenda
4 Dispatch the agenda, which will serve as a notice, to the directors, with a draft of the minutes of the last meeting and any other papers for consideration at the meeting
5 Prepare board room
   (*a*)   Pads and pencils
   (*b*)   Attendance book
   (*c*)   Agenda for the chairman with special notes if necessary
   (*d*)   Minute book
   (*e*)   Company seal if it is to be used
   (*f*)   Memorandum and articles of association
   (*g*)   Documents for production–bank statement, etc
   (*h*)   Spare copies of papers circulated for consideration
   (*i*)   Cigars
6 At the meeting, quietly draw attention of the chairman to any irregularities; produce documents as required; draft resolutions, if necessary, and take notes for minutes
7 After the meeting
   (*a*) Ensure documents are properly signed and sealed
   (*b*) Effect any decisions of the board–dispatch dividend warrants, etc
   (*c*) Comply with any statutory requirements–returns to Registrar, etc
8 Accumulate papers and items for submission to next board meeting

AGENDA FOR THE FIRST BOARD MEETING AFTER INCORPORATION

Agenda for the first meeting of Directors to be held on Friday 24 April 1975 at

10.30 at. 346 Middle Grosvenor Steeet, London W1.

1   Report incorporation. Production of certificate of incorporation and memorandum and articles of association
2   Report directorate (probably named in articles or appointed by subscribers)
3   Appointment of chairman (clause 101 of Table *A*)
4   Appointment of secretary (*s*177 of Act and clause 110 of Table *A)*
5   Appointment of auditors (*s*159(5) of Act)
6   Fix situation of registered office (*s*107 of Act)
7   Appointment of bankers and opening of bank account (clause 85 of Table *A*)
8   Adoption of common seal (*s*108 of Act)
9   Disclosure of directors' interests (*s*199 of Act)
10 Approval and execution of agreement purchasing business (if any)
11 Dates for subsequent meetings

Some of these items are dealt with in the specimen board resolutions that follow.

SPECIMEN BOARD RESOLUTIONS

Minutes

That the minutes of the board meeting held on 23 May 1975 be and they are hereby confirmed.

Interim dividend

That an interim dividend of 10 per cent, less tax, on the ordinary capital of the company, be and is hereby declared payable on 5 June 1975 to shareholders recorded in the register of members at the closing of the books on 26 May 1975.

Approval of new seal on change of name

The secretary reported that as a result of the change of name of company it was necessary to adopt a new common seal. *It was therefore resolved:*

   That the seal produced to the meeting, an impression of which shall be made in the margin of the minutes of this meeting, be and is hereby adopted as the common seal of the company and *that* the secretary be and is hereby instructed to ensure that the die of the seal bearing the previous name of the company is thoroughly defaced and destroyed.

Appoint director / managing director / secretary / other officer

That Mr Harold Heath be and is hereby appointed a director/managing director/ secretary/other officer of the company.

Transfers

Audit report number 217 dated 14 March 1975 relating to the undermentioned documents was produced, and *it was resolved that* transfers numbered 1241–1283 be passed and that the sealing of new share certificates numbered 4147–4179 in respect thereof be authorized.

Annual/extraordinary general meeting

That the/an annual/extraordinary general meeting be held on Wednesday 24 May 1975 at Thames House, Victoria Embankment, London EC4, at 11 00, for the ordinary business of the company and/or for the purpose of considering and if thought fit passing the following resolution (as a special resolution):
That . . . .

Execution of lease or other document

That the seal of the company be impressed upon the lease—now produced— by A B Properties Limited to this company in respect of the fourth floor of Kingscote House, Block Street, London EC3, for a period of ten years from 1 January 1976 at an annual rent of £12 000.

Approval of accounts

That the balance sheet as at 31 December 1974 and the profit and loss account for the year ended on that date together with the directors' report—now produced—be approved, that the balance sheet be signed by Messrs Bread and Dripping, two of the directors, and that the directors' report be signed by the secretary of the company.

Appointment of a committee

That pursuant to Article 71 of the company's articles of association a finance committee be and is hereby constituted, that Messrs Skin, Flint and Scrape be appointed members thereof, that Mr Screw be and is hereby appointed secretary and that the following functions be and are hereby delegated to such committee:

1   To consider . . . .
2   To authorize . . . .

3   To deal ....

Reporting directors' interests

Pursuant to s199 of the Companies Act 1948 a letter was read from Mr I M Hardup dated 27 March 1970 declaring that he is a partner in Fish and Co.

Allotment of shares

That 200 shares of £1 each in the capital of the company for which payment in full had been received be allotted to Mr J Smith and that share certificate number 23 in respect of such shares be sealed and issued.

Appointment of alternate director

The secretary reported that a letter had been received from Mr T Pot appointing Mr B Hive to act as his alternate director during his absence or inability to act as a director.

(If board approval also necessary). *It was resolved that* the appointment by Mr T Pot of Mr B Hive as his alternate director be and is hereby approved.

Approval and issue of prospectus

That the prospectus of the company which has been considered at this meeting be dated 31 July 1975 and be signed by the directors now present, and sent to each other director named therein for signature by him or his authorized agent and that the same when so signed by all the directors named therein be delivered forthwith to the Registrar of Companies for registration and that immediately thereafter the prospectus be issued and advertised.

Appointment of representative to attend general meetings

That this company being a member of Bacon Curing Company Limited hereby appoints Mr A Smoke or failing him Mr J Ham (or the secretary of the company for the time being) to represent this company at any general meeting of Bacon Curing Company Limited and at any and every adjournment thereof.

Closing tranfer books

That the transfer books of the company be closed from 1 March 1975 to 13 March 1975, both days inclusive.

Denumbering shares

That the 15 000 issued shares in the capital of the company which are credited as fully paid and rank *pari passu* in all respects, do have no distinguishing numbers.

Making a call

That a call of £0.10 per share be made upon the members registered in the books at the close of business on 31 May 1975 payable on the 21 June 1975 to Left Bank Limited, Threadneedle Street, London EC2.

Forfeiture of shares

That Mr W Glover, the registered holder of 100 shares of £1 each in this company, having failed to pay the instalment of £0.25 per share due on the said shares on 31 March 1975, and having failed to comply with the notice served upon him dated 24 May 1975 the said shares be and are hereby forfeited.

ORGANIZATION AND PROCEDURE FOR AN ANNUAL GENERAL MEETING

Before the meeting

1   Agree date for meeting bearing in mind statutory time-limits and in liaison with those responsible for production of accounts, etc
2   Arrange suitable accommodation well in advance
3   Agree agenda and draft procedure for meeting with the chairman
4   Finalize drafts and arrange printing (after informal approval of board) of
    (*a*) Notice of meeting
    (*b*) Directors' report
    (*c*) Chairman's speech (if desired)
    (*d*) Accounts
    (*e*) Two-way proxy forms (if quoted)
5   Board meeting to formally approve and authorize signing of directors' report and audited accounts, convene AGM and authorize dispatch of notices. (Inform Stock Exchange of any dividend declaration or recommendation if quoted.)
6   Dispatch notices, report and accounts, and so on—twenty-one clear days—copies to Stock Exchange if quoted
7   Summarize proxy position just before meeting and be prepared for a poll
8   Ensure in advance that a quorum will be present
9   Prime those who will take part—proposers, seconders, stewards, tellers, commissionaires
10 Check accommodation on day prior to meeting—reception area

for members, seating, heating, loudspeaker system, parking place for chairman's car, etc.
11   Assemble appropriate papers and reference books—register of directors' interests, memorandum and articles of association, Companies Acts, major agreements, general meeting minute book, etc

At the meeting

12   Members (in person or by proxy) and press to show admission cards or sign attendance sheets
13   Check that quorum is present
14   Secretary to produce register of directors' interests, read notice (unless taken as read) and auditors' report
15   Chairman to take report and accounts as read
16   Chairman addresses meeting and calls for members to move and second adoption of report and accounts (and dividend)
17   Chairman to invite questions
18   Chairman puts motion adopting accounts to meeting and declares result
19   Chairman refers to election of directors and calls for members to move and second motion(s). Two or more directors may be appointed by a single resolution only if a private company or if no member present objects
20   Chairman puts motion(s) electing directors to meeting and declares result
21   Chairman refers to remuneration of auditors and calls for members to move and second motion. (No resolution needed to reappoint auditors.)
22   Chairman puts motion fixing auditors' remuneration to meeting and declares result
23   Chairman refers to any other motion for which proper notice has been given and calls for members to move and second motion; chairman puts motion to meeting and declares result
24   Members to move and second vote of thanks
25   Chairman responds and closes meeting

After the meeting

26   Prepare minutes
27   Action subsequent to any change of directors—Registrar of Companies, bank, Stock Exchange, etc
28   File resolutions (if any) with Registrar of Companies
29   Pay dividend (if any)

30 Inform press unless present at meeting—and Stock Exchange if quoted
31 Prepare annual return

Protests at annual general meetings

It can no longer be assumed that the annual general meeting of a public company will be the usual thirty-minute formality. It was at annual general meetings in the spring of 1971 that chairmen of Barclays Bank Limited and Imperial Chemical Industries Limited faced groups of articulate young people, protesting against alleged support for the apartheid policy of South Africa. Shareholders arriving for the meeting were met outside by young people brandishing banners and leaflets and inside others attempted to question the board, move resolutions and generally harass the proceedings so that, in the case of Barclays Bank, the meeting was extended to about three hours. Many other meetings have been similarly disturbed since then.

Recent issues rousing protest have covered such predictable topics as pollution, equal pay, board representation for workers and the shipment and sale of arms but of all issues, that of racial discrimination is likely to be the most emotive in the future. No public company with interests in South Africa, for example, can afford to neglect the possibility that its next annual general meeting may be chosen as a target for protest. Although the disturbance of meetings in the United Kingdom is not yet the highly organized business that it is in America, public companies are well advised to approach future meetings rather more cautiously and a careful review of procedures is not now inappropriate.

The following reasonable precautions are being taken by some public companies and in the present still moderate climate they should prove sufficient to ensure that company officials retain the initiative in all currently envisaged situations:

1 Assume that protesters will be present when preparing for a meeting
2 Consider tightening admission procedures so that only shareholders (including, of course, their proxies or representatives) and any other invited persons obtain admission. This obviously will not exclude protestors who are genuine shareholders, nor persons who have become shareholders or proxies merely to obtain admission for protest purposes, but it may well exclude some unwelcome visitors. A small room or separate table at one side of the admission area could be a useful facility for interviewing doubtful cases without impeding the flow of other shareholders. If the formal checking of each person's right to attend appears to be too onerous a task it is worth

bearing in mind that even a mere semblance of control may deter some. Other entrances to the meeting place should be sealed off from the outside except that it may help if the platform party and important guests could use a separate and less conspicuous entrance

3   Advise the local police that the meeting is due to take place and agree with them the procedure for obtaining their help if required. One responsible steward should locate in advance the telephone nearest to the meeting place and be prepared with appropriate coin (if necessary) and telephone number so that he can summon instant police help at an agreed signal from the chairman. The presence of a uniformed police officer outside the meeting place may have a tranquillizing effect on some

4   Arrange the seating in manageable blocks so that every seat is reasonably accessible to stewards for the purpose of distributing poll cards, handling microphones and reaching troublemakers

5   Ensure that a good number of well-briefed and strategically placed stewards are seen to be present. Badges help to create an official atmosphere and the more timid protesters may be deterred. Stewards should know the whereabouts of fire buckets and brooms so that they can deal expeditiously with such phenomena as stink bombs

6   Ensure that a competent official is in charge of the amplifying system which ideally should be designed so that the chairman is always in a position to dominate proceedings and that where questioners are provided with individual roving microphones each can be switched off from a control point if necessary

7   Draft the agenda so that formal business is transacted as quickly as possible in the first part of the meeting. By firmly following a carefully worked out agenda a chairman will more easily be able to rule questions out of order if they are not strictly within the scope of the item being dealt with. If an unusually large number of questions are expected it may help to inform the meeting that there will be ample time for general questions at the end of the formal business

8   Ensure that the chairman is supplied with necessary facts, figures and possibly prepared statements in advance so that he is in a position to answer all foreseeable questions competently. Some chairmen appreciate an opportunity to rehearse the formal agenda and to answer dummy questions with a few officials present prior to the actual meeting

9   Check that the procedure for conducting a poll is as simple and streamlined as possible. Protesters may successfully demand a poll on every resolution in an attempt to lengthen the meeting and if

one poll card is designed to cover all possible resolutions considerable time will be saved in not having to distribute and collect cards at each poll

10   If it is normal practice to reappoint several directors by a single resolution (no one member voting against the initial resolution permitting such action), consider re-electing each director by a single resolution voluntarily rather than be forced to do so by one protester being unhelpful

11   On the assumption that advance warning has been received, consider the possibility of the chairman inviting representatives of the protesters to meet him privately before the shareholders' meeting. It could be that private assurances from the chairman would satisfy the protesters.

A serious factor which must be borne in mind in planning any important meeting is the possibility that the meeting place may be chosen as a target for a bomb or bomb scare causing the meeting to be abandoned before essential business has been transacted. In this connection the services of the company's security officer becomes essential and in some large companies the security officer has become an important member of the team preparing for the meeting. He will coordinate all aspects of security and safety for the meeting, including the ejection of troublemakers if necessary and the procedure in the event of a speedy evacuation being necessary. He will make himself responsible for surveying the meeting place before the meeting, familiarize himself with all the objects inside and outside, and all means of escape. He will ensure that, as people arrive, no packages of doubtful content are brought in without first being examined. Obviously it could be expensive and embarrassing for a shareholders' meeting to have to break up or perhaps not even get started with the consequence that the meeting would have to be reconvened, and at least one large public company in London has for several years gone to the trouble of booking and preparing a second meeting place to which the meeting could be rapidly adjourned if necessary. From the shareholders' point of view the declaration of the dividend is probably the most important item of business and some companies have taken the precaution of dealing with this item first to ensure that at least that part of the business is dealt with.

SPECIMEN NOTICES FOR MEETINGS OF SHAREHOLDERS

Notice for an annual general meeting

ROBERT ROBERTSON AND SONS LIMITED

Notice is hereby given that the fifth *annual general meeting of ROBERT ROBERTSON AND SONS LIMITED* will be held at 20 King's Terrace, Aberdeen, on Thursday 3 June 1976, at 12 30 in the afternoon to transact the ordinary business of the company.

20 King's Terrace
Aberdeen
8 May 1976

By order of the board
Binder and Looseleaf
Secretaries

Any member entitled to attend and vote at the above meeting may appoint one or more proxies to attend and vote instead of him. A proxy need not be a member of the company.

This notice is being sent to all members but only holders of ordinary shares are entitled to attend and vote at the meeting.

Notice for an annual general meeting followed by a class meeting

THAMES AMENITIES LIMITED

Notice is hereby given that the *annual general meeting* of the members of Thames Amenities Limited will be held at Liberty House, Greenfriars, London EC4 on 13 April 1976 at 10 00, for the following purposes, namely:

1   To receive and consider the accounts and balance sheet and the reports of the directors and auditors thereon
2   To declare a dividend on the ordinary stock
3   To elect directors
4   To approve the auditors' remuneration

Notice is hereby also given that at the conclusion of the business of the annual general meeting a separate general meeting of the holders of the preference stock of the company will be held for the purpose of appointing a director to represent such holders.

A member of the company entitled to attend and vote is entitled to appoint one or more proxies to attend and vote instead of him. A proxy need not also be a member.

Dated 21 March 1976
Liberty House,
Greenfriars, London EC4

By order of the board
E A DEADWOOD Secretary

Notice of an extraordinary general meeting

ASSOCIATED SYNDICATIONS LIMITED

Notice is hereby given that an *extraordinary general meeting* of Associated Syndications Limited will be held at the Holt Hotel, Bread Street, Chester, Cheshire, on Friday 28 May 1976 at 10 30 in the forenoon, for the purpose of considering and, if thought fit, passing the following resolutions of which that numbered 1 will be proposed as an *ordinary resolution* and that numbered 2 as a *special resolution:*

RESOLUTIONS

1   That the whole of the issued ordinary stock in the capital of the company be converted into fully paid ordinary shares of £0.25 each and that each of the unissued ordinary shares of £1 each in the capital of the company be subdivided into four ordinary shares of £0.25 each

2   That the company's articles of association be altered by deleting '£1' in article 70 and substituting '£0.25' therefor

The Rookery
Oak Drive,
Chester, Cheshire
4 May 1976

By order of the board
B A Mackenzie
Secretary

Any member entitled to attend and vote at the above meeting may appoint a proxy to attend and vote instead of him and a proxy need not be a member.

MEETINGS IN A WINDING-UP

Members' voluntary winding-up

1   Board meeting to
   (*a*)   Authorize statutory declaration of solvency (*s*283(1))
   (*b*)   Convene extraordinary general meeting (*s*278(1))
2   Initial EGM (or AGM) to
   (*a*)   Pass appropriate resolution (*s*278(1))
   (*b*)   Appoint liquidator (*s*285(1))
3   General meeting at end of each year to receive accounts (*s*289(1))
4   General meetings at any other time to

(*a*)   Replace liquidator (*s*286(1))
(*b*)   Empower liquidator to accept shares etc (*s*287)
(*c*)   Transact any other business (*s*303(1), *s*306 etc)
5   Final meeting to
(*a*)   Receive accounts (*s*290(1))
(*b*)   Dispose of books (*s*341(1)(*b*))
(*c*)   Assign undisclosed assets

The normal provisions about notice and quorum apply in meetings 1 to 4 above. Notice for meeting 5 is governed by *s*290(2)—one month's notice in the *London Gazette*. There is no provision for individual notice for meeting 5 although it is usually sent—especially if business is more than that required by *s*290(1).

If in a members' voluntary winding-up the liquidator is at any time of the opinion that the company will not be able to pay its debts in full within the period stated in the declaration of solvency, he must summon a meeting of creditors and *s*299 and *s*300 will then apply in place of *ss*289 and 290. Although creditors' meetings are called, the winding-up remains a members' voluntary winding-up.

Meetings in a creditors' voluntary winding-up

1   Board meeting to
(*a*) Convene EGM (*s*278(1))
(*b*) Convene creditors' meeting (*s*293(1))
(*c*) Appoint chairman of first creditors' meeting (*s*293(3)(*b*))
(*d*) Approve statement for creditors' meeting (*s*293(3)(*a*))
2   Initial EGM (AGM) to
(*a*) Pass extraordinary resolution (*s*278(1)(*c*))
(*b*) *Nominate* liquidator (*s*294)
(*c*) *Nominate* up to five members of committee of inspection (*s*295(1))
3   Initial creditors' meeting held on day of EGM or next day to
(*a*) Nominate and *appoint* liquidator (*s*294)
(*b*) Appoint committee of inspection (*s*295(1))
4   General meetings of members and of creditors at end of each year to receive accounts (*s*299)
5   General meetings of members and/or creditors (or committee of inspection) at any other time to
(*a*) Replace liquidator (meeting of creditors, see *s*297)
(*b*) Empower liquidator to accept shares, etc (*s*298)
(*c*) Transact any other business (*s*303(1), *s*306, etc)
6   Final meetings of members and creditors to
(*a*) Receive accounts (*s*300(1))
(*b*) Dispose of books (creditors per *s*341(1)(*b*))

(*c*) Assign undisclosed assets

In a creditors' voluntary winding-up the provisions about notice, quorum and chairman are a little complicated but may be summarized as follows:

Meetings 1 and 2.   Normal provisions.
Meeting 3.   *Notice* by post (with notice of meeting 2 (*s*393(1)) in *Gazette* and at least two local newspapers (*s*293(2)).
Quorum.   Three or all if less than three (Rule 138 of the Companies (Winding-up) Rules 1949).
Chairman.   A director (*s*293(3)(*b*)).

Meetings 4 and 5.   *Notice.* Normal provisions for members; creditors, seven days by post, in *Gazette* and at least one local newspaper (Rule 129).
Quorum. Normal provisions, for members; creditors, as for meeting 3.
Chairman. If summoned by liquidator, him. If by someone else the meeting elects a chairman (Rule 133).

Meeting(s) 6.   *Notice.* One month's notice in *Gazette* (*s*300(2)). No provision in Act for personal notice to members or creditors but usually sent.
Quorum. As for meetings 4 and 5 but if not present appropriate return sent to Registrar (*s*300(3)).
Chairman. Liquidator.

FURTHER READING

F. Shackleton, *The Law and Practice of Meetings,* Sweet and Maxwell, London, 1967. (To be revised in 1977).
T.P.E. Curry and J.R. Sykes, *The Conduct of Meetings,* Jordans, London, 1975.
Talbot's Company Meetings, Stevens
Nelson's Table of Procedures, Oyez Publications, London, 1971.
The City Code on Take-overs and Mergers, Issuing Houses Association, London, 1976.
Handling Protest an Annual Meetings, Conference Board, 1971.
Sir Sebag Shaw and Dennis Smith, *The Law of Meetings,* Macdonald and Evans, London, 1974.

PART TWO

Accounting and Financing

5

The Annual Accounts

W P Ridley

I Accounting Requirements of the Companies Acts

Anyone interested in the management of a company, whether he takes an active part or merely has capital invested, needs to have financial information of two kinds concerning the company: where the capital is invested (shown in the balance sheet) and what return is being obtained on that investment (shown in the profit and loss account). Those in active management can call for accounts to be designed according to their requirements. But, for investors, forms of balance sheet and profit and loss account have been laid down by Acts of Parliament, and together with a directors' report these documents must be sent to each member of the company, debenture holder and certain other interested parties at prescribed intervals.

The final accounts in the prescribed form, together with the directors' report, must also be filed with the Registrar of Companies.

Note that filing of accounts does not imply an inspection of such accounts by the Registrar or the Department of Trade. It means exactly what it says—the documents are filed. Such filing, however, involves laying the documents open to public inspection at Companies House. A search fee is payable before the accounts and report can be inspected. These accounts, however, are likely to be markedly different from management accounts, particularly the profit and loss account. The contrast between typical management accounts and accounts prescribed for shareholders is shown in Figures 5.1 and 5.2.

	£'000	£'000
SALES		5000
less		
Purchases of raw materials	2000	
Manufacturing wages	1500	
Foremen's wages	50	
Factory expenses	150	
Depreciation of plant and machinery	60	3760
GROSS PROFIT ON SALES		1240
add		
Investment income from:		
quoted investments	10	
unquoted investments	5	
Rents	300	
Profit on sale of sports field	40	355
		1595
less		
Directors' fees	10	
Directors' remuneration	80	
Salaries	600	
Rent	10	
Rates	12	
Insurance	20	
Property repairs	100	
Provision for renewal of office building	5	
Depreciation of office equipment	2	
Telephone and postage	6	
Provision for doubtful debts	11	
Bad debts	25	
Interest on bank loans	6	
Interest on debentures	8	
Plant hire	2	
Auditors' remuneration	1	
Loss on sale of investment	80	978
NET PROFIT BEFORE TAXATION		617

Figure 5.1 Profit and loss account of a limited company as presented to its management

	£'000	£'000	£'000
TURNOVER			5000

NET TRADING PROFIT after charging the amounts inset below   452

	£'000
Directors' emoluments:	
fees	10
salaries	80
Provision for depreciation of fixed assets	62
Provision for renewal of office building	5
Plant hire	2
Auditors' remuneration	1
Interest on bank loans	6
Interest on debentures	8

add

	£'000	£'000	£'000
Income from investments:			
quoted	10		
unquoted	5		
Rent receivable from land, after deducting ground rent, rates and other outgoings	190	205	
Profit on sale of sports field		40	245
			697

less

	£'000
Loss on sale of investments	80
NET PROFIT BEFORE TAXATION	617

Figure 5.2   **The accounts shown in Figure 5.1 in the form to be filed with the Registrar**

THE COMPANIES ACTS

The form of the published accounts and the directors' report is set by the Companies Acts. The most recent of these is the Companies Act 1973, but this Act must be read in conjunction with the previous major Acts on the subject dated 1948 and 1967.

    The Companies Acts do not limit the information to be presented, but they set out what must be included in the final accounts and directors' report, including any notes which may be required for clarification. Such information is termed the minimum legal requirements. In fact, the Companies Acts select the information that needs to be filed. The full final accounts must therefore be adapted to meet the needs of the Acts. The balance sheet and profit and loss account of a company based on this selected information are termed the statutory accounts.

Growth of information required

The information required for the statutory accounts has grown enormously during the past sixty years, owing to pressure from investors, the government and the general public. The pressure from investors for more information has grown with their increasing separation from management in industry and commerce. This separation has led to a need of investors to learn as much as possible of the state of companies, in order to assess the security of their investment. The general public, which in this connection includes creditors and potential investors, are concerned to know how companies are being managed, and whether they are financially sound. (This demand for information becomes especially apparent when public confidence in company administration has been shaken by a well-publicized fraud.) Successive governments have responded to these two pressures in their legislation.

The government itself may wish to have more information made public if it feels this will have a beneficial effect upon industry or commerce as a whole. Thus the publication of export figures by each company, for example, can have the effect of increasing emphasis on overseas sales and thereby stimulating trade. As a result, the successive Companies Acts tend to set increasingly stringent requirements for company disclosure.

STATUTORY PRESENTATION

Figures 5.1 and 5.2 highlighted typical differences between management and shareholder information. However, the accounts shown were not comprehensive since they took company information only to the stage of profit before taxation. After this point there is no difference between the information required by the Companies Acts and that normally presented to the management. The balance sheet designed for management is also broadly similar (in most cases) to that which is required by the Companies Acts to be presented to the investors and filed with the Registrar.

Full details of a statutory profit and loss account are given in Figure 5.3, covering all information that would have to be published if relevant to the company concerned. Figure 5.4 details the tax information that has to be provided in statutory accounts and Figure 5.5 gives an example of a statutory balance sheet.

Directors' emoluments

In addition to the information shown in Figure 5.3, certain information concerning directors' emoluments must be given, either in the accounts or in a statement attached to the accounts. All directors' remuneration and past directors' pensions, paid by the company or by any other person, either for their services as directors or for services in other capacities must be shown. Likewise the statement or accounts must show any compensation paid by the company or any other person to past or present directors for loss of office. In addition the statement must show the number of directors who have waived their rights to emoluments and the aggregate amount that has been waived. The chairman's emoluments must be shown, and also those of the highest paid director if these are in excess of the chairman's emoluments.

The numbers of directors must be shown, broken down into income groups; that is, the number of directors whose emoluments do not exceed £2500; the number whose emoluments exceed £2500 but do not exceed £5000; and so on for each successive integral multiple of £2500. For each of these items, the term 'emoluments' does not include contributions paid by the company for the benefit of directors under any pension scheme.

Taxation items

The more detailed requirements about disclosure of taxation items are covered by the layout shown in Figure 5.4.

Notes on Figure 5.5

The paragraph numbers 1–6 following refer to the corresponding bold figures shown in the balance sheet, Figure 5.5, and provide full explanation of the statutory requirements for information.

1 The following items, so far as they have not been written off, must be disclosed. It is suggested that they be deducted from reserve at this point in order to give the amount of the shareholders' funds represented by assets.

(*a*) Preliminary expenses
(*b*) Expenses of issuing shares or debentures
(*c*) Commission paid in respect of shares or debentures
(*d*) Discount on debentures
(*e*) Discount on shares

2 The word 'valuation' may include the net book amount at 1 July 1948, in respect of any fixed assets for which figures of cost or provisions for depreciation relating to the period prior to that date cannot be obtained without unreasonable expense or delay.

	£	£	£
TURNOVER (unless it does not exceed £50,000)			x
NET TRADING PROFIT after charging the amounts inset below	£		x
Directors' emoluments:			
for services as directors	x		
for services in executive capacities	x		
(Details required to comply with s196 of the 1948 Act and ss6 and 7 of the 1967 Act might best be dealt with in a separate statement attached to the accounts. See Directors' emoluments, p.111			
Provision for depreciation of fixed assets	x		
Provision for renewal of assets	x		
Sums paid for hire of plant and machinery	x		
Auditors' remuneration	x		
Interest on:			
bank loans	x		
overdrafts	x		
loans repayable within five years of balance sheet date:			
repayable otherwise than by instalments	x		
repayable by instalments	x		
other loans	x		
add			
Income from investments:			x
quoted			x
unquoted			

For fixed assets shown at valuations, the year in which the valuations were made must be disclosed. For fixed assets valued during the last financial year, the names or qualifications of the valuers and the bases of valuation they used must be given.

Freehold land must be shown separately from leasehold land, and land held on a long lease (one having not less than fifty years to run) must be distinguished from that held on a short lease (having less than fifty years to run).

There must also be shown (i) the aggregate amount of fixed assets acquired during the year; and (ii) the book value at the date of the last balance sheet of fixed assets disposed of during the year.

Rent receivable from land (if material) after deducting ground rent, rates and other outgoings   x

Exceptional or non-recurrent profits   x   x

less

Exceptional or non-recurrent losses   x   x

NET PROFIT FOR THE YEAR BEFORE TAXATION   x   x

less (see Figure 5.4)

Corporation tax (based on profits for the year)

NET PROFIT FOR THE YEAR AFTER CORPORATION TAX   x   x

add

Balance of unappropriated profit brought forward   x   x

Adjustments to balance brought forward   x   x

less

Amounts transferred to reserves   x   x

Dividends (before deduction of income tax):   x   x

    paid

    proposed

BALANCE OF UNAPPROPRIATED PROFIT CARRIED FORWARD   X

Figure 5.3 Format of the statutory profit and loss account

If the detail to be disclosed is considerable it might best be given on a statement attached to the accounts, reference thereto being made in the balance sheet.

3 As with other fixed assets, for long-term investments it is necessary to show the cost of valuation and the aggregate amount written off, except in the case of:

(*a*) Shares in subsidiaries which may be shown as a single figure–but it is necessary to state the basis on which the amount was arrived at, as illustrated in the balance sheet;

(*b*) Quoted investments and unquoted investments, provided the value as estimated by the directors is shown either as the amount of the investments or by way of note.

Taxation based on profits for the year:	£	£
Corporation tax at 52% (1972 40%)	*x*	*x*
less Relief for overseas taxation	*x*	*x*
Taxation on dividends payable	*x*	*x*
Overseas taxation	*x*	*x*
less Prior-year adjustments	*x*	*x*
add Tax on chargeable capital gains	*x*	*x*

Figure 5.4   Presentation of taxation details

For any investments in the form of unquoted equity shares in respect of which the estimated value is not given, there must be disclosed:

(*a*) The year's gross income from those investments;

(*b*) The company's share of the profits (or losses) both before and after taxation, for the last accounting period of the bodies in which the investments are held;

(*c*) The company's share of the undistributed profits (or losses) accumulated by those bodies since the investments were acquired;

(*d*) The manner in which any losses incurred by those bodies have been dealt with in the company's accounts.

4 If, in the opinion of the directors, any of the current assets will have a lower value upon realization in the ordinary course of the company's business, than the amount at which they are stated, a note must be given that the directors are of that opinion.

5 Strictly, all provisions (other than for the fall in value of assets) should be grouped together in order to show the aggregate total. This aggregation is not thought to be necessary, however, if such items are clearly described as 'provisions'.

6 If the tax is not due for payment within one year of the balance sheet date, show this item either at this point or as an additional source of funds after share capital, reserves and loans. If it is due for payment within one year, show it as a separate item under current liabilities and provisions.

LIABILITIES   £   £   £

SHARE CAPITAL

Authorized and issued for each class of share x

(Give notes of:
1   Earliest and latest dates of redemption of any
     redeemable preference shares;

2   Whether the shares must be redeemed in any event
     or are liable to be redeemed at the option of the
     company;

3   Whether any, and if so what, premium payable
     on redemption;

4   Any capital on which, and the rate at which,
     any interest has been paid out of capital during
     the year under *s*65 of the 1948 Act.)

RESERVES

Capital redemption reserve fund	x		
Share premium account	x	x	
Other reserves	x		
Balance carried forward from profit and loss account	x	x	x

SHAREHOLDERS' FUNDS (1) x

DEBT FINANCE

Loans not repayable within five years of the balance
sheet date (with a note of the terms of repayment and
the rate of interest) x

Loans or other amounts due to subsidiaries (under
current liabilities of short term) x

Debentures and other (long-term) loans x x

TOTAL LIABILITIES T

Figure 5.5   Format of the statutory balance sheet

ASSETS

FIXED ASSETS (Other than investments) **(2)**

	AT COST £	AT VALUATION £	DEPRECIATION £	£	£	£
Freehold land and buildings				*x*		
Leasehold property:						
long lease				*x*		
short lease				*x*		
Plant and machinery				*x*		
Other	___	___	___	*x*	*x*	

Goodwill, patents and trade-marks: at cost less amounts
written off   *x*   *x*

INVESTMENTS (any short-term items should be shown under current assets) **(3)**

Quoted investments   *x*
Unquoted investments   *x*   *x*

CURRENT ASSETS **(4)**

Stocks and work in progress (if the amount is material
a note must be given of the manner in which these items
were computed)   *x*
Debtors (after deducting any provision)   *x*
Balances at bank, and cash   *x*   *x*

less
CURRENT LIABILITIES AND PROVISIONS **(5)**

Bank loans   *x*
Bank overdrafts   *x*
Taxation currently due   *x*
Creditors   *x*
Dividends proposed   *x*   *x*

WORKING CAPITAL   *x*   *x*

TOTAL ASSETS   *x*

less
Corporation tax on profits for the year (due . . .) **(6)**   *x*

     T

The bold figures in parentheses refer to the notes on p.111.

Figure 5.5 (Continued)

Other items required

Other matters to be disclosed in the published accounts (by notes if not otherwise shown) include:

(a) The corresponding figures for the preceding year;

(b) The nature and amount, or estimated amount, of any contingent liabilities not provided for;

(c) The amount or estimated amount of any contracts for capital expenditure, so far as not provided for, and of any capital expenditure authorized by the directors but not yet contracted for;

(d) The bases on which foreign currencies have been converted into sterling;

(e) Any special circumstances affecting the company's taxation liability for the current or succeeding financial years;

(f) The number of employees (other than directors of the company) whose emoluments for the year (from the company, its subsidiaries or any other person in respect of services to the company or its subsidiaries)—

exceeded £10 000 but did not exceed £12 500
exceeded £12 500 but did not exceed £15 000
exceeded £15 000 but did not exceed £17 500

and so on in successive integral multiples of £2500.

(g) The information required by s3 of the 1967 Act concerning each of the company's subsidiaries.

(h) The information required by s4 of the 1967 Act.

(i) Where the company holds equity shares in another company (other than a subsidiary) exceeding one-tenth of the nominal value of the issued equity capital of that other company, or

(ii) Where the company holds shares in another company (other than a subsidiary) which, in the investing company's balance sheet, are shown at an amount exceeding one-tenth of the investing company's assets (as stated in its balance sheet).

(j) Under s5, a subsidiary has to give the name and country of incorporation of its ultimate holding company.

THE DIRECTORS' REPORT

The directors' report must accompany the balance sheet and profit and loss account filed with the Registrar of Companies, and must be sent to all members of the company, debenture holders and other interested parties.

The report, which is presented by the board of directors, contains much relevant information concerning a company's activities, and its minimum contents, summarized below, are considerably extended by the Companies Act

1967. It should be especially noted that these minimum contents are required by legislation and are not subject to directors' choice any more than the information contained in the statutory accounts.

Minimum contents of directors' report

Review. A review of the company's affairs during the period covered by the accounts.

Dividends. The amount(s) recommended to be paid by way of dividend.

Reserves. The amount(s) proposed to be transferred to reserves.

Activities. The principal activities of the company and significant changes in these activities.

Directors. The names of all directors who acted in such a capacity at any time during the period under review.

Changes in fixed assets. Significant changes in the company's fixed assets. If the market value of land is substantially different from the value shown in the balance sheet, an indication of the difference in value.

Share and debenture issue. The reason(s) for making any issue of shares or debentures during the period under review, and details of classes issued and amounts received in each class.

Contracts. Contracts with the company (except service contracts) in which a director of the company has an interest; the parties to the contract, the director involved, the nature of the contract, and the nature of the director's interest must be specified.

Arrangements between company and directors. Any arrangement whereby the directors are able to obtain benefits by the acquisition of shares or debentures in the company or any other body corporate.

Directors' interests. Directors' interests (at the beginning and end of each year) in shares or debentures of the company. This requirement is extended to include the directors' spouses and infant children (the directors' 'family interests').

Matters showing the state of the company's affairs. Particulars of any matter required for an appreciation by its members of the state of the company's affairs, so long as in the opinion of the directors the publication of such information would not be harmful to the company.

Relative profitability of different activities. Turnover and profit or loss of each class of business carried on by the company, if such classes differ substantially.

Persons employed. The average number of persons employed in the UK by the company (on a weekly basis) during the year, and the aggregate remuneration paid or payable to such persons in respect of that year. This information is not required where a company has fewer than one hundred employees.

Political and charitable contributions. The amount of contributions, if exceeding £50, given for political or charitable purposes, and the identity of the political party concerned.

Exports. The turnover from exports when the value exceeds £50 000, and a note where no goods are exported.

Previous year. The corresponding amounts in each section for the immediately preceding year.

ORGANIZATION OF INFORMATION

It is clear that the company's book-keeping systems must be designed to ensure that this statutory information can be easily obtained. This requires an analysis for each category of data that has to be published under the relevant Acts of Parliament. Careful organization on these lines can avoid a great deal of end-of-year panic, which so often delays preparation of final accounts. It will also give the directors of the company a better opportunity of reviewing their progress, thus facilitating a more meaningful review of their activities and management of the funds under their control.

II How a company is judged from its accounts

Reports by a company to its shareholders are regulated in detail by law. As a result, outside assessments of the financial standing of a company are almost inevitably based on the information given in these reports (normally issued annually) rather than on other publications of the company or on its trade reputation. Increasingly it is being realized that this outside assessment is important to the company—in raising finance, whether by loan or equity, in merger discussions with other companies, or in trading negotiations. It is therefore advisable for senior company executives to consider in detail the standards against which their company's financial performance—as set out in the fully audited report to shareholders—will be judged.

PROFIT AND LOSS ACCOUNT

This chapter takes the abridged accounts of a company called Pangloss Limited to highlight information on which a financial examination is based (see Fig. 5.6).

In the year to 31 March 1975, Pangloss earned £1.4m, before a charge of £0.4m for depreciation; depreciation is singled out because it does not represent a direct cash outflow but an accounting adjustment to the value of fixed assets—some of which are likely to have been bought many years before. Therefore when considering the cash resources available to the company both the level of depreciation and retained profits will be taken into account. The trading surplus net of depreciation gives pre-interest profits—an important indicator of company trading performance, see Figure 5.8—of £1.0m.

Interest charge

The interest charge depends on the amount of loans and overdrafts outstanding, which is an integral part of the financing of the company's assets, rather than of current trading. It is therefore of prime significance to those providing finance whether as lenders or investors. From the point of view of a potential lender, the relation of the interest charge to the level of pre-interest profits gives some indication of the security for loans; in this case with interest at £0.3m he is likely to be deterred by the relatively high ratio of 30 per cent of pre-interest profits (of £1m) already absorbed by interest. From the point of view of the equity investor, this ratio represents the gearing given to the amounts available to ordinary shareholders. Thus if pre-interest profits increase by 70 per cent to £1.7m with interest remaining at £0.3m, pre-tax profits will double to £1.4m, while if they fall by 70 per cent pre-tax profits will be reduced to nil. So the element of gearing offers both opportunity for increasing the return to shareholders where the company is successful and additional risk if trading returns fall. The degree of gearing that investors are prepared to accept varies according to the industrial risk and this must be borne in mind by the company executive when negotiating loans, overdraft facilities or equity finance.

YEAR TO 31 MARCH 1976

		£m
	Trading surplus (before depreciation)	1.4
Less:	Depreciation	0.4
	Pre-interest profits	1.0
Less:	Interest	0.3
	Pre-tax profits	0.7
Less:	Tax	0.3
	Available to shareholders	0.4

Figure 5.6   Abbreviated profit and loss account of Pangloss Limited

Tax charge

The tax charge depends not only on the rates of tax ruling in the countries where profits are earned, but also any special allowances or grants offered. Where the charge appears abnormal it will be analysed to ascertain whether this is due to temporary or permanent factors. The tax charge shown for Pangloss however of £0.3m on £0.7m represents a tax rate of 43 per cent which is unexceptional. This leaves £0.4m available for distribution to shareholders which will be evaluated by investors with reference to the number of shares issued.

YEAR ENDED 31 MARCH 1976

Earnings for the year to 31.3.70 = £0.4m or £0.2 (20%) per share*
Recommended dividend   = £0.2m or £0.1 (10%) per share*

Retained profits   = £0.2m

*Issued capital 2 million ordinary shares of £1

Figure 5.7 Earnings, dividends and retentions of Pangloss Limited

RETURN TO SHAREHOLDERS

Earnings of £0.4m on 2 million shares (see Figure 5.7) are equivalent to £0.2 per share in Pangloss. The value of the share is normally directly related to this figure; thus if the share price is £1, an investor will consider whether it is reasonable to buy or sell the share given that £1 is equivalent to five times the earnings attributable to that share (that is a p/e ratio of 5). The dividend may also be considered but normally only by small investors who are concerned with income in the short term. At a price of £1, the dividend of £0.1 per share represents a 10 per cent net return on the investment; because tax is already deducted, the dividend is free of tax to the standard rate in the hands of the recipient. The 10 per cent return is therefore worth 15 per cent in gross terms to the standard taxpayer at current rates of tax . But it is the trading prospects rather than dividend that remains the first criterion for investors in examining the record of the company.

TRADING PROSPECTS

The ultimate strength of Pangloss must be assessed not only against last year's earnings and dividend but also in relation to the trading prospects of the company and the assets employed in the business. Figure 5.8 shows the ratios normally applied to the results published in the accounts to judge the management's ability in running the trading of the business.

INDUSTRIAL AVERAGE		YEAR ENDING 31 MARCH		
		1973	1974	1975
	Pre-interest profit (£m)	0.8	0.9	1.0
	Turnover (£m)	8.0	8.0	9.0
11%	Margin on sales	10%	11%	11%
	Capital employed (£m)	10.0	11.0	11.0
11%	Return on capital	8%	8%	9%

Figure 5.8   Pangloss performance ratios

Performance

Figure 5.8 shows Pangloss's performance measured against sales and capital employed. These criteria are used as a guide to management efficiency, as they allow comparison with other companies in the same industry, as well as to the underlying viability of the company. In this table, pre-interest profit (taken because it excludes interest which depends on the method of funding of the capital employed) has advanced by a quarter from £0.8m in 1973 to £1.0m in 1975; with turnover (up from £8m to £9m) and capital employed (up from £10m to £11m) both rising less fast, margins on sales and return on capital have increased over the period. Margins at 11 per cent in 1975 are the same as for the industry as a whole, which therefore indicates normal trading returns and one without volatile fluctuations; return on capital however at 9 per cent is well below the industry level of 11 per cent indicating that the amount of capital employed is high compared with other companies in the industry. Moreover, since the return of 9 per cent falls below the general level of interest rates, it is insufficient to justify the use of new capital in the business; indeed disposal of the existing assets or a change of management—whether through merger or staff recruitment—could be justified in these conditions. For the business cannot justify to its shareholders the employment of funds which could be better invested elsewhere. Thus return on capital forms a key element in the financial assessment of a company; capital in this context however has to be carefully defined and this is considered in detail with reference to the Pangloss balance sheet.

BALANCE SHEET

Pangloss's balance sheet is given in abbreviated form in Figure 5.9.

Values of shares

The first point of interest raised by the balance sheet is the book value of the shares. Of the £11m capital employed in Pangloss at the end of the 1975-76 year, £6m is shown to be financed by shareholders' funds giving a book value of £3 each for the 2m shares. (This allows for the assets of the company fetching the £11m shown and thus providing £6m surplus after paying off the debt finance of £5m.)

Scope for raising funds.

Secondly the balance sheet gives an indication of the scope for raising further finance. In this case with borrowing at £5m against £11m capital employed, it is unlikely that lenders would be interested in advancing further funds to Pangloss. In addition to checking the company's ability to service the interest charge out of current profits, lenders are concerned with the asset backing for loans. It is rare for a company to obtain half its funds from borrowing. Within the £5m debt the £3m 4 per cent debenture explains the relatively low interest charge given in the profit and loss account. However since it falls to be redeemed in 1975, it can be considered, with the bank overdraft, as short-term finance; the refinancing of the debenture could well be at a rate of interest of 18-per cent

		£M
Sources of Finance		
Share capital 2 million ordinary shares of £1		2
Retained profits		4
Shareholders' funds		6
Debt finance		
4% Debenture 1976	3	
Bank overdraft	2	5
Total funds		11
Assets Employed		
Fixed assets		
Property	5	
Machinery	1	
Vehicles	1	7
Net current assets	—	4
Total assets		11

Figure 5.9 Abbreviated 1975 balance sheet of Pangloss Limited

instead of 4 per cent, increasing the interest charge by £420 000 from £120 000 to £540 000. Thus the funding problems of the Pangloss Company are clearly likely to discourage investors; for shareholders will expect to be asked to contribute further equity finance.

Assets employed

However, close   attention must also be paid to the assets shown in the balance sheet. For the value attributed to these assets is critical to measuring the efficiency of the company through the rate of return on capital and the potential debt finance that they can secure. In particular the value given to the property must be considered; for if the book figure represents cost or an out-of-date valuation, the current value may be considerably higher provided the property is freehold or on a long lease. The annual report must therefore be examined for details of the basis of valuation of the property; if the up-to-date value of the Pangloss property was for instance £8m against £5m shown, the total assets employed come to £14m; and with pre-interest profits of £1m, return on capital is little over 7 per cent, indicating that higher rewards could be gained by investing the money in gilt-edged stocks. (This assumes the machinery, vehicles and current assets, which include stocks and debtors net of creditors, raise their book value of £6m.) On the other hand the prospect of raising debt finance is clearly less forbidding; not only does property tend to appreciate but legal rights to it can be granted to lenders. As a result up to two-thirds of the value of the property can commonly be raised by debt finance and—provided it is invested at a rate of return that exceeds the interest charge—this offers opportunities for expansion. Property may make Pangloss attractive as a takeover prospect whether on a break-up basis or on the prospect of improving the present returns.

Assets other than land have to be treated more cautiously; the value of the plant may be minimal on a break-up basis, while current assets, such as debtors and stock, may not fully realize their book values—particularly if the company does not impose sufficient financial control. The trend of these assets to turnover will therefore be examined closely to see whether normal business standards are being achieved. On a forced realization, these assets may recover much less than their book value if standards have not been maintained.

Other information

There is much other information that can be taken from the report, for instance on the extent of capital commitments, or the subsidiaries and associated companies of the group. These do not however affect the key standards applied to the balance sheet and profit and loss account that have been examined here. These standards are used for assessing the company from several standpoints. For the shareholder the attraction of the company may be measured by the trend in earnings per share. Potential lenders will look at the cover for the interest charge, the proportion of capital funded by loans and the type of security offered. Management will be gauged by the margin on sales and return on capital secured. The significance of the information given in the Annual report is therefore of fundamental importance to a company in any assessment of its financial standing and the efficiency of its management.

ACCOUNTING FOR INFLATION

The forward prospects of a business are increasingly tested by using techniques which adjust standard accounts for inflation. There are two objectives in making these adjustments:

1   To check whether the equity on the business is being maintained in real terms; this is achieved by relating all figures to the value of the pound at the year end

2   To test the ability of a firm to finance the replacement of its assets and thus ensure the business can maintain its current level of activity

Both these objectives are sensible, and offer a useful addition to traditional historical accounting; but they are not entirely compatible.

The first—which has been proposed by the main accountancy bodies—is achieved by producing a supplementary balance sheet which adjusts the value of physical assets to allow for the change in the value of money (the movement in the retail price index is used to measure this change), but leaves monetary assets and liabilities at book value since they are fixed in monetary terms.

The profit and loss account is also subject to adjustment, mainly with regard to stocks, depreciation and debt. The value of opening and closing stocks have to be adjusted for the change in money values since purchase. Similarly, the depreciation charge is based on the cost of assets after adjustment for the fall in money values. Sales and other costs are normally adjusted to 'year-end pounds' by assuming they accrue evenly through the year and therefore have to be increased by a half-year movement in the retail price index. A further significant adjustment is made in the case of loans; since the repayment is fixed in monetary terms, the borrower gains by the effective reduction in the cost of meeting the repayment. This gain is measured by calculating the extra cost of the debt that would have been incurred if repayment was adjusted for inflation. The benefit is included in the profit and loss account to offset the interest charge—which also tends to rise with inflation.

Typically these adjustments taken together tend to show companies in a financially weaker position (surveys of public companies show on average profits 20 to 25 per cent lower after adjustment for inflation than before). However, companies with a large property base or substantial gearing in fact benefit since in the first case the gain from asset adjustment is not offset by higher depreciation charges, while in the second case the effective saving on the debt is substantial.

It is immediately evident that these adjustments must be treated with caution; as 1973 and 1974 indicated, property may fall in value even in monetary terms, making the inflation adjustment utterly misleading; while the gain from the effective reduction in the cost of debt repayment is a 'book' gain which in no way improves the liquidity or cash flow of the firm. The first problem has to be countered by relying on the judgment of the directors to substitute a valuation of assets if the inflation adjustment is irrelevant. The latter problem, however, only highlights a traditional accountancy theme – profits must always be distinguished from liquidity. It is this approach that is of concern to Merrett and Sykes in their plea for 'replacement cost' accounts. The argument put forward is that profits should indicate the level of dividends that can prudently be paid out by the directors without undermining the financial base required by the company to maintain its activities.

On this basis the finance needed to replace fixed assets and stocks at current levels of cost must be provided for before calculating profit; moreover, book profits on property revaluation are irrelevant unless the property can be sold without affecting the activities of the business. This approach assumes that business should be maintained regardless of changes in its economics and that, therefore, replacement is realistic; however, to take one example, when airlines need to replace their aircraft it is likely that the cost of new planes will be dimensionally different in operating terms from the former ones, as a result of the depreciation factor. In such cases, to calculate profit after allowing for replacement assumes not only that new investment is justified but that distinction can be drawn between 'improvement' and direct replacement—if only the latter is deemed to be a charge against profits.

There are, however, fewer problems in allowing for the replacement element in stocks since these cover standard commodities; moreover, the cost of these stocks can vary sharply, given the volatile movements recorded by commodities. It is therefore reasonable for companies to declare profits after allowing for the actual cost incurred of replacing stocks; this can be done by the LIFO (last in, first out) system which charges against profits the cost of stocks based on most recent purchases. This system is not quite 'replacement' since it is based on costs incurred, not on costs ruling at the year end; it is, however, a reasonable substitute which can be readily prepared from a company's books.

Recent government action on taxation concessions for stock increases supports a move towards use of this type of accounting. However, technical difficulties—for the Inland Revenue as well as companies—on assessing replacement costs is likely to mean that some form of 'indexing' will be required to calculate inflationary effects. Whatever changes in techniques are adopted, auditors will increasingly provide supplementary accounts adjusted for inflation—and these accounts will be studied with care to gauge individual companies' susceptibility to inflation.

FURTHER READING

C. Knight, *Realistic Tax Reform,* Chatto and Windus, London, 1971.

L.E. Rockley, *Capital Investment Decisions,* Business Books, London, 1968.

A.J. Merrett and A. Sykes, *Finance and Analysis of Capital Projects,* Longman, London, 1973.

W.G. Nursaw, *Purposeful Investment,* Hutchinson, London, 1965.

R.J. Lister, *Studies in Optimal Financing,* Macmillan, London, 1973.

J. Morgan and M. Luck, *Managing Capital Investment,* Mantec, Rugby, 1973.

6

Procedures for Raising Capital

Stephen Badger

In theory three sources of wealth are available to a company—land, labour and capital. These are not wholly interchangeable, but to some extent the balance in any given company can be changed by the entrepreneur; land can be turned into capital by sale and leaseback (see Long-term facilities, below) or a given process can be made more capital-intensive and so generally require less labour (or vice versa). These decisions are within the scope of management, one of whose functions is to optimize the balance between the different factors of production. The first step before raising capital is therefore to ensure that it is really capital that is required.

WHY CAPITAL MAY BE REQUIRED

Capital is required to finance the conduct of the business. When a manufacturing business is first established for instance factory and office premises will be needed and plant and machinery and transport vehicles. These can either be bought outright or hired; in the first case the expenditure represents capital permanently invested in the business (for the second see Medium-term facilities, below). In addition funds will be required to finance production from the initial purchase of raw materials until the sale of the finished product to an external purchaser, to pay wages and to meet overheads; these funds are known as working or revolving capital. As the business expands, fresh injections of both permanent and working capital will be required. If on the contrary it contracts (or is merely run more efficiently) capital will be freed for alternative uses. When the original fixed assets need replacing, more expenditure will be needed. This should have been adequately provided out of profits by depreciation provisions over the life of the assets, but in times of inflation there may well be a shortfall which will need an injection of new capital.

Capital may also be required for acquisitions (see Chapter 9).

TYPE OF CAPITAL REQUIRED

Capital is conventionally described as short-term, medium-term or long-term. The distinctions are not rigid, but short-term capital may be regarded as any liability repayable within one year; medium-term as being repayable between one and ten years in the future; and everything else as being long-term capital (this covers both the proprietors' ordinary risk capital, or equity, and long-term borrowings, or debt capital). In general, working capital requirements should be financed by short-term capital and capital permanently invested in the business should be long term. Medium-term capital is useful to give added flexibility and balance to the overall financial structure; if a project is expected to generate sufficient cash flow to repay the initial investment within say seven years, medium-term financing may be appropriate.

This chapter deals primarily with long-term capital (both debt and equity), but sources of short and medium-term funds are considered in outline.

SOURCES OF LONG-TERM CAPITAL FOR UNQUOTED COMPANIES

The types of capital available to a company that is not quoted on a stock exchange are much the same as those for one that is. The difference in the two situations is that the unquoted company is restricted to a much narrower range of sources, since many potential lenders or shareholders will be unwilling to put up funds if their investment is unquoted and so not marketable. In addition, if the company is private in the legal sense there will be restrictions on the total number of shareholders and on any invitation to the public to subscribe for shares or debentures.

In the first place an unquoted company will rely on the permanent capital put up by its promoter and his friends and relations, supplemented by bank borrowings. But in due course, if the company expands faster than retained earnings by themselves allow, there will come a time when these individuals are unable to find all the funds required; or they may wish to realize part of their investment. If the company has not yet reached a stage where a public flotation is appropriate, it should be possible to find one or more institutions to put up more capital (consisting either of ordinary shares or a mixture of ordinary and loan capital) on the basis that a flotation will take place within a few years so that the institutions will then be able to realize their investment if they wish.

This type of investment is referred to as venture capital and there are a number of specialist institutions providing this kind of finance, such as Industrial and Commercial Finance Corporation, a subsidiary of Finance for Industry which is owned by the Bank of England and the clearing banks. The merchant banks are also active in this field, and insurance companies and pension funds may participate in a placing if the company is large enough.

GOING PUBLIC

The procedure for obtaining quotation on the Stock Exchange is explained in the appendix to this chapter. This is a most important step in any company's development, but at the end of 1970 there were a total of almost 559 500 companies registered in the UK. Of these, over 542 800 were private companies in the legal sense and only just over 3000 were quoted on the Stock Exchange. Many companies will therefore never reach the stage at which a quotation is appropriate, or their proprietors may for various reasons not wish to seek a quotation; taking in new shareholders provides an additional source of capital but at the same time involves added responsibilities towards those shareholders typified by the Stock Exchange's requirements on disclosure. The interests of 'outside' shareholders may at times differ from those of 'family' shareholders and the future management of the company must reflect the new spread of interests represented.

The reasons for going public are usually some of the following:

1   To make the shares marketable and hence more valuable
2   To diversify the family investment holdings and so to reduce the degree of risk
3   To provide funds to meet estate duty liabilities when necessary
4   To make acquisitions of other companies for shares practicable
5   To raise new funds once the resources of the existing shareholders cease to be adequate

This chapter is concerned with the last of these, but it is important to realize that going public does not necessarily involve raising new money for the company—the shares sold to the public are often existing shares being sold on behalf of existing shareholders.

Where money is being raised for the company the procedure is normally to use an offer for sale made by a merchant bank or a firm of issuing brokers. The offer will be underwritten (see p.136) so that the money will be available even if sufficient public subscriptions are not forthcoming. But it is most important for the company's future capital-raising ability that the issue should be successful, which means that it should be fully subscribed, that the shares should open at a premium and that a free after-market should be maintained. To achieve this it is essential that the company should have continuity of good management and attractive prospects and that large shareholders should not continue selling frequent blocks of shares once the offer for sale is complete. The amount of money that can be raised initially will depend primarily on the present and future profit levels of the company and hence on its ability to pay reasonable dividends on the increased capital. The Stock Exchange will not grant quotation unless the company as a whole is expected to have a market value of at least £500 000 (which probably involves after-tax profits of at least £75 000), but in practice it is probably not worth a company going public until it is several times this size since the amount of money raised will otherwise be relatively small, the proportion of it consumed by the expenses of the issue will be unduly high and an adequate after-market is unlikely to result.

SOURCES OF LONG-TERM CAPITAL FOR QUOTED COMPANIES

Once a company has taken the important step of going public it can seek to raise funds from the whole range of investors, both private and institutional, without restriction.

In recent years private investors have tended to an increasing extent to channel their saving through life assurance policies, pension schemes and unit trust purchases rather than making direct investments in securities themselves. Figure 6.1 illustrates this by showing, for recent years, selected uses of funds by

	PERSONAL USES OF FUNDS		USES OF FUNDS BY FINANCIAL INSTITUTIONS		
	Investment in company securities	Life assurance and superannuation funds	Corporate loan capital	Ordinary shares	Land, property and ground rents
1965	−670	1163	336	316	174
1966	−494	1241	381	410	174
1967	−586	1372	280	468	198
1968	−462	1508	299	747	269
1969	−459	1507	301	393	359
1970	−831	1763	180	639	346
1971	−1248	1930	211	961	341
1972	−1225	2601	230	1833	323
1973	−2075	2957	87	454	664
1974	−1310	3115	−19	−291	788
1975	−1325	4420	55	1966	790

Figure 6.1 Uses of funds by individuals and institutions
(In millions of pounds.) *Source:* Central Statistical Office

the personal sector and by financial institutions (other than the banking sector). This shows that there has been a steady net divestment of corporate securities by individuals, whereas financial institutions have been substantial net purchasers. They have also increased their rate of investment in property significantly. Any company wishing to raise funds therefore has to try to issue the sort of security that will appeal to this type of investor—primarily insurance companies, pension funds and unit and investment trusts.

Figure 6.2 shows some of the ways in which companies have in fact raised finance over the same period. It can be seen from this that bank lending plays a very important role, since banks are the first (and often the cheapest) source of finance to which all companies turn. Even more important in the overall picture are internally generated funds: the figures in Figure 6.2 must be viewed in the perspective of a total figure for undistributed income (before providing for depreciation or stock appreciation) of £8682 million in 1975.

	BANK BORROWING	OTHER LOANS AND MORTGAGES	UK CORPORATE ISSUES Ordinary shares	Fixed interest (net)	ISSUES OVERSEAS
1966	187	106	123	452	4
1967	333	24	65	350	32
1968	569	111	298	184	48
1969	664	211	177	335	11
1970	1126	295	44	159	40
1971	732	274	160	215	75
1972	2988	156	326	290	118
1973	4504	805	107	51	113
1974	4411	31	43	−56	11
1975	710	462	966	56	34

Figure 6.2 Selected sources of capital funds for industrial and commercial companies
(In millions of pounds.) *Source:* Central Statistical Office

Types of security

The types of security usually issued are the following:

1   Ordinary shares
2   Preference shares
3   Debentures, secured either by a floating charge or a specific mortgage

4   Unsecured loan stocks
5   Unsecured loan stocks with conversion rights or warrants attached
6   Foreign-currency bonds

Ordinary and preference shares. The distinction between ordinary and preference shares is explained on p.30. Issues of preference shares have become a little more popular in recent years, but even so only £40.1 million was raised in this way in 1975.

Debentures and loan stocks. The other types of capital are generically referred to as loan capital, which may be either secured or unsecured.

A debenture, according to s455 of the Companies Act 1948, includes debenture stock, bonds and any other securities of a company whether constituting a charge on the assets of the company or not; but in stock exchange parlance the expression debenture normally means a secured stock while unsecured loan stock is used to refer to a stock which is not secured. This is the terminology used here.

Unlike shareholders, holders of a debenture or unsecured loan stock are not members of a company, simply its creditors. They are therefore entitled merely to receive the agreed rate of interest (which is normally paid semi-annually) and to receive repayment of capital on final maturity. Their rights will be incorporated in the trust deed constituting the stock which will be made between the company and (usually) a trustee on behalf of the stockholders. It is a requirement of the Stock Exchange that there must be such a trustee if the stock is to be quoted; the trustee will normally be one of the insurance companies or investment trusts which specialize in this type of work.

Investors in fixed-interest stocks have historically required a long life to final maturity. In fact most stocks issued in the London market have a term of twenty to twenty-five years, although more recently some medium-term issues have been seen. There is usually a period of five years before final maturity when the company can repay the stock without penalty and the average life of the stock may be reduced by the operation of a sinking fund. Since the creditworthiness of a company, and even the nature of its business, can change materially over an interval of this length the trust deed constituting the stock will impose certain restrictions on the company. These will vary from case to case, but they may include limitations on such things as disposing of more than a certain proportion of the business, changing the nature of the business and giving security. An unsecured loan stock deed will also contain a permanent limit on the overall borrowings of the company and its subsidiaries and a separate limit on the borrowings of UK subsidiaries. A debenture deed will not impose a continuing limit but will require the presence of a certain level of cover in terms both of income and of assets before any further issue of another tranche of the stock can be made. In general, debenture stock holders, since their claims are supported by security, will require rather less in terms of restrictions than the holders of an unsecured loan stock who merely rank alongside trade and other unsecured creditors. But in either case the trustee will have the power to declare the stock immediately repayable if interest is not paid or if the company defaults on certain other obligations.

Convertible and warrant stocks.   These are a compromise between borrowing and equity. A convertible is an unsecured loan stock which initially merely carries a fixed rate of interest but which, on specified dates or within a specified period, may be converted, at the option of the holder, into ordinary shares of the company at a fixed ratio. Warrant stocks are stocks which are not convertible but which are issued together with warrants which entitle the holder to subscribe for ordinary shares of the company at specified times and at a specified price. Convertible stocks have been popular for a long time, but warrant stocks are only beginning to become familiar in the UK.

The advantage to a company of issuing convertible stock is that for the initial period it can service the stock at a lower rate of interest than would be necessary for a stock that was not convertible, that when it is finally converted the effective price of issuing the resultant shares will be higher than it could have been initially, and that in the interval the interest payments (unlike ordinary dividends) will have been an allowable expense for tax purposes. A warrant stock gives the company a long-term borrowing (at a lower rate of interest than a simple borrowing), and when the warrants are exercised there is a further inflow of cash into the company. Both kinds of stock will impose the same sort of restrictions on the company as an ordinary unsecured loan stock with additional provisions to protect the holders' rights to convert or exercise their warrant rights.

Foreign-currency bonds.   Only the very largest companies will want long-term loans in foreign currencies. In the great majority of cases, the UK market will be amply sufficient as a source of capital and in general it is unwise to incur a foreign-currency liability unless one has corresponding assets in that currency. Moreover only the largest companies would be well enough known to attract the interest of foreign lenders. However, in the 1960s a substantial international capital market developed in eurodollars (US dollars deposited outside the USA, but not necessarily in Europe, and so not subject to any national restrictions on capital flows). A large number of US, and a smaller number of European, companies have taken advantage of this to raise quoted eurodollar loans (both fixed interest and convertible) and there have also been issues in Deutschemarks, Swiss francs and artificial units such as the European unit of account. Unlike domestic issues, eurodollar issues usually have a life to final maturity of not more than ten years – their average life is considerably shorter. UK companies have to apply for Bank of England consent before they are permitted to incur a foreign-currency liability.

METHODS OF ISSUE WITH QUOTATION

The four chief methods of making an issue for cash on the Stock Exchange are:

1 Offer for sale
2 Rights issue
3 Open offer
4 Placing

Offer for sale

In this case all members of the public are invited to subscribe for the issue by advertisements inserted in the press. The offer is usually made at a fixed price. Sometimes an offer for sale by tender is used where only a minimum price is fixed and applicants decide themselves how much they are willing to pay; a striking price is then fixed at a level at which the issue will be fully subscribed and the shares issued at that price to all applicants who applied at that price or above. In either case, only a fixed number of shares are available for issue and, if a greater number of applications are received, each application is scaled down proportionately. Priority is sometimes given to existing shareholders or employees who are sent special application forms.

An offer for sale is normally used when a company goes public for the first time, as described earlier. It may also be used in an issue of loan capital where the amount of capital required is very large or where it is necessary to appeal to a particularly wide circle of investors for some other reason. In most cases, however, a placing is preferred because of its speed and simplicity (see overleaf). By comparison an offer for sale involves significantly larger advertising and administrative costs.

Rights issue

In a rights issue new ordinary shares or other securities are offered to existing shareholders of the company *pro rata* to their holdings. Shareholders can then choose between taking up their entitlement (their rights) by subscribing the set amount per share, or they can sell some or all of their rights in the market if these are quoted at a premium. If they choose to sell they of course receive money rather than paying it out, but their percentage holding in the company is reduced so that in theory the effect is the same as if they had sold some of their existing shares. From the company's point of view the subscription money will still be received from the purchaser of the rights.

It is a requirement of quotation on the Stock Exchange that new equity shares (or other securities involving an element of equity) should only be issued for cash to existing shareholders of the company in proportion to their holdings (unless they consent otherwise in general meeting). As a result, issues of ordinary shares or convertible stocks are normally made by way of rights so that shareholders have the opportunity of maintaining their proportionate stake in the company.

Open offer

An open offer is an offer of loan capital restricted to shareholders (and possibly the holders of loan capital) of the company making the issue. However, the offer is not made *pro rata* to their holdings. Each shareholder can apply for as much stock as he wishes or for none; if more applications are received than stock is being issued, each application will be scaled down proportionately. This method of issue is relatively infrequent, but it may be used if it is thought that the stock being issued may attract a large premium and the benefit of this should accrue to shareholders. It is appropriate only where the company has a large number of shareholders, but in that case the effect is very similar to an offer for sale but without the attendant advertising costs.

Placing

In a placing, stock is offered direct to a relatively small number of large institutional investors who are the principal holders of fixed interest stock; it is therefore a quick and effective method of issue which allows the most precise pricing. Placing for an unquoted company was considered under Sources of Long-term Capital. Stock Exchange permission must be obtained for a placing with quotation and it is a condition of such permission that a proportion of the stock should be available publicly in the market. As already noted, a placing of new equity issued for cash is only possible with shareholders' consent but, because of its simplicity, placing has become the most usual method of raising loan capital for UK companies.

Underwriting and expenses of an issue

Once a company has decided that it needs money, it will clearly wish to be assured of that money as soon as possible, come what may. Rather than making an issue itself it will therefore go to a merchant bank or issuing broker who, in addition to advising on the documentation and terms of the issue, will arrange for it to be underwritten; that is, the issuing house will undertake to subscribe or find subscribers for the issue on the terms fixed in so far as it is not fully subscribed by the public or shareholders as the case may be. In return for accepting this risk and for its overall coordinating work on the issue, the issuing house normally charges a total commission of 2 per cent, 1¼ per cent of which is passed on to the subunderwriters, that is the institutions who agree to take up different amounts of the issue *pro rata* to the extent that it is not fully subscribed. In the case of a placing, however, the stock is placed directly with a number of the same institutions. Accordingly, no subunderwriting commission is required and only a placing commission of perhaps ¾ per cent (varying with the size of the issue) is payable; however, the issue terms will be slightly worse so that the net proceeds receivable by the company will be much the same. The other major expense of an issue of share capital is capital duty levied at a rate of 1 per cent on the value of the shares being issued. Duty is no longer payable on the issue of loan capital but, in the case of a convertible stock, capital duty arises on conversion. By comparison the administrative costs of an issue, especially in a placing, are small.

OTHER METHODS OF SUPPLEMENTING CASH FLOW

The main methods of raising long-term capital with a quotation have now been outlined. It remains to consider briefly the various other possible methods of supplementing cash flow, which are of course open to quoted and unquoted companies alike. Some of these can provide relatively long-term finance, but the majority are short-term.

Long-term facilities

These include mortgages, sale and leaseback transactions and public authority and specialist institution lending. The main sources of mortgage and sale and leaseback finance are the insurance companies and pension funds. In the case of a mortgage loan, a single lender will advance up to two-thirds of the value of a building for a specified term on the specific security of that building—the borrower retains the ownership of the building but his rights are subject to a mortgage charge for the term of the loan. In a sale and leaseback transaction he will actually sell the building (and so forfeit any appreciation in value) in return for a capital sum and at the same time lease the building back for his own use from the purchasing institution for a long period at a specified rent. Other sources of relatively long-term facilities include the Department of Industry (for specified purposes in development areas and in accordance with such schemes as may be in effect from time to time), local authorities where employment is being created in their areas, and various specialist semi-official organizations such as Finance for Industry, Agricultural Mortgage Corporation, Commonwealth Development Finance Company and National Research Development Corporation, all of which exist to lend for certain purposes. The present government has initiated a very considerable expansion of Finance for Industry's medium-term lending and has also established the National Enterprise Board, which has powers both to make loans and to subscribe for share capital. Similarly Equity Capital for Industry has been formed as a vehicle through which insurance companies and other institutions can subscribe new share capital in certain circumstances.

Medium-term facilities

These include leasing, hire-purchase, export finance, project finance and term loans.

Leasing and hire-purchase are most appropriate for items such as vehicles, plant, machinery and office equipment. In leasing, the ownership of the item remains with the lessor, but the lessee is entitled to the use of it for a specified term in return for regular payments under the lease. This is not strictly a borrowing at all and it is often referred to as off-balance-sheet finance since it need not be shown in the company's balance sheet. In a hire-purchase transaction the purchase price of the item and interest thereon is paid in instalments over a set period, at the end of which ownership of the item does pass to the hirer. There are a large number of finance houses which specialize in these activities.

Export finance (which may be either short or medium-term) is made available by the clearing banks, by agreement with the government, at preferential rates to finance exports or specific medium-term export projects. Insurance against political and commercial risks is provided by the governmental Export Credits Guarantee Department. In large transactions, a negotiating bank will undertake to coordinate all aspects of the deal for the exporting company or consortium.

Similarly, merchant and other banks may undertake to arrange finance for a specific project where there is no export element. This will involve tapping a number of different sources of finance in accordance with the cash flow requirements of the individual project and is a particularly flexible form of financing.

Finally, banks sometimes engage in term lending for periods up to five or even ten years. A term loan could come from a single bank or it might be syndicated among a number of different banks. It might be at a fixed rate of interest or on a roll-over basis; that is, with interest fixed periodically at the prevailing rate. In the latter case it is also possible to arrange for drawings to be made in different currencies at different times.

Short-term facilities

These include bank overdrafts and loans, bank acceptance credits, bills of exchange, trade credit, invoice discounting and factoring. Of these, bank overdrafts and loans are the most common and are used universally by companies as Figure 6.2 shows. They may be supplemented by acceptance credits, where a bank undertakes to accept approved bills of exchange up to a certain limit so that the bills can be discounted at the finest rates. Alternatively, bills of exchange can be used as a form of trade credit, whether or not discounted with a bank or discount house, or various arrangements may be made between buyers and suppliers as to the length of credit given in payment for goods. Finally, invoice discounting and factoring are undertaken by various specialist institutions. Invoice discounting means financing the collection of specific invoices (at the risk of the selling company). Factoring involves making immediate payment against invoiced debts which are then normally collected at the factor's own risk for an appropriate charge. All these methods have in common that they finance relatively small revolving trade transactions, but in aggregate they provide the finance of a vast amount of business on a continuing basis.

Current trends

The willingness of lenders to lend for long periods will depend on their being able to foresee a reasonable rate of return in real terms. In times of high inflation there is therefore a reluctance to tie up funds in this way except at rates so high as to be unacceptable to many borrowers. Equally, companies may prefer to borrow for relatively short periods in the hope of being able to refinance their obligations later at a lower rate. For these reasons, there has been a considerable shift in recent years away from long-term issues to more flexible short-term borrowing. This has been encouraged by the greater availability of bank credit following the new monetary policy adopted by the Bank of England from 1971 onwards in its new approach to competition and credit control.

LOOKING AT THE OVERALL CAPITAL STRUCTURE

We have now outlined the chief avenues open to a company wishing to raise new capital. Before raising any new capital a company should consider what the capital is needed for, whether it is permanent or likely to be repaid out of cash flow within a period and what rate of return it is likely to earn. One can then go on to decide how it can best be supplied. For instance in the case of an investment with a high degree of risk the best source of finance is likely to be equity (or risk) capital; but, if it is a relatively risk-free long-term investment, loan capital may be more appropriate. If it is a specific project of medium-term duration, project finance should be considered, while if it is a working capital requirement, bank overdraft facilities are likely to be the answer. In all cases the various methods of supplementing cash flow in other ways must be borne in mind so as to minimize the amount of new capital actually required. Finally, the rate of return must be set against the cost of the capital to ensure that an adequate margin exists to justify the investment.

One of the most important considerations is to preserve a proper balance between debt and equity in the company's financial structure. This relationship is described as the company's financial gearing; if the company's source of income is reasonably stable and assured (such as the rental income of a property company) it is safe for it to be highly geared, but if it is operating in a cyclical industry (such as machine tools) it is prudent to keep the gearing (ie the element of borrowing) at a low level, for interest on borrowings has to be paid in adverse as well as favourable times and if a temporary set-back combined with high interest charges results in the company making a loss, its overall status will suffer. The degree of gearing will depend both on the absolute amount of borrowing and the extent to which any of this borrowing is at fluctuating interest rates which may rise faster than the company's income. In inflationary times, borrowing at a fixed cost can be most advantageous to a company. But the closer the company gets to what is thought to be an unduly high level of borrowings, the more reluctant lenders will be to provide new funds and the more the equity interest of existing shareholders will be endangered.

The object of company financial administration should be to see that the company has adequate funds at the lowest cost consonant with all these factors and so to seek to maximize its earnings for ordinary shareholders.

FURTHER READING

The author is not aware of any books directly covering the same ground as this chapter, but the following may be useful.

Merrett, Howe and Newbould, *Equity Issues and the London Capital Market,* Longmans, London, 1967.

Admission of Securities to Listing, Stock Exchange, London, revised 1973.

Report of the Committee on the Working of the Monetary System (Radcliffe Report) (Cmnd. 827), HMSO, London, 1959.

'Competition and Credit Control', Bank of England, reprinted in *Bank of England Quarterly Bulletin,* June 1971.

Report of the Committee of Inquiry on Small Firms (Cmnd. 4811), HMSO, London, 1971.

J.H.C. Leach, 'The Weight of New Money—Two Years Later', *Investment Analyst,* December, 1969.

J.H.C. Leach, 'The Role of the Institutions in the UK Ordinary Share Market', *Investment Analyst,* December, 1971.

'New Capital Issues Statistics', *Midland Bank Review,* commentary published annually in February edition.

R.A. Brealey and C. Pyle, *Bibliography of Finance and Investment,* Elek Books, London, 1973.

Appendix

Listing on the Stock Exchange

The Stock Exchange Public Relations Office

A listing on the Stock Exchange is sought through a stockbroker alone or in conjunction with one of the issuing houses, which are specialized concerns or departments of the merchant banks. They are known as sponsors. With the help of chartered accountants, the company's finances, its profit and loss accounts, balance sheets, book-keeping and costing systems are examined. The assets and future prospects of the company are the main factors in determining its capital structure and the method of issuing the shares.

The full requirements of the Stock Exchange when a listing for new securities is sought are available in *Admission of Securities to Listing,* published by the Stock Exchange. General requirements are:

1 No application will be considered unless the company will have an expected market value of at least £500 000 and any one security for which listing is sought will have an expected market value of £200 000.

2 All applications and documents to be considered or approved by the Stock Exchange should always be submitted at the earliest possible opportunity. Although it is possible for the draft prospectus to be first submitted only fourteen days before publication such a short interval is rarely practicable. Moreover, application to make a placing or an introduction of securities of companies not already listed will usually need to be made at least two or three weeks before the draft prospectus is submitted. When reading documents submitted to it for approval and considering applications, the prime concern of the Stock Exchange is to ensure that sufficient information is revealed to enable a fair view to be formed of the worth of the securities involved. The Stock Exchange is also concerned with certain practices and procedures relating to the

distribution of securities.

3 The Bank of England exercises control of the timing of issues, where the amount of money to be raised is £3 000 000 or more, in order to maintain an orderly new issue market; in such cases it is necessary for the sponsoring broker to apply to the government broker for a date known as 'impact day'—that is, the first day on which the size and terms of the issue may be made known to underwriters, placees and the market.

4 Before grant of listing all companies must sign a Listing Agreement that they will provide promptly certain information about their operations and that they will follow certain administrative procedures. However, a number of the Stock Exchange requirements may be varied if the Stock Exchange is satisifed that any of its requirements should not apply in the circumstances of the particular case; specific approval must be obtained.

Where it is proposed to increase the authorized share capital, the directors must state in the explanatory circular or other document accompanying the notice of meeting whether they have any present intention of issuing any part thereof. Where 10 per cent or more of the voting capital will remain unissued (disregarding shares reserved for issue against exercise of subsisting conversion rights or options), the directors must undertake that no issue will be made which would effectively change the control of the company or nature of its business without the prior approval of the company in general meeting.

Methods of issue

Securities may be brought to the Stock Exchange by any one of the following methods:

1   An offer to the public, by or on behalf of a company or other authority, at a fixed price (*prospectus issue*)
2   An offer to the public, by or on behalf of a third party, at a fixed price (*offer for sale*)
3   An offer to the public, by or on behalf of a company or other authority, or a third party, by tender (*offer by tender*)
4   Placing
5   Introduction
6   Rights offer to holders of existing securities
7   Open offer to holders of existing securities
8   Capitalization issue to holders of existing securities
9   In consideration of assets acquired
10   In exchange for or conversion of other securities
11   In exercise of options

PROSPECTUS ISSUES, OFFERS FOR SALE, OFFERS BY TENDER

The Stock Exchange must approve the prospectus before it is issued and the prospectus must be advertised in accordance with the Companies Acts and the Stock Exchange's requirements which are, in the interests of investors, more stringent than those of the law. Any abridged particulars or preliminary announcement of a public offer must not include any information that does not or will not appear in the prospectus. If none of the company's securities is already listed on the Stock Exchange, the Stock Exchange must also approve the memorandum and articles of association. Preferential treatment on allotment must be approved prior to publication of the prospectus and must normally be limited to 10 per cent of the amount offered and then only to employees or shareholders. Prior approval must also be obtained for any part underwritten firm; this must be strictly limited, the amount depending upon the proportion of the total amount of the security being offered for subscription.

The Stock Exchange must be satisfied about the procedure for determining the price and basis of allotment in the case of offers by tender, particularly where listing is sought for securities of a company no part of whose capital is already listed.

CONTENTS OF PROSPECTUS

1   The full name of the company.
2   A statement as follows:

> This document contains particulars given in compliance with the Regulations of the Council of The Stock Exchange for the purpose of giving information to the public with regard to the company. The directors collectively and individually accept full responsibility for the accuracy of the information given and confirm, having made all reasonable enquiries, that to the best of their knowledge and belief there are no other facts the omission of which would make any statement herein misleading.

(Where listing is being sought for securities of one company guaranteed or secured by a second company not being its subsidiary, and the prospectus gives material information with regard to the second company, the directors of the second company should make a statement accepting a similar responsibility regarding the information given about their company.)

3   A statement as follows:

> Application has been made to the Council of The Stock Exchange for the securities to be admitted to the Official List.

4(*a*) The authorized share capital, the amount issued or agreed to be issued, the amount paid up and the description and nominal value of the shares.

(*b*) A statement that (apart, where applicable, from issues or proposed issues specified in the prospectus) no material issue of shares (other than to shareholders *pro rata* to existing holdings) will be made within one year without prior approval of the company in general meeting.

(*c*) In a case where 10 per cent or more of the voting capital (unclassified shares being regarded as voting capital) will remain unissued (disregarding unissued shares reserved for issue against exercise of subsisting conversion rights or options), a statement that no issue will be made which would effectively alter the control of the company or nature of its business without prior approval of the company in general meeting.

5   In relation to the company and its subsidiaries:

(*a*) Particulars of loan capital (including term loans) outstanding, or created but unissued, and of all mortgages or charges, or an appropriate negative statement.

(*b*) Particulars (as at the latest date reasonably practicable) of other borrowings or indebtedness in the nature of borrowing, including bank overdrafts and liabilities under acceptances (other than normal trade bills) or acceptance credits, hire-purchase commitments, or guarantees or other material contingent liabilities, or, if there are no such liabilities, a statement to that effect.

Inter-company liabilities within the group should normally be disregarded, a statement to that effect being made, where necessary (see Note iv).

6 The full name, address and description of every director and, if required by the Committee, particulars of (*a*) any former christian names and surname, (*b*) his nationality, if not British, and (*c*) his nationality of origin if his present nationality is not the nationality of origin.

7 The full name and professional qualification (if any) of the secretary and the situation of the registered office and transfer office (if different).

8 The names and addresses of the bankers, brokers, solicitors, registrars and trustees (if any).

9 The name, address and professional qualification of the auditors.

10 The date and country of incorporation and the authority under which the company was incorporated. In the case of a company not incorporated in the UK, the addresses of the head office and of the principal place of business (if any) in the UK.

11 If the application is in respect of shares:

(*a*) The voting rights of shareholders.

(*b*) If there is more than one class of share, the rights of each class of share as regards dividend, capital, redemption, and the creation or issue of further shares ranking in priority to (or *pari passu* with) each class other than the lowest ranking equity.

(*c*) A summary of the consents necessary for the variation of such rights.

12 The provisions or a sufficient summary of the provisions of the articles of association, by-laws or other corresponding document with regard to:

(*a*) Any power enabling a director to vote on a proposal, arrangement, or contract in which he is materially interested.

(*b*) Any power enabling the directors, in the absence of an independent quorum, to vote remuneration (including pension or other benefits) to themselves or any members of their body.

(*c*) Borrowing powers exercisable by the directors and how such borrowing powers can be varied.

(*d*) Retirement or non-retirement of directors under an age limit.

13 Where listing is sought for loan capital, the rights conferred upon the holders thereof, and particulars of the security (if any) therefor.

14 The general nature of the business of the company or group and, in cases where the company or group carries on two or more activities which are material, having regard to profits or losses, assets employed or any other factor, information as to the relative importance of each such activity. If the company or group trades outside the UK, a statement showing a geographical analysis of its trading operations.

15(*a*) In regard to (i) every company whose results are, or are proposed to be, dealt with in the consolidated accounts, and (ii) other investments which are material in relation to the company, particulars of: the name, date, country of incorporation, whether public or private, general nature of business, issued capital and the proportion thereof held or about to be held.

(*b*) In regard to the company and every subsidiary or company about to become a subsidiary, particulars of: the situation, area and tenure (including in the case of leaseholds the rent and unexpired term) of the factories and main buildings, the principal products and approximate number of employees.

16 A statement showing the sales turnover figures or gross trading income during the preceding five financial years which should contain a reasonable breakdown between the more important trading activities. In the case of a group, internal sales should be excluded.

17(*a*) A statement as to the financial and trading prospects of the company or group, together with any material information which may be relevant thereto, including all special trade factors or risks (if any) which are not mentioned elsewhere in the prospectus and which are unlikely to be known or anticipated by the general public, and which could materially affect the profits.

(*b*) Where a profit forecast appears in any prospectus the principal assumptions, including commercial assumptions, upon which the directors have based their profit forecast, must be stated. The accounting bases and calculations for the forecast must be examined and reported on by the auditors to the company, and any reporting accountants joined with the auditors in their report, and such report must be set out. The issuing house, or, in the absence of an issuing house, the sponsoring brokers must report in addition whether or not they have satisfied themselves that the forecast has been stated by the directors after due and careful inquiry, and such report must be set out.

(*c*) Where listing is sought for fixed income securities, particulars of the profits cover for dividend/interest, and of the net tangible assets.

(*d*) A statement as to any waiver of future dividends.

18 A statement by the directors that in their opinion the working capital available is sufficient, or, if not, how it is proposed to provide the additional working capital thought by the directors to be necessary.

19 Where the securities for which listing is sought were issued for cash within the two years preceding the publication of the prospectus, or will be issued for cash, a statement or an estimate of the net proceeds of the issue and a statement as to how such proceeds were or are to be applied.

20 A report by the auditors of the company:

(*a*) With respect to the profits or losses of the company in respect of each of the five completed financial years immediately preceding the publication of the prospectus, or in respect of each of the years since the incorporation of the company, if this occurred less than five years prior to such publication; and, if the report is in respect of a period ending on a date earlier than three months before such publication, a statement that no accounts have been made up since that date.

(*b*) In the case of an issue by a holding company, in lieu of the report in (*a*), a like report with respect to the profits or losses of the company and of its subsidiary companies, so far as such profits or losses can properly be regarded as attributable to the interests of the holding company.

(*c*) As to the rate of dividend and the amount absorbed thereby for each class of shares during each of the five financial years preceding the issue of the prospectus with details of any waiver of dividends in such years.

(*d*) With respect to the balance sheet of the company and in the case of an issue by a holding company, a like report with respect to the consolidated balance sheet of the company and of its subsidiary companies, in each case at the end of the last accounting period reported upon.

(*e*) With respect (and in summarized form, if desired) to the balance sheet of the company or, if the company is a holding company, the consolidated balance sheet of the company and of its subsidiary companies at the end of each previous accounting period reported upon and at the beginning of the first such period.

(*f*) With respect to any other matters which appear to the auditors to be relevant having regard to the purpose of the report.

In making such a report the auditors shall make such adjustments (if any) as are in their opinion appropriate for the purpose of the prospectus.

21 If, after the latest date to which the accounts of the company have been made up and audited, the company or any of its subsidiaries has acquired or agreed to acquire or is proposing to acquire a business or shares in a company which will by reason of such acquisition become a subsidiary, and no part of the securities of that company is already listed, a report made by qualified accountants who shall be named in the prospectus with respect to:

(*a*) The profits or losses of the business or to the profits or losses attributable to the interests acquired or being acquired in respect of each of the five completed financial years immediately preceding the publication of the prospectus, or in respect of each of the years since the commencement of the business or the incorporation of such company if this occurred less than five years prior to such publication; and if the report is in respect of a period ending on a date earlier than three months before such publication, a statement that no accounts have been made up since that date: provided that where any such company is itself a holding company the report shall be extended to the profits or losses of that company and its subsidiary companies which shall be ascertained in the manner laid down in sub-paragraph (*b*) of paragraph 20.

(*b*) The assets and liabilities of the business or, where appropriate, the balance sheet of such company and where such company is itself a holding company, the report shall be extended to the consolidated balance sheet of that company and of its subsidiary companies in the manner laid down in sub-paragraph (*d*) of paragraph 20.

(*c*) Any other matters which appear to the accountants to be relevant having regard to the purpose of the report.

In making such report the accountants shall make such adjustments (if any) as are in their opinion appropriate for the purposes of the prospectus.

22 Particulars of any capital of the company or of any of its subsidiaries which has within two years immediately preceding the publication of the prospectus

been issued or is proposed to be issued fully or partly paid up otherwise than in cash and the consideration for which the same has been or is to be issued, or an appropriate negative statement (see Note (iv)).

23 Particulars of any capital of the company or of any of its subsidiaries, which has within two years immediately preceding the publication of the prospectus been issued or is proposed to be issued for cash, the price and terms upon which the same has been or is to be issued and (if not already fully paid) the dates when any instalments are payable with the amount of all calls or instalments in arrear, or an appropriate negative statement (see Note (iv)).

24 Particulars of any capital of the company or of any of its subsidiaries which is under option, or agreed conditionally or unconditionally to be put under option, with the price and duration of the option and consideration for which the option was or will be granted, and the name of the grantee, or an appropriate negative statement (see Note iv). Provided that where options have been granted or agreed to be granted to all the members or debenture holders or to any class thereof or to employees under a share option scheme, it shall be sufficient, so far as the names are concerned, to record that fact without giving the names of the grantees.

25 (*a*) Particulars of any preliminary expenses incurred or proposed to be incurred and by whom the same are payable (see Note (i)).
(*b*) The amount or estimated amount of the expenses of the issue and of the application for listing so far as the same are not included in the statement of preliminary expenses and by whom the same are payable.

26 Particulars of any commissions, discounts, brokerages or other special terms granted within two years immediately preceding the publication of the prospectus in connection with the issue or sale of any capital of the company or any of its subsidiaries (see Notes (iv) and (v)).

27 A statement showing:

(*a*) Any alterations in the share capital of the company within the two years preceding the publication of the prospectus.
(*b*) The interests of each director in the share capital of the company appearing in the register maintained under the provisions of the Companies Act 1967 (or which would be required so to appear if the company were subject to the provisions of that Act) distinguishing between beneficial and non-beneficial interests, or an appropriate negative statement.
(*c*) Particulars of any interest, other than that of a director, in any substantial part of the share capital of the company and the amount of the interest in question, or an appropriate negative statement.

28 (*a*) Details of directors' existing or proposed service contracts with the company or any subsidiary, excluding contracts expiring, or determinable by the employing company without payment of compensation (other than statutory compensation) within one year, or an appropriate negative statement (see Note (iv)).

(*b*) The aggregate emoluments of the directors during the last completed financial period together with an estimate of the amount payable to the directors, including proposed directors, for the current financial period under the arrangements in force at the date of the prospectus.

29 (*a*) Full particulars of the nature and extent of the interest, direct or indirect, if any, of every director in the promotion of, or in any assets which have been, within the two years preceding the publication of the prospectus, acquired or disposed of by or leased to, the company or any of its subsidiaries, or are proposed to be acquired, disposed of by or leased to the company or any of its subsidiaries, including:

(i) the consideration passing to or from the company or any of its subsidiaries;

(ii) short particulars of all transactions relating to any such assets which have taken place within two years immediately preceding the publication of the prospectus;

or an appropriate negative statement (see Notes (i) and (iv)).

(*b*) Full particulars of any contract or arrangement subsisting at the date of the prospectus in which a director of the company is materially interested and which is significant in relation to the business of the company and its subsidiaries, taken as a whole, or an appropriate negative statement. In determining what contracts are to be disclosed in compliance with this requirement, reference should be made to Note 39, Chapter 2 of the document *Admission of Securities to Listing* published by The Stock Exchange (see Note (iv)).

30 A statement that the company or any of its subsidiaries has or has not (as the case may be) any litigation or claims of material importance pending or threatened against it (see Note (iv)).

31 (*a*) The name of any promoter; and (if a company) the Committee may require a statement of its issued share capital; the amount paid up thereon; the date of its incorporation; the names of its directors, bankers and auditors; and such other particulars as the Committee think necessary in connection therewith (see Note (i)).

(*b*) The amount of any cash or securities paid or benefit given within the two years immediately preceding the publication of the prospectus, or proposed to be paid or given to any promoter and the consideration for such payment or benefit.

32 Where the prospectus includes a statement purporting to be made by an

expert, a statement that the expert has given and has not withdrawn his written consent to the issue of the prospectus with the statement included in the form and context in which it is included.

33 When relevant, in the absence of a statement that income-tax, surtax and shortfall clearances as appropriate have been obtained, a statement that appropriate indemnities have been given. (The Committee may require such indemnities to be supported by continuing guarantees.)

34 When relevant, in the absence of a statement that estate-duty and capital transfer tax indemnities have been given, a statement that the directors have been advised that no material liability for estate duty or capital transfer tax would be likely to fall upon the company or any subsidiary. (The Committee may require any indemnities to be supported by continuing guarantees.)

35 The dates of and parties to all material contracts (not being contracts entered into in the ordinary course of business) entered into within two years immediately preceding the publication of the prospectus, together with a summary of the principal contents of each contract including particulars of any consideration passing to or from the company or any subsidiary (see Notes (iii) and (iv)).

36 A statement that for a period (being not less than fourteen days) at a named place in the City of London [or such other centre as the Committee may determine] the following documents (or copies thereof) where applicable may be inspected: The memorandum and articles of association; trust deed; each contract disclosed pursuant to paragraphs 28(a) and 35 or, in the case of a contract not reduced into writing, a memorandum giving full particulars thereof; all reports, letters, or other documents, balance sheets, valuations and statements by any expert any part of which is extracted or referred to in the prospectus; written statements signed by the auditors or accountants setting out the adjustments made by them in arriving at the figures shown in their reports and giving the reasons therefor; and the audited accounts of the company and its subsidiaries for each of the two financial years preceding the publication of the prospectus together with all notes, certificates or information required by the Companies Acts (see Notes (ii) and (iv)).

NOTES

(i) In the case of a company which has carried on the same business for more than the two years immediately prior to the publication of the prospectus, application may be made to the Committee to dispense with the requirements of paragraphs 25(a) and 29(a), in so far as they relate to interests in the promotion, and with 31(a).

(ii) In the case of foreign companies, the documents to be offered for inspection will be the documents corresponding to those above mentioned in the case of British companies, and where such documents are not in the English language there must be available for inspection transla:ions either notarially certified or made by a person certified by a solicitor, qualified to practise in any part of the UK or in the Republic of Ireland, to be in his opinion competent to make such translations.

(iii) In cases where it is contended that contracts cannot be offered for inspection without disclosing to trade competitors important information the disclosure of which might be detrimental to the company's interests, application may be made to the Committee to dispense with the offering of such documents for inspection.

(iv) Under paragraphs 5, 22, 23, 24, 26, 28 (*a*), 29, 30, 35 and 36, reference to subsidiaries is to be construed as including any company which will become a subsidiary by reason of an acquisition falling within paragraph 21.

(v) In the absence of confirmation under paragraph 26, an appropriate negative statement must be supplied in the form of a letter addressed to the Department.

(vi) The requirements stated above are in general applicable to an industrial company. The Committee will require additional or alternative information for companies engaged in other enterprises. In the case of a company whose activities include exploration for natural resources reference should be made to pages 150-2 of the Stock Exchange publication, *Admission of Securities to Listing.*

LISTING AGREEMENT (COMPANIES)

1 To notify the Department in advance of the date fixed for any board meeting at which the declaration or recommendation or payment of a dividend is expected to be determined upon, or at which any announcement of the profits or losses in respect of any financial period or part thereof is to be approved for publication.

2 To notify the Department immediately after the relevant board meeting has been held of:

(*a*) Any preliminary profits announcements for any year, half-year or other period.
(*b*) All dividends and other distributions to members recommended or declared or resolved to be paid and of any decision to pass any dividend or interest payment.
(*c*) Short particulars of any proposed change in the capital structure, or redemption of securities.

3 To notify to the Press the basis of allotment of securities in prospectus and other offers and, if applicable, in respect of excess applications, such notice to appear not later than the morning of the business day next after the allotment letters or other relevant documents of title are posted.

4 To notify the Department without delay of:

(*a*) Particulars of any material acquisitions or realizations of assets comprised in the definition set out in the chapter on Acquisitions and Realizations contained in *Admission of Securities to Listing.*

(*b*) Any information required to be disclosed to the Stock Exchange under provisions of the City Code on Take-overs and Mergers.

(*c*) Any changes in the directorate.

(*d*) Any proposed change in the general character or nature of the business of the company or of the group.

(*e*) Any information required to be notified to the company under Section 33 of the Companies Act 1967 (or which would be so required if the company were subject to the provisions of that Act).

(*f*) Any change in the status of the company under the close company provisions of the Income and Corporation Taxes Act 1970 (and of any amendments thereto).

(*g*) Any other information necessary to enable the shareholders and the public to appraise the position of the company and to avoid the establishment of a false market in its securities.

5 To send with the notice convening a meeting of holders of securities to all persons entitled to vote thereat proxy forms with provision for two-way voting on all resolutions intended to be proposed.

6 To forward to the Department copies of:

(*a*) Proofs for approval (through the company's brokers), of all circulars to holders of securities, notices of meetings, forms of proxy and notices by advertisement to holders of bearer securities.

(*b*) All circulars, notices, reports, announcements or other documents at the same time as they are issued.

(*c*) All resolutions passed by the company other than resolutions concerning routine business at an annual general meeting.

7 To notify the Department of an explanation for the delay in any case where no annual report and accounts have been issued by the company within the six months following the date of the end of the financial period to which they relate, at the same time indicating when it is expected that such report and accounts will be published.

8 To prepare a half-yearly or interim report which must be sent to the holders of securities or inserted as paid advertisements in two leading daily newspapers not later than six months from the date of the notice convening the annual general meeting of the company.

9 To circulate with the annual report of the directors:

(*a*) A statement by the directors as to the reasons for adopting an alternative basis of accounting in any case where the auditors have stated that the accounts are not drawn up in accordance with the standard accounting practices approved by the accountancy bodies.

(*b*) A geographical analysis of turnover and of contribution to trading results of those trading operations carried on by the company (or group) outside the UK.

(*c*) The name of the principal country in which each subsidiary operates.

(*d*) The following particulars regarding each company in which the group interest in the equity capital amounts to 20 per cent or more:

(i) The principal country of operation.

(ii) Particulars of its issued share and loan capital and, except where the group's interest therein is dealt with in the consolidated balance sheet as an associated company, the total amount of its reserves.

(iii) The percentage of each class of loan capital attributable to the company's interest (direct or indirect).

(*e*) A statement as at the end of the financial year showing the interests of each director in the share capital of the company appearing in the register maintained under the provisions of the Companies Act 1967 (or which would be required so to appear if the company were subject to the provisions of that Act), distinguishing between beneficial and non-beneficial interests; such statement should include by way of note any change in those interests occurring between the end of the financial year and a date not more than one month prior to the date of the notice of meeting or, if there has been no such change, disclosure of that fact.

(*f*) A statement showing particulars as at a date not more than one month prior to the date of the notice of meeting of an interest of any person, other than a director, in any substantial part of the share capital of the company and the amount of the interest in question or, where appropriate, a negative statement.

(*g*) (i) A statement showing whether or not, so far as the directors are aware, the close company provisions of the Income and Corporation Taxes Act 1970 (and of any amendments thereto) apply to the company and whether there has been any change in that respect since the end of the financial year.

(ii) In the case of an investment trust a statement showing the status of the company under the provisions of the Income and Corporation Taxes Act 1970 (and of any amendments thereto) and of any change in that status since the end of the financial year.

(*h*) Particulars of any contract subsisting during or at the end of the financial year in which a director of the company is or was materially interested and which is or was significant in relation to the company's business.

(*i*) Particulars of any arrangement under which a director has waived or agreed to waive any emoluments.

(*j*) Particulars of any arrangement under which a shareholder has waived or agreed to waive any dividends.

10(*a*) To procure that any service contract granted by the company, or any subsidiary of the company, to any director or proposed director of the company not expiring or determinable within ten years by the employing company without payment of compensation (other than statutory compensation) must be made subject to the approval of the company in general meeting.

(*b*) To make available for inspection at the registered office or transfer office during usual business hours on any weekday (Saturdays and public holidays excluded) from the date of the notice convening the annual general meeting until the date of the meeting and to make available for inspection at the place of meeting for at least fifteen minutes prior to the meeting and at the meeting copies of all service contracts, unless expiring or determinable within one year by the employing company without payment of compensation, of any director of the company with the company or any of its subsidiaries and, where any such contract is not reduced to writing, a memorandum of the terms thereof.

(*c*) To state in a note to the notice convening the annual general meeting that copies or, as the case may be, memoranda of all such service contracts will be available for inspection or, if there are no such contracts, to state that fact.

11 To certify transfers against certificates or temporary documents and to return them on the day of receipt or, should that not be a business day, on the first business day following their receipt and to split and return renounceable documents within the same period.

12 To register transfers and other documents wthout payment of any fee.

13 To issue, without charge, certificates within:

(*a*) One month of the date of expiration of any right of renunciation.
(*b*) Fourteen days of the lodgment of transfers.

14 To arrange for designated accounts if requested by holders of securities.

15 Where warrants to bearer have been issued or are available for issue:

(*a*) To issue certificates in exchange for warrants (and vice versa if permitted) within fourteen days of the deposit of the warrants (or certificates).
(*b*) To certify transfers against the deposit of warrants.

16 In the absence of circumstances which have been agreed by the Council to be exceptional to obtain the consent of the company in general meeting prior to issuing for cash:

(*a*) equity capital or capital having an equity element, (*b*) securities convertible into equity capital, or (*c*) warrants or options to subscribe for equity capital;

otherwise than to the equity shareholders of the company and, where appropriate, holders of other equity securities of the company entitled thereto.

17 In the event of a circular being issued to the holders of any particular class of security, to issue a copy or summary of such circular to the holders of all other listed securities unless the contents of such circular are irrelevant to such other holders.

7

Taxation

J C Craig

Tax law is mainly based on the Income and Corporation Taxes Act 1970, the Taxes Management Act 1970, the Capital Allowances Act 1968 and annual Finance Acts. The three named Acts brought together the combined effects of the Income Tax Act 1952 and subsequent Finance Acts to 1969 with the principal exception of personal capital gains tax; this is still governed by the Finance Act 1965 as amended by subsequent Finance Acts.

Each year (sometimes more frequently), following the budget speech, a Finance Act is introduced, so it is always necessary to look at the accumulated effect of amendments when examining a tax problem.

Interpretation of the law follows the standard pattern of court decisions, and there are now more than two thousand references to decided cases, each of which is binding on everyone in similar circumstances—unless reversed by a subsequent enactment.

RETURNS AND ASSESSMENTS

Every individual who receives income of any kind is under statutory obligation to complete a return of income each year; the senior partner deals with the form for a partnership; and the officers for a limited company. Personal responsibility for making correct returns cannot be avoided even if an agent is employed to complete the return form.

Tax assessment

Assessments for tax are made by local Inspectors of Taxes in accordance with the return of income and supplementary figures supplied by the taxpayers, including a copy of the annual accounts of a business. Where necessary, an assessment may be altered within six years of the end of the accounting period to which it relates, for example if a mistake is discovered by either the Revenue or the taxpayer. However, there is no time-limit to the correction of assessments which were wrong because of the fraud, wilful default or neglect of the taxpayer. A case heard in 1970 (Rose *v* Humbles) referred to assessments stretching back to 1942.

Appeals against assessment

Where the taxpayer does not agree with the Inspector's assessment, he may appeal in writing within thirty days. Usually the appeal is settled by correspondence or at a meeting with the Inspector, with or without professional advice. If agreement cannot be reached the taxpayer may have the appeal heard by either:

1   General Commissioners, who are leading local citizens, unpaid, not Civil Servants and not specialists in tax, but hear each case on its merits and aim to give a fair decision according to the facts; or
2   Special Commissioners, who are Civil Servants concentrating wholly on the complexities of tax and therefore better able to unravel an argument of a complex nature.

It tends to be more costly to ask for the appeal to be heard by the Special Commissioners because though no charge is made, it may be necessary to travel some distance with professional advisers for the appeal to be heard.

A decision of the Commissioners is binding on both Revenue and taxpayer unless it can be shown that the query is based on an interpretation of the law, when permission may be asked to appeal to the High Court.

Further appeals may go beyond the High Court to the Court of Appeal and then to the House of Lords, if it can be shown there is still doubt as to whether the law has been interpreted correctly. A decision of the Lords cannot be disturbed, but a new clause in a Finance Act may alter the law for the future.

Appeals are an expensive, troublesome activity. A good working relationship between the company's management, its auditors who commonly handle the tax returns, and the local Inspector of Taxes, with the management taking a close personal interest in the tax computations, is recommended as the most practical approach to tax.

(a)

INCOME

Gross trading profit	200,000
Rent from industrial premises let to tenants	20,000
Interest from bank deposit account	6,000
Dividends from shares held	10,000
Interest from debentures held (gross)	4,000
	240,000

EXPENDITURE

Depreciation	26,000	
Salaries, wages, employer's contributions to national insurance and graduated pensions	60,000	
Directors' salaries and fees	10,000	
Bad debts	300	
Specific provision for the bad debt of a named customer	100	
General provision for bad debts	800	
Legal expenses	200	
Rent, rates and insurance	3,000	
Superannuation (company's contribution to an approved scheme)	2,000	
Heating and lighting	1,000	
Travelling expenses	2,000	
Entertainment expenses	600	
Distribution costs	20,000	
Sundry expenses	3,000	
Loss on sale of machinery	1,000	
		130,000
NET PROFIT		110,000

(b)

Net profit shown in the accounts		110,000
add back items not allowable		
Depreciation	26,000	
General provision for bad debts	800	
Entertainment expenses	600	
Loss on sale of machinery	1,000	
		28,400
		138,400
deduct items, either not taxable or		
taxable under different headings		
Rent	20,000	
Interest income	6,000	
Dividends	10,000	
Interest	4,000	
		40,000
		98,400
less		
Capital allowances (in lieu of depreciation)		28,400
CASE I INCOME		70,000

(c)

Case I income -- business profits adjusted	70,000
Case III income -- untaxed income from bank deposit interest	6,000
Schedule A income -- rent	20,000
Income received subject to deduction of income tax at	
source -- debenture interest but *not* dividends	4,000
	100,000
Corporation tax at 52% on £100,000	52,000
	48,000
Dividend income, not liable to corporation tax,	
is not part of the computation	10,000
Remainder, which may be retained or paid out as dividend	58,000

Figure 7.1 Example of a corporation tax computation—
(a) Profit and loss account, (b) Adjustment for corporation tax purposes, (c) Calculation of corporation tax

ADJUSTMENT OF PROFIT AND COMPUTATION OF AMOUNT LIABLE TO TAX

The normal pattern for an industrial or commercial business is to measure and adjust the income from all sources, to arrive at the total on which corporation tax is payable as shown in Figure 7.1.

In making the adjustment of profit to arrive at the amount liable to tax, the starting point is the profit shown in the ordinary profit and loss account. Expenses not allowable must be added back; income which is either not taxable or taxable under a different Case or Schedule must be deducted, to arrive at the Schedule D, Case I (or Case II) adjusted profit.

Apart from advance corporation tax paid to the Collector of Taxes following the payment of dividends (dealt with later), the balance of the liability to corporation tax (the 'mainstream' liability) is due for payment nine months after the end of the accounting period except in the case of companies which carry on the same trade as they did prior to 1965. Such companies have a longer interval—normally they pay their mainstream liability on 1 January in the fiscal year following that in which the accounting period ends.

Rate of tax

The rate of corporation tax is announced for each 'financial year', which runs from 1 April to the following 31 March, in the Chancellor's end-of-year budget. For the financial year 1974 which ended on 31 March 1975, the rate of 52 per cent was announced in the budget on 15 April 1975.

Accounting year

If the company's accounting year spans two financial years in which the percentage differs, the profits are apportioned on a time basis. In, for example the accounting year ended 31 December 1974, three-twelfths of the profit, for January, February, March 1974 is taxed at the rate announced in 1974, and the remaining nine-twelfths at the rate announced in 1975.

ALLOWABLE EXPENSES

For any expense to be allowable, it must have been incurred 'wholly and exclusively' for purposes of the business. Certain forms of expenditure are disallowed, either by definite statements in the Acts, or as a result of cases decided by the courts. It would be impossible to give an exhaustive list here, particularly as many of them concern only a restricted range of industries, but a selection of the more common ones is given below.

General advice is: when in doubt, check with the detailed tax textbooks; if these do not settle the doubt, claim the expense is allowable and see the Inspector's reaction. There is no penalty for this approach provided the true nature of the expense is stated openly and honestly.

Salaries and wages

Salaries and wages of employees are normally allowable in full. Since April 1969 this has applied to directors, the former restrictions having been cancelled, except that excessive payment to part-time directors are liable to be restricted if the Inspector is not satisfied that the amount is reasonable considering the services rendered. This does not prevent large fees from being paid, or from being taxed as earned income in the hands of the directors, but simply means they are added back in the corporation tax computation.

Entertaining

Entertainment expenses are *not* allowable, except for entertaining overseas customers, and even in this case the amount must be reasonable considering the potential business arising. An agent for a foreign customer who is resident in the UK is not within the scope of what is allowable.

'Entertainment' includes gifts of food, drink and tobacco, for example as Christmas presents.

When a senior employee is reimbursed for the cost of entertaining UK customers, the amount is not treated as part of his personal income, but if he is given an allowance to cover entertaining, among other expenses, it becomes part of his earned income from which he cannot deduct any part of the cost of the entertaining.

Bad debts

A general reserve for bad debts is not allowable, but actual bad debts and a specific provision for the bad debt of a named customer are allowable.

Depreciation

Depreciation is not allowable, but capital allowances are given in appropriate cases.

Capital expenditure

No kind of capital expenditure is allowable. Capital profit or loss on the sale of an asset would be excluded from the computation of business profit, but may be subject to a separate calculation for capital gains tax.

Legal expenses

Some legal expenses are and some are not allowable, the distinction being broadly that they are allowable if they relate to a transaction of a revenue nature but not if they are of a capital nature. For example the preparation of a service agreement for a manager, or the collection of debts, or the renewal of an existing short lease are revenue, but the purchase of freehold premises or a long lease is capital.

Retirement benefits

Retirement benefits for employees are allowable whether they are direct pensions or contributions to a superannuation scheme approved by the Inland Revenue. A moderate lump sum to an employee on his retirement would be allowable, but an exceptional lump sum to a superannuation fund would be spread forward over future years.

RELIEF FOR INCREASE IN STOCK VALUES

In a time of inflation, an increasing amount of cash becomes tied up in trading stock, causing cash-flow problems. To alleviate these difficulties, a stop gap stock relief has been introduced. Relief was first granted by the Finance Act 1975, and was extended by Finance (No.2) Act 1976. A more permanent relief is provided for in the Finance Act 1976: broadly, the taxable profit for an accounting period is reduced by the increase in the value of stock held less 15% of the case 1 or 11 profit which would otherwise be liable to tax. In any period in which there is a decrease in the value of stock held, then taxable profit is increased by the amount of the fall or the amount of unrecovered past stock relief, whichever is smaller.

THE NECESSARY BOOK-KEEPING

Adjustment of profit and computation of tax payable are made outside the double-entry book-keeping system, but settlement of the tax requires three ledger accounts:

1 Corporation tax account (including advance corporation tax and tax credits)
2 Income tax account for unfranked investment income
3 Income tax account for PAYE deducted from employees' income

The foundation for accounts 1 and 2 is that a company suffers corporation tax but not income tax on its own income. Income tax which has been deducted at

Corporation tax account	with double entry in:
Debit:	
(a) adjustment for overprovision of last year's liability	Profit and loss (appropriation) a/c
(b) Excess tax suffered on unfranked investment income tax	Unfranked investment income a/c
Credit:	
(a) Estimated tax on the profits for the year now ending	Profit and loss (appropriation) a/c
(b) Adjustment for under provision for last year's liability	Profit and loss (appropriation) a/c

Tax on Unfranked Investment Income Account	
Debit:	
Income tax suffered at source on unfranked investment income received	Unfranked investment income a/c
Credit:	
Tax retained when paying out debenture interest and other annual interest payments	Accounts for debenture, etc. interest paid
Where credit is greater than debit, the difference is settled by paying tax to the Collector	Bank a/c
Where debit is greater than credit, the difference is settled by transfer to corporation tax a/c	Corporation tax a/c

Advance Corporation Tax	
Debit:	
Tax credit accompanying franked investment income received	Memorandum only— not passed through books of account
Credit:	
ACT paid when paying out dividends (debited to corporation tax account) bank a/c	

Figure 7.2 Entries to make in the tax accounts

source from investment income received by the company may be offset against income tax deducted from payments made out by the company, and the net balance is payable to the Collector of Taxes. It is important to keep franked items separate from unfranked, and PAYE separate from both.

The necessary entries are summarized in Figure 7.2.

CAPITAL ALLOWANCES

Capital allowances exist on seven main types of fixed assets used wholly and exclusively for purposes of the business:

1 Industrial buildings
2 Plant and machinery
3 Agricultural land and buildings
4 Mines and oil-wells
5 Capital expenditure on scientific research
6 Patents
7 Know-how

Only the first two types will be considered in detail here.

When any asset which qualifies for allowances is purchased, the first allowances are given in full for the company's accounting period no matter how late in the period the asset was obtained. This rule may need to be modified where the accounting period is shorter than twelve months.

It is important to consider the overall position before deciding whether or not, or to what extent capital allowances should be claimed.

Industrial buildings

The nature of the business must be industrial as distinct from commercial, retailing or wholesaling, or professional. Even for an industrial company the allowance is not given for offices and showrooms, except where these form an integral part of a factory and account for less than 10 per cent of its whole cost.

The allowances to the first owner are now:

1   Initial allowance which has been 40 per cent since April 1972 (previously it varied up to 30 per cent). The initial allowance was increased to 50 per cent on expenditure from 12 November 1974
2   Writing-down allowance of 4 per cent of the cost price (or 2 per cent if the building was erected before November 1962)

In the year of disposal, instead of the writing-down allowance there is a balancing allowance or balancing charge to bring total allowances into line with net cost. Where the building is sold for more than it cost, the balancing charge cannot exceed the total of allowances already received. (There may, however, be a taxable capital gain in addition to the balancing charge.)

On sale of a factory built before November 1962 there is no balancing adjustment if it is sold after it is fifty years old, and for factories built since November 1962 none after they are twenty-five years old.

Cost price includes: the building, plus the architect's fees, plus cost of tunnelling, levelling and preparing the land; installing main services, fences, perimeter walls and roadways on the site.

It does *not* include: the cost of land, legal and estate agency fees; preparation of a lease; purchase price of a lease; demolition of a former building.

When a building is demolished, the cost of demolition is added to the original cost before working out the balancing adjustment.

For the second and subsequent owners, the allowances are equal to the residue of cost spread over the remainder of twenty-five or fifty years. An example is given in Figure 7.3. The importance of distinguishing between land and buildings is vital, with seller and buyer having opposing interests.

Example

Original cost to first owner, 1967		£10,000
Initial allowance in first year 15%	£1,500	
Writing-down allowance 4% a year for 4 years	1,600	3,100
Written-down value in 1970 (end of year)		6,900
Sell on 1 January 1971 for		7,350
Balancing charge on first owner		450

Second owner: residue of cost is £7,350
             balance of 25 years is 21 years
             so annual allowance is £350 a year

Check £350 x 21 = £7,350

Figure 7.3   Example of allowances for expenditure on industrial buildings

Plant and machinery

Allowances may be claimed by any type of business assessed under Case I or Case II of Schedule D, or against Schedule A assessments on income from real property, or in respect of assets owned by an employee and used by the employee for his employer's business, or against profits of a trade assessed under Schedule D Case V.

The definition of 'plant and machinery' spreads remarkably wide to include office and canteen equipment, furniture, dry docks and virtually every type of fixed tangible asset which is not 'building'.

There are two scales of allowances now in the process of being integrated:

1   Assets bought on or after 27 October 1970 take:

(*a*) In the year of purchase a first-year allowance, the balance of the cost being carried forward to the next year

(*b*) In each subsequent year the brought-forward balance of cost for all the different assets is combined and there is a single writing-down allowance of 25 per cent on their total ('the pool').

(*c*) When an asset is sold or scrapped, its disposal price is deducted from the total figure on which writing-down allowances are being calculated.

2   From the first accounting period ending after 5 April 1976, the balance of pre 27 October 1970 expenditure is to be aggregated with the 'pool' of past 26 October 1970 expenditure. (Previously, writing down allowances at various percentages of the written down value brought forward were granted, depending on the nature of the asset.)

The first-year allowance began at 60 per cent but was increased to 80 per cent for machinery bought between 20 July 1971 and 21 March 1972. For assets bought after 21 March 1972, the first-year allowance was increased to 100 per cent. It is given in full no matter how late in the accounting year the machine may have been bought.

It is possible for the company to take any smaller amount of five-year allowance and so take a correspondingly larger writing-down allowance in subsequent years. The allowance applies equally to new or secondhand assets unless a secondhand machine is bought from a connected company mainly with a view to obtaining a larger allowance, in which case the first-year allowance is restricted.

There is no first-year allowance on private cars or on assets bought for purposes of business entertainment, nor on any machines which have qualified for investment grants (if they were ordered before grants were discontinued in October 1970).

Private cars costing over £5000 (£4000 prior to April 1976) are kept separate from other assets, qualifying only for a writing-down allowance at 25 per cent of the written-down value but restricted to a maximum of £1250 per year, starting in the year of purchase and with a balancing adjustment for the year of sale.

For assets acquired on hire-purchase, allowances are given on the equivalent of the cash price, and the hire charge is treated as an allowable revenue expense in the years in which it is paid. For assets on straight hire, contract hire or lease, there are no capital allowances but the rental is fully allowed as a revenue expense in the years in which it is paid (the lessor will normally be eligible for capital allowances like any other trader).

Expenditure incurred on the provision of a new ship is eligible for 'free' depreciation in that any part of the 100 per cent first-year allowance not claimed in the year of purchase may be claimed at the discretion of the tax-payer in any subsequent year. This contrasts with other plant where allowances not claimed merely augment the balance eligible for 25 per cent writing-down allowance.

LOSSES

Setting losses against profits

A trading loss in one accounting period may be set against:

1   Other sources of profit in the same accounting period in which
     the loss is suffered
2   The trading profit of the accounting period immediately
     preceding
3   Other sources of profit in that preceding accounting period

To the extent that a trading loss has been created by first-year allowances it may be set against profits in the three years preceding the year of the loss.

Claims for relief in this way are optional. If they are not made, or if they leave a balance of loss still unrelieved, the remaining loss may be set against the first available future profits from the same trade, but *not* against future profits from other sources.

The right to carry forward any losses is ended when a majority of the shares changes hands and there is a major change in the nature or conduct of the trade being carried on. The effect of this restriction has been virtually to end the sale of tax-loss companies.

An example of a normal loss claim is given in Figure 7.4.

Terminal loss relief

A loss suffered during the final twelve months up to the time a trade is discontinued may be carried backwards and set against the trading profits of the three preceding years. An example is given in Figure 7.5.

RS Ltd. will have a terminal loss claim of £80 000 which will successfully be offset to the extent of £65 000 against the profits of 1970, 1971 and 1972. TU Ltd. has no terminal loss because the loss was not made in the final twelve months. and so will only be able to use normal loss claims against 1972 (£10 000) and 1974 (£5000).

Note particularly that to make a terminal loss claim it is sufficient that the *trade* has been permanently discontinued. This is not necessarily the same as winding up the company, as a company may have more than one activity and its existence may continue without the discontinued trade, or a fresh trade of a different nature may be started after the loss-making enterprise has been discontinued.

PQ Ltd   Accounting period to 31 December annually:

Trading results – 1973 profit	£20,000
1974 loss	60,000
1975 profit	8,000
Unfranked investment income – 1973	5,000
1974	7,000
1975	6,000

Set-off of loss

1 Other income in 1974	7,000
2 Profits in 1973 (£20,000 + £5,000)	25,000
3 Trading profit in 1975	8,000
4 Carry forward against future trading profits	20,000
	£60,000

Unfranked investment income in 1975 is taxable as it cannot be set against the loss. Corporation tax payable for the year to 31 December 1973 would be cancelled, or if already paid it will be refunded.

Note the cash flow advantage of submitting promptly the figures for 1974, and the claim for loss relief.

Corporation tax will be payable on the 1975 investment income, while the remaining £20 000 of 1974 loss is being carried forward to 1976.

Figure 7.4 Example of normal loss relief

Profit for year to	RS Ltd £	TU Ltd £
31 December 1970	40,000	40,000
31 December 1971	15,000	15,000
31 December 1972	10,000	10,000
31 December 1973 loss	(80,000)	(80,000)
RS closed trade at 31 December 1973		
31 December 1974		5,000
TU closed trade at 31 December 1974		

Figure 7.5 Example of terminal loss relief

For explanation see p.165.

Directors' remuneration as it affects loss

It will be seen that skill is needed in arranging a company's affairs in the way to take the best advantage of the many variations of the loss-relief rules. For example, even in a small private company it may be sound policy to pay the directors at least a portion of their customary remuneration, even though this makes the loss larger. Otherwise the directors might be without income from which to offset their personal tax reliefs.

Example. Williams is sole director and principal shareholder of WL Ltd. He customarily draws £4000 a year from the company as director's remuneration and leaves the company with no profit to suffer corporation tax. In 1976/7, trade is poor and before paying himself any remuneration there is trading loss of £1000. If Williams foregoes remuneration his personal reliefs will be wasted, so he declares himself £2200 and leaves the company showing £3200 loss.

His personal income then is
from which he takes: £2,200

personal allowance	£1,085	
child allowance, 3 younger children	900	
dependent relative relief	100	2,085
		£ 115

Income tax payable by Williams will be only:

£115 at 35% = £40.25

The company's trading loss will go forward to set against future 1975 trading profits, as Williams is confident he can restore the profit-making basis of the trade. His personal reliefs would have been wasted had he not taken any remuneration, as they cannot be carried forward.

ADVANCE CORPORATION TAX

On the occasion when a company pays a dividend (or other distribution to members), it is required to make a payment of advance corporation tax (ACT) to the Inland Revenue. The rate of ACT is fixed annually and applied to the actual or net dividend but is equivalent to income tax at the basic rate on the gross of the dividend plus the ACT. Payment of ACT is due quarterly and must be made fourteen days after the end of the quarter in which the dividend is paid. When the dividend is paid, the member is given a tax credit for the ACT in respect of the dividend.

TREATMENT OF SHAREHOLDERS

Every individual who receives a dividend and tax credit can treat the tax credit as if it were a voucher for income tax paid. If he is liable at the basic rate of income tax, no further liability will arise; if he is liable at more than the basic rate, he will be required to pay only at the excess of his higher rate over the basic rate. If his income is so small that he pays no income tax, he will recover the tax credit.

Where a company receives a dividend with a tax credit the sum of the two will be treated as 'franked investment income', ie income which has already borne corporation tax and therefore income upon which no further tax is payable. The company may set the amount of the tax credit against an obligation to pay ACT in respect of its own dividends, and pay only the balance to the Inland Revenue

Treatment of ACT by company paying dividends

In respect of dividends paid during an accounting period, ACT is treated as a payment to account of the corporation tax liability for that accounting period and only the balance (or mainstream liability) is payable nine months after the balance date (or later in respect of certain companies—see Adjustment of profit, above). The ACT must, however, be set against corporation tax on income—it must not be set against tax on capital gains—and the maximum which may be set off is the ACT on a distribution such that the sum of the two is equal to the income charged to corporation tax. Any ACT not relieved in this way may be carried back for two years and any balance still not relieved may be carried forward. An example is given in Figure 7:6.

During the year to 31 March 1974, when the rate of corporation tax was 52 per cent and of ACT three-sevenths, Z Ltd. had the taxable profits shown in Figure 7.6.

GROUPS OF COMPANIES

There are special concessions in the taxation of groups of companies, their main effect being to reduce or cut out the tax on intercompany transactions within the group. It requires considerable skill to arrange group affairs to take the best advantage of these arrangements, and the administrator should either make a specialized study or else form a regular practice of consulting the group's professional advisers before making transfers of assets or dividends within the group.

For example, for some purposes a 'subsidiary' is one in which the parent company owns more than half the ordinary shares, for others the minimum is 75 per cent of the ordinary shares, and for yet others 75 per cent of the whole

Trading profit, Schedule D Case I	£120,000
Unfranked investment income	20,000
Capital gains £52,000, less excluded £22,000 (see section on capital gains tax, below)	30,000

In May 1973, Z Ltd paid a dividend of £105,000 on which ACT amounted to £45,000

The mainstream liability is computed:

Taxable profits –

Income (£120,000 + £20,000)		£140,000
Capital		30,000
		170,000
Corporation tax at 52%		£ 88,400
ACT for set-off	£45,000	
Restricted to tax on gross dividend of £140,000, ie to		42,000

(since £98,000 + ACT thereon of £42,000 = £140,000)

Mainstream liability	£ 46,400

Figure 7.6 Example of set off of ACT

equity capital including certain non-commercial loans.

The main advantages of group taxation are:

Subsidiaries. A subsidiary may pay dividends to its parent company with or without paying ACT thereon. It may be valuable to pay the dividend without ACT when the parent company is not making distributions to its own shareholders, or when it has other sources of franked investment income receivable net and no trading income of its own.

Loss in one company against profit in others. When one company has suffered a trading loss, this may be set off against the profits of any one or more members of the group. It should be noted that this concession does not extend to capital losses, so where possible any assets likely to show a capital loss on disposal should be transferred to a company which will be showing a capital gain on other transactions, before selling them outside the group.

Transfers of capital assets.   No chargeable gain arises when capital assets are transferred between members of a group.   Care is required however when a company which has received an asset leaves the group within six years of the transfer.

CAPITAL GAINS TAX

A capital gain made by a company suffers corporation tax which is collected along with the corporation tax in the same computation. A proportion of the capital gain is excluded from the assessment at the full rate of corporation tax to bring the effective rate of corporation tax on capital gains down to 30 per cent—the normal rate for individuals. It is fair to say that any form of profit not caught under some classification as 'income' is sure to be taxed as capital gain, the following exceptions apart:

1   Wasting assets with a predicted life of less than fifty years, if they are chattels (tangible movable objects) but excluding assets (other than cars) which have qualified for capital allowances
2   For assets held since before April 1965, there is no tax on the gain prior to April 1965
3   Gains on certain government securities
4   Winnings from betting or lotteries
5   Gains on discharge of liabilities (eg the repayment of debentures at less than their issue price)

This list does not include assets such as dwelling houses for which the gain may be exempt if made by an individual.

When a capital gain made by a company has suffered tax and the balance is paid out to shareholders, a further round of tax is deducted. For example, if it sells its premises and goes into liquidation the position is as shown in Figure 7.7. This example has been simplified to illustrate the principle, which in an actual company would be clouded but not overthrown by the existence of other assets.

Underlying capital gains

A company with an underlying capital gain in its assets is always better sold as a going concern than put into liquidation, and to the purchaser it is a matter of indifference whether he obtains ownership of the valuable assets in the one way or the other. He is not obliged to run the company as a trading concern when he has acquired its shares.

For the concern shown in figure 7.7, from the buyer's angle:

1   Purchase price of asset, £400 000, is absorbed into his own business as a fixed asset, or

Sell the asset and then go into liquidation:		Alternatively sell the company's shares for	
Selling price 1975	£400,000	for =	£400,000
Cost price 1965	300,000	Cost price 1965	300,000
Capital gain	£100,000	=	£100,000
Tax at effective rate of 30%	30,000		
Balance distributed to shareholders	70,000		100,000
Less personal capital gains tax 30%	21,000		30,000
Net remainder in the hands of shareholders	£ 49,000		£ 70,000

Figure 7.7   Sale as a going concern is better than liquidation when assets have appreciated

2   If he buys the shares, the asset will thence be treated as a subsidiary of the buying company. It may subsequently be sold to the parent company which may declare a dividend to dispose of its capital gain without suffering any tax; alternatively, the proceeds may simply be lent to the parent company.

The directors of a private company should give thought to the chances of 'retirement exemption' before disposing of their shares. The first £20 000 of gain will be exempt if they have been full-time directors for not less than ten years and hold either:

1   Not less than 25 per cent of the voting share capital in own right
2   Not less than 10 per cent in own right, and members of immediate family own sufficient to bring the total of family holding up to 75 per cent

The exemption is restricted to the gain on underlying chargeable business assets.

Replacement of assets

Deferment of tax on capital gains may be claimed where the asset is replaced by fresh assets (not necessarily of a similar nature, or even serving the same function) if they are of one of the following classes:

1   Land, buildings, plant, machinery
2   Ships
3   Aircraft
4   Goodwill
5   Hovercraft

It is important that the replacement is bought within twelve months before or three years after the sale of the previous asset. These time-limits may be extended at the discretion of the Inland Revenue.

Deferment continues indefinitely if the replacement asset is permanent, but if a 'depreciating asset' is bought it will continue only for ten years. If the depreciating asset is sold within less than ten years and replaced by a fresh permanent asset, the permanence of the deferment is restored, but if it is replaced by a fresh depreciating asset the deferment ends immediately.

Depreciating assets are assets with an expected life of less than 60 years, ie they are wasting assets, or items which will become wasting assets within ten years. The most common example is fixed plant.

Full deferment is given only where it is requested and where the whole proceeds from sale of the previous asset are used for the purchase of the replacement. Where only a portion of the sale proceeds are used, the amount on which deferment can be claimed is restricted.

THE COMPANY AS A TAX COLLECTOR

Although the company does not itself pay any income tax, it is obliged to serve as an unpaid collector by withholding income tax when making payment of:

1   Wages and salaries, for the PAYE system
2   Annual interest, the most common example being debenture interest

The amount of PAYE deducted in a month has to be passed to the Collector of Taxes on the nineteenth of the month next following. For example, month from 6 April to 5 May: tax to be paid on 19 May. Income tax on annual interest is payable quarterly, fourteen days after the end of the quarter.

Extension for close companies. When a close company does not pay a sufficient dividend, part of its income may be treated as if it had been distributed by the company and income tax thereon at the higher rates applicable to its members may be recovered from the company.

CLOSE COMPANY DISABILITIES

1   If money is lent to a 'participator', an amount equal to income on the grossed-up amount of the loan is payable by the company

2   Where a substantial part of the capital takes the form of loans from directors, there is a strict limit on the amount of interest allowable for corporation tax

3   Where a close company fails to make an adequate distribution out of income, tax may be payable as if such a distribution had in fact been made. The amount of the shortfall in distributions is apportioned to members and the appropriate income tax is computed; this income tax may be paid by the members or by the company.   A trading company may retain up to 50 per cent of its trading and estate incomes—more if the requirements of the business justify further retentions

For apportionment purposes, the trading and estate income is disregarded if it is below £5000; or if it is between £5000 and £15 000 it is abated by one-half of the amount by which the income falls short of £15 000.

It is always open to a trading company to justify a smaller distribution, on the ground that the company needs to retain more of the profit to meet the requirements of its business—to finance improvements, modernization or expansion and to repay short-term loans; but not to pay off the original loan capital or to finance the acquisition of its first business.

Negotiations with a view to ensuring there will be no apportionment of income should be opened by an approach to the Inspector backed by a clear statement of intentions such as the forecast of sources and application of funds which forms part of the management accounting routine of most companies.

CONTRAST BETWEEN LIMITED COMPANY AND PARTNERSHIP

Partners pay income tax at graduating rates on the whole of their profit, which is regarded as earned income in their hands, except in the case of a limited (or 'sleeping') partner whose share is treated as investment income for tax purposes.

In a limited company, whether private or public, corporation tax is payable on the profit after deducting remuneration of its directors, who are classed as employees. Profit remaining in the company after paying corporation tax is not subject to further tax but if it is withdrawn as dividend this may be liable to income tax at the higher rates as personal investment income of the shareholder.

In a small business where a few individuals share both management and ownership, there is no important difference in the overall effect of tax between limited company and partnership, unless profit is appreciably higher than £8000 a year per individual. Where the profit is larger, the limited company has the advantage so long as profits retained in the business are needed to finance expansion. However, where there are shareholders who are not concerned in managing or working for the company, there may be tax drawbacks in paying them a return on their capital.

Examples. Three men share the ownership and management of the business.

A. Profit before paying the three men is £15 000
Limited company. The whole profit is taken as directors' remuneration and they pay income tax on it as earned income. No corporation tax.
Partnership. The whole profit suffers income tax as earned income. Difference between the two forms—none.

B. Profit before paying the three men is £84 000.
Limited company. Take £10 000 each man as directors' remuneration, suffering income tax as earned income. Remaining £54 000 suffers 52 per cent corporation tax − £28 080 − balance of £25 920 escapes further tax if it is retained in the company.

Partnership. Whole profit suffers income tax − £28 000 each man. The profit is taxed as earned income but the personal tax rates rise to 83 per cent on the top slice. Difference: worthwhile tax saving with limited company. This would be somewhat curtailed if the directors were obliged to pay dividends to avoid an apportionment of income.

There are many powerful legal advantages for running a limited company and these often far outweigh the importance of tax differences. The larger the business and the more involved its ownership, the more important it becomes to operate it as a limited company. On the other hand certain undertakings, such as most of the professions, are not allowed to operate through limited companies.

CHANGES IN PERSONAL AND CORPORATION TAX

From 1973-4, income tax and surtax were replaced by a single unified tax, but the change was one of administration. It did not alter the total tax liability, the only real difference to the taxpayer being that the new high rates of tax on large incomes are payable more promptly than the surtax they replaced.

Changes in the corporation tax system were effected from 1 April 1973 when the system was changed from a 'classical' one (corporation tax on profits, with income tax deducted from dividends) to an 'imputation' one (corporation tax on profits, part of the tax being passed on as a credit to the recipients of dividends). The object of the change was to make the corporation tax on retained profits as heavy as the combined tax on distributed profits. This reduces the incentive to retain profits for reinvestment in expansion of the company's business, the plan being strangely at odds with the then government's supposed encouragement to increase industrial investment.

DEFINITIONS OF SOME PHRASES USED IN THE CORPORATION TAX RULES

Accounting date.   The date to which a company makes up its accounts.

Accounting period.   The period for which corporation tax is charged: this will normally be a period for which a company makes up its accounts but it may be a shorter period and must not exceed a year.

Close company.   A UK resident company under the control of five or fewer participators, or any number of participators who are directors, or if more than half of the company's income could be apportioned for tax purposes among five or fewer participators or among any number of participators who are directors. However, any company in which shares carrying at least 35 per cent of the voting power are held by the public is excluded from the definition provided such shares have been dealt in and officially listed on a recognized stock exchange within the preceding twelve months.

Participator in a close company.   Primarily a person who is a shareholder or has an interest in the capital or income of the company.

Distribution.   Any dividend paid by a company, including a capital dividend. It also includes any other distribution out of the assets of a company, whether in cash or otherwise, except for a repayment of capital or any amount for which new consideration has been given.

Franked investment income.   Income from a source which has already suffered corporation tax and is consequently not liable to further corporation tax in the hands of the receiving company. Dividends from British companies are the most common example.

Unfranked investment income.   Income from a source which has not suffered corporation tax and is therefore to be included in this company's total income for corporation tax purposes. Debenture interest from other companies is the most common example.

FURTHER READING

The aim in this chapter has been to highlight those aspects of a company taxation which appear to be of most consequence to administrators. All the rules are hedged round with ifs and buts which make it imperative to check details *before* making major decisions.

Useful explanatory booklets may be obtained free from the Revenue. These include Corporation Tax; Capital Gains Tax; Directors' Benefits and Expenses; Capital Allowances on Plant and Machinery.

The taxation of banks, insurance companies, building societies and other financial organizations, and of agricultural concerns, is outside the scope of this work. The following books may prove useful.

K.S. Carmichael, *Spicer and Pegler's Income Tax*, HFL (Publishers), London, 1975.

J.M. Cooper and P.F. Hughes, *Key to Income Tax*, Taxation Publishing Company London, 1975.

T.L.A. Graham and P.F. Hughes, *Key to Corporation Tax*, Taxation Publishing Company, London, 1975.

B.J. Ruffels, *Barclaytrust Guide to Unified Tax*, Sweet and Maxwell, London 1973.

K.R. Tingley and P.F. Hughes, *Key to Capital Gains Taxation*, Taxation Publishing Company, London, 1975.

Whiteman and Wheatcroft on Income Tax, Sweet and Maxwell, London, 1976.

8

Administering Value Added Tax

Lindsay Duncan

Important though the administrative aspects of VAT are, it must be accepted that they are secondary to the changes in both political and economic philosophy which preceded the introduction of the tax in 1973 and subsequent amendments. In this country, we have only recently conceded that public expenditure is likely to continue its upward trend and this has meant that further taxation has to be levied on the whole of the population and not merely on the wealthier sectors. Other countries discovered before us that the only substantial source of revenue not tapped was the broad base of consumer expenditure. Value added tax is the best means known of raising substantial sums of revenue without at the same time twisting the economy and destroying the potential for growth. The VAT we now have is a very small tax indeed in comparison with what is to come, and one can confidently predict that the yield of the tax will double by perhaps the end of the present decade. This is not to say that the rate will be doubled but rather that the base will be greatly extended. This is a fundamental matter which should be borne in mind by company administrators and they should always ensure that whatever systems they introduce are sufficiently flexible to take this expansion into account.

Change will come from another direction, namely the need to harmonize our VAT with the structures of the other members of the EEC. The United Kingdom will of course have a strong say about the form of the common VAT but it is probable that in one respect at least we shall have to alter our system. The broadened base of the tax will almost certainly involve other positive rates in addition to the standard rate. This is a matter which companies ought to plan for in advance.

We have lived under a very distorted market-pricing structure for over thirty years and to a substantial extent these distortions will be eliminated as the base of the tax is broadened. Over a period of time this will mean that relative price differentials will change. We have seen this to some extent already in that the removal of purchase tax at the top rates and their replacement by VAT at the standard rate caused price reductions; equally we have seen price rises where previously tax-free goods and services have come into the VAT net. The new pricing structure will clearly give rise to different levels of demand. Where the demand for a company's product rises, the company must decide how to react. Will it let its own prices rise to choke off the extra demand (and one has to bear in mind the prices and incomes policy) or will the company increase its production to satisfy the extra demand or will it import extra goods and if so from where? If demand falls, the company's reaction will be in the reverse direction but a decision will have to be made as to whether to cut prices, limit production or export more. It may take several years for the effects of a broad-based VAT to work their way through the economy but the way in which a company responds to the new demand patterns will clearly have a decisive effect on the company's profits.

THE ARITHMETIC OF THE TAX

Strictly speaking, value added tax is not a tax on value added in the true economic sense. Rather it is a tax on consumption, collected at each stage in the economy, on the difference (broadly) between the purchase price of goods and services acquired to make the product and the sale price of that product. Purchases are called inputs, and the tax which a business pays on buying those inputs is called input tax; sales are called outputs, and the tax which a business charges on its customers is called output tax. The excess of output tax over input tax is payable by the business to Customs and Excise, who are responsible for administering the tax, but if the input tax exceeds the output tax the difference is repayable by Customs and Excise to the business. Assuming then that a business is wholly within the VAT system, the business bears no VAT itself but recovers all the tax it pays on its inputs either by way of deduction from its output tax or by way of repayment from Customs and Excise.

RATES OF TAX

With effect from 1 April 1973, two rates of VAT were introduced—the standard rate of 10 per cent and the zero-rate. The standard rate was changed to 8 per cent from 29 July 1974, petrol was charged at 25 per cent from 18 November 1974 and certain electrical appliances, boats, aircraft, furs, jewellery, etc. at 25 per cent from 1 May 1975. As from the 12 April 1976 the rate is reduced from 25 per cent to 12½ per cent.

The introduction of the new 25 per cent rate (which has now been reduced to 12½ per cent) caused very considerable problems especially in the retail sector and many taxpayers using the special retail schemes have had to elect to use different schemes to reduce their VAT bills. Television rental arrangements were in a state of chaos for months.

RELIEFS

Our VAT conflicts with the provisions of EEC Directives on VAT in a number of respects. Possibly the most important of these is the extent of the relieving provisions. These are of two kinds:

Zero-rating. References should be made to the Finance Act 1972, Schedule 4 (as amended) for a list of zero-rated items. These are principally food, books, newspapers, periodicals, news services and advertisements, fuel and power, the construction of buildings, services to overseas traders, transport and certain drugs and medicines. In addition, the export of all goods and most services is zero-rated. This ensures that no VAT enters into the price of any export.

Exemption. Exemption is of two kinds:

1   Finance Act 1972, Schedule 5 (as amended) gives exemption to a list of items of which the most important are land, insurance, postal services, certain financial services (mainly banking), education and health
2   Small traders whose turnover of taxable supplies does not exceed £5000 per annum are exempt but they may elect to come within the system if it is to their advantage to do so

The difference between zero-rating and exemption is that a business dealing in zero-rated supplies charges VAT at the rate of zero per cent but is nevertheless fully within the system; thus it can recover from Customs and Excise any input tax which it has paid on its purchases. Exemption on the other hand is generally a less favourable status in that, whereas the business cannot charge VAT on its supplies, it cannot recover the VAT on its purchases; thus the exempt business must either bear any input tax itself or, if it can, pass it on in the form of higher prices.

Many businesses are taxable on some part of their sales (whether at the standard rate or zero-rate) and exempt on another part. In these cases an apportionment of the input tax is made, and only that part considered to be referable to taxable sales is deductible. This is the situation of the part-exempt business.

THE LEGAL FRAMEWORK

Value added tax is by its nature a very practical tax. Whereas it is generally possible to calculate within very narrow limits the precise corporation tax liability of a business, this is seldom possible in the case of VAT without negotiation with Customs and Excise. The most important source-material on VAT is as follows:

The statutes.   The basic law on VAT is in the 1972 Finance Act as amended by subsequent Finance Acts.

Statutory instruments.   The 1972 Finance Act gives extensive power to the Treasury and to Customs and Excise to amplify and to change the Finance Act provisions by way of statutory instrument. These statutory instruments are subordinate to the Finance Act provisions in that a statutory instrument is only valid if made under the authority of a statute.

Customs and Excise Notices.   The way in which Customs and Excise administer the law is set out in a series of Public Notices which are available from VAT offices. Those issued to date are as follows:

364	Awards for distinction—relief
368	Legacies—relief
700	General guide (revised September 1973)
701	Scope and coverage (revised February 1975)
702	Imports (revised October 1973)
703	Exports (revised November 1973)
704	Retail export schemes (revised November 1973)
705	Tax-free sales of motor vehicles to tourists, etc
706	I Partial exemption (revised September 1973)
	II Self-supply (stationery) (revised September 1973)
708	Construction industry (revised June 1973)
709	Hotels and catering
710	Supplies by or through agents (revised October 1973)
711	Secondhand cars
712	Secondhand works of art, antiques and scientific collections
713	Secondhand caravans and motor cycles
714	Young children's clothing and footwear (revised July 1973)
715	Construction industry: alterations and repairs and maintenance
716	Changes in the rate of tax
718	VAT: reduction of the standard rate
745	Preparation for additional rates
746	Pearls, semiprecious stones, precious stones (other than

diamonds) and postage stamps

749   Local authorities and similar bodies covered by Section 15,
       Finance Act 1972

It is important to make sure that the latest version is used.

Appeal cases.   The president of the VAT tribunals has issued two explanatory leaflets: on appeals and practice notes. These are not statutory notices.

Case law.   A large number of cases involving points of dispute between Customs and Excise and taxpayers have been heard by VAT tribunals and these are reported in VAT Tribunal Notices issued periodically by the Stationery Office.

Customs and Excise leaflets.   Information of interest only to particular trades, etc, publicized through trade associations or other organizations concerned.

Leaflet No	*Title*
2/74/VLB	Young children's clothing: supplies by manufacturers, wholesalers and importers
3/74/VLB	Ships' managers and port agents
4/74/VLB	Gross tonnage of unregistered ships and boats
5/74/VLB	Taxis and hire cars
6/74/VLA	Estate agents: charges for advertising
9/74/VLD	Value added tax
	(*a*) Aids for chronically sick or disabled persons
	(*b*) Talking books for the blind and handicapped; wireless sets for the blind
10/74/VMF	Indemnities under property lease agreements
11/74/VMG	VAT return (form VAT 100): guidance to finance houses and insurance companies on how certain types of supply should be shown in Part B of the form

VAT News.   Periodic issues of this newsletter amend Customs and Excise Notices and give general guidance.

THE SCOPE OF THE TAX

The tax is chargeable on the supply of goods and services in the UK and on the importation of goods (but not services) into the UK. The tax will be charged only where the supply is a taxable supply and where the goods or services are supplied by a taxable person in the course of a business which he is carrying on. The tax is payable by the person supplying the goods or services. Tax is chargeable on the importation for goods whether for business purposes or not and the tax is payable whether or not the importer is carrying on a business. The supply of goods includes not merely sales but also the letting of goods on hire and the making of certain gifts or loans of goods. The supply of services is taxable only where it is made for a consideration. In certain cases, the supply of goods to oneself in the course of a business is taxable.

TIME OF SUPPLY

In order to determine which VAT accounting period a transaction falls into, the time of supply has to be ascertained. Broadly the time of supply is as follows:

Goods

1   If the goods are to be removed the basic tax point is the time when they are removed
2   If the goods are not to be removed the basic tax point is the time when they are made available to the person to whom they are being supplied
3   There are special rules for sale or return and for certain other transactions. A hire-purchase transaction is deemed to be a sale. The construction industry is subject to special rules
4   Where a tax invoice is issued within fourteen days after the basic tax point, the invoice date becomes the tax point unless the taxpayer elects to use the basic tax point instead. The fourteen-day period may be extended by agreement with Customs and Excise
5   If a tax invoice is rendered before the date of the basic tax point or if payment is received in respect of a supply before the basic tax point, the earlier of the invoice date and the payment date becomes the tax point. The taxpayer in this case has no option to elect for the tax point in 1 or 2 above

Services

1   The basic tax point in the case of the supply of services is when those services are performed
2   If a tax invoice is issued within fourteen days after the basic tax point (extendable by negotiation with Customs and Excise), the invoice date is the tax point unless the taxpayer elects to the contrary
3   In other cases, the tax point is the earlier of the tax invoice date and the date on which payment is made for the services
Businesses should ensure that where an option is open they choose the best tax

point for their accounting and administrative systems

PLACE OF SUPPLY

A supply is taxable only if it is made within the UK or if goods are imported into the UK. Broadly, if goods are supplied within the UK for use in the UK, the supply is a taxable supply. If goods are supplied in the UK and exported, the goods are still a taxable supply but at the time of export are zero-rated. Goods supplied outside the UK but imported into the UK are liable to VAT at the time of importation. There are special accounting rules for VAT purposes which are designed to ease the cash flow problems of importers. A supply of goods made outside the UK but not imported into the UK is outside the VAT altogether; this applies whether or not the goods are ordered from the UK.

The rules regarding the place of supply of services are in some respects inconsistent with EEC Directives and may therefore be expected to change during the next few years. As matters stand, a supply rendered and enjoyed within the UK is liable to VAT. On the other hand, services rendered in the UK for the benefit of someone outside the UK are generally zero-rated. A service performed outside the UK but used in the UK is not within the VAT; neither is a service performed outside the UK for use outside the UK. Problems are already emerging regarding the liability to VAT on services where there is an international aspect.

THE TAX INVOICE

No special form of tax invoice is laid down but certain minimum requirements have to be met. In particular every tax invoice must show an identifying number, the date of the supply, the name and address and VAT registration number of the supplier, the name and address of the person to whom the supply is made, the type of supply (ie sale, lease, etc), a description of the supply, the price for each supply before the addition of VAT, any discount offered and the rate and amount of tax chargeable.

An abbreviated form of tax invoice may be used in some cases; these are generally small transactions at retail level.

It is not necessary, unless requested, for a retailer to issue a tax invoice. Tax invoices need not be rendered where the transaction is zero-rated. In the case of exempt transactions it is not legally possible to issue a tax invoice.

DISCOUNTS

Where a discount is offered for prompt or immediate payment, VAT should be shown on the tax invoice as though the discount had been earned by the person to whom the goods or services are being supplied. If in the event the discount is not earned no recalculation of the VAT should be made. Where a trade discount is offered, VAT should similarly be calculated on the discounted price. Where on the other hand a contingent discount is offered which will be available, for example, when a certain level of purchases have been achieved by the customer, the VAT should be calculated on the assumption that the volume target will not be reached.

RETROSPECTIVE ADJUSTMENTS

Where a downwards adjustment to the price charged for a supply is made, the VAT on the original invoice will be overstated. This may be corrected by showing VAT on a credit note issued to the customer; the VAT must be at the same rate as that originally charged by the supplier. Retrospective adjustments of any kind can be made by the use of the credit-note mechanism.

BAD DEBTS

No relief is available for VAT on bad debts. Thus a supplier of goods or services who is not paid for those supplies loses not merely the value of those supplies but also the VAT on their price. The draft EEC Sixth Directive proposes that relief should be given for VAT on bad debts and it is likely that in due course the UK will adopt this Directive.

SECONDHAND GOODS

In principle secondhand goods are treated in the same way as new goods. There are, however, special schemes for second-hand works of art, antiques, precious stones, postage stamps, scientific collections, cars, motor cycles and caravans. The effect of these schemes is to make liable to VAT only the dealer's margin rather than the full sale price.

CAPITAL GOODS

In principle, capital goods are treated in the same way as any other items and there is no question of spreading the input tax over the life of the asset or indeed in any other way. Thus, heavy purchases of plant within a short period may put a business into a temporary repayment position. The effect on cash flow ought to be studied before engaging in large-scale plant acquisitons.

DISALLOWANCES OF VAT

Powers are given to Customs and Excise to disallow certain amounts of input tax even though the expenditure is for the purposes of a taxable business. The two main disallowances at the present time are for business entertaining (other than of overseas customers) and the purchase price of business cars.

APPORTIONMENTS

Reference has been made above to the part-exempt business. A business whose outputs are part-taxable and part-exempt may have a disallowance of some part of its input tax.

Special apportionment schemes are prescribed for retailers. These are somewhat complicated and Public Notice No 727 (as amended) should be consulted.

GROUPS

Provision is made so that groups of commonly controlled companies can be treated as one single VAT-paying entity. Transactions within companies in such a group are then ignored for VAT purposes and a single return is made by the 'representative member' of the group to Customs and Excise. Not all members of a Companies Act group need be grouped for VAT purposes, and the cash flow of a Companies Act group can be improved if the correct selection of companies is made.

DIVISIONS

A company organized in divisions may request to have each division treated separately for VAT.

ACCOUNTING PERIOD

The basic VAT accounting period is three months but a company which is in a habitual repayment position may elect for a one-month period. This minimizes the delay between the payment of input tax by a business and its recovery from Customs and Excise.

ACCOUNTING RECORDS

The quarterly VAT return (form VAT 100), which has to be submitted to

Customs and Excise, requires information to be extracted from the accounting records of the registered person in such a way that the trader can make his own .assessment.

For VAT recording purposes, the accounts will have to provide the following figures:

1   VAT – output tax
2   VAT – tax on imports
3   VAT – deductible input tax

This should not present any problems, but the quarterly return requires, in addition to the above details, the following categories of inputs and outputs to be shown separately:

1   Outputs chargeable at the standard rate
2   Exports
3   Other zero-rated taxable outputs
4   Exempt outputs
5   Total taxable inputs including zero-rated inputs

It is very important therefore to ensure that the accounting records are maintained in such a form that the tax return can be completed with the minimum of additional work.

Although accounting for VAT is a burden on most businesses the quarterly return imposes a discipline on the accounting function and should be used as a method of providing up-to-date information for the trader, and thus result in increased efficiency.

RETENTION OF RECORDS

Invoices both in and out should be retained for a minimum period of three years to enable Customs and Excise to perform their periodical audit of the business's VAT position. By agreement with Customs and Excise, invoices may be kept in microfilm or any other form. Invoices should be stored and recorded in such a way that the periodical VAT return can be completed without difficulty.

The amount of record-keeping which has to be done is likely to be far greater than many businesses are used to.

CASH FLOWS

The combination of the rules on the tax point and the date on which tax is payable to Customs and Excise gives rise either to cash-flow advantages or disadvantages. Thus a business which secures a long period of credit on its purchases will very likely not have to pay the VAT on the purchase price until after it has received credit for the tax on the purchase. On the other hand, a business which allows long periods of credit on its sales may find that it has to pay the appropriate output tax to Customs before receiving payment of that tax from the customer. The rule must therefore be that the maximum credit should be obtained from one's suppliers but the minimum credit should be given to one's customers. Equally important is the most advantageous use of the provisions for tax-point elections.

APPEAL PROCEDURES

Large numbers of disputes have arisen between businesses and Customs and Excise. If agreement cannot be reached with the local VAT office, it is usually prudent to seek a ruling from Customs and Excise head office in London. If agreement is still not possible, an appeal may be lodged to a VAT tribunal. These are presided over by lawyers, and meet in various parts of the country. Their proceedings are sometimes publicized and sometimes not; in so far as they are not, Customs clearly have an advantage over the taxpayer. A determination by a tribunal on a question of fact is final but on a question of law there is a right to appeal first to the High Court (in England), then to the Court of Appeal and (with permission) to the House of Lords.

PROFESSIONAL ADVICE

It is evident, in an area of taxation which is a mixture of law and administrative practice, that the taxpayer is at a disadvantage in dealing with Customs and Excise. It is important, therefore, to take professional advice not merely in negotiations with Customs and Excise but also in the handling of appeals.

RECENT DEVELOPMENTS

Changes in VAT policy have made it necessary to include a section in recent developments.

Public expenditure continues to rise and there is no immediate prospect that it could be controlled much less cut. The resulting inflation has meant that the VAT is now being applied to a much larger base of consumer expenditure. It is now thought probable that the yield of VAT will, by 1976, be almost double the yield for 1973.

Unfortunately the Government, by introducing the new 25 per cent rate, is effectively perpetuating the pattern of distortion which was a characteristic of purchase tax and selective employment tax and one of the main virtues of VAT, namely its non-distortive characteristic, is being destroyed. Those countries of the EEC which have a multirate VAT system know from bitter experience that the problems of administering VAT increase vastly as each additional rate is added. In the UK it has already been found necessary to recruit a further 3000 VAT officers to cope with the recent changes.

The recommendation that VAT systems set up by taxpayers need to be flexible is therefore stressed. Further Customs and Excise notices have been issued as follows:

719   Refund of VAT to do-it-yourself housebuilders
727   Special schemes for retailers
728   Trading stamps issued with sales of petrol—a change in retail scheme output calculations
741   The higher rate of VAT
742   Scope and coverage of the higher rate schedule

Further Custom and Excise Leaflets have been issued as follows:

Leaflet No	*Title*
12/74/VLB	Zero-rating of certain kinds of protective boots and helmets
15/74/VMG	Group registration; return form VAT 101
16/74/VMF	Sales at fresh fruit, flower and vegetable markets
17/74/VCL	Borderline between alteration and repair or maintenance as applicable to roads and other civil engineering works
19/74/VLC	Wood logs, firewood and firelighters
1 /75/VLC	Apportionment of subscriptions to clubs, associations and societies
2 /75/VLB	Freight forwarding services in connection with international movement of goods
3 /75/VLB	Offshore oil and gas installations
4 /75/VMC	Changes in the arrangements for business promotion schemes
5 /75/VMC	New arrangements for retail pharmacists
6 /75/VMF	Exhibitions and the supply of exhibition stands
7 /75/VMD	Sub-contractors in the construction industry: zero-rating of certain supplies and exemption from registration

Finally, the authority given to the Treasury whereby they can alter the rates by 20 per cent up or down without legislation has been increased to 25 per cent.

FURTHER READING

Commission on Industrial Relations Report No 31, HMSO, London.
The City Code on Takeovers and Mergers.
EEC Memorandum on Industrial Policy
Report of the Monopolies Commission

P.E. Hart, M.A. Utton and G. Walshe, *Mergers and Concentration in British Industry,* Cambridge University Press.

C. Layton, *Cross Frontier Mergers in Europe,* University Press, 1971.

A. Vice, *The Strategy of Takeovers,* McGraw-Hill.

R. Jones and O. Marriott, *Anatomy of a Merger,* Pan.

R. Moon, *Business Mergers and Takeover Bids,* Gee, London.

P.F. Barratt, *Human Implications of Mergers and Takeovers,* Personnel Management, London.

D. Brooks and R. Smith, *The Human Effect of Mergers,* Acton Society Trust.

After the Takeover—A Study of Employee Reactions, National Institute of Industrial Psychology, London

A. Jay, *Management and Machiavelli,* Hodder & Stoughton, London, 1967

S. Ellon and T.R. Fowkes (eds), *Applications of Management Science in Banking and Finance,* Gower Press, Epping, 1972.

M. Doctoroff, *Company Mergers and Takeovers,* Gower Press, Epping, 1972.

9

Managing Mergers and Acquisitions

Leonard H Verreck

Mergers have been likened to marriages with somewhat similar programmes consisting of a period of search, a period of courtship, a solemnization, a honeymoon period and finally, one hopes, a settling down. In seeking a marriage partner, certain inherited and intuitive instincts prevail to create a course of action which follows in general a familiar plan. The individual learns by observation and from experience, while there is no shortage of experts with their own particular brand of advice.

Despite all this, some marriages fail and the divorce courts are available to put an end to the partnership. The process is not painless and it can be costly and time-consuming. No such comparatively easy disengagement is possible when it is a 'business marriage', although the original causes may be similar, such as ill-matched partners, immaturity, inadequate planning and instruction. The incidence of failed mergers is very much higher than that of marriages and the failure can have a much wider and more serious effect on the community.

There is no reliable or accepted method of assessing success or failure of mergers and one must concede that the number of cases of divorce is no guide to the rate of unhappy marriages! It is, however, authoritatively estimated that some 60 per cent of mergers either failed or did not reach expected results: the figure has been put as high as 80 per cent. Which quite simply means that four out of every five mergers were either badly planned or badly carried out, whilst some of these should never have been contemplated in the first place.

There are no rules for mergers in the conception and planning stage, though there are laws, recommendations and instructions laid down in the public's interest for the remaining stages. Probably the most significant factor in many current mergers has not been growth by acquisition, as was usually the case, but merger to avoid bankruptcy or redundancy. Economic forces may create conditions under which positive, if disagreeable, action needs to be taken and which *per se* may create a viable organization.

In the past two years and under conditions of stress, a number of such mergers are showing some success which it is hoped will be maintained on a return to normality.

A further development of late has been the takeover, often with government assistance, of a factory by employees threatened with redundancy.

This chapter can only introduce the reader to the subject of mergers generally, and recommend the study of case histories of both successful and not so successful mergers, while stressing the importance of both short-term and long-term planning. There is value to be gained from the expertise of others including the use of specialist consultants but even this requires a high degree of selective skill. The past few years has seen an increase in the literature on the subject and further reading is advisable. Recent years have also seen remarkable, if not totally unexpected developments over the whole field of acquisitions. Some of these developments have been of a legislative nature, but research has been carried out particularly on the aspect of human relations, with case histories accordingly being written up and often quite critically.

Few business terms in common usage cause the reaction that seems to follow the words 'mergers' and 'acquisitions'. This emotional attitude is not confined to any one section of the community and there has been a marked degree of sensationalism in the step-by-step reporting of a number of cases. An attitude almost of fear has sometimes developed and this is not unreasonable when one appreciates the element of secrecy often necessary in the conduct of negotiations which may have an effect on the lives of many people. It is also unfortunate that much more coverage is given to the difficulties and problems of failed mergers and very little may be written of the successes. The general reader could easily believe that the practice of merging and acquiring was a recent innovation, whereas it has certainly been with us in a formal way since the 1862 Companies Act.

Mergers and acquisitions should be seen to be normal processes of corporate evolution. If a company is to develop, or indeed remain in being, it must constantly be searching and probing. It can never stand still except for temporary consolidation. It must closely examine its future and must do so in the light of ever-changing patterns of commerce whether local, national or international.

Shareholders and employees have the right to expect that the board of directors are taking all possible steps to protect the company and *inter alia* their security. Planning for merger should be high on the list of priorities and adequate planning will of itself prove both defensive and offensive.

Planning of this nature will be incorporated in the overall corporate plan, and management responsible for outward development through merger or acquisition must provide defensive tactics. Such tactics do not imply a negative attitude or an admission of defeat—they are an acceptance that the company must be placed in a position of strength if and when it is necessary for the board to report to the shareholders following a takeover offer.

DEFINITIONS

The term 'merger' is used in this chapter in a broad sense to include both mergers and consolidations. Both have the object of combining the assets, liabilities, organization, rights and business of one or more units into one corporate body. In a merger the company absorbing the assets, and so on, retains its identity, but a consolidation involves the formation of a new company which acquires the assets and liabilities of the constituent companies. The term merger is also used for straightforward acquisitions, as the latter term denotes basically the same operation.

There are various formulas employed in merger situations but for simplicity these can be reduced to the following outlines:·

Acquisition by purchase of equity.   The acquiring company offers to purchase the capital stock from the owners of the company and is prepared to make payment in cash or other negotiable instrument. The acquired company usually retains a separate identity but is operated as a subsidiary.

Acquisition by purchase of assets.   The tangible assets, as well as possible goodwill or patent rights, are purchased and payment is made in cash or in equity of the purchasing company or much more frequently in a combination of cash and equity. Liabilities of the acquired company are often assumed by the purchasing company, although it is not uncommon for the latter to insist on the exclusion of certain types of indebtedness. Some cash element is therefore essential in order that the sellers can settle such claims on their own terms.

Takeover bids.   Certain writers have considered that a 'takeover' is not a merger as it is usually a unilateral process, as the name seems to imply. But in the context of this chapter, I prefer to suggest that this is not necessarily correct. A form of agreement between the principal shareholders or the boards of directors of both companies has often been reached before the bid is made. The takeover tactic is employed quite often to acquire a controlling interest in a publicly quoted company and bids are made to existing shareholders for their stock at a price usually above that prevailing on the market. The price can be one of many combinations, as in a purchase of assets, and this can make it difficult to assess the true value being offered.

Other common expressions include:

Conglomerate mergers. These involve combination of two or more companies engaged in seemingly unrelated activities. The activities may however be similar in relation to production but based for instance on different markets.

Vertical mergers (or integration). These aim to bring successive stages of manufacture under common ownership. Such a merger can be carried out as a protection against a competitor or to deny him access to supplies essential to his operation.

Horizontal mergers. Involve possibly the unification of two or more companies engaged in similar manufacture, services or perhaps markets. A notable form of this type of merger in the past few years has been evident amongst brewers as well as in the hotel industry.

Reverse takeover. This term is used increasingly today. It is the process whereby one company, usually the stronger, is taken over by another but payment in equity gives the seller control of the purchaser. Control may be gained of the management of the purchasing company without of necessity having control of stock. This technique is particularly valuable as a means of obtaining quotation without the considerable cost of going public.

The high incidence of this form of merger is partly due to the number of public companies formed under looser regulations some years ago and which have failed to grow in line with the rest of the economy. Others have lost their real objectives possibly by mergers, and are now little more than shells. A certain number of companies being used as the 'purchaser' in this form of financial exercise may have been the outcome of failed mergers.

European merger. A further form of merger has been taking place in EEC countries, and British companies have been involved in a number of such actions. Time has unfortunately shown that some of these have not proved the success originally anticipated and one reason advanced is the lack of a true pan-European form of enterprise.

The Rome Treaty originally sought to curb monopolies while removing trade barriers. A change has taken place since 1969 and the EEC Commission produced in 1970 a memorandum which plainly encouraged cross-border mergers. Later it went further by giving assistance to the setting up of a common merger 'marriage' agency which would act as a catalyst in bringing together likely partners. Other encouraging steps were also taken (further reading is advisable).

If some transfrontier mergers have not proved successful, the reasons could be legal or fiscal. Or they might be historical or industrial. This should have been appreciated at the outset.

A number of European firms have demonstrated marked success through joint ownership of a common operation across frontiers and with shared responsibilities—Shell, Unilever, Gevaert-Agfa, etc. Mutual interest, a willingness to share management, similarity of objectives are probably some of the reasons for the progress such companies have made and which incidentally, has also made them powerful competitors of US multinationals.

REASONS FOR MERGERS

It is unfortunately true that the reasoning for some acquisitions has seemed obscure, while financial circles have not been slow in accusing certain company directors of going into the market place with a mentality more akin to that of a 'campaign medal collector' or possibly, as one writer caustically remarked, 'adding glitter to the company Christmas tree'.

Assessment of merger success is not easy and certain authorities place the success rate as low as 20 per cent, although I should prefer to place it nearer 40 or even 50 per cent. This optimistic assessment still leaves a somewhat depressing image and it is incontestable that many of the failures would never have left the drawing board if serious consideration had been given at the early planning stage not only to the reasons for contemplating the merger but equally to the alternatives.

The reasons or motives for seeking a merger or an acquisition are many and there are invariably more than one for each situation. The following is only a representative list:

1   Diversification—a useful reason because it can cover so much
2   Elimination of competition—sometimes a costly process
3   The acquisition of skilled management or personnel
4   The acquisition of production facilities
5   The acquisition of patent rights, etc
6   Gaining greater collateral
7   Improving the rate of growth
8   To avoid seasonal underproduction, etc
9   To exploit a raw material or process
10   To inject profits before further capitalization
11   To rationalize or regulate marketing
12   Cost reductions—mainly of specific functions, such as administration
13   To cut costs by localized production
14   To penetrate a protected market
15   For the benefit of tax losses
16   Asset acquisition and eventual disposal
17   By combining two or more companies to make possible the obtaining of a Stock Exchange listing
18   Similarly, to obtain a quote by merger with an existing quoted

company (see reverse takeover)

PROGRAMME

The need to evolve a programme, as well as the importance of including some form of preparation for merger situations in the company's corporate activity, has already been stressed. Responsibility for this function should be at board level and incorporated in strategic decision making.

The programme can be divided into four parts which in turn are sectioned according to the activity contemplated and the various skills or professional acumen required.

Planning stage

Various alternatives are considered followed by research of the selected choice. This will involve undercover activities and the amount of information obtained will depend upon sources. In general much of this stage is concerned with financial data of markets, of products, of weaknesses, of strengths, etc.

Approach and negotiations stage

This follows once the planning stage provides an affirmative response. In theory they could be looked on as two separate stages but in practice are concurrent. The skills required for successful approach are often those of the diplomat and different from those required for negotiating, which are those of the financier-cum-psychologist. The planning stage will have revealed some economic data and the accountant will have no difficulty in arriving at a number of valuations using different formulas, and this knowledge will be useful to set low and high values during early stages of negotiation.

The price to be paid is obviously a vital factor in any negotiation but many acquisitions have failed to get off the ground because (a) the approach was wrong and (b) too little attention was paid to future organization and the effect on the human side of the enterprise. Asset values seldom seem to have much relevance to the price except where the assets have not as yet started to show any real profitability such as in the case of a fairly new enterprise or when they could be substantially surplus to requirements and easily realized.

Profit record is currently used and today's trends seem to indicate that the buyer is looking for a return in the range 17 to 24 per cent. Prices based on such easy formulas are more commonly used when there is general agreement to buy and sell, whereas a good deal of bargaining may otherwise be necessary. The reaction of institutional shareholders and the opinion of the financial press also become vital factors.

Procedural activities

These would be started during the stage of negotiation but get really under way once general agreement has been reached. Really competent advice is necessary as the planning and realization of this stage are invariably linked to a tight schedule.

Briefing of accountants and solicitors is essential at an early stage, together with any other experts whose assistance may be required.

On reaching agreement, the proposed contracting parties will draw up a simple memorandum stating the basis (or terms), and that such agreement is subject to approval of respective boards and of their shareholders. It will also allow for access by the buyer to properties, assets, books of account, and so on and will possibly stipulate a certain date by which completion is to take place. Agreement will also have been reached with reference to disclosure and some provision made for operations during the interim period. Most of us who have been involved with this stage have usually found that the completion date seemed impossibly narrow but long-delayed completions can create problems from which the new corporation may suffer for long after the merger takes place. Careful planning, efficient communications and wise allocation of responsibilities are the answer.

It is perhaps appropriate to suggest that the reader should by now have made a study of the Merger and Monopolies Act 1965, together with certain other publications issued by professional and other bodies, including the 'City' Code on Takeovers and Mergers.

The procedural activities can now be summed up:

1   Final agreement and contract prepared by legal advisers for the buyer in close touch with those for the seller
2   An audit of the financial accounts with adjustments made for any variance in accounting practice
3   An examination of deeds of title, contracts of service, etc. copyrights, debentures, and similar memoranda
4   An investigation of contingent liabilities, of long-term commitments, of possible legal actions, bad debts, etc.
5   Some investigation, possibly on behalf of the seller, of the financial situation and prospects of the buyer

Financing

The method to be employed will in practice have been discussed and agreed upon at an earlier stage and we have already suggested various methods of carrying out the acquisition.

It is rare that a suitable financing arrangement cannot be planned, to permit the acquisition to proceed. Financing the arrangement is unlikely to be the main consideration but it should not be assumed that it is going to be straightforward. Each situation involves particular conditions, personal and domestic obligations and special factors.

The size of the acquiring company compared to that of the seller needs to be considered. If the seller is large, this may affect the acquiring company's results. A side-by-side study of the respective balance sheets carried out at an early stage can often avoid late pitfalls, particularly if proper regard is being given to the future.

'Consideration' can take a number of forms and the first that often springs to mind is 'cash' but this has become less attractive in the United Kingdom since the introduction of capital gains tax. This form of consideration probably raises fewer problems of financing than most as it is relatively easy to raise funds, although advice is essential on the most suitable and cheapest way of obtaining the money.

An important amendment was made in September 1971 to the City Code on Takeovers and Mergers. The relevant section should be studied but briefly the point at issue was whether an offeror who purchases for cash, through the market or otherwise, holdings of a size which may materially affect the outcome of a bid should, in certain circumstances, be required to offer a cash alternative to the remaining holders. The City panel decided in favour and introduced a new rule (29A) and an amendment to Rule 16.

The panel now has specific authority to require a cash alternative in exceptional circumstances where it feels that this is necessary in order to ensure that General Principle 8 of the Code is observed. Provision for exemption is made in certain circumstances.

Other forms of consideration could be debentures, loans, preference stock, equity, or a combination of some of these, together perhaps with cash. One particular method which has found favour in certain situations is the issue of convertible preference shares.

Equity holders will prefer to exchange for similar shares and will not favour other forms of stock but personal considerations are important, for instance if there is a need to maintain some kind of assured income which would be available from preference shares or debentures. But again there may also be a wish to remain involved in the running of the business and to participate in any capital growth.

Capital gains tax must remain a prime concern of the vendor. He may appreciate that there is little possibility of total avoidance but will want to postpone payment of the tax.

A further issue will be the strain on the purchasing company's resources and on its borrowing powers if a cash consideration is proposed. Obviously the relative size of companies is to be considered as is the future capital requirements, hence the need for planning. The level of anticipated profits should be accurately forecast if new capital is going to incur a servicing charge.

In general, equity consideration is desirable for the acquiring company if profits are likely to be unsteady, while some form of loan stock would be preferable if stable profits are anticipated. If, on the other hand, it is expected that satisfactory profitability will be slow to materialize, the offer of stock with conversion rights might prove attractive.

Mergers have come unstuck because an *ad hoc* solution has been provided to rush a deal through without regard to the financial position of the consolidated group.

PEOPLE AND MERGERS

Takeovers, mergers or acquisitions have been receiving, and will receive, growing attention not only from the national government but also from the European Commission and Parliament. Much of this interest will be concerned with the influence of such activities as they affect the lives of employees and of the public, rather than with political implications. Apart from the Monopolies Commission which has already been mentioned and the City Code on Takeovers and Mergers a study should be made of the findings of the Watkinson Commission, of the Fair Trading Bill, of the Redundancy Payments Act and even of the Contracts of Employment Act 1972. Much fuller reference will be found in other chapters of this book. The timing and release of information is relevant; while the City Code is concerned with the mechanics of communication at various stages of acquisition, no mention is made of the employees' interests. The Commission on Industrial Relations however advocates early consultation, though recognizing that there may be practical and ethical reasons for caution.

Trade unions have shown growing concern but have at times demonstrated a realistic appreciation of the economic necessity for certain mergers, though regrettably there have been other cases when the short-term interest of their members—often at the local level—has taken precedence over long-term security.

In practice, a wise manager will institute a plan which will allow for reasonable communication at both pre- and post merger stages. The relevance of the information given must be judged from the local standpoint but sensibly should prevent employees, shareholders or public, receiving from a secondhand source, news which affects their lives. Responsibility for the creation and implementation of such a plan of communication should rest with a member of the main board—it is in any case assumed that an efficient company will place the personnel function at that level—and such a plan must cover personnel of both companies, at least at the postmerger stage.

MANAGEMENT AND MERGERS

During the course of mergers and acquisitions, problems are met and decisions need to be taken which are often far more complex than most of those faced ordinarily by management. Generally, there is a lack of earlier experience, training is minimal and few companies carry staff qualified to examine, analyse and carry out preliminary investigations, follow-up negotiations and further planning. The help of organizations with specialist skills is often desirable. Banking institutions including merchant banks and finance houses are prepared to put at disposal the services of their advisory departments while certain firms of solicitors and accountants also have a considerable background of experience. In some cases, it can be helpful to bring in a firm of management consultants but care is required in the selection and definition of the assignment.

Throughout this chapter 'people' have figured prominently. It has been suggested that communication and information should be adequate, and we have emphasized that all the processes of a satisfactory operation depend on the participant people.

A merger is not merely the acquisition of the assets of another firm or company. The board of the acquiring company have to assume fresh responsibilities as well as new relationships. Will the new team operate efficiently? Will personalities clash? Have they the intellectual capacity to manage a larger unit? Can they accept a more challenging role?

These are just some of the questions which should be asked—and answered. It is in the board room that strains and tensions become dangerously acute and yet top management's ability to manage mergers is seldom questioned. Some critical reading of published case histories will demonstrate this fact.

Management at all levels is under strain during a merger activity and many will come under unusual scrutiny. Their future should be adequately defined for them from the outset, if full collaboration is desirable — as of course it is.

To conclude: first define objectives, develop a policy, examine alternatives, seek advice, study fiscal and legal considerations, inform and communicate, have adequate management skills and resources, set a time for completion, revise the corporate plan, consider postmerger situation, examine new organization critically and, in particular, its boardroom ability.

FURTHER READING

Commission on Industrial Relations Report No 31, HMSO, London.

The City Code on Takeovers and Mergers. HMSO, London.

EEC Memorandum on Industrial Policy. HMSO, London.

Report of the Monopolies Commission. HMSO, London.

P.E. Hart, M.A. Utton and G. Walshe, *Mergers and Concentration in British Industry,* Cambridge University Press.

C. Layton, *Cross Frontier Mergers in Europe,* University Press, 1971.

A. Vice, *The Strategy of Takeovers,* McGraw-Hill.

R. Jones and O. Marriott, *Anatomy of a Merger,* Pan.

R. Moon, *Business Mergers and Takeover Bids,* Gee, London.

P.F. Barrett, *Human Implications of Mergers and Takeovers,* Personnel Management, London.

D. Brooks and R. Smith, *The Human Effect of Mergers,* Acton Society Trust.

After the Takeover—A Study of Employee Reactions, National Institute of Industrial Psychology, London.

A. Jay, *Management and Machiavelli,* Hodder & Stoughton, London, 1967.

S. Ellon and T.R. Fowkes (eds), *Applications of Management Science in Banking and Finance,* Gower Press, Epping, 1972.

M. Doctoroff, *Company Mergers and Takeovers,* Gower Press, Epping, 1972.

PART THREE

Commercial Functions

10

Law of Contract

Alan Hobkirk

ESSENTIAL ELEMENTS OF A VALID CONTRACT

Six essential elements must be present in any valid contract: offer and unconditional acceptance, genuine agreement between the parties, intention to create legal relations, capacity of the parties, legality and possibility and consideration or form.

Offer

1   May be made to a definite person or a member of a group or even to the world at large
2   Must not be vague, for example, selling a car on 'usual hire purchase terms' was regarded by the court as being too vague in Scammel *v* Ouston (1941)
3   Must be distinguished from an invitation to treat, for example, goods displayed in shop windows
4   Must be communicated to the offeree
5   Must state all the terms of the offer
6   May be terminated at any time before it is accepted by revocation, lapse of time, death or rejection

Acceptance

1   Must be unconditional, otherwise it is regarded as a counter offer

(Northland Airliners *v* Ferranti (1970))

2   Must be made within a reasonable or stipulated time
3   Silence cannot amount to acceptance; compare inertia selling methods and the case of Felthouse *v* Bindley (1862). Felthouse wrote to the owner of a horse, offering £30 for it and saying that if he did not hear from the owner within a day he would assume the horse was his. The owner did not reply to Felthouse but tried to halt the auctioning of the horse by Bindley who refused and sold it. Felthouse sued Bindley for conversion, that is denying his ownership of property. The court held that Felthouse never owned the horse because his offer had not been expressly accepted
4   Must be communicated to the offeror, although the following are exceptions to this general rule
     (*a*) Acceptance may be implied from conduct
     (*b*) Communication may be waived by offeror
     (*c*) Where an acceptance is made by post, the contract is regarded as being completed at the moment of posting, not at the time of receipt by the offeror. The so-called postal rules apply also to telegrams but not to telephones or telex.

Genuine agreement between the parties

It is essential that there should be real consent to the contract by the parties to it otherwise there is no *consensus ad idem* or meeting of the minds. Factors such as mistake, fraud, misrepresentation, duress and undue influence may affect the genuineness of consent.

Mistake may involve the subject matter of the contract, the identity of the parties, the nature of the instrument. If the mistake is fundamental, the contract will normally be rendered void. This is a complex topic, however, and there is a great deal of case law involved.

Fraud, if proved, allows the injured party to avoid the contract with or without seeking damages.

Misrepresentation falls into two classes: fraudulent or innocent. Before the 1967 Misrepresentation Act it was more essential to distinguish between the two classes since the remedies available were quite distinct. The position regarding remedies is as follows:

Fraudulent misrepresentation. Here the aggrieved party may either avoid the contract with or without seeking damages or alternatively affirm the contract and seek damages or specific performance.

Innocent misrepresentation. The main remedy is to avoid the contract, but damages may now be awarded even after performance has taken place or after title in goods has passed—Misrepresentation Act 1967.

Misrepresentation and its remedies is another complicated subject and the above outline is only to be regarded as a broad simplification of the position. Duress has been defined as 'actual or threatened violence to or imprisonment of the party coerced' and, at common law, any contract induced by duress is voidable. Undue influence, on the other hand, has been defined as 'pressure on or coercion of a party to a contract, *not amounting* to duress, whereby he is precluded from the exercise of free judgement'. A contract which has been induced by undue influence is voidable at the court's discretion.

Intention to create legal relations

Albeit that an agreement may be in existence this will not be enforced by the courts unless it can be shown that the parties intended it to have a legal effect. There are two main presumptions as regards intention:

1 In domestic or social agreements the court usually decides that there was no intention to create legal relations
2 In business agreements the court presumes that there was such an an intention although this presumption is rebutted by express provision such as that which appears on football coupons

Capacity of the parties

This topic is dealt with in more detail in the next section, but suffice it to say at this stage that before an agreement made with the intention of creating legally binding relations can be enforced, it is essential that the parties involved should have had proper capacity to contract.

Legality and possibility

At the time of its formation, it is fundamental that the contract should be capable of being performed; where reasonable to do so, however, future difficulties should be anticipated and provided for in the contract, for example the possibility of delay through labour difficulties—Davis Contractors *v* Fareham Urban District council (1956). The contractors attempted to prove that their contract for building houses had been frustrated by bad weather and labour troubles, which had turned their quoted price into a loss, but they failed.

A contract which is illegal at formation is devoid of legal effect; where a contract is legal when made and subsequently becomes illegal because of a change in the law, such a contract will usually be discharged on the ground of frustration.

Contracts may be illegal because they are forbidden either by statute or by common law. Examples of contracts contrary to statute are:

1   Gaming and wagering contracts (various Acts from 1845 onwards)
2   Moneylenders Acts 1900 and 1927
3   Resale Prices Act 1964
4   Trading with the Enemy Act 1939

Examples of contracts contrary to common law are:

1   Contracts for an immoral purpose
2   Contracts interfering with the course of justice
3   Contracts in restraint of trade (see p.221)
4   Contracts to defraud the Revenue

Consideration or form

Apart from contracts incorporated in deeds conforming to certain formal requirements such as being signed, sealed and delivered, the general rule in English law is that unless something of value is given in exchange for a promise or undertaking, the promise cannot be enforced against the promisor. Consideration may be regarded, therefore, as the element of bargain in a contract and at its simplest involves a *quid pro quo*. The classic definition of consideration was given in the case of Currie *v* Misa (1875): '...some right, interest, profit or benefit accruing to the one party, or some forbearance, detriment, loss or responsibility, given, suffered or undertaken by the other'.

   The following are some of the principal rules relating to consideration but it is stressed that many exceptions to these rules have arisen over the years as a result of case law decisions:

1   Every simple contract requires to be supported by consideration
2   The consideration must move from the person to whom the promise is made. This rule is to some extent connected with the doctrine of privity of contract which at its simplest means that only those who are parties to the contract acquire rights and obligations under it
3   The consideration must be something beyond the promisor's existing obligations to the promisee
4   The consideration must be legal
5   Consideration must not be past—this means that a promise made in return for some past benefit or service is usually unenforceable. Where it can be shown that services were rendered at the express or implied request of the promisor, however, the courts take the view that this is sufficient consideration to support a subsequent

promise to pay. Also by the Bills of Exchange Act 1882 (s27), a bill of exchange can be supported by an antecedent debt

6   The consideration must be real but need not be adequate since it is up to the parties to make their own bargain

CONTRACTUAL CAPACITY

The principles relating to contractual capacity will be dealt with below as they affect various groups both of natural and artificial persons who suffer either limitation or impairment in their ability to enter into contractual relations. Particular emphasis will be placed on the position of the companies.

Infants

Since the Family Law Reform Act 1969 the age of majority has been reduced from twenty-one to eighteen; anyone below eighteen is classified in English law as infant. For their protection, infants have limited contractual capacity and although, as a general rule, they can enforce contracts against other people, they cannot have contracts enforced against them. To this general rule, however, there are certain exceptions and the following are examples of contracts which can be enforced against infants:

1   *Contracts for necessaries.* Defined by s2, Sale of Goods Act 1893, as 'goods suitable to the conditions in life of the infant and to his actual requirements at the time of sale and delivery'. The tests both of utility and relativity will usually be applied and, if the goods are deemed necessaries, the infant will be obliged to pay a reasonable price for them and not necessarily the contract price

2   *Contracts for the infant's benefit.* Educational, service or apprenticeship contracts, provided it can be shown that the fundamental purpose of such contracts is for the infant's ultimate benefit—Doyle *v* White City Stadium (1935)

3   *Voidable contracts.* These are contracts under which an infant usually acquires an interest of a permanent nature, for example acquisition of shares in a company. Unless the infant takes active steps to avoid such a contract during his minority or within a reasonable time of reaching his majority, such a contract will bind him—Steinberg *v* Scala Limited (1923)

By statute (Infants Relief Act 1874) certain contracts are void and cannot therefore be enforced against an infant. Void contracts include the following:

1   Contracts for the repayment of money lent or to be lent

2   Contracts for goods supplied or to be supplied, other

than necessaries

3   All accounts stated—for example, IOUs

Mentally disordered persons

The general rule is that contracts made with persons of unsound mind are valid except in the following cases:

1   If the other contracting party is aware of the mental disability, the contract is voidable at the option of the mentally unsound person. The onus of proof lies with the person claiming insanity and he must prove both that his disability prevented him from understanding the consequences of the transaction and that the other party knew this

2   In cases where the property of the mentally ill person has been placed in the court's control under the Mental Health Act 1959, any contract involving disposal of the property does not bind the patient

Despite the two exceptions above, the effect of $s2$ of the Sale of Goods Act 1893 should be noted as regards the supply of necessaries. $S2$ provides that 'where necessaries have been sold and delivered...to a person who by reason of mental incapacity...is incompetent to contract, he must pay a reasonable price therefor'.

Drunkards

Since it is not unknown for contracting parties to facilitate their negotiations by the administration of liberal doses of alcohol, the possible effect of such ministrations on the capacity to enter into binding contractual relations should be understood. The contract is voidable at the option of the party who was drunk if he can prove both that he was incapacitated temporarily through intoxication and also that the other party was aware of this.

The drunkard is liable, of course, if he ratifies the contract when he becomes sober. Again, under $s2$ of the Sale of Goods Act 1893, a drunkard is liable to pay for necessaries.

Bankrupts

Although a bankrupt is not devoid of contractual capacity, certain limitations are imposed upon him under the Bankruptcy Act 1914. For instance, it is an offence for him while undischarged and without disclosing his position to obtain credit beyond £10 or to trade under a name different from that under which he was adjudged bankrupt.

In circumstances where, after formation of the contract, one of the parties to it becomes bankrupt, the rights and obligations under the contract pass to the trustee in bankruptcy who in certain circumstances may exercise his right of disclaimer and thereby abandon the contract.

Corporations

The contractual position of the following types of corporation aggregate requires to be considered.

Common law corporations.   Such corporations are formed by the granting of a royal charter which sets out the objects. The better view appears to be that a contract with this type of corporation will be binding if it is unauthorized or even forbidden by its charter although in such cases the Attorney General is empowered to initiate proceedings for the revocation of the charter and a member can restrain such contracts by injunction.

Statutory corporations.   These corporations are created by special Acts of Parliament which specify their powers. The *ultra vires* doctrine applies to this type of corporation and basically any contract entered into beyond the scope of the defined powers of the corporation will be void.

Registered companies

The contractual capacity of a limited company is governed by the contents of its memorandum of association and to a certain extent its articles of association. In this respect, UK law has been altered by entry into the EEC so as to make our law conform with Directive 151/1968. This is effected by the European Communities Act 1972 (*s*9). There are nine subsections and it is proposed to deal with each:

Section 9(1)   To understand the provisions of the subsection it is necessary to examine the *ultra vires* doctrine and the rule in Royal British Bank *v* Turquand as applied up to 31 December 1972:

On the formation of a limited company two documents are necessary: The Memorandum of Association which is a document of external management and affects the relationship between the company and outsiders dealing with it and the Articles of Association—a document of internal management affecting the company's relationship with its shareholders, directors and employees. Both these documents are a matter of public record, and knowledge of their contents is imputed to everyone. A company's capacity to contract is found in the objects clause of its memorandum of association. The objects clause specifies in detail the business that the company is empowered to carry on. There is very little scope for satisfactorily amending the objects clause once the company is incorporated (*s*5 Companies Act 1948). Further, because of the restrictive interpretation by the courts of the *ultra vires* doctrine, it has become the practice to draft the objects clause to provide for the widest possible area of operations. However, in view of the Court of Appeal's decision in Bell Houses Limited *v* City Wall Properties Limited (1966), the need for this practice is not now important so long as the objects clause contains a Bell Houses type of 'sweeping up' object. Any contracts within these objects are said to be *intra vires* and valid, whereas contracts outside these objects are *ultra vires* and void. Either the company or an outside contracting party can plead that a contract is *ultra vires* and void.

Powers of directors or employees to contract on behalf of company. A person negotiating with an outsider on behalf of a company is acting as agent for the company whatever his position inside the company. Assuming the contract to be within the powers of the company, the question is how far can the company deny liability if a director, manager or employee negotiates and completes a contract without authority. So far as the outsider is concerned—provided he does not know of the lack of authority—he is entitled to assume that a director, manager or chief officer has ostensible authority to do such acts as would normally be expected to be given to such agents ... Rule in Royal British Bank *v* Turquand (1856). Until recently a company's secretary was assumed not to have any ostensible authority to bind the company in contract. However, in Panorama Developments (Guildford) Limited *v* Fidelis Furnishing Fabrics Limited (1971) the Court of Appeal held that a company's secretary had ostensible authority to bind his company on contracts connected with the administrative side of company affairs such as employing staff and ordering cars.
*S*9(1) provides as follows:

In favour of a person dealing with a company in good faith, any transaction decided on by the directors shall be deemed to be one which it is within the the capacity of the company to enter into, and the power of the directors to bind the company, shall be deemed to be free of any limitation under the memorandum or articles of association; and a party to a transaction so decided on shall not be bound to enquire as to the capacity of the company to enter into it or as to any such limitation on the powers of the directors, and shall be presumed to have acted in good faith unless the contrary is proved.

From the wording of *s*9(1), it is clear that the effect of the *ultra vires* doctrine and the rule in the Royal British Bank case are modified but only so far, as they affect an outsider dealing with the company in good faith. Neither doctrine has been abolished. As between the company, its directors and shareholders, both doctrines still apply and one can envisage a case where, because of the acts of the directors, a company incurs liability to an outsider on an *ultra vires* contract, it can claim reimbursement from the defaulting directors personally for compelling it to act *ultra vires*. Directors ought to consider the inclusion of an indemnity clause in their contracts of service to exclude their personal liability in this respect.

The effect of *s*9(1) so far as the outsider is concerned can be summarized as follows:

1   Any lawful transaction decided by the directors will be deemed to be within the capacity of the company and within the ostensible authority of the directors. It seems the outsider can plead *ultra vires*, but the company cannot

2   Although the memorandum and articles are public documents, the outsider is not bound by constructive notice of their contents—and he is not under obligation to find out the objects of the company

3   The outsider is only protected if he deals with the company in good faith. There is a rebuttable presumption that good faith exists and the onus is on the company to rebut it, eg by showing that the outsider had actual knowledge that the transaction was outside the scope of the objects of the company or outside the scope of the ostensible authority of the directors. This presumption will be difficult to rebut, as the outsider is expressly relieved of the obligation to inspect and therefore to investigate the capacity of the company or the authority of the directors. One possible way is to show that the outsider was put on inquiry by suspicious circumstances and deliberately refrained from inquiring

4   Even an express prohibition of activities in the memorandum or on the authority of directors in the articles will not exclude a company's liability under the section: '....and the power of directors to bind the company shall be deemed free of restrictions under the memorandum or articles.'

5   The transaction must be decided upon by the directors collectively even though acted upon by one of them or by an executive of the company. It thus seems that *s*9(1) will afford no protection to an outsider if the transaction is dealt with by a manager, the secretary or director without the collective approval of the directors; in these cases the original *ultra vires* doctrines and the original rule in the Royal British Bank case still apply

Section 9(2). Again we must examine the law as it stood up to 31 December 1972. The general rule is that a company comes into existence as a legal entity on being incorporated and has no legal personality before incorporation. Therefore it could not enter into a pre-incorporation contract nor could it, after incorporation, ratify such a contract purported to be entered into on its behalf by the promoters or other persons. However, this rule created problems as to what rights or obligations, if any, such pre-incorporation contracts created and the parties that are bound by such contracts. In Newborne *v* Sensolid (Great Britain) Limited (1954), Mr Newborne signed a contract in the name of a company about to be incorporated, adding his name as a director under that of the company. It was held that neither company nor Mr Newborne could be bound by the contract and that it was in fact a nullity. However, in Kelner *v* Baxter (1867), the directors of a company about to be formed signed a contract in their own names 'as agents for' the company whose name was added after their signatures. In this case it was held that the directors were personally liable under the contract as principals. This unsatisfactory state of UK law has now been removed by *s*9(2) which provides:

> Where a contract is purported to be made by a company or by a person as agent for a company, at a time when the company has not been formed, then subject to any agreement to the contrary, the contract shall have effect as a contract entered into by the person purporting to act for the company or as agent for it, and he shall be personally liable on the contract accordingly.

The effect of this provision is to abolish the decision in Newborne *v* Sensolid and to extend the decision in Kelner *v* Baxter to cover all pre-incorporation contracts by making the purported agent personally liable in all cases unless the contract provides to the contrary. However, it seems that the company still can not ratify such contracts but obviously there is no objection, if it wishes, to the company entering into a new contract on the same terms.

Sections 9(3) and (4).   Before the coming into force of these provisions, the Companies Act required the company to file certain documents or information at the Registry of Companies or maintain registers at its registered office containing information of certain of the matters dealt with in the provisions. In other cases the Companies Acts required the Registrar of Companies to issue certificates to a company. The effect was to place the onus on an outsider to inquire at the registered office of the company or make search at the Companies Registry to ascertain that certain events had taken place, eg a company had been incorporated as a limited company, its memorandum or articles had been altered and so on. *S*9(3) now places a duty on the Registrar of Companies on the receipt or issue by him of certain documents to advertise notice of this fact (stating the name of the company, the description of the document and the date of receipt or issue of the document) in the *London Gazette* for English companies and the *Edinburgh Gazette* for Scottish companies. Such an advertised notice shall constitute 'official notification'. The documents set out in *s*9(3) are as follows:

1   Any certificate of incorporation of a company

2   Any document making or evidencing an alteration in the memorandum or articles of association of a company

3   Any return relating to a company's register of directors or notification of a change among its directors

4   A company's annual return

5   Any notice of the situation of a company's registered office, or of any change therein

6   Any copy of a winding-up order in respect of a company

7   Any order for the dissolution of a company on a winding-up

8   Any return by a liquidator of the final meeting of a company on a winding-up

The significance of 'official notification' as defined in s9(3) is that the company cannot rely against other persons on the happening of any of the events listed in s9(4)

'...if the event had not been officially notified at the material time and is not shown by the company to have been known at that time to the person concerned or if the material time fell on or before 15 days after the date of official notification and it is shown that the person concerned was unavoidably prevented from knowing of the event at the time'.

Consequently the company can only safely rely on the events listed in s9(4) after the expiration of fifteen days of the notice in the *London Gazette*. The events listed in s9(4) are as follows:

1   The making of a winding-up order in respect of the company, or the appointment of a liquidator in a voluntary winding-up of the company; or

2   Any alterations to the company's memorandum or articles of association; or

3   Any change among the company's directors; or

4   (As regards service of any documents on the company) any change in the situation of the company's registered office.

Sections 9(5) and (6).   The first affects statutory alterations to a company's memorandum and articles—as such statutory alterations are extremely rare it need not affect or concern most of the incorporated companies in the UK. In addition, a second part of the subsection makes available to the public an up-to-date copy of the company's memorandum and articles. Thus, where a company's memorandum or articles is altered after 1 January 1973 and the company is required by s9 of the European Communities Act, or otherwise, to file a copy of the document making the alteration, a printed copy of the memorandum or articles as altered must be filed at the same time, eg s10

Companies Act 1948 enables a company by special resolution to alter its articles and s143 of the same Act requires special resolutions to be filed within fifteen days of their being passed—such a resolution will be the 'document making or evidencing an alteration in the company's articles' (s9(5))—and it must be filed together with a printed copy of the articles as altered. The provisions in s9(5) do not apply to alterations to the objects clause in a memorandum since s5 of the Companies Act 1948 already imposes on the company the duty of filing a copy of the memorandum as altered when the special resolution is passed to alter the objects clause. Whereas s9(5) deals with alterations to the memorandum or articles made after 1 January 1973, s9(6) provides *inter alia* that where an alteration had been made in a company's memorandum or articles in any manner before the coming into force of the subsection (ie before 1 January 1973) , and a printed copy of the memorandum or articles as altered has not been sent to the Registrar of Companies, it shall be sent to him within one month after the enforcement of this subsection. This provision applies to all alterations made at any time since incorporation and affects a considerable number of companies both private and public which have made changes in their memoranda (eg in the capital clause) or articles since incorporation and had not previously been required to deliver a printed copy of the memoranda or articles as altered.

In default of compliance with s9(5) and (6) the company and any responsible offer thereof will be liable to a fine.

Section 9(7).   Under s201 Companies Act 1948, unless a company is exempted by the Department of Trade and Industry, it must show on its business letters, trade catalogues, circulars and showcards its directors' names and nationalities if not British—if any director is a corporation, the corporate name must be shown. S108(c) provides that every company must have its name mentioned with the word 'limited' as the last word of the name (unless exempted by Departments of Trade or Industry) in all business letters, notices, official publications, cheques and various other documents or papers. In addition, s9(7) European Communities Act now itemizes the following matters, details of which must appear in 'all business letters and order forms' of a company:

1   The place of registration of the company
2   The company's registered number
3   The address of its registered office
4   If exempt for the use of the word 'limited' in its name, the fact that it is a limited company
5   If, in a company having a share capital, its stationery carries reference to the amount of share capital, such reference must be to paid-up capital—not authorized or nominal share capital

Non-compliance renders the company and any of its officers authorizing the issue of stationery not complying, to a fine not exceeding £50 each.

Subsection 9(8). This extends the provisions of *s*9 to unregistered companies and certain unincorporated bodies entitled by letters patent to privileges under the Chartered Companies Act 1837.

REMEDIES FOR BREACH OF CONTRACT

The following are the remedies which may be available in the event of a breach of contract:

1 An action for damages
2 A *quantum meruit* claim
3 An application to the court for a decree of specific performance
4 Application to the court for an injunction

Damages

An award of damages by the court is intended to be compensatory and not punitive. If a legal right has been infringed, therefore, yet no actual loss has resulted, the court will award nominal damages only. Furthermore, the injured party must take all reasonable steps to mitigate the extent of the damage and he will be unable to claim compensation for loss which is really due to his own failure to act in a reasonable manner after the occurrence of the breach.

Some limitation requires to be imposed on the extent of the defendant's liability for the losses occasioned by the breach and certain rules have evolved as regards remoteness of damage. These rules, which were stated in the leading case of Hadley *v* Baxendale (1854), are as follows. If the results of the breach were:

1 Such as could fairly and reasonably be considered to the natural consequences of the breach
2 Such as could reasonably be supposed to have been in the contemplation of both parties at the time of the contract

—then the resultant damage will be recoverable.

A distinction requires to be drawn between liquidated and unliquidated damages. In the former case, these are damages agreed upon by the parties at the time of entering into the contract. Only the fact that a breach has occurred need be proved and no proof of loss is required. Unliquidated damages are those which are awarded by the court in cases where no damages are provided for in the contract itself, and obviously proof of loss is required.

To be enforceable by the court, however, liquidated damages must be shown to be a genuine pre-estimate of loss and not a penalty inserted as a threat of punishment to follow in the event of a breach. If the court concludes that the prearranged sum is in fact a penalty, it will not be awarded but unliquidated damages based on normal principles will be awarded instead.

The following rules, which were established by the case of Dunlop Tyre Company Limited *v* New Garage Limited (1915), will normally be applied by the court to determine whether or not a penalty is involved:

1   The words used by the parties are not conclusive.
2   The essence of a penalty is a payment which is stipulated *in terrorem* in an attempt to frighten the defaulter into carrying out his side of the bargain. The essence of liquidated damages is a genuine pre-estimate of the likely loss
3   If a single sum is payable as damages for any one of several breaches, varying in gravity, there is presumption that it is a penalty
4   If the sum involved is extravagant or unconscionable it is a penalty

Quantum meruit

The meaning of this expression is literally 'as much as has been earned, and a claim on this basis is for reasonable remuneration distinct from a claim for compensation for loss which would be the basis of an action for damages. The following are the circumstances where a *quantum meruit* claim would be appropriate:

1   Where work has been carried out under a contract which subsequently turns out to be void, as damages cannot be awarded for breach of a void contract
2   Where substantial performance of the contract has taken place
3   Where, although no agreement as to remuneration was made, there was an express or implied contract to render services
4   Where the original contract has been replaced by a new implied contract

The above information is of necessity very generalized since this particular remedy can be used both contractually and quasi-contractually, the latter being out of the scope of this chapter. At its simplest, a *quantum meruit* claim may offer an alternative course to a plaintiff in preference to an action for damages.

Specific performance

This is an equitable remedy which formerly was only available in the courts of equity but which is now available in any court. It is not available as of right and is awarded only at the discretion of the court.

The discretion exercised by the court is not an arbitrary one, however, and reliance will be made on the following established principles:

1   Action must commence within a reasonable time in accordance with the maxim 'delay defeats equity'
2   The plaintiff's conduct will also be considered by the court as 'he who comes to equity must come with clean hands'
3   A decree of specific performance will never be granted where damages would be an adequate and appropriate remedy
4   Where the contract is one for personal services, specific performance will not be awarded
5   If it is not possible for the court to supervise the contract, a decree for specific performance will not be granted—for example, the granting of such a decree is very rare in the case of building contracts
6   A promise unsupported by consideration and even if made under seal is not specifically enforceable
7   Where undue hardship would be caused to the defendant, specific performance will not be awarded
8   Where the contract is not binding on both parties—for example, infants' voidable contracts—specific performance will not be awarded

Injunction

Injunction is another equitable remedy which the court may award especially in cases where damages would neither be an adequate nor an appropriate remedy. Its application by the court is governed by the same guiding principles as outlined in the preceding paragraph. There are several forms of injunction: interlocutory, prohibitory, perpetual and mandatory. At its simplest, an injunction is a court order restraining either an actual or contemplated breach of the contract in question

Limitation Act 1939

In conclusion, it should be noted that there are time-limits within which actions for breach of contract must be initiated. The time-limits are as follows:

Simple contracts.   No action may commence after the expiration of six years from the date on which the cause of action accrued

Specialty contracts.   An action cannot be commenced after the expiration of twelve years from the date on which the cause of action accrued. A specialty contract is one made under seal

TRANSFER OF OWNERSHIP AND RESPONSIBILITY FOR ACCIDENTAL LOSS OR DAMAGE

The underlying purpose of a contract of sale of goods is of course the transfer of the ownership of the goods from seller to buyer. The legal distinction between possession and ownership must be kept in mind—although one of the parties to the contract may have physical possession of the goods, this does not necessarily mean that he is the legal owner. The Sale of Goods Act 1893 sets out various rules regarding the transfer of ownership of the goods and these will be examined later. The reason it is important to know the precise moment of time at which the ownership of the goods passes from seller to buyer is that (*a*) if the goods are accidentally destroyed, it is essential to know which party has to bear the loss, and (*b*) in the case of bankruptcy of either party or liquidation of a limited company it is necessary to know whether the goods belong to the trustee or liquidator or not.

The rules governing the transfer of ownership depend on whether the goods are unascertained or specific. S16 (Sale of Goods Act 1893) provides that unless and until the goods are ascertained then no transfer of ownership is made to the buyer. S17, dealing with specific goods, states that transfer of ownership will take place at such time as the parties intend it to take place. The parties' intention may be determined from the terms of the contract itself or from the conduct of the parties but recognizing that in many cases such intention will not readily be determinable, the Act in *s*18 specifies the following rules for ascertaining when ownership is transferred, unless a contrary intention appears:

1   In unconditional contracts for the sale of specific goods in a deliverable state, the ownership is transferred when the contract is made, irrespective of the date of payment or delivery

2   Where sales of specific goods are involved and the seller is bound to do something to the goods to put them into a deliverable state, the ownership does not pass until such thing is done and the buyer has notice of it

3   In sales of specific goods in a deliverable state, where the seller is bound to weigh, measure, test or do some other act or thing with reference to the goods for the purpose of ascertaining the price, transfer of ownership does not take place until such thing is done and the buyer has notice thereof

4   Where goods are delivered to the buyer on 'approval' or on 'sale or return', or other similar terms, the transfer of ownership takes place
    (*a*) When the buyer signifies his approval or acceptance to the seller or does any other act adopting the transaction
    (*b*) If the buyer does not signify his approval or acceptance but retains the goods without giving notice of rejection, then, if a

time has been fixed for the return of the goods, on the expiration of such time, and if no time has been fixed, on the expiration of a reasonable time. What is a reasonable time is open to interpretation

5 (*a*) Where there is a contract for the sale of unascertained or future goods by description, and goods of that description and in a deliverable state are unconditionally appropriated to the contract, the ownership of the goods thereupon transfers to the buyer. The consent may be express or implied and can be given either before or after the appropriation

 (*b*) Where, in pursuance of the contract, the seller delivers the goods to the buyer or to a carrier or other bailee or custodier—for example, warehouse owner—whether named by the buyer or not, for the purpose of transmission to the buyer, and does not reserve the right of disposal, he is deemed to have unconditionally appropriated the goods to the contract

Apart from the above rules, the effect of *s*20 should be noted since it provides that, unless otherwise agreed, the goods remain at the seller's risk until ownership has been transferred to the buyer and furthermore where such transfer does take place, the goods are at the buyer's risk, whether delivery has been made or not. There are two provisos to *s*20:

1 Where delivery has been delayed by the fault of either buyer or seller the goods are at the risk of the party in default as regards any loss which might not have occurred but for such fault

2 Nothing in the section is to affect the duties or liabilities of either seller or buyer as a bailee or custodier of the goods of the other party. In other words, irrespective of fault, the party who has physical possession of the goods must exercise due care of them

Although the general rule as provided by *s*20 Sale of Goods Act 1893 is that the risk of accidental loss follows ownership, this is not the case in cif (cost, insurance, freight) contracts where once the goods are delivered to the ship, the risk of loss passes to the buyer. So far as Fob (free on board) contracts are concerned it is usual that once the goods are shipped the ownership and risk passes to the buyer.

CONTRACTS IN RESTRAINT OF TRADE

At its simplest, a contract in restraint of trade is one in which a person's freedom of action to carry on business or to be employed is restricted. Such contracts may be classified under three distinct heads:

1 Agreements whereby the vendor of a business undertakes not to

set up in competition with the purchaser (see below)

2   Agreements in contracts of employment which restrict the freedom of movement of the employee after leaving his employer's service (see below)

3   Agreements regulating trade and involving restrictive practice (see below)

Before considering in more detail the three groups of restrictive agreement outlined above, we must mention the following general rules which apply to all types of restrictive agreement:

At common law, every agreement in restraint of trade is *prima facie* illegal and void.

Despite the initial presumption against validity, however, the court will look into the question of reasonableness and will apply two major tests: (i) is it reasonable between the parties to it, and (ii) is it reasonable from the point of view of the public interest? In the cases of agreements classified under (1) and (2) above, the question of extent—both of time and of geographical area—will be taken into consideration. The person seeking to enforce the agreement will also be required to show that he has given valuable consideration for the promise which he seeks to enforce, even if the contract is under seal.

Agreements in connection with sales of businesses

Since the purchase price of the business normally includes a substantial sum in respect of goodwill, the court tends to enforce those agreements which are intended primarily to protect a proprietary interest. The question of reasonableness is fundamental and, provided the agreement is no wider than is reasonably necessary to protect the interest, is not against the public interest and is not unreasonably restrictive as regards the party involved, it will be enforceable.

Agreements imposing restraints on employees

The court is usually very reluctant to enforce this type of restrictive covenant and the tests of reasonableness which will be applied are normally much stricter than those involved in agreements between vendors and purchasers of businesses. It is clearly established that a covenant which is concerned primarily with restricting competition after the employee has left his employer's service will be void. Factors such as the type of employment, the area of restraint, the period of the restriction, will all be taken into account by the court. Furthermore the court will normally require to be satisfied that the employee has received some valuable consideration in return for his undertaking to be restricted.

Agreements involving the regulation of trade

Fundamentally, these are agreements between manufacturers and suppliers relating to the conditions under which they will produce, market or fix the price of goods. Unlike the other forms of contracts in restraint of trade, this particular category is very much subject to statutory regulation, in particular the Restrictive Trade Practices Act 1956 and the Resale Price Act 1964.

In broad terms, the 1956 Act covers agreements under which producers, suppliers or exporters of goods restrict the manufacture, supply or distribution of these goods by means of collective agreements. Unless such agreements are registered with the Registrar of Restrictive Trading Agreements, they will be void. After registration, the Restrictive Practices Court will then consider the validity or otherwise of the agreement.

The Resale Prices Act 1964 prohibits resale price maintenance except where it can be shown to be in the public interest.

Since 1973, restrictive trading agreements come within the province of the Director of Fair Trading and reference should be made to Chapter 14.

FURTHER READING

Cheshire and Fifoot, *Law of Contract,* Butterworths, London, 1975.

Smith and Keenan, *Essentials of Mercantile Law,* Pitman, London, 1965.

A.H. Boulton, *The Making of Business Contracts,* Sweet and Maxwell, London, 1972.

Charlesworth, *Mercantile Law,* Sweet and Maxwell, London, 1972.

R. Brazier, *Cases and Statutes on Contract,* Sweet and Maxwell, London, 1973.

11

Negotiation

P D V Marsh

NATURE OF THE NEGOTIATING PROCESS

Purpose of negotiation

Negotiation is a dynamic process by which two parties, each with their own objectives, confer together to reach a mutually satisfying agreement on a matter of common interest. This definition establishes the four essential elements of the negotiating process:

1   The process of negotiation takes place within a defined time-scale which will impose limitations on the objectives of the negotiators. This time-scale may extend to include the next occasion on which the parties contemplate doing business
2   Each party will have its own objectives which it must strive to achieve
3   The parties must be motivated towards reaching agreement which is recognized by both as mutually satisfying their essential needs: imposition by the stronger of his will on the weaker, regardless of the latter's interest, is not negotiation
4   The end-product of the negotiation is a matter of common interest: this could be the construction of a new factory, or, in a labour negotiation, the continued existence of the firm as providing a source of worthwhile employment to its employees and of profit to its shareholders

Distributive and integrative bargaining

Distributive bargaining refers to the process in which two parties bargain over the allocation between them of a fixed resource. Their interests are in total conflict since the gain to one is a loss to the other. Bargaining between employer and union over a simple pay increase with no productivity strings attached, or between buyer and seller on the price of an article, are examples of this type of bargaining.

Integrative bargaining describes the situation in which, through a joint exercise by the parties, a solution can be found to a problem which provides both with some benefit.

An example of such a bargaining situation was where a union and management were in dispute because few long-service employees were being promoted. The union proposed that long service be given greater weight in judging promotion suitability; the company stated that it could judge promotion suitability only on the grounds of ability and skill. The solution found was for the company to institute a scheme for helping long-service employees to obtain the necessary skills through further education. Both sides achieved their objective. The union obtained better promotion opportunities for their members; management retained the prerogative of determining the criteria for promotion decisions.

Negotiation as a matter of progressive commitment

Negotiation is an exercise in progressive commitment. As the negotiation proceeds, both parties will leave their initial positions and move towards each other so that, with each move made, the area remaining for further movement is automatically reduced. Only exceptionally will a negotiator be able to increase his area of movement by withdrawing from a position previously conceded, while at the same time retaining his integrity. No position should therefore be established or movement made until the degree to which the company is willing to be committed has been determined.

This would apply, for instance, where a firm is asked to give a budgetary quotation. Whatever figure is put forward will in practice represent the maximum price the firm will be able to obtain. The buyer will only expect the price to move one way from the budgetary figure—and that is downwards.

PLANNING THE NEGOTIATION

Value and scope of planning

Success in negotiation depends primarily on the skill and care with which the negotiating plan has been prepared. Tactics at the negotiating table can help but they too need to be planned in advance. Planning should commence before any offer is made, or responded to, and continue the whole way through the negotiation until final agreement is reached and recorded. In this activity, planning and action are partners; successive stages of a single process the third stage of which, monitoring and review, completes the activity cycle as illustrated in Figure 11.1.

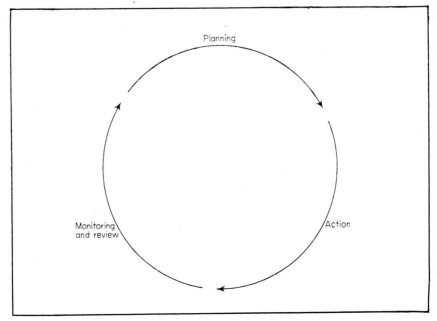

Figure 11.1   The activity cycle

In the course of a single negotiation this cycle will be repeated many times. The review and planning stages may be the subject of a formal review meeting held away from the negotiating arena, or a quick ten-minute adjournment part-way through a negotiating session. Whatever their form the purpose of such meetings must be to ensure that:

1   The timing and extent of movement are in accordance with the degree to which the management of the company are willing to be committed
2   At all stages the moves have been fully prepared for in advance, the facts established and the strategy selected

If these objectives are not met then the negotiators should not continue or they will be drawn into making unscheduled concessions or establishing unwanted precedents, from neither of which will it be possible for them later to withdraw.

Selection of the objective

The starting point for the preparation of any negotiating plan should be an explicit statement of the target objective. Vague generalizations should not be accepted. The objective should be quantified as for example

> Our gross margin after an allowance for contingencies of 5 per cent and based on recovery of full shop costs and overheads should not be less than 30 per cent.

The next step is the analysis of the target objective in relation to the three critical factors which will affect its achievement:

1 Strength of negotiating position
2 Competing objectives of other projects
3 Resource requirement and availability

These three factors within the time-scale for an individual negotiation have a single total value so that an increase in the value of one can be secured only at the expense of a decrease in the value of one or both of the others. Negotiating strength can be increased if all competing objectives are abandoned and the whole resources available are concentrated on the one project. Equally, if the resources required are greater than those which can be made available without interfering with other projects, then either a reduction in negotiating strength must be accepted or one or more competing objectives abandoned. What should never be allowed to happen is that the available resources are spread across so wide a range of objectives that the negotiating strength on each is reduced to the point at which success is achieved on none.

Assessment of the negotiating position

Three typical negotiating situations will be discussed:

1 Bid submission
2 Procurement
3 Dispute

The factors which will primarily influence the company's negotiating position in each situation and which need to be considered in preparing the negotiating plan are as follows:

Bid submission
1 Probability of the company being successful
2 Desirability of the company securing the business

3   Resources required both for bidding and contract execution
4   Alternative opportunities open to the company for the employment of its resources

Clearly factors 1 and 2 are interrelated. Thus the company might increase its success probability by taking a lower margin or shortening the delivery but either of these steps would lead to a reduction in bid desirability since the profit would be less and the risk of penalty greater.

A simple method of presenting the negotiating position to management would be to require the sales department to prepare a quantified assessment of both the success probability and the bid desirability and by taking the product of these two figures arrive at an expected value of the bid. This expected value could then be compared with the norm established by the company for the product line in question.

Two other propositions are put forward:

1   If the bid desirability as a percentage is below some guide-line figure established by management then no tender should be submitted, irrespective of success probability
2   If the business desirability is positive then the extent of resource employment which is justified is related directly to the expected value of the bid. The employment of additional resources because the expected value is high is valid only to the extent that these increase proportionately the success probability

Procurement.   Three basic procurement situations exist:

1   Continued demand by two or more buyers which is large enough to stimulate competition and maintain two or more suppliers in the market. This may be further subdivided into situations where:
     (*a*) One major buyer predominates
     (*b*) No single buyer predominates
2   Continued demand by a single buyer large enough to stimulate competition and maintain two or more suppliers in the market
3   Demand insufficient to maintain more than one supplier in the market or one supplier has established a monopoly

Within the framework of these three basic situations, the buyer can improve or worsen his own negotiating position according to the manner in which he specifies his requirements.

In cases 1(*a*) and 2, the specification is set by the buyer and the suppliers have no alternative if they wish to stay in business but to respond. The buyer should therefore draft his inquiry in such a way that it can be responded to by the maximum number of qualified firms at the minimum economic price level.

Reduction in competitiveness will arise if the buyer specifies higher technical standards than are really needed or imposes technical or commercial conditions which can be met only by a limited number of firms.

In the other two cases, the buyer does not possess the negotiating advantage. In 1(*b*), he must accept the specification standards generally prevailing in the industry or else pay a much higher price for a special whatever the total value of his purchasing bill. Again in 3, it is often the buyer himself who contributes towards the monopolistic nature of the supply position, by the detailed descriptive manner in which he defines the item or service required. If he would limit himself to describing the service or function which he wishes to have performed then he would widen the competitive field.

Dispute. The strength of a party's negotiating position should be assessed under three headings:

1   Contractual
2   Financial
3   Commercial

A checklist divided into three sections under these headings is set out on p.244. From an appraisal of the answers to these questions a schedule should be prepared of the losses and gains which can be expected from each possible course of action. There are at any stage in a negotiation three courses open to either party:

1   Accept the terms proposed by the other
2   Seek to negotiate improved terms
3   Refer the dispute to law or arbitration

A balance sheet should therefore be drawn up utilizing the items and values listed in the schedule, and the results compared so as to arrive at the course of action which shows the maximum expected value. The balance sheet should show for each item:

1   Its estimated value
2   The probability of that value being realized
3   Its expected value (item 1) x (item 2)

Although the details of the checklist have been prepared for a contract dispute, a similar list could be prepared for an industrial relations dispute and the principles of the method proposed and of selecting the act with the maximum expected value would equally apply.

Choice of negotiating strategy

There are two basic negotiating strategies which a party can employ:

1   Quick kill
2   Hold back

Quick kill is the strategy of selecting an offer which the recipient will accept without further negotiation or of responding to an offer by accepting it without bargaining.

Hold back is the strategy of selecting an offer which is sufficiently attractive to the recipient that he will not reject it out of hand, but which at the same time contains a margin for negotiation which is adequate:

1   To enable the party submitting the offer to meet the recipient's anticipated demands
2   To ensure that at the end of the negotiation the party submitting the offer obtains a return which he considers to be adequate

To the recipient, it is the strategy of bargaining with the party or parties submitting offers until terms are secured which the recipient considers to be the most advantageous he can obtain.

Strategy selection for bid submission and procurement.   The parties will be in one of the three negotiating states relative to each other:

Party	*Opponent*
Domination	Subordination
Subordination	Domination
Uncertainty	Uncertainty

Domination.   This exists:

1   For the seller, if the buyer must so far prefer some feature in the seller's offer that this preference outweighs any advantages which are possessed by the competing offers and this is known to the seller
2   For the buyer, if he knows for certain he will obtain at least two genuinely competing offers either of which would be acceptable to him and this is known to the sellers

The correct strategy for the party to select if he is dominant is quick kill.

Subordination. Subordination exists if the strategy of the person submitting the offer must be that which is dictated by the wishes of the recipient. Two basic examples would be:

1   Tendering to a strict public authority which is debarred by its own rules from post-tender negotiation. The bidder must adopt quick kill

2   Tendering to a purchaser who is known to bargain whatever offer is submitted to him. The bidder in this event must select hold back

Uncertainty. In many negotiating situations neither party will possess enough knowledge to be certain of the competitive situation or the other's intentions. In a state of uncertainty which strategy should each party select?

This position can be represented in a game-theory type matrix as set out in figure 11.2.

In this matrix the expected value to the seller of the outcome of each combination of his strategy with that of the buyer is determined in accordance with the following equation: EV = Conditional value of strategy if successful × probability of success + conditional value of strategy unsuccessful × (1−success probability)

		BUYERS' STRATEGIES	
		Quick kill	*Hold back*
		b_1	b_2
	Quick a_1	$\left.\begin{array}{l}4 \times 0.7 \\ -1 \times 0.3\end{array}\right\} 2.5$	$\left.\begin{array}{l}4 \times 0.2 \\ -1 \times 0.8\end{array}\right\} 0$
SUPPLIERS'	*kill*		
STRATEGIES			
	Hold a_2	$\left.\begin{array}{l}6 \times 0.2 \\ -1 \times 0.8\end{array}\right\} 0.4$	$\left.\begin{array}{l}5 \times 0.7 \\ -1 \times 0.3\end{array}\right\} 3.2$
	back		

Figure 11.2   Strategy selection for bid submission (figures in thousands of pounds)

The values shown are based on the following assumptions:

1   Normal profit margin is £4000. To this is added £2000 as negotiating margin when hold-back strategy is employed

2   Variable tendering costs which would be lost if bid not successful: £1000

3   In $a_1 b_2$ the supplier does not reduce his price, therefore there is a high probability that he will lose the bid

4   In $a_2 b_1$ he has a lower probability of success due to the addition of

the negotiation margin
5   In a_2b_2 the success probability of 70 per cent is based on the
supplier conceding 50 per cent of his negotiating margin

The seller will select hold back since the expected value of the holdback strategy
is £3600 as compared with £2500 for the quick kill, and hold back maximizes
his security against either strategy used by the buyer.

A similar analysis can be prepared for the buyer as shown in Figure 11.3. The
buyer estimates the price at which he will have to purchase for each alternative
and in the absence of any better information thinks it equally likely that all or a
majority of suppliers will adopt a quick kill or holdback strategy. It is obvious
that again the buyer will select hold back.

| | | SUPPLIERS' STRATEGIES | |
		Quick kill b_1	Hold back b_2
	Quick a_1 kill	$40 \times 0.5 = 20$	$42 \times 0.5 = 21$
BUYERS' STRATEGIES	Hold a_2 back	$38 \times 0.5 = 19$	$41 \times 0.5 = 20.5$

Figure 11.3 Strategy selection for bid procurement

In a state of uncertainty, therefore, the strategy of both parties should be
hold back. Outcome a_1 b_1 will *not* be reached by both parties acting
independently of one another, but only if there is cooperation between them to
the extent that both have complete confidence in the strategy which will be
selected by the other, so that the situation is no longer one of uncertainty.

Strategy selection for a dispute.   Two cases can be distinguished: tangible and
intangible.
Tangible.   Party's case is based wholly on factual evidence capable of
proof. Dealing with a rational opponent, Party's strategy should be quick kill.
Any attempt to pad by adding a negotiating margin would only weaken his case
by making Opponent lose confidence in Party's integrity once the padding was
discovered. In industrial relations a comparable strategy would be that of
Boulwarism as practised by General Electric of America in which the company
having made a thorough study of the situation both from their own and their
employees' viewpoints, put forward a detailed package which is a genuine
attempt to meet both sides but on which they refuse to negotiate with the union
on any significant issue.

The danger in this type of approach is that by preventing Opponent's negotiators from being seen to do their job this makes them hostile and resentful. In this condition emotional abuse is likely to replace rational argument. Party should anticipate this reaction and be at pains to show when putting forward his case that he has taken note of Opponent's views to modify his first proposals. In this way he will enable Opponent's negotiators when reporting to their own management or union committee to achieve credit for having caused Party to improve his offer.

Intangible.   Party's case is based on factors of subjective judgment. Opponent will therefore negotiate to test Party's strength and both will employ a holdback strategy.

NEGOTIATING AREA AND THE INFLUENCE OF TIME

Identification of the negotiating area and resistance points

The level of the first offer to the party who submits it is critical in that it establishes the maximum benefit which that party will derive from the negotiation on the assumption that the recipient of the offer behaves rationally and does not make a mistake.

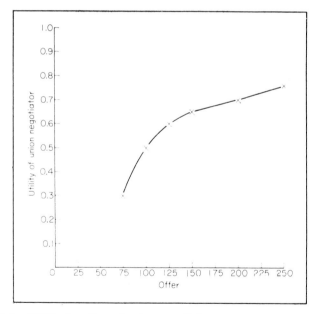

Figure 11.4   Utility function of union negotiator

If the negotiating strategy of the party making the offer is quick kill then the initial offer should be put forward at a level which maximizes that party's expected value.

Assume that a union negotiator was putting forward a proposal for an increase in the basic wage rate which is at present £20 per week. He estimates the minimum demand likely to be just acceptable to his members as 75p and the maximum he could possibly hope to obtain would be £2.50. The curve of his utility function against possible increases could be of the shape shown in Figure 11.4.

Increments up to 75p are valued very positively; increments over that and up to £1.25 are still valued positively but of rather less importance; over £1.25 each marginal increase becomes of less and less significance. Assume that a strike would have a disutility cost of 3 against the above scale and the negotiator subjectively assesses the probabilities of a series of offers as in Figure 11.5. The final column in the table shows the expected value of each offer to the union negotiator.

OFFER	UTILITY	PROBABILITY OF ACCEPTANCE	DISUTILITY COSTS	PROBABILITY OF REJECTION	EXPECTED VALUE
75p	3	0.9	−3	0.1	2.4
£1.00	5	0.8	−3	0.2	3.4
£1.25	6	0.7	−3	0.3	3.3
£1.50	6.5	0.5	−3	0.5	1.75
£2.00	7	0.2	−3	0.8	−1.0
£2.50	7.5	0.1	−3	0.9	−1.95

Figure 11.5   Expected value of offers to union negotiator

If the union leader was bidding on a final-offer-first basis then he would select a bid at £1.00.

If, however, he were expecting to bargain then he would use the above table to establish both his target objective and his points of resistance. Realistically on the above scale these would be:

Target	£2.00
First resistance point	£1.25
Final resistance point	£0.75

Assuming now the company negotiators similarly assessed their position and came up with the following:

Company preferred level	£1.00
Company maximum acceptable level	£1.50

The negotiating area could then be represented as shown in Figure 11.6.

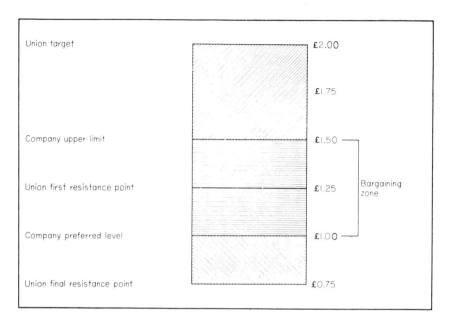

Figure 11.6   Bargaining zone in management—union negotiation

The real bargaining zone would be the hatched area between £1.50 and £1.00 and the likely point of settlement between £1.50 and £1.25. The union could be expected to resist strongly any attempt to reduce below £1.25. As this is below the company's maximum it is probably the minimum figure at which a bargain will be agreed.

Movement within the negotiating area relative to time

The advantage in negotiation lies generally with the party who is under least pressure for reaching agreement by a deadline. Either party can therefore bring pressure on the other by creating an artificial deadline. 'We must have an answer from the company by Friday midnight or we strike', or by deliberately showing that he is not bothered by time, like the sales negotiator who lets the overseas buyer know he has booked his hotel for an indefinite period and has an 'open' return air ticket.

In most negotiations both parties will be aware at some stage that there is a defined time-limit. Over the period remaining it is to the negotiator's advantage:

1   In the initial stages to move as little as possible from his original position. He will gain tactically by keeping the gap deliberately wide and cause his oponent to lose confidence and become uncertain. He must however be prepared to suffer a

certain amount of abuse!

2   At the penultimate stage:

(*a*) If he is dominant again to make only a minor adjustment to his position leaving it to his opponent to concede, or

(*b*) If he is less than dominant to move sufficiently to persuade his opponent also to move so that at the final stage the gap left between them is such that both will recognize the point at which to cordinate their expectations and reach a bargain.

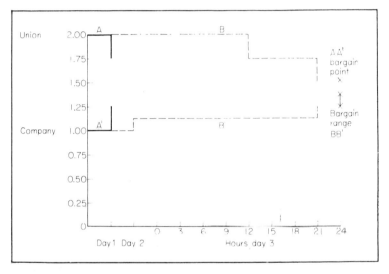

Figure 11.7   Influence of time on negotiation

Assume in the example in the previous part of this section the negotiating period left before expiry of the union's strike ultimatum was three days.

Line AA′ in Figure 11.7 shows the pattern as it might be if both sides made the mistake of moving too early. By the end of day one there is only a gap of £0.50 between them and however long the negotiations last a 50/50 split of this seems inevitable. The gap is too small relative to the time left for it to be otherwise. This would mean a final bargain at £1.50, the company's maximum figure.

Supposing however that the company recognizing that it had only £0.50 to negotiate with and three days to go increased its offer only marginally at the beginning of day two by £0.25. The position could then be as shown on line BB′. After its initial move the company stays firm until the union drops to £1.50. The company has learnt something of the shape of the union's utility curve through the negotiation and does not believe that the union will use its threat. Finally the company offers £1.25 shortly before the deadline. The union may accept or possibly come back with say £1.35. In either event the company will have made a significant saving.

NEGOTIATING TEAMS

Size and constitution of the team

The following guidelines should be observed in the selection of a negotiation team:

1   The team should never consist of one but equally should not be too large. One person on his own cannot be expected to present his case, listen to his opponents' arguments, develop counterarguments, take notes and finally achieve the most favourable bargain. He must have support without which any effective negotiating tactics are impractical. At the same time three is probably the maximum number that can function effectively as a negotiating team at any one period
2   The characters who form the team must be compatible and prepared to work together
3   The team should have equal status to that of the opponent's and equal competence on technical matters such as law, accountancy or engineering
4   Technical experts on a team must be prepared, however senior their personal position may be in the organization, to act only as advisers. Even though they are members of the team it may be preferable for certain negotiating sessions that they remain in the background since their presence may inhibit Opponent from making a commercial deal

Appointment and duties of the team leader

Someone must be selected to act as team leader and there can only be one leader for any negotiation. His authority must be recognized and respected by the other team members even though within their particular functions they may be senior to him in the company hierachy. The duties of the team leader include:
1   Preparation of the negotiating plan
2   Ensuring the availability of all necessary data, files and so on
3   Conducting the briefing meeting before the negotiation starts: he must allow adequate time for this
4   Ensuring that all necessary authority has been obtained from company management and that individual team members have authority to act for their departments
5   Checking that all administrative and security arrangements

appropriate to the negotiation have been made

6   Selecting the negotiating tactics
7   Opening Party's case
8   Responding to Opponent's case
9   Calling on other team members to make their individual contributions but personally summing up after each one
10   Holding further briefing sessions as necessary; revising the negotiations plan and obtaining any additional authority required from company management. The team leader should be the only person who communicates with company management during the course of the negotiation
11   Allowing any necessary concessions
12   Making the final bargain
13   Ensuring a written record of the negotiation is made and agreed with Opponent
14   Signing or initialling the written record
15   Reporting on the negotiation to management. This report should include a list of follow-up action points with the names of those responsible for carrying them out

OPENING STAGES

The objective in the opening stage is to expose the whole of the area which you as the negotiator wish to cover, and to identify the strength of Opponent's case including the degree of his opposition to or acceptance of your ideas. Until this has been done no concession should be made, even if you agree with his point of view, since to do so would deprive you of a bargaining counter which you may need in the future. The table of Do's and Don'ts in Figure 11.8 summarizes the way in which the negotiator should handle the opening of the negotiation.

When a written statement has been submitted by the other side

DO	DON'T
1 Challenge each point asking why he has made it.	Speculate on his reasons or put words into his mouth.
2 Appear ignorant, even if you are not, and let him justify his case.	Try to be clever and show how much you know by answering your own questions.
3 Note his answers and reserve your position.	Agree immediately even if you know you will in the end, no matter how reasonable his proposal. You may need that 'concession' later.

Figure 11.8 Do's and don'ts for negotiator handling opening stages

DO	DON'T
4 Make certain you have fully understood each point and his motives even if this means going over the ground more than once. This applies particularly if your native languages are not the same.	Snatch at what appears to be a favourable bargain or interpretation of his views.
5 Test out the strength of his views on each point so that later on you can assess the probability of his sticking to his position under pressure, and formulate a possible overall bargain.	Be drawn into lengthy arguments on any individual point at this stage in which it may be difficult to avoid offering or accepting a compromise solution on that point alone.
6 Be aware of interrelationship between different contract points and the possible counterarguments which will be developed against you if you succeed or are allowed to do so, on any one. For example, if as a contractor you suggest that the buyer should have a liability for additional costs in which you may be involved, if items supplied by him prove defective, you must expect that he in turn will ask you to accept some measure of consequential liability for defective items of your supply.	Be conscious only of the particular point under negotiation and of the immediate benefits to be derived from succeeding on that point alone.
7 Appear calm and quiet and keep your thoughts to yourself.	Betray your feelings by showing anger, surprise or delight at his remarks.
8 Correct him if he is proceeding on a false belief as to a factual position for which you are responsible.	Improve his judgment unless it is to your advantage to do so.

When you have submitted a written proposal

DO	DON'T
1 Limit your answers to his questions to the minimum and seek to persuade him into talking again as soon as possible.	Elaborate at length on your motives.
2 Test out the strength of his objections by seeing if he will withdraw without requiring any corresponding concessions from you.	Concede anything or be drawn into trade-off negotiations before all points have been discussed.

3 Behave generally as described in points 6, 7 and 8 above.

When no written statement has been submitted by either party

DO	DON'T
1 Identify all the points to be discussed.	Let the discussions ramble on without any defined order.
2 Cover each point in sufficient depth for both sides to be aware of each other's position.	Concentrate the discussion on one point to the exclusion of all others.
3 Keep the discussions exploratory—you	Be drawn into definite commitments either

Figure 11.8 (Continued)

DO   DON'T
can confirm your position in writing   in the form of making a firm concession or
later.   taking up a position from which it will be
                                                                 difficult later for you to withdraw.

4   Behave generally as described in points 6, 7 and 8 above.

Conclusion of the initial presentation

The initial phase of the negotiation is preferably limited therefore to an overall review and
an identification of the differences between the parties. It should end in the establishment
of the means by which these differences are to be resolved.

   The situation at the conclusion of the initial phase will fall into one of the following
three broad categories:

1   The issues will be sufficiently simple and the gap identified between the
     parties will be sufficiently narrow for the negotiators to move straight into
     the decision phase
2   The issues will be more complex and/or the differences wider so that
     further discussions are required on specific issues to be followed by a final
     bargaining session
3   It will be apparent that the gap is so wide that the result must either be a
     'no-bargain' or, if an agreement is to be reached then one, or perhaps both,
     sets of negotiators must concede further than they are permitted to do by
     the terms of their negotiating authority. Accordingly before meeting again
     they must refer back for revised instructions

Follow-up

Resolution of the gap between the parties to the point at which a bargain can be identified
may be accomplished in the following ways:

1   Establishment of small working parties from each side consisting of one or
     two experts to deal with specific issues
2   Each side is assigned to give further study to and prepare draft proposals on
     the controversial issues. These drafts are then exchanged and used as bases
     for further discussion between full negotiating teams
3   Through informal contact between the chief negotiators for each side or
     their respective specialists on an exploratory basis
4   By referring the issue to a third party whose judgment is respected by both
     sides

These methods are not mutually exclusive. On a major contract negotiation all four may be
used.
   The principal problem facing the team captain for each side at this stage is to retain
overall control. He must identify and make sure all his team are fully aware of:

1   Any issue so vital that the company would prefer 'no-bargain' to conceding
     from their present position
2   The interrelationship between specific issues, particularly if these are going
     to be discussed by different pairs of specialists for example inspection,
     testing and time for delivery, penalty
3   The limits to which at any stage the team leader is willing to be committed
     on any issue.

Figure 11.8 (Continued)

NEGOTIATING TACTICS

Offensive tactics

Final offer first.   Taking the initative by making a complete presentation to Opponent to which he can make no major objection. Can be extremely effective provided Party has done a complete and thorough job of preparation and had limited his case to that which he knows cannot be faulted. Carries with it however the risk of causing resentment from Opponent which may lead to an emotional outburst. Party must either be ready for this, or if he believes the emotional response will be serious should abandon the use of the tactic.

Pressurizing Opponent.   Pressure is brought to bear on individual members of Opponent's team who are vulnerable for some reason. This could be because of their past actions or position in the company or organization concerned; for example a junior member of a functional department who is standing in for his chief. He can be attacked: 'We have always dealt with your Mr X before and he has never taken that line—are you sure about this?' Alternatively he may be flattered: 'We would like your opinion on this, after all you are the expert in the field here: can you tell us how we should approach this?' Again, while it may be initially effective the use of this tactic can cause lasting resentment.

Putting on a show of strength.   Party deploys a team of experts under the leadership of a senior manager or director whose status level is higher than Opponent would normally expect for the type of negotiation concerned. Often used in association with the 'final-offer-first' tactic in order to lend credence to its authority.

Arbitrary behaviour.   Sheer obstinacy or the threat of harmful action can sometimes be a more potent means by which Party can get his own way than logical argument; provided that the threat is accepted by Opponent as credible. Party must not however bluff and be caught. His commitment to carry out the threat should be graded therefore to the degree to which he is prepared to carry it out in practice should the necessity arise.

Making opponent appear unreasonable.   By taking Opponent's line of argument to the extreme, Party shows that as a matter of principle it cannot be supported. Opponent is then put on the defensive and compelled to justify the particular case as an exception to the general rule. Party is then in a position to demand acceptance of one of his points as the price Opponent must pay for Party agreeing to the 'exception'.

Fishing tactics.   A proposition is deliberately overstated by Party to make Opponent respond by disclosing his true position and the reasons why he is adopting that position. After hearing Opponent's explanation and going through the argument, Party can then make a 'concession' in return for one from Opponent.

DEFENSIVE TACTICS

Keeping quiet.   A minimal response by Party to a proposition put forward by Opponent to which he is seeking Party's agreement will often result in Opponent feeling compelled to go on talking and offer more and more justification for his proposal. In so doing he is likely to reveal more of his genuine motivation than he intended and provide Party with a basis on which to mount a counterattack.

Pretended misunderstanding.   By pretending to misunderstand Opponent's case, Party may again cause Opponent to show more of his hand than he intended. Experts in particular can rarely miss the opportunity to display their knowledge.

Yes-but technique.   Rather than an outright denial of a proposition put forward by Opponent, which may cause antagonism and a break-down in communication, Party will often obtain better results by indicating that he has some sympathy or support for Opponent's position but cannot see its application or relevance to the present negotiation. 'Yes, I see what you mean and there could be a problem here, but I don't see how what you propose will provide any real solution.' The only admission Party has made with that reply that 'there could be a problem' which was probably evident anyhow; otherwise Opponent is back where he started from. At the same time he cannot accuse Party of being non-cooperative.

Calculated incompetence.   If Party does not wish to discuss a particular issue, or at any rate not for the moment, he can deliberately avoid doing so by ensuring that his expert on that subject is not available.

Taking Opponent into your confidence.   It is much easier for Opponent to be agressive and demanding when he is not in possession of sufficient facts. If for example Opponent is insisting that Party complete certain work by a date which is impossible of achievement Party should table his own internal production or construction schedule and invite Opponent to consider this and see where he could suggest improvements. This at once calms down the discussion and can easily lead to the negotiators for Opponent becoming supporters of Party's position against their own management. This same type of tactic can be used in industrial relations negotiations. By taking the union leaders into the company's confidence on such matters as the state of the order book, overseas competition, profit margins, economies being made in staff 'perks', it is made much more difficult for those leaders to press unrealistic wage claims.

IDENTIFYING, MAKING AND RECORDING THE BARGAIN

Tacit and explicit coordination

The way in which an offer is presented will have a significant effect on the final outcome. The following general propositions are made:

1   People coordinate on round numbers. The most obvious is the 50/50 split. In order to reach agreement, it is often easier therefore to deal in principles rather than to calculate out actual sums or contributions where these would result in figures which people would not coordinate. Hence the frequent use of percentages.

2   Multiples of five or their halves are preferred as negotiating steps, for example 2½, 5, 7½ and 10

3   Natural boundary lines exist associated with particular price levels for particular propositions. For example, if a car is offered for sale at £1 283, there is every chance that the parties would agree almost immediately to a price of £1 250. A simple boundary line in contract negotiation is formed when the contractor says 'I will not accept any liability for consequential damages'. If he allows himself to be driven off that line then there is no 'natural' boundary left.

Determining the point at which agreement is reached

It has already been indicated that the negotiator should not snatch at the bargain too early; equally, however, he must not wait beyond the point at which he senses that his opponent is willing to settle. The negotiator for Party should observe Opponent for any outward signs that the tension of negotiation is bringing him to the settling point; excessive fidgeting, anxious looks at the time, hurried private consultations by Opponent's negotiator with his colleagues, feeble last-minute proposals to try to stave off the inevitable or gain a little comfort to sustain him on the journey home. Once Party is convinced that Opponent is willing to agree, he should restate the terms of the bargain and make it clear that this is final agreement.

Avoiding the rethink

Once Party has Opponent's agreement, whether this is to the whole bargain or any significant item on the agenda, he should ensure that there is no further discussion on the matter. No opportunity must be given to Opponent to raise the matter again. In particular Party must avoid such statements as 'Thank you for agreeing to that point this will now enable us to....' and then go on to give the reasons why he was so anxious to secure Opponent's agreement. At once this gives Opponent the chance to say 'Just a moment we had no idea that was what was behind your proposal. I am afraid that puts the matter in a totally different light...'

The agreement which has perhaps taken many hours to obtain has now vanished. This is one point where the discipline of the team leader must be absolute.

Recording the bargain

As the negotiation proceeds, both sides should take notes of any items on which agreement has been reached or any points on which some further definite action has been agreed, for example set up a joint working party to investigate and report. At the end of each day or negotiating session, these notes should be agreed and signed or initialled by the two team leaders.

Once the negotiation has been concluded the essential terms of the agreement reached should be recorded and similarly signed or initialled. The practice of one party preparing minutes subsequent to the negotiation and sending these to the other to agree should be avoided even if this means prolonging the negotiation. Minute-writing, in the way you would have liked the meeting to go, not the way it did go, is an ancient art and one that causes a great deal of trouble. Never leave a negotiation without an agreed written record of the outcome.

CHECKLIST: CONTRACT DISPUTE

Contractual

1   Has a legally binding contract been formed? By what law is it governed?
2   What are the contract documents?
3   What are the rights given expressly by the contract documents? Note, in answering this question make sure that all the contract documents are looked at as a whole. These may include preliminary correspondence in which representations were made
4   To what extent are these rights supplemented or modified by the general legal system by which the contract is governed?
5   Have the rights available under 3 and 4 been waived either in whole or in part by the conduct of either of the parties?
6   To what extent are the rights available under 3 and 4 exercisable in practice? This will depend upon:
    (*a*) Which court or tribunal has jurisdiction
    (*b*) Whether such court or tribunal is independent or open to influence

(*c*) The time which such proceedings are likely to take

(*d*) The availability of local lawyers and their freedom to practise in the court or tribunal

(*e*) The costs which are likely to be incurred and the extent to which these may be recovered from the other party in the event of the proceedings being successful

7 What is the measure of damages which may be recovered or other legal remedy available?

8 To what extent may any judgment obtained be enforced in practice against the other party? This will depend upon:

(*a*) What are the assets of the other party situated within the jurisdiction of the court or tribunal? If none, can a judgment be enforced within a territory where the other party does have assets by registration without re-examination of the merits of the case?

(*b*) Is there any political immunity of the other party from process either in theory or practice?

(*c*) Where the defendant is resident overseas, can any sums awarded easily be transferred or can they be blocked under exchange control or taxation legislation?

Financial

9 What payments if any are outstanding, when are these payable and how are they secured?

10 Is there a performance bond covering the performance of any contractual obligations, if so under what circumstances can it be encashed and by what procedure? Note that a bond can often be cashed by simple notice to the bank without the necessity of the holder of the bond having to prove contractual default.

11 What retention monies are held and when are these due to be released?

12 Are there any goods or plant which may be seized or are liable to be seized and either held as security or sold?

13 Are there payments due under any other contract between the parties which may be used as offset?

14 On an export contract, is there any insurance cover against default by the buyer in payment and if so is such cover still valid?

Commercial

Possible action by purchaser

1 Is there another tender from the supplier under adjudication by the purchaser which he may refuse to accept or use as a

bargaining counter?

2   Are there other contracts in existence between the parties on which it is possible for the purchaser to claim damages or otherwise strictly enforce his contractual rights?

3   Are there concessions which the purchaser normally allows to the which the purchaser can restrict or suspend?

4   Are there concessions which the purchaser normally allows to the contractor on this and other contracts, for example on inspection and testing, which it would be open to the purchaser to withdraw?

5   Could the purchaser blacklist the supplier for future work and, if so, could this extend to associated companies or other firms/administrations with which the purchaser has contact?

Possible action by supplier

1   Could the supplier suspend work even without any contractual right to do so?

2   Is the supplier in a position to refuse to tender for other of the purchaser's requirements?

3   Could the supplier bring pressure through his government, trade association or Member of Parliament?

CASE STUDY IN NEGOTIATION

Scene. The Purchasing Manager's Office—Magnum Corporation Ltd.
Present. The Purchasing Manager, John Standish, and Mary his secretary.
Time. Wednesday 9 30am.
John Standish. OK Mary that's all for the moment. Ask young Malcolm to come in with the Jimjam file and let Mr Brown and Mr Henderson know we're ready to start. We've got an hour and a half before the Ace representatives arrive. When they do, let me know and hold them in reception. Coffee as soon as they come and you've booked lunch in the visitor's room for one o'clock; right?
Mary. Yes, that's all organized.
Exit Mary. Enter Malcolm Taylor, Mr Standish's young assistant.
Malcolm. Good morning Mr Standish.
Standish. Morning, Malcolm. Got the Jimjam file all organized?
Malcolm. Yes there's a short brief here. (*Hands Mr Standish some papers.*)
Standish. Fine. We'll wait to discuss it until George Harrison from production and David Brown from marketing arrive.
Enter George Harrison and David Brown.
Standish. (After introductory pleasantries.) OK, we've an hour and half before the Ace people arrive. Malcolm, you've done the spadework perhaps you would

take us through it.

Malcolm. The only issue is price. Mr Harrison has confirmed quality of the present order is good. In conjunction with Mr Harrison, I have prepared a short table summarizing the position:

TERM	PRESENT CONTRACT	OUR PROPOSAL	THEIR OFFER
Period	January to December 1975	January to December 1976	
Quantity	120 000 at 10 000 per month	144 000 at 12 000 per month	
Price	100p each	112.5p	130p

We have obtained a check quote from Duncans which was 120p

Ace have told us their price increase breaks down into two parts; 20 per cent (ie 20p) for escalation and 10p for amortization of new machinery costs. This is to meet the new production rate. We believe they have loaded all the costs into one year. Our proposal is 10 per cent uplift for escalation (ie 10p) and 2.5p for machinery costs, ie spreading them over four years.

Standish. OK Malcolm, that's very clear. You agree, George?

Harrison. Yes, Malcolm and I have been through the figures together and we both arrive at the same conclusion.

Standish. From Marketing's viewpoint, David, how do you see the position as regards future sales of products using Jimjams and the price you can accept?

Brown. Sales prospects are good, both the products are on the upward part of the growth curve, but we must be competitive on price. I've checked on the costings and we can accept up to 122-123p. Also we could just tolerate the delivery; but only just.

Standish. If they accept four-year amortization, that brings the price down on your figures, Malcolm, to 122.5 even taking their escalation. But we'll have to give them a carrot—how about a two-year contract with minimum quantity for the second year equal to that for 1975. Can you accept that, David?

Brown. If the price is right, yes.

Standish. Assuming we settle for, say, 30 per cent escalation over the two years, that would give you a price in '76 of 132.5p. That OK?

Brown. Yes, we would be happy at that.

Standish. Good, that gives us the strategy then. We insist on a four-year spread and offer them a two-year contract; it seems a fair sharing of the risk. If they buy that then we seek to contain escalation to a maximum of 30 per cent over the period so the prices would be 117.5 in year one and 137.5 in year two. Any problems?

Chorus of no's.

Mary. The Ace representatives are here, Mr Standish.

Standish. Right, show them in.

Enter Paul Dickinson, marketing manager and Bill Draper, sales manager, of Ace Products Ltd. Standish and Dickinson know each other well. After the usual introductions:

Standish. I'll start Paul, if I may. We've had your quote and frankly it looks very high. Can you explain what it's all about?

Dickinson. Yes, We have suffered with rising costs like anyone else and we reckon next year will be no better. Additionally you have increased the quantities. Now, although that helps in one way, it does mean that we will have to automate the test facilities. That's going to be fairly expensive and we only need that gear for Jimjams. Since you're the only buyer for them we can only recover from you.

Standish. Can you break the increases down between the two, Paul?

Dickinson. Yes its about 2/3 escalation; 1/3 test facilities.

Standish. Over how many years are you spreading the test gear costs then?

Dickinson. We have charged them all to this year. We have really no alternative. The year after next you may not want any Jimjams or you may go elsewhere.

Standish. Sorry Paul I just cannot accept that—how many years have you been supplying us now, five, and the demand's gone up consistently. There is further growth to come, too, but you've got to take some risks to earn your profit and this is one of them.

A general discussion follows for about three-quarters of an hour which John Standish finally ends by saying:

Standish. Let me state our position very clearly, Paul. We are willing to go to a two-year contract, if you'll spread over four years—I think that's a fair division of risk. If you can agree to that then we can turn to the escalation issue which we ought to be able to settle fairly easily. If you can't agree then I'll have to ask you to take it back to your board and time's running out if you want an order this week. If you want to think it over, there is a spare room next door.

Dickinson. That's your final word, John.

Standish. Yes.

Dickinson. We would get escalation of course, for the second year?

Standish. We would have to agree on a fixed price for the second year today but I would have thought we could do that.

Dickinson. If we agree, that would make our offer for year one 122.5 and we would have to think about year two. But it would include the same 2.5p for amortization.

Standish. Yes, I agree with that.

Dickinson. (Hesitates for a moment—looks at Draper and then says) OK we agree.

Standish. Good, then I suggest we go to lunch and deal with escalation afterwards.

After lunch.

Standish. I'll let Malcolm do the talking now, he's more familiar with the detail.

Malcolm presents his arguments for 10 per cent escalation, not 20 per cent, taking into account the increased volume, and the discussion continues until about 4 o'clock. At this point Mary comes in with the tea and Standish breaks in.

OK let's see where we are. You are asking for 122.5 for year one and 146.5 for year two. We are offering 112.5 for year one and 122.5 for year two. In order to settle today I would be prepared to go to 116.5 for year one and 131.5 for year two. That's meeting you I think very fairly considering the increase in volume. If you can agree, Malcolm has had the order prepared on the basis of a two-year contract while we have been talking and we could both sign tonight. How about it Paul?

Dickinson. I think Bill and I had better talk it over for a few minutes.

Exit Dickinson and Draper.

Standish. (While the others are out.) We may have to give them a little sweetener—say 117 for year one. That's just over half the difference on their original figure and say round it to 132 for year two . That's within our original plan. All agreed?

Chorus of assent. Dickinson and Draper re-enter.

Dickinson. We are not very happy, John. Although I could accept 117 for year one, I am more concerned about year two. It's not just ordinary labour and material increases that worry me. There are other things—taxation and government action. I don't see how I could agree to less than 135p for year two.

Standish. That's too much, Paul, but we could write something in to cover you against exceptional statutory increases. We're taking a risk on this as well you know. I'm prepared to round our offer to 132 and put in a clause, which Malcolm will draft now for you to agree, on government action. I'll also accept your 117 for year one.

Dickinson. Let me see if I have got it right. Your final offer is 117 for year one and 132 for year two. *(Pauses).* You're not making things easy John, sure there's nothing more you can do?

Standish. That's as far as I can go Paul. *(His face as he says this is completely impassive and he looks straight at Paul.)*

Dickinson. (Hesitates for a moment and looks at Draper.) OK, Bill and I will probably get the sack but we'll take it.

Tension relaxes.

Standish. Thanks, Paul. Now, as soon as Malcolm has got the papers ready including the new clause we can get it all signed up.

Key points brought out in the case study

1   The careful preparation by Standish including the involvement of other departments
2   Making Dickinson state his case in detail even although Standish

knew most of it already. This puts Dickinson on the defensive

3   The two occasions on which Standish takes the initiative on each occasion using a natural break to his advantage

4   Standish taking a hard line on amortization to convince Dickinson he meant what he said but giving Dickinson a strong hint he would not be so tough on escalation. Dickinson could judge from this what the final bargain was going to be

5   Dickinson, by repeating Standish's proposition and clarifying it, indicates he is likely to accept. Standish by keeping his answers to a minimum brings maximum psychological pressure to bear on Dickinson

6   Standish deliberately lets the discussion go on after lunch for a long time so as to start to bring time pressures to bear on Dickinson coupled with the promise of the order if he will agree. Then he makes his initiative but still keeps a little in hand. Notice he again checks with his colleagues while the other two are out of the room

7   As soon as the bargain has been reached Standish insists that it is put down in writing and signed and Malcolm had made preparations for this

8   Standish has also used the session as a training experience for Malcolm

12

Debt Collection

G Metliss

No matter what type of business one is involved in, a time will come when the normal approaches to a customer to settle his account become exhausted and one has to look elsewhere for its collection. Whether a debt can be classified as bad at that stage must depend on the particular circumstances of the case, but it would be prudent to make provision for it to be written off as 'doubtful' once its collection has to be placed in other hands. Once an account has reached this stage there are only two alternatives open for collection: either to place it in the hands of a debt collector, or to employ a solicitor.

DEBT COLLECTORS

A multiplicity of debt collection agencies exists, ranging in size from those agencies that form part of large companies dealing with trade protection in general down to those that are little more than individual 'door-to-door knockers'. Clearly one must exercise a great deal of care in choosing a debt collector and a correct choice can save a creditor both time and the expense of legal proceedings. Debt collectors however do not have the power to issue proceedings and if they are unsuccessful in collecting an account then solicitors will have to instructed and much valuable time will have been lost. The efficiency of agencies does, of course, vary widely as does the efficiency of solicitors. It would seem prudent from a creditor's point of view that, in the event of debt collectors being instructed, a firm that specializes in the creditor's particular trade is employed. A number of trade protection associations exist which operate in certain trades, and bodies also exist that specialize in the hire-purchase and mail-order fields.

The fees charged by debt collection agencies vary according to the efficiency of the service provided. It is fair to say that the higher the charge, the better the service is likely to be. Few agencies charge other than a nominal registration fee unless they recover the debt, when they normally charge a percentage of the amount recovered. At this stage the employment of a debt collector can prove expensive as some agencies are known to charge up to twenty per cent in addition to any legal fees which may have been incurred. Low rates, however, are often charged where large sums are recovered.

An advantage of using a debt collector is that information is often available which is not available to a solicitor. In addition, most collectors offer a tracing service where debtors have disappeared.

SOLICITORS

If a creditor does not wish to employ a debt collection agency then his only alternative is to employ a solicitor. Again, it is essential to choose carefully and it is advisable, in these days of specialization, to select a firm that is a specialist in this type of work. There are few firms now that wish to involve themselves exclusively in collection work but those that do have organized themselves almost on factory lines so that both speed and comparative cheapness of service are achieved. Most of these firms are closely associated with trade protection associations, insurance companies, factoring companies or debt collection agencies. Solicitors will normally charge a fee which is based on the amount of work done, whether the debt is recovered or not. The basis of charge is for negotiation between the creditor and the solicitor, and some firms specializing in this type of work will be prepared to agree a percentage charge of what is recovered.

COURT ACTION

If it becomes necessary to instruct a solicitor then, prior to issuing any proceedings, he will wish to make formal application to the debtor for payment. It is only in exceptional circumstances that he will dispense with a letter before action: firstly, because there is usually a fair chance that the debtor will respond in some way to a letter and secondly, because the Law Society advises that a letter before action should be written lest it should be thought that, by not doing so, a solicitor is incurring a debtor in unnecessary costs.

The solicitor, in order to be able to act quickly and effectively, will require certain information from the creditor. He will need to know the exact name and address of the debtor and precise details of the account he is being asked to collect. Clearly the debtor will take advantage of any error or omission in order to prevaricate and so delay payment. Much valuable time will be lost if the creditor gives his solicitor incorrect information, and in particular it is important to identify the debtor accurately. It is little use to the solicitor if he is told that the debtor is a partnership when in fact the debtor is a limited company as any proceedings commenced would require amendment and reservice thus causing great delay.

Proceedings can be commenced in either the High Court or a county court depending on the amount of the debt. The High Court has jurisdiction throughout England and Wales but a county court is limited geographically to its particular area. The High Court has jurisdiction for the issue of proceedings up to any amount, but a writ issued for a sum of less than £150 does not entitle the plaintiff to be paid his costs by the defendant, as such a writ is not endorsed with any scale costs. Costs are payable by a defendant in respect of proceedings commenced for sums over £150 provided that they are issued before payment by the defendant. It sometimes happens that a defendant will pay the debt after issue of the writ but before service upon him: he is still liable for payment of the scale costs of the writ. The county court is limited to the issue of proceedings of sums up to £1000 and its general jurisdiction and procedure and governed by the County Courts Act 1959 and the County Court Rules 1936, as amended.

COUNTY COURT PROCEEDINGS

Proceedings must be brought either:

1   In the court of the district where the defendant resides or carries on business; or
2   In that in which the cause of action wholly or in part arose

The action will commence with the issue of a default summons, service of which is normally effected by the county court bailiff. A default summons may be issued in respect of any debt or liquidated claim. A form of notice of defence, admission, set off or counterclaim is appended to all summonses when served and an admission or defence must be filed by the defendant within fourteen days of service. If an admission and offer are delivered in a default action and the offer is not acceptable to the plaintiff, then the court will fix a day for disposal; at the disposal the plaintiff will be expected to produce evidence of the defendant's means and the onus will be upon him to show that the defendant is able to pay more than the amount of the instalments offered. If no defence or admission and offer is filed, then the plaintiff may enter judgment in default of appearance at which time the whole of the debt becomes payable and the judgment may be enforced.

Debts arising under hire-purchase agreements, moneylending transactions and in cases where the debt is the subject of an assignment, fall within a different category and an ordinary summons must be issued. Although served in the same way as a default summons, judgment in default of appearance cannot be obtained if the defendant fails to appear, as the case is given a fixed hearing date and the plaintiff is required to attend and formally prove his debt. Personal attendance may now be avoided by producing proof in the form of an affidavit which is filed with the court prior to the hearing.

HIGH COURT PROCEEDINGS

All proceedings in the High Court are governed by the Supreme Court Practice in which are incorporated the Rules of the Supreme Court (Revision) 1965 and the Queen's Bench and Chancery Masters Practice directions and forms. Proceedings commence with the issue of a writ of summons which must be served personally on a defendant, unless service is accepted on his behalf by his solicitor. Service is effected by handing to the defendant a copy of the writ, and by producing to him the original. A writ may be served at any time of the night or day, and on any day but a Sunday. The plaintiff must make his own arrangements for service unlike the position for a county court summons and usually a professional process server is employed.

Partners, if named individually on the writ and not sued in the firm's name must be served individually. If, however, they are sued as a firm, the writ may be served upon any one of them or at the firm's principal place of business on any person having at that time the control of the partnership business. Service upon a limited company may be effected by post upon the company's registered office.

If the defendant wishes to defend the proceedings, he should enter an appearance to the writ after which he has fourteen days, inclusive of the day of service, in which to serve a defence. Should the defendant not enter an appearance, the plaintiff may enter judgment in default of appearance after the fourteen days have elapsed. In the event that the defendant enters an appearance, he then has a further fourteen days in which to file his defence, although this time is often extended by agreement between the respective solicitors. It is not necessary for the plaintiff's solicitors to wait these fourteen days for a defence to be entered, particularly where it is clear that the defendant has only entered the appearance to gain further time. In that case, he can issue a summons for summary judgment under the provisions of Order 14 of the Rules of the Supreme Court. Under this procedure, the plaintiff or his solicitor will depose to an affidavit briefly setting out the facts, and a summons will be issued and served on the defendant four clear working days before the hearing, which is before a Master in chambers. If on the hearing the defendant satisfies the Master that he has a bona fide defence, and the defendant will require to produce an affidavit as well, then he will be given leave to defend the action. Otherwise, the

Master will allow the plaintiff to enter judgment for the amount endorsed on the writ.

ENFORCEMENT OF JUDGMENT DEBTS

A party who has successfully obtained a judgment may well find, particularly if there has been no active participation by the defendant in the proceedings, that he has gained only half a victory. The court will not normally take any initiative, in civil cases, to enforce the judgment and it will be for the plaintiff's solicitor to advise the best method of enforcement dependent upon the information available. To assist in coming to a proper conclusion it is obviously desirable to have as much information as possible regarding the defendant's assets. If insufficient information is available, then an inquiry agent might be employed to make investigations as a matter of urgency. Searches might also be made at this stage in the register of bills of sale kept in the Central Office of the Law Courts, in the Land Charges Registry, in the Register of Deeds of Arrangement, or in the register of bankruptcy proceedings kept at Thomas More Building, Royal Courts of Justice, Strand, London, WC2, as information may be revealed from any one of these sources which would avoid fruitless and time-consuming proceedings. If a defendant company is the subject of winding-up proceedings or an individual the subject of bankruptcy proceedings, then an uncompleted execution against goods would be ineffective and any money recovered by the sheriff would stand to be returned to a liquidator or trustee in bankruptcy for the benefit of all creditors.

In order to gain information, it is possible to summon the defendant, or in the case of a limited company, any officer thereof, before an officer of the court to be examined orally. The court may also order production of any relevant books or other documents.

Execution against goods

There are numerous methods of execution of a money judgment both in High Court and county court, but the commonest method is by means of a warrant of execution against goods, known technically as a writ of *fieri facias*. This method may be used in both High and county court and is generally the most effective, although it will fail where goods belong to third parties, for example where they are subject to hire-purchase agreements. The sheriff is bound to treat the warrants in the order in which they have been lodged with him, and it is therefore imperative that no time is lost in enforcing a judgment in this way, as it becomes a question of 'first come, first served'.

Garnishee proceedings

It is not infrequent to find that having obtained a judgment, the creditor is unable to enforce it easily. A process is available in both High and county courts which enables a judgment creditor, as one of his remedies, to attach money due to the judgment debtor by way of garnishee proceedings. Application is made to a Master *ex parte* on affidavit stating that some other person is indebted to the defendant and is within the jurisdiction. On this application an order is made attaching the debt due from the third person (called the garnishee) and ordering the garnishee to appear before the Master to show cause why he should not pay the amount he owes the defendant, or so much as will satisfy the judgment debt and costs, direct to the judgment creditor. This order is called an order *nisi*, and must be served on the garnishee and on the judgment debtor seven days before the hearing to make the order *nisi* absolute.

Charging order

This method of enforcing a High Court judgment may be used to charge the defendant's beneficial interest in any property, stock, shares, debentures, funds or annuities and any dividends or interest payable thereon.

Attachment of earnings

It was formerly possible to issue a judgment summons in order to obtain an instalment order in the defendant's local county court and if the defendant failed to make payment, he could eventually be committed to prison for contempt of court provided that court was satisfied that the defendant had the means to pay but had neglected, or refused, to do so. Since the Administration of Justice Act 1970 came into force on 2 August 1971, the power to commit to prison for civil debt based on a judgment is no longer available and it is no longer possible to issue a judgment summons.

It is now open to a judgment creditor to obtain through the defendant's local county court an attachment of earnings order pursuant to the Attachment of Earnings Act 1971. The Act sets out the power of the courts to attach earnings and the consequences of the issue of an order, on both the employer and the employee. The procedure for obtaining an order is governed by the County Court (Amendment No 2) Rules 1971 (SI 1971/836 (L 20)).

Bankruptcy and winding-up proceedings

Strictly, proceedings in bankruptcy or for compulsory winding-up are not proceedings by way of execution of a judgment. In practice however, such proceedings, or the threat of them, are commonly used as a means of extracting payment and are therefore worthy of mention. Service upon a judgment debtor of a bankruptcy notice or a demand upon a company for payment pursuant to *s*223 of the Companies Act 1948, often leads to payment, or a proposal for settlement, and as such may now be regarded as a method of practical enforcement of a judgment.

MORATORIA

When a business finds itself without sufficient working capital to carry on trading, it is open to it to obtain what is known as a moratorium from all of its creditors. The effect of a moratorium, if granted by the creditors, is to 'freeze' those debts existing at the time for an agreed period of time. As a moratorium must essentially refer to and be agreed upon by all creditors, its main advantage is that no creditor obtains preference over any other and the business may continue, probably under the general supervision of a committee elected by the general body of creditors, so that the assets are realised to their best value.

As a moratorium is an informal arrangement it does not have any statutory requirements. Any formalities would be dealt with, in all probability, at an informal meeting of the creditors called to approve the moratorium. At the meeting, creditors should insist upon a proper statement of affairs, deficiency account and list of creditors, and an explanation of why the business has failed. Creditors would then be advised to appoint a small committee from among themselves to investigate the position and make a recommendation to the general body of creditors. It should be suggested that any director's loan accounts should remain frozen until after creditors' claims had been paid in full; that a new bank account should be opened and the old one frozen pending the period of the moratorium; that all small debts, say those below £50, should be paid in full forthwith in order to avoid the possibility of one of them proving difficult and wrecking the scheme; and that a professional trustee be appointed to generally supervise the running of the moratorium. The object of a moratorium is to ensure equality of treatment to all creditors and these measures should, to a large extent, ensure it.

A creditor is not bound to accept an informal arrangement of this kind and he can take steps, if he does not wish to accept it, to present a petition for compulsory winding-up or bankruptcy. If, however, the general body of creditors decides to accept it then the dissenting creditor might find that all the other creditors will oppose a winding-up petition and defeat him. In order to bind creditors to an arrangment of this nature, a company may present a scheme for approval by the court pursuant to the provisions of s206 of the Companies Act 1948. A petition for such a scheme provides for the convening of a meeting of creditors at which the creditors present vote either for or against it. A report is made to the court by affidavit by the chairman of the meeting and if three-quarters of those creditors present and voting approved the scheme, then the court will sanction it and it will become binding on all creditors. This type of procedure is not recommended however, as it is both costly and long drawn-out.

LIQUIDATION

There are three types of liquidation of limited companies; members' voluntary winding-up, creditors' voluntary winding-up and compulsory winding-up by the court.

Members' voluntary winding-up

Where a company believes itself to be solvent and wishes to cease trading either for reasons of reconstruction or because the members wish it to close down so that they may realize their investment, a resolution for voluntary winding-up may be passed. A statutory declaration is then filed by the directors which states that a full investigation has been made into the company's affairs and that the company will be able to pay all its debts in full within a period of twelve months. This declaration is called a declaration of solvency and there are fairly severe penalties imposed for making a false declaration.

Creditors' voluntary winding-up

The directors will call a meeting of creditors pursuant to the provisions of $ss293$, 294 and 295 of the Companies Act 1948, if they have reason to believe, or are advised, that the company is insolvent. At the meeting, the creditors will have placed before them a statement of affairs together with a list of the creditors' names and the amounts owed to each of them. Prior to the creditors' meeting, a meeting of the shareholders of the company will pass a resolution for voluntary winding-up and may appoint a liquidator of their own choice to realize and distribute the assets. The main purpose of the creditors' meeting is to endorse the shareholders' resolution and nomination, although this does not often happen as creditors will usually wish to nominate a liquidator of their own choice as an alternative. The creditors' choice prevails over that of the shareholders. It is not uncommon for joint liquidators to be appointed.

The liquidator's fees are payable out of the assets of the company and are voted to him by a committee of inspection which is normally appointed by the creditors to assist the liquidator. A liquidator's fees may be fixed in advance at a certain sum or he may retain a percentage of the assets realized and distributed.

Compulsory winding-up

It has been previously stated that a judgment creditor may present a petition for compulsory winding-up and also that a creditor may serve a statutory demand under $s223$ of the Companies Act 1948, upon which a petition may subsequently be based. A petition may also be presented on the grounds that it is just and equitable that the company should be wound up.

The court will hear the petition on an appointed day, after it has been served upon the company's registered office and advertised once each in the *London Gazette* and a newspaper circulating in the district where the company's registered office is situated. On the evidence before it, and depending on the number of those creditors appearing either to support or oppose the making of a winding-up order, the court may either make a winding-up order, dismiss or adjourn the petition. If a petitioner is paid off by the company, then it is open to any creditor supporting the petition to apply for an order substituting him as petitioner in place of the original petitioner.

Upon the making of a winding-up order, the company ceases to trade and the directors no longer have any powers to act. They must attend upon the Official Receiver and submit to him a statement of affairs. The Official Receiver becomes the provisional liquidator of the company and he will call meetings of the creditors and shareholders as soon as possible so that the creditors may decide whether they wish to appoint an outside liquidator or not. If the latter case, then the Official Receiver remains liquidator and proceeds to realize the assets and distribute them to the creditors under the court's supervision.

BANKRUPTCY

The law and procedure relating to bankruptcy is contained in the Bankruptcy Act 1914, as amended, and the Bankruptcy Rules 1952. Proceedings may be taken either in the High Court or whichever county court has jurisdiction for bankruptcy purposes.

Before bankruptcy proceedings can be commenced, the debtor must have committed one of a number of statutory bankruptcy offences. The most common of these is failure to comply with the terms of a bankruptcy notice within seven days, excluding the day of service. A bankruptcy notice is issued for a liquidated sum and must be based on a judgment debt which is unfettered in any way. If, within the seven days after service, the debtor has failed to pay the sum demanded, then the debtor has committed an act of bankruptcy upon which a bankruptcy petition may be presented. If the petition is accepted by the court then a receiving order is made against the debtor the effect of which is to vest the debtor's possessions in the Official Receiver in Bankruptcy pending the possible appointment of a trustee in bankruptcy by the creditors.

The debtor is required to submit a statement of affairs to the Official Receiver within seven days of the making of the receiving order and subsequently a public examination is held at which creditors may examine the debtor regarding his financial affairs and conduct generally. Within fourteen days of the making of the receiving order, the Official Receiver will summon a meeting of the creditors at which a resolution will be passed either adjudicating the debtor bankrupt or at which a proposal for a composition will be put forward. In the event of adjucation, creditors will also vote for the appointment of a trustee who will then begin the realization of the estate.

A bankrupt suffers severe disabilities until such time as he obtains his discharge. For example, he cannot obtain credit for more than £10 without disclosing that he is an undischarged bankrupt; he may not become a director or the secretary of a limited company; he may not engage in trade on his own account. As a general rule creditors cannot expect to receive any dividend and it would be prudent to write the debt off.

Fraudulent preference

This most complicated subject is one of the most difficult branches of English law. In principle the law says that no one creditor should be preferred to another in event of an insolvency and that all available assets should be distributed proportionately among them, save for the claims of secured and preferential creditors as set out in *s*319 Companies Act 1948. If a debtor pays off one creditor in preference to the others with the intention of preferring that creditor, then that payment could amount to a fraudulent preference. Whether it does will depend on the facts, and above all, on the debtor's intention at the time. A fraudulent preference may be investigated if committed either six months prior to the act of bankruptcy in the event of an individual, and up to six months prior to liquidation in the event of a company. The effect of a fraudulent preference will be to make it void or voidable at the instance of the trustee or liquidator, who will then apply to the court for an order to have the transaction reversed.

13

Patents and Trade-marks

G A Bloxam

Letters patent for inventions ('patents' for short) have a long lineage in England. They were being granted by the Crown, along with other monopoly rights, in pre-Tudor times, but the first legislative enactment was the Statute of Monopolies of 1623, which made all monopolies void except (under *s*6) those granted for fourteen years (now sixteen) in respect of 'any manner of new manufacture'.

INVENTION

This is still defined in the current statute (Patents Act 1949—referred to in this chapter as 'the Act') as 'any manner of new manufacture' (*s*101), but these words, archaic in themselves, derive their present meaning from case law. This evolution has inevitably been piecemeal and there is no comprehensive definition in present-day English. As a rough-and-ready guide, one can say that an invention is a new article or substance, or a new machine, or a new method or process of carrying out an industrial operation—the word 'industrial' including agriculture and horticulture and, by a very recent decision, a treatment of the human body for a non-medical (in the case in question, contraceptive) purpose. The protection of computer programmes is in a state of evolution. It is likely that the Whitford Committee on Copyright will recommend a form of copyright protection for new computer programmes.

THE PATENT SPECIFICATION

The grant of a patent can be regarded in a sense as a contract between the Crown and the patentee under which the Crown grants the patentee a sixteen-year monopoly in making or using the invention in return for a disclosure to the public of the invention and how to put it into practice. The vehicle for this disclosure is the patent specification—a document printed and published by the Patent Office as a prerequisite to every granted patent.

The claim

Besides disclosing the intention, the specification has another essential function; the definition of the area of monopoly to which the patentee claims to be entitled, this being contained in the *claim* of the specification.

It has long been recognized that to confine the patentee's monopoly exactly to his invention would stultify the whole system, since a competitor could evade the monopoly simply by making an inconsequential variation. The patentee is therefore allowed to include in his monopoly a range of constructions or processes centred on the original invention but in return he must delineate by exact wording the total range to which he claims to be entitled. This wording is the claim of the specification.

A simple example will help to clarify this rather difficult concept. Suppose the invention is a ball-cock for a cistern. It is a piece of mechanism which includes a float in the form of a hollow sphere. If the patent monopoly were confined to the exact mechanism as conceived by the inventor, a competitor might be able to evade it quite easily by replacing the sphere by an egg-shaped float or even perhaps a rectangular one. So the patentee does not refer in his claim to a 'hollow spherical float' but to a 'hollow body serving as a float' or perhaps just to a 'float'.

The extent to which the inventor can extrapolate from his original invention is dealt with in the Act by the provision that the claim must be 'fairly based' on the matter disclosed in the specification ($s32(1)(i)$), but what is a fair basis can in the last analysis only be a subjective judgment by the tribunal or Patent Office examiner considering the matter.

Explaining the nature and function of patent claims is not made any easier by the fact that the word 'invention' is used not only as above to mean the concrete article or process devised by the inventor but also in the quite difference sense of 'the invention claimed'—that is the area of the monopoly. Although these two meanings are hallowed in the Act and by time-honoured usage generally, the word will in this chapter be used only in the first of the above senses, thus removing at least one semantic obstacle from the reader's path.

WHAT A PATENT IS

We can now consider what sort of thing a patent is. A simple analogy may be helpful. A patent can be likened to a fence erected round an area of technology and bearing the sign 'trespassers will be prosecuted'. The area of technology will be recognizable as the claim discussed above, while somewhere near the middle of the area is the 'invention'.

By way of illustration, let us vary the theme from a ball-cock to a chemical process—say a process for making sulphuric acid by passing sulphur dioxide over a catalyst at a temperature of $x°$C. The patentee will probably have been allowed to include in his claim a range of catalysts and a range of temperatures on either side of x. The fence delimits these ranges.

It will be observed that the fence in itself does not prevent anyone from trespassing on the forbidden area, or *infringing* the patent as it is called. But once the fence is crossed the patentee has a cause of action in the High Court claiming damages and (usually much more significant) an injunction to stop the infringer from doing it again. A patent thus belongs to the species of property known in law as a chose-in-action but it has one peculiar feature: although it is a right granted by the Crown after due administrative process, the validity of the grant is not only open to challenge in the courts but such challenge is quite likely to succeed.

VALIDITY OF PATENTS

There is nothing in the Act which states explicitly what makes a patent valid, but $s32$ lists twelve grounds on which a patent may, on a petition to the court, be revoked; that is, twelve grounds of invalidity. Only the most important of these can be dealt with here. Two have already been discussed:

1   That the alleged invention is not a 'manner of manufacture' as that term is currently interpreted by the courts
2   That the claim is 'not fairly based' on the disclosure in the specification

Prior art

The most fundamental ground of invalidity is that, at the priority date (see p.269) of the claim, the invention was not new because it was part of the *prior art*. Prior art means knowledge available to the public and includes documentary material and known uses of inventions (see overleaf).

Documentary material is considered to be part of the prior art if it is available as of right to an interested member of the public. Its existence and location must be ascertainable by the relevant expert, even if they are rather obscure; language is not likely to be a bar nowadays—especially if it is that of a developed country such as Japan or Russia. A significant source of this documentary material consists of prior patent specifications which are received by the library at the Patent Office from most countries of the world. The date from which UK and foreign specifications become effective for this purpose is discussed on p. 269.

Prior use

Prior use is a much less usual ground of lack of novelty. Its effect depends on whether or not it was 'secret', this term being used to include even a normal works operation provided the public are not admitted. If the use was 'secret' it is only effective if it was not 'by way of reasonable trial and experiment'. Commercial use will thus normally be effective.

Obviousness

The commonest ground of invalidity is probably that the invention is 'obvious and does not involve any inventive step' having regard to the prior art. This means that while there is some difference between the invention and the prior art, so that it can properly be described as new, the difference is such as would have been obvious to the 'man skilled in the art' such as, for instance, a 'mere workshop variant'. To justify a monopoly the inventor must have taken an 'inventive step'. This need not be of breakthrough proportions; quite the contrary. In one case it was held that a 'mere scintilla of invention' will suffice. What is certain is that there is no definition of what it consists of. As in the case of the phrase 'fairly based' discussed above, it is a matter of the subjective judgment of the tribunal considering the case. It is possible by a study of the decided cases to arrive at various generalizations to assist in judging particular cases but such a study would not be appropriate here.

There is, however, one criterion which is worth discussing as it enters in one form or other into most arguments on obviousness. Let us take as an example, the mixing of two well-known fungicides. One's first reaction is likely to be that this cannot be inventive, especially as it is generally well known to mix biocidal agents in order to enlarge their 'spectrum' of activity. If, however, the inventor shows that the fungicides have a marked synergistic effect on each other, so that the mixture is more effective than the sum of the components, it is very difficult to say that it was obvious to make the mixture. The incentive was there, but nobody before the inventor thought of doing it. That the invention produces an *unexpected advantage* is thus often decisive in justifying a finding of inventiveness, although it must be emphasized that it is not an indispensable condition.

One point of detail on obviousness needs making for the sake of accuracy. Prior secret use has been included above for convenience in the term 'prior art'. However, this particular form of prior art cannot be deployed to found a case of obviousness, only of lack of novelty. Thus it is sufficient if the invention differs at all from the secret prior use (leaving aside *de minimis* considerations) even if the difference is an obvious one.

Inadequate specification

The only other grounds on invalidity we need mention (apart from 'prior claiming', which is dealt with later in this chapter, are that the specification does not adequately describe the nature of the invention or how to carry it out, and that the patent was obtained on a false suggestion or representation, for example a false allegation of a result obtainable by the invention. Clearly either of these shortcomings would go to the root of the consideration for the grant of the monopoly.

The whole of the above discussion on validity needs qualifying in view of our determination not to use the word 'invention' in a double sense. To understand the point it may be helpful to return to the analogy of a fence round an area of technology—defined with precision by the words of the patent claim—and think of the area as covering a whole range of articles or processes roughly centred on the invention. Then everything which has to be satisfied by the invention to make the patent valid must also be satisfied by the whole range of variants included in the fenced-off area. It is this which is the main factor in restraining the inventor from claiming too great an area, for the bigger the area, the more chance there is that some variant near the periphery will contravene one of the requirements for validity. In that event the whole claim is invalid—patent claims cannot be like the curate's egg, good in parts.

EMPLOYEES' INVENTIONS

The ownership of an invention made by an employee is a matter of contract, but under common law any service agreement which is silent on the point is deemed to include an implied term that inventions made by the employee 'in the course of his employment' belong to the employer. This phrase conceals two requirements; first, that the employee's job is of a kind in which innovations in his employer's business are liable to arise, for example a research worker or a development engineer; second, that the particular invention in question did arise out of the job.

The employing company cannot be an inventor, but it may apply for a patent provided the right to apply has been assigned by the inventor. This assignable right was first created by the 1949 Patents Act and there was some dispute at the time about the form the assignment should take, but it is thought to be generally accepted now that a simple declaration by the inventor of his assent in the making of the application, for example as set out at the end of the official patent application form, operates as a valid assignment of the right to apply. It should be noted, however, that this goes only to the legal title and has no effect on the beneficial ownership of the invention.

If the case is one to which the common law doctrine referred to above applies, an assignment of the beneficial ownership is not strictly necessary, although it is prudent to secure one by way of acknowledgment.

It is, of course, possible to make terms with an employee different from that implied under common law. For example a prospective employee in a particularly strong bargaining position may be able to negotiate for a royalty payment for any invention he makes in the course of his employment. However, although the Act (s56) provides machinery for resolving disputes between employer and employee including making an apportionment between them, the House of Lords has held that only a legally enforceable agreement will enable the Court to make such an apportionment, otherwise the invention belongs wholly to the employer if made in the course of employment or wholly to the employee if not.

In some countries, notably Germany and the Scandinavian countries, the employee inventor is automatically entitled to a reward for his invention. There is some political urge in this country in favour of such a provision but those with experience of these matters tend to feel that a patentable invention in modern industry is nearly always part of a team effort to which a range of other employees contribute directly or indirectly, and that to single out the 'inventor' for special treatment would only lead to bad feeling.

INFRINGEMENT OF PATENTS

A patent is infringed by anyone who makes, uses or sells an article or machine protected by the patent, or uses a process protected by the patent, or sells the direct product of such a process. To decide whether a given article is protected by the patent it is necessary to construe the definition constituted by the patent claim and determine whether the article falls within or without the definition.

British patent law is strict in holding the patentee to the words of his claim but there are two qualifications. The first is that the *de minimis* rule (that the law takes no account of trifles) applies as always. The second is the doctrine of *equivalents* or 'pith and marrow', according to which a man infringes a claim if he substitutes an element of it by an equivalent (as for instance a non-spherical float in a ball-cock claim confined to a spherical float) so as to take the pith and marrow of the claim even if it is not within its exact wording. This doctrine grew up in the days before the patentee was required to delineate the boundary of his monopoly by an accurately drafted patent claim. Today the doctrine is given lip service but is hardly ever applied.

Court action

If the patentee wishes to go to the limit in enforcing his patent against a supposed infringer, he must issue a writ for infringement in the High Court. If he cannot tell from any product sold by the alleged infringer whether what the latter is doing infringes the patent (as in the case of a chemical process, for example) he can ask the Court for an order for discovery and inspection on the basis of a reasonable suspicion.

It is routine in an infringement action for the defendant to counter-claim for revocation of the patent on the basis that it is invalid on one or more specified grounds. The question at issue at the trial is therefore whether any *valid* claim of the patent has been infringed.

Threats

An important practical point is that unlike most other legal causes, it is actionable for the patentee or anyone else to threaten anybody with an action for infringement of a patent (s65). Thus an incautious word or letter may land the person uttering it in court. However, there is a complete defence if it can be proved that a valid claim was in fact being infringed.

PATENTING PROCEDURE IN THE UNITED KINGDOM

Each country has its own system of patent law and administrative procedure. In broad outline the principles set out in the preceding sections, although directed primarily to the UK law, are valid for overseas countries, with a few important exceptions which will be referred to later. Administrative procedures, however, differ substantially from country to country. Those obtaining in Great Britain will be considered first.

Application

The first step in obtaining a patent is to file an application at the Patent Office. The applicant must be either the inventor (who cannot be a corporate person) or his assignee. An assignment, for example from an employee inventor to his company, of the right to apply for a patent can be effected by signature of a *declaration of consent* to the assignee's making the application.

The application must be accompanied by a specification which may be *provisional* or *complete.* A provisional specification must be followed within twelve months by a complete. A complete specification must include the claim or claims which the applicant thinks he is entitled to make.

Examination

When the complete specification has been filed, the application is remitted to an examiner who makes a search among existing UK patent specifications and informs the applicant of any which may be relevant to the novelty of the claims. He also has discretion to cite any other type of relevant document of which he may be aware.

Let us imagine that the applicant thinks he is entitled to claim a ball-cock with any kind of float, but that (surprisingly) an elliptical float is especially advantageous in some way. The examiner cites a specification describing a ball-cock with a spherical float. This clearly destroys the novelty of the broad claim to any kind of float but not of a claim limited to the case in which the float is elliptical. To cater for this (very common) type of situation the law provides that the applicant can make a whole series of claims directed to successively smaller fenced-off areas, each within the confines of the previous one, and that in litigation the validity and infringement of each claim is to be considered separately. In our case claim 1 would include any kind of float and claim 2 would be restricted to an elliptical float; so that on being notified of the examiner's citation, the applicant would simply strike out claim 1 and accept the grant of a patent based on claim 2.

The examiner's remit

If, however, the examiner had missed the ball-cock specification in his search, so that a patent was granted containing claim 1 as well as claim 2, and this was challenged in litigation by a defendant who managed to discover the prior specification the examiner had missed, the court would hold claim 1 invalid but might hold claim 2 valid. If then the defendant had made a ball-cock with an elliptical float, the court would order an injunction and (subject to a defined discretion) damages for infringement of claim 2, at the same time ordering the cancellation of claim 1.

This shows that because of a mistake the Patent Office can grant an invalid patent, but it goes much further than that. The examiner's remit in fact only touches the fringe of the possible objections to a patent. First, any of the world's literature which reaches the UK (and that means most of it) can be used to invalidate a patent but the examiner only searches the quite small sector represented by UK patent specifications.

Secondly, the Act (*ss*6, 7 and 8) explicitly confines the examiner to consideration of only a few of the possible grounds of invalidity. In particular he must consider novelty but may not consider obviousness. The reason behind this is that some of the grounds such as obviousness depend on evidence from the expert in the art, and this is not available to the examiner.

The result of these limitations on the examiner's activities is far-reaching. The uninstructed layman assumes that short of making a mistake, the Patent Office will not grant invalid patents, but this is far from being the case, since some of the important grounds of invalidity will not have been considered at all.

Publication, opposition and grant

When the examiner is satisfied that the applicant has overcome all objections, he accepts the application and passes it for publication. Until this time all the papers are secret and if the application is abandoned, they will remain so. On publication, the complete specification is printed and is open for opposition (s14 of the Act) by any interested third party. The opponent can ask the Comptroller at the Patent Office to refuse the grant of the patent on grounds which are in a sense intermediate between those available *ex parte* to the examiner and those available in the High Court. The case is heard by the Comptroller or his delegate and there is an appeal to a patents appeal tribunal.

If there is no opposition, or it is resolved in favour of the applicant, a patent is granted or 'sealed' and the Letters Patent document is issued to the patentee. Within a year of the grant an interested party may apply to the Comptroller to revoke the patent (s33 of the Act). These proceedings are usually known as 'belated opposition', as the procedure and grounds are the same as in opposition before grant.

Priority dates

It has been mentioned that to be effective against a patent claim, an item of prior art must have been dated before the priority date of the claim. If the application for a patent was filed with a complete specification in the first instance, the priority date of its claim is simply the date of the application. (This needs qualifying if the application was filed under the International Convention—see next section.) If, however, the first specification was provisional, any of the claims of the eventual complete which are 'fairly based' on the provisional take the priority date of the original application, while any others take the date of filing of the complete. It is further possible to file more than one provisional during the twelve months before a complete is due on the first provisional, and combine or *cognate* the provisionals in a single complete. It is then necessary to sort out which claims can take the priority date of which provisional. It will thus be seen that the function of the provisional specification is to establish the inventor's priority. To make sure that it does this to the best effect, it is prudent to include as much material in it as possible, so that it is virtually as full as a complete specification though without any claims. Then, when the time comes to prepare the complete, it is only necessary to add any fresh material and a set of claims.

Prior claiming

The whole procedure, from filing the application to publication, takes a considerable time—usually about two or three years—but it is only on publication that the specification counts as 'prior art' against a third party's patent. What then is the position if B files an application after A has filed one in respect of the same invention but before the publication of A's specification? The basic principle is easily stated but difficult to apply. It is that the Crown will not grant the same monopoly twice. Since the monopolies are defined by the respective claims, any difference in wording, even an adventitious one, between A's claim and B's claim makes them different whereas as a matter of substance they may be directed to the same subject-matter. The resolution of the problem: how different must the claims be to avoid 'prior claiming' of B by A has given rise to a lot of argument and case law, some of it difficult to follow. No attempt will be made here to explain the current situation; the main point to remember is that the effect of A's prior 'concurrent application' on B is much less severe than if A's specification had actually been published before B's priority date. Furthermore, A's claim will not count at all for prior claiming unless a patent has been sealed on his application. It should also be noted that foreign patent specifications have no prior claiming effect and are thus only effective from their publication dates.

PATENTS ABROAD

The diversity of law and procedure and the expense of obtaining patents abroad are usually obstacles to obtaining protection in the range of countries where there is a commercial potential for an invention. There is a great deal of activity towards harmonization and unification, notably the Patent Cooperation Treaty for unifying the initial steps and the searching procedure and the European Patent Convention which provides for a European Patent Office in Munich which will grant a European patent effective in nearly all Western European countries according to their respective laws. Negotiations have also been in progress between the EEC countries for a second Convention under which the European Patent Office will be able to grant a single patent effective throughout the EEC. These treaties have been signed but not yet ratified and the only important treaty at present in force to which the UK adheres is the International Convention for the Protection of Industrial Property which dates from 1883 and now includes all the industrial countries of the world.

The main provisions of the Convention are:

1   That the laws of a Convention country will be applied equally to citizens of all Convention countries
2   That if a patent application for an invention is filed in one Convention country and within twelve months an application for the same invention is filed in one or more other Convention countries, then such other applications will have the priority date

of the first one. Hence it is very desirable for a UK applicant to file foreign applications within twelve months of his British application. Thus if the latter was accompanied by a provisional specification, the filing of the complete in the UK normally coincides with the filing of foreign 'Convention applications'

If an applicant (usually from abroad) files a Convention application in the UK, he files a certified copy of the original foreign application and this serves to establish his priority in much the same way as a British provisional specification does for a British applicant in the UK. Thus there is no provision for filing a provisional specification with a Convention application, but only a complete.

Diversity of laws

It is not possible here to touch on the different procedures in different countries and only salient differences in substantive laws can be mentioned.

In the USA and Canada, the inventor's priority does not stem from the date of filing a patent application, but from the date he 'conceived' the invention.

No country except the UK and some of the old commonwealth countries has the provisional specification system.

The examination to which a patent application is submitted before grant varies as follows:

1   Full examination of all possible grounds of invalidity—for example, the USA, Japan, Germany and other northern European countries
2   No examination at all—for example, Italy, Belgium, Spain and Latin countries generally. France has provision for an official search, although it is left to the applicant whether to take action on the search report or not.
3   The compromise 'British' system of partial examination—for example, the UK and Australia
4   Germany, Holland, Australia and Japan have adopted the system of 'deferred examination' whereby a 'provisional' patent (not to be confused with the British provisional specification) is automatically granted for a specified period and is not examined unless the patentee or an interested party requests it within the specified period, failing which it lapses

There is a fundamental difference in the way the UK, on the one hand, and the civil law countries and most of the rest of the world on the other (with USA somewhere in between but nearer the UK) approach the questions of definition of the monopoly area and validity. To take Germany as a typical example, there is no definition of the monopoly area in the claims or the rest of the specification or in any other document. Whether any particular manufacture is within or without can only be a matter of subjective judgment after considering the specification and claims in the light of the prior art and any statements made by the patentee to the Patent Office to persuade them to grant the patent. On the other hand, the validity of a patent once issued tends to be taken for granted unless a challenger brings up fresh facts such as items of prior art which were not before the examiner. This is somewhat the reverse of the British position where the monopoly is tightly defined by the claims and the question of validity is almost completely open.

Renewal fees

In all countries except the USA and Canada, annual renewal fees have to be paid to keep a patent in force. These vary greatly in amount and usually increase with the life of the patent. In West and, more especially, East Germany the fees are particularly onerous.

LICENSING

Instead of using his 'fence' to keep out the competition, the patentee may decide to exploit it by allowing one or more parties in for a consideration. A licence in its simplest form is a promise not to sue the licensee for infringement if he enters the forbidden territory. If at the same time the patentee agrees not to let anyone else in, and to stay out himself, the licence is 'exclusive'. An exclusive licensee has most of the rights and privileges of the patentee, including the right to sue for infringement.

If the patentee undertakes to grant no further licences, but does not exclude himself from working the invention, the licence is known as a 'sole' licence. This carries none of the statutory rights of the exclusive licence.

Territory

The effect of a licence is to give the licensee permission to do something which would otherwise be an infringement of the patent. This may be limited to a part only of the technology covered by the patent and to a part only of the UK, though the latter is probably rare in these days. If there are corresponding patents in other countries, the agreement may include a licence in one or more of these other countries. A not uncommon arrangement would be to grant a British company an exclusive licence to make, use and sell in the UK and a non-exclusive licence to sell in other countries where there are patents, thus leaving it open for manufacturing licences to be granted to other companies abroad. The licensee does not need a licence to sell in countries where there are no patents, but he may agree collaterally *not* to sell in specified countries.

Financial arrangements

The consideration for the grant of a licence is normally monetary, and may take the form of a royalty based on use of the invention, an annual minimum payment and/or a down payment. The royalty can conveniently be expressed as a percentage of the sales value of an article, or the product of a process, covered by the patent. If, however, the article is a machine, for example for making shoes, it is difficult to get a fair return by charging a percentage of the value of the machine unless the percentage is an intimidatingly high figure. It is more realistic to charge a small percentage on the value of the shoes made by the machine. Similar considerations arise if the invention is for example a mixture of petrol and an additive present in very small quantities, in which case a royalty based on the value of the petrol has a more realistic appearance than one based on the value of the additive.

If the licence is exclusive, the patentee has a prime interest in ensuring adequate performance by the licensee. This is usually provided for by requiring the licensee to make up the royalty payment to a stated annual minimum payment. The licensee for his part is willing to do this since he is effectively buying a monopoly as well as a right of entry. The licensee may either covenant outright to pay the annual minimum or he may reserve the right not to pay it in which case he submits to a penalty such as termination of the licence or conversion to a non-exclusive one.

A down payment is appropriate if the deal includes the initial transmission of technical information such as drawings, to enable the licensee to commence manufacture.

Miscellaneous terms

If the licensee wishes to be able to grant sublicences, he must be given this right explicitly in the agreement.

It is part of the common law that a licensee cannot challenge the validity of the patent, but this is usually spelt out in the agreement.

The question of infringement usually arises during negotiations. There are two quite distinct issues: what is to happen if a third party infringes the licensed patent, and infringement of a third-party patent by the licensee. On the first issue, the licensee is justified in objecting to pay royalty if an infringer is operating for nothing. The agreement can therefore provide that the payment of royalty shall be suspended until either the infringement is stopped by the patentee or the infringer is granted a licence (assuming the original licence was non-exclusive). What is not reasonable in view of the high cost and uncertainty of patent actions is to expect the patentee to covenant to sue an infringer.

The question of infringement of a third party's patent by the licensee is really quite unconnected with the licence, and the licensor is justified in refusing to take any responsibility. The fact that a licensee's operation is covered by two patents, one of them being the subject of the licence and the other belonging to a third party, is in no way derogatory of the former. A patent gives no right to anyone, even the patentee, to manufacture the subject of the patent, as can be seen if we remember the fence analogy. To revert to the ball-cock example, if *A* gets a patent with a claim worded widely enough to cover any kind of float, but in which the specification describes only a spherical float, and later *B* discovers that an elliptical float has a special unexpected advantage, *B* may be able to get a valid patent for that particular variant and this would in no way reflect on the validity of *A*'s patent. If *B* grants a licence to *C* there is no reason why *B* should be responsible for the fact that in operating under the licence *C* will infringe *A*'s patent. It is up to *C* to make terms with *A* (with the sanction of a compulsory licence in the background if *A*'s terms are so unreasonable as to frustrate exploitation of *B*'s invention).

The duration of a licence is normally for the life of the relevant patent and it is provided in the Act (*s*58) that it shall be terminable by either party when the patent expires.

Technical information and improvements

It often happens, especially if an exclusive licence is contemplated, that the parties agree to transmit know-how and improvements to each other. The point to note here is that an essential part of such an agreement is an exact definition of the technological field. If this is to be coterminous with the fenced-off area of the patent, the agreement should say so; it is not, as if often believed, an accepted meaning of the word 'improvement'. The agreement should also be clear about what rights will accrue in respect of patentable improvements. Possibly each party will get the benefit of these in his own territory.

Another important point is the right to use the know-how after termination of the agreement. In the absence of an explicit provision there is no such right, and this can have very serious consequences for the recipient of the know-how.

Forbidden terms

In English law the parties can negotiate a patent licence in any terms they please provided it is not in restraint of trade—a common law doctrine of fairly narrow compass—and does not contravene *s*57 of the Act. This provides that the patentee shall not extend his monopoly right by making it a condition of a licence that the licensee shall buy from the patentee unpatented raw material—for example, unpatented phosphoric acid for use in a patented metal-finishing process. This is in fact frequently done, but the patentee is risking the enforceability of his patent if the practice ever comes to light.

In the USA this matter comes in the province of the antitrust laws, which are being applied with ever more stringent effect to restrict what a licensor and licensee can lawfully agree. It is impossible here to go into any detail on this subject, but readers will be aware of the importance of not falling foul of these laws.

Somewhat similar provisions are included in Common Market law. This part of the law is still in a state of evolution but there is no doubt that it is being strictly applied by the EEC Commission in Brussels and the European Court of Justice in Luxembourg.

Trade-marks

It has for long been part of the common law that if *A* has a reputation in a trade name or trade-mark and *B* sells his goods in association with the trade-mark in such a way as to lead the public to believe that his goods emanate from *A*, then *A* has a cause of action against *B* for 'passing off' his goods as *A*'s. In such an action, *A* has the onus of proving both the reputation of his mark and the confusion caused by *B*'s use of it.

By the Trade Marks Act of 1875, the owner of a trade-mark was given a new right: to enter his mark on a Register of Trade Marks, thereby gaining an entitlement to stop anyone else from using the mark—always assuming that the registration was valid.

An essential part of the system is that the registration must be in respect of a specified range of goods on which the owner uses or intends to use the mark, and that the registration is infringed only by use of the mark in connection with goods within this 'specification of goods'.

The Register

The Register of Trade Marks is kept by the Registrar, who is in fact the same person as the Comptroller of Patents. As in the case of patents, an application to register a trade-mark is examined to see if it complies with requirements of the statute, currently the Trade Marks Act 1938, but in the case of trade-marks the examination extends to almost all the grounds on which a registration could be held invalid. The guiding principle is that the mark must be distinctive (in the sense that it distinguishes the owner's goods from those originating elsewhere) either inherently or because past use has in fact made it distinctive. The former is in effect a subjective judgment by the examiner or tribunal considering the matter while the latter is determined by evidence furnished by persons in the relevent trade. There are, however, two categories which are difficult to register no matter how much distinctiveness is proved, namely words of which the ordinary significance is either a geographical name or a surname, (*s*9 of the Act). The opposite of a distinctive mark is one which is descriptive of the goods in question. This fact, coupled with the overriding requirement (*s*11) that the mark must not be deceptive, shows the narrow path which has to be trodden in many cases. For example, 'Silico' for polishes might be held descriptive if they contained silicones but deceptive if they did not.

All goods are divided into thirty-four classes and separate applications must be made for goods in different classes.

Conflicting marks

A further requirement of registration (s12) is that the mark must not resemble too closely a mark already on the Register for the same or similar goods, unless the applicant for registration can prove 'honest concurrent use' of the two marks for a period of some years. In borderline cases the Registrar will accept the consent of the owner of the mark already on the Register as justification for allowing the marks to coexist. Whether the consent is given and if so, subject to what conditions, is a private matter between the two parties, but in practice consent is often given gratis on the assumption that the consenting party may want the same favour from the other on some future occasion.

Opposition and rectification

There is provision for opposition to the registration (s18) and for an action to 'rectify the Register' by removing an existing registration (s26). One ground of removal which will not have been considered at the registration stage is that the owner had no bona fide intention to use the mark and has not in fact used it; or that he has not used the mark for a continuous period of five years.

Licensing

The right to use a trade-mark (whether registered or not) can be licensed by the owner but he must be careful to require the licensee to adopt his standards of quality for the goods in question, since otherwise the public may be deceived, with the result that the owner will lose his rights in the mark. It is advisable in the case of a registered trade-mark to get the official seal of approval on the terms of the licence by making the licensee a 'registered user' under s28 of the Act. This has the further advantage that use of the mark by the registered user counts as use for the purpose of s26.

International

Trade-marks are included in the International Convention for the Protection of Industrial Property, but the priority period is six months as distinct from twelve months in the case of patents. The trade-mark laws and practice of other countries differ from each other about as much as they do for patents, the main point to watch being that in some countries, notably France, there is no concept of ownership of a trade-mark until and unless the mark is registered, prior use being of no consequence. Hence a company that has failed to register a valuable mark in France can see it lost to a third party simply by registration.

FUNCTION OF PATENT AGENTS

Patent agents have a function in relation to patent law and practice which is analogous to that of solicitors in relation to other branches of the law. Owing to the technological subject-matter involved, a patent agent has to have achieved at least GCE *A* level standard in a science or engineering subject, and usually has a university degree, before sitting for the qualifying examinations which the Chartered Institute of Patent Agents administers on behalf of the Department of Trade.

There is a contradiction between the difficulty of the concepts underlying the patent system and the familiarity of its main visible product—the patent specification. In many industries, patent specifications are an important if not the main source of information on recent developments and they are constantly handled by technical personnel of all grades. This means that laymen who are familiar with 'patents' (as they incorrectly term patent specifications) as items of technical information are unlikely to learn the underlying concepts of the system but substitute a rough-and-ready version which usually has little relation to reality. There are, in fact, very few matters connected with patent law or practice in which it is safe to proceed without consulting a patent agent.

It is usual for patent agents to include trade-marks in their practice, some training in trade-marks being necessary in order to pass the patent agent's qualifying examinations. Although this is elementary compared with the training in patents, a patent agent will either have acquired a full understanding by assisting an expert or will employ a fully qualified trade-mark agent in his practice. Unlike the profession of patent agency, that of trade-marks is not closed, but there is an Institute of Trade Mark Agents which administers a rigorous examination as a condition of membership. Many patent agents are members of both institutes.

The bread-and-butter work of the patent agent is the preparation of patent applications, the main part of which is the patent specification, for filing in the UK and abroad in accordance with the various local procedures; dealing with objections raised by the various examiners and with any oppositions; securing the grant of a patent; and ensuring the renewal fees are paid on it as long as the patentee requires. To do this job properly the patent agent ought to be in *direct* touch with the inventor in any particular case.

Analogous work arises in relation to trade-marks and here the agent should be in *direct* touch with the relevant marketing executive. Trade-mark matters sometimes seem simple, but in fact this is deceptive and the agent needs to have direct access to the principal actually involved just as much as he does in patent matters.

COSTS

The costs of obtaining and maintaining patents contain two components: government fees and professional charges. The Patent Office in each country has to carry out a number of clerical and technical operations on each patent application, the latter requiring skilled manpower, and the objective is to charge applicants and patentees enough to make the Patent Office self-supporting. The fee in the UK for an application with a provisional specification is still at the nominal figure of £1 but a complete specification is charged at £60. The patent agent's charges depend on the nature of the job but they are not likely to be less than £40 for a provisional specification and £100 for a complete. Much higher charges may be made for lengthy or complex work.

The costs for foreign applications vary a good deal from country to country. A large fraction of the costs in foreign-language countries goes for translation. An idea of the order of magnitude of the costs and of their range can be given by quoting estimates of £100 for an average case in India, and of £280 in West Germany.

It is impossible to estimate the cost of prosecuting an application since it depends on the nature of the subject-matter, the procedure of the country concerned and the objections the examiner happens to turn up. The cost can vary from a few pounds in some countries to hundreds of pounds for a difficult American case.

The annual renewal fees necessary to maintain a patent in force also vary enormously from country to country and over the life of the patent, generally increasing with its age. In USA and Canada no renewal fees are payable and among the principal countries they are probably heaviest in West Germany, varying from about £25 to about £320 (including agents' charges) over the life of the patent. The UK is on the inexpensive side with a range of about £40 to £108.

In addition to these main costs there are one or two smaller fees to be paid at certain stages in the life of a patent application, again depending on the country concerned, but these are generally of the order of £10 or less.

Charges for trade-mark work follow a similar pattern but on a lower scale, perhaps a quarter to a half of the charge for analogous patent work. Renewal fees are required only at relatively long periods, for example in the UK every fourteen years after an initial period of seven years.

The Chartered Institute of Patent Agents publishes guides to charges for various kinds of patent and trade-mark work, which can best be obtained from your patent agent.

FURTHER READING

J.W. Baxter, *World Patent Law and Practice,* Sweet and Maxwell, London, 1968.

B.I. Cawthra, *Industrial Property Rights in the EEC*, Gower Press, Epping, 1973.

T.A.. Blanco White, *Kerly's Law of Trade Marks and Trade Names,* Sweet and Maxwell, London, ninth edition, 1966.

L.W. Melville, *Precedents on Industrial Property and Commercial Choses in Action,* Sweet and Maxwell, London, 1965.

A. Turner, *The Law of Trade Secrets,* Sweet and Maxwell, London, 1962.

T.A. Blanco White, *Patents for Invention and the Registration of Industrial Designs,* Sweet and Maxwell, London, third edition, 1962.

14

Fair Trading

Ivor Hussey

THE MEANING OF 'FAIR TRADING'

A businessman could well consider that a chapter on 'fair trading' in a company administration handbook would constitute a provocative incursion into ethics. There is, however, no intention here to try to tell those who administer companies how a company should ethically conduct its business operations. The object of this chapter is to explain the law relating to what can conveniently, although by no means accurately, be described as fair trading.

The description is convenient because the expression has been brought into general use for a limited range of purposes: the Fair Trading Act 1973 created the appointment of Director General of Fair Trading and gave him specific responsibilities and powers. His functions and the substance of the Act's main provisions will be outlined and explained below.

The description is also convenient as a means of indicating what lies behind and in a variety of other Acts of Parliament and an increasing number of so-called voluntary codes of practice. These will be covered on p291.

But the term is also inaccurate. A concept of 'unfair trading' is recognized in the business and legal systems of many countries, where it is given definite existence through both legislation and pronouncements by courts: the United Kingdom is not among these countries. And, despite the adoption in the United Kingdom of the term 'fair trading' in the titles of a major statute and of an important public official (as noted above), neither in this country nor anywhere else in the world has a concept of 'fair trading' even begun to be worked out, either in law or in business practice.

Moreover, the limited range of the provisions of the Fair Trading Act and the consequent and similar limited range of the powers and responsibilities of the Director General of Fair Trading mean that to interpret the expression 'fair trading' generally in terms of the content of that Act is both inadequate and misleading. Any rational definition of the expression would necessarily include, for example, particular reference to the relationship between companies doing business with each other; yet nothing in the Act has any relevant reference to such a relationship. Nor, indeed, is there much in the way of such a reference in the other legislation with which this chapter will deal.

THE FUNCTIONS OF THE DIRECTOR GENERAL OF FAIR TRADING

It would be reasonable to expect that a statute which begins by announcing that 'the Secretary of State shall appoint an officer to be known as the Director General of Fair Trading' would include, early in its statements of that officer's functions, at least some mention of promoting and upholding the principles of fair trading as such. But the Fair Trading Act contains no further mention of fair trading until in its definition ($s137$) it says that the Director General of Fair Trading is referred to in the Act as 'the Director' (which is how he will be referred to also for the rest of this chapter) and then until in its final section it states its own title. Consequently it cannot be said, in so many words, that the Director has responsibilities concerning fair trading.

The Director has statutory responsibilities and powers in four areas. Under the Act, he is concerned with the protection of consumers; with the examination of monopolies and of proposals for mergers of firms; and with the control of restrictive trade practices. Under the Consumer Credit Act 1974, he is in addition concerned with the organizations and control of matters relating to consumer credit.

The staff which works for and advises the Director operates as the Office of Fair Trading. The Office has four main divisions, each of which looks after one of the areas in which the Director is involved. It is a statutory body wholly financed from public funds, and all its staff (though not the Director himself) are Civil Servants. More than half the senior posts, however, were filled originally by recruitment from outside the Civil Service. The first and present Director was a career industrialist until his appointment.

CONSUMER PROTECTION

Understandably, the Director's responsibilities and powers in relation to the protection of consumers have received more publicity and general attention than have any of his other functions. The Fair Trading Act enjoins him to keep under review the carrying on of commercial activities in the United Kingdom which relate to the supply of goods or services to consumers, and to collect information about such activities and about the traders who carry them on. He is required to do this with a view to his becoming aware of, and ascertaining the circumstances relating to, practices which may adversely affect the economic interests of persons in the United Kingdom—although in this context the Act clearly uses 'persons' to mean 'consumers'. What the Director does to carry out these functions may affect trading companies, and those who administer them, in any of three ways.

First, although it is no part of the Director's functions to act directly in any way for any individual consumer, he has power to take action against an individual firm or trader. If he has reason to believe that such an individual has, in the course of his business, adopted and persisted in a course of conduct which—in the words of the Act—is both 'detrimental to the interests of consumers in the United Kingdom' (and these interests need not be merely economic) and 'to be regarded as unfair to consumers' in the light of certain indications stated in the Act, he shall 'use his best endeavours' to obtain from the individual a satisfactory, written assurance that the undesirable course of conduct will be abandoned.

Should the assurance not be forthcoming, or should it be given but not honoured, the Director may seek a High Court order against the individual firm or trader, and breach of the order would be punishable. The Director would base his original approach to the firm or trader, and any later action, on evidence derived from complaints coming to the Office from members of the public and consumer organizations and on reports to him by Trading Standards Officers and other local authority bodies. In practice, and although one assurance was secured during 1974, the Director is unlikely to have cause to make use of these powers: their importance is in their very existence as a deterrent to a firm or trader tempted to operate shady forms of business in the provision of consumer goods or services.

Secondly, the Director's duties under the Fair Trading Act include encouraging trade associations and similar bodies 'to produce, and to disseminate to their members, codes of practice for guidance in safeguarding and promoting the interests of consumers in the United Kingdom'. The Director is known to regard this part of his functions as of major importance, and the Office is working in accordance with this as speedily and energetically as staff resources permit. Particular interest is taken in the arrangements within industries generally and companies individually for efficient handling of complaints made by dissatisfied purchasers of the goods or services supplied. Administrators of companies trading in the supply of consumer goods or service should be prepared, in any event, to join in the development of codes of trading practice by national trade associations and local Chambers of Commerce.

The third way in which the Director's consumer protection activities may affect trading companies is more remote. The Act requires him to consider possibilities that consumers will be adversely affected by 'consumer trade practices'. It defines a consumer trade practice as being, in effect, any practice carried on by a trader supplying consumer goods or services which is connected with marketing or selling. If, after preliminary investigation, the Director forms the opinion that any such practice might adversely affect the economic interests of consumers, and especially if he considers that it misleads or confuses consumers or puts pressure on them or is inequitable to them, he may make a formal reference about the practice to an independent body called the Consumer Protection Advisory Committee.

This Committee, set up as an independent body under the Fair Trading Act, has the sole function of considering such references and, in appropriate circumstances, consulting the Secretary of State about using the powers which the Act gives to legislate by means of orders so as to control or end any consumer trade practice so referred. During 1974 the Director made two references of this kind, accompanying each with a recommendation that there be legislation by order. It is desirable that individual firms in consumer industries should, directly or through their trade associations or Chambers of Commerce, ensure that they are aware of any reference made by the Director to the Committee in this way: any interested firm or organization is entitled to make representations to the Committee about a reference, and firms may well find that, in consequence of the issue of an order by the Secretary of State after a reference has been made and reported on, they have to make changes in their trading practices and methods.

CONSUMER CREDIT

The law relating to hire-purchase and credit sale and to consumer credit generally has for some years been complex and detailed, and is unlikely to be simplified. An attempt to summarize it would be out of place in this book: an administrator of a company which, in the course of its business, grants credit to consumer customers by means of express agreements will need specialist information and advice at all times. All that need be said here is that the Consumer Credit Act 1974 made a number of changes in the law, one of the most important of which in practice was to make the Director responsible for the licensing and control of arrangements by which consumers are given credit facilities.

MONOPOLIES

The Fair Trading Act replaced and in some respects altered the previous law on monopolies. The investigation of actual or suspected monopolies remains the responsibility of an independent statutory Commission (now named the Monopolies and Mergers Commission), which has wide powers to require information to be supplied to it. It cannot, however, make an investigation on its own initiative but can act only on a reference being made to it in accordance with the Act. Neither has it power to take any action otherwise than in direct connection with the process of investigation: its findings and conclusions are reported to the government.

A monopoly situation giving rise to a reference to the Commission may occur in connection with the supply of goods or services in the whole or any part of the United Kingdom or in connection with the supply of goods for export, and may be a monopoly by a single supplier or a single purchaser, or by a group of suppliers or purchasers as the case may be. If the monopoly is or may be that of a group, it is immaterial that the firms constituting the group may, in the words of the Act, be acting 'voluntarily or not' or 'by agreement or not'.

For the purposes of the Act, control of the supply or purchase of one-quarter of the goods or services under consideration constitutes a monopoly situation. Thus, so far as the Act is concerned, the existence in a small town of only one retail bookseller or two hairdressers or three builders or four petrol stations would just as much create a monopoly supply situation likely to qualify for investigation as does the predominance nationally of the suppliers of a variety of commodities. who have already been subjected to investigation by the Commission in its previous forms and under earlier statutes. The 1973 Act did not introduce this principle; it did, however, change the 'share' criterion from one-third to one-quarter.

The Act requires the Director to keep under review all commercial activities in the United Kingdom, and to collect information with regard to those activities and the persons by whom they are carried on, with a view to his becoming aware of and ascertaining the circumstances relating to monopoly situations. This provision is similar to that mentioned above regarding the Director's consumer protection function, but it has the important addition here that in carrying out his duties regarding monopolies he is both required and empowered under the Act to call upon firms to provide him with information. He may call for such information about what a firm supplies or what it buys, and may do so in the course of considering whether in the circumstances which he is investigating a monopoly situation might exist. Failure to provide information as required by the Director, or provision of false information, could lead to prosecution and a fine.

References to the Commission can be made by the Director or by the government. Either can make a reference relating to goods or services supplied or purchased by private industry, but only the government can make one involving nationalized industries or other public sector bodies. A monopoly reference directs the Commission to ascertain whether a monopoly situation exists in regard to specified goods or services and, if the Commission finds that it does, to comment on whether it operates or may be expected to operate against the public interest. The Commission has power to call for information, documentary or oral, relating to any reference made to it; failure by a firm to respond to such a call could result in prosecution and a fine.

The Commission's proceedings take place in private, and in general the information which it obtains is not made available to any party involved in the investigation. The evidence which it receives is not made available either to the public or to the government except in so far as it may be incorporated in the report which in due course the Commission puts to the government. The report is made to the government even if the original reference was initiated by the Director; the Commission's reports are always subsequently published. The government is under no statutory or other obligation to accept the report or the recommendations made by the Commission. In practice, though, the government has invariably agreed with what the Commission says and has sought to take whatever remedial action is appropriate by means of reaching agreement in discussion with the firm or firms concerned, perhaps also securing formal undertakings.

The Fair Trading Act gives the Director responsibility for having such discussions and obtaining suitable undertakings if (as is highly probable) the government requests him to do so for it. Should he in such circumstances find himself unable to obtain an appropriate undertaking, he may advise the government to take action by making an order. It is in any event the Director's duty under the Act to follow up the outcome of a reference to and report by the Commission on a monopoly situation.

MERGERS

Because mergers between companies are quite likely to create monopoly situations, the law about mergers has developed in close association with the law concerning monopolies. The Fair Trading Act thus also replaced and in some respects altered the previous law on mergers. Investigation in appropriate circumstances is carried out by the Monopolies and Mergers Commission, but (as with monopoly investigations) only when a specific reference is made to it. The Commission has the same powers when investigating a merger reference to require the provision of information as it has for the investigation of monopoly references, and the same absence of powers to take any action otherwise than in direct connection with the process of investigation. Its conclusions in merger references are reported to the government.

A merger situation qualifying for investigation under the Act occurs when two or more firms of which one at least is a United Kingdom firm, engage in, negotiations which will result in their ceasing to be what the Act describes as 'distinct enterprises', and when in addition either the value of the assets to be taken over exceeds £5m or a consequence of the conclusion of the negotiations will be the creation of a situation in which a single firm will control one-quarter of the market in any description of goods or services in the United Kingdom, either as supplier or as purchaser.

The Director has a duty under the Act to 'take all such steps as are reasonably practical for keeping himself informed about actual or prospective arrangements or transactions which may constitute or result in the creation of merger situations qualifying for investigation'. He does not, however, have any obligation or power to obtain any information from firms about plans for mergers which they may be making or contemplating.

In practice, he does not need any such powers. This is because no firm would let itself get into an 'investigatable' merger situation without having already entered into discussions with the Office of Fair Trading with the intention of securing clearance for the merger plans. Under the previous legislation, such discussions were initiated with the Board of Trade and, later, with the Department of Trade and Industry. The practical reason for firms to have such discussions was (and still is, now that the Office has taken over the relevant functions which the Board and the Department used to have) that the result of the government making an order if a merger were to be completed without the Commission having the opportunity to consider it could be quite devastating.

In this context, clearance means being formally told that a reference about the proposed merger will not be made to the Commission. The discussions which firms will accordingly have with the Office will enable the Director to fulfil his duty of keeping himself informed and also equip him to carry out another duty under the Act—that of making recommendations to the Secretary of State about referring or not referring a merger proposal to the Commission. It has been and will probably remain unusual for the discussions to fail to bring about a situation in which, perhaps after the original plans have been adjusted or undertakings have been given, the Director cannot then recommend to the Secretary of State that no reference to the Commission is necessary.

Nevertheless, the Act provides—as it must—for the Commission to be directed by the Secretary of State to investigate and report on whether a proposed merger would create a situation such as described in the second paragraph of this section, and if so, whether the creation of such a situation would, or may be expected to, operate against the public interest . Little more consideration need be given here to merger references to the Commission: it is almost universally accepted that any such reference effectively puts an end to the merger plans. When a reference is made, the procedures are essentially the same as those described earlier for monopoly references.

RESTRICTIVE TRADE PRACTICES

This term is almost as inaccurate, though rather more usual and less convenient that the description 'fair trading' discussed at the beginning of this chapter. The part of the law to which the term 'restrictive trade practices' relates is more accurately referred to as that concerned with restrictive trading agreements, ie agreements between firms which relate to trading and which have the effect of restricting freedom of action and competition. The relevant legislation is in the

Restrictive Trade Practices Acts 1956 and 1968 and the Resale Prices Act 1964, and was modified and extended by Parts IX and X of the Fair Trading Act 1973.

The essence of the legislation is that retailers may not be put under a contractual obligation to their suppliers about selling goods at a minimum retail price; that suppliers may not decline to accept an order from a retailer solely on the ground that the retailer is considered likely to sell the goods at a lower retail price than the supplier would wish; and that agreements between two or more firms carrying on business as manufacturers or suppliers of goods which have the effect of restricting freedom of action or competition are valid only if they have been approved by the High Court. The Director has duties under the the 1973 Act in connection with the last point, and the Act prepares for the extension of the law about restrictive trading agreements so that it will eventually apply also to agreements relating to services.

By definition under the 1956 Act, as amended, a restrictive trading agreement is an agreement limiting the freedom of the parties or competition between them with regard to the prices which they will charge or pay for goods or work on goods; the prices which, as suppliers, they will recommend retailers whom they supply to charge for the goods; the terms on which they will buy or sell goods or work on goods; the quantities or descriptions of goods which they will buy or sell; the processes which they will apply in doing work on goods; or the suppliers or customers with whom they will do business. The legislation is concerned with any such agreement, however informal. Acceptance of any of the restrictions or limitations of the types listed by the members of a trade association or similar body is deemed by the legislation to be an agreement between the members.

Every such agreement has to be notified to the Director (who, by the 1973 Act, took over the functions which under the earlier legislation had been performed by the Registrar of Restrictive Trading Agreements) and, unless it falls within one of the categories specified in the legislation as giving entitlement to exemption, will be registered and referred by the Director to the Restrictive Practices Court for a decision on whether the restrictions in the agreement are contrary to the public interest. If the court finds that they are (and it has only very rarely found othewise), it will order the parties to give up their observance of the restrictions.

The examination of matters referred to the Restrictive Practices Court is conducted wholly judicially and in public. One consequence is that well-documented case law has developed since the 1956 Act was passed, so that it is fairly clear that (very few) characteristics of a restrictive trading agreement are likely to be found by the court not to be contrary to the public interest. Firms considering making agreements which might be classed as restrictive trading agreements can therefore quite readily obtain guidance from the Office of Fair Trading on the advisability of including or omitting particular provisions. Guidance can also be obtained on whether an agreement would be eligible for any sort of exemption from the full investigation laid down.

During 1975, a start was made on calling up for examination those agreements which incorporate restrictions on the supply or purchase of services, similar to those defined above, under the 1956 Act. The Secretary of State is empowered to make orders to this end, under the provisions of the Fair Trading Act.

THE SECRETARY OF STATE

This chapter contains some references to action by 'the government' and others to action by 'the Secretary of State'. The references to government are made when the action could be taken by any of several Departments or their respective Ministers. In the context of fair trading, references to action by the Secretary of State necessarily indicate that the only appropriate Department is (at the time of writing) that headed by the Secretary of State for Prices and Consumer Protection. This requires some explanation.

From the earliest relevant years until 1974, all the legislation referred to in this chapter (with exceptions as specified) came within the province of the President of the Board of Trade, or, for a few years at the end of the period, the Secretary of State for Trade and Industry. When the Fair Trading Act came into operation in 1973, a fair trading division to administer it and associated legislation was set up in the Department of Trade and Industry by the (then Conservative) government. It was in everybody's interests that this division should cover within the government precisely the same range of functions as the Director General of Fair Trading was to cover as an independent statutory authority.

After the General Election of 1974, the Labour Government divided up what had been the Department of Trade and Industry. The whole of the fair trading division was allocated to the newly created Department of Prices and Consumer Protection. It thus came about that the Secretary of State for Prices and Consumer Protection has responsibilities not only for consumer protection, which is only to be expected, but also for monopolies, mergers and restrictive trade practices, for sale of goods and trade descriptions and for unsolicited goods and services, even though these are each at best only in part 'consumer' matters and would seem each to be more logically associated with the Department of Trade.

SALE OF GOODS

One of the oldest pieces of legislation relating to fair trading is the Sale of Goods Act 1893. This remained almost in its original form until changes in trading methods were recognized and covered by amendments to some of its provisions in the Supply of Goods (Implied Terms) Act 1973. As most businessmen will have developed their ways of doing business in probably unknowing accordance with the original provisions of the 1893 Act, the changes made by the 1973 Act must be treated here as important.

In fact the principles of the law remain substantially as they were in the 1893 Act, namely that in all transactions of sale and purchase of goods the seller has three main and fundamental obligations to the buyer. These are that he will give the buyer good title to the goods being sold; that the goods shall be fit for their obvious purpose and of a quality appropriate to their description and price; and that the goods shall be reasonably fit for any purpose for which the buyer has told the seller he intends to use them, the seller having done nothing to give a contrary indication. These principles remain of general validity notwithstanding that, clearly, in some situations the conduct of buyer and seller—or discussions between them—may effect modifications. Because of the provisions in the 1893 Act regarding these principles, it has for more than eighty years been incorrect for reliance to be placed on the principle of *caveat emptor*.

The 1973 Act made a major change in what the law will allow and recognize in the way of agreement between the parties to absolve the seller from having these basic obligations. There was provision in the 1893 Act whereby, in effect, the buyer could waive the 'fitness for the purpose' obligations set out in the preceding paragraph. (The 'title' obligations were always, and still are, unavoidable.) As a consequence of this provision, sellers developed the use of 'exclusion clauses' in documents of sale, whose effect was to oblige the buyer to agree, as a term of the contract of sale, to waive these obligations. The increasing use of such clauses is now regarded as contrary to the public interest.

The 1973 Act severely reduces the possibilities for an arrangement whereby a seller does not have the 'fitness for purpose' obligations. It provides that in no circumstances can the seller be relieved in any way of these obligations when the sale is a 'consumer sale', ie a transaction when the goods sold are of a type ordinarily bought for private use or consumption, when the seller is acting in the source of a business, and when the buyer is a private individual. It also provides that a contract term in a transaction between two parties, both acting in the course of business, which constitutes an agreement that the seller shall be relieved of his 'fitness for purpose' obligations will be enforceable only if to rely on it would in all the circumstances be fair and reasonable. The Act illustrates the considerations to be taken into account in assessing what would be fair and reasonable.

TRADE DESCRIPTIONS

The Merchandise Marks Act 1885 was an even earlier piece of 'fair trading' legislation, replaced and brought up to date by the Trade Descriptions Act 1968 which in turn was supplemented by the Trade Descriptions Act 1972. The purpose of all the Acts was and is to punish, by fine or imprisonment, traders who promote the sale of their goods or services in such a way that purchasers are misled.

The 1968 Act introduced some innovations. By far the most important was the provision that local weights and measures authorities were to have positive responsibility for enforcing it: no such responsibility was attributed by previous legislation. As a consequence the committees and officials of local authorities have taken a most active interest in carrying out inspections and issuing warnings and prosecutions about sales promotions generally. The Weights and Measures Departments of local authorities have expanded and become Trading Standards Offices and even Consumer Protection Divisions, and the professional body to which members of the weights and measures service belong has changed to being the Institute of Trading Standards Administration.

The basic provision of the 1968 Act, like the 1885 Act before it, is to declare that an offence (punishable by fine or imprisonment) is committed by any person who in the course of a trade or business applies a false trade description to goods, or supplies goods to which a false trade description is applied. An extensive definition is given of the expression 'trade description', by way of illustrations, and the Act provides that a trade description can be applied to goods not only (as under the previous legislation) by being shown on the goods or their packaging but also (and these are innovations) by an oral statement about the goods or by an advertisement for them. Two other important innovations are that the Act makes it an offence for any person to make knowingly or recklessly a false statement about the provision or nature of services offered or provided, and that it is designed, though under somewhat complex provisions, to prevent purchasers from being misled about actual or comparative prices for goods.

The 1972 Act applies only to situations in which goods of non-British origin are marketed under what it calls a 'United Kingdom name or mark'; its purpose was to prevent purchasers from being allowed wrongly to infer that such goods were of British origin. It therefore provides that the actual country of origin shall be shown on goods which are of foreign origin but are marketed in this country under a 'United Kingdom name or mark'. Failure to comply may result in prosecution and a fine; local weights and measures authorities have the duty to ensure that the Act is otherwise enforced.

MISREPRESENTATION

Any consideration of fair trading must obviously include an assumption that no party to a transaction will knowingly permit another party to labour under an important and relevant misunderstanding. Such a misunderstanding can arise from an inadvertent failure to pass information over or from a lack of knowledge of a material fact at a material time; in either event there is likely to have been what the law calls 'innocent misrepresentation'. The Misrepresentation Act 1967 (which came from the Lord Chancellor's department and is not among the concerns of the Secretary of State for Prices and Consumer Protection) provides remedies for situations which arise when a transaction has been completed but would not have gone through had all concerned known all the material facts at the material time.

UNSOLICITED GOODS AND SERVICES

Much annoyance is caused to many company administrators (and, it seems, an adequate income is acquired by some people) through the process known as 'inertia selling' and variations on it and through the operation of the 'directory racket' and its variations. Both come into the category of unfair trading, and the Unsolicited Goods and Services Act 1971 was passed in an endeavour to make them illegal and bring them to an end. To deal with inertia selling, the Act relieves from any obligations to the supplier a person who receives a delivery of goods which he has not ordered. To deal with bogus directories, the Act contains detailed provisions about the requirements for a valid order for the inclusion of an entry in a trade directory or similar publication. The Act has not succeeded in its object, and company administrators and their staffs continue to be taken in by practitioners of these forms of selling. The only effective defence is continuing vigilance, coupled with strict adherence to careful systems of (1) controlling and limiting the members of a company's staff who may sign documents presented by outsiders, and (2) scrutinizing all invoices and similar documents received from outside and making payment only of those which can be associated with the company's own properly authorized purchase order.

VOLUNTARY CODES OF PRACTICE

Although they do not—and usually could not—have any legal force, the provisions of voluntary codes of trading practice are in general at least as important to fair trading as is any piece of parliamentary legislation. Company administrators should be aware of any codes operating in their own company's industry (usually through a trade association) or locality (through a Chamber of Commerce) and should try to keep themselves informed about any nationally applicable codes such as, in particular, the Code of Advertising Practice. Industry or local codes of course have to avoid becoming restrictive trading agreements and should be actively developed because of the specific reference to them in the Fair Trading Act.

PART FOUR

Office Administration

15

Managing Office Equipment

John Ashton

Office mechanization has been taking place since the early nineteenth century, but the advent of electronic computers has created a new technology in offices. Research and development in transistorized, micro-miniaturized circuitry, with electronic impulses transmitted at the speed of light, has changed the face of office machines in recent years.

All machines need some form of input, whether in the form of keys that are depressed, characters that can be read automatically or impulses that can be transmitted directly into a machine. Human control is required at some stage. In the office the basic clerical operations undertaken by humans are:

1   Communicating
2   Writing
3   Copying
4   Calculating
5   Sorting
6   Checking
7   Filing

It is difficult to mechanize sorting and checking except in the sense that punched-card machines and computers can sort data and check it. Filing cannot be mechanized, except by sophisticated automated microfilm retrieval systems, or by a computer. Information, if suitably coded, can be stored in the form of magnetic tapes or cards, punched cards and tape, magnetic film, discs or electrical impulses.

There are automated retrieval units on the market able to handle most filing media but there is nothing that will actually file, classify, extract and replace documents mechanically.

Summarizing and coding are a combination of sorting, checking and copying, and sometimes calculating. The remaining clerical operations of communicating, writing, copying and calculating can be dealt with by office machinery.

COMMUNICATING MACHINES

Considerable development is taking place in the field of data transmission. The more that is found out on how to use computers, the more they are likely to be used, and this will mean faster and larger machines. More data traffic than voice traffic will be carried in the future over the telephone and telegraph networks. Organizations will want to collect and process information from different locations more quickly than can at present be done either by hand or by post. The British Airways real-time airline seat reservation booking system is an example of this. Access to large computers will be available to firms of all sizes to enable them to process data and programs.

Apart from data-transmitting equipment, other machines are used in the preparation and transmission of written messages, such as dictating machines, facsimile transmitters, electrowriters and teleprinters.

Centralized dictating systems are usually of the 'bank' or 'tandem' variety. The 'bank' system involves a battery of dictating machines wired to an internal telephone network. Staff may dictate to these machines from their offices by using their internal telephones. The supervisor of the audio typing bureau will then allocate work to her staff by changing the medium—for example a cassette—after the dictation has taken place and allocating it to an audio typist, who will play it back on her own transcribing machine sited on her desk. The 'tandem' system retains the personal touch because each audio typist has both a recorder and a transcriber. The office staff can dial straight through to a particular typist who may be familiar with certain classes of work. The typist can then transfer the dictating medium (cassette or magnetic or plastic belt) from the transcriber and play it back on her recorder.

The installation of dictating systems requires careful planning as staff must not only be trained to use the equipment properly, but they must sometimes be persuaded to use it. Many firms have had more trouble with staff when they installed centralized dictating systems than they had when they installed a computer. Considerable savings can be achieved by eliminating shorthand typists, although it is prudent to pay audio typists at the same rate as shorthand typists—after all, audio typists must be good at English if they are to transcribe accurately.

Facsimile transmitters allow documents and photographs to be transmitted over the telephone using electronic scanning methods. It is now possible to transmit particulars of a wanted criminal by radio to a moving police car, by use of the latest facsimile equipment.

Other machines that can be grouped in this section include ancillary equipment used to prepare communications for the post, or for mail handling after receipt—for example, letter openers, folding machines, envelope sealers, inserting machines and permutations of these. Collators can also be included in this section.

WRITING MACHINES

In recent years, equipment has been developed to capture data automatically, as a by-product of another operation. Data capture is the first stage in the supply of information through a data processing system. Punched paper tape or cards can be obtained as an automatic by-product of normal work—for example, an acknowledgement of an order could be typed using edge-punched cards in an automatic typewriter with the tape punch switched on. The tape punch would automatically generate punched paper tape for input into a computer for further processing in the field of production control. Attempts are being made to eliminate card and tape as they are slow computer-input media. Optical character recognition (OCR), magnetic-ink character recognition (MICR), and mark-reading equipment have been introduced to try to eliminate this expensive, error-prone input. Machines used for data capture include adding, accounting and electronic invoicing machines, cash registers, typewriters and automatic typewriters. Word processing machines (automatic typewriters) have undergone radical changes, and many manufacturers have dispensed with punched paper tape and have now introduced varying degrees of storage such as magnetic-tape cassettes, magnetic discs and cards, and video display units with the ability to update a tape cassette using the visual display unit as a real-time terminal.

There are many different kinds of typewriters but basically there are two types: standard models and special models; these can be either electric or manual machines. In the USA, two electric machines are sold for every one manual. In Britain, one report suggests that only one electric typewriter is sold to every three manual machines: they require less effort to operate, they give a clear, even impression on every stroke, and, it is claimed, they can increase output by up to 20 per cent. They are invaluable for the preparation of stencils and offset masters because of the evenness of the type.

Special typewriters include flatbeds (permitting typing in a bound book), front-feed machines (simultaneous preparation of correlated forms—eg cheque and cash book, statement, ledger card and journal—when linked to an adding or calculating machine) and a variety of attachments for continuous stationery, including automatic line finders and automatic feeds.

Addressing machines, and franking, numbering, cheque writing, cheque-signing and perforating machines come into this category.

COPYING MACHINES

Copying includes making copies of an existing document, and preparing a master from which further copies can be obtained either by duplicating or by photocopying. The history of major developments in copying can be plotted roughly as follows:

Offset duplicating	c1800
Stencil duplicating	c1800
Spirit duplicating	c1900
Dyeline photocopying	1935
Reflex photocopying	1946
Thermofax photocopying	1952
Diffusion photocopying	1953
Electrostatic photocopying	1960
Adherography photocopying	1967
Colour photocopying	1968
Plain paper photocopying	1973

It will be seen from the above that the duplicating processes are the oldest, and today they are still the cheapest systems to run. Photocopying machines are making strong inroads on the duplicating market as the machines are much easier to use. As the cost of photocopying becomes lower this trend will doubtless continue.

Duplicating involves taking copies from a specially prepared master—for example, spirit (hectograph), stencil (wax or electronic), and offset-litho. Electronic stencil cutters have been introduced for the automatic preparation of stencils from an original or a copy. Once the master has been prepared the benefits of low-cost duplicating may be enjoyed. Of all the duplicating processes, offset-litho gives copies of the highest quality. An excellent combination of equipment is an electrostatic photocopier for short-run copying and an offset-litho machine for long-run work. Masters for the offset machine can be prepared by photocopying an original using the electrostatic machine—paper plates are loaded in the electrostatic photocopier instead of copy paper.

Originals can be photocopied without special preparation of the original by using the reflex, thermofax or diffusion, as well as the electrostatic and adherography processes. Special preparation of a master is necessary in the dyeline process.

Recent developments in photocopying machinery include the introduction of plain-paper photocopying machines many of which can be bought outright instead of paying meter charges for copies used. Recent shortages of coated paper have boosted sales of plain-paper copiers.

Photocopies in colour can now be obtained on both electrostatic and dyeline machines. An application here would be the provision of coloured drawings for electrical engineers, showing electrical circuits in colour, or coloured plans for architects.

CALCULATING MACHINES

The main classes of calculating machines are:

1   Those that can be used for calculating and writing the results—adding and listing machines, printing calculators, electro-mechanical and electronic accounting machines and visible-record computers and cash registers
2   Those where the results are read from the dials of the machine and must be written down as a separate operation—adding and listing machines, calculating machines (key-driven, rotary and electronic)
3   Those calculators that give both a print out on a tally roll and a displayed answer

Adding machines

Adding machines are of two types: listing and non-listing. Both types can have either abridged or full (bank) keyboards. They can be manual or electric. Most machines will subtract as well as add but not all machines will show a true credit balance.

Calculators

There are four main types of calculator and the difference between these machines and adding machines is that calculators can also multiply and divide. The four types are:

1   Key-driven machines—eg, a comptometer
2   Rotary calculators—eg, a barrel calculator, Facit, Odhner, Marchant
3   Printing calculator—electromechanical and electronic—eg, Monroe Epic, Olivetti Programma 101
4   Electronic calculators—Anita, Muldivo, Canola, Sharp

The trend is towards electronic calculators since these machines are fast, silent and easy to operate. Prices have dropped drastically in recent years and pocket-size calculators are now available for less than £5.

    More kinds of electronic printing calculators have come on to the UK market since the introduction of value added tax, meeting the needs of many organizations who require a print-out.

    The link-up of an electronic calculator, to an electric typewriter in the form of an electronic invoicing or billing machine is now well established.

Book-keeping and accounting machines

There are three basic types of book-keeping and accounting machines:

1   Electromechanical
2   Electronic accounting
3   Visible-record computers

As with adding machines, the keyboards are either full or abridged.

While the conventional electro-mechanical book-keeping machine is still available in the UK the move is towards electronic machines, which are faster, more powerful and more reliable. Improved storage facilities are available and an electronic machine can add, subtract, multiply and divide as well as print, which makes it much more versatile in application. An electromechanical machine would cost less (eg Addo or Daro) but such machines basically only add, subtract and print.

Visible-record computers continue to be popular in the UK and as new technology becomes available in the form of video display units, magnetic discs and high-speed printing terminals, all interfaced with the machine, they are likely to attract widespread interest in the future—particularly as manufacturing costs of electronic equipment must come down.

SOURCES OF INFORMATION

The field of office machinery is very large. In organizations big enough to support a management services division or an O & M department the responsibility to evaluate office equipment will normally be delegated to them. As the vast majority of firms in this country employ less than 100 people, this job will usually be the responsibility of the office manager or the company secretary.

In some O & M departments, the manager will allocate to individual officers under his control the responsibility for keeping abreast of developments in particular classes of machines and equipment. It is impossible to become expert in all aspects of office machinery, therefore the appropriate officer can be consulted by colleagues as required during assignments. Even the knowledgeable O & M officer should familiarize himself with the uses to which machines are put, rather than become involved in the technical intricacies.

A useful starting point for the newcomer to office machinery and equipment is to read as many books on the subject as possible. As there is a time-lag in the publication of books on this subject, articles are an excellent source of up-to-date information and are to be found in publications such as:

Business Systems and Equipment
Office Equipment News
Business Equipment Digest
Index to Office Equipment and Supplies
Office Management
Office Equipment Selector
Management in Action
Computer Management
Professional Administration

The BEE is to be renamed The International Business Show and the next exhibition will be held at the National Exhibition Centre in Birmingham in October 1977 and will be well worth visiting. One of the best ways of acquiring up-to-date information about office machinery and equipment is to see them demonstrated at exhibitions. A salesman will always be pleased to demonstrate his equipment since this is the chief method by which he sells it. Although it can be an exhausting business, large exhibitions are the only places where all competing machines are under one roof, and this makes it convenient to compare them.

Much can be learnt from the office equipment representative. He is an expert in his field and will advise his customers and contacts of any developments that are taking place. Businessmen can call in the representative to help them. No representative worth his salt will attempt to mechanize a system that will not do the job properly.

The *Business Equipment Buyer's Guide* (from Digest Data Books, Park House, Park Street, Croydon) is an excellent reference, as it contains very comprehensive information about office machines, their specifications and prices, together with details of suppliers—all cross referenced. Members of the Business Equipment Trade Association are noted with an asterisk in this publication.

REASONS FOR MECHANIZATION

Offices are mechanized for a variety of reasons, but usually to reduce costs, as labour is the largest single expense in any office. If carefully selected, machines can reduce these costs by an amount greater than the investment in the machine. Machines are often introduced at the expense of increased costs because they are good investments if they produce needed information. In most parts of the country high-calibre office staff are hard to come by. In London, the shortage is particularly acute and many organizations are being forced to mechanize because of this.

Information may not be available by manual methods or may be rendered useless when available because it has taken too long to obtain. Mechanized methods can produce records in a much better condition and in much less time than manual or semi-mechanized systems.

Machines can introduce specialization into offices, and this in turn increases speed and reduces costs. Before mechanizing his sales ledger, a Midlands coal merchant employed a staff of six, dealing with 12 500 accounts. Statements were being dispatched to customers up to three months late, and contained many inaccuracies. Bad debts were over £3500 a year. After mechanizing his sales ledger with an accounting machine used in conjunction with a dyeline photocopying machine to copy his translucent ledger cards, his accounts were sent out on time each month. He was able to reduce his office costs to such an extent that the equipment was paid for in savings in seven months.

Monotonous work can be made more interesting by installing office machinery. The operator takes a pride in using the very latest equipment although intense mechanization can have the opposite effect. One firm installed a battery of electronic invoicing machines on which the operator typed the invoice and extended and totalled it using the electronic calculating section of the machine (obviating the need to use a comptometer). Operators were impossible to keep because of the resultant boredom of the job.

Errors in clerical work can be greatly reduced and sometimes virtually eliminated, or at any rate more easily detected, with office machinery. Some machines, such as chequewriters, can prevent fraud. Check-digit verifiers linked to tape-punching machines can eliminate all errors except certain types of random errors. This ensures a 'clean' perforated paper tape for subsequent computer input. Security is another reason for mechanizing office procedures. Microfilming bulky records can provide an opportunity of safeguarding vital records against fire since fire-resistant cabinets and safes can house the reduced media. Shredders can effectively deter the industrial spy whilst intruder alarms using electronic microwave techniques are particularly effective. Static and mobile guardian services have expanded rapidly in recent years and insurance companies are insisting on strong security precautions against a background of increases in fire damage, theft and rising criminal activities.

CRITERIA FOR CHOICE OF EQUIPMENT

It is difficult to decide which machine to buy when pushed from all sides by competing salesmen who claim that theirs is the best. It is necessary to consider the main purpose for which the equipment is required, since some machines have additional features that are not required but are included in the basic machine price. The rule is: do not buy features on machines that you do not really need.

Before any steps are taken to purchase a machine, it is vital to undertake a review of the entire procedure in order to simplify it. It is pointless mechanizing an obsolete or unworkable system. A machine cannot solve a problem that cannot be solved manually.

Assuming that work simplification has been carried out, the next step is to call in the equipment representatives who will soon indicate if the job can be mechanized. Demonstrations of the machines will be arranged and it is up to the prospective purchaser to decide which machine to buy.

The representative will quote references, and it is a good idea to take them up. A prospective buyer can then see an actual installation of the equipment and question the operating and managerial staff. There is no reason why independent references should not be found, for this will possibly confirm impressions gained so far.

Many decisions to buy office machines are made intuitively because it may appear too difficult, too costly or simply not possible to weigh alternatives systematically. Dominant factors such as attitudes and emotions in a particular situation may render qualification useless or too costly in relation to the importance of the decision. The businessman has to consider what costs would be incurred if the alternative is implemented and would not be incurred if it is not adopted. A given quantity of material may be typed in less time by using an electric typewriter but no real saving will accrue unless the time freed is used productively for some other purpose. On the other hand, one may not be able to engage a secretary unless an electric typewriter is provided, so the importance of the qualitative factor should not be overlooked. Cost calculations make it possible to express the net effect of a number of factors as a single figure and therefore the number of factors to be considered is reduced.

A simple example of costing alternative methods would be to take the writing of 1000 names and addresses on envelopes each week. Each address consists of four lines; the name, street number and name, town and postal code. The same names and addresses are written each week. There are several different ways of completing this work.

By hand: about 15 hours
By manual standard typewriter: about 12 hours
By electric typewriter: about 10 hours
By manually operated addressing machine: about 2 hours
By electrically operated addressing machine with automatic feed: about 15 minutes

The approximate costs of the above methods would be as shown below:

Cost of addressing 1000 envelopes

METHOD OF PREPARATION	CAPITAL COSTS	ANNUAL LABOUR COSTS
Hand	nil	£293
Manual typewriter	£94	£235
Electric typewriter	£159	£195
Manual addressing machine	£150	£20*
Electric addressing machine with automatic feed	£2500	£5*

*Not including platemaking

The hand-operated addressing machine appears to be a very attractive proposition particularly when, for an extra £15, an envelope ejector would increase output by 30 per cent. Depreciation charges would also be negligible.

The selection of one particular method of duplicating from another can be simplified by the adoption of selective criteria, such as cost, speed and quality, although not necessarily in that order. The cost per copy using offset-lithography machinery is less than that produced by photocopying processes, including electrocopying. In so far as speed is concerned the electrocopying (high-speed) process is fastest for a duplicating run of about 200 copies but after 200 copies the offset process is the fastest of all.

The quality of copying varies considerably between processes and also within the photocopying processes. The clearest copies are given by the offset process, although it is fair to say that etched masters from an electrostatic master preparation unit cannot be touched up to give the top quality which one normally associates with offset printing. The quality of the electrocopy is next in order of quality with stencil and spirit duplicating coming near the bottom of the list. There is no doubt that the offset process gives a higher-quality copy on ordinary paper than any other office copying or duplicating process on the market.

The reputation of the supplier

This is important since office machinery manufacturers and distributors have a reputation to maintain and those who want to stay in business will ensure that the equipment they are marketing is reliable. There is a famous American cartoon depicting a tramp on a railway line, belongings tied in a bundle on the end of a walking stick held across his shoulder, with the caption: 'I used to give the biggest discount in town'. Discounts can be valuable, but their value is reduced if the after-sales service offered is substandard.

After-sales service

Most reputable suppliers will guarantee service within twenty-four hours. This will obviously vary according to circumstances but most suppliers take immense pride in their servicing facilities. In many instances a call made for service before noon will be answered the same day, and a request for service made in the afternoon will be met the following day.

Flexibility

Many machines can be used for more than one operation—for example, an electronic invoicing machine can be used to post a ledger and can be most useful for calculating the gross pay of an employee—usually more difficult than the subsequent calculation of net pay. An accounting machine can be used for posting all the ledgers including sales, purchases, nominal and payroll, apart from stores ledgers, stock records and various types of analyses, simply by changing the program on the machine. A dyeline machine can be used to produce statements and remittance advices by photocopying translucent ledger cards in addition to reproducing plans and other documents.

Durability

An office manager will want to know if the machine will stand up to constant hard work. Independent references are again useful here, for some large organizations buy new machines in batches, test them for six months and then get their own office engineers to strip the machines down and assess wear. If the machines come through the examination satisfactorily such firms will standardize on them.

Noise

A quiet, smooth-running machine is a joy to operate. It is the practice in many offices to segregate noisy machines. Replacing conventional machines by noiseless typewriters used to reduce the noise level by as much as 75 per cent; it is unfortunate that they are no longer being manufactured. Noise can be reduced by placing rubber or felt mats underneath machinery. Even electronic machines can be very noisy if they are fitted with electro-mechanical printing heads, and a special room may have to be allocated to them. Rotary and certain printing calculators are noisy in operation, hence the popularity of the new breed of electronic calculators which are silent and swift.

Styling and design

Good styling often means good design and in a modern office the machines must not only be good, but must look good and harmonize with their surroundings. Good styling and design will usually give ease of operation, and if the machine is easy to operate, few operator problems will be experienced and training time will be minimized.

Accommodation

Room has to be found for the machine, the operator and any peripheral machinery and equipment—for example, ledger trays, trolleys, punched-card files. If the machine is electrically operated there must be adequate power points provided, together with necessary telephones. Special facilities may be required such as adequate ventilation for dyeline machines using ammonia.

Training

Training of operators is usually provided in the price of the machine and is given on the job by trained demonstrators. The quality of training is obviously very important and independent checks help. Normally one or two operators are trained free of charge and the customer is charged for subsequent training. A demonstrator will not leave a trainee until he or she is quite familiar with the machine and can operate it to everyone's satisfaction. It is not so much the routine operation of the machine that is important as what to do when errors are made. Facilities offered by the supplier should be examined, for off-the-job training schemes are very useful although perhaps most expensive to the customer. Installation facilities vary from one firm to another. A reputable supplier will ensure that adequate training is given to operators and that both management and operating staff have confidence in the equipment before the demonstrator leaves. It is better to have subsequent operators trained by fully qualified demonstrators rather than to leave them in the hands of a person who is about to leave, since bad operating habits may be passed on.

Portability

If the machine is likely to be used in several locations throughout the firm it must be portable. Staff cannot be expected to carry around heavy office machines. A trolley should be provided.

Operating costs

Special stationery—for example, magnetic ledger cards, edge-punched cards, offset ribbons, opaque ribbons for dyeline use, kimball tags, spot-carbonized forms—can be expensive additional costs often ignored when a project is being examined.

Additional equipment

A visible-record computer may require peripherals such as punched-card readers, a paper-tape punch and a magnetic-card reader and perhaps additional core storage facilities in order to handle an application effectively. An accounting machine may require extra program bars, a trolley for the ledger posting trays, a machine stand and a special chair for the operator. it may also require a pinwheel platen for continuous stationery, none of which are included in the basic machine price. These extras must be taken into account when considering the feasibility of installing a mechanized system.

Simplicity of operation

Machines need operators to work them and machine operators cost money. The simpler the machine, the less expensive the operator. An offset-litho operator would normally expect more pay than a stencil-duplicating machine operator, because offset machines are more difficult to operate than the stencil machine and consequently it takes more time to become fully conversant with them.

Maintenance

Log books can be issued to machine operators in order to obtain machine performance statistics. This record could indicate breakdowns, stoppages, parts fitted by service engineers, as well as information concerning throughput of data.

There is little point in purchasing equipment that cannot be serviced properly. One useful guide is whether or not the supplier of the equipment is a member of the Business Equipment Trade Association, 109 Kingsway, London WC2. Only manufacturers and sole concessionaires are admitted to membership, and the Association lays down stringent standards concerning after-sales service which must be nationwide. Members must have substantial capital and should be established, stable organizations. Sometimes guarantors are required before admittance to membership. This is not to say that anyone who is not a member of the Association will give bad after-sales service. Many local organizations give good service in the areas in which they operate.

Maintenance of office machinery is as good as the service manager and his staff in any particular area. Some machine suppliers operate on a break-even basis with their service department and others work on a profit-making basis. Some machines are more expensive to buy than others but the annual service charge may be less than that of a less expensive machine. The service agreement should be examined carefully since what you get for your money varies considerably. Some agreements do not cover electric motor replacement but others do. One agreement may offer three annual calls for cleaning and adjustment where another supplier offers four such calls. In the case of electronic equipment, one supplier may insist on immediate payment of a service charge since no guarantee is given with the machine. Another may guarantee the machine for three months. Another will make no charge for maintenance service in the first year or the first 2400 hours' use of the equipment, from the date of the commencement of the service, whichever ends earlier. One manufacturer may say that the service charge will be a certain percentage of the total purchase price of the machine. Programming costs may amount to an additional $33\frac{1}{3}$ per cent on the machine costs, so it may be possible for the following situation to develop:

Basic machine price	£4500
Programming costs	£1500
Total	£6000

Annual service charge 7½%

7½% x £6000   = £450

A good service agreement may contain the following clause:

> In consideration of the payment in advance of the maintenance fee, the supplier will provide maintenance service for one year from the date of commencement of this agreement. This service will include four service inspections per year and at each inspection the equipment will be cleaned, lubricated and adjusted as necessary. All necessary repair parts and labour required to keep the equipment in good operating condition will be supplied and fitted free of charge and this will include all intermediate service calls unless calls are made by the user without good reason. The repair of damage caused by fire, water, accident or abuse is not covered by this agreement.

It is useful to be shown round a service department of a prospective supplier. This is helpful in assessing the efficiency of the after-sales service. Independent references are always valuable in this respect.

METHODS OF ACQUISITION

Medium-term financing may be used to purchase or acquire office equipment and the methods available are:

1 Outright purchase
2 Equipment leasing and renting
3 Hire-purchase

Outright purchase

The technique of discounted cash-flow analysis should be applied before the acquisition of any office equipment involving a substantial outlay of capital.

  Cash used to purchase equipment could be employed more usefully elsewhere in the business. For this reason many firms turn to the second option.

Equipment leasing and renting

Most major companies and public undertakings lease some of their equipment. A financing house will buy equipment chosen by its customer (who may choose from any supplier he wishes) and lease it to him over a number of years, ranging from three to seven, with an option to renew thereafter for a nominal annual rental. Maintenance services are not normally included in the leasing charges.

During the period of the lease, the charges will recover the cost of the equipment. The leasing company receives any investment grant and the customer may debit his profit and loss account with the leasing charges as an allowable expense for tax purposes.

Leasing facilities offer a useful alternative to costly medium-term borrowing. Renting is similar to leasing except that maintenance of the machine is normally included in the rental charges.

Leasing rates vary from one leasing company to another and it pays to shop around to obtain the best rates.

Rentals can be paid monthly, quarterly or annually to suit a firm. Leasing tends to be used for total purchases over the value of £1000, although a leasing firm is not likely to refuse business involving smaller items.

The rates charged per £1000 vary according to the purchase price of the equipment. The higher the value of the machine to be leased, the lower the rates are. For example, the monthly repayment rate per £1000 for a machine costing £15 000 on a five-year lease would be £22.10, whilst the rate for an electronic calculator would be £22.45 and the rate for a computer costing £200 000 would be £21.15 per £1000 for the same period of lease.

An example of the leasing rates charged by one organization for the acquisition of a visible-record computer costing £15 000 over five years would be as follows;

Cost of machine	£15 000
Leasing period	5 years
Leasing rate of £22.10 per month per £1000	
Annual leasing charges	£3978
Total paid over five years	£19 890

At the end of a leasing period, a company may wish to terminate the leasing agreement and usually the lessee is required to arrange for the machine to be returned to the lessor at the lessee's expense.

A leasing company is normally anxious to retain the account and will sometimes appoint the lessee as its agent to negotiate the sale of the old equipment. In return, the leasing company will usually return much of the proceeds of the sale back to the customer in the form of reduced rentals on further equipment leased.

Hire-purchase

Industrial hire-purchase is available to assist organizations to buy equipment, although this facility is used less than renting or leasing. Unlike leasing and renting, a deposit is normally required. The size of the deposit may be a limiting factor when cash is in short supply.

In the office equipment field, hire-purchase is normally used for items costing under £5000 that will have a reasonably long life, such as calculating machines, typewriters and accounting machines. Most hire-purchase companies will fix a credit limit for their customers which will determine the total amount of hire-purchase they can commit themselves for over a certain period. Hire-purchase rates are very competitive and, again, it pays to shop around.

An example of the acquisition of an electronic invoicing machine using hire-purchase is as follows:

Purchase price	£3000		
Deposit (25%)	750	£2250	
Interest charges over 3 years (at the rate of 11% per year)	742	£2992	
Total amount paid, not including maintenance charges			£3742

Leasing a similar machine would be as follows:

Purchase price	£3000
Leasing charges over three years, not including maintenance, at the rate of £1198.80 per £1000 over 3 years	£3595

Leasing may appear to be very attractive for one organization particularly when important technological advances are taking place and it is essential to keep ahead or abreast of competitors. Another organization may prefer to use hire-purchase because of the lower annual charges payable once the deposit has been found.

FURTHER READING

J.C. Denyer, *Office Management,* Macdonald and Evans, London.

Mills and Standingford, *Office Administration,* Pitman, London.

Mills and Standingford, *Office Organisation and Method*, Pitman, London.

M. Symes, *Office Procedures in Management,* Heinemann, London.

H.H. Longman, *How to Cut Office Costs,* Anbar Publications, London, 1967.

J. Ashton, 'An Introduction to Office Machinery', *O & M Journal,* June 1967.

J. Ashton, *Profiting from Mechanisation,* Paper presented to PERA Conference, Melton Mowbray, December 1970.

16

Reducing Office Costs

L G Titman

Over the past forty years, the population of this country has increased by roughly a quarter. During this time the number of people working in factories has increased by a slightly lower percentage. However, the number of people working in offices is now two and a half times the level of forty years ago.

This vast growth in the number of office workers reflects the increasing complexity of administration. It is also a vivid reminder of the increasing amount of money nowadays involved in administration. Moreover, it is in many ways more difficult to contain administration costs than factory costs. Consider a company that makes and sells chocolate Easter eggs. If one year the company manufactures 100 000 unwanted eggs then this fact is obvious for all to see. If in the same year the company processes 100 000 unnecessary memos then all that happens is that they get filed. But the cost of 100 000 unnecessary memos may be the same as the 100 000 unwanted Easter eggs.

PHILOSOPHY OF COST REDUCTION

Mechanization

The underlying philosophy behind office cost reduction has evolved greatly over the years. At one time, the predominant aim was mechanization. It was felt that since machines were reliably impersonal, they should be introduced as often as possible.

It is now realized that mechanization as an end in itself may hold severe pitfalls. A company was recently uncovered that possessed fourteen photocopying machines—these fourteen machines were producing 3 000 000 photocopies a year. In fact, photocopies can present a considerable challenge to those trying to contain administration costs. Some firms are putting multiple locks on their photocopiers; each lock is released by a key which belongs to a departmental manager who has the relevant photocopying cost deducted from his budget.

Other firms are transferring certain procedures away from their computers on to more simple methods. This is both to save money and also to increase flexibility.

Method study

The next stage in the evolution of cost reduction philosophy saw an emphasis being placed on 'work simplification' and 'method study'. People looked for the 'one best way' of carrying out each task in the office. The search was for greater efficiency. In some instances, however, even this proved insufficient. A work study department in a large organization received a considerable bundle of statistics every Friday from central accounts. A work study engineer filed this information (very efficiently) because he had been told that central accounts were very short of filing space. Meanwhile, the people in central accounts prepared the statistics every week with a Friday deadline. They did this very efficiently; they had been told that the work study department needed the statistics. Thus these statistics were prepared at considerable cost for the sole benefit of the filing cabinet manufacturer.

Effectiveness

The third and final stage in the evolution of cost reduction philosophy is the present emphasis on 'effectiveness'. This has not been accompanied by a rejection of mechanization or work simplification or efficiency in any way. It is rather a further evolution in philosophy. The search for effectiveness follows two paths.

The first path is to look at major items of expense and to ask what benefit is being obtained from each—the cost of each item and its effectiveness. For example, what do fringe benefits cost us and are they what the employees want? How much did the O & M and Work Study departments cost and what benefits did we actually gain in return?

The second path is to look at the paperwork in a concern and to regard this paperwork as being a flow of information. We can then ask what information is being provided, what does it cost and at that cost is it worth having? A sales director told the computer manager what information he needed each week; the first week that the computer went on stream it took two men to push on two trolleys all the print-out required. On the other hand, a large car manufacturer now charges divisional managers with programmers' time so that value is obtained. This path to improving effectiveness is shown in Figure 16.1.

THE O & M DEPARTMENT

For many concerns, the main agent for reducing costs will be the O & M department. This being so, it is important that this department should itself be made effective.

Every job that an O & M team is given should have an objective and a set time for completion. For example, the objective might be to reduce the money, outstanding on the sales ledger by seven per cent in forty working days. It is relatively easy to put a standard cost per day to the actual working time of the members of the O & M department—when all costs are included this *usually* lies in the range of £40-50 per day. If in the above example the cost per day is £45, then forty working days will cost £1800. The decision to be made then becomes, should we spend £1800 to reduce the outstanding debtors by 7 per cent? It

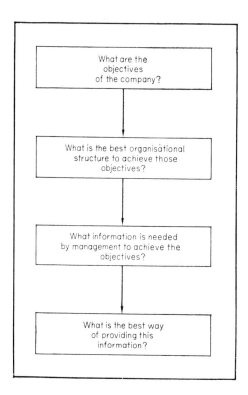

Figure 16.1 Path to improving effectiveness
The final questions are: What does this item cost? How effective is it?

may be that we would get an even better return by getting the O & M department to tackle a different area.

Certain jobs will be tackled that do not result in any financial savings. Such jobs should still be given a time allocation since this will allow a clear judgment to be made on the job's importance in relation to the cost. We are not restricting freedom of choice—we are however indicating a clear decision that has to be made. Shall a particular job be done if it is going to cost x hundred pounds?

Once a year, the O & M department should present a report. This report will contain:

1   Highlights of the year's work
2   Total cost of the O & M department including rent, typing, printing, etc
3   Total of money saved
4   Annual ratio of money saved to money cost

Appendices can show jobs completed in more detail. The method of allocating money saved on any long-lasting improvements must be agreed in advance. A good compromise is to take 100 per cent of the money in the first year, two-thirds in the second year, one-third in the third year and nothing thereafter.

This report should be distributed to top management. As far as the O & M department is concerned it can become a first-rate piece of 'public relations'. As far as top management is concerned, it acts as a form of control. If an O & M department cannot save every year an amount equal to its cost, does it have any right to exist?

The objectives and organization of the O & M function are treated in detail in Chapter 18.

WORK MEASUREMENT

The basic idea of measuring work is not of itself new. There is a record of an interesting 'oath of allegiance' which a particular work measurement engineer had to take in the eighteenth century. By then, a manufacturer of pins had already used standard times to build up standard costs for his product. By the middle of the nineteenth century, the British Treasury was using work measurement techniques—in Ireland the amount of food received by certain labourers on relief depended upon the amount of work completed in road-laying.

However, what is rather new is the application of work measurement techniques to administrative staff. At one time this was perhaps considered undignified for white-collar people. There are several reasons for the change in attitude that has occured. First, the gap between white and blue collar people has changed. Secondly, during periods of wages restraint, government departments have demanded proof of increased productivity before sanctioning pay rises. Thirdly, greater union activity is increasing the incidence of productivity deals.

Work measurement in the office can have many uses. Some of these are:

1   To provide management with the means of knowing the size of staff needed for different workloads. For example suppose that an increase in sales of fifty per cent is expected—how many more staff must be engaged and trained, and what skills will they need?

2   To form the basis of cost comparisons between alternative methods. For example, an entrepreneur was considering setting up a computer-based information service. He then considered the alternative of using straightforward manual methods—a cost comparison was only possible by using work measurement.

3   To provide management with the relative costs of obtaining different levels of management information. A chain of retail shops placed 300 000 orders a year with suppliers, many of the orders having several lines. It was the habit to provide buyers with printed details of all purchase orders including standard mark-ups. Was this level of information worth having at the cost involved?

4   To provide a yardstick for personal or group performance. This may or may not then be used for incentive purposes.

Work measurement techniques

There are a number of work measurement techniques that can be used in the office. It is very important that flexibility be retained in the choice of technique. Anybody pinning his faith to one technique alone will not be as effective as the person who uses different techniques in different situations. The particular technique to use will depend on:

1   The economics of measurement. A different technique is needed if the group size is four compared with 150 people all performing the same task

2   The use that is to be made of any standards

3   The ease of defining the units of output (for example telephone calls, memos)

4   The size of the units of output (for example a design drawing as compared with a short calculation)

5   The needs of management

The main techniques that are in use are:

Time study.   This long-established technique involves the timing of a task as it is being performed. At the same time, an assessment is made of the effective rate of working which is compared with a standard rate. The time actually taken is then converted to the time which would be taken at the standard rate. In factories, a stop-watch is used for timing. It has been found that in offices a wrist watch is usually more appropriate. For example, if a job actually takes one minute when performed by somebody working at ninety per cent performance, then the standard time would be:

$$\frac{90}{100} \times 60 = 54 \text{ seconds}$$

To this time must be added certain allowances for possible contingencies and for personal needs.

Activity sampling.   This is the application of sampling techniques to work activities. A number of instantaneous observations are made of people and/or machines over a period of time.

At each observation, a note is made of the activity taking place (for example typing, telephoning, awaiting work). At the end of the study, the percentage of time that a particular activity was observed is a measure of how often this activity is occurring in the office. An example is given in Figures 16.2 and 16.3.

Clerical standard data (CSD).   There are certain tasks which occur in a precisely similar manner in many offices (such as using a particular machine). A standard time for a task can therefore be used in such a situation.

Various proprietary systems have been developed to this end, one of which is Clerical Standard Data.

Predetermined motion time system (PMTS).   There are certain basic human movements (such as reaching, taking hold, letting go). These movements are used repeatedly in all human activities. A standard time for a task can therefore be built up by using a predetermined time for each of these very small motions.

Various systems have been developed to this end, one of which is Clerical MMD. This resulted from an international research project and incorporates the better features of several previous systems.

All the basic standard values for Clerical MMD are contained on a white card measuring 150mm x 100mm. These values are coded. Suppose we wish to time somebody getting up from a desk, moving four paces to a filing cabinet, opening and closing a drawer, returning to the desk and sitting down (ignoring for this example what is done to the filing when the drawer is open).

Moving the chair back from the desk when getting up and moving the chair into the desk when sitting down are covered by the element coded *SCM.* The walk is of eight paces or steps—coded *S.* Opening and closing a filing cabinet drawer is coded as *ODF.* We now have:

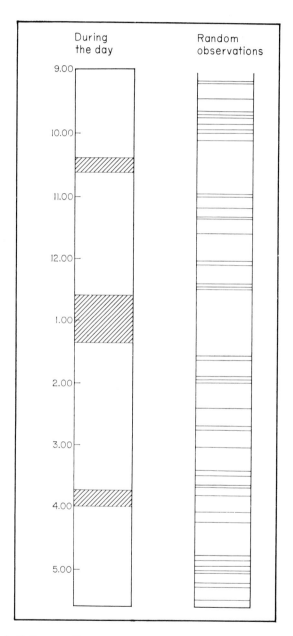

Figure 16.2 Activity sampling
Observations are made at random, at the times shown in the chart. The results are shown in Figure 16.3

ACTIVITY SEEN	NUMBER OF TIMES SEEN	PERCENTAGE OF TIME SPENT
Awaiting work	78	26
Out of office	12	4
Telephoning	63	21
Meetings	94	31
Dictating	32	11
Reading	15	5
Calculating	6	2
	300	100

Figure 16.3 Activity sampling

ELEMENT	CODE	TIME
Move chair	*SCM*	86
To filing cabinet and return	8*S*	72
Open and close drawer	*ODF*	35
		193

The time is given in milliminutes (1/1000 minute), so that the total time is 0.19 minute or nearly 12 seconds.

Presentation of work measurement data

Having selected the combination of work measurement techniques to be employed, the method of presentation must be decided upon. This will depend upon:

1   Nature of the work
2   Variability of the work
3   Length of time that management has been using work measurement in the office
4   Incidence of machinery
5   Needs of management

There are alternative methods of using work measurement techniques, and of presenting the data. The main ones include:

Job values.   This is the commonest type of presentation. Using one of the work measurement techniques, a standard time can be built up for a particular job or task. These standard times can then be used to discover the workload for an office.

Categorized work values. The tasks in an office are listed in order of approximate length of time required for each one. This list is divided into a smaller number of groups so that the operations in each group do not differ excessively in amount of time needed. A task in each group is timed precisely to act as a 'benchmark' for the whole group. Each group is allotted a single work value and all operations in a group receive the same time.

Synthetics. This technique builds up the total time for a job by adding together times for parts of the job which have been obtained from various sources. This technique is of particular use when dealing with office machinery. Most managements find that they can build up their own 'synthetics' which are special for their particular enterprise.

Controls

There are a number of ways in which the work measurement techniques can be used. The methods chosen will depend upon:

1   Nature of the work
2   Degree of control contemplated
3   Agreements made with staff assocations and unions
4   Need for exact timetables and schedules
5   Needs of management

The alternative methods of control which may be selected include:

Group assessment. Group assessment programmes (such as Group Capability Programme) give a broad supervisory control where a group of people are carrying out a separate clear-cut set of tasks. The need for detailed standards, which may be needed for individual control, can be reduced by controlling on a group basis. The group should be 4–12 people. Incentives are usually not recommended for group assessment systems.

Short-interval scheduling. This is a method of control based on work standards. The work is divided into batches, each one of which is to be completed in a target time (say, two hours). The batches are distributed to the staff who return for the next batch when the previous one has been completed. The supervisor controls the work flow and individual performances.

Incentives. There are monetary and non-monetary incentives. For both types, work measurement can provide a valid, meaningful basic tool. Incentives are not an inevitable consequence of work measurement.

Management controls.   Clerical work measurement must aim to produce a comprehensive and relevant system of management controls. The basic principles for such controls are constant although the precise details vary with the needs of management. A practical example is given in Figure 16.4.

Office: Accounts C						
Date	Standard numbers	Actual numbers	Variance	Statistics		
				Invoices	Queries	Owing—£
7:9:74	24	26	+2	5700	80	128 000

Figure 16.4 Management controls

The choices available in work measurement are summarized in Figure 16.5.

INCENTIVES

We should query incentives on the grounds of cost and effectiveness just as we query other items of expenditure. What are our incentives supposed to be for? To reduce costs, to make people get to work on time, to increase output? Could we attain these ends in other ways at less cost?

Fringe benefits.   The question of incentives can be very confused, especially in the field of employee benefits. Employee benefits can add 25 per cent to clerical labour costs; they can include free BUPA, sports clubs, on-site dentists, help with children's education. The whole question of employee benefits is discussed in detail in Chapter 24 but the point being made here is that they can be expensive. Nowadays, their effectiveness as incentives for higher output is considered minimal. They are often retained since they are a sign of good management practice rather than being major incentives.

Campaigns and lotteries.   A second group of incentives are those known as 'campaigns'. These have very specific aims, cost relatively small amounts of money and have measurable results. An example in this group is 'zero defects' which is an incentive for people not to make mistakes. This is done by building up the right atmosphere and by motivating people rather than by just giving them money. Another example is that used by a company that holds a lottery every week. Everybody's name goes into the lottery provided that they have an absolutely clean attendance and time-keeping record for the previous week (illness is no excuse). The winner of the lottery gets £50. One of the major car manufacturers started the same idea using a car as the prize. In both cases, the

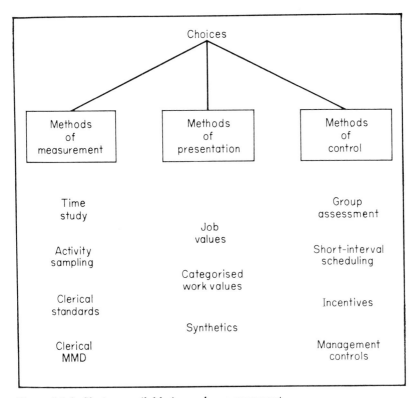

Figure 16.5 Choices available in work measurement

firm was convinced that the lottery paid for itself several times over in better time-keeping and reduced absenteeism.

Profit-sharing.   A third group of incentives is the 'profit-sharing' idea. The best known of these is probably the ICI scheme in which shares in the company are distributed to employees. Other firms using profit-sharing are the John Lewis Partnership and, in a very different philosophical approach, Scott-Bader. Although once very popular, it is usually admitted nowadays that profit-sharing is not the strongest form of incentive to reduce costs. However, many firms use it as part of their general management philosophy.

Competitions.   A fourth group of incentives is the competition. For example, a large firm can offer a prize to the office supervisor that reduces his costs of say, photocopying, by the largest amount. There are some concerns that specialize in running these competitions on behalf of an employer. For example, Thomson use one of their package holidays as a prize—the idea of a fortnight's sun-bathing in Majorca can be a powerful incentive. Care must be taken that prizes do not attract income tax—this usually happens if a recipient earns more than a certain amount in his regular job.

Bonuses.   The fifth group of incentives is that based on work measurement. It is possible, using clerical work measurement, to set a certain level of output as being a norm. If output exceeds this, the payment of a bonus is made for all extra work. For example, an audio typist may be paid her basic salary for producing 800 lines of typewriting per day. Output above this level can be paid for at the rate of so much per fifty lines up to a maximum of say 1250 lines per day. This type of incentive is particularly appropriate for typists, computer-punch operators and verifiers.

Management.   The final incentive is 'management'. Just that. The part played by straightforward management ability and leadership is often overlooked. It is in fact the most important single incentive and motivator there is.

The field of incentives can now be expressed briefly thus:

	TYPE OF INCENTIVE	OBJECTIVES	AMOUNT OF MONEY INVOLVED	ARE THE RESULTS MEASURABLE?	EXAMPLE
1	Fringe benefits	General	High	No	Sports club
2	Campaigns	Specific	Low	Yes	Zero defects
3	Profit-sharing	General	Medium	No	Trusts
4	Competitions	Specific	Low	Yes	Holidays
5	Work measurement based	Specific	Medium	Yes	Clerical MMD
6	Management	General & specific	Medium	Yes	Personal ability

REDUCING THE COST OF SPACE

There are four basic ways of reducing the cost of office space.

Using space effectively

The first approach is to ensure that the correct number of rooms and people are employed within the office. This assessment will normally be based on the work measurement techniques already described. This is reinforced by looking critically at each function and considering whether it would be better to replace it by outside contracts. For example, should the tea ladies' kitchens be replaced by vending machines? Would the staff prefer luncheon vouchers to the existing canteen facilities? Should bulky files be microfilmed and/or deposited with a firm specializing in paperwork storage?

Lower-cost buildings

The second way of reducing costs is to reduce the cost per square metre of the office accommodation. This involves moving part or all of the staff to a lower-cost building. Such a move is a major event and must be treated with care. The alternatives usually lie between:

1   Moving all or part of the office away from a high-cost area (eg central London)
2   Moving into purpose-built offices which are more suitable for one's needs
3   Converting a building (eg a modern warehouse) to one's own special needs, provided 'change of use' permission can be obtained
4   Putting widely dispersed offices all together in one location

The feelings of the key staff must be carefully sounded out. Sometimes as few as 15 per cent of staff want to move although senior personnel will usually be willing and flexible.

In this field, a further possibility that should be considered is selling the building and retaining the offices needed on a leaseback basis. The attraction of this manoeuvre depends on the current financial situation.

Reducing cost of furniture

The third way of reducing costs is to get value for money in the field of furnishing, decorations, carpeting, and so on. One firm spent nearly £100 per desk in one office and paternalistically congratulated themselves. The staff however were appalled. Not only did they feel that this was wasteful ('I'd rather have it in my salary') but they did not like the furniture anyway. It is therefore worth asking people what furnishings they want—in practice, people do not take advantage of this situation. For example, it is usually found that typists in a typing centre are happy with utilitarian desks but appreciate carpeting or curtains.

Office layout

The fourth way of reducing office costs is in better office layouts. This is a subject about which numerous books have been written but here we are concerned with the cost of various alternatives and their respective effectiveness. One of the current trends is towards some form of open-plan office instead of having many separate 'cells'. An example of this is 'Bürolandschaft' or office landscaping. An analysis of scores of books and articles on office landscaping leads to the following areas of agreement:

1   The minimum dimension of a landscaped office should be 18m
     (60ft) in either direction
2   Employees should have a minimum of 4½m² (50ft²) per person.
     For creative work the minimum distance between people should
     be 4m (13ft)
3   Some background noise is necessary and a level of 55dB is
     recommended
4   Separate areas should be provided for snacks, vending machines,
     and so on

It is claimed that open offices save money because of the reduced cost of moving
groups of people and the greater feeling of working together.

ASK THE STAFF

As has been previously hinted at in this chapter, a potent method of saving costs
is to ask the staff what they want. Employee questionnaires are being used by
more and more concerns to ask people for their opinions. For example, do
people want a sports ground?

One company asked its staff this sort of question. The answer came back that
what the men would really appreciate would be a petrol filling station near the
entrance—not, it should be noted, to get cheap petrol, but just for the
convenience.

Other companies are experimenting with flexible hours for the staff. For
example in Germany (where this idea is called 'gleitende Arbeitszeit'),
Messerschmitt allow staff to arrive between 7 a.m. and 9 a.m. and leave between
4 p.m. and 6 p.m. The staff clock on and off to make the official working week
of 43⅔ hours. When the scheme started it was feared that employees would take
advantage of the scheme and 'run into debt' with their hours worked. In point of
fact, in the first month, the staff ran up 26 000 hours credit.

SUMMARY

The secrets of reducing office costs can be summarized as follows:

1   Decide what information is needed by management and provide
     this information at optimum cost
2   Investigate all major items of expenditure and decide on their
     effectiveness
3   Ask the staff for their help

FURTHER READING

H.H. Longman, *How to Cut Office Costs,* Anbar Publications, London, 1967.

Victor Lazzaro, *Systems and Procedures,* Prentice-Hall, Englewood Cliffs, New. Jersey, 1959.

Bursk and Chapman, *New Decision-making Tools for Managers,* Harvard University Press, Cambridge, Mass., 1963.

R. Townsend, *Up the Organization,* Michael Joseph, London, 1970.

17

Setting Up
a New Office

Peter Lebus

Setting up a new office is an infrequent and complex operation for most companies. However, it presents a rare opportunity for creating a major and long-lasting influence on company efficiency and overhead costs. On all these counts, therefore, thorough planning and close management attention are amply rewarded.

A project of this nature should be under the direct control of a senior member of the company to ensure that decisions are taken quickly and that all the cost implications are recognized. For the purposes of control, the project can be split into a number of overlapping stages:

1   Establishment of requirements
2   Building assessment
3   Furniture
4   Implementation
5   Continuing administration

The time required for each stage will vary from project to project, but the same logical sequence should always be followed.

ESTABLISHMENT OF REQUIREMENTS

The first step in the planning operation is to collect together the data on which all else will be based. The ultimate success of the project will depend on a proper balance being reached between individual needs and corporate objectives after a careful analysis of each.

In order to ensure that the information is comprehensive, staff questionnaires and selected interviews can be used. It is very important at this stage to obtain a complete and unbiased picture of the type of work that is undertaken by each individual. Questions should be phrased so as to elicit information in the form which will be most useful. For instance, it is not enough to know that someone is an engineer, an accountant, or a typist. The questionnaires should highlight the activities which are carried out for a significant portion of the time—such as reading, writing, telephoning, meetings and so on. The number of visitors that can be expected and their frequency of arrival is important, as well as the degree of confidentiality of the work that is being performed. Communication patterns should be analysed for departments, sections and individuals, and the need for furniture, storage and equipment should be calculated.

In addition to individual needs, staff numbers today and for at least five years into the future must be established. It should be remembered that these figures need not be the same as those used for normal budgeting purposes. It is not unusual for management to reduce budget figures in order to provide a target for each department to aim for. The figures that should be used for office planning purposes should relate to a less restrained estimate of what will actually happen. It is rare to find that a company overestimates its future staff numbers. The penalty of underestimation is that the new offices become overcrowded and inefficient within a relatively short period of time. Forecasts should also be made of the possible changes in company organization, office systems and equipment over this period. It would be unrealistic to expect a high degree of accuracy but the range of options should be identified.

Thus far, the information has been gathered in company terms, which are of little use when looking for or assessing potential new offices. Therefore it must be translated into an accommodation specification. In order to achieve this, a process of analysis must be carried out to determine space requirements, relationship patterns, layout types, service requirements and working environment. All facets of the company's needs must be established and expressed as accommodation requirements. In many cases it is advisable to use professional assistance during this phase, to ensure the most economic solutions.

Space requirements

In order to establish space requirements, a set of standards must be developed for individuals and functions. These should be based on the analysis of a number of factors:

> Work content
> Furniture and equipment
> Storage

Need for privacy
Type of layout
Number of visitors or meetings
Access

Space standards should also be developed for facilities such as meeting areas, common storage, reception, computer and catering. The sum of all these needs is the total net usable space requirement for the company. It is most important that this figure is not confused with the net lettable area quoted for a building. The difference between these figures is discussed in the next section.

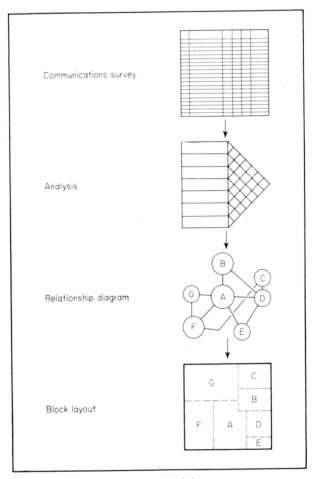

Figure 17.1   Creation of a block layout
This shows the four steps in the analysis of communications which are used to determine the relationship pattern within an organization and the optimum layout of departments or functions

Relationship patterns

The relationship pattern within the company can be established by the sequence of steps illustrated in Figure 17.1. A survey is carried out to determine the existing pattern of telephone calls, paper flow and visits. This can be done by individual record, sampling, estimate or observation. The results should be summarized into a matrix which will show the comparative figures. Any major

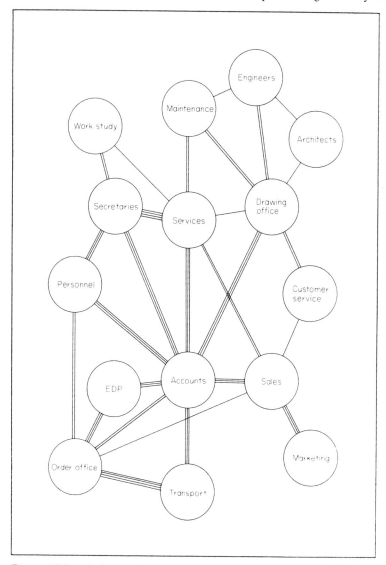

Figure 17.2   Relationship diagram
This shows the volume of communications between departments.
This can reflect the present situation or be used to show future
intentions

bias resulting from the present location of departments or individuals should be known from interviews. It is common to find that some personal communication links have grown up for no other reason than that the people are housed in adjacent areas, and conversely that departments which should be working closely together have a weak link as a result of being based on different floors, or in different buildings. Adjustments can be made to the matrix in order to correct this or to reflect company policy. By this means, specific communication links in the new building can be strengthened and others weakened.

The modified matrix should be used to create a relationship diagram (Figure 17.2), which will be the basis for locating activities. The thicker lines denote the stronger relationship links and therefore should be kept as short as possible. In due course, when space requirements have been finalized and the shape and size of the accommodation is known, the relationship diagram is developed into a block diagram allocating space to each department (see Figure 17.1).

Layout types

There are several types of layout in common use which should be considered. The choice will depend on an analysis of departmental and individual needs, with the twin objectives of an efficient office and good staff relations. Figure 17.3 illustrates a means of determining the most appropriate layout. Each layout has a number of advantages and disadvantages and they are graded accordingly. However, each department or function will have a particular set of priorities and these must be matched with the layout factors in the table. Thus an advertising department may well need considerable flexibility and good communications but little privacy, whereas a personnel department would put a very high rating

	OPEN SPACE	OPEN PLAN	CELLULAR INDIVIDUAL	SHARED	HALF-HEIGHT PARTITION	CARREL
Privacy	**		***	*	*	**
Freedom from distraction	**	*	***		*	**
Communication	***	***		*	**	*
Flexibility	***	**		*	*	*
Supervision	**	***		*	*	
Work flow	***	***		*	*	
Space utilization	***	***		*	*	**

Figure 17.3   Characteristics of office layouts
This table shows the relative merits of six types of layout. The greater the number of asterisks, the better is the result

on privacy but might need little flexibility.

The six layouts listed in Figure 17.3 are all in common use in offices throughout the country. A layout which is currently much in fashion is the open-space or landscaped office. This type of layout gives an informal appearance whilst being based on an analysis of departmental requirements. No fixed partitions are used and individuals are grouped by section or department. Figure 17.4 shows a typical open-space office. A high degree of flexibility is achievable and the reorganization of departments can be accomplished by moving a few pieces of furniture. Shoulder-high freestanding screens and boxes of indoor plants are used to provide privacy and freedom from undue distraction. Communications are good as there are few barriers to inhibit conversation or discourage meetings.

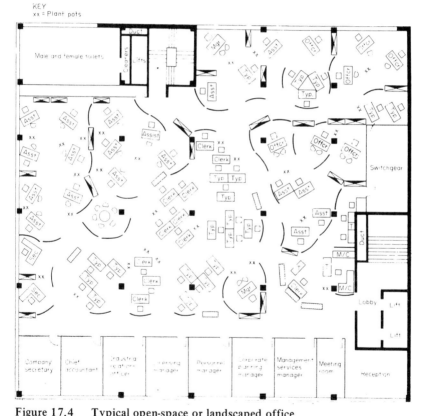

Figure 17.4 Typical open-space or landscaped office
This illustrates the informal layout and the use of screens and plants
to define groups and individuals

Acoustics play an important part in the success of this type of layout. Noise levels must be such as to provide adequate masking without creating too much distraction. This will be promoted by using a large room which is as deep as possible and can accommodate at least fifty people. Nevertheless, several successful open-space offices have been created for as few as twenty people. The minimum number of people which is acceptable will be influenced by the number and intensity of noise sources and the individual need for freedom from distraction.

Figure 17.5 illustrates an open-plan office, which is particularly appropriate for many routine paper-handling departments or drawing offices. No fixed partitions are used and there is little if any screening. Space utilization can be very high and the flow of paper is good; however, it is difficult to achieve any degree of privacy. It is usual with this layout to accommodate managers in separate offices so that they will not have undue distraction. In drawing offices, the bulky furniture that is used tends to break up the pattern of sound and the drawing boards provide some degree of screening.

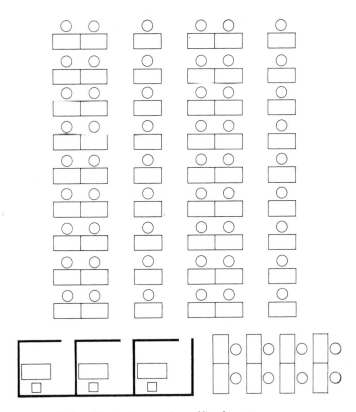

Figure 17.5   Typical open-plan office layout
This shows the straight lines and high space utilization.
There is little privacy

Cellular offices when used by individuals achieve a high degree of privacy and freedom from distraction. However, communications are not good and relationships tend to become more formalized. Flexibility of use is low, and any change of office staff may require a large number of partition moves. Space utilization is usually poor when the building module dictates large offices. Spare space is often wasted when it becomes available in the wrong part of the building.

A cellular office which is shared by several people has the worst of all worlds. It has the disadvantages of inflexibility, poor space utilization and bad communications. At the same time, because of its small size, it gives the highest levels of distraction and lack of privacy. However, the design of the building or special company requirements may dictate its use.

The half-height partition layout is a compromise between the cellular and open-plan office. Fixed partitions from four to six feet high are installed and staff work in the boxes which are created. This layout tends to give a false feeling of privacy.

A new type of layout, which is being promoted by many furniture suppliers is the carrel. This consists of a number of individual or paired work stations. The furniture is designed to provide an integrated system of work top, storage and screening, which forms two or three sides of a square. Some systems are designed as a complete square or rectangle with a small entrance way. This provides more flexibility than a cellular layout, and more privacy than an open plan. Considerable storage is close at hand, but communications are not good, which indicates that this is more appropriate for research or similar activities.

Service requirements

The provision of services is often one of the last items to be considered when companies move to new offices. Consequently telephone and power outlets are often in the wrong place or unavailable, causing undue expense and inconvenience. The planning of the telephone system should be started early in the project as delivery of equipment can be very long. During the initial investigation into individual requirements, it is important to determine the detailed telecommunication needs of each department and function. The Post Office and other equipment suppliers undertake surveys or telephone traffic to form a basis for the future planning. There are now so many systems and new developments in this field that some time spent in discussion with suppliers or other experts will be well repaid.

Working environment

The introduction of the Offices, Shops and Railway Premises Act in 1963 has made management much more conscious of the influence of environmental conditions on staff efficiency and welfare. However, the standards that are set out in the Act have been overtaken by current good practice. When determining environmental requirements for new offices, it is sensible to set two standards. A target standard should be established which would create good working conditions for the staff. In addition, a threshold level should be set, below which there is a significant drop in office efficiency or staff acceptance. If a proposed office does not meet the minimum standard then it should be rejected. On this basis a target figure can be used when looking for new accommodation, and the threshold level is known so that unsuitable offices can be identified at an early stage.

Figure 17.6 lists in a simplified form many of the standards that are commonly used. This list is only a general guide, as it may be possible or even desirable to depart from these figures under some circumstances. An example of this variation is shown in the tables. Noise levels need to be adjusted in line with the type of activity that is being performed. For instance, a typing pool can usually tolerate a noise level of 55dBA, whereas a private office will probably have a noise level of about 35dBA. Professional advice should be used for setting these standards, and for ensuring that they are met.

	CELLULAR OFFICE		OPEN-SPACE OFFICE	
	Threshold	*Target*	*Threshold*	*Target*
Temperature (°F)	68–80	68–75	68–80	68–75
Ventilation (cubic feet of fresh air/hour/person)	750	1200	750	1200
Humidity (per cent)	35–60	40–55	35–60	40–55
Lighting (Lux)	400	450	600	750–1000
Acoustics (average noise level in dBA)	35–60	30–50	55	45

Figure 17.6   Environmental standards
This table lists outline standards in a simplified form. The threshold figure is the limit beyond which staff efficiency suffers

Timing

The preparation of a specification of requirements is often undertaken in two phases. In the first, sufficient information must be assembled for a search to be made for new accommodation and to assess its suitability. This is usually a matter of some urgency. During the search period, there is then time to assess the company needs in full, so that detailed planning can start as soon as a building is found.

Information required for the building search can be summarized as:

1   Net usable space requirement
2   Types of layout
3   Departmental relationship patterns
4   Main service requirements
5   Outline environmental requirements
6   Location requirements
7   Special facilities such as computer room, catering area or banking hall

This information is used as a basis for the selection of a short list of buildings. These would be separately assessed and a final selection made.

BUILDING ASSESSMENT

The selection of a new office building commits the company to it for a number of years. It is imperative therefore, that the company's short and long-term requirements are used as the basis for comparison between alternatives. This requires an analysis of the building design and facilities to ensure the most cost-effective result.

The assessment may be best illustrated by the example summarized in Figure 17.7. Company requirements have been established in outline showing that during the next five years a total of 250 staff will have to be accommodated. In order to provide adequate working areas, together with space for other office functions and circulation, 37 500 square feet of net usable space is required. This has been calculated on the basis of 70 per cent of the area being used for open offices and 30 per cent for cellular offices. A number of service requirements and environmental standards have been fixed at both the target and threshold levels.

During the five-year period of occupation, it is anticipated that 10 per cent of the staff will move each year because of internal reorganization. It is also considered desirable to have additional space available for a 20 per cent expansion after the five-year period. This additional space may be in the form of floors that have been sublet on a short-term lease or areas which have not yet

	COMPANY REQUIREMENTS		BUILDING 1	BUILDING 2	BUILDING 3	BUILDING 4
Staff	250					
Net usable area (square feet)	37 500		41 000	37 000	39 000	47 000
Net lettable area (square feet)			45 000	39 000	42 000	54 000
Layout						
70 per cent open			*	—	—	*
30 per cent cellular			*	*	*	*
Services						
Telephone grid			—	—	—	*
Power grid			*	—	—	*
Environment:	THRESHOLD	TARGET				
Temperature (°C)	68–80	68–75	Threshold +	Target	Threshold +	Target
Ventilation (cubic feet/hour/person)	750	1200	Threshold +	Threshold +	Threshold +	Threshold +
Humidity (per cent)	35–60	40–55	Threshold +	Target	Threshold +	Target
Lighting (lux)	600	850	Target	Threshold +	Target	Target
Acoustics (dBA)	55	45	Threshold +	Threshold +	Threshold +	Target
Flexibility			*	*	*	*
10% Annual change						
20% Expansion after 5 years —			*	*	*	*
Initial costs						
Conversion			£270 000	234 000	336 000	810 000
Fitting out			£202 500	175 500	189 000	243 000
			£472 500	409 500	525 000	1053 000
Annual costs						
Interest on capital at 12%			56 700	49 140	63 000	126 360
Rent			337 500	409 500	231 000	162 000
Running costs			27 000	29 250	25 200	40 500
Maintenance costs			9 000	7 800	8 400	10 800
Staff cost differential			15 000	22 500	22 500	7 500
Total annual cost			£445 200	518 190	350 100	347 160

Figure 17.7 Building assessment

This illustrates in a summarized form the factors to be considered. The environmental standards that can be achieved in each building are shown as meeting the target level or the threshold level. The asterisks indicate that the building meets the specified requirement been converted for use.

Four buildings are considered in this example. Buildings 1 and 2 are conventional postwar offices which have been built by a developer. Building 3 is a prewar office which was designed for another occupant. Building 4 is a warehouse which can be converted to office use.

The net usable area is calculated on the basis of company requirements and individual space standards, as described earlier.

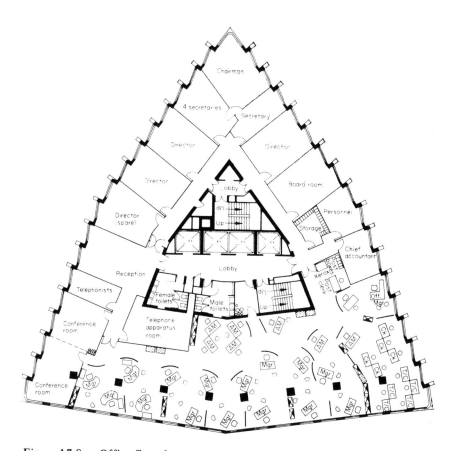

Figure 17.8   Office floor for a company headquarters
This illustrates how the design of the building influences space utilization. The window module is 8 feet. The directors' offices are 16 feet x 20 feet

The net lettable area within a building is the total area inside the walls excluding the service areas and vertical circulation, and is the figure usually used for lease documents.

These two figures are not directly comparable, and a utilization factor must be used to convert 'lettable' to 'usable'. This factor is normally between 80 and

95 per cent, but it is not uncommon for it to be as low as 70 per cent. The size of this factor is controlled by the internal shape and layout of the building, the partition modules and inactive space. This is illustrated in Figures 17.8 to 17.10.

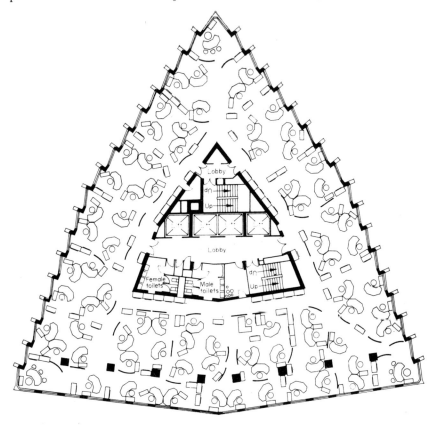

Figure 17.9   Open-space layout
This shows a much higher space utilization than that of the layout in Figure 17.8

Figure 17.8 relates to layouts used on a floor of an office building in Wembley. The requirements for the chairman and directors of this company are for offices of 200 square feet each, plus 35 square feet for corridor space, making a total of 235 square feet. In practice, because of the internal dimensions of the building and the necessity for a one-sided corridor, the directors have offices of 320 square feet with corridor space of 80 square feet making a total of 400 square feet. Thus there is a loss of 165 square feet for each director which is reflected in the availability of space. Figure 17.9 shows an open-space layout on a lower floor of the same building. In the latter case 79 people have been accommodated at an average of about 105 square feet per head, whilst on the upper floor there was room for only 56.

The building illustrated in Figure 17.10 has a more conventional shape and size than the previous example. The internal building depth is 45 feet and the window and partition module is 5 feet. On this basis, offices can be constructed with widths which are multiples of 5 feet. Because of the internal depth of the building, the individual offices will be 20 feet deep. Therefore the smallest usable office is 200 square feet. Increments can be made in steps of 100 square feet only. These figures are most unlikely to coincide with the company space standards which would have been previously established. An additional loss of space can be created in the shaded area of the plan, which can be used only for meetings or storage. However, it is likely that the requirement for these facilities would be spread in an uneven fashion throughout the building with a consequent waste of space.

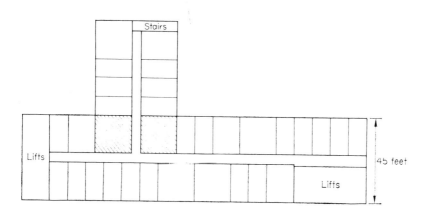

Figure 17.10   Cellular office layout
This shows a typical office building with individual offices 20 feet deep and 10, 15 or 20 feet wide. The shaded areas cannot be used for staff as there is no external light

These two examples illustrate the necessity to calculate a utilization factor when assessing the suitability of a building. If this is not done then it will probably be found that the new building does not provide enough space for all the activities which are to be accommodated. The process of establishing the utilization factor can be complex and should be undertaken with great care.

In the comparison illustrated in Figure 17.7, each building area has been reduced by this factor to establish the net usable area.

The estimated capital cost for preparing each building for occupation has been calculated in this example on the basis of £6 per square foot for buildings 1 and 2, £8 per square foot for building 3 and £10 per square foot for building 4. This would provide lighting, power, telephones, other services, partitions and so on. The fitting-out cost for internal fittings, furniture and equipment has been estimated at £4.50 per square foot for each building.

Annual costs are based on interest and amortization charges, rent, power, heating, cleaning, maintenance and other running costs. In order to compare the buildings on a common basis, a staff cost differential should also be calculated. This is a reflection of the greater efficiency that can be expected from the provision of good working conditions for staff. If it is assumed that a new building has been designed to optimize working conditions and provide the most appropriate layout and staff space standards, then existing buildings will incur additional cost as a result of any variation. Information in this field is not yet conclusive, however there is evidence to suggest that this differential can be as high as 5 per cent of staff costs. For the purpose of this example, differences of 1, 2 and 3 per cent have been used.

The totals for the annual costs give a cost comparison for the four buildings. This, together with the comparison of facilities, services and other factors, forms the basis for choosing the most appropriate course of action. In practice it is likely that these cost calculations would be based on discounted cash flow or other sophisticated accounting techniques.

FURNITURE

At an early stage in any project, the vexed question of whether to buy new furniture or retain the old is raised. In many cases, this question answers itself when the furniture is old and in a bad state of repair. In others, arguments are heard about the need for a uniform appearance or a good design image. Valid as these arguments may be, in most companies it all comes back to economics—is there an economic case for investing a significant sum of money in new office furniture and equipment? In this light, a decision can be reached based on facts and estimates instead of opinions and hunches.

During the early part of the project, considerable information will have been gathered about the methods of operation within departments and sections, and individual requirements. When selecting furniture a number of factors have to be considered.

Working surface

The size and shape of this is determined by the needs for reading, writing and meetings. The large majority of functions require space for reading and writing, no more than 36 inches by 24 inches. When additional reference material is used, this can rise to 60 inches by 30 inches. These sizes assume that suitable storage is available to each person which removes the need to use the work surface for storing papers, files, books or equipment.

If there is a need for meetings to be held at the work place, this should be reflected in the design of the work top. The conventional rectangular design is most appropriate for formal discussions between a small number of people. It is possible to encourage a more informal and relaxed atmosphere by the use of a table which is circular or hexagonal. The more a person is surrounded or protected by his furniture, the more this creates a barrier between him and his visitor.

Storage

The first requirement of any system is that all items can be easily retrieved. This means not only that retrieval must be physically simple but also that the items should be readily identifiable. An efficient system ensures that items are stored in batches and that marker tags are visible so that the information can be identified quickly.

The amount of space available for storage is critical. Too little space results in overcrowding and the use of the work top for storage purposes. This leads to inefficiency and delay for other activities. Too much space encourages bad storage discipline. Many items are kept which should be destroyed or placed elsewhere, and important items are lost in the crowd.

The speed with which each category of information is needed and the use of storage by other people must be established. These factors can be used as the basis for deciding which items should be stored at the work place and which stored elsewhere.

Communication

This factor is often overlooked when choosing furniture, although it can have a significant effect on design. For instance, the carrel type of furniture layout mentioned earlier, which consists of a small screened area with the work top and storage hung on the screen, is an efficient means of providing storage. However it discourages person-to-person contact on an informal basis. Therefore the needs for working space and storage must be balanced against the individual requirement for communication.

General

Consideration should be given to the ergonomic and anthropometric suitability of each design. In other words, it must function efficiently and easily, and it should fit the range of anatomical measurements for office staff. Both the British Standards Institution and the Furniture Industry Research Association have published data on this subject.

An analysis, as set out above, makes it possible to compare the overall advantages of different designs of furniture, and to compare them in turn with the existing furniture already in the office. It should be remembered that it requires a very small increase in staff efficiency to repay the cost of furniture. For instance, a 1 per cent increase in efficiency would save £15 to £20 per year for each junior member of the staff, and this can be much more than doubled for middle and senior staff.

IMPLEMENTATION

Layout planning

Once the furniture has been chosen, a building leased and all detailed requirements established, it is possible to carry out the detailed layout planning. This also serves as the basis for the allocation of services, the erection of partitions, and the design of all the interior.

The first step in the detailed planning process is to create a block diagram for the building. This allocates all the available space to individual departments, functions and reserve areas.

This is followed by the development of a detailed layout, which is a very critical phase. It is at this point that the immediate working environment for each individual in the organization is decided, and the result will have a significant influence on his ability and inclination to be efficient. For instance, if distraction is too high he will certainly work more slowly or make more mistakes. In a shared office, the layout for each person has an influence on all those others adjoining him, and therefore each individual's need for privacy or freedom from distraction must be considered.

When preparing the layout, it is most important to visualize it in all three dimensions. The height of screens and storage units can be forgotten when viewed on a normal two-dimensional plan. It is quite common to provide totally inadequate privacy for this reason. Another point to remember is that no one within the office will ever see the layout from the same bird's eye view as is shown on the plan. Therefore the temptation to create pretty patterns or strict regularity should be resisted. Groups must be identified clearly so that each person feels part of the team, but at the same time a feeling of individual treatment must be retained.

The layout will be affected by the availability of services such as telephone and power, as well as the interior dimensions of the building. Thus a number of priorities—some of which may be in conflict—must be balanced, as the result has a major influence on staff efficiency.

Control

In order to prepare the offices for occupation, the layouts and other planning decisions must be defined carefully in the form of a specification, so that contracts can be negotiated. If the work is likely to cost more than £10 000 it is advisable to use the services of a professional office planner or interior designer. He should check the feasibility of the company's decisions, carry out the detailed planning and design work, negotiate contracts with suppliers and other contractors, and supervise the completion of the work on time and within the cost estimates. However, before employing a professional adviser, it is important to establish clearly with him that the cost of his services will be more than recovered by the development of more cost-effective design solutions, the negotiation of larger discounts or an increase in staff efficiency.

A number of contractors and suppliers provide a design and planning service which can be used by client companies. These services are often supplied free of charge, and their cost recovered through the sale of goods. Therefore it is most important when considering the use of such advisers that the total cost of the contract including services is established at an early date.

The move

The week of the move can be a traumatic experience with lost files, damaged equipment and disgruntled staff. However, this need not be if proper planning has been done. In the first place the layout and location of departments must be settled well in advance, and all staff notified. Visits to the new building by members of the staff can go a long way to winning their cooperation during the very sensitive period prior to the move.

At an early stage in the project when filing and storage requirements are first being determined, the entire company should be directed to examine all their filing to see what items can be disposed of or put into an archive store. This will usually reduce the total requirement by at least 25 per cent. This initial operation is likely to have taken place six to twelve months before the move date. If in the week immediately before the move the exercise is repeated, it is probable that an additional 10 per cent can be saved.

The layout plans for the new offices should be clearly marked with room numbers and floor codes. If large open offices are used, a coded grid should be devised so that each desk or other piece of furniture can be located by a map reference code. Each member of the staff should then be notified of the code for his new location in the building and all items of furniture, equipment and paperwork should be clearly marked with this code. This will enable the removal team to assemble items together and ensure that they are taken to their right location. It is almost inevitable that some items will go astray during the move and this coding system will enable them to be rerouted.

Throughout this period, it is most important that a senior member of the staff has overall control of all operations and is present throughout the move.

CONTINUING ADMINISTRATION

The planning and other work that has been carried out should have resulted in the efficient occupation of the building. However, it must be remembered that this is right only for this company and at this point in time. Every company is constantly changing in size, organization and techniques. Therefore within a relatively short period of time, a number of changes will be necessary in order to ensure continuing efficiency. These changes must be closely controlled or the result can quickly deteriorate into a form of accommodation anarchy. It is of the utmost importance that a senior man, probably the office manager, has direct responsibility for all alterations to furniture, layout and services. He should have been closely involved during the planning of the new offices, so that he is fully aware of the planning philosophy and operational requirements for each department. If individual departmental managers are allowed to make major changes to their own accommodation this can affect the accommodation of other departments and is almost certain to result in a reduced space utilization.

The office manager has a major effect on company overhead costs. An office is a very expensive and highly complex management tool which must be used with intelligence and foresight. It is important that every member of the staff knows how to use the furniture and equipment they are given. It is rare to see desk drawers being used effectively, or chairs being adjusted to the right height. The office manager's role should be much closer in attitude to the production manager's role than is normally the case. He must be aware of the cost effectiveness of the decisions which he takes and he should not necessarily go for the cheapest solution. For instance, the cheapest item may also be the one which will wear out or break down first, or the cheapest service facility may have an adverse effect on staff efficiency. All these considerations must be taken into account if the new offices are to continue to meet the long-term requirements established at the beginning of the project.

FURTHER READING

Planned Open Offices (Cost Benefit Analysis), Department of the Environment, Whitehall Development Group, London.

B. Robichaud, *Selecting, Planning and Managing Office Space,* McGraw-Hill, New York, 1958.

P. Manning (ed), *Office Design* (A study of environment), Pilkington Research *Office Building (Architects Journal* handbook), series published 1973–5.

M. Mogulescu, *Profit through Design,* American Management Association, New York, 1970.

18

Role of O & M

R H Reed

Good organization of a company is as essential to its success as is the particular technical, professional or other expertise on which the company is based. Similarly, a company requires more or less complex systems and procedures for handling the information which is used to control operations and in making decisions. The administration of a company depends on these two factors: organization—by which work is divided among individuals or groups and the working relationship between them is defined; and the office—which in its widest sense is the means of handling the information of a company and which provides the system of communications by which it is controlled. A company has to adapt its organization to its changing needs and circumstances and will correspondingly find it necessary to adapt its office systems and methods. Failure to do so may limit its success or its growth.

WHEN IS AN O & M DEPARTMENT NECESSARY?

In a very small company, problems of organization and method, while not unimportant, are relatively minor. The lines of communication are short, most communication is direct and relationships are face to face and unformalized. Paperwork tends to be at a minimum and the boss and his few aides may run the company with only the most elementary of systems and little in the way of formal procedure. As a company grows in size its operations usually become more complex. The organization necessarily becomes more defined and formalized even though it may be structured in such a way as to retain as far as possible the advantages of flexibility of the smaller concern. The office functions which prove necessary to this increasing size are accompanied by defined systems and procedures and more sophisticated methods of processing information whether in handling orders, keeping the accounts or planning production.

A company reaches a point at which office work accounts for a significant number of employees, where its managers need to be competent at administration as well as their own jobs and there needs to be someone in the company who as part of his job has an overall responsibility for office work, staff and systems, including staff productivity. Beyond this stage when a company becomes large its main structure and detailed organization require no less attention than its main activities do. It is likely to be using costly office machinery and employing specialists to analyse and design its systems, and anything approaching a reasonably detailed knowledge of the whole organization and its systems may well be beyond the capacity of any one individual.

Whatever its size or stage of development, to be efficient a company needs to keep its organization and methods under regular review. It should, in addition, make a complete reappraisal every few years. The means by which this is done are likely to depend on the size of the company concerned. In the smaller company it may well be a responsibility of the secretary, accountant or office manager. Larger companies will probably employ a full-time specialist in organization and methods whose job is to advise the management of the company in this field. In the largest companies and groups there is likely to be a management services department acting as an internal consultancy service and including on its staff specialists in general organization and methods, operational research, computers and data processing, and management accounting and control.

There is a considerable difference in practice between the continuing review and improvement and the periodic major review and reorganization. The former tends to deal with only a section or department at a time or with partial aspects of an overall system. The latter, however, to be effective, must be concerned with the business as a whole and it follows that the scope and level of the work involved may be substantially different. Both kinds of review, but especially the latter, should be carried out by someone who has the necessary general knowledge and experience of business and the specialist knowledge of organization and methods, office machinery and equipment and work measurement. He should also be able to take the time needed to study problems in depth and be so placed as to be able to give independent advice on matters which affect the company as a whole. This is the role of the O & M man.

A company of sufficient size will employ its own O & M department or management services department which will deal with the process of continuous review and improvement, and, provided it is of the right calibre and is properly placed, will also undertake major reviews. Smaller and medium-sized companies which are members of a larger group may have access to a central O & M or management services department. In those which have to rely on their own resources it is advisable that a person in a position of senior administrative responsibility, for example the company secretary or accountant, should be charged with the responsibility to keep abreast of developments in the field of O & M and maintain a continuous review of the company's organization and office methods not only to ensure that improvements are made but to recognize when there are problems or opportunities which require either the time or specialist knowledge which cannot be made available from within. In these circumstances such assistance and advice can be sought from external consultants.

O & M and management services departments can, as a rule, be supported only by the larger companies. It is nevertheless a fact that the larger companies commission most of the work done by external consultants. In spite of the impression of the predominance of large businesses in Britain, the majority of companies in the country are small to medium-sized and employ a large proportion of the working population. For this reason, the rest of this chapter is written primarily with the needs of small and medium-sized companies in mind. It will tell the larger company little that it does not already know. It is intended to convey to the small and medium-sized company an appreciation of the subject to enable it to judge whether and when to set up an O & M department and how to organize it, and to know how to go about using consultants.

ORGANIZING AN O & M DEPARTMENT

The way in which an O & M department comes into being will vary from one company to another. In some companies it has grown out of a department having some special concern with office systems and methods such as internal audit. In others it has been set up from scratch as a result of a recognition by the board of the need to improve administrative efficiency and not infrequently following a recommendation by consultants.

Preliminary considerations

The way in which O & M is first set up is likely to influence considerably the scope of its work, the level at which it subsequently operates and, at least initially, the acceptance of its role in the company. It is essential, as with any other function, that it should not be set up in accordance with preconceived ideas or in imitation of another company. It should be set up to meet the particular needs of the particular company and although different companies will frequently have similar needs, they will seldom be identical. It follows that before setting up O & M the board should thoroughly understand what O & M is and should have a clear idea of the kind of work and scope of operation for O & M in their particular company. In particular they should decide whether their need is to improve the management structure and overall administration of the business, to redesign major company systems, to improve the methods and organization of work in individual departments or sections, to improve the productivity of clerical employees, or to do all of these.

It is difficult to generalize about when a company can or should set up an O & M department and the number of staff that will be required. Some quite large companies have simple organization structures and employ relatively few office staff. In contrast the organization of some small companies is very complex and the office employees may in some cases outnumber the manual and technical employees. In practice it is unlikely that a company having say twenty office employees could use a full-time O & M officer; a company with eighty office employees might well justify one and it would be exceptional if a company with 200 office employees could not profit from the services of a full-time practitioner.

Placing the department

The placing of O & M in an organization plays a large part in enabling it to operate effectively. The best placing will differ from one company to another. It is important that O & M should report to a sufficiently senior person so as to enable it to operate through all departments; it is unwise therefore to attach it to any particular department where it might be used only as a tool for that department and where its impartiality might be questioned. O & M needs to be sponsored preferably by a board member who understands the role and scope of the function and who can ensure that it is given the chance to operate at the required level. He should keep a watch on general progress and ensure that the climate and working relationships are right but should not concern himself with the detail of the work undertaken by O & M for the different parts of the business. In practice the sponsor may be the managing director or some other senior official having an interest in overall administrative efficiency such as the administrative or financial director or company secretary.

The main value of O & M, as with all advisory work, is the ability to take a fresh and independent view of a problem and to take the time to study it properly. O & M must therefore be advisory in character but should wherever possible be involved in implementing proposals that have been agreed.

Relationships with other management services

The O & M man is the general practitioner in the field of improving office and administrative efficiency. He may be working alone in a company or he may be one of a team comprising a management services department which may include work study, operational research, data processing or other specialists. In either situation as general practitioner, he should be able to recognize when problems or situations require specialist treatment and he will frequently find himself needing the assistance of, or working with, such specialists. A common situation occurs in the company which has both an O & M department and a data processing department. This may present problems, but given sensible organization it need not. It is a mistake to approach problems with the firm intention of finding a computer solution to them, and this is more likely to occur where a data processing department employing only computer specialists is the senior partner in the systems field. It is advisable that there be close liaison between both units and that each has a clear understanding of the role and function of the other. How this is achieved will depend on the particular set-up and the individuals concerned.

Selecting staff for O & M

When setting up O & M for the first time, the choice of man to start and establish the function is more critical than the subsequent selection of staff. Where a department is being established as a result of recommendations by consultants, it is likely that they will advise on the choice of man and will assist in establishing the department in its early operations. Where O & M is being set up in response to some particular major problem or development, such as the installation of data processing equipment, the need for specialist knowledge or experience will influence the choice. In all cases a sound general practitioner experience coupled with breadth of outlook will prove most valuable in the long run. Subsequent staffing may be both from outside and from the company's existing personnel.

It is seldom wise to employ a man in O & M until he has had several years of practical business experience; not for the particular experience, but in order that he shall have gained a reasonable background of how business is organized, a knowledge of commercial procedures and an understanding of and maturity in dealing with people at work. People in O & M coming from different backgrounds in terms of education, training and experience can, given the opportunity to acquire the particular knowledge and expertise, do equally well. What characterizes the successful O & M man is more his personal qualities than his specialized expertise. Personal qualities to be sought are common sense, a real interest in solving problems and improving the way things are done, good power of observation with the requisite analytical ability and the feel for a constructive and workable solution, the tact to deal with people at all levels and, finally, clarity of thought and expression and the ability to sell his ideas but to negotiate to a realistic compromise when necessary.

For many people nowadays, a few years spent in O & M or some other branch of management services is looked on as a useful means of enlarging their experience and giving them a wider view of a company. Others may wish to make their careers in management services and after a few years in a company may wish to move on to greater responsibilities in a larger concern or join a firm of consultants. Whenever practicable it is of advantage to employ both kinds and to anticipate and provide for movement into and out of the department.

Training staff

O & M is an intensely practical job and formal training is no substitute for sound and varied experience in the field. Such experience is normally best obtained by working on assignments with a senior practitioner or as a member of a small project team. This kind of training may be difficult to arrange in a small company but may be compensated to an extent by the range of problems likely to be encountered in a shorter time. Further training in general O & M and in specific techniques can be obtained through courses run by technical colleges, professional institutes and consultants. Such training should be supplemented by attending exhibitions of machines and equipment and the meetings of professional societies and institutes. Visits to other companies and exchange of experience with other practitioners are of great value.

USING CONSULTANTS

The use of management consultants by all kinds of business, commerce and public service, has been increasing year by year. The reasons for seeking their services are as diverse as the assignments they undertake and their contribution to the continuous improvement in the standards of business management and to increasing productivity has been considerable.

Firms of consultants range in size from the one-man concern or small partnership to the handful of very large firms which employ several hundred consultants. Some are general management consultants covering the whole field and of these some are particularly strong in certain fields or techniques. Some are primarily specialists, but may offer supporting services in related areas. Several of the well-known firms of accountants have established management consulting branches. In addition there are also consultants who specialize in dealing with the smaller company.

Apart from dealing with technical, manufacturing or marketing activities, consultants are frequently employed to advise on organization, administration and office methods, computers and the use of techniques such as clerical work measurement. The circumstances in which consultants may be called in might include:

1   To deal with a specific problem area such as the installation of better production control or management accounting methods and systems

2   To improve staff productivity by improving methods and using clerical work measurement

3   To undertake an overall review of offices and administration when a company has outgrown its present systems and these require major change including possibly installation of data processing

machinery

4   To carry out a general audit of the administration of the company on the basis of a periodic check-up, possibly as part of an overall review of the company

5   To carry out a specific project when the company has no staff of its own having either the time or the expertise

Consultant's fees amount to a significant expenditure by the company that decides to employ them. It is therefore important to choose carefully, to know what can be expected of them and, no less important, to know what the client should do in order to make best use of them.

The decision to seek the help of a consultant should have been preceded by thorough and careful consideration of the problem to be dealt with and should be agreed by the whole board. The reason for seeking their advice should be set out clearly to provide a firm basis on which preliminary discussions can be carried out.

Unless there is prior knowledge of the particular consultants best suited to the job, it is wise to get in touch with two or three firms. The problem should be clearly stated, followed by a discussion of what their approach to it would be. This discussion should also elicit some indication of their previous work. Consultants do not advertise. The Management Consultants Association, of which not all are members, gives general advice on the basis for selecting a consultant and a list of member firms. Gower Press publishes the *Register of Management Consultants* which includes details of nearly 1000 organizations. The BIM and CBI maintain a register of consultants but neither of these bodies will recommend a particular firm. It is, however, usually possible to find companies which have used particular consultants and get an appreciation of what kind of work was done and how well it was carried out.

The consultants initially approached should be given the opportunity to make a preliminary survey, which may take from a few days to a few weeks, and should be asked to submit outline proposals of how they would handle the assignment, how long it would take and their estimate of the costs, savings and benefits. They should also say what staff they would assign to the project. The proposal should set out their terms which are usually based on a time rate either hourly, weekly or monthly and normally includes the cost of supervision. It should also set out the arrangements for cancelling the assignment at short notice.

To get the maximum benefit from consultants, it is essential to appreciate that their role is primarily advisory and that their main value to the client is in taking the time to study a problem fully, in giving an independent view and in having appropriate specialist knowledge and supporting resources. The client should therefore, following necessary preliminary survey and discussion, set down the agreed terms of reference clearly and ensure that these are thoroughly understood by both parties. Before the consultant starts, the staff should be briefed about the nature, purpose and scope of the assignment and it is usually advisable to appoint a senior staff member to look after liaison and generally assist the consultant in making the internal arrangements necessary to smooth working. There should be regular discussion on progress and regular progress reports and meetings.

Best results come from a partnership between client and consultant and where the recommendations emerge and are agreed during the study, rather than coming entirely in the final report. It is advantageous to both client and consultant that the consultant should himself assist in implementing whatever proposals are agreed and that the criteria by which the success of the project are to be judged should be clear. Where practicable the consultant should be given the opportunity of maintaining contact after completion to assess the success of the project.

FURTHER READING

J.M. Pfiffner and F.P. Sherwood, *Administrative Organisation,* Prentice Hall, Engelwood Cliffs, New Jersey, 1960.

W. Puckey, *Organization in Business Management,* Hutchinson, London, 1963.

G.E. Milward (ed), *O and M–A Service to Management,* Macmillan, London, 1957.

M. Symes, *Office Procedures and Management,* Heinemann, London, 1969.

B.H. Walley, *Management Services Handbook,* Business Books, London, 1973.

19

Design and Control of Documentation

P M Smith

Forms design and control is valuable not primarily because it is a money saver, but because a properly designed form assists users and can create a favourable image to recipients. Savings there are, but except for printing costs they are usually intangible.

Forms control is becoming more vital in industry and commerce for several reasons, not least of which is the paper explosion caused by the increased use of computers, and by increased government documentation. The most important reason for it, however, is that it is the centre around which methods and systems can be controlled. If it is known what forms exist, then it is possible to achieve common systems throughout the company, and to streamline the organization. Through forms control, new systems can be designed around existing documentation.

FORMS CONTROL

Generally, forms control is the elimination of forms not needed and the elimination of two or more different forms serving the same purpose. Forms control and systems control frequently become related.

FORMS DESIGN

Forms design is more superficial. It relates to such aspects as uniform design standards; adequate appearance; layout compatible with the clerical procedure. The latter is also an aspect of forms control.

CONSIDERATIONS BEFORE SETTING UP DESIGN AND CONTROL

Forms design and control alone will bring no great savings. There may be an initial saving from the elimination of unnecessary forms, but continual review will cost money. Forms control can be beneficial if a system requires changing or if a new system has to be designed, since existing forms may be usable. Lack of forms control may mean that suitable forms were not known to exist. The first consideration, therefore, is a realization that substantial savings will not accrue unless forms design and control is allied to systems control.

The next consideration is whether the management is prepared to set up machinery to review all forms used, to investigate all requests for forms, and to maintain an adequate forms register. The department responsible for control and design must be reasonably conversant with printing methods, paper qualities required and the economics of make-up of form sets.

Thirdly, it is possible that forms design and control can create systems awareness amongst staff. This can be double-edged. If management appreciates the effort required, and if it considers the return adequate, then it can institute design and control.

APPROACH TO FORMS DESIGN

Assuming design and control has not existed, it would be foolish to go the whole way in one go. In the first place the amount of work would be great, and secondly, needless opposition—both practical and emotive—would be aroused.

Forms design is the correct starting position, progressively obtaining a grip on the subject. For example, start on new forms only and requests for amendments to existing forms. This will bring gradual acceptance of new paper sizes, new type faces, and new methods of making up form sets. The way is thus paved for greater control.

Next begin the redrawing and simple redesign of existing forms. This can be achieved by obtaining agreement from the stationery store and the buyer to refer all forms as they come up for reorder. Above all, decide if a form is needed.

Forms register

Immediately control of design begins, a forms register must be introduced. This minimizes later pains. The structure of the register must be as simple as possible. At all costs, avoid a register classification based on who uses a form. The function of the form should be the base of the classification. The register should contain a numerical listing of all forms and a copy of each form filed by form function, together with a copy of the form specification sheet. A form specification sheet is shown in Figure 19.1. The purpose of the sheet is to give sufficient information regarding form users, print orders, printing instructions, copies used and other details.

A suggested form classification method is shown at the end of this chapter. Always try to get people to quote form numbers since this assists the forms designer to locate the correct form. Filing forms by function also assists in standardizing form titles and in searching the file to ascertain if similar forms can be used in conjunction with new form requests.

APPROACH TO FORMS CONTROL

Assuming that forms design is now accepted by staff, forms control can be introduced. This is far more difficult than control of forms design, requiring as it does knowledge of the company procedures. It must involve delving into procedures and the way people work. In its simplest element, forms control must have the ultimate objective of creating common systems within the organization and eliminating unnecessary forms.

Two examples will be sufficient to show the need for control. A company had three operating divisions on one site, and it was found that six different forms existed concerning the loan of cars. Moreover, each division had a separate short packings and pilferage procedure. Another company also had three operating divisions on one site. Two of the divisions manufactured similar products, and each division had its own stores record and issue procedures, and its own goods received procedure.

These are extreme cases requiring considerable reorganization, but in each case, control of documentation in the different divisions would have resulted in considerable savings. Essentially, this is what forms control is about. Essentially also, these examples indicate how forms control and systems control become related. It is when these forms of control *are* related that savings can become great.

Again, decide if a form is needed. Far too frequently purpose-designed forms are designed when notebooks, memo forms or letterheads can be used.

The premium for ordering small quantities is considerable and therefore such requests should be discouraged. In any case, give little time to justifiable requests for forms to be used in very small quantities. Also, when someone requires, say, a standard letter, just tell them to put it on a letterhead and have it duplicated.

IDEAS RELATING TO SYSTEMS AND FORMS

This section is designed to stimulate thought in the direction of creative forms design. Some practical examples are listed overleaf:

					Form specification sheet

Form title   **Form number**

Form details

Type of set	Serially numbered	Number of copies	Copies reproduced by	Punching. hole centres and position

Copy number	Current revision	Paper size	Paper weight	Paper colour	Ink colour	Perforation	Distribution

Miscellaneous details

Usage details

Annual consumption	Reorder level	Reorder quantity	Charge printing to

List those departments completing the form

Supplier details

Printed by

Figure 19.1   Form specification sheet

Original system for orders. The customer sent an order to the supplier. The supplier typed the order details on to his own documents which formed part of a computer system.

Revised system. This is illustrated in Figure 19.2. The supplier gave his customers printed order forms, consisting of four-part sets interleaved with one-time carbon, for the customer to complete. The customer retained the bottom two copies and sent the top two copies to the supplier.

The supplier returned one copy as acknowledgement of the order and from the remaining copy made sufficient internal copies by dye line machine.

An incentive to customers can be provided by supplying prepaid addressed envelopes.

Advantages. No transcription by the supplier eliminated errors. The main job left for the supplier's clerks comprised product coding when this was introduced in 1970. Savings of over £1000 per year were achieved on only 1200 orders per year.

It is quite feasible to develop an integral system of making works order copies, dispatch notes, advice notes and invoices all from the one copy left in the supplier's hands.

Machining a shaft. In an engineering concern, a shaft was to be machined, involving seventeen different machining operations. A separate job ticket was needed for each operation, each job ticket containing the following repetitive information:

1   Job number
2   Drawing number
3   Drawing item
4   Item description
5   Number of items to be machined

In an organization where each job ticket was individually typed, the repetitive information was repeated eighty-five times (with all the risks of error) followed by the particular machining operation. A line-selection spirit duplicator, costing £500 was installed to duplicate the information, and the clerical staff was immediately reduced by two.

The system is very simple and is illustrated in Figure 19.3. All repetitive (fixed) information is entered on the top of a sheet of paper, followed by a description in list form, of each machining operation. Behind the paper is a sheet of carbon. When all machining operations have been entered on the sheet, the fixed information section is separated from the machining description section. Both parts are put into a duplicating machine. The machine mechanism produces a job ticket for each machining operation. The ticket contains the fixed information and the machining operation instruction.

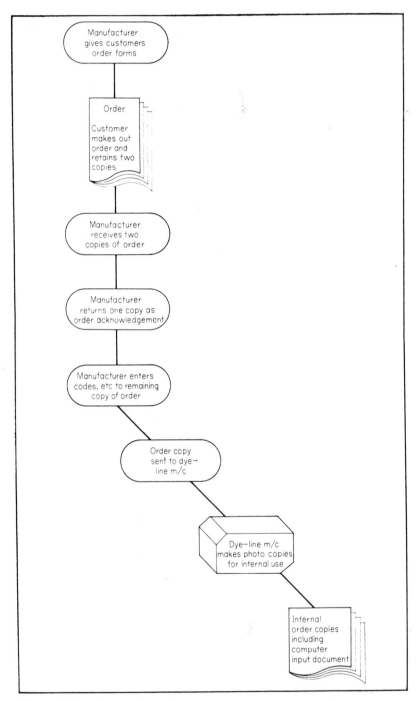

Figure 19.2   System for orders

Job tickets can also be made using Addressograph equipment. This method is only viable when the operations are repeated over and over again and not as part of a jobbing machine-shop activity.

Work with copying machines.   Many firms have not realized the potential of these machines. In fact, such machines are economical for some applications but prohibitive for others. Basically, all the systems use overlays.

Assume you have an order form in a magazine or a newspaper and the form is completed by the customer. Using overlays over the order it is possible to make

1   The order acknowledgement
2   The warehouse copy
3   Dispatch note
4   Delivery note

The cost would be much less than making your own documentation. By stacking the orders correctly, the bank paying-in slip can be made on the machine as well as the cashbook sheet. All these documents can be made for a cost of between 10p and 15p, error free and cheaper than conventional clerical methods. The method of operation is illustrated in Figure 19.4.

Forms work using address plates.   Much can be done with address plates such as those marketed by Addressograph. Payroll is one example. Address plates are used to provide the payroll list each week. These plates contain embossed details of employees' names and fixed weekly deductions. The rest of the payroll is effected by accounting machine or by clerical means.

Control of maintenance of machines can also be dealt with by such methods. Some jobs need doing weekly, others monthly, others quarterly. Instead of writing a ticket by hand each time, this work can be done by address plates. Work required is put on to the address plate. At the appropriate time, the address plate is used to make the job ticket.

There are endless possibilities for this type of equipment—credit transfers, listings of credit transfers, dividend warrants. With the latter, the warrants can be made out even with the value entered.

MADE-UP FORM SETS

Much recent form design has been in the field of form sets using one-time carbons and copying machines.

If we take an example involving three separate documents such as an order acceptance, an advice note and a purchase requisition, one form can be designed to eliminate repetitive work by duplicating information.

The two sheets of carbon paper contain specific cut-out sections so that

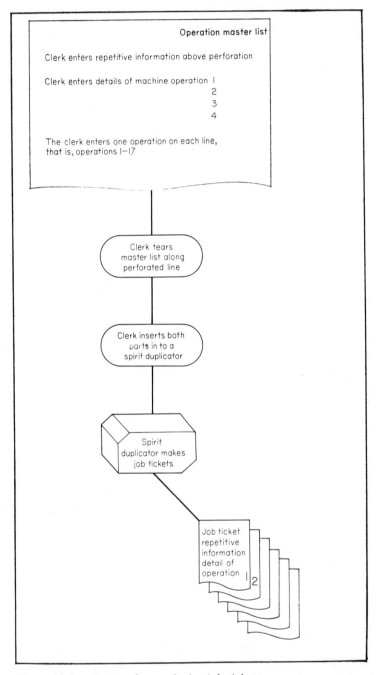

Operation master list

Clerk enters repetitive information above perforation

Clerk enters details of machine operation 1
2
3
4

The clerk enters one operation on each line,
that is, operations 1—17

Clerk tears
master list along
perforated line

Clerk inserts both
parts in to a
spirit duplicator

Spirit
duplicator makes
job tickets

Job ticket
repetitive
information
detail of
operation 1 2

Figure 19.3   System for producing job tickets
Seventeen job tickets are made. Each ticket contains the
repetitive information and details of one machine operation

certain information required on the top copy is not transmitted to either the centre or bottom copies. The same principle can be used for information on only the top and bottom copies or any other combination required. If this system is used correctly it can help prevent both repetitive writing and errors, while at the same time providing a faster turnround of documentation. A considerable cost saving in clerical time is thereby achieved.

DESIGNING THE FORM

The aims of forms control and design have been set out as well as suggestions regarding systems applications. This section briefly states some design considerations. Forms control and design procedure are discussed later in the chapter.

Use of the form

First, ensure that the use of the form is understood. Secondly, determine what entries—including length of entry—are needed. Do not put in entry spaces just in case they are needed. However, do try to design a form allowing for flexibility and change in statutory requirements such as changes in the rate of VAT.

Determine who needs the form and how it will be completed (hand or machine). This investigation work is frequently best done in conjunction with a forms control sheet (see Figure 19.5). Design should not start until these questions have been answered.

Layout and printing

The printer must be given a drawing, either a rough sketch or an accurate drawing. Accurate drawings are not difficult if a designing grid is used. Two examples are shown in Figures 19.6 and 19.7, one of which can be obtained from the Stationery Office.

Layout, type sizes and type faces are important, as well as paper and ink colours. Always have the company name and a title on the form. The forms design specification sheet (Figure 19.1) is an excellent example of good layout. Note how vertical lines are justified and compare against the example of bad layout in Figure 19.9. Note the correct positionings of entries in the specification sheet. All headings for entries are left-hand justified and not centralized. Again, compare against the bad layout example.

Always put the company name and the form title on the form. Headings should be readily understood to prevent confusion by those completing the form.

If you have your own printing department, very adequate art work can be drawn internally with a Rotring pen and a typewriter with small elite type face. Concerning print sizes when the work is printed by an outside printer, use

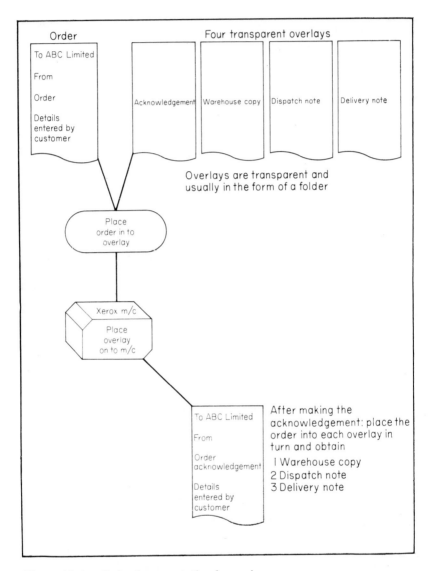

Figure 19.4   Order documentation by copier
When several orders are received at one time, the work can be batched by first making all the acknowledgements, then all the warehouse copies and so on

Forms design control sheet		

Form request

Department	Person	Date

Forms design control sheet

Design by	Form title

Design data

Form entries by	Form used for
Hand	
Typing	
Other (describe)	

	Copies made by
	One-time carbon ☐ Sensitised paper ☐ Duplicating ☐
Number of copies made	Loose carbons ☐ Dye-line ☐ Photocopy ☐

Form make up   Filing

Loose sheets, pads or sets (state)	Filing requirement (State yes/no)
	Left hand Top Holes

Annual usage   Completion frequency

Total number of copies	Daily ☐ Weekly ☐ Monthly ☐
	Quarterly ☐ Other ☐ ☐

Form distribution (state who)   Form used by recipients for

Can existing form be modified to suit?

Yes/no	If no, Why?

Entry spaces on recipients' copies

Would these assist?

Completion method and sequence of completion

Method change advantageous (Yes/no)	Reason for answers
Sequence change advantageous (Yes/no)	

Figure 19.5   Forms design control sheet

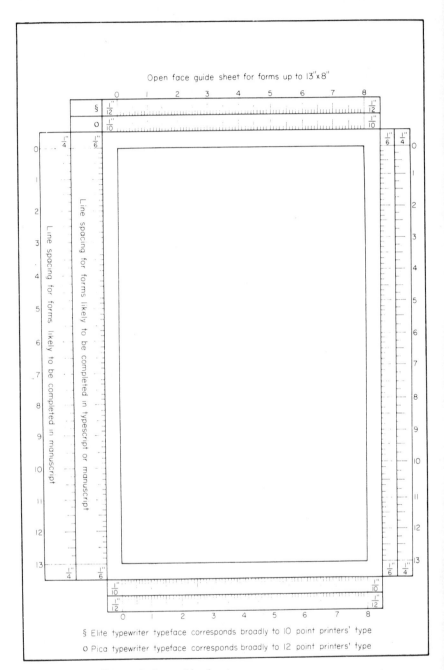

Figure 19.6   Forms design guide sheet
Reduced to one-third of the original size. These sheets are available from the Stationery Office

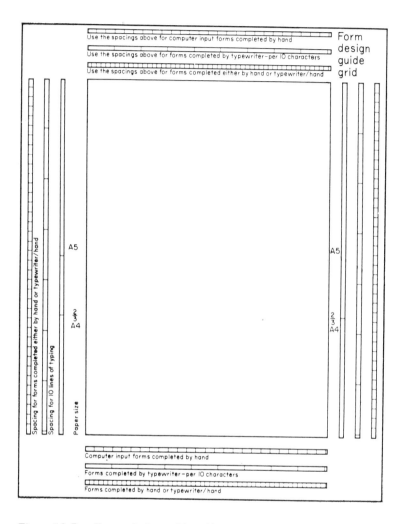

Figure 19.7   Forms design guide grid
Reduced to one-third of the original size

no more than two sizes on one form. For form headings, 13-point or 20-point type face is usually adequate. The remainder of the form should be 9-point type face. Univers and Gill Sans are suitable type faces. Examples are shown in Figure 19.8.

In regard to paper colour and ink colour, avoid red and other colours which tire the eyes, and colours that affect copying machines. Some colours will not copy. In most cases wove paper is suitable, but consult your printers who can be helpful. Always consult the form user, and remember that shiny paper is difficult to write on. Do not expect a typist to be able to type a 12-part set and obtain readable copies.

Gill Bold (275)

8D ON 9 PT.
When jobs have type sizes fixed

12 PT.
When jobs have type sizes fixed

18 PT.
When jobs have type sizes fixed

Univers 751-75

8 PT.
The P16 computer

12 PT.
The P16 computer

18 PT.
The P16 computer

Figure 19.8   Examples of type faces suitable for use in forms
When emphasis is required, use the same type size but in bold

Colour coding between departments

Some firms use different paper colours or ink colours to denote that one colour goes to Dept A, another colour to Dept B and so on. Such methods increase print costs and bring no clerical savings.

Pads and sets of forms

Should forms be made up into pads or sets as part of the printing process? Without doubt these methods are valid at times but the increases should be justified, particularly that of padding. Forms made into sets are frequently useful and of value when the forms are printed on sensitized paper. For example, if an invoice is in a five-part set it is much easier for the user to pick a set out of a box than to collate separate sheets.

Regarding sensitized paper, ensure that the paper is suitable for the job by testing it. Note particularly the following points:

Will a copying machine copy it?
Does the paper soil the fingers? (Important if the form has to be
handled frequently)
Are copies readable?
Is it possible to write notes on the paper?
Do filed copies curl?
Will exposure to light affect copies?
Remember that qualities will vary from one supplier to another

PAPER SIZES AND FORM ENTRY-SPACE DIMENSIONS

International (DIN) sizes are rapidly becoming accepted. In any case metrication
will automatically bring universal acceptance. The two sizes for normal forms are
Size A4—210mm x 297mm (8¼″ x 11¾″)
Size A5—148mm x 210mm (5⅞″ x 8¼″)
Increasingly $\frac{2}{3}$A4 is used for some applications. The standard entry-space
dimensions are:

METHOD OF ENTRY	SPACING	DIMENSIONS
Typewriter	Horizontal	1/10″ per character
	Vertical	1/6″ for each line
Typewriter/hand writing	Horizontal	1/8″ per character
	Vertical	1/3″ between lines
Hand written (not computer-input forms)	Horizontal	1/8″ per character
	Vertical	1/4″ between lines
Hand written computer-input forms	Horizontal	1/6″ per character
	Vertical	1/4″ between lines

Forms completed by typewriter should never be horizontally lined unless such
lines indicate divisions between different entry spaces. Forms completed by
hand or typewriter/hand must always have horizontal guiding lines.

FORMS CONTROL IN OPERATION IN A LARGE ORGANIZATION

This section describes a forms design and control system designed some years
ago. The system uses metric measurements only.
The system description is in four parts:

1   Forms Design Specification Section I which is available and issued to all departments
2   Forms Design Specification Section II which is available only in the systems department
3   Systems Department Operating Instruction which is available only in the systems department
4   Forms Control Specification which is available only in the systems department

The idea is to encourage any person to design the forms he needs and then submit them for approval. Hence Section I is of a general nature readily understandable by all. The remaining sections are more technical and aimed at knowledgeable forms designers. Therefore these sections are retained in the systems department as they are not likely to be fully comprehended elsewhere.

Forms design specification—Section I

Design of forms.   Any person may design and draw a form. Forms must not be used before the form has been approved and a form number allocated.

Objectives of forms design

1   To ensure that all forms are designed to one standard layout
2   To ensure a high standard of appearance consistent with correct layout
3   To ensure that the layout is compatible with the clerical procedure, that form entry spaces are in correct sequence and that the entries are readily seen and understood

Purpose of specification.   This specification formalizes the standards against which forms must be designed.

Approval of form.   Design approval is given by the chief O & M systems analyst and the head of department using the form. Details will be shown on a form design specification sheet which must accompany each form for approval.
     The chief O & M analyst may refuse approval to print, on control grounds. These grounds are outlined in the forms control specification.

General design details.   In the top lefthand corner of each form will be a logo. In the top right hand corner will be the form title on the same baseline as the logo. A solid logo must be used if the form is sent outside the company and an outline logo when the form is internal. The logo will be lefthand justified with a column heading and not with a line or margin ruling.

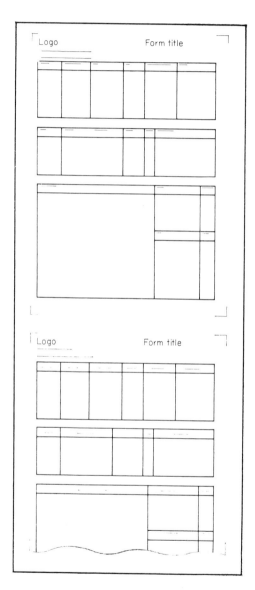

Figure 19.9 **Permissible and impermissible form designs**
The top (permissible) design has: headings in top left corner, vertical lines justified one below the other and headings justified one below the other. The bottom (impermissible) design has: headings not in top left corner, vertical lines not justified one below the other and form title not justified above a heading

All form titles will be justified with the wording of a column heading on the righthand side of the form.

All headings must be lefthand justified, that is as far to the left as possible and in the top corner if boxes are used. The points discussed in both this paragraph and the previous paragraph are illustrated in Figure 19.9.

The first letter of a title must be in upper case (capital letter) and the remainder lower case except proper nouns when the first letter must always be upper case.

Points for guidance.   Establish the need for the form. Check that there is no existing form suitable.

Evaluate source material (for example: how is the material submitted to the person completing the form? Is the source material in the same sequence as the sequence of the material required by recipients of the form?)

Examine how the information entered on to the form is used.

Design details.   Entry-space dimensions must be as follows:

FORM COMPLETED BY	SPACING	DIMENSION
Typewriter	Horizontal	23mm per 10 characters
	Vertical	42mm per 10 lines single spaced
Typewriter/hand writing	Horizontal Vertical	4mm per character lines spaced alternately 8mm and 9mm apart
Handwritten Computer-input forms	Horizontal Vertical	6mm per character lines spaced 8mm apart
Other handwritten forms	Horizontal Vertical	4mm per character lines spaced 8mm apart

Normally, entry spaces should be a little longer than the expected entry requires. Otherwise, the form may be difficult to complete and it may have an overcrowded appearance after completion. Entry spaces on computer input documents must be dimensioned to accept only the permitted number of entries.

Headings and title positions must be lefthand justified. Figure 19.9 gives correct and incorrect examples.

Alignment of lines: Figure 19.9 gives correct and incorrect examples. Dividing lines must be aligned, where possible, with those above. Rectangle (boxes or panels) entry spaces are preferred but this is not mandatory.

Permissible paper sizes.   Only DIN (international) paper sizes are permitted. The three usual sizes are:

A4=210mm x 297mm
A5–148mm x 210mm
B4–250mm x 353mm
A4 is intended to replace quarto and foolscap
A5 is intended for forms approximately half quarto
B4 is for those foolscap forms which cannot be condensed to **A4**

Paper quality.   Systems department will advise the most suitable paper to be used.

Drawing the form.   Drawings submitted should be drawn on the forms design grid. Copies of the grid are obtainable from systems department. Systems department are responsible for the final drawing to either internal print department or outside printers.

Forms design specification–Section II

Investigation of request for a form.   Establish the purpose of the form and cycle of operations.
    Before doing any design work, use a forms design control sheet and:

1   Establish the purpose of the form
2   Study how the form is completed
3   Where does the information entered on to the form come from, and in what form

Establish the contents of the form:

1   The entry space needed and those parts not needed
2   How data entered on the form is submitted
3   The constant information that can be preprinted
4   The method of form entry–manual or machine or both
5   The average length and maximum length of entries
6   The average number and maximum number of entries
7   The frequency of maximum entries (continuation sheets or two sheets may be more suitable than a large sheet if the maximum entries are infrequent)
8   The sequence of entries

Drawing the form.   The method of printing (internally or outside) determines the type of drawing made. In any case, the form must be drawn on a form design grid. If the form is printed outside, a pencil drawing with handwritten entries is sufficient. The drawing must show all dimensions, perforation instructions, numbering instructions, type sizes, and colour.

If the form is printed internally, a full-size pen-and-ink drawing will be made on to which will be typed form headings and title using a microface typewriter.

Type sizes used (where artwork is prepared outside).   No more than two type sizes shall be used on one form. The type sizes to be used are:

Univers 689 8D on 9 point for address and column headings, unless emphasis is required, in which case Univers 693 8D on 9 point shall be used. Univers 693 18D on 20 point or 12D on 13 point must be used for form titles unless a bolder title is required when Univers 696 shall be used.

Permitted paper weight (thickness).   61 gsm weight paper shall, normally, be used unless multiple copies are required.

49 gsm weight paper or combinations of 49 gsm and 61 gsm will be used for mutlipart forms.

Permitted paper qualities.   Three paper qualities (types) of paper are commonly used:

1   Plain
2   Sensitized (NCR, Corafax)
3   Translucent

The principles listed in Figure 19.10 shall be observed in selecting papers.

Forms control specification

Introduction.   The objective of forms control is:

1   To eliminate duplication of forms
2   To eliminate duplication of clerical effort
3   To eliminate forms not needed
4   To ensure that forms show the information required at the time of completion and any other information required later

Forms control will extend to all forms except:

1   Forms used entirely within a particular department, unless the usage exceeds 250 per year
2   Letters and memos that can be classified as circulars and which have little or no space for insertion of entries after printing,

PAPER TYPE	WHERE PRINTED	WRITING QUALITIES	SHELF LIFE	COPYING	TINTS AVAILABLE	STABILITY
Plain	Internal, 49 gsm and above	Satisfactory	Good	Good	Yes, but remember it is not possible to copy when some tints are used	Good
Sensitized (See note below)	Outside only	Not possible with some papers	Limited, in some cases Some are sensitive to daylight Some require special storage	Not good, in most cases	Some papers	Limited in some cases
Translucent	Internal, with care	Satisfactory	Good	Good	No	Good

Examples of sensitized papers are:

1) NCR
2) Diazo
3) Corafax
4) Duscript
5) Action

Some sensitized papers are dirty to handle and some display a tendency to curl. Such papers should, therefore, be selected with care.

Figure 19.10 Notes on paper types

duplicating or copying

Definition of a form.   A form is a printed, duplicated or copied document on which entries are made after printing, duplicating or copying.

Approval of forms.   Forms will only be printed when they have the approval of the chief O & M analyst. Each form will be allocated a form number to indicate the approval of the chief O & M analyst. The chief O & M analyst will not approve any form not agreed by the head of the user department.

Method of control.   When approval for a form is requested, the chief O & M analyst will decide:

1   If a detailed investigation will be made before the form is approved
2   Whether to accept the request and print the form without detailed investigation

The chief O & M analyst will investigate all cases when forms have not been printed after six months.

Requests for new forms or changes to forms can be submitted verbally or in writing and can be accompanied by a sketch, a list of requirements, or a final design.

At this point, the chief O & M analyst will decide if a detailed investigation will be made. In any case, a search will be made to check if an existing form is suitable.

Responsibility for form control.   Responsibility for form control and design resides in:
Department requiring the form.   The department requiring the form is responsible for submitting to systems department the purpose of the form and its contents, together with expected usage and number of copies needed.

The department requiring the form can submit a sketch or final design.
Systems department.   Systems department is responsible for the layout of the form, agreeing the form content, submitting drawings to printers or internal print department and deciding the paper qualities.

Determining if an existing form is suitable. A new form will not be provided if an existing form is suitable.

Making final drawings of all forms which printing department cannot print for technical reasons.

Giving supply department dimensioned drawings and specifications to allow quotations to be obtained for forms which printing department cannot print for technical reasons. Approving the artwork and proofs of these forms.

Providing an artwork drawing service when this is required by printing department.

Requesting quotations from outside printers for comparisons against printing department costs.

Maintaining a register of all forms by form number and by form title. Systems department will standardize form titles so that similar forms will have the same basic title. This will assist in bringing about form uniformity.

Printing department. Making artwork for all forms which it is technically possible to print in printing department.

Deciding where such forms shall be printed, internally or outside.

Approving such printers' artwork and forms.

Advising chief O & M analyst of any forms not printed after six months.

Stock of forms. Stationery department will not keep stocks of forms unless the forms are used by two or more departments. User departments will keep sufficient stocks to cover their immediate needs and the time needed to obtain fresh supplies.

The maximum stock kept should not exceed six months' usage. New supplies should be ordered when stock levels fall to two months' usage.

Obtaining supplies of forms. Normally, printing department will not accept standing orders and will only print supplies on receipt of a stationery requisition.

Systems department operating instructions

Designing the form. The systems department clerical assistant will record each form request on a forms design control sheet—form C2024. The clerical assistant will detach the tear-off portion and retain it for progress purposes.

The forms design control sheet will be passed to the person allocated to design the form. The designer will complete the relevant parts of the control sheet and then design the form. To do this, it will be necessary usually to discuss the form with the department requiring the form.

When the form is designed and approved by the user department, complete a form specification sheet—form A052/7 and pass both documents and the form to the clerical assistant.

Registering the form. The clerical assistant will register the form in the forms book and enter the form number onto all documents.

The clerical assistant will file, in numerical sequence a copy of the form and a copy of the form specification sheet.

The form design control sheet will be filed by 'Title' in a classification file and the tear-off portion then destroyed. Form titles will be classified and the control sheet will be filed by document number within the appropriate classification. The classification categories to be used will be:

1   Forms for cash received or to be received
2   Forms for cash paid or to be paid
3   Forms that advise or instruct movement
4   Forms that instruct
5   Forms that advise
6   Forms that record
7   Other forms

To obtain the correct classification for a form; scrutinize from category one the seven classifications. The correct category is the first classification which describes the form purpose. It is not permissible to classify a form in more than one classification.

FURTHER READING

The forms design book published by HM Treasury O & M Division and obtainable from the Stationery Office.

Applications of O & M edited by G.E. Milward for the Organisation and Methods Training Council, published by Macdonald and Evans, London, 1964.

How to Cut Office Costs by H.H. Longman, published by Anbar Publications, London, 1967.

The latter book is particularly worth while, because of its suggestions for clerical routines.

20

Electronic Data Processing

Michael Blee

One of the most important developments, if not the most important, that has occurred in business management is the introduction of the electronic digital computer. Today even businesses having an office staff of only two or three book-keepers find that they are able to benefit from electronic data processing techniques. Manufacturers, of course, are only too happy to supply the equipment and in many cases they will provide free appreciation courses.

Computers can be powerful management tools. In the right hands they are rapid and accurate and can be instrumental in reducing business operating costs. However, if they are misapplied they can be expensive white elephants capable of causing chaos and even bankruptcy. By far the most common cause for such dramatic failure is the lack of direct involvement of the company's management in the project.

Today managements are becoming increasingly aware of the part the computer can play as a management tool in every aspect of business control. Luckily they are also beginning to realize that the success or failure of a computer installation is directly dependent on their own personal involvement in all stages of designing and running the project.

COMPUTERS: DEFINITION

Today equipment credited with the title 'computer' is available at prices ranging from about £200 to over £3 million. Such price variation reflects a wide divergence in performance, capacity and application, but in broad terms, whatever the configuration or application the basic principles of computer operation remain constant.

The secret of the computer's ability to perform complex calculations is its power of carrying out a repertoire of a few simple operations at very high speed and with 100 per cent accuracy. Any computer system will have to fulfil three basic functions. It must be able to perform operations according to instructions—this is the job of the *central processor* which contains the arithmetic unit.

The second basic capability is that of being able to store data and instructions. This is achieved by the *main memory* (housed in the central processor and composed usually of a network of ferrite cores—hence the term *core store*) or the *backing store* (magnetic tapes, drums or discs).

Third, it must be possible to get data into the computer and receive the results of its calculations in a readily intelligible form. This is achieved by input and output devices such as paper-tape readers, punched-card readers, card punches and line printers. Such units are often referred to as *peripherals*.

This collection of devices is known as the computer *hardware*. This comprises only part of the total computer system, however, for the machine is absolutely useless unless it is provided with instructions telling it what to do. The list of instructions is the computer *program*, and the total of all the programs of a particular installation is called the *software*.

Input date is often prepared as a separate operation by transferring data from documents such as conventional order forms into a coded format on magnetic tape or punched cards by special data-preparation devices equipped with a keyboard.

USES OF A COMPUTER

What will the introduction of electronic data processing do for a company?

Provided the installation is efficiently implemented and well managed, the following are some of the benefits that may be expected:

1   Elimination of the delays in producing management information
2   The provision of information not possible by other methods
3   Increased accuracy of records
4   A reduction in the cost of processing data

These are not all, nor even the most common reasons for installing a computer, but the order is deliberate. We hear so much about the 'information revolution' which is supposed to be taking place in business life that it can come as no surprise to find that two of the favourite reasons for installing a computer—speed and accuracy—have to a large extent been replaced by the desire for an increase in the quantity and quality of information for helping management with the day-to-day running of the company.

One example can be seen in the numerous commercial concerns, some of them comparatively small, that are producing detailed monthly accounts within a few days of the end of the month. Only a few years ago, such firms were finding difficulty in producing similar accounts on an annual basis within two months of the end of the year. The fact that managements now have the right tools available can be attributed largely to the ability of the computer to store an immense amount of data and to process it at electronic speeds.

TYPES OF COMPUTER

Naturally as the equipment becomes more powerful the cost increases. At first sight it may appear that a ratio of power to cost would be an extremely useful one in assessing the value of particular equipment. In practice, however, it is an extremely difficult value to determine. Taking the central processor in isolation, there is no problem in determining the throughput, or the speed at which information is processed. But in commercial data processing this is rarely the critical factor, the throughput of the system often being dependent on one of the input or output peripherals such as the punched-card reader or the line printer. Thus for the addition of, say, an extra line-printer at a relatively modest price increase, the effective power of the system for a particular application may be doubled.

Another difficulty is the comparatively costly item known as the core storage of the central processor. An increase in the store size is unlikely to result in more than a marginal increase in speed of any program, its main purpose being to accommodate larger, and thus more complex programs.

It is impossible to make general recommendations about which equipment should be bought by a potential user. The selection must depend on the requirements of the job in question.

Simplest form

For many years, installing the simplest form of business computer would involve a company in a capital outlay in the order of £50 000. More recently however, manufacturers have been realizing that today's small business is likely to be the user of tomorrow's large computer installations; thus they have been turning their attention more and more to the lower-cost end of the market in an effort to secure the loyalty of the customer early in his business career. Now, the company with £20 000 to £80 000 to spend can have a wide variety of computer equipment from which to choose.

Potential users of these small systems though, should pay particular attention to the provisions made for expanding the hardware capabilities. Although most ranges of computer are expansible there are some smaller systems on which this is not as simple as it may appear at first sight.

There are too many variations in the type of equipment available to develop this theme further and discuss what one would expect of systems in excess of £100 000. Obviously, faster peripherals, more powerful processors and more extensive backing store are some of the features of the more expensive equipment.

Software

The software which a manufacturer can offer with a particular equipment configuration is as important as the hardware. Though the various hardware units may look good in theory, without good software to control them the high-performance characteristics may never be achieved.

In the computer's early days, manufacturers offered all the compatible software for a particular hardware configuration for a single inclusive hardware/software price. Today, however, more and more manufacturers are selling the software separately from the hardware so that the potential user buys only the software which he thinks he will need. Such a practice is not necessarily cheaper for the user in the long run.

HOW TO PAY FOR THE COMPUTER

Purchase prices have been quoted in the previous paragraphs rather than rental rates because most people think in these terms when making comparisons. Computer men think in terms of what you get for £50 000-worth of computer and how much more you get for £100 000. However, most computers today are obtained through rental, leasing or hire-purchase, with rental from the manufacturer being the most widespread of these practices. Most manufacturers base their monthly charges on 1/48 of the equipment's cost but often make an extra charge if the computer is to be used for more than one shift per day. This basic charge includes maintenance.

It can be a good deal cheaper to lease the computer from one of the specialized computer leasing companies. These organizations offer equipment to the user at a monthly charge of about 1/72 of the capital cost of the equipment, and frequently make no extra charge for second shift working. This they are able to do because they reckon that the life of a computer is much longer than the four-year write-off period used by the manufacturer.

FURTHER COSTS

The costs do not end with the hardware; in fact that is where they begin. The means proposed for housing the installation must be examined very carefully.

Many computers require stringently controlled environmental conditions and will not only require a special room but may even require a specially constructed building if suitable space is not available for conversion.

Before the installation begins to operate there is much expensive work to be done. Most important of all, the system must be evolved and the programs written. Often manufacturers give an allowance of consultant assistance and program trial facilities as part of an inclusive service, but such supplies are not infinite, neither is the amount of training in computer methods which the user's staff can receive without extra charge.

Once the machine is running the monthly rental cost becomes only a tiny part of the budget of running the computer department, being swamped by the cost of staff, extra software and supplies for daily running such as punched cards, paper and magnetic tape, discs and so on.

FEASIBILITY STUDY FOR A COMPUTER INSTALLATION

Long before any manufacturer is approached, the potential user should make a thorough examination of his business procedures to determine whether in fact computerization is feasible. In the case of newcomers to data processing, it may well prove advisable to seek the help of specialist consultants even at this stage. The first task is to determine the objectives which the introduction of a computer is hoped to achieve and then examine the possibility of applying a computer towards these ends given the conditions of that particular company.

The result of this survey should be an outline of a possible computer system which carries such details as an estimate of the volumes of data to be processed, the frequency of particular operations and so on. With this information to hand, the company is in a position to ask a number of manufacturers to tender.

Difficulties in evaluating proposals

In evaluating computer hardware, the prospective user may find it hard going to plough through the many pages of standard material that most manufacturers seem to use to describe their proposals. It is unfortunate that many representatives seem incapable of putting themselves in the other man's shoes and asking themselves what the potential buyer will be looking for in the various proposals.

This point may be illustrated by a proposal that was recently made by a leading computer manufacturer for the installation of some £80 000-worth of equipment. Well over half of its bulky proposal consisted of standard pages describing the detailed features of the machine and its accompanying programs. This was supported by a further dozen technical booklets. The effect of this was to strike fear into the heart of the potential customer who was quite incapable of digesting the majority of the information. The software available was described in great detail but its relevance to the applications under consideration was vague and gave no indication of the benefits which would come from use of the manufacturer's standard application packages. Each application had been considered in detail and the processing methods fully explained but no timings were given. Although these can be misleading if they are taken in isolation, they are essential for comparison purposes. If one manufacturer is proposing more powerful equipment it is essential that he should quantify, in terms of time taken, the reasons for so doing.

Perhaps the most glaring omission was any reference to the time-scale for implementation. A figure was suggested for the number of analysts and programmers who would carry out the work (no doubt these were considered the standard number for this particular equipment) but this in itself implies a time-scale. If the company wished to transfer all its existing punched-card applications by a certain date, a much higher staff level would be required. No attempt had been made at the investigation stage to find out the company's opinions on this and no suggestions had been made as to how the changeover could best take place.

Getting out specifications, inviting manufacturers to tender, and examining proposals is not a simple business. It is a job for experienced and skilled people and if they are not available within the company they must be found outside. Some people still regard the use of consultants as an expensive luxury, but the really expensive part of the exercise is to choose equipment which is inadequate for the designated tasks.

Qualifications necessary in discussions with manufacturers

Discussion with a manufacturer should should be carried out by someone who is technically competent and capable of assessing the relative merits of various proposals. This may seem obvious, but unfortunately some people seem to think that by the very nature of his position the company secretary or the chief accountant automatically qualifies for the job. If a person of the right calibre is not available from within the organization, the use of consultants should be given serious consideration.

However, calling in consultants is no signal for the potential user's management to sit back and let the computer specialists fight things out between themselves. For the project to be a success the closest cooperation between computer specialists and company representatives is essential at all times.

APPLICATIONS SUITABLE FOR PROCESSING

A vital question for the potential user is what applications are suitable for computer processing and where should the exercise begin?

There are several schools of thought on the matter. Many would advocate aiming straight away for the area which will give the maximum payoff and there are many situations in which this approach has worked well. For complete newcomers to data processing, however, it often makes sense to begin with a simple self-contained operation which can be implemented in a relatively short time. In this manner the company is introduced as soon as possible to living with a computer and, if the process proves successful, the staff in general are much more ready to give the real assistance in the construction of larger, more ambitious systems.

It cannot be stressed too strongly that the fullest cooperation of all levels of staff is essential if potential disaster is to be avoided.

Necessity for overall plan before considering installation

It is, of course, difficult to generalize about the best approach, but one or two hints may be useful. Perhaps the most important is so obvious that it scarcely deserves mention, but many companies have ignored it with disastrous results. It is simply this—never start without an overall plan. In days when fully integrated systems are aimed for, this is of the utmost importance. The attitude, so common a few years back, 'let's work on the payroll first then see where we go', has almost inevitably led to difficulties. For example, when the requirements of cost control and personnel records are later taken into consideration, extensive modification of the initial application may be needed.

Quite often where an overall plan does exist it has been drawn up by the O & M or data processing departments. By this road lies disaster. It is for top management to decide the fundamental requirements of a business; the O & M department's job is to determine how to meet these requirements.

Systems analysis

Having got the overall plan in place a start can be made on the detailed planning of the individual procedures to be processed. Existing methods of performing the task in question must be investigated in detail to discover their real objectives, their raw materials and their end-products. This investigation is the task of the systems analyst. Obviously he must work closely with all levels of staff concerned with a particular activity and must be capable of obtaining their full cooperation without ever losing his objective viewpoint.

The results of his searches are considered in the light of any new requirements that may be planned for the computerized system, and a skeletal system is designed. This is usually in the form of flow charts which can then be passed to the computer programmers for translation into computer terms.

Danger of overloading the system

A word of warning should be given to companies, which, having installed their first computer, feel that as much as possible should be loaded on it to justify the expense. It is very often true that the more applications involved, the lower the return of each successive application. Acceptance of the principle of marginal cost without considering how high the marginal cost can be, has often resulted in companies buying their own equipment when, if they had done their homework thoroughly, they would have opted for bureau working (see p.385), at least initially.

NEED FOR LIAISON BETWEEN DEPARTMENTS

There are differing views among the experts as to the extent to which the data processing department is responsible for systems definition in the various departments of an organization. Often the computer group design the system and then attempt to sell it to line management. This is not always a good idea. Naturally there is suspicion of new ideas, and this tends to be increased if the whole of the design has been carried out by people inexperienced in the operating procedures of the department in question. Conversely, if the latter are left to develop their own requirements, their lack of experience of data processing can result in an impractical scheme, which, at best, has to undergo considerable modification.

More enlightened organizations have come to recognize that a compromise of the two schemes is the best approach. Capable people from the user departments are assigned full-time to the project to work alongside the trained systems design team. In some cases, a top person from the user department becomes the project leader with overall responsibility for the implementation of the scheme. Although this may not meet with universal approval, many people have obtained successful results by this method.

PROVISION OF STAFF

Another problem area which requires careful consideration by the potential user of electronic data processing systems is the shortage of people adequately trained in the appropriate skills. It was discovered early on that data processing skills could be transferred between different companies, as well as different types of businesses. The result was that neither the computer man nor the company he worked for worried very much about a career structure, for if the employee wanted more money he could simply go to the firm around the corner and get it. More recently, though, companies have been realizing that even in the computer department a little company identification would be no bad thing, while from the employee's point of view, more recessive economic climates encourage him to look a little more kindly on the hand that feeds. Thus today's computer man need not stand quite so much in awe of the high turnover in the computer room as did his predecessor of the sixties.

Choice of staff

Space does not allow the detailed listing of the qualities required for each of the various types of job in the data processing department, and in any case it is not certain that the reader would have learnt much from such a list, because even the experts are still to a certain extent in the dark with regard to the particular talents that are likely to lead to success in programming and systems design. Aptitude tests are frequently employed, and many people favour their use, but they are at best only a guide and serve a negative rather than positive function. Success at the best-designed aptitude test cannot guarantee success as a programmer, but a poor result on such a tests shows that the person is unlikely to succeed in data processing work.

Happily the tendency to buy ready-trained staff from the outside market instead of trying to retain existing employees is far less strong than it was a few years ago. Seeking to recruit a portion of the computer staff from existing forces makes sense not only because it improves company morale and tends to produce programmers and analysts with a greater identification with the company, but the firsthand knowledge of company procedures that such individuals can introduce into the computer department can be invaluable.

Of course some ready-trained experts are necessary but there is no need to ignore altogether those people already in the firm.

Salary levels

As one would expect, there is an enormous variation in salary levels and any quotation of figures should not be taken too seriously. However, a recent survey found that the average annual salary for programmers was £3200, for operators it was £2300 and for data processing managers £4400. In data processing as in everything else salary levels will be found to vary with factors such as the location and the nature of the company's business. Thus the best way of discovering prevailing rates is to inspect the situations vacant columns of the national or the specialized press.

COMPUTER SERVICE BUREAUX

Although the time is rapidly approaching when almost any commerical concern will have some active interest in computing, it is unlikely that a firm whose turnover is less than £500 000 will be able to afford £50 000 or even the equivalent rental of a full electronic computer system. Such a firm may well, however, have data processing problems which cannot be adequately solved with anything less. Hence the growth of the computer service bureau industry. Its development has been one of the outstanding features in computing. The principle is first-class, since it brings the power of a large computer to a small business at a price that it can afford.

There are now many computer service bureaux throughout the country that provide facilities for small companies to use big computers. They also provide facilities for large companies to offload their excess work or to make use of some available package program, but most of their customers are small companies unable to justify the cost of their own equipment.

The bureau's function as a good starting ground for a novice company cannot be ignored either. Through a bureau, a company can gain firsthand knowledge of using a computer without incurring immediately all the frightening initial costs of operating one's own installation.

In addition to the batch processing bureau, which takes raw data from a client to present him with the processed results at regular intervals, there are time-sharing services, which install on the client's premises a computer terminal that can be connected over Post Office telephone lines, to a large central computer at the time-sharing company's headquarters. Once connected with the computer, it appears to the user, that he is the sole user of the machine.

Originally, this type of service was confined mainly to scientific and technical applications which require little input and output but high processing capabilities. With the development of the remote batch processing bureau though, the time-sharing principle has been applied to commercial tasks as well. In a typical remote-batch situation, a user will have a terminal for transmitting data to the bureau and a line printer for printing his own results, but all processing will be done on the bureau's computer, some distance away, at the end of a telephone line.

Package and custom-built programs

Some bureaux specialize in the 'package' or standard approach to the problem, others deal entirely with custom-built programs. It is a question of cost and objectives. A custom-built sales analysis for example will probably cost of the order of £2000-£3000 to program. If it can be adapted to one of the many standard packages available, it is likely to cost about one-third of this figure. However, in accepting this, one may be accepting certain limitations also. It may be that all the required print-out information is available but not in the format desired, or certain information which is highly desirable but not essential may not be provided. For example, deviations from budget may be provided in actual pounds whereas they are more meaningful to the user when expressed in percentages. It is unlikely that a bureau will be ready to modify its package to user requirements, except at a price similar to that which would be charged to program the job from scratch to meet those requirements.

Dangers of bureau operation

One of the greatest dangers of bureau operation can result from the lack of involvement of the company's staff. Because the work is to be processed, and in all probability programmed, on the bureau premises it is easy to adopt the attitude of leaving everything to them, sometimes with disastrous results. It is essential that some of the user's staff become involved with the systems design, and that once operational running has begun, one man is responsible for all liaison with the bureau and control of all incoming and outgoing data.

SMALL-SCALE COMPUTERS

Some of the most exciting developments in modern computer technology have been aimed at the smaller-business user.

The popularity of computers designed specifically for the smaller business was really established by the visible-record computer, of which there are many varieties on the market today. Most are logical extensions of adding and accounting machines, thus it is not surprising that they were first thought of basically as equipment for the job of invoicing. Since their introduction, however, they have well proved themselves in many fields of business application.

Magnetic ledger cards

One of the main reasons for the success of the visible-record computer is its ability to use magnetic ledger cards. These documents are so designed that they can not only carry a comprehensive account history of a particular customer in the traditional written way but, because of a magnetic stripe on the card, can also hold the same accounting information in magnetic form so that it can be fed directly to the computer's central processor. Similarly, for example, in payroll application, the magnetic stripe can be used to carry details of an employee's standing deductions and code number, and even in some cases his name.

Small disc-based systems

For some time, visible-record computers—with or without magnetic ledger cards—had the office computer market pretty much to themselves. In recent years, however, their supremacy has been seriously challenged by small systems whose main storage medium is a magnetic disc similar to that of the large-scale computer installations. In these systems, though, the actual file record cannot be read as from a written ledger, a cathode-ray tube display facilitating inspection of the disc-held file contents more or less at will.

CHOICE BETWEEN OFFICE COMPUTERS AND FULL-SCALE SYSTEMS

Until recently, the application areas of office computers and their large brethren were clearly defined. The introduction of magnetic discs, automatic input and output, large-scale memories, multiconsole units, and line printers has clearly filled the gap between them and created a situation where the choice between them needs careful consideration. Often it is purely a question of cost, but choosing between a minimum full-scale system and a sophisticated office computer system of about the same price, £30 000 to £40 000, can be difficult. Obviously the full-scale system is better able to cater for expansion both of work volumes and future application, but there are many advantages in the office system, particularly to newcomers in the field of electronic data processing.

Simplicity

One advantage of the office system is simplicity of operation, and few will dispute that, whether systems be manual or mechanized, simplicity makes a contribution to its effectiveness.

Compared with their larger brothers they are remarkably tolerant of variations in their environmental conditions. Air-conditioning is not required and there are no worries about installing items such as raised flooring.

Training operators in the use of a keyboard system can often be much simpler than training for a full-scale magnetic-file installation.

Flexibility

This is a favourite word of advocates of the smaller-scale systems. It mainly implies adaptability to change: an area where large computers often fail. A system costing £5000 to design, promote and develop is unlikely to be changed afterwards except as a matter of extreme necessity.

Immediacy

The third, and probably the biggest advantage of the office computer is best summed up in the word 'immediacy'. The final result is usually accomplished within seconds of the original keyboard entry. Updating a particular record may be delayed for hours by the organizational structure of a large-scale batch system.

Accessibility

The accessibility of each individual record should not be overlooked. The fact that a visible-record computer does produce discrete records which can be read directly by the human eye has been an important attraction to many who are willing to sacrifice the additional power of the full-scale computer system for the simplicity and accessibility of its smaller brother.

Further applications

Twenty years ago, the commercial computer was a new, bulky and very expensive machine for the exclusive use of the adventurous and wealthy. This is a far cry from today's office computers, the majority of whose users are small to medium-sized commercial concerns. These machines offer, at a modest price, what has hitherto been an expensive service. So far, activities have largely been concentrated on the more mundane office routines such as ledger, stock control and payroll, but there is a growing tendency to use the office computer in the production of management information involving operational research and forecasting techniques.

PART FIVE

The Company and its Employees

21

Employment Law

F W Rose

A contract of employment is subject to the general principles of the law of contract, thus the essential elements of a contract must be satisfied, namely agreement (offer and acceptance), intention to create legal relations, consideration, capacity, legality and compliance with formal requirements.

If the contract is reduced to writing, the terms of employment may be set out in a lengthy document, stipulating numerous conditions. Any employee signing such an agreement is then bound by the terms embodied therein, even if he did not read them or properly appreciate their significance. If an employee asks for the contractual terms to be explained to him, great care is required, for any misrepresentation may nullify the effect of a given term.

DETERMINATION OF DISPUTES

Most legal problems connected with employment are dealt with by the ordinary courts, but there are some exceptions. Tribunals established under s12 of the Industrial Training Act 1964 are empowered to deal with issues arising under:

1 The Industrial Training Act 1964
2 The Redundancy Payments Act 1965
3 The Equal Pay Act 1970

4   The Contracts of Employment Act 1972
5   The Trade Union and Labour Relations Act 1974, in relation to
     unfair dismissal (Schedule I, paragraph 16), other provisions of
     this Act are referred to the ordinary courts of law
6   The Employment Protection Act 1975
7   The Sex Discrimination Act 1975

Each tribunal has a legally qualified chairman appointed by the Lord Chancellor
and two lay members, one with knowledge and experience in business and
another with knowledge and experience of trade union interests. Appeal lies on
a question of law to the Employment Appeal Tribunal comprised of High Court,
Court of Session and Court of Appeal Judges and other members with special
knowledge or experience of industrial relations.

An employee may complain to an industrial tribunal alleging unfair dismissal,
sex discrimination or infringement of the provisions of the Employment Protection Act 1975 intended to safeguard individual rights. The issue may be passed
on to a conciliation officer if both parties to the complaint agree, or if the
conciliation officer considers that he has a reasonable prospect of successfully
intervening. Additionally, either party to the issue may refer it direct to the
conciliation officer without first referring it to a tribunal.

CONTRACT OF EMPLOYMENT

A contract of employment is not a contract *uberrimae fidei* (of utmost good
faith), consequently there is no obligation on the employee to inform his prospective employer of factors that might result in the employer declining to
make any offer of employment. It is the duty of the employer to discover the
facts for himself by question and inquiries.

Minority

A contract of service or apprenticeship is binding on a minor if it is substantially
for his benefit at the time when it is made, on the ground that it enables him to
earn his livelihood. Where a contract contains onerous terms, the minor is
nonetheless bound if after examining the whole agreement it appears to be for
his benefit.

Illegality

If a contract of employment is illegal neither party thereto can enforce it by
legal action, for this would be contrary to public policy. In Napier *v* National
Business Agency Limited (1951), Napier was employed by The National
Business Agency at a salary of £13 weekly from which tax was deducted, plus £6

weekly for expenses from which tax was not deducted. Both parties knew that expenses rarely exceeded £1 a week. This agreement to avoid payment of income tax was contrary to public policy and illegal, consequently Napier's action for wages of £13 in lieu of notice, failed.

Contracts of Employment Act 1972

A contract of employment may be oral, written, or partly written and partly oral. It is important, however, that the employee knows the precise terms of his contract of employment, thus s4 of the 1972 Act as amended by the Employment Protection Act 1975, requires every employer, within thirteen weeks after the beginning of the employee's period of employment, to give the employee written particulars of his work, unless contained in a written contract of which the employee has a copy or reasonable access to a copy. These particulars must state:

1   The parties to the contract
2   Date of commencement of employment
3   Details of the employment as at a specified date, not more than a week before the statement is given covering remuneration, hours of work, holidays (including holiday pay), sickness and sickness pay, pensions and notice
4   The title of the job which the employee is employed to do
5   Details of any disciplinary rules applicable to the employee or reference to a document, which is reasonably accessible to the employee, specifying those rules
6   Reference to the person to whom the employee can apply if dissatisfied with any disciplinary decision relating to him, and also the person to consult when seeking redress of any grievance relating to his employment and the manner in which such applications should be made. Details must be given of further steps to follow if such an application is made, or reference to a reasonably accessible document to explain them.

An employee must also be informed within one month of any changes to the particulars of employment. If there is merely a change in:

1   The name of an employer, but without any change of identity, for example, where the name of a limited company is changed
2   The identity of an employer, without causing any break in the continuity of the employee's period of employment, then a further statement of particulars need not be given.

This written statement given in compliance with s4 is neither a contract of employment, nor conclusive evidence of the terms thereof. If the terms of the written contract differ from the particulars in the written statement, the former probably prevails.

An employee may report failure to observe s4 to an industrial tribunal to determine what particulars ought to have been given.

Certain employees are not entitled to written particulars under the Act:

1   Those whose employment is for less than sixteen hours per week
2   Dockworkers, seamen
3   Crown servants
4   Employees engaged on work mainly or wholly outside Great Britain
5   Husband or wife of the employer

RACE RELATIONS ACT 1968

At common law the employer is free to contract with whom he wishes, but such freedom may cause hardship. This statute makes it unlawful to discriminate on grounds of colour, race or ethnic or national origins in the hiring, promotion or dismissal of employees or in the conditions of employment. 'Discrimination' denotes treatment less favourable than that given to other persons, in those matters covered by the Act. Separate but equal treatment amounts to less favourable treatment. If an employee, such as a personnel officer interviewing applicants, shows discrimination, his employer is liable unless reasonably practicable steps have been taken to prevent such conduct. This principle also applies to an act of sex discrimination discussed below.

There are exceptions to these rules:

1   Discrimination in employment is lawful if 'done in good faith for the purpose of securing or preserving a reasonable balance of different racial groups'
2   It is lawful to employ only employees of a particular nationality where they possess special qualities essential for a particular position, eg Indian waiters in an Indian restaurant
3   The Act makes no provision for discrimination on grounds of religion, language or length of residence

Complaints concerning discrimination must be made to the Secretary of State for Employment, the Race Relations Board or a conciliation committee. Injunction and damages are available by civil action, at the instance of the Board, if conciliation fails.

SEX DISCRIMINATION ACT 1975

Although intended to prevent discrimination against women, the Act also covers discrimination against men. Direct sex discrimination arises where the employer treats a woman on grounds of her sex less favourably than he treats a man, after comparing her treatment with that of a man with comparable experience and qualifications. Indirect sex discrimination arises where on seeking a job the employer applies certain qualifying conditions to both men and women applicants, but the number of women able to comply is considerably less than the number of men able to do so. The woman applicant is treated detrimentally if the qualifying conditions are unjustifiable. For example, a general office worker may be male or female. An employer wishing to engage only male employees cannot advertise for clerks who are at least six feet in height, knowing that the condition would exclude most women. A woman refused a job as a clerk because of her height may claim indirect sex discrimination. An advertisement for a job vacancy with a description carrying a sexual connotation, such as 'sales girl', is evidence of an intention to commit an unlawful discriminatory act, unless the advertisement states that the job is open to both men and women.

It is also unlawful to discriminate in relation to the terms and conditions of work offered, or by refusing, or deliberately omitting to afford access to, opportunities for promotion, transfer, training or other benefits. However, where work for an employer is done exclusively or mainly by one sex, it is lawful to provide facilities for training in that work to members of the other sex and encourage them to take advantage of the opportunities so offered.

Victimization is a separate, unlawful act, arising where the employer treats another person, male or female, less favourably than he treats other persons, because the person victimized has brought proceedings or given evidence against the discriminator, or anyone else, under the Sex Discrimination Act or Equal Pay Act. Less favourable treatment of a person who made a false allegation in bad faith is not victimization.

Discrimination against married persons is also unlawful. Direct discrimination arises where the employer treats a married person, male or female, less favourable than an unmarried person of the same sex where the discrimination is based on marital status; for example, refusing to engage a married woman on the ground that her domestic duties may impede her work performance. Indirect discrimination against married persons, as already defined, is also unlawful.

Lawful discrimination

An employer may concede special treatment to women in connection with pregnancy, childbirth, death or age of retirement and payment of pensions.

Sometimes a person's sex is a genuine occupational qualification for a particular job, then men only, or women only, need be engaged, for example:

1   Where the essential nature of the job requires either a man only or
    a woman only for physiological reasons, other than physical
    strength or stamina, for example, modelling clothes or perform-
    ances in the entertainment media
2   Where there are considerations of decency or privacy because the
    job involves contact with persons of one sex only in a state of
    undress or using sanitary facilities
3   Where welfare, educational or similar personal services can be most
    effectively provided by a man only or a woman only
4   Where legal restrictions prohibit employment of women, for
    example, men may be engaged on late-night shifts at factories

Remedies

A successful complainant to an industrial tribunal may be awarded:

1   Compensation reflecting expenses incurred and other losses, up to
    a maximum of £5200
2   An order declaring the rights of the parties
3   A recommendation that the employer takes a particular course of
    action, for example, stating that a woman should be promoted to a
    higher grade. Compensation may be awarded for failure to follow
    the recommendation or compensation already awarded may be
    increased. The limit is £5200

MATERNITY RIGHTS

These rights are contained in the Employment Protection Act 1975. An
employee absent from work because of pregnancy or confinement is entitled
to maternity pay for a six week period provided that:

1   She continues in employment until eleven weeks before the baby
    is expected
2   On that day she has been continuously employed for at least two
    years
3   She informs her employer of her claim at least three weeks before
    the beginning of the payment period, or, if this is not possible then
    as soon as is reasonably practicable. The intention of returning to
    work after the confinement must also be stated
4   She specifies the expected date of confinement, by producing a
    doctor's certificate, if the employer so wishes

Maternity pay claimable is 9/10th's of a week's pay, less the maternity allowance
payable by the State, even though the employee cannot claim full State benefit

because her contribution record is insufficient. An employer making maternity payments to his employee may reclaim the whole sum from a national fund controlled by the Secretary of State.

Return to work

The employee may return to work up until the end of a 29 week period beginning with the date of confinement, under her original contract of employment, on terms as favourable as those that would have prevailed if she had not been absent. If this is not practicable she is entitled to re-engagement by her employer, or associated employer, in another occupation on suitable terms and conditions appropriate for her in the circumstances. The new contractual provisions as to her capacity and place of employment must not be substantially less favourable to her than if she had returned to work under her original contract of employment. At least one week's notice must be given to the employer, or associated employer, of the proposed date of a return to work. The employer may postpone the proposed return by up to four weeks, provided the employee is so notified. The employee may postpone her return for a similar four week period by producing a medical certificate supporting her incapacity to return.

Unfair dismissal based on pregnancy

Where an employee has exercised her right to return to work, but has not been permitted to do so, she may claim compensation for unfair dismissal and also a redundancy payment, as if continuously employed up until the date notified by her for a return to work. An employee dismissed for some reason connected with her pregnancy, may claim compensation for unfair dismissal, where for example she has become incapable of adequately discharging her contractual duties, unless the employer offers suitable alternative work. If such work is not available the dismissed employee is still entitled to maternity pay and reinstatement after the birth.

WAGES

Quantum meruit

The employer is obliged to pay the agreed remuneration. This is usually fixed by the parties following negotiation and is often a principal term of the agreement.

Where there is an express or implied contract to render services, but no agreement concerning payment, the court decides what is reasonable (*quantum meruit*, what it is worth) and this sum is then payable.

The Truck Acts 1831-1940

The work 'truck' means the payment of wages in kind, whereby the employer supplies the employee with goods or services in place of a monetary payment.

The Acts do not protect all employees, only *workmen* engaged in manual labour under a contract of service, excluding domestic or menial servants. The test seems to be whether manual labour forms a substantial part of the employment; if so the employee is protected by the Act, but not if manual labour is merely incidental to his work.

A contract will be illegal, null and void, if it provides for the payment of the wages of a workman in any other form than cash. The provision of goods or services by the employer in part payment of wages due is illegal, and the workman may claim the balance due to him in cash and also retain the goods, even though he consented to the deduction from his wages.

An employer cannot deduct a sum awarded to him by a court of law for an employee's previous breach of contract.

If a workman is entitled, whether by custom in the trade or by agreement with his employer, to receive an advance of his wages before the fixed time for payment of the full sum, then it is illegal for the employer, either to refuse to make an advance or to charge interest for so doing.

The employer cannot deduct from a workman's wages the price of goods supplied to him by a person ordered to do so by the employer. The person supplying the goods cannot sue the workman for payment.

It must not be a condition of the workman's employment that he shall spend his wages, or part of his wages, at any particular place, or in any particular manner, or with any particular person, nor can the workman be dismissed for not doing these things.

The Truck Acts do not prevent the employer and workman from entering into an independent contract for the sale of goods in which the employer deals, which are often sold to employees at cost price. Similarly, the workman may buy shares in the company that employs him. In both cases, however, the contract of employment must not compel an agreement of this kind and any debt incurred by the workman must not be deducted from his wages direct.

If an employer regularly pays his employees a bonus, a usual occurrence at Christmas time in some firms, the danger for the employer is that the bonus may become, by implication, a part of the workman's wages, which must then be paid in cash. If, on some occasion, the bonus payment is not made at all, or made in a form other than cash, it becomes an illegal deduction.

If the workman requests the employer to pay his wages or part of his wages to a third party, any deduction and payment to that third party by the employer is legal. An example is the payment of trade union subscriptions. The workman must authorize this deduction in writing, whether it be for a single occasion, a stated period of time, or to remain effective until revoked. An employer cannot even make deductions for wages overpaid on a previous occasion, but if the workman refuses to refund the money, the employer may sue him.

Deductions permitted by the Truck Act 1896. The Act authorizes an employer to make a deduction from a workman's wage, or require a payment to be made to him by the workman for:

1   A breach of discipline, by imposition of a fine
2   Bad or negligent work, or damage to property of the employer
3   Use or supply of materials, tools, machines, standing room, light, heat or any other thing to be provided by the employer in relation to the work of the workman

In each of the above three situations the deduction or payment is permissible if the following conditions have been satisfied by the employer:

1   The terms of the contract allowing the deduction or payment are either in writing and signed by the workman, or alternatively, embodied in a notice that is continuously and conspicuously displayed, where it may be seen, read and copied by any person affected. The acts or omissions for which the deduction or fine may be imposed and the amount must be stated
2   Any deduction or payment made must be in accordance with that contract
3   The amount deducted or paid must be fair and reasonable
4   The workman must be informed in writing of the acts or omissions in respect of which the deduction or payment is imposed, together with the amount involved on each occasion when a deduction is made

The fine imposed under the contract must be in respect of some act or omission which either actually causes, or is likely to cause damage or loss to the employer. The most common offence for which an employer will deduct a fine from his workman's wages is late arrival for work.

Many employers hand out a rule book to their workmen, which clearly states the disciplinary offences for which a fine will be levied. The workman is then required to sign a statement whereby he agrees to the imposition of the fine in the circumstances set out in the rule book. This action makes it difficult for him to establish lack of knowledge of any relevant details if an offence is committed at a later date.

Deductions for bad or negligent work or damage to the employer's property must not exceed the actual or estimated damage or loss suffered by the employer.

Deductions or payments in respect of materials supplied must not exceed the actual or estimated cost to the employer.

Method of paying wages

Payment by cheque, money order or postal order, or payment direct into a bank account is permissible under this Act, if the employee makes a written request to this effect. Payment by the chosen method must be discontinued on request. Wages, in the form of a money or postal order, may be posted to an employer where he is:

1 Absent from work, through illness or injury
2 Working at a place away from the normal place of payment

unless the employee has objected to this method in writing. Calculation of the wages due must be specified in writing and sent by the employer to the employee (Payment of Wages Act 1960).

On or before receipt of wages or salary every employee is entitled to a written itemized pay statement stating:

1 The gross amount
2 Deductions made and for what purpose
3 The net amount
4 Where different parts of the net amount are paid in different ways, the amount and method of payment of each part payment

The employer may give a written, standing statement of fixed deductions, together with the purpose for which, and intervals at which, they are made, to avoid having to give such details on each appropriate pay statement. This standing statement must be re-issued at intervals not over 12 months, incorporating amendments notified in the meantime (Employment Protection Act 1975, Sections 81–2).

Equal Pay Act 1970

Equal treatment. The Act eliminated on 29 December 1975 discrimination on grounds of sex, in respect of remuneration and other terms and conditions of employment.

It is a term of a woman's contract of employment that there be equal treatment for men and women, where they are engaged upon:

1 The same or similar work, or
2 Where the woman's job, though of a different nature to the man's, has been rated as equivalent thereto following job evaluation, taking into account the demand on the worker of effort, skill and decision

In the absence of an express term securing these rights, a term will be implied. Employment wholly or mainly outside Great Britain is excluded.

Where:

1　Terms and conditions of a woman's employment are affected by compliance with the law regulating employing of women in general, or
2　They are specially treated in connection with birth, expected birth, retirement, marriage or death

then to that extent equal treatment for men and women is not required.

Disputes. Either party to a 'dispute' may refer the matter for a decision to an industrial tribunal. The term 'dispute' covers any claim respecting the operation of an express or implied term in a woman's contract of employment, including:

1　A claim for arrears of pay
2　Damages for failure to comply with an equal pay clause

The Secretary of State for Employment may so refer issues respecting an employer's failure to comply with an equal pay clause.

A court dealing with an equal pay clause dispute may, on its own initiative or that of a party to the proceedings, refer the matter to an industrial tribunal, if that body might dispose of it more conveniently.

Claims respecting an equal pay clause shall not be referred to an industrial tribunal, except if the woman has not been employed in that employment within six months preceding.

Damages or arrears of pay cannot be recovered for failure to comply with an equal pay clause for any period over two years before the date on which proceedings were instituted.

The onus of proof is on the employer to show that pay difference between the sexes results from material differences (except sex) between their cases.

Collective agreement. Where clauses of a collective agreement apply to men only or women only, then any party thereto or the Secretary of State may ask the Central Arbitration Committee to make necessary amendments to remove any discrimination. Any contract of employment dependent upon that collective agreement is then effective subject to those amendments.

Wages orders. Any such order containing provisions applying to men only or women only may be referred by the Secretary of State to the Central Arbitration Committee so that any necessary amendment may remove the discrimination. He may refer either:

1   On his own initiative, or
2   If requested by either an employers' association or trade union entitled to nominate members to the wages council or statutory joint industrial council.

The order is then effective subject to the amendments, where the Secretary of State so directs by statutory instrument, within five months of the Committee's decision.

Assimilation of wages and working conditions

The conditions of work and wages for a large number of employers and employees engaged in a given type of job may have been settled by collective agreement. Under Schedule 11 of the Employment Protection Act 1975 failure by a particular employer to observe these generally recognized working conditions may be reported in writing to the Conciliation and Arbitration Service ('The Service'). The claim must show that the employer concerned is imposing conditions of employment less favourable than:

1   Those usually conceded in comparable employment in that particular job either nationally or in the region where he operates. The complaint may be made by an employers' association or an independent trade union that has determined the usually accepted conditions of work
2   The general level of working conditions observed for comparable workers engaged by other employers engaging persons in the same trade or industry in the same district. The complaint may be made by an employers' association with members engaged in that trade or industry in the district to which the claim relates, or by a trade union recognized as having negotiating rights for a body of workers which includes the worker whose working conditions are being considered.

If a claim is deemed to be partly or wholly justifiable, an award will be made requiring the employer concerned to grant either the generally recognized terms and conditions, or the general level of terms and conditions, as the case may be, in relation to those employees specified. The award will become an implied term of the individual employee's contract of employment and as such directly enforceable by him against the employer.

The fair wages clause

A resolution passed by the House of Commons in 1946 states that in all government contracts a fair wage clause should be inserted requiring contractors to:

1 Pay wage rates and observe hours and conditions not less favourable than those commonly accepted in the district; and in the absence of a commonly accepted standard, then terms equal to those observed by other employers in the industry concerned
2 Comply in respect of all employees, not only employees directly engaged on the government contract. Before being placed on the list of firms invited to tender for government contracts, the contractor must show compliance with those terms for the preceding three months
3 Allow their workers to join a trade union
4 Display a copy of the resolution in every workplace used by the contractor during the continuance of the employment
5 Ensure the observance of the resolution by subcontractors employed by them in performance of the government contract

Any dispute concerning the implementation of the clause must be referred to the Secretary of State for Employment and if it is not settled a further reference to arbitration is necessary.

GUARANTEE PAYMENTS

Under the Employment Protection Act 1975 an employee is entitled to a guarantee payment for any working day, or part thereof, if the employer fails to provide work because of lay-off or short time. The guarantee payment is the employee's normal daily earnings, up to a maximum of £6 a day for up to 5 days in a calendar quarter beginning 1 February, 1 May, 1 August, 1 November, provided:

1 He has been continuously employed for at least 4 weeks previously
2 He has not refused to do suitable, alternative work, though it was outside the scope of his contractual duties
3 He has complied with reasonably imposed requirements to ensure that his services are available, such as attending the work place during slack periods to ascertain whether there is alternative work
4 Lack of work is not caused by a trade dispute involving employees of the same or an associated employer

EMPLOYEE'S IMPLIED OBLIGATIONS

Where the express terms of the contract of employment do not deal with some particular point, the court may be prepared to include some terms by implication, by reference to:

1   The presumed intention of the parties (terms implied in fact)
2   Custom
3   Other implied terms that are essentially legal duties in a contractual
    disguise (terms implied by law)

Many obligations imposed at common law concern working conditions and are
fully covered in Chapter 2, but obligations not dealt with there will now be
discussed. The duties to be discussed in this section are implied by the common
law, unless the contract of employment contains an express provision to the
contrary.

Obedience

A lawful order must be obeyed by the employee, otherwise he may be dismissed
without notice or payment of wages in lieu of notice. If he is required to act
beyond the scope of employment the order becomes unlawful, as where the
employee is exposed to the risk of physical injury or serious infection by
obeying an order. An isolated act of disobedience may justify dismissal, if it is
serious, as where an insurance risk is underwritten in defiance of a definite order
not to do so. A single act does not always suffice. In Laws *v* London Chronicle
(1959), Laws disobeyed an order from the chairman of the company not to
follow her boss after the latter had left the room in a fit of temper. Her
subsequent dismissal, without proper notice, was held to be unlawful.

Duty of care

When accepting employment, an employee implies possession of the skill and
care necessary for the performance of his work. The nature of the employment
determines the extent of the skill and care required. In the significant House of
Lords decision of Lister *v* Romford Ice and Cold Storage Company Limited
(1957), a lorry driver carelessly backed his lorry, thereby injuring a fellow
employee, who then recovered damages from his employer. The employer
successfully sought full indemnification of damages and costs from the driver
responsible, on the ground that his contract of employment embodied an
implied term that his duties be performed with proper care.

   If the employer is negligent as well as the employee, damages may be
apportioned. In Jones *v* Manchester Corporation (1952), a hospital patient
died because of the negligence and carelessness of a doctor selected by the
hospital board. Damages were apportioned: the hospital was liable for four-
fifths and the doctor one-fifth.

Secret profit

An employee must render proper and complete accounts to his employer. He
must not make any secret profit or take bribes from customers. Acceptance of

gratuities may be allowed by convention. In Reading *v* Attorney General (1951) (House of Lords), Reading, an army sergeant stationed in Cairo, secured £20 000 by wearing his uniform while accompanying lorries carrying illicit spirits, thereby preventing police inspection. Following release after conviction, he tried to recover the money, but it was held that it belonged to his employer, the Crown.

Confidential information

There is an implied duty binding the employee not to divulge confidential information or trade secrets entrusted to him by the employer during employment, where it was stated to be confidential. To protect secret processes or methods of working, it is advisable to include an express term in the contract restricting later disclosure to any rival, because the courts will not always restrain disclosure where it is difficult to prove that the employee knew the matter to be secret.

Fidelity

An employee owes a duty of loyalty to his employer to render faithful service, which is itself dependent upon the nature and circumstances of the work done. The courts will interfere where the use of knowledge and skill acquired by the employee harms the employer. In Hivac Limited *v* Park Royal Scientific Instruments Limited (1946), without Hivac's permission or knowledge its employees worked, in their spare time, for one of Hivac's rivals on work similar to that done for Hivac. Although there was no evidence that confidential information had been passed on, the employees were restrained from so acting.

The Patents Act 1949 allows only the true and first inventor (or his assignee) to apply for a patent in respect of an invention. This will be the employer, if as a result of guided research under instruction, an invention is made by an employee. Though the employee be the true and first inventor, he cannot claim the benefit of any patent where:

1   He agrees under his contract of service to assign inventions to the employer while so employed
2   In the absence of express agreement it would be disloyal for the employee to so act, as where making inventions
   (a)   Is his job
   (b)   Is a by-product of work he is employed to do
   (c)   Results from the provision by the employer of necessary facilities

There are similar principles applicable to the copyright of a literary work written by an employee.

Provision of work

In general the employer is not under a duty to provide work for his employee, but there is an implied obligation to do so in certain cases; first, where the employee's remuneration is dependent on the work done for the employer, as where he is employed on a piecework basis; secondly, where the employment enables the employee to further his career by acquiring experience, publicity and reputation, eg actors, journalists.

TERMINATION OF THE CONTRACT OF EMPLOYMENT

The contract of employment may contain an express term which states that the employment is to continue for a given period, or until the task specified in the contract has been performed. The contract will be terminated automatically at the end of the period specified, or when the task is completed, but not before. Thus neither party can terminate the agreement by giving notice.

Many contracts of employment do not specify the period for which the contract is to last, since the parties contemplate a continuing relationship until some event occurs which brings the agreement to an end, such as dismissal, giving notice, or death of the employee. This section on the common law right to terminate employment must be read in the light of the statutory protections against unfair dismissal (see Chapter 28).

Notice

Where the contract of employment may be terminated by either party giving notice to the other, the length of notice required is usually fixed by an express term in the contract. In the absence of any such provision, reference may be made to any custom in the trade or industry applicable to persons in the same position as the employee. If a custom does not exist then a 'reasonable' period of notice must be given, which is determined by an examination of factors such as the employee's status in the concern employing him, whether the employment was temporary or permanent, and the intervals between wage payments.

Contract of Employment Act 1972

This Act as amended by the Employment Protection Act 1975 stipulates the minimum periods of notice that an employer must give his employee in order to terminate employment. The contract of employment may, if required, provide for a period of notice that is longer than the period set out in the Act. Where the employer and employee have not expressly agreed upon a period of notice, an employee may claim that the minimum period of notice stipulated by the Act is shorter than that required by custom or the period that is 'reasonable' in the circumstances.

Under the Act, the employer must give the following periods of notice:

1 One week to an employee with continuous employment of four weeks or more, but less than two years
2 Not less than one week's notice for each year of continuous employment where the period of continuous employment is two years or more, but less than twelve years
3 At least twelve weeks notice must be given if the period of continuous employment is twelve years or more

An employee who has been continuously employed for four weeks or more must give one week's notice. The employer's common law rights of dismissal without notice remain unaffected.

Dismissal without notice

An employer may terminate the contract immediately by paying wages in lieu of notice, but it is not necessary to compensate for the loss of benefits in kind, like board and lodging.

Summary dismissal

Either party may summarily terminate the contract where the other commits an act undermining the essential purpose of the contract. The employer should inform the employee of the reason for the summary dismissal at the time it occurs or shortly afterwards. The right to dismiss is waived by continuing to employ the employee after the alleged dismissal.

Misconduct

This depends upon the nature of the employment, and the duties of the employee, a higher standard being expected where there is close personal contact with the employer. In general it means behaving in a way that is inconsistent with the standard of conduct expected. Behaviour outside working hours is considered as well, if this affects the confidence placed in an employee during working hours. Dishonesty usually justifies instant dismissal, as where an employee without permission takes money from the till, intending to replace it and in fact replacing it, but knowing that the employer would disapprove of such conduct.

Disobedience

See above: Employee's implied obligations.

Incompetence

Summary dismissal is justifiable if an employee claims to be able to do a certain kind of work, and this proves to be untrue, but not for inability to do work that he never claimed that he was competent to perform.

Illness and injury

An employee's illness may make him permanently incapable of discharging his contractual duties. The commercial purpose of the contract of employment is frustrated and the employee may be dismissed without notice or wages in lieu of notice. On the other hand the employer cannot claim damages from the disabled employee for breach of contract, though the monetary loss incurred may be considerable where a highly paid employee has special skills.

With a prolonged illness it may not be clear precisely how long the employee will be away, though the disability is not sufficiently serious to preclude the possibility of returning to work at some time in the future. A temporary disability will discharge the contract of employment only in those situations where the incapacity goes to the root of the contract, making performance when it is resumed fundamentally different to that originally contemplated. The express terms of the contract of employment may provide for its termination if absence through illness extends beyond a given length of time. In the absence of such a clause, the court may consider various criteria to ascertain whether the contract of employment has been frustrated, including the following:

1   The expected duration of the incapacity. Dismissal based on prolonged absence is fair under the Trade Union and Labour Relations Act 1974 (Schedule I) if the employee has been warned of this possibility unless he resumes work by a given date. In most types of job it is unreasonable to dismiss until the expiration of six months' sick leave, unless it is immediately obvious on becoming ill that the employee will be away for more than six months, then he may be dismissed immediately, even though eventually he will be fit to work again at the same job

2   The employee's length of service with the employer. A long-standing relationship is less easily destroyed than is a short one

3   The status of the employee and the nature of his work, the higher the status of the employee, the longer the period of absence that should be allowed before asserting that the contract of employment has been frustrated

4   Whether a substitute must be engaged immediately, if so, this suggests frustration of the absent employee's contract of employment. Often existing staff can cope with extra duties on a short-term basis.

Position of the employee

An employee may leave his employment without giving notice and regard the contract as discharged in circumstances, such as:

1 The employer's misconduct (assaulting staff)
2 Employer's death
3 Illness among fellow employees where there is a risk of infection
4 Wilful neglect to carry out the contract properly (as by not paying wages due or providing satisfactory working conditions)

Remedies for breach of contract

Damages.   For breach of contract, whether by the employer or the employee, the usual remedy is damages for loss suffered, if it was contemplated in the circumstances. Damages are either:

1 Liquidated: where the amount has been determined by the parties themselves in the agreement. Such damages are recoverable by the innocent party irrespective of the loss actually suffered
2 Unliquidated, in which case they are determined by the court

If the agreed damages in the contract are excessive and do not represent a true and fair estimate of the loss likely to be suffered by the innocent party, they are considered to be a penalty, then only unliquidated damages are recoverable. The general rule is that compensation is payable for the financial loss caused by the defendant's breach of contract. An employee wrongfully dismissed may recover damages for the wages he would have earned during the period of notice that he was entitled to, but he must seek alternative employment and try to mitigate his loss. If the employee leaves his employment without giving notice, the employer must try to fill the vacancy. The cost of finding a replacement is the reasonably foreseeable loss suffered that may be recovered by way of damages. Substantial damages may be claimed where a responsible post is vacated in this way.

A breach of contract may be anticipatory, occurring before the date agreed upon for performance of the contract, and then the party detrimentally affected can sue for damages immediately. It is unnecessary to wait for the due date of performance.

Injunction and specific performance. A contract of employment is not directly enforceable at the employer's request. The court will not order an employee specifically to perform those tasks that he has contractually bound himself to undertake. It would be impossible for the court to supervise effectively the actions of the employee to ensure that he observed a decree of specific performance. Further, it is undesirable to keep persons tied together in a business relationship when the tie has become odious, thus turning a contract of service into a contract of servitude. The employer is limited to a remedy in damages.

Contracts of employment for a fixed period of time often embody positive promises, such as a promise to carry out various duties stipulated. There may also be negative promises, such as a promise not to work for competitors for the duration of the contract. If the employee refuses to carry out his positive promise, a decree of specific performance will not be granted to make him carry out his work. On the other hand an injunction may be granted to prevent him working for his employer's competitors until the period of the contract expires.

Injunctions are usually issued only against an employee with specialized skills earning a high salary, such as a director, engineer or designer. For example, a company may employ a highly qualified and well-established engineer for a fixed period of time, say five years, to assist in a proposed scheme of expansion. He may be contractually bound to give the whole of his time to the company's business and not to work for any other person as an engineer while the contract of employment is in existence. This contract will not be specifically enforced. Further, any injunction granted to restrain his breach of contract by preventing him from working for the employer's competitors, during the period of the contract of employment, must be limited in its effect to the type of work specified in that contract, namely engineering. The engineer is free to engage in other remunerative activities, though presumably less highly paid, during the period of restraint. There is a reluctance to grant an injunction the effect of which is to compel the employee to perform his contract or starve. Since the employee will usually wish to work only on his own specialized field, he will be induced to fulfil the original contract of employment.

If an employee agrees to give the whole of his time to his employer during the term of his employment, a clause that is not unusual in many contracts of employment, this is a purely affirmative contract for personal services. A negative promise will not be implied to prevent the employee from serving another employer in his spare time, provided such work does not compete with that of his employer.

TESTIMONIALS

An employer is not under any duty to provide an employee with a reference or testimonial, unless there is a term in the contract to that effect. If a reference is given, however, the employer must not defame the employee. A statement is defamatory if it tends to lower the plaintiff in the estimation of right-thinking members of society. The person making the defamatory statement may be liable for damages in tort, for either slander, in respect of spoken words, or libel, if the defamation is in some permanent form, like writing.

To succeed in any action, the employee has the burden of proving that the statement was defamatory and that it referred to him. There must also be publication, that is communication to a party other than the person defamed. No action lies for defamation in an open reference handed to the employee personally, for any subsequent publication must be by the employee himself. In cases of slander there is the additional burden of showing either an imputation of incapacity in relation to the employee's trade, profession or occupation, or alternatively special loss, such as loss of a position that might otherwise have been secured.

Defences to an action for defamation

The employer may have one of the following two defences to any action, and if the defence is successful it will negative liability: first, that the statements made about the employee were substantially true, for no one is entitled to a reputation that is unwarranted. This is a defence of justification. Secondly, there is the more usual and useful defence of qualified privilege, where, for example, an employer provides a reference for the guidance of a potential employer who might offer the employee a situation. Here the statement is made to someone having a justifiable interest in receiving it. An employer will not be in breach of duty to his employee, if the reference is not entirely true, provided it was not made maliciously. The defence of qualified privilege is lost, however, if the employee establishes malice, as by proving one of the following factors, that the employer did not himself believe the statement to be true, or that he made a false statement with spite, or that it was published to someone with no justifiable interest in receiving it.

If an employer gives a good reference, but later rescinds it, the second communication is also privileged. Where the employer supplies a reference unrequested he will have to bring in stronger evidence to show good faith than in cases where a reference is requested.

Liability for a false reference

An action in deceit will lie if an employer recommends an employee by making untrue statements fraudulently, that is knowing of their untruth, or without belief in their truth, or recklessly not caring whether they were true or false. The misconduct of the employee recommended renders the employer at fault liable, though the employer acted without malice or hope of gain. Further, following the House of Lords decision in Hedley Byrne and Company Limited *v* Heller and Partners Limited (1963) liability is established where a reference is merely misleading, if for example it contains careless mis-statements, causing monetary loss to the person relying on the reference.

VICARIOUS LIABILITY

This section deals with torts committed by an employee for which his employer may be responsible. A *tort* is a civil wrong committed by one person that causes harm to another person, giving rise to an action in damages as compensation for the loss suffered. For example, a negligent act causing personal injury. The person causing the loss is the *tortfeasor* and the wrongful act is referred to as a *tortious* act.

Throughout this section, the terms 'employer' and 'employee' will be used. An alternative terminology frequently used is that of 'master' and 'servant', but the principles involved remain the same.

Liability of employer and employee

If an employee causes injury to a third party by his tortious act, then an action lies at the instance of the third party against both:

1   The employee responsible, as the actual tortfeasor
2   The employer, if in the circumstances he is deemed to be vicariously liable for his employee's act

The injured party may prefer to sue the employer, since he is more likely to be able to satisfy any award of damages made.

The employer's responsibility for a wrong that he did not commit personally is justifiable on the following grounds:

1   He is in a position to control the actions of his employee
2   He derives the profit from his employee's work, thus he should also bear the losses consequent upon the employee's tortious acts
3   He should choose only those persons as employees who will discharge their duty with care. If they are not careful this is the fault of the employer, who must then pay damages to the party injured

To protect himself against the consequences of vicarious liability, it is usual for an employer to take out appropriate insurance.

Exclusion of liability

The employer wishing to exclude liability for his employees' acts may include an exemption clause in any contract he makes. It must be stressed, however, that this exclusion is only effective if:

1   There is, in the majority of cases, a contractual relationship with the party claiming, and
2   Notice of the existence of the clause is effectively brought to the attention of the party whose rights are so limited

The employee will not usually be a party to any contract excluding liability, consequently he remains liable to the party injured as the result of his conduct.

Establishing vicarious liability

To establish vicarious liability the following must be proved:

1   That the relationship of employer and employee existed under a contract of service, as opposed to a contract for the services of an independent contractor
2   That the employee committed the wrongful act in the course of his employment

If the employer expressly authorized the employee's wrongful act then he is liable for issuing wrongful instructions. It is not a case of vicarious liability.

Express prohibition by the employer of the wrongful act

If the employee is carrying out those tasks that he is employed to do, even though he is doing them in a wrongful manner, it is no defence for the employer to show that he had expressly forbidden the act in question. For example, where contrary to his employer's instruction, a bus driver injured a third party by racing with buses run by rival companies in an attempt to be first at the bus stop to pick up passengers waiting there.

If this defence were possible, an employer could frequently evade liability in tort by giving restrictive instructions to his employees.

Employee's acts outside the scope of his employment

Where the employer has expressly ordered his employee not to act in a stated manner, the employee's failure to observe this direction may mean that he acts outside the scope of his employment. The employer is not liable to a third party for injury suffered as a result of the employee's wrongdoing if his acts are independent of and distinct from his employment, as when he either:

1   Does something alien to the job he is employed to do, for example, where a bus conductor drives the bus and causes injury to a pedestrian, or
2   Stops working to indulge in an act for his own personal

convenience, eg where a driver parks his employer's vehicle and causes an accident while crossing the road to take refreshment at a roadside cafe

An employee's improper performance of his duties

The employer is liable for the employee's tort, if it is within the scope of his employment, even though it is a negligent and improper way of performing the duties he is employed to perform. For example, when a driver delivering petrol lit a cigarette and caused an explosion that wrecked a garage. Lighting a cigarette is a personal act for the employee's own convenience, but the employer is responsible for the harm caused where the act is committed by the employee simultaneously with the execution of his duties, rather than separately and distinctly after employment for the day is over or during a meal or rest break.

Employer's duty to insure against vicarious liability

An employer is under a legal duty to insure vehicles used in the course of his business in respect of death or bodily injury to passengers and third parties, caused by an accident in which the vehicle is involved (Road Traffic Act 1972 *ss*143 and 148(3)). Any agreement between the passenger and its owner is ineffective if it attempts to negative or restrict liability for injury or death to the passenger in the event of an accident. It is a criminal offence not to take out compulsory insurance, the penalty being a fine up to £50 and/or imprisonment up to three months. The owner and driver of the vehicle, if they are different persons, are both liable to prosecution. An employee driving a vehicle in the course of his employment is not liable if he neither knew nor suspected that the vehicle was not insured against the risks in question. If an employee is sued by a third party or passenger for injuries caused while driving his employer's uninsured vehicle, then he may claim an indemnity from the employer for any compensation payable.

Where compulsory insurance is required by law, the third party or passenger injured in an accident involving a vehicle driven by an employee in the course of his duties may require the insurer to meet any loss suffered where the employer has been sued and been judged vicariously liable for the injury caused. The employer's liability to pay must be for a compulsory risk covered by the policy. The insurer is not liable to pay the third party or passenger if, when the accident occurred, the vehicle was being used by the employee for a private purpose, but insured only for business purposes. In such cases the employee is personally liable to the injured person, but not the employer, since the employee was acting outside the scope of his employment at the relevant time.

The employer may be vicariously liable to a third party for damages to his property caused by a vehicle driven by an employee acting in the course of his employment, unless he has taken out a comprehensive insurance policy to cover the risk. There is no legal requirement to insure against this type of risk. The employee alone is liable if the damage was inflicted while he was driving his employer's vehicle, but acting outside the scope of his employment at the relevant time. The employee may take a journey in the course of his employment, but then deviate from the direct route most appropriate. It is then a question of degree as to how far the deviation could be considered to be a separate, unauthorized journey, such that the employer is not vicariously liable for damage to the property of a third party during that deviation. If the employee's journey while using his employer's vehicle is private and unauthorized, its character is not changed if during that journey he performs some act benefiting the employer, as by collecting goods on his employer's behalf.

An employer is still liable for an employee's torts committed in the course of employment when the employee uses his own vehicle in execution of his duties, even though he was ordered to use the employer's vehicle. If the employee's vehicle is uninsured, the employer is liable for any loss suffered by a third party.

If an employee is driving his own vehicle to or from his place of work along a public road and carrying a fellow employee as a passenger, any injury to that passenger, driver or a member of the public caused by negligent driving will be the employer's responsibility only if it can be proved that the employees were acting within the scope of their employment at the relevant time.

Assaulting a third party

Any assault on a person by the employee while carrying out his employer's business will render the employer liable in damages for the injury suffered by the person harmed in circumstances where:

1   The employee is overzealously executing his duties, for example, where a railway porter instructed to ensure that passengers travel on the correct trains forcibly removed a passenger from a train in the mistaken belief that he was on the wrong train
2   The employee is protecting the employer's property from damage or theft, even though the precautionary measures are excessive in relation to the danger and outside the scope of the employee's normal duties

On the other hand if the employee acts outside the scope of his duties by assaulting a third party after an argument, but acting from motives of spite and personal vengeance for his own satisfaction, then the employer is not liable in damages to the person injured.

Criminal and fraudulent acts

An employer is liable at civil law for injury suffered by a third person because of his employee's criminal or fraudulent conduct in the course of employment though the wrong is committed solely for the employee's personal and proprietary benefit, where, for example, goods are stolen by an employee entrusted with them in the course of his employment. In Lloyd *v* Grace, Smith and Company (1912, House of Lords), at the instance of Sandles, a managing clerk employed by a firm of solicitors, Lloyd — an elderly lady — signed papers believing that this would enable her property to be sold. In fact the documents were conveyances to Sandles, who then sold the property and absconded with the proceeds. The firm was held liable in damages in respect of Sandles's fraud since, by advising Lloyd, Sandles was fulfilling the job he was employed to carry out.

Joint liability

The injured party may sue either the employer only or the employee only, but he can if he wishes bring an action against both of them jointly. If, in these circumstances, judgment is given in favour of the injured party, then:

1   The full amount of the damages awarded may be entered against both employer and employee, and
2   Execution for the whole amount (or any part thereof) may be levied against either employer or employee, provided not more than the total amount awarded is recovered

Separate actions.   If the injured party successfully sues one joint tortfeasor only (the employee), this does not bar a later action against the other joint tortfeasor (the employer) (Law Reform (Married Women and Joint Tortfeasors) Act 1935 *s*6(1)(*a*)). A second action is useful if the first judgment cannot be satisfied because of lack of funds. The total amount recovered must not exceed the total amount awarded in the first action.

Contributions between joint tortfeasors

By virtue of *s*6(1)(*c*) of the above-mentioned Act, if the injured party recovers the full amount awarded by way of judgment from the employer, then a contribution may be claimed from the employee by way of a separate action, so that the employer wholly or partially recoups himself for the loss suffered. The employer could when sued by the injured party join the employee as a codefendant to avoid the necessity of a separate action later.

The contribution of each tortfeasor is a matter of discretion for the court. It is a just and equitable sum having regard to the extent of the responsibility for the damage caused.

Indemnification

See above.

INDEPENDENT CONTRACTORS

Many common law and statutory rules exist to regulate the relationship between the employer and employees working for him from day to day on a permanent basis. For some purposes however, such as building an extension to existing work premises, the employer cannot rely on the services of his employees. He must engage an independent contractor for a fixed period of time until completion of the stipulated task, after which the relationship between the parties will terminate. The mutual rights and liabilities of the employer and a person working for him will depend on the status of the worker, whether in law he is an employee or an independent contractor, and for this reason it is vital to draw a distinction. For example:

1 The Redundancy Payments Act 1965 applies to employees but not independent contractors, consequently only an employee may claim a redundancy payment from his employer
2 The Contracts of Employment Act 1972 is inapplicable to an independent contractor, thus the person engaging him is not obliged to give written details of the main terms and conditions covering his employment, though a written contract usually exists setting out such details
3 The precise sum payable as a contribution for Insurance varies with the status of the insured person, whether he is an employee or an independent contractor
4 An employer is liable in tort for damages for injury caused to members of the general public by the negligent acts of his employee committed during the course of his employment. Subject to some important exceptions. There is no corresponding general liability for the negligent acts of the independent contractor
5 There is a general rule, subject to important exceptions, that an independent contractor cannot claim damages for injuries suffered because working conditions on the employer's premises are unsafe, though employees would have a claim in similar circumstances
6 An employee can claim industrial injuries benefit from the state in relation to any injury he suffers at work, provided he falls within the scope of the detailed regulations governing the payment of such benefit. A claim cannot be substantiated by an independent contractor injured during the course of his work on the premises of the person engaging his services

When is a worker an independent contractor?

An employee engaged by an employer under a contract of service has been defined by Salmond as a person 'subject to the contract and direction of his employer in respect of the manner in which his work is to be done'. An independent contractor engaged by an employer under a contract for services has been defined by the same writer as 'a person engaged to do certain work, but to exercise his own discretion as to the mode and time of doing it – he is bound by his contract, but not by his (employer's) orders'.

In many cases it may be obvious whether a person is working as an employee or as an independent contractor, but sometimes it is difficult to reach a clear-cut decision either way, though it may be essential to do so in order to determine and enforce the respective rights and obligations of the parties. The simplest solution is for the parties themselves to label their agreement as one 'of service' or 'for services' in accordance with their wishes, but this is rarely done. Even in such cases it is always open to the court to draw their own conclusions on the matter after examining the substance of the agreement reached.

A number of tests or guiding principles have been devised to assist the court in its task, though a decision in any given case will depend on the peculiar, individual facts that have arisen and the application of whichever test appears to be most appropriate and helpful in the circumstances.

Tests used by courts

A person is deemed to be an employee if he is controlled by his employer as to the time, manner and type of work he carries out. Although the 'control' test can be effectively applied to unskilled work, many employers, like hospital boards, lack the specialized knowledge necessary to instruct staff in the exercise of their professional skills.

In the last twenty-five years, other tests have been applied though the element of control retains special significance. Under the 'multiple' test, reference may be made to four criteria, namely, who exercises the power of appointment and dismissal, who pays wages earned and who controls the work carried out.

Under the 'organization' test, persons who are integrated into an undertaking are considered to be employees, but not those performing related work. This test depends upon whether a person is part and parcel of the organization, whereas the previous two tests depend on whether he submits to orders: but the test has not been widely accepted and applied. In Whittaker v Ministry of Pensions and National Insurance (1967) a trapeze artiste, injured during her performance, was held entitled to industrial injuries benefit as an 'employed' person, on the ground that she was contractually bound to act, *inter alia*, as an usherette as well. She could not act independently, but was an integral part of the circus company while under contract.

Other relevant criteria

In addition to the various tests set out above, the task of determining whether a particular worker is an employee or an independent contractor may be facilitated by considering the following factors:

1   A person will usually be an employee if the number of hours he works, the period during which he works, his entitlement to holiday, and the period during which it may be taken, are fixed by the person engaging him. An independent contractor will probably be able to make his own arrangements on these matters

2   A person who always works on the premises of the party engaging him is often an employee, for example, a factory hand working one specific machine. In contrast, the independent contractor may be able to work partly or wholly on his own premises, eg an engineer constructing machinery to meet the employer's own specifications, prior to its installation

3   Where one party provides large-scale plant, machinery and equipment for another party to use this in indicative of employment under a contract of service. On the other hand a person is probably an independent contractor if he supplies his own equipment when executing those tasks he has been engaged to carry out, especially if his remuneration depends on his own efficiency, and the risks of a business failure rest on him.

Liability for torts of an independent contractor

When an employer has engaged an independent contractor to complete an agreed project, it may be necessary to determine who is responsible for any damage caused by the negligent acts of persons employed by the independent contractor to execute the task in hand. As a general rule an employer engaging an independent contractor is not liable for collateral or casual acts of negligence committed by employees working for that contractor in the course of the work they are employed to do, subject to the exceptions discussed below.

The employer of an independent contractor may be liable for the contractor's torts, if committed in the following circumstances:

1   Where the tort is authorized or later ratified by the employer

2   Where an incompetent contractor is chosen

3   Where the full information necessary to complete the task properly has not been given to an otherwise competent contractor

4   Where the employer is under a statutory duty to fulfil a task in a given manner, because the responsibility for its completion cannot be transmitted to an independent contractor

5   Where the employer has failed to take adequate safety precautions
    where work delegated to an independent contractor is of a danger-
    ous nature
6   Where the employer personally interferes with the completion of
    the work
7   Where the employer coordinates the work of several subcontractors,
    he must provide a safe system of work; thus he is liable in respect
    of foreseeable injuries suffered by the employees of the subcon-
    tractors

Although the employer is liable to third parties injured, he may claim an
indemnity from the independent contractor in respect of the latter's torts.

FURTHER READING

Aitkin and Reid, *Employment, Welfare and Safety at Work*, Penguin,
    Harmondsworth, 1971
B.A. Hepple and P. O'Higgins, *Individual Employment Law*, Sweet and Maxwell,
    London, 1971
J.C. Wood, *Cooper's Outlines of Industrial Law*, Butterworth, London, 1972
F.W. Rose, *Personnel Management Law*, Gower Press, Epping, 1972

22

Working Conditions

Pat George

HEALTH AND SAFETY AT WORK ACT 1974

One of the main purposes of this Act is to provide a comprehensive and integrated system of law to deal with the health, safety and welfare of people at work. Based on the concept of a general duty of care, the Act has been drawn up in such a way that it can be changed, expanded and adapted to cope with risks and problems in industry for many years ahead. It has been described as the most significant statutory advance in this field since Shaftesbury's Factory Act of 1833. The Act applies to all people working in any capacity: employers, employees (except domestic servants in private employment), self-employed and to certain members of the public.

The basic obligations of all employers and all employees, which the Act deliberately couches in very general terms, are given below.

Basic obligations of employers

The employer must ensure, so far as is reasonably practicable, the health, safety and welfare at work of all his employees. This duty includes the provision of (and maintenance of, as appropriate):

1   A safe, healthy working environment with adequate facilities and arrangements for welfare at work
2   A safe healthy place of work with safe means of access and egress
3   Safe healthy plant and systems of work

4   Means, etc to use, handle, store or transport articles and
     substances without risk to health or safety
5   Information, instruction, training and supervision necessary to
     ensure the health and safety of his employees
6   Written statement of his general policy for the health and safety
     of his employees, and the organization and arrangements for
     carrying out that policy

Directors will be required to give information in their annual reports to
shareholders on what their companies are doing in this field. The Companies Act
1967 was amended accordingly by s79 of the Health and Safety at Work Act on
1 April 1975.

When regulations have been made, employers must, in specified
circumstances, allow their employees to appoint their own safety
representatives, consult with them and, if so requested, set up safety
committees.

Basic obligations of employees

Every employee has a duty to take reasonable care for the health and safety of
himself and of others who may be affected. He must cooperate with his
employer to enable the duties and requirements of the Act to be carried out.

Specific processes or activities are likely to be governed in the future by
regulations or approved codes of practice. In general, contravention of the
appropriate regulation will be an offence. A person will not however be open to
criminal proceedings for failing to observe a particular code of practice but in
the event of criminal proceedings any relevant code of practice is admissible in
evidence.

The Health and Safety Commission, Executive and Inspectorate

In general, the Commission is responsible to the Secretary of State for
Employment for making whatever arrangements are appropriate for the general
purposes of the new legislation. It has an information, education and advisory
role and the power to carry out investigations and inquiries within the health
and safety field.

The Health and Safety Executive, responsible to the Commission, is its
operational arm and has been set up to carry out the Commission's functions
under the Commission's direction. In its turn, the Executive is empowered to
appoint inspectors to carry out its enforcement and advisory functions.
Inspectors of factories, mines and quarries, nuclear installations, alkali and clean
air and explosives have been transferred to the Executive for this purpose.

Improvement and Prohibition Notices. An inspector will be able to issue

Improvement and Prohibition Notices.

Improvement Notice.   Requires the employer to remedy a contravention of Act or a regulation under it within a specified period.

Prohibition Notice.   Requires the employer to stop (immediately if necessary) any activity which carries risk of serious personal injury.

There is a right of appeal to an industrial tribunal, within seven days, against these Notices. Improvement Notices will be held in abeyance pending the appeal but Prohibition Notices will remain in force unless the employer satisfies the tribunal to the contrary, by application prior to the hearing.

Employment Medical Advisory Service

Part II of the Health and Safety at Work Act re-enacts the Employment Medical Advisory Service Act 1972 with minor changes. Apart from its advisory role, the Act authorizes a medical adviser to carry out a medical examination of any employee whose health is believed to be in danger because of his work, provided the employee himself consents. The Act also requires an employer to inform the local careers office when recruiting a person aged less than eighteen and to specify the nature of the work he will be doing.

Disclosure of Information

The Commission can serve a notice on any person to reveal information affecting health and safety.

An inspector can in appropriate circumstances inform the employees at a workplace of matters affecting their safety, health and welfare.

Building Regulations

Part III of the Act, which will be the responsibility of the Secretaries of State for the Environment and for Scotland, extends the power to make building regulations governing the structure of buildings.

Enforcement of the Act

The Executive is required to make adequate arrangements for enforcement except where regulations made by the Secretary of State place the duty on local authorities or other bodies.

Responsibility for fire prevention and fire precautions. S78 amends the Fire Precautions Act 1971 so that the fire authorities and the Home Office can deal with general fire precautions (means of escape in case of fire, fire-alarm systems, fire-fighting equipment and so on) under the Act. The Commission and

Executive will remain responsible for control over risks of fire associated with particular processes or the use of particular substances, and for all fire precautions in certain scheduled premises (which will include major hazard factories).

Offences.   S33 lists the offences and the type of penalty which may be imposed for each: fines and/or imprisonment.

Action by management.   Management should:

1   Prepare and issue a written safety policy statement
2   Set up an accident prevention programme
3   Provide training in safety policy and practice
4   Designate line and functional responsibilities for health, welfare and safety

The main provisions of the Act came into force on 1 April 1975 and largely replace most of the existing law on safety and health in industry. Among the major Acts which will eventually be replaced or mainly replaced are the Factories Act 1961, and the Offices, Shops and Railway Premises Act 1963.

THE FACTORIES ACT

The Factories Act 1961 and the regulations made under it remain in force for the time being. The Act applies to all factories as defined in s175 of the Act, as well as to certain other premises, such as building sites, which are not factories in the normal sense of the word. For the purposes of the Act, a factory is defined as a place to which the employer has right of access or of control and where two or more persons are employed in manual labour, by way of trade or for the purpose of gain in any of the following operations:

1   Making any article or part of an article
2   Altering, repairing, ornamenting, finishing, cleaning, washing, breaking up or demolishing any article
3   Adapting any article for sale
4   The slaughtering of cattle, sheep, swine, goats, horses, asses or mules
5   The confinement of such animals while awaiting slaughter at other premises, provided those premises are not maintained primarily for agricultural purposes and do not form part of the premises used for holding of a market in respect of such animals

Furthermore, whether or not they fall within this general definition, s175(2) specifically applies the Act to the following groups of premises, provided that persons are employed in manual labour:

1   Packing articles, washing or filling bottles or containers incidental to the purposes of the factory
2   Sorting articles prior to work in a factory
3   Printing or bookbinding carried out as a trade or incidental to a business
4   Sorting of articles prior to work in a factory
5   Making up or packing of yarn or cloth
6   Laundering carried on as an ancillary to a business or public institution. (Ordinary commercial laundries are factories within the general definition quoted above.)
7   Constructing, reconstructing or repairing vehicles, locomotives, or other plant used for transport purposes, when ancillary to a transport, industrial or commercial undertaking (other than running repairs to locomotives)
8   Production of films. (It would be wise to assume that the production of recordings on videotape might be treated as coming within this definition, though the point could lead to much legal argument.)
9   Making or preparing articles for the building, fishing and engineering industries, the theatre and for films
10 Dry docks in which ships are constructed, repaired or broken up
11 Gas holders of over 5000 cubic feet

Certain sections of the Act also apply to electrical stations and substations, warehouses, docks, wharves, ships and sites where building and civil engineering are carried on.

Premises that come under the definition of a factory but are used by public authorities or charitable institutions may still be subject to the Act even though they are not actually operated 'by way of trade or for the purpose of gain'. The same applies to factory premises occupied by the Crown or a local council.

A place sited within the factory precincts is not a part of that factory if it is used solely for a purpose different to the processes carried on in the factory, eg the office buildings in the factory may not be part of the factory.

The principal matters legislated for under the Factories Act are:

1   Cleanliness, overcrowding, temperature, ventilation, lighting, sanitary conveniences, washing facilities, drinking water, seating, accommodation for clothing and the provision of first-aid facilities.
    Cleanliness
    Dirt and refuse must be removed daily from floors and benches in workrooms and from staircases and passages.

Workroom floors must be washed or otherwise cleaned at least once per week. All inside walls, partitions and ceilings must be periodically washed, painted, whitewashed or otherwise treated as prescribed by the Factories (Cleanliness of Walls and Ceilings) Regulations 1960. Factories must be kept free of effluvia from drains, sanitary conveniences, etc.

Overcrowding

Workrooms must not be so overcrowded as to be dangerous to health. The employer must allow at least 410 cubic feet ($11.3m^3$) of space for every person employed, excluding any air space more than 14 feet (4.27m) from the floor.

Temperature

The temperature must be reasonable. If a substantial proportion of the work in a particular room is done sitting and does not involve serious physical effort, the temperature must be at least $15.5°C$ ($60°F$) after the first hour.

Ventilation

Fresh air must be circulated to provide adequate ventilation, and measures taken to protect employees from inhalation of dust, fumes or impurities which may be injurious or offensive.

Lighting

The minimum standard is set out in the Factories (Standard of Lighting) Regulations 1941. Windows and skylights used for lighting workrooms, etc must be kept clean inside and out and free of obstructions, but may be whitewashed when necessary to prevent glare.

Sanitary conveniences

The Statutory Rules and Orders 1938 No 611 setting out the minimum requirements for factories can be obtained from the Stationery Office. The conveniences must be maintained, kept clean and effectively lit. The general scale is one convenience for every twenty-five men or twenty-five women but when employing more than a hundred this scale may be varied by the substitution of urinals for water or chemical closets.

Washing facilities

Must include a supply of clean, running hot and cold or warm water, soap and clean towels or other suitable means of cleaning or drying and be suitable and adequate for the number employed.

Drinking water

The employer must provide an adequate supply of drinking water, with an upward jet convenient for drinking or with suitable drinking vessels and facilities for rinsing them.

Seating

The employer must provide suitable seating where an employee (male or female) has reasonable opportunities for sitting without detriment to his/her work.

Accommodation for clothing

Adequate and suitable accommodation must be made for clothing not worn during working hours, with arrangements where practicable for drying such clothing. The risk of theft is an element which must be taken into account in deciding whether accommodation is suitable.

First aid

A box or cupboard containing first-aid requisites (one for every 150 employees or fraction of that number) must be provided in every factory. The First Aid Boxes in Factories Order 1959 stipulate the minimum contents. Such boxes must be in the charge of a responsible person. Where more than fifty persons are employed, there must be at least one person who has been trained in first aid. In addition a notice must be placed in every workroom stating the name of the person in charge of the box or cupboard provided in respect of that room.

2   Precautions against fire: There must be means of escape in case of fire, adequate in regard to the circumstances and the number of people employed, and there must be suitable fire-fighting equipment available.

All but the smallest factories must be certified by the fire authority as being provided with proper means of escape for employees. Application for the certificate must be made by the occupier of the premises.

3   Safety: There must be

Safe conditions of workplaces, including floors, stairs, passages and gangways, and the means of access to places where people have to work. The requirements for handrail and fencing are stipulated for means of access, for workplaces, and for openings in floors

Precautions against dangerous fumes, dust and other health and safety hazards, protection of eyes, restrictions on lifting heavy weights

Fencing on dangerous machinery and parts of machinery which are in motion or use, restriction on cleaning machinery by persons under eighteen and women, training and supervision of young persons required to operate certain machines

Safe construction and safe operation of cranes, hoists and other plant with special hazards

4   Restrictions on the employment of women and young persons, including limitations on normal hours, overtime and holiday work.

5   Statutory registers kept and statutory reports made, eg regarding
     accidents and industrial diseases, inspection of factories and other
     administrative matters.

In addition to the requirements of the Factories Act itself, many specific
processes are subject to special regulations made by statutory instrument under
the Act. These include detailed requirements for certain types of machinery, eg
woodworking machinery and for certain types of industrial employment for
example, building operations and works of engineering construction.

OFFICES, SHOPS AND RAILWAYS PREMISES ACT

The Offices, Shops and Railways Premises Act 1963 is in force for the time
being. It extended to such premises some of the requirements formerly applied
only to factories. $S1$ details what premises are covered but these can be briefly
summarized as follows:

Office premises: A building which is used solely or principally for office
purposes from filing to the preparation of material for publication. Premises
used in connection with office premises, such as storerooms or canteens, are also
subject to the Act even if they are not physically part of the office premises.

Shop Premises: In addition to a shop of the ordinary kind, the term is defined
to include any building or part of a building
  — of which the sole purpose or principal use is the carrying out of
    retail trade, eg the sale to the public of food or drink for
    immediate consumption, retail sales by auction and the lending of
    books or periodicals for the purpose of gain
  — occupied by a wholesale dealer or merchant who keeps goods
    there for sale
  — which members of the public visit to deliver goods for repair, etc
    or to carry out repairs, etc for themselves
  — used to sell solid fuel

The Act does not apply to:
    Offices in which the total number of man hours worked does not
    exceed twenty-one a week
    Movable office structures in which people work for less than six
    months
    Permanent buildings in which persons work for less than six
    weeks

The Offices, Shops and Railway Premises Act is mainly concerned with the
following:

1   Physical working conditions
     Cleanliness, ventilation, lighting, drinking water, seating,

accommodation for clothing and provision of first-aid requisites. Overcrowding: the employer must allow at least 40 square feet of floor space for each person normally employed in a room, or where the ceiling is lower than 10 feet, 400 cubic feet per person. Furniture, fittings, machinery and other such items should be ignored when measuring the size of the room.

Temperature: unless the room is used by the public and it is impracticable to do so, a reasonable temperature must be maintained. Where a substantial proportion of the work does not involve severe physical effort the temperature must not be less than 16°C (60.8°F) after the first hour. The employer must provide a thermometer on each floor in a conspicuous place for the use of the employees.

Sanitary conveniences and washing facilities: the Sanitary Conveniences Regulations 1964 and the Washing Facilities Regulations 1964 lay down the minimum requirements.

2   Constructing, maintaining and keeping reasonably free from obstruction floors, stairs, passages and gangways.

3   Precautions against fire—somewhat similar to those under the Factories Act.

4   Restrictions on lifting heavy loads.

5   Fencing dangerous machinery, restricting the cleaning of certain machines by persons under eighteen and training and supervising persons using certain prescribed machines which are registered as particularly dangerous.

6   Registration of offices and shops with the local council, obtaining a fire certificate from the fire authority, and other administrative matters.

7   Eating facilities for those working in shops.

OTHER MAJOR LEGISLATION COVERING WORKING CONDITIONS

As noted earlier, many regulations have been made for special processes and industries. There are too many to quote here, and most apply only to a few specialized processes, but mention should be made of the regulations for building operations, and canteens, and the code of practice for noise.

Building operations

Regulations apply not only to the erection of new buildings but to the repair and maintenance of existing buildings, including redecorating, repointing and external cleaning of buildings. They thus affect firms who, without being engaged in the construction industry, employ their own teams of maintenance workers. The requirements for such operations are contained in four sets of regulations:

The Construction (Working Places) Regulations 1966
The Construction (Lifting Operations) Regulations 1961
The Construction (General Provisions) Regulations 1961
The Construction (Health and Welfare) Regulations 1966 and
    Amendment 1974

Canteens

Staff and works canteens are included under Food Hygiene (General) Regulations 1970, made under the Food and Drugs Act. These regulations include provisions for cleanliness (and personal cleanliness) and other precautions against the contamination of good. A canteen within the curtilage of a factory and used by employees working on the manufacturing process is also subject to the Factories Act. A staff canteen used by office workers, whether part of the office premises or not, is subject to the Offices, Shops and Railway Premises Act.

Noise

The Code of Practice covering noise was published in 1972. It applies to all persons employed in industry who are exposed to noise and sets out recommended limits to noise exposure.

CHEKLIST OF NOTICES TO BE POSTED

In the following list of statutory notices which have to be displayed, where relevant, the numerical references are to the sections of the Factories Act (FA) and the Offices, Shops and Railway Premises Act (OSRPA) in which the requirement appears. An asterisk against an item indicates that the notice displayed has to be in a prescribed form, copies of which can be obtained from the Stationery Office.

1   *Prescribed abstract of the Factories Act (FA 138)
2   *Prescribed abstract (or a copy) of any statutory regulations made under the Factories Act and applicable to the premises (FA 139)
3   *Prescribed abstract of the Offices, Shops and Railways Premises Act, unless every employee affected has been given a copy of the prescribed booklet containing the same information (OSRPA 50)
4   *Notice in each factory workroom showing the maximum

number of persons permitted to work in that room unless the factory inspector exercises his power to exempt a factory from this requirement (FA 2)

5   Notice showing the name of person in charge of the first-aid box for the workroom or office (FA 61 and OSRPA 24)

6   The address of the employment medical adviser for the area (Health and Safety at Work Act Part II)

7   Notice showing the addresses of the inspector of factories for the district and the superintending inspector for the division (FA 138)

8   *Notice of any exemption applied for or granted under the Offices, Shops and Railway Premises Act (OSRPA 46)

9   Notice showing the hours of work, times of meal breaks, etc for women and persons under eighteen (FA 88, 90, 94 and 115)

10 Notice specifying the clock, if any, by which the period of employment of women and young persons is regulated (FA 138)

11 *Cautionary placards required to be displayed under regulations for certain special processes, eg chromium-plating and power-press regulations

12 Placards showing the recommended treatment for electric shock—if electricity is used at voltages above 125v ac or 250v dc

13 Notice in sanitary conveniences used by persons handling food, requesting them to wash their hands (this is a requirement of the Food Hygiene Regulations 1960)

14 Notice showing the piecework rates payable for certain prescribed operations (FA 135) and orders made under the Act)

15 Fire regulations and drill

It is an offence for any person to deface or pull down a notice displayed under the Acts.

CHECKLIST OF NOTICES TO BE SENT TO FACTORY INSPECTOR OR OTHER AUTHORITY

The following notices must be sent to the district inspector of factories, unless otherwise stated. The numerical references are to the relevant sections of the Factories Act (FA) and the Offices, Shops and Railway Premises Act (OSRPA). An asterisk against an item shows that the notice must be sent on a prescribed form obtainable from the Stationery Office.

1   *Notice that premises are to be used as a factory (FA 137)

2   *Notice to local council that premises are to be used as offices or shops (if the offices are to be on factory premises, the notice

must be sent to the factory inspector instead; if at a mine or quarry it must be sent to the inspector of mines and quarries) (OSRPA 49)

3   *Application to the fire authority for a fire certificate for a factory, office or shop (FA 40 and OSRPA 29)

4   Notice to fire authority when material structural alterations are made to premises, or number of employees materially increased, after fire certificate has been granted (FA 41 and OSRPA 30)

5   Notice that it is intended to use mechanical power on factory premises where it was not previously used (FA 137)

6   Notice to the local careers officer of the Youth Employment Service when recruiting a person under eighteen (a requirement under the Health and Safety Act Part II)

7   *Notice of any fatal accident and any accident which keeps the victim away from his normal work for more than three days. Factory accidents are notified to the factory inspector, accidents in offices to the local council (FA 80 and OSRPA 48)

8   *Notice of a factory accident which, while not causing death or injury, is of the type specified in the Dangerous Occurrences Regulations 1947

9   *Notice to factory inspector and also to appointed factory doctor of any cases of industrial disease. These diseases are prescribed in ,s82 of the Factories Act and in various orders made under it

10   *Notice of intention to employ women or young persons on overtime (FA 90)

11   *Notice of intention to employ women or young persons at different times from those stated on routine notice posted in factory (FA 88)

12   *Notice of intention to take advantage of permitted exemptions to the legal hours for women and young persons allowed in certain industries (FA 99 to 112)

13   *Notice of intention to employ persons in an underground room ie one with at least half its height below ground level (FA 69)

14   *Biannual return to local council (in February and August) of any outworkers working on any of the processes named in the Home Work Order 1911 and the Home Work Orders Variation Order 1938

15   *Intention to begin building operations or works of engineering construction expected to last for six weeks or more (FA 127)

The special regulations for certain processes also contain the requirement that the use of such processes shall be notified to the factory inspector.

CHECKLIST OF REGISTERS TO BE KEPT

All the following records and registers must be kept on the prescribed forms, published by the Stationery Office.

1   General factory register. This is in five parts and provides a record of young persons employed, periodical painting or limewashing of the factory, accidents and dangerous occurrences, cases of industrial disease, testing of fire-warning systems, and any exemptions granted by the factory inspector concerning the hours worked by women and young persons (FA 140)

2   Certificates, etc attached to general register. Reports and certificates of the various examinations and tests of plant required by the Factories Act and regulations made under it are, in most cases, required to be entered in or attached to the general register. The fire certificate issued by the fire authority must also be attached to the general register

3   Accident book kept under the Industrial Injuries Act. This book (form BI 510) must be kept by every factory and on all other premises where more than ten persons are employed. It is separate and distinct from the accident book which forms part of the general register and is provided so that an injured workman, or someone acting for him, may record details of any accident which might lead to a claim under the Industrial Injuries Act

4   Health registers. The regulations for certain special factory processes require the medical examination of workers engaged in them; the results of these examinations must be recorded in the prescribed health register for the process

5   Register of overtime. This must be used to record overtime worked by women and by persons under eighteen (FA 90)

6   Record of hours worked by van boys, etc. This must be used to record the hours worked by young persons employed outside the factory on business connected with the factory, eg as van boys or messengers (FA 116)

Detailed information about the responsibilities of employers in regard to working conditions and liability to employees will be found in the following standard works.

I. Fife and E. Anthony Machin, *Redgrave's Factories Acts,* Butterworth, London 1972. Gives the full text of the Factories Act and regulations made under it, with legal references and explanatory notes.

I. Fife and E. Anthony Machin, *Redgrave's Offices and Shops (together with Agricultural and Railway Safety),* Butterworth, London, 1965. A companion volume to the above, giving text and notes for the Offices, Shops and Railway

Premises Act and the Agriculture (Safety Provisions) Act.

A. Allsop (ed), *Encyclopaedia of Factory, Shops and Office Law and Practice,* Sweet and Maxwell, London; and W. Green, Edinburgh. The annotated texts of the Factories Act and the Offices, Shops and Railway Premises Acts, with the regulations made under them, bound in loose-leaf form to accommodate periodical revised pages supplied under a follow-up service.

J. Munkman, *Employer's Liability at Common Law,* Butterworth, London, 1971. A comprehensive work dealing with general common law obligations and the effect, in civil actions, of breaches of statutory duty.

R. McKown, *Comprehensive Guide to Factory Law,* George Godwin, London, 1968. Detailed summaries of the Factories Act, the Offices, Shops and Railway Premises Act, and certain other relevant legislation, arranged for quick reference by subject.

Sir W. Mansfield Cooper and J.C. Wood, *Cooper's Outline of Industrial Law,* Butterworth, London, 1972. Designed primarily as a textbook for students, it also provides a useful introduction to the subject for members of industrial managements.

The Stationery Office publish the texts of all Acts and regulations, the prescribed forms, and various advisory booklets. Details are given in Section List 18, obtainable free from the Stationery Office, PO Box 569, London SE1.

23

Salary and Wage Management

Irene Innes

I Salary Management

NEED FOR A SALARY POLICY

Companies which employ up to fifty staff normally have an informed salary policy – and rightly so. However, when total staff exceed this number, anomalies begin to appear in the system and some form of framework is necessary. This is particularly so when rapid expansion is taking place.

Although there must be an overall coordinator, the responsibility for salary management is that of line management. What is needed therefore is a salary policy laying down administrative perimeters within which discretion may be exercised and providing salary ranges based on simple job evaluation.

Involvement of line managers at this point is essential in order that they recognize the need for regularizing salary management and make a positive contribution to drawing up a salary policy.

Example of a salary policy statement

Introduction. The aim of this document is to set down the company's policy with regard to salary. It is the responsibility of all who apply it to explain it fully to their subordinates.

Aims. The aims of the company's policy are:

1   To recognize the value of all jobs relative to each other within the company and in comparison with similar jobs outside

2   To recognize the value of the individual to the company and to
     relate this to the salary range applicable to his or her job
3   To maintain the purchasing power of each individual salary

The foregoing is subject to Government legislation, as appropriate.

Salary structure.   The salary structure will be based on job evaluation. Each
job will have a declared minimum and maximum salary range and it is the
company's policy to pay at least the minimum for each job.

Job evaluation.   It is the policy of the company to ensure that staff are fully
involved in job evaluation, including representation on the job evaluation
committee.
     Job evaluation is a continuing process and once salary grades have been
established, the committee will meet regularly to deal with re-evaluation existing
jobs as well as evaluating new jobs.

Initial salary.   In determining an individual's salary on appointment, no
differentiation is made on the grounds of sex.   In addition, the following
features are taken into account:

1   The value to the company of the relevant experience he or she
     brings
2   The individual's value in the outside market
3   The individual's value in comparison to existing staff who hold
     similar jobs

Staff appraisal.   An integral part of salary is the regular appraisal of staff. This
is an aid to management to spot early potential. Equally important, it is the
basis on which management counsel individuals in order that everyone has
maximum opportunity to develop his or her own potential.   In order that
individuals utilize their abilities to the full, short and longer term objectives will
be mutually agreed with management.

Salary reviews.   It is the policy of the company to review quarterly the salaries
of all staff under the age of eighteen years. At age eighteen years and over, all
staff salaries will be reviewed annually. Performance increases, if any, will be
paid effective from 1 April.

Promotion.   When an individual is promoted to higher-grade work, his or her
salary will be increased 10 per cent. If the individual fails to measure up to the
needs of the new job, he or she will be made aware of his or her shortcomings
and given an opportunity to improve and, failing this, to move to a more suitable
job. If the individual is required by the company to take work of a lower grade,

there will be no salary decrease. Instead there will be a salary standstill until the rate for the new position equals that of the old.

Progression within salary range. Everyone will know the salary range for his or her job. Those who do their job particularly well will reach the maximum for their salary range within four years.

Long-serving staff who are already on their salary ceiling will be subject to a salary review every third year to a maximum of six years.

Grievance procedure. Anyone who feels that his salary indicates that an injustice has been done has the right to appeal first to his manager and then to the managing director. The individual has a right to bring along a colleague to help support his or her appeal.

Communication

As important as the preparation of a salary policy is the need to communicate it to everyone concerned: indeed there is no reason why every staff member should not have a copy of the actual policy statement.

By far the best way of passing on information is for each departmental manager to call a briefing meeting with all his staff to explain what the policy covers and, more important, how it will affect each individual. Care should be taken that each employee's questions are answered sympathetically and honestly.

JOB DESCRIPTIONS

In every company there are formal and informal arrangements about who reports to whom and how work is done. It is important, therefore, to establish and seek agreement on an organization or accountability chart. Job titles can be very misleading and some renaming may be necessary. This in turn involves the writing of *job descriptions*.

A job description is a basic statement covering such features as:

Job title
Department
To whom responsible
Date
Task/areas of responsibility
Job titles of subordinates
Training and/or experience required for job

The completed description must be agreed by both the job holder and his supervisor. (Where disagreements arise, the grievance procedure should be operated.)

A specimen job description follows.

Specimen job description

Position: Secretary to Chief Mechanical Engineer
Department: Project Engineering

Date:
Agreed by: Chief Mechanical Engineer
Responsible to: Chief Mechanical Engineer

Overall Aim: To provide a complete secretarial service to Chief Mechanical Engineer by organizing the routine aspects of his work

Daily tasks:
1   On receipt of mail, sort into order of priority, attach previous correspondence, if any, and type routine letters for signature
2   Take dictation from Chief Mechanical Engineer and deal also with urgent correspondence dictated by senior mechanical engineers
3   Against a tight timetable, type complicated statistical tables connected with department's project work. Master copies are produced on stencils or Multilith masters
4   Deal with department's travel arrangements and prepare travel itineraries
5   Maintain simple time records concerning progress of experimental projects. Ensure that progress charts are kept up to date
6   Act as an assistant to Chief Mechanical Engineer by dealing with the more routine aspects of his work
7   Act as a 'shield' by dealing with callers personally and on the telephone

Weekly tasks:
1   Prepare for accountant short summary of personal expenses incurred by department during previous week, and allocate to individual projects

Monthly tasks:
1   Collect brief reports prepared by senior engineers on their respective projects and type draft of progress report for the Project Engineering Director

Six-monthly tasks:
1   Transfer old files to basement and make out new files for next six months

Annually:

1   Type statement of account showing income over expenditure on previous year's projects

Minimum age:	Twenty-one years
Educational qualifications:	Five 'O' levels (including English language) and secretarial college training
Experience:	Three years' practical office experience including one year in a similar firm
Induction:	Three months
Other information:	The Chief Mechanical Engineer is frequently off site and the job holder is expected to deal with all routine problems arising during such absences

JOB EVALUATION

Many companies avoid installing job evaluation because they feel it is either too costly or too sophisticated. This need not be the case. Two methods should be considered as practicable:

1   Ranking
2   Job classification

Ranking involves the study of each job description and placing it in order of importance. Note that it is the *job* which is being graded and *not* the person doing it. Here is a likely plan of attack.

1   Constitute a committee of, say, three people who have a good knowledge of all the jobs being covered
2   Select about 15–20 jobs as being representative of all the jobs being covered. These are the bench mark or key jobs and form the basis of job evaluation
3   Separately rank these jobs in order of importance and seek agreement with other committee members
4   Design a job questionnaire (see Figure 23.1)
5   Brief all employees on how they should complete the questionnaires (see Specimen briefing notes overleaf)
6   Ensure that all questionnaires are agreed by the respective supervisors
7   The committee finally slot in jobs according to benchmarks to reach an overall ranking

Specimen briefing notes

Introduction.   Job evaluation is a method of looking objectively at jobs and ranking them in order of importance. By comparing them one with another, each job will be placed in a salary grade relative to its worth. However, it must be stressed that it is the *job* which is being examined and *not* the individual.

A job evaluation committee has been formed under the chairmanship of Andrew Brown, the company secretary. The other members of the committee are Alan Garnett and Jill Pepperell.

The scheme.   After a great deal of investigation, the committee has decided to use a nationally accepted job evaluation scheme designed by the Institute of Administrative Management. Those who wish to study the scheme in depth may find it helpful to borrow from their public library the IAM book on the subject entitled *Clerical Job Grading and Merit Rating.*

Completing the questionnaire

1 *Overall objective.*   One sentence will normally suffice here. It should be concise and give the reason for the job's existence in order that the committee has 'something to hang its cap on' before looking at the job in depth. For example:

> Process all orders ensuring that departmental computer data codes
> are included and that the VAT figure is correct

2 *Family tree.*   A clearer picture of your job is given if you draw up a family tree of your department showing your job in relation to all other jobs

3 *Job description.*   It is always difficult to write one's own job description: consider therefore that you are transferring to another department in the company and that you must prepare a note for your successor covering the main elements of the job. Describe the job as it is now and not how it should be. Do not be afraid to go into detail. It is better to give too much detail than too little.

Write down the area headings first, such as correspondence, planning, queries, staff; and describe the responsibility involved under each heading. For example:

> Correspondence — on receipt of mail, decide what can be dele-
> gated to subordinates and retain non-routine letters. Where
> necessary give instructions regarding the handling of particular
> letters

4 *Supervisory responsibility.*   Supervisory responsibility can only be assessed fairly by examining carefully the job descriptions of those jobs under his or her jurisdiction. By looking at the situation as a whole, the supervisory aspect should be accorded its proper degree of responsibility.

Job title _____

Department _____

Responsible to_____

Agreed by _____ Date_____

1 What is the overall objective of the job?

2 Draw up a family tree showing the job in perspective

3 Give a concise description of the main areas of responsibility in the job. Take it area by area and stress the important features

Daily tasks

Weekly tasks

Monthly tasks

Quarterly tasks

Figure 23.1   Job questionnaire

Half-yearly task
Annual tasks
4   Give the titles of the jobs which you *directly* supervise
5   Contacts – With what levels of people in other departments and/or outside the company do you have contact in order to carry out the job effectively? Is contact by telephone or in person? Comment on the reason for contact *Internal*
External
6   Comment on the qualifications and/or previous experience necessary to do the job effectively
7   Other information

Figure 23.1   Job questionnaire (continued)

5 *Contacts.* The strength of the company lies in the service given to customers. This does not diminish the value of internal contacts. What is important is the level at which contact is normally made and the reason for contact in the first place.

6 *Qualifications and/or experience.* Comment should be made here regarding the minimum qualifications and/or experience which must be brought to the job *before* it can be done effectively. It may be possible to state an actual qualification or the job may simply call for 'an aptitude for figures'. Experience required must be quite specific. For example: six months' practical experience in credit control.

7 *Other information.* No questionnaire can possibly cover all aspects of a job and since it is important that every member of staff has the opportunity to comment on all areas of the job which are important, space is provided for this. For example:

Large proportion of work is concerned with meeting tight time schedules

These comments should cover features which are an integral part of the job and not temporary difficulties.

Completion date for questionnaires. All questionnaires must be completed and returned to Jill Pepperell by Monday 29 January.

Completion date for job evaluation exercise. With the cooperation of everyone, the committee hopes to complete the evaluation exercise by 15 March.

Right of appeal. Any member of staff who feels his or her job has not been fairly evaluated has the right to appeal to the committee through his or her head of department. The individual can then expect to be invited, along with his or her head of department to discuss his or her job in detail with the members of the committee.

Paired comparisons

An extension of ranking – *paired or forced comparisons* – is easier to use administratively. Each job is compared with every other job and a decision is made about which job is the more important. An example of a paired comparison is given in Figure 23.2.

A word of warning. Fifty jobs is the maximum number of jobs which can be evaluated manually.

Once this is done, a matrix is drawn up showing the jobs in rank order (see Figure 23.3).

	Accounts clerk	Invoice typist	Receptionist/ telephonist	Wages clerk	Messenger	Costing clerk	Director's secretary	Shorthand typist	Stock clerk	Sales clerk
Accounts clerk	X	1	0	0	2	0	0	0	1	0
Invoice typist	1	X	0	0	2	0	0	0	1	0
Receptionist/ telephonist	2	2	X	1	2	1	0	1	2	1
Wages clerk	2	2	1	X	2	1	0	1	2	1
Messenger	0	0	0	0	X	0	0	0	0	0
Costing clerk	2	2	1	1	2	X	0	1	2	1
Director's secretary	2	2	2	2	2	2	X	2	2	2
Shorthand typist	2	2	1	1	2	1	0	X	2	1
Stock clerk	1	1	0	0	2	0	0	0	X	0
Sales clerk	2	2	1	1	2	1	0	1	1	X

Figure 23.2   Ranking chart
Reading from the left, compare each job in turn with every other job shown along the top. If the job is more important, insert 2; if equally important, insert 1; if less important, insert 0. For example in this chart an accounts clerk is considered less important than a receptionist, more important than a messenger and the same as an invoice typist

Job classification

The best known method of job classification is that produced by the Institute of Administrative Management. This particular system is used and understood nationally and apart from being simple to use, it provides a common language when making external salary comparisons. In addition to this, IAM produce a comprehensive salary survey annually covering the whole country.

The IAM system is designed for classifying all clerical jobs up to and including supervisory level. Job descriptions are written task by task and further broken down into task frequency, that is daily, weekly, monthly. The actual grades range from A to F, A being the lower end of the scale. Some companies may feel that the IAM grade descriptions are not quite tight enough for their needs and a slightly expanded version may have to be designed to meet the company's needs, for example:

Director's secretary	2	2	2	2	2	2	2	2	2
Receptionist/telephonist		2	2	2	2	1	1	1	1
Wages clerk		2	2	2	2	1	1	1	1
Costing clerk		2	2	2	2	1	1	1	1
Shorthand typist		2	2	2	2	1	1	1	1
Sales clerk		2	2	2	2	1	1	1	1
Invoice typist							2	1	1
Stock clerk							2	1	1
Accounts clerk							2	1	1
Messenger									0

Figure 23.3   Job evaluation matrix
Derived from the ranking chart shown in Figure 23.2

Expanded IAM grades description

Grade A.   Tasks are simple and each one is individually allocated. No training or experience required. Continually supervised.

Grade B.   Tasks are simple and conform to clearly laid down procedures. All written work and calculations are checked. Up to a few weeks' training required.

Grade C.   Tasks are subject to laid-down procedures but can involve a limited measure of initiative. Work subject to systematic checking. Up to six months' training or experience required.

Grade D.   Tasks are carried out and decisions made in accordance with standard procedures, subject to infrequent supervision. Routine contact, external and internal, up to own level to obtain and provide information. Probably minimum of two years' experience.

Grade E.   After specific direction, plans and arranges work within main work programme with little or no supervision. Only non-routine problems referred to superior. May have supervisory responsibility. Can have contact at higher level than own, external and internal, to obtain and give information which may be of a confidential nature. Specialized knowledge may be required. Probably five years' experience.

Grade F.   After general direction, plans and arranges work with little or no supervision. Tasks can involve work of a non-routine nature requiring an original approach as to planning and method. Would normally have contact at a higher level than own, external and internal, to obtain and give information which may be of a confidential nature. Can be required to make decisions as to daily action and direct work of subordinates. More than five years' experience required.

There is a tendency for companies to combine grades *A* and *B* because few people retain a grade *A* job for longer than a few weeks. Each task is allotted a grading by matching the task description with the grade description. When the evaluation is completed, the number of each classification accorded is totted up and a decision made by the team regarding the overall grading.

SALARY GRADES

Following a ranking exercise, the decision to group the jobs into salary grades is largely arbitrary. Five grades ought to suffice up to and including supervisory level.

To have more will mean that differentials between grades will be reduced and staff will see little financial advantage in taking on more responsibility. Alternatively, the salaries coordinator will be faced with an excessive number of appeals for upgrading each time there is a slight increase in responsibility.

In general, jobs will tend to fall into broad groups but there are bound to be some jobs which will cause much soul-searching. The establishing of grades completed, the jobs on either side of the line must be scrutinized carefully to ensure they are in the right group. In the event of appeals being raised, it is likely that they will spring from this grey area.

Salary ranges

Now comes the problem of allocating actual cash to each band or grade. A number of structures is possible, but a structure like that in Figure 23.4 is recommended for its flexibility.

Grade	*A/B*	£1000 – – – – – £1300			
	C	£1150 – – – – – £1535			
	D		£1350 – – – – – £1800		
	E			£1600 – – – – – £2250	
	F				£2200 – – – – – £3300

Figure 23.4   Salary structure
Overlapping salary ranges based on IAM grades

As will be seen, the salary ceiling is roughly a 30/50 per cent addition on the base figure and the base for the next grade starts at approximately the midpoint of the previous grade. This means that on promotion an employee may move easily from one grade to another. It also recognizes that an employee on his or her ceiling on a grade *D* job is worth more than one about to start on grade *E* work with less experience.

SALARY SURVEYS

Although salary comparison is a continuing exercise, a particular effort must be made to obtain factual information when designing a new salary structure. This can be done in four ways:

1   By consulting the IAM annual salary survey or the quarterly salary survey published by the Alfred Marks Bureau which is particularly useful for London-based companies. In addition to this, members of the Institute of Administrative Management can obtain information at any time on up-to-date salary trends in any part of the country
2   By telephoning your opposite number in other companies in the area and exchanging information
3   By sending to selected companies a job description from each grade, complete with proposed salary range and asking for a comparison. (It is wise to telephone personally to inquire if the company is willing to take part.) This must be followed up by sending to the participants details of the survey but excluding actual company names
4   By inviting four or five opposite numbers in your area to form a Salary Comparison Club with the first meeting on your premises. An agreed agenda should be drawn up stating the jobs to be discussed in order that salary information is forthcoming

Even at this point, the salary ranges cannot be thought conclusive until a thorough internal costing is completed.

RATE FOR AGE

Although many companies find it useful to retain a rate-for-age scale, the trend is to move away from this. It is the experience of a large number of organizations that the inflexibility of such a system, even with merit rating on top, can result in a rapid turnover among staff of high potential.

It is helpful, however, to draw up a range of offering salaries linked to age lest the internal organization is upset by offering a salary which is higher than it should be in comparison to existing staff with similar potential. The IAM grading system is used as the base for the structure shown in Figure 23.5.

If however a rate-for-age scale is maintained, care must be exercised to ensure that, on the eighteenth birthday, recognition is made of both the increase in social security contributions and rail travel (if applicable).

GRADE	AGE	MINIMUM	AVERAGE	MAXIMUM
A/B	15/16	850	900	950
	17	900	950	1000
	18	1000	1050	1100
C	16	975	1050	1125
	17	· 1050	1125	1200
	18	1150	1225	1300
D	17	1250	1350	1450
	18	1350	1450	1550

Figure 23.5   **Rate-for-age scale**
Starting salaries: based on IAM grades

SALARY ANOMALIES

Once salary grades have been established, it will be found that the majority of staff will be on a salary within the new grades. However, there will probably be a number of staff who are either over or underpaid. Those underpaid should be brought up to at least the minimum for the grade. Apart from explaining the situation to those staff who are over the maximum for their job grade, the following should be considered:

1   Promotion to higher-grade work
2   Rearrangement of job content in order that some higher-grade work is included
3   Salary standstill until the new rate catches up with the old

EMPLOYEE BENEFITS

The subject of employee benefits is covered in Chapter 24, but it is worth while to mention that when constructing a new salary structure, consideration must at the same time be given to the adequacy of existing employee benefits. When conducting a salary survey, therefore, employee benefits must also be taken into account.

Staff accept fringe benefits as a fact of life but different social groups within the company and indeed within the area will view different benefits with varying degrees of interest. Young people are more attracted to a company by the promise of a realistic salary than by the offer of a generous sick pay or pension scheme. Assisted house purchase, membership of a hospital scheme and profit sharing is likely to appeal to management.

In designing the salary structure, therefore, it is important to consider how much influence employee benefits need have on the salary ranges.

TOTAL REMUNERATION PACKAGE

Although still a new concept, there is a growing interest in the total remuneration package. The principle is that the director or senior manager may elect to have an individually tailored remuneration package. Those employee benefits available each have a value as also will his total salary package, which is his worth to the company. He may decide that he will take a lower salary in exchange for 'top hat' pension arrangements, private use of the company flat or a bigger car, for example. In the past the real benefit lay in tax advantages to the individual concerned, thereby enhancing the actual value of earnings. However the present Government will likely enact legislation to limit this aspect.

DEPARTMENTAL BUDGETS

Every department should have a budget and within this, there should be an agreed figure for salaries. This should be decided one year in advance and should take into consideration staff retirements (with recruitment on a lower salary level), promotions and increases in staff complement. It should also take into account a figure to be set aside for salary increases. This can either be an arbitrarily agreed lump sum or, more usually, something like 3—4 per cent, excluding cost-of-living increases.

SALARY REVIEWS

Staff over the age of eighteen should have their salary reviewed annually: staff under eighteen should have their salary reviewed six-monthly or even quarterly.

A review does not necessarily mean that all staff get an increase. If a particularly good increase is given and no increase is planned for the next review, the individual must be told that the next review period has been anticipated.

The timing of reviews is important. A review coinciding with Christmas should be avoided if possible. The festive spirit can overcome the managers' commonsense. October and/or April are useful periods to consider. A salary review sheet is shown in Figure 23.6.

Salary review — 1 April 1976											
Confidential							Department				
1 Name	2 Job title	3 Age at 31 March	4 Service at 31 March	5 Date of last performance increase	6 Amount	7 Present salary	8 Grade	9 Maximum salary	10 Proposed increase	11 New salary	12 Remarks
Total											

Figure 23.6   **Salary and review form**

MANAGEMENT SALARIES

Salary management is based on job evaluation and this is difficult when a small number of managers is involved. Furthermore, their jobs will tend to expand considerably if the company is in course of rapid growth. Individual managers are therefore paid a figure which represents their individual worth to the company. It is unlikely they will have a salary ceiling unless the company's growth is fairly static.

Salary surveys are still necessary though best handled at director level.

Once a company employs fifty managers, including supervisors, then is the time to rationalize management salaries.

II WAGE STRUCTURES

SETTING A COMPANY WAGE POLICY

The wage structure must be linked to what the company is trying to achieve. It is not unusual to find a company with a wage structure in direct conflict with the company's overall objectives. For example, a company may plan to produce a high-quality product while at the same time have a direct incentive geared to quantity. These questions must be asked:

> Apart from profit, what are we in business for?
> Where are we going during the next two to three years; in the next five to ten years?
> How do we plan to get there?
> What influence will these plans have on our wage structure?
> How can the wage structure aid the company in meeting its objectives?

From this a corporate plan is built up, in simple terms, expressing the company's short and long-term objectives and how these will affect specific areas. It may be, for example, that in two years' time a massive capital investment is planned. In terms of human resources this will probably affect the way work is organized, manning arrangements and job demands. Care must be taken, therefore, to ensure that the new wage structure will form a satisfactory springboard to cater for future developments. Consideration must also be given to the spin-off which will affect the whole company.

Management style

It is necessary to identify what the company's management style is. Is it autocratic, paternalistic, participative or *laissez-faire*? Incompatibilities arise if a wage structure is implemented in isolation of this major consideration. An autocratic management style for instance is in conflict with a Scanlon/Rucker plan. Since the pay structure expresses to employees how the company values them, a real attempt must be made to draw up a declared wage policy. A framework for a policy statement is given on p.471.

CHANGING A WAGE STRUCTURE

The desire to change a wage structure usually springs from an existing structure which management no longer controls. Common features are that the present structure suffers from wage drift, that it has numerous rates which are inequitable in terms of individual contribution and there has been a gradual build-up of 'special' allowances.

Most companies, when faced with the need to change their wage structure, begin by looking for alternative incentives. In reality this is prejudging the issue. The first step should be an initial investigation to ascertain the pressure points which exist in the present structure. Only by discovering the 'lumps and the bumps' in the present system will the way ahead seem clear. A discussion with the senior wages clerk will be an enlightening experience since he, more than anyone else, is fully aware of the inadequacies and inequities of the existing system.

Wage analysis

This should be based on a thorough examination of the gross pay earned department by department for, say, a 'typical' week at two points in the year. All special allowances should be examined and the totals expressed as a percentage of labour cost. Consideration should be given to the effectiveness of the incentive element.

Overtime

The number of hours overtime should be broken down and scrutinized to see what indicators exist. Excessive overtime working usually means an unrealistic basic hourly rate. What, for example, would be the result if overtime working were curbed? If overtime earnings were consolidated in the basic rate on the understanding that productivity was maintained, would the need for overtime working cease? And would this be socially acceptable in your locality?

Work study

One of the main reasons why a company decides to change its wage structure is because work study values have worked loose and wage drift has become a dominant feature. For example, is the pace of working closely related to that shown on the time sheets? Too often top management assumes that because performances are high on paper, all is well. If the company's present work study team cannot cope with the situation, the use of consultants should be considered. An alternative is to employ experienced work study personnel on a short-term contract.

Labour turnover

Annual figures should be produced and broken down by department. These figures are normally associated with the social aspects of employment but it is not by any means unknown for a definite correlation to be established between them and the method of payment. For example, it is possible that a very low labour turnover linked to a very high rate of absenteeism indicates that earnings may be unusually high for the area but working conditions are intolerable, leading to low morale: the employees cannot afford to leave. In other words, it is just as problematic to grossly overpay people as to underpay.

Age and sex

On a departmental basis, figures should be produced for both men and women grouping them by age, for example 16–18, 19–25, 26–40, 41–45, 46–50, 51–56, 56–60, 61–65, 65+. Men and women in particular age groups have different attitudes to work and how their pay packet should be made up. Additionally, they will have fairly specific ideas about what they are prepared to do to earn £x per week. It is doubtful, for example, whether a middle-aged male work force would be enthusiastic about the introduction for the first time of direct incentives.

Attitude survey

Ideally an attitude survey should be made to ascertain what needs have to be satisfied through a wage structure. What are the employees' attitudes towards the current pay structure and what are their deeper expectations? The pay structure to a large extent determines and reinforces attitudes. Two of the areas a survey ought to highlight are the reasons why employees work for a particular company and what motivates them. Every company has a reputation as an employer and if it has achieved, for example, a 'quick buck' image, it will attract a particular type of employee. Thought must therefore be given to the kind of image the company wants to have and how it plans to achieve it.

What motivates people in your geographical area? What kind of incentives are socially acceptable, for instance? The whole of the Midlands is almost incurably on direct incentives and a firm that works otherwise is viewed with suspicion. In a free bargaining situation, a company introduced a new incentive scheme which theoretically should have increased take-home pay — and the impact was nil! An investigation highlighted the fact that the social custom was for young people to lay their unopened pay packet on the kitchen table each pay day and to receive in turn a fixed amount of pocket money. A little unusual in the 1970s, perhaps, but knowledge of this factor would have saved the company much time and trouble.

The survey should be done by an outside specialist in order to gain the confidence of the work force.

Influence of production method

Insufficient consideration is normally given to the link between the technological aspects of production and how people are paid. It is obvious that this is important and yet many operatives in a machine-controlled situation are on direct incentives intended to make them work faster! Similarly, it is not unusual for a company specializing in one-offs to have a direct incentive scheme which entails on-the-spot bargaining between, say, a rate fixer and a shop steward for every unit produced: the result is a hardening industrial relation climate.

These questions should be asked:

1   Are runs short, long, one-offs?
2   How important is quality, quantity, accuracy, consistency?
3   Is the operation operator- or machine-controlled?   And what happens in *practice*?
4   What are the capital investment plans for the next 3—5 years? Will   these   developments   influence   pay   structure?
5   What are the market pressures?   Are there seasonal fluctuations?
6   Can buffer stocks be kept or is the product perishable?
7   How much is lost through scrap? (If the material is reconstituted, cost this.)

JOB EVALUATION

Job evaluation is an essential exercise if a company is to be truly in control of its wage structure.   Certainly it is the only answer to leapfrogging pay claims and escalating special allowances.

Job evaluation can be as difficult or as expensive as a company likes to make it.   However, it must be done by a full-time committee (thereby reflecting management commitment) under the chairmanship of a line manager respected for his integrity and there must be continuing involvement on the part of job holders.   Ranking is quite satisfactory: the basis of job evaluation is ranking anyway and all other methods are, in simple terms, administrative systems which are an aid to maintaining the original rank order of the benchmarks.   Points rating is the most commonly used system, however.

The gnawing question is whether or not shop stewards should form part of the committee. The straight answer is that unions should be as involved as much as both management and unions can stand.   It depends to a large extent on the industrial relations climate.   If there is a well-established participative management style, there is no reason why stewards should not do the evaluation by themselves.   After all, management's prime concern ought to be centred round the total wage bill: provided the job holders feel the evaluation is fair, there is no reason why management should taken an overactive interest in how it is distributed.

At the other end of the industrial relations scale, however, is the multi-union situation, or long-established union militancy, or a combination of both. In such a situation, the unions should be consulted regarding their role but they will probably prefer to let management make all the decisions while they reserve the right to object on behalf of their respective members. In any case, such unions are probably accustomed to an autocratic management style and a large dose of participation is just as difficult for the unions to countenance as for line management. Obviously, union participation simplifies the situation but involvement does not guarantee instant success: there will still be appeals. In point of fact, most companies fall somewhere between these two points. In a free bargaining situation therefore, the introduction of job evaluation is frequently a joint exercise. What is important is that job evaluation is regarded as a quite separate situation from negotiating actual rates.

LEGISLATION

Two Acts of Parliament are intended to safeguard, among other things, women's wage rates and how they are established:

Equal Pay Act, 1970
Sex Discrimination Act, 1975

In simple terms the legal framework gives an individual right of appeal, depending on the case, to an Industrial Tribunal or, through his or her union to the Central Arbitration Committee, for a decision. To avoid such a situation, the following points should be observed:

1   Job evaluation should have been carried out
2   Each job grade should 'contain jobs carried out by either sex
3   The jobs in each grade should be 'the same or broadly similar' to each other

COSTING

The basis of a carefully considered wage structure is sound costing. The company accountant, therefore, has an important role to play. Here are the major areas to be scrutinized for key indicators:

1   Budgeted labour cost for the coming year
2   Trend of total labour cost over the last five years
3   General breakdown of cost of the various wage components which contribute to the total labour cost for, say, the last two years
4   Earnings distribution for each department for 2 typical weeks

5   The unit cost of producing each selling line and the proportion of
    labour cost attributed
6   Cost of employee benefits. Frequently overlooked, these benefits
    are nonetheless part of the total labour cost
7   Cost of labour turnover. As a rule of thumb, a routine factory
    worker who leaves after, say, three months, has probably cost the
    company approximately £200. This figure includes recruitment
    costs, interviewing time (allowance must be made for the average
    number of interviews to fill each job), initial training and a scale
    linked to the likely contribution an individual will make as his
    skill and know-how increases. A new employee does not begin to
    function as a member of a team until one or two weeks have
    elapsed
8   Cost of absenteeism. (Absenteeism is being used in a wider context
    than simply illness.) It is a useful pulse to take: if, say, absentee-
    ism is running at a steady 20 per cent, possible causes are overman-
    ning, overpaying or simply low morale. The cost of morale is not a
    balance sheet item but it is nonetheless an important hidden cost
    which must not be ignored.

FINANCING THE WAGE STRUCTURE

It is inflationary to set out to design and implement a new wage structure
without first agreeing with the unions concerned that the increase in the wage
bill must be found from within the company's resources. The actual cost of
changing a wage structure is about 5 per cent of the wage bill, excluding cost-of-
living for example. At first glance this figure will appear to be high: in effect a
redistribution of cash and control is taking place with a short-term gain for the
operatives involved and a longer-term gain for management. In a stable
economy, no matter how sophisticated a company's techniques and know-how,
it is possible to find savings to cover this cost. Of prime importance at the
beginning of the exercise is agreement by management and unions on how the
savings are to be achieved and shared.

Running concurrently with the initial investigation should be the operation of
productivity groups bent on finding savings. These groups should comprise
operatives meeting on a sectional or departmental basis during working hours or
at the end of a shift (on overtime). Their remit should be a broad one where
they may discuss every aspect of the organization and planning of the work in
their immediate working area and make recommendations to a coordinating
committee which will cost and evaluate each proposal.

While the structure of the groups will depend on the size of the section or
department, the numbers meeting at any one time should not exceed eight to
ten. By rotation everyone should have an opportunity to contribute to the

group's findings. A simple record of decisions made should be kept by each group for the sake of continuity and an effort made to communicate this within the group. Each group should appoint its own chairman. Obviously, short training courses will be necessary to help the groups to assess each problem and devise a probable solution. Many companies underestimate the wealth of untapped potential which exists at shopfloor level. However, companies who have attempted a similar exercise have discovered that operatives are quite capable of using simple method study and costing techniques, for example. Provided the groups understand in essence the services provided by, say, the company's work study or value engineering specialists, the groups will ask for expert advice if the need arises.

The supervisor's role must not be overlooked. He is primarily a member of the management team. While a supervisor may, by invitation, act as a catalyst within his own section, he ought to be involved in the knottier problems being investigated by management.

DESIGNING THE WAGE STRUCTURE

Having established the realities of the existing structure, the next step is to design one which will meet the company's needs. The trend is for a company to have a three-tier wage structure: a basic hourly/job rate tier accounting for 80—85 per cent of the wage bill; an incentive tier (if any) accounting for 15—20 per cent; and a factory wide share-of-prosperity element.

Number of grades

The trend is to have six grades covering all factory personnel. The more straight-forward the production process, the less reason for numerous grades. Without prejudicing the situation in the early stages of the investigation, there should be at least £3.00 per week differential between each grade. To have less will act as a disincentive to internal promotion. In effect this means reducing the number of grades to a point where the differential is a significant demonstration that work in a higher grade really is more important to the company. If the pay steps are too small, management will be faced with numerous requests for regrading jobs every time a fraction of responsibility or a grain of dirt is added to the job.

The decision regarding the break point for each grade is largely arbitrary. It will probably be a negotiating point. On the whole, jobs tend to fall into homogeneous groups but no matter where the break points are made, 'grey area' jobs on either side of the line will give rise to much tooth-sucking. It is from this area that job evaluation appeals usually spring.

As an aid to deciding where the break points might be, it is useful to produce some scattergrams showing how, for example, the results of job evaluation compare in relation to job holders' basic rates as well as gross pay (see Figure

23.7). The next step is to determine the 'line of best fit': in simple terms a line is drawn through the centre of the points already plotted. It is then possible to determine roughly what the pay steps might be. In practical terms this is a quite considerable exercise and it may be that a 30 per cent sample, say, of all jobs might suffice.

Yet another statistical aid is the use of bar graphs. In most companies the bulk of the jobs will be in the middle two grades with roughly the same number in the bottom and top grades.

Deciding the basic rate

Traditionally, manual workers have been in a position where the ratio of basic rate to incentive was 2:1. However, this ratio now tends to be nearer 4:1 largely because companies moving towards single (staff) status are rightly challenging the concept that a manual worker's earnings should fluctuate with the company's production throughput.

The case for greater security of earnings should therefore be considered as a matter of course. If nothing else, a proportion of 2:1 is a prime cause of wage drift. Theoretically, a wage survey should be conducted with other firms but since the make-up of gross pay is so variable from company to company, it is difficult to establish any meaningful form of parity. A company must examine its own costing system in terms of budgeted labour cost and the relationship this bears to unit cost. In other words, management must decide how much of the budgeted labour cost should be attributed to basic rate and how much to incentive, if any. Since this is negotiable, management should also know in advance the influence on unit costs of different break points or alternative basic rates.

One company employing about 1000 people avoided this problem by taking the budgeted labour cost for the coming year and giving to the unions concerned three different 'mixes' of total wage cost. This was broken down into 3, 5 and 7 grades complete with incentive calculated at 80, 90 and 100 BSI. (80 BSI is a good average rate of working.) The unions were told that they could produce another option still coming to the same total if they so desired. The company in question, while unused to this level of participation, had a history of good industrial relations. Obviously some unions will question the budgeted labour cost but this does not detract from the principle proposed.

Dealing with anomalies

Once the job evaluation exercise is completed and new basic rates determined, a scattergram will pinpoint those jobs which are likely to be over or underpaid in relation to the new rates. Provided the old structure was not completely out of control, the bulk of the jobs will be just about right with roughly the same number over as underpaid. The options open to management are:

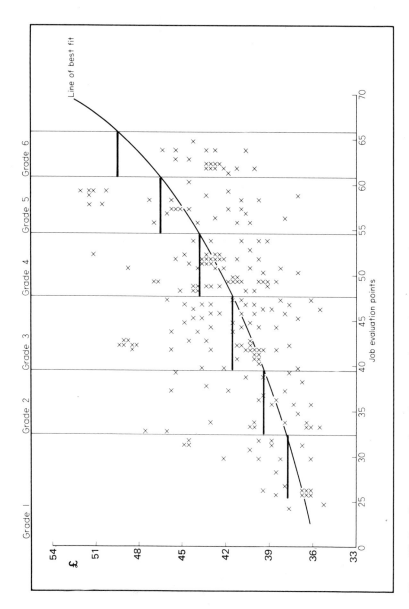

Figure 23.7   Scattergram of total earnings (excluding overtime) related to job evaluation points as well as possible break points between grades and new pay steps

For overpaid employees

1   Retrain the individuals concerned in order that they can take on
    work of a more responsible or skilful nature and therefore justify
    the new level of payment
2   Make the difference between the old rate and the new a personal
    allowance which would be eroded each time a new basic rate was
    agreed. In time the new rate would catch up with the old
3   Buy out anomalies by paying a lump sum comprising the differ-
    ence multiplied by a negotiated figure. This is a strong negotiating
    area. While a number of companies advocate this for seemingly
    sound business reasons, a marketplace bargaining environment is
    unlikely to be conducive to improved industrial relations. What
    must be considered rather is the percentage of employees involved
    and the fact that the majority of differences will be swallowed up
    within twelve to eighteen months anyway

For underpaid employees.   There are no options here: the individual's pay
must be brought into line.

INCENTIVE ELEMENT

The word 'incentive' is synonymous with the word 'effort' in the minds of
many. But this is not so. An incentive is some form of financial encouragement
recognizing a particular contribution made by the work force. It is, in effect, a
sum of money additional to the basic rate which a company pays to ensure that
its most important production aspects are being optimized. For example, a
capital-intensive company might have an incentive linked to machine utilization;
a company making diamond-tipped drilling bits might put particular emphasis on
a low scrap value while still maintaining quality. Nonetheless many companies
insist that effort is the only factor to recognize despite the fact that automation
is very much with us.

   Thought must be given to the *cost* of maintaining any one incentive: how
many work study personnel, bonus clerks, tally clerks and inspectors are
required to maintain standards? Can it be done in a more simple, effective way?
Need there be an incentive? Will people only work on a carrot and stick basis?
Will you, the reader, only work on this basis or are you different? What
contribution does first-line supervision make to motivating people? Will the
system encourage or stifle the growth of tomorrow's supervisors?

   The basic decisions to be made about the incentive element are whether or
not it is going to be individual, group, area or company based or a combination
of these. The other important feature is whether the incentive is to be based on
a straight-line formula (the more units produced the more earned *ad infinitum*)

or on a curve where rather less is earned proportionately the more units produced, sometimes with a cut-off point to limit production and thereby restrict bonus. Yet another approach is to have a cut-off point beyond which any bonus earned is placed in a common pool. This in turn is used to help finance basic rates when these are renegotiated.

Direct incentives

Definition. A method of payment whereby a bonus is paid in direct relation to effort. It is based on the concept that man is motivated by money alone.

Advantages
1 Appropriate where a high level of physical effort is necessary and it is difficult to supervise workers effectively
2 Can generate substantial motivation as payment occurs shortly after achievement
3 Flexibility in allocating added reward for added effort
4 Introduction can mean a reduction in labour
5 Simple and easy to administrate
6 Can be useful in the short term to increase the pace of working as an interim step to moving on to a more sophisticated system

Disadvantages
1 Management is not in control of production
2 Tendency to ignore avoidance of waste
3 Supervisors in time may earn less than their subordinates, skilled less than semi-skilled
4 People learn how to achieve earnings without undue effort, for example by qualifying for special allowances, avoiding promotion to non-lucrative jobs, embarking on slow-downs during 'testing' of new rates
5 Can ruin industrial relations
6 Mobility of labour becomes virtually impossible
7 Supervisors become good progress chasers but rarely good managers

Measured daywork

Definition. Measured daywork is a stabilized payment system where the incentive element is consolidated in the basic rate, thereby achieving a high, non-fluctuating weekly wage or salary.

It is based on sound training, sophisticated work measurement techniques and sound management. It is still payment by results except that the underlying philosophy is one of trust — that an individual will work at an agreed pace provided work is available for him or her. The most common types are:

High day rate, which is suitable in an assembly-line situation. Each new employee is fully trained before starting work on the factory floor. He or she will be expected to produce work of a specified standard and to maintain a fixed working pace of, say, 90 BSI. The aim is to achieve a controlled work flow: those individuals who have a naturally high pace of working would normally be transferred to indirect work. Those who have a naturally slow pace are subject to warnings and then either transferred to indirect work or dismissed, following reasonable warning.

Advantages
1 Simplified pay structure usually based on job evaluation
2 Considerable operating flexibility
3 Trust and responsibility given proper emphasis
4 Management is in control of production and uses work study standards as a condition of employment as well as for management information

Disadvantages
1 Not always possible to elicit acceptable levels of performance without the 'pull' of a direct incentive
2 Sophisticated control techniques, such as daily computer data, are necessary
3 High calibre of supervision is essential
4 Disputes can be tougher than in direct incentive plants as employees can slow down without impairing earnings

Philips premium pay plan is suitable where individuals can control the pace of work. The same principles as those for high day rate apply except, perhaps, the problem of disputes since PPP is based on individual effort.

The pay structure is a simple one, usually based on job evaluation, but unlike high day rate, it is graded in steps according to the pace of working (see Figure 23.8). Each individual contracts through his supervisor to work for a period of

SALARY AND WAGE ADMINISTRATION

GRADE	80 BSI	90 BSI	100 BSI
	£	£	£
I	54.00	58.00	62.50
II	50.00	53.50	57.50
III	46.50	50.00	53.50
IV	43.00	46.00	49.00
V	40.00	43.00	46.00

Figure 23.8   Example of a wage structure of the Philips premium pay plan type

three months at a particular pace. If he does not maintain this pace and the fault is not that of management, he is warned. If his pace of working does not meet the agreed standard during the following three months, he is either retrained or moved back to a lower pay band. If he is unable to maintain an acceptable pace, he is liable to dismissal.

Group/area incentives

Definition. A method of payment whereby a bonus is paid either equally or proportionately to individuals within a group/area as a result, of, say, *output achieved* over an agreed standard.

Advantages
1 It encourages team spirit
2 It breaks down demarcation lines
3 The group disciplines its 'slackers'
4 Job satisfaction is achieved through seeing the complete operation within the group area

Disadvantages
1 Management is not in control of production
2 The bonus ceases in time to be an incentive and management might as well consolidate the rate
3 Individual effort is not rewarded

Plantwide incentives

There are three main types:

Factory throughput. Linked to, say, tons leaving the factory, the bonus is distributed either equally or porportionately according to skill. Basic concept is that workers become more closely associated with the company's aims.

Advantages
1 Improved atmosphere
2 Demarcation less pronounced
3 Employees are aware of the production targets the company plans to achieve

Disadvantages
1 Individual effort is not recognized
2 Employees find it difficult to associate themselves directly with the bonus

3   To safeguard against bad weeks/months, companies sometimes
    maintain a bank, so that the bonus becomes an employee benefit
4   If a bad week/month is experienced it's always the fault of 'other'
    departments

Scanlon plan.   An alternative name is share of production plan. The nub of
the system is the formation of a joint management–union productivity team
which has *executive authority.*   The bonus is based on productivity improvements and is usually calculated monthly.

Rucker plan.   An alternative name is cost reduction plan. The basic theory is
that there is a constant relationship between wages and production or added
value.   A joint management–union productivity team is formed but it has
advisory authority only.   Savings made by reducing costs are shared either
equally or proportionately and are usually distributed on a monthly basis.

In a nutshell, Scanlon is strong on industrial relations and weak on mathematics and Rucker vice versa. In practice, the best of both methods is adopted. The
share-out is usually about a third of total savings. The basic concept for both is
that manual workers have very much more to offer to a company than simply
effort.

Advantages of Scanlon/Rucker plans
1   Can encourage better use of resources and raw materials and there-
    by produce substantial savings
2   Focuses attention on cooperation and teamwork to reduce costs
3   Trust and responsibility given proper emphasis
4   People accept change more readily
5   Normally covers direct and indirect workers and can include staff
    directly linked with production
6   Work group has a stake in how well management performs – and
    has freedom to criticize poor decisions: it therefore keeps manage-
    ment on its toes

Disadvantages of Scanlon/Rucker plans
1   Cannot in itself create a willingness to cooperate or a management
    capable of exploiting cost reduction
2   Some groups have more control over results than others and some
    contribute more than they receive
3   Parochialism can result: good communication is essential
4   Success largely hinges on sophisticated cost control techniques over
    a long period – and deciding on the 'right' calculation for distribu-
    tion of savings

Profit-sharing

Definition. On the basis of company profits, employees either receive an annual cash bonus or actual company shares. Basic concept is paternalism/participation.

Advantages
1 Thrives in non-union firms
2 From management's point of view, extra rewards are allocated only when they can be afforded
3 Improved teamwork and cooperation. However, to optimize this, management must communicate the economic facts of life
4 The system is self-adjusting although the method by which profits are calculated or the form in which the money is distributed may come under attack

Disadvantages
1 Workers have little control over final profit achieved
2 An industrious worker does not necessarily achieve extra payment
3 Tendency to withhold part of the profit to be shared against less fortunate times, thus making it a handout or employee benefit
4 Many schemes do not pay sufficient money to make an impact on motivation

Merit-rating

Definition. A method of payment based on management decisions about an individual's personal *qualities and aptitudes*. Basic concept is that management reserves the sole right to pay people individually.

Advantages
1 Supervisors regularly consider each subordinate's contribution
2 A counselling interview gives both supervisor and supervised an opportunity to plan constructively for the future
3 Method of payment is flexible
4 Employees feel they are being treated as individuals

Disadvantages
1 Supervisors are expected to be amateur psychologists
2 Because it is usually a subjective assessment, it is difficult to discuss problem areas without an element of emotionalism — always supposing they are discussed at all
3 Economic pressures often result in the system being bent with everyone ending up at the top end
4 Supervisors find it easier to pay everyone the same so that it effectively becomes an employee benefit

PRODUCTIVITY ELEMENT

The third tier, the productivity element, is a means of jacking up the wage structure while maintaining differentials between grades.

It is a well-established fact that in a stable economy there is an almost constant relationship between labour costs and added value. It follows, therefore, that this provides a useful formula on which to calculate savings: these in turn are used to fund annual wage increases on a plantwide basis.

For example, assume that unions and management agree (as a result of information provided by the company's auditors) that over the last five years labour cost has been 34 per cent of added value.

		£
Sales		100 000
Less raw materials		55 000
Added value		45 000
Labour cost		15 300
Labour cost: Added value		34%

It is agreed that any savings made in labour cost beyond this reference point of 34 per cent will be shared equally between management and unions.

Assume that sales increase 20 per cent with no additional increases in the cost of raw materials and that labour costs increase by 10 per cent. The situation would appear thus:

		£
Sales		120 000
Less raw materials		66 000
Added value		54 000
Labour cost		16 830
34% x £54 000		18 360
Saving in labour cost		1 530
Proportion contribute to plantwide increases		765

A total of 4.5 per cent on the total wage bill

It will be obvious that companies will be required to open their books if the operation of the added-value concept is to maintain credibility. Set against this is the fact that the more information which can be produced prior to negotiation, the less conflict there will be between management and unions. Approximately half of all disputes leading to stoppages are caused by friction over wage rates.

A removal in part, even of some of the reasons behind these stoppages would give both management and unions more time to contribute to other important areas.

PRODUCTIVITY AGREEMENTS

A productivity agreement is a statement jointly agreed by management and unions on how work and people may be more effectively organized to mutual benefit. Two types of agreement are:

1 An agreement using the 'buying out' principle on the basis of *quid pro quo*. In effect, this type of agreement covers immediate wage increases in exchange for relaxation of rigid demarcation lines; elimination of tea breaks; forfeiture of mates; reduction in total labour force
2 An agreement which lays down a framework for allowing savings to be accumulated over six to twelve months. These savings are normally shared equally between management and shop floor employees

In a nutshell, the difference between the two is 'jam today or jam tomorrow'. In selecting the right approach, a company must consider what will best match its industrial relations climate *and* its overall company objectives. It may be that its lack of operating flexibility demands a 'buying out' agreement in the short term but its longer-term objectives require phased steps towards a position where greater participation will fund wage increases as well as strengthen the company's future. But it must be *planned*.

In times of high unemployment, productivity agreements of the buying-out type are not popular with unions. In any case, it is narrow to assume that increased productivity can *only* be achieved through a reduced labour force: there are numerous options which are equally valid. For example, what would be the effect of better machine utilization, improved work flow, reduction in scrap value, introduction of shift work? It is rather a question of selecting the right tools in order to make the best use of human resources.

Whatever form the agreement takes, it is, in effect, a *statement of intent* signed by both parties: what must not be overlooked is that it is not a once-and-for-all effort but a document calling for positive action throughout its term with regular progress reviews properly communicated. All too often companies negotiate excellent productivity agreements but fail to follow them through.

SINGLE STATUS

Employee or fringe benefits provide an element of security, a security which up until the last few years was the preserve of staff and management only. With the trend towards narrowing the differences in conditions between blue and white collar workers, unions are becoming increasingly aware of the value to their members of negotiating, for example, increased holidays. This is further emphasized in the Industrial Relations Code of Practice. If the incentive element influences employee attitudes, how much more that of employee benefits? Sometimes overlooked, the Equal Pay Act requires equality in particular employee benefits as well as pay. If single status is the ultimate aim, a phasing operation must be planned in order that costs may be absorbed. The point being made is that employee benefits are part of the total labour cost and must be taken into account when looking at overall pay and conditions. This last point is also underlined in the Code.

COMMUNICATION

An important area not stressed sufficiently is the need to communicate effectively. *The need to know* what is happening must be satisfied. Managers are often as starved of information as operatives! Will your present system cope? It is not the shop stewards' job to communicate management's intentions. Can your supervisors brief their subordinates face to face? What can you do to help them? Above all, every individual affected by the new pay structure must *understand* how it works. Could a simple booklet be produced? These are the main points concerning communication but since it is vital to the success of the whole project, readers are strongly advised to read the Industrial Society's booklet on 'Communication' in the *Notes for Managers* series.

SUPERVISORY STRUCTURE

Because many companies are attempting to move away from direct incentives, it is wise to comment on the need to investigate the existing supervisory structure and to consider the calibre, in effect, of first-line managers. Whatever management decides in terms of a new structure, first-line supervisors will be required to manage more effectively. Apart from training needs, the span of control must be examined. If a supervisor is to manage effectively, the most he can control and motivate is twenty operatives. The successful implementation of a new wage structure hinges on how carefully this aspect is handled.

EXAMPLE OF A WAGE POLICY STATEMENT

It is the intention of management that this document is issued to every employee whom it concerns. It is the responsibility of first-line management to explain it fully to their subordinates. Should anyone feel that any aspect of this policy is not operating in practice, he should ensure this is discussed by the Joint Consultative Committee.

Aims. The aims of the policy are:

1 To recognize the value of all jobs in relation to each other within the company
2 To take account of wage rates paid by companies of similar size, product and philosophy
3 To ensure stable earnings
4 To enable individuals to reach their full earning potential
5 To ensure employees share in the company's prosperity as a result of increasing efficiency

Job evaluation

The basis of a sound wage structure is job evaluation. It is in the interest of both unions and management that this is carried out on a joint basis.

Job evaluation is a continuing process and therefore must be maintained if it is to retain its usefulness. To ensure that the scheme is still relevant, it will be reviewed jointly by unions and management at the end of its third operating year.

Wage structure

In designing the wage structure, the company aims to make the best use of people in order to achieve the company's short and longer-term objectives. By achieving these objectives the company is able to remain a leader in its field, thereby ensuring greater job security for all concerned.

Rate for the job

No one will be paid less than the recognized rate for the job. Equal pay is in force on the basis of 'equal pay for work of equal value'. While the company recognizes the right of the unions' joint negotiating panel to negotiate on behalf of its members, management believes that first and foremost rates should be linked to the company's prosperity.

The company does not aim to pay the top rates in the area but rather to place the emphasis on good working conditions, security of employment and an atmosphere in which individuals may reach their full potential. Nonetheless the company aims to be in the top 15 per cent as far as total earnings are concerned. (Total earnings includes employee benefits.)

Number of grades

The number of grades will be as few as possible in order that differentials are of a sufficiently high level for real differences in responsibility and/or skill to be recognized.

Incentives

The company does not accept that its employees will work only on a carrot and stick basis: neither does it believe that its employees will give of their best if earnings fluctuate from week to week. This policy is reflected in the company's wage structure which is based on measured daywork.

Every employee should, through training, have the opportunity to reach maximum earnings for his grade. Provided work is available, employees are expected to work at a mutually agreed pace. Where work is not immediately available, employees will not lose financially but will be expected to move to alternative work in order to maintain production.

Where individual targets are not maintained, and management is not responsible, an employee must expect to be counselled, disciplined and, as a last resort, dismissed.

Work measurement

The basis of the wage structure is work measurement. The company aims to use the most advanced methods available. However, it does not intend to wrap these methods in a jargon not easily understood. All production managers (including first-line supervisors) and shop stewards will attend jointly sponsored appreciation courses in order that any disagreement over standards is discussed in full knowledge of how the system works.

Indirect workers

Indirect workers such as maintenance, cleaning and catering employees play an important support role in the overall production process. It is not possible to apply work measurement techniques to indirect jobs at an economic cost. An enhanced day rate will therefore be payable to employees in this category.

Minimum earnings

No employee will receive less than £40.00 for a 40-hour week. This ensures that lower-paid employees are paid a 'living wage', but employees in other grades must not expect that established differentials will necessarily be maintained.

Overtime

The wage structure is designed to ensure that excessive overtime is both unnecessary and unattractive. Overtime is a requirement which will only arise in very exceptional circumstances. Since it is management's responsibility to plan work effectively and determine manning requirements, 72 hours' notice will be given of the need for overtime working, except in very exceptional circumstances.

Promotion

The company operates a policy of internal promotion, wherever possible. When a promotion takes place, the individual will immediately take the 'rate for the job'. However, if the individual is on maximum earnings for his old grade, he will retain the old rate for three months until he has established himself in the new grade.

In exceptional cases where the individual fails to maintain a satisfactory level of performance, he will be transferred to lower-grade work. He will, however, retain the higher rate until the annual negotiation of wage rates when his personal rate will be eroded.

A similar policy operates for staff promotions.

Single status

It is company policy to remove progressively all differences in employee benefits for blue and white collar employees. To this end, the cost of such benefits will be included in overall labour costs. The ultimate aim is to move towards a 'package' concept negotiated annually.

Share of prosperity

The company believes that employees have a right to share in the company's prosperity. It also believes that increases in its labour bill should not be passed automatically to its customers. An accounting formula has therefore been agreed between management and unions whereby all savings made as a result of shopfloor participation will be divided on a 50/50 basis and used to finance increased wage costs.

Cost of living

The company believes that it has as much responsibility to maintain the purchasing power of its employees' earnings as it has to ensure that shareholders get a fair return on their investment. The company is in favour of a 'threshold' cost-of-living increase provided this is not passed automatically to its customers.

Negotiating information

The company believes that only by providing unions with sound, factual information can a positive industrial relations climate be fostered.

Quarterly figures will be issued to the joint negotiating panel concerning the share-of-prosperity formula. These figures will be subject to audit in the usual way.

No additional information requested by unions will be unreasonably withheld.

CHECKLIST: CHANGING A WAGE STRUCTURE

The following checklist is intended to provide a starting point for discussion before installing a new wage structure. The list is by no means exhaustive but answering such questions should enable managers to decide the direction in which they plan to go in the short and longer term.

Company objectives

1   Apart from profit, what are you in business for?
2   Where are you going during the next two to three years; in the next five to ten years?
3   How do you plan to get there?
4   What influence will these plans have on your wage structure?
5   How can the wage structure aid the compamy in meeting its objectives?

Product

1   Are runs short, long, one-offs?
2   How important is quality, quantity, accuracy, consistency?
3   Is the process operator- or machine-controlled?
4   What are the capital investment plans for the next three to five years? Will these developments influence the pay structure?
5   What are the market pressures? Are there seasonal fluctuations?
6   Can buffer stocks be kept or is the product perishable?
7   How much is lost through scrap? (If the material is reconstituted, cost this.)

Government legislation

The foregoing is conditioned, as appropriate, by current Government legislation.

Work measurement

1 Are measurements loose, tight or a mixture of both?
2 Is pay related to effort? Is this what you want anyway?
3 To what extent are you subject to wage drift, that is, increasing labour costs with little or no increase in productivity?
4 Do your supervisors and shop stewards understand the principles of work measurement?
5 Have you enough industrial engineers to ensure that three separate studies are made before each standard is decided?
6 Are your existing studies sufficiently accurate to allow you to consider the introduction of synthetic ratings?
7 How about method study?
8 Will it be necessary to employ contract work-study personnel? Or experienced industrial engineers on a short-term contract?

Wage analysis

1 How many wage rates exist?
2 Where do national agreements fit in?
3 Is there a 20 per cent differential between supervisors' pay and the gross pay (less overtime) of those they supervise?
4 What is the budgeted labour cost for the coming year? Does it include the cost of employee benefits?
5 What is the trend of *total* labour cost for the last five years?
6 How many elements make up gross pay? How many of these do you wish to consolidate?
7 What is the earnings distribution for each department for two, separate, typical weeks?
8 What trends are indicated from a breakdown of overtime worked?
9 What is the cost of producing each selling line and the proportion of labour cost attributed?
10 What is the cost of labour turnover?
11 What is the cost of absenteeism?

Job evaluation

1 What is the simplest possible method you could use which would satisfy the company's and the job holders' needs?
2 Should there be a joint job evaluation team or one comprising managers only?
3 Should it be a full or part-time exercise?
4 To what extent can you involve the job holders?
5 Who should write the job description? The job holder, a job analyst or a member of the job evaluation committee?

6   How much information are you prepared to give to job holders
    about the scheme?   Do you mean, for example, to tell each job
    holder the number of points allocated to his job?   Could you give
    everyone concerned a copy of the scheme?

7   Will your existing appeals procedure match the needs of a job
    evaluation exercise?

8   Could you time and cost in advance the implementation of job
    evaluation?

Financing the wage structure

1   Can you finance from within the increased cost of the new wage
    structure?

2   Could you negotiate initially the share-out between company and
    employees of any savings made?

3   How can you communicate effectively the aims of the exercise?

4   What training will have to be undertaken?

5   How can you involve your supervisors in order that they make a
    major contribution to the exercise?

Social aspects

1   What is the age and sex distribution by job and department?

2   What motivates your employees?   What are their aspirations?
    Would an attitude survey be useful?

3   What kind of image does your company have?   Is it what you want?

4   What kind of incentives are people used to in your geographical
    locality?   Would your proposals cut across the expectations of your
    employees?   What can you do to engineer the change?

5   How do you rate your industrial relations?   How can this exercise
    improve them?

6   What is the company's management style?   Will the new wage
    structure alter this in any way?   How can you involve middle and
    senior management in order that they are party to the proposals?

7   What plans have you regarding such things as security of employ-
    ment and earnings; single status?

8   How important is a stable work force to the company?   Is it
    company policy to promote from the shop floor?   Will the new pay
    structure influence or detract from this?

Designing the wage structure

1   From scattergrams of the existing situation, what anomalies exist?
    How many of these can you hope to get rid of first time around?

2 Using the scattergrams, how many grades ought you to have in the short term? What are you aiming for in the long term?

3 How can you involve your company accountant in order that the exercise is properly costed?

4 Is an alternative incentive planned? Do you need incentives anyway? If you do, will they be individual, group or company based? Or a combination of these?

5 What effect will the incentive element have on your products, the way you plan work, the way you manage people, employee attitudes?

6 Could you work out three possibilities for, say, a 3, 5 or 7 grade structure complete with differentials and incentive element, if any, each coming to the total budgeted labour cost?

7 How competitive would these rates be locally?

8 What is your policy on equal pay?

9 What will your unions be expecting at the negotiating table? To what extent can you consult them in the actual design of the structure before negotiation?

10 What kind of productivity agreement do you need? To what extent can you make it a charter for the future?

11 How far can you go in giving information to your unions in order that negotiation may be constructive?

12 How will you handle pay anomalies?

13 How can you provide simple information on a regular basis to all concerned regarding the productivity element?

Implementing a wage structure

1 How can you improve your methods of communication in order that everyone *understands* what is happening?

2 Do senior managers understand how the new pay structure might affect them? Marketing and sales, for example?

3 What training can you give to your supervisors in order that their status and respect is strengthened and not weakened by the demands of the new pay structure?

4 Is your supervisory structure adequate in relation to the needs of the new pay structure? Can you give your supervisors more scope for decision-making without reference to the next level? Is their span of control about right in view of the demands which will be put on them?

5 What training should you give to shop stewards in order that they are aware of the implications of the new structure?

24

Pensions and Employee Benefits

Betty Ream

The last few years have seen a marked increase in employee benefits and of the importance they play in what is known in current jargon as the 'total remuneration package'. Many benefits were originally given by philanthropic employers as a reward for loyalty and long service, the majority being limited to staff employees whose closer association with those at the top made their contribution to the organization more easily recognized. Today, not only is the gap between blue and white collar workers disappearing at an unprecedented rate but employees at all levels are coming to consider certain basic privileges as an essential norm, as a right instead of a privilege.

REASONS FOR DEVELOPMENT

In the past, employee benefits have received most attention when the economy has been booming and when employers and employees have not been primarily caught up with the struggle to maintain adequate base rates. Today, inflation means that there will be continuing representations about the size of the pay packet itself and this cannot but remain the major concern in any negotiating situation. Nevertheless there are certain other influences which have stimulated the demand for benefits, both to cover more people and be more generous in themselves and to offer a variety of provisions not considered ten or twenty years ago. These influences are likely to remain with us indefinitely.

Firstly, those who have managed to achieve a reasonable standard of living no longer accept an outworn assumption that this standard should drop markedly when they are unable to work, often through no fault of their own—in sickness, old age, after a redundancy and so on. All of us, in an increasingly insecure world, are looking for buffers against circumstances which we can in no way control. Society now gives the majority an existence substantially above subsistence level, the lot of so many in the past, and while the State sets out to protect against fundamental hardships, employees are now looking increasingly to their employers to play their part in addition.

Secondly, in an economy such as our own with a high level of taxation, benefits in kind or which guarantee income when it might otherwise have been withdrawn may well give a much better return than a straight cash payment. Again, the levels obtaining in other European countries and the possibility of compulsory observance of certain common employment conditions have added to existing pressures.

COST OF BENEFITS

An inevitable consequence of this development in benefits is that they now involve a cost which represents a very considerable percentage of the payroll. Estimates vary but a survey carried out by The Industrial Society towards the end of 1974 showed, over a small sample, an average cost of 23.45 per cent of the payroll. For organizations in the commercial world in particular, the cost may very well be much higher. Figures for the same year for the EEC as a whole suggest a percentage of 30.5 per cent of the payroll, and in both areas, there was every indication that costs are increasing.

The costs of benefits is considerable but there are, of course, advantages to the company, whether they be direct or indirect. Thus, a company car can well save considerable time, an attractive, subsidized midday meal may help output in in the afternoon and so on. Moreover, few organizations will be able to build up a responsible work force in the long term if they fall behind levels generally obtaining.

A substantial sum of money is involved, but so often an investigation will show that those affected have no idea of the amount the company is spending on them in this way and are also unaware either of the value of the benefit to them or even that they are covered by it at all. Accordingly, a number of organizations in this country—but as yet too few—are introducing the practice, more common in the USA, of giving employees an annual statement of their benefit entitlement.

NEED TO REVIEW AND INVESTIGATE

The last few years have seen a change in thinking about social security payments from the State so that now the aim is to relate them, in general, to earnings rather than to provide a universal base rate. This means that, for many, the amount from the State has increased considerably and may increase still further in the future; any company scheme should therefore be flexible so that the payments can be taken into account. The employee too is paying his share of the cost and there is no sense in overproviding for certain needs at the expense of others, especially if this puts an undue contribution burden on either side.

Again, social attitudes, needs and philosophy vary and a benefit that is relevant and appreciated in one decade may be an anomaly in the next. Accordingly a benefit programme should be reviewed at regular intervals to ensure that it is apposite and up to date. Today's emphasis on participation should mean that there is no need to stress the value of consulting those affected, both so that their views and values are taken into account and so that, through joint consultation, the benefit is seen to have worth and meaning.

PENSIONS

The importance of pension provision has been spotlighted over many years by stormy debates in parliament and outside, over successive governments' proposals to widen the scope and extent of the national insurance scheme and reduce drastically the number of those dependent on means-tested supplementary benefits. All parties accept the principle of earnings-related benefits and earnings-related contributions on top of a minimum base rate: all also accept that it is right to rely on a partnership between state and occupational schemes, the State providing a basic pension for all, supplemented either by an additional, fallback, state scheme, separately funded, or by an occupational scheme which has been recognized as guaranteeing certain essential minima.

Occupational schemes were acknowledged in the 1974 White Paper 'Better Pensions' as being socially valuable and economically important and as representing an important element of personal savings and investment. While the best of them have in-built safeguards against known problems and are intrinsically generous, others are limited in their coverage or provide amounts that give little significant help to the financial problems of old age. Thus, legislation has been devised to encourage inadequate schemes to achieve a higher standard or to give additional coverage elsewhere to those with insufficient provision.

Though on the surface it would appear to be an expensive commitment, a recognized occupational scheme offers the organization certain advantages which may well justify any difference in cost between its operation and that of compulsory membership of the supplementary state scheme. It can, firstly, be designed to meet the particular needs of the organization, whether it be an earlier-than-normal retirement age or the assurance of a substantial life cover. It can be used to ensure a measure of flexibility and can more quickly reflect changing needs and expectations.

Type of scheme

In designing a pension scheme, the organization will first agree what it wants to achieve, determining the priorities and, with specialist help, calculating the cost. It may decide to operate a self-administered scheme if adequate actuarial, investment and administrative services are available or it may prefer to introduce an insured scheme through one of the many life offices in the field. It is, of course, quite possible to take advantage of both, using the self-administered scheme for the general provision while insuring with an outside office either the life cover or an increased entitlement (a 'top hat' scheme) for senior staff. If the decision is a difficult one, a pension consultancy firm may be called in to give impartial advice.

Originally, and to a small continuing extent, a number of pensions were awarded on an *ex gratia* basis and were not funded but paid out of current income. This type of arrangement, because of its inherent insecurity, being dependent on goodwill and having little safeguard in the event of mergers or bankruptcies, will not allow contracting-out of the second tier state cover.

Protection against inflation

Most schemes today relate pensions to average or basic earnings in the last year, or last few years, of employment. In the case of employees whose earnings are not necessarily maintained towards the end of their working life, the calculation may be made on the best three years during the last ten years' service. Salary grade and other types of scheme which purchase fixed amounts of pension for each year spent in a specific salary bracket, or which guarantee a uniform sum for each year of service, no longer represent a realistic proportion of a man's earnings at the point when he retires. Final salary schemes, therefore, give the best safeguard against continuing inflation during working life though, by the essential nature of things, it is more difficult to anticipate the actual costs involved.

Inflation, too, can not only affect the proportion of salary awarded as a pension but causes extreme anxiety among pensioners themselves. The last few years have seen a growing number of occupational schemes either make a specific commitment to a percentage annual increase to compensate for falling money values ('inflation-proofing', 'dynamizing' or 'escalating') or promise in general terms to review the position and take action as and when this is called for and possible.

The most recent proposals of governments of both parties have recognized the need to ensure some guarantee of the maintenance of the value of pension rights and indeed this was a major emphasis of the 1975 legislation. Recognizing the extent of the problem and the open-ended cost of any worthwhile guarantee, the State has now undertaken to provide for the guaranteed minimum pension, as defined in the Act, to be increased in line with national earnings levels, thereby underwriting a very expensive but vitally important form of protection.

Changes authorized by the Finance Act now make it possible for many more occupational schemes to offer the opportunity of commuting a given proportion of the pension. Those with financial skills or good financial advice see this as a right which offers another opportunity of maintaining money values. Others will welcome the chance to acquire a substantial lump sum which may help them in some way adapt to retirement, whether it be by moving to a smaller house or flat, or by the purchase of labour- or cost-saving equipment. Some quite frankly take a lump sum to enable them to satisfy some unachieved ambition before they settle down to the pattern of retirement.

Preservation of pension benefits

One of the main changes brought about by the Social Security Act 1973 was the compulsory preservation of pension rights for those in occupational schemes who were aged twenty-six and over and who had five years' pensionable service (or service carrying pension credits) with the organization in question. Those who meet these qualifications may now no longer receive a refund of contributions on leaving employment but will receive at normal pension age the amount of pension earned during service, secured in one of a variety of ways. Service before April 1975 is not included in the calculation if the employee does not want this, but nevertheless, he has the right to ask for it to be assigned.

Pensions may be preserved (frozen) in the scheme in question, or rights bought out by the purchase of an insurance policy or annuity if the scheme rules allow. Alternatively, again if scheme rules provide, rights may be transferred to the new employer's scheme if the latter is empowered to receive them. Compulsory transferability has been mooted for some years as being a desirable ideal. The concept is both complex and difficult to implement but what, increasingly, is becoming the practice on a voluntary basis may before very long be made obligatory.

Contracting out of the state scheme

It will be open to employers to contract occupational scheme members out of the second part of the state scheme, which will come into operation in 1978, if their occupational scheme satisfies certain minimum standards. Those include levels of basic pension and the overall requirement that at the end of the day the pension is no less than the state scheme would have provided – the guaranteed minimum pension. Widow's pensions at 50 per cent of the husband's entitlement are also an essential. Those who are contracted out will pay a lower contribution to the state scheme.

The decision whether or not to contract out is complex, and calls for specialist advice. It will depend among other things on the investment return that can be obtained from the difference in contributions and on the age structure and characteristics of the population involved. The wishes of those concerned should also be taken into consideration, for a provision will lose part of its value if it is not welcomed.

SICK PAY

The problem of maintaining normal standards of living during prolonged periods of absence is very real, and at present the responsibility is shared by the State, those employers who have made commitments to ensure that their employees have an adequate income when they are sick and employees themselves who, like employers, pay part of the cost through their national insurance contributions. While there has been some discussion about the possibility of making employers wholly responsible for payments during the first few weeks of any illness, to cut down the administrative time involved in the operation of two distinct systems, there is as yet no indication that this will become a major issue.

Amount of coverage

It has always been impossible to generalize about the amount of sick pay allowed and the length of time during which it is payable, for variations from industry to industry and company to company have, in the past, been very great. Some, and in particular white collar workers, have normally received allowances calculated to give them the whole or a high proportion of their salary when national insurance benefits are taken into account. Many manual workers on the other hand have been granted weekly payments on a fixed-sum basis which have had no direct relationship to their wage packets or to the difference in skills and take-home pay within an organization.

As with pension arrangements, so with sick pay schemes there has been a steady move to relate benefits to earnings, and the state scheme itself introduced an earnings-related element in 1966. Moreover, continuing inflation has meant that any amount quoted in actual money terms has had a rapidly decreasing value and this has undermined any sense of security those covered by fixed-sum schemes might otherwise have had.

More important still have been the strong pressures to remove the marked differences between the conditions of white and blue collar employees, differences which are of historic origin but which are increasingly difficult to justify in today's conditions. Here again, the influence of the EEC countries—in France, for example, the mensualization programme has quickly affected a substantial proportion of the working population—has given an impetus to our own thinking, and time-limits for action.

In establishing its sick pay scheme, a company must first decide what it wants to achieve through its sick pay policy. Is its main concern to look after those in senior jobs or with long service? Does it wish to offer attractive conditions from the start, to enable it to recruit and retain staff? Does it feel an overall sense of responsibility for anyone on its books or does it believe that it is for employees first to make their contribution to prosperity over a defined period?

It is then possible to consider a few general guidelines to current practice without indicating length of time which should be covered, save to say that provision is steadily getting more generous. Most organizations will take into account national insurance payments and allow salary less the amounts receivable, believing both that it is unnecessary to overcompensate and that it is putting a temptation in people's way if they are better off in sickness than in health. Practice varies over payment for uncertified absence and waiting days (ie days during which national insurance is not payable) and in this respect manual employees have been treated, and often continue to be treated, less generously than staff.

Service is a concept about which ideas are slowly changing and this may well be the result of today's greater mobility. At one time, sick pay scales were very much more generous to those with longer service and this continues to be today's general pattern. Nevertheless, there are those who say that employees contribute to company prosperity as soon as they begin a new job, and many indeed bring with them skills and knowledge from elsewhere which are particularly valuable in the new situation. Some unions are firmly against differentiation, and this is an area in which the pattern may well change in the future.

Long-term disability

There has been growing concern for those—and they are mercifully few—who have long and serious illnesses which take them outside the cover provided by the normal sick pay provisions. This has resulted in the introduction of long-term disability schemes underwritten by an insurance company and paid for by the employer and which guarantee weekly sums, often for an indefinite period, to those who have been ill for a given number of weeks.

Legal obligations and controls

The granting of sick pay is entirely a matter for the organization's discretion unless it is specifically provided for by an industrywide agreement or wages council. Nevertheless, if there is no payment scheme in operation, this should be stated clearly—not only do the requirements of the Contracts of Employment Act make this essential but there is legal presumption that where there is no clear evidence of an intention to the contrary, the employer should continue to pay wages unless the illness is so serious that a contract can be considered to have been frustrated.

Experience has shown that the introduction of a sick pay scheme where one has not existed before may well result in an increase in sickness absence. This rise will normally level off and statistics have also shown a decrease in the duration of longer-term illnesses. It is obviously essential to keep a tight control on the position, and the concerned discipline of a good supervisor should in all cases be supplemented by rules to ensure immediate advice of absence, adequate records and at times the right to a second medical opinion.

Maternity leave

Again, practice in this country has been affected by the European position and by a growing realization of the contribution that women can make to the work force. The public sector led the way in allowing leave of absence with promises of reinstatement to those who wish to return, and the Employment Protection Act now guarantees reinstatement and continuity of employment to women who have two years' service. The payment of six weeks' salary to those who qualify will probably be compulsory in 1977.

HOLIDAYS

It may come as a surprise to many of the younger generation to know that, while clerical staff have been more generously treated over the years, there are still a considerable number of manual employees who can remember the time when paid annual or public holidays were unknown. Unlike his counterpart on the continent, the British employee has no statutory right to paid holiday, except for certain minimum provisions laid down in wages council regulations, and has therefore always had to look to collective bargaining or to initiatives taken by his employer. Here too, the greatest advance has been made in times of prosperity and full employment, the most significant in this respect being the two postwar periods and the late 1960s onwards.

Entitlement

Right to a specified period of paid holiday may be laid down in industrial agreements or wages council enactments or by an undertaking written into the individual employment contract on a basis established within the company. The written statement of terms and conditions of employment required by the Contracts of Employment Act must also refer to the actual amount of pay and to the entitlement on leaving.

The length of holiday in this country has increased considerably during the past two decades and the counter-inflationary legislation of 1973-4 encouraged employers to improve the lot of those receiving less than three weeks' annual holiday, by that time already an insignificant number. In 1974 the Department of Employment established that 61 per cent of all manual workers—less favourably treated overall than their staff colleagues—were receiving more than three weeks and that this figure included 7 per cent whose entitlement was four weeks or more. Industrial and other agreements made but not then effective would produce a further increase in the following months.

The norm for staff would appear to be approaching four weeks, with senior staff and those with longer service beginning to regain the differential they had more commonly when the basic figure was lower.

Pay

For many years, payment for holidays for manual workers was calculated on base rates, with the exception of the building and construction industries where the stamp scheme was, and still is, operated. Today, however, pay is coming to be related to average earnings so that merit and bonus are taken into account. Guaranteed, but not usually non-contractual overtime, may at times be included. The payment of holiday bonuses is far less common in this country than in Europe and so far there appears to be little change in practice.

Closedown or staggered holidays

A close-down period will help to avoid a prolonged period when loss of efficiency is inevitable, when waiting time may well result from an unbalanced labour force and when costs escalate through the use of temporary labour and the switching of employees to jobs to which they are not accustomed. It will also allow certain essential maintenance to be carried out without disruption. On the other hand, certain organizations will—by their very nature—have to give a continuing service to customers or may carry out processes which are uneconomic to close down. Equally important is the fact that failure to offer flexible dates will inconvenience employees, most of whom have a variety of domestic and social obligations to consider.

RECREATIONAL FACILITIES

One of the oldest established employee benefits is the sports and social club, which provides opportunities for the extension of contacts made during working hours. Originally intended to help foster a greater sense of unity within an organization, it also provided recreational facilities which were not available for, or beyond the means of, the average employee. Social clubs now vary greatly in the interest they attract, for while some are enthusiastically supported, the increase in travelling time for so many, the pull of television and the extension of social opportunities generally mean that in large towns in particular their attraction is beginning to wane.

Administration

Most clubs have a contributory membership and to the subscription income a company will often add a stated amount as a guaranteed yearly sum or on a percentage basis.

Control is normally vested in a members' committee, and there may, if size warrants, be a full-time secretary either on the payroll of the company or paid direct by the club. Subcommittees can be appointed to run specific sections which have their own budgets and raise their own funds, the latter possibly being supplemented by a grant from central resources. This kind of help from the centre is often limited to the purchase of equipment or to special development projects.

The capital cost of providing club premises is substantial and the proportion of employees who use them comparatively low—often as little as 10 per cent—with an even smaller percentage prepared to take an active interest. It is important to consider from time to time what it is hoped to achieve by such an expenditure and whether the aims are being fulfilled. Nevertheless a truly successful club can contribute much to morale and to the maintenance of a good public image.

CATERING AND FOOD SERVICES

There is no legislation requiring an employer to cook and sell food (the Canteen Order disappeared with the Defence of the Realm Act) but there are some messroom requirements in certain industries and some special regulations for women workers in factories. Two world wars, however, emphasized the importance of feeding people at work, and a food service now operates in over 25 000 companies in the UK and is available to probably over 60 per cent of all employees in industry. The remaining employees are employed in the main in smaller companies, and are issued with luncheon vouchers or are part-time employees who might, for example, be working in the mornings or afternoons only.

The provision of employee food services depends to a large extent on local factors—the availability of alternative eating arrangements, the length of the meal break, the demands of shift working and the amenities offered by other companies in the district. Although the proportion of employees who buy meals from the service varies considerably from company to company, where services are available a third of all employees on average buy a main meal each day, and a half buy a sandwich, filled roll or cake. The majority buy one or more cups of tea, coffee or a cold drink.

Refreshment services

While the main methods of serving refreshments during mid-morning and mid-afternoon breaks still include vending machines, trolleys and dining-room counters, a survey carried out by The Industrial Society in 1974 showed that approximately 60 per cent of companies were using vending machines. The change probably arises from the cost and non-availability of canteen labour and the introduction of new working patterns.

Level of catering subsidies

In these days of higher wages, the advisability of food services being self-supporting is often discussed, but this would be tantamount to asking the employee to bear an abnormal cost because of the conditions in which these services operate—at times which are uneconomic, within a very short period, etc. The level of subsidy will be influenced substantially by the prices charged, the style of service, provision for shift workers and method of food production. It will also be affected by the numbers involved and geographical factors within the unit concerned. The Industrial Society's 1974 survey reported a direct quarterly subsidy of £4.14 per employee on the site but with the current rate of inflation, this figure is already well out of date.

Administration

Canteen administration may be entrusted to a manager recruited by and on the payroll of the company, or alternatively, it may be passed to a contractor. The latter will be paid a fee for his services and be reimbursed the cost of providing food, snacks and beverages.

TRANSPORT

Company cars

Among senior employees in particular the provision of a company car, for which there may be a salary abatement in token of its use for private motoring, is becoming a normal perquisite. Others who use their own cars on official business receive a mileage allowance which takes into account petrol consumption, depreciation and, in some instances, a proportion of the insurance policy. Company-owned cars are usually maintained and serviced at the company's expense, a facility which is occasionally extended to some privately owned vehicles.

Transport to bring staff to work

Subsidized transport may be provided to bring in employees from areas difficult of access or to add to the attractions of employment. Such transport may be operated by the company itself, entirely at its own expense or paid for wholly or in part by a charge levied on individuals. If a charge is made it is, of course, necessary to obtain a public service licence and to remember that, while there are no restrictions affecting clerical and administrative employees, the Truck Acts prevent an employer from deducting the charge from the wages of a manual worker, even though the latter has signed an authority to do. There are no problems if the transport is run by a third party or if a volunteer collects the fares in cash from his colleagues.

HOUSING

While housing remains a constant national problem and a matter of basic individual concern, emphasis has changed from the practice of providing company houses at a modest rental or abatement of salary to the offering of greater facilities for house purchase. Not only are employers increasingly unwilling to allow substantial sums of money to be tied up in this way, but in a much more mobile society, employees themselves look for a greater measure of security in their domestic affairs.

Housing loans may be made at low rates of interest—this is more common in parts of the commercial word—or arrangements made for favourable terms with building societies and insurance companies. Help, on a loan basis may be given to meet the difference between the mortgage available and the purchase price of the property.

When relocation takes place, a company may arrange with the local council for an allocation of public housing and will normally pay the removal expenses of those employees it wishes to take there. These expenses will not only cover legal and removal costs, but will often also include a disturbance allowance to compensate for the fact that new curtains, carpets and so on will be required. Companies may decide to run their own hostels when young employees in particular have to be brought from other districts or when there are special requirements, such as those of shift workers, that would deter potential landladies.

OTHER BENEFITS

There are in addition, a multitude of other benefits, some of which are widely available while others may be related to the company's products or services or arise from an anxious and determined effort to provide an additional attraction to employment. Equally, they may come from a genuine concern to supplement national provisions or to add in some way to health and comfort.

Medical and educational services

Medical services may range from the provision of a surgery staffed by a full or part-time doctor, trained nurses and ancillary staff such as physiotherapists and chiropodists, to a company convalescent home or free membership of one of the insurance schemes covering the cost of private treatment. Educational benefits may not only include the whole range of facilities now being introduced to encourage general or vocational training but may be extended to provide scholarships for employees' children or the payment of membership fees of professional bodies.

Shops, laundries and other benefits

Some arrangements are made with the special interests of women in mind, and include shops and laundries, creches etc. Hairdressing is available for more men than women but the sale of company products at special rates may be of value to both, as will specialist advice from a company solicitor or accountant. Suggestion schemes not only help the company to get practical advice from the man actually doing the job but enable those who put forward ideas to receive a cash reward for constructive thinking.

FURTHER READING

C. Hymans (ed), *Handbook on Pensions and Employee Benefits,* Kluwer-Harrap, London, 1973.

J. Moonman, *The Effectiveness of Fringe Benefits in Industry,* Gower Press, Epping, 1973.

D. Gilling Smith, *The Manager's Guide to Pensions,* Institute of Personnel Management, London, 1974.

M. Pilch and V. Wood, *Managing Pension Schemes,* Gower Press, Epping, 1974.

Betty Ream, *You and Your Pension,* Industrial Society, London, 1975.

Fringe Benefits for Executives, Information survey 148, British Institute of Management, London, 1970.

Catering Prices, Costs, Subsidies and Other Information, Survey No 192, Industrial Society, London, 1974-5.

Employee Benefits Today, Survey Report No.19, British Institute of Management, London, 1974.

25

National Insurance

Information Division
Department of Health and Social Security

Britain's social services grew up piecemeal and it was not until the 1940s that the various schemes were reviewed by a committee under the chairmanship of the late Lord (then Sir William) Beveridge and remodelled on the recommendations contained in his report. The present social security schemes have, therefore, existed only since the end of the Second World War. The present unified system began in 1948 – the National Insurance Act 1946 unified all state insurance and improved the benefits; the National Insurance (Industrial Injuries) Act 1946 replaced the old system of workmen's compensation; the National Health Service Act created a medical service – including doctors and hospitals – for all; and the National Assistance Act was designed to help financially all persons unable to maintain themselves and whose needs could not be met by the insurance schemes.

Since 1948 the schemes have undergone considerable modification and extension in the light of experience. In 1961 a graduated addition to flat-rate retirement pension was introduced and in October 1966 a system of earnings-related supplements to unemployment and sickness benefit and widow's allowance began.

In September 1971, more favourable rates of payment for the chronic sick were introduced. An attendance allowance for severely disabled people was introduced in December 1971.

The Social Security Act 1975 introduced, from 6 April 1975, a new system of national insurance contributions to replace the previous system of flat-rate and graduated contributions. From 6 April 1975, Class 1 contributions are related to the employee's earnings and are collected with PAYE income tax, instead of by affixing stamps to a card. Class 2 and Class 3 contributions remain flat-rate, but, in addition to Class 2 contributions, those who are self-employed may be liable to pay Class 4 contributions on profits or gains between certain figures, which are assessable for income tax under Schedule D. Class 3 contributions are voluntary and may be paid only to secure entitlement to certain benefits.

In August 1966 a new Ministry of Social Security was set up to administer the existing schemes of national insurance, industrial injuries, family allowances and war pensions. The Ministry also became responsible for a new scheme of supplementary benefits and the National Assistance Board was abolished. On 1 November 1968 the former Ministries of Social Security and Health were merged to form the Department of Health and Social Security.

The National Health Service.   Provides hospital, medical, dental and other services for all, whether insured or not, and is paid for mainly out of general taxation although there is a separate national health service contribution which is collected with the national insurance contributions.

There are fourteen regional health authorities in England appointed by, and directly responsible to, the Secretary of State for Social Services. They are concerned in the main with the strategic planning and the development of health services.

Responsibility for the day-to-day administration of health services is in the hands of ninety area health authorities throughout the country, and they include the hospital services, health visiting, home nursing, midwifery, vaccination and immunization, family planning and activities in connection with the prevention of illness. They are also responsible for providing medical and dental inspection and treatment facilities in schools. With the exception of London and the larger areas, where a metropolitan service is provided by the regional health authorities, they also run the ambulance services.

Area health authorities match the local government non-metropolitan county councils and metropolitan district councils on a one-for-one basis, but in London they may match one or more of the boroughs. This matching was created to encourage collaboration between local government and personal social services and education and the NIIS.

Each area health authority has established a family practitioner committee which is responsible for running the family practitioner services, and their responsibilities include family doctors and dentists, and pharmaceutical and optical services. Each committee can also deal with any complaints about these services.

An entirely new kind of body has recently been established – the Community Health Council. There are more than 200 in England, each of them serving a health district and designed to represent the views of people living in the distrct to the health authority.

Cost of the health and personal social services.   The total cost of health and personal social services in England in 1975 amounted to £4107m, most of which is met from general taxation. The separate national health service contribution is estimated to produce about £230m in 1974—5 (in Great Britain). Other sources of income are local rates and health service charges for such things as prescriptions, spectacles, dentures and dental treatment.

Administration. To provide people with ready access, the nation's social security benefits are at present administered by 570 local offices of the Department of Health and Social Security grouped for control under ten regional offices in England, with central offices for Scotland and Wales, with a controller in charge of each. The local offices deal with claims for benefit and give advice on social security problems.

Unemployment benefit offices run by the Department of Employment act as agents of the Department for the payment of unemployment benefit. Careers offices provided under local authority schemes perform this function for those under eighteen years of age.

A central office at Newcastle houses the central records of British social insurance. Within the central office a records branch contains social security details of every contributor. Before 6 April 1975, cards bearing stamps or other details of the flat-rate contributions were sent in annually for clerical recording on record sheets. Graduated contributions were collected with PAYE income tax on the deduction card and recorded in a computer system. From 6 April earnings-related Class 1 contributions will be similarly collected with PAYE income tax, on deduction cards, which will be forwarded at the end of each income-tax·year by the employer. These contributions will be recorded by a highly mechanized system — using magnetic tape and microfilm and will be stored in a computer — Class 2 and Class 3 contributions may still be collected by means of stamped cards but the contributions are to be recorded in the computer.

WHO IS COVERED BY THE SCHEMES?

National insurance extends to practically the whole population aged 16 or over and under pension age. Arrangements are made for children reaching school-leaving age to be allocated a national insurance number. Persons over school-leaving age are liable for contributions where they are employed and earning £13 a week or more or are self-employed. If they are non-employed they can pay contributions voluntarily, to establish entitlement to certain benefits. An employer also pays contributions once an employee's earnings reach £13 a week. The State supplements the contributions paid by employees and employers, from general taxation. Contributions and supplement together with interest on investments form the income of the National Insurance Fund from which benefits are paid. There are four classes of contributions:

Class 1. (Payable by employed earners and their employers). Employed earners are:

1 Persons gainfully employed in Great Britain under a contract of service or in an office (including elective office) with emoluments chargeable to income tax under Schedule E
2 Certain persons who are treated as employed earners by the regulations; this includes anyone who is employed:

   (*a*) As an office cleaner or in any similar capacity
   (*b*) Through an agency where the agency has a continuing financial interest in the employment and the person supplied to do the work is subject to supervision, direction or control or to the right of supervision, direction or control in the manner of the rendering of the service
   (*c*) For the purpose of trade or business by his or her spouse

   A company director, being an office holder, is included in the category of 'employed earners' where his emolutions are chargeable to tax under Schedule E

Class 2. (Payable by self-employed earners.) A self-employed earner is one gainfully employed otherwise than as an employed earner whether or not he is also an employed earner in relation to some other employment

Class 3. Payable voluntarily by earners and others for the purpose of providing entitlement to certain benefits

Class 4. Payable by the self-employed in respect of a limited range of profits or gains taxable under Class I or II of Schedule D.

NATIONAL INSURANCE CONTRIBUTIONS FOR EMPLOYEES

National insurance contributions for employees are related to their earnings and are collected under the income-tax PAYE procedure. They are payable, whether or not the employee actually works during a week, if earnings are paid eg during sickness.

Employee's contributions are at one of three rates:

1 Standard rate payable by most employees and
2 Reduced rate payable by certain married women and most widows entitled to national insurance widow's benefit
3 Nil rate where the employee is a national insurance retirement pensioner or is otherwise treated as retired for national insurance

purposes. In such cases, only the employer's contribution is payable

Employer's contributions are at the same rate regardless of whether the employee is liable for the standard rate, reduced rate, or the nil rate.

Liability of both employees and employers is limited by both lower and upper earnings limits.

Where earnings do not reach the lower limit, there is no liability for contributions from either employee or employer. If earnings equal or exceed the lower limit, contributions are payable on the whole of the earnings up to the upper earnings limit.

The contribution rates and earnings limits for the 1976–7 tax year are as follows:

Employee's Contributions	
Standard rate	5.75%
Reduced rate	2.0%
Employer's Contributions	8.75%
Earnings Limits	
Weekly lower limit	£13.00
Weekly upper limit	£95.00
Monthly lower limit	£56.33
Monthly upper limit	£411.67
Annual lower limit	£675.96
Annual upper limit	£4940.04

Special groups

Married women and widows. The Social Security Pensions Act 1975 abolishes the right of married women and certain widows to pay reduced contributions. It is intended to allow women to continue to have reduced liability after April 1978 if by then they are married women or widows who already have current elections to pay contributions at the reduced rate, provided that they do not have a break of two or more complete tax years in either employment for which contributions are due, or self employment. The effect of this is that if a woman wishes to pay only reduced rate contributions she must be entitled to make an election from *6 April 1977* and must register her choice *no later than 11 May 1977.*

Persons over pension age. Persons over pension age (65 for a man and 60 for a woman) who retired, are treated as retired, or who did not satisfy the contribution conditions for a retirement pension at that age, are not liable for contributions. An employee who is over pension age and has no liability should obtain a certificate of earner's non-liability to give to his employer.

Calculation of Class 1 contributions

Class 1 contributions are always calculated on gross pay. Normally this will be the same as the amount of pay entered on the deduction card for income-tax purposes. But where a net pay scheme is operated for tax purposes, the national insurance contributions should still be calculated on the gross pay. Details of what should and should not be included in gross pay figures are given in the Employer's Guide to Pay as You Earn (P7) and in the Employer's Guide to National Insurance Contributions (Leaflet NP15).

The contribution payable depends on the date the payment of earnings is made (not the period over which it was earned) and the length of the shortest regular earnings period. If the employee is regularly paid weekly, the earnings period is a week; or if monthly, a month. If an employee works for more than one employer then contributions are payable in each employment, but there are provisions which enable the employee to obtain a refund of contributions paid in excess of a prescribed annual maximum. The employer's contributions, however, are not refundable.

The employer is responsible in the first instance for meeting the whole cost of the contribution payable by himself and the employee. The employer may recover the employee's contributions provided he deducts it from wages or salary at the time the wages are paid. Where, however, an under-deduction is made he may recover such underpayments during the current tax year so long as the total deduction is not more than twice that which would normally be made from that payment of wages.

An employer may calculate contributions either (*a*) exactly by applying the prescribed percentages (see page 495), or (*b*) by reference to contribution tables supplied by the Department of Health and Social Security. He may use only one method for any employee during a tax year, unless otherwise authorized.

Exact calculation. An employer who uses this method must calculate the employee's contributions separately from his own, and round each calculation to the nearest penny (£0.01), ½p being rounded down.

Contribution tables. Tables are provided covering earnings periods of one week and one month. There are three tables each bearing its own distinct category letter.

> *Table A* is for use where the employee is liable for standard-rate contributions
> *Table B* is for use where the employee is liable for reduced-rate contributions

Table C is for use where the employee is not liable and only the employer's contributions are payable

Instructions on the calculation of national insurance contributions and use of the tables are given in leaflet NP15 and on form P8 (Blue Card).

Recording contributions

At the beginning of the income-tax year (or employment), the identifying letter of the contribution table must be entered on the deduction card in the space provided. If the table has to be changed during the tax year, the contributions paid under each table must be shown in sequence in the Totals box on the deduction card. Where annual cards (P11(5)) are used, the details must be recorded separately in the pay records so that the deduction documents can be completed at the end of the tax year.

The employee's contribution and the total of the employee's and the employer's contribution should be entered on the deduction card.

Employers may use privately designed deduction documents instead of the official standard forms provided they are approved and authorized by the Inspector of Taxes.

Monthly payment to Collector of Taxes

At the end of each income-tax month, the employer must pay to the Collector of Taxes the employees' contributions deducted during the month together with the employer's contributions and any income tax deducted under PAYE procedure. A single remittance can cover both payments but the P30 remittance card must show the national insurance contributions separately.

At the end of income-tax year

At the end of each income-tax year, the employer should see that every deduction card is properly completed:

1   Ensure that the employee's national insurance number, surname and first two forenames are correctly entered at the top of the card
2   Check that each contribution table category letter and corresponding totals of contributions have been correctly recorded

and send them together with completed forms P35 and balance of contributions or tax due to the Collector of Taxes. Leaflet NP15 gives full details.

Form P60.   The employer is required to give every employee for whom he holds a deduction card, a certificate of pay and tax deduction (form P60 or P60 substitute) after the end of the income-tax year.

National insurance numbers

The Department of Health and Social Security allocates national insurance numbers to all contributors. Generally, young people will have a national insurance number allocated to them on reaching school-leaving age and will be given a national insurance number card. Anyone who has not been given a number must, when he comes liable for contributions or wishes to pay Class 3 voluntarily, apply to the local social security office.

Employers should ask any new employee to produce evidence of his national insurance number. If he is unable to do so, he should be told to apply to his local social security office. New employees changing jobs will normally produce a form P45 on which his national insurance number should have been entered by his previous employer.

If an employer is unable to obtain the national insurance number of a new employee, he should not delay sending form P46 to his Inspector of Taxes, who will endeavour to trace the number from his records or from Department of Health and Social Security records. *It is essential that the correct national insurance number is obtained and entered on all deduction cards for employees so that the contributions can be posted to the employees' accounts in the computer.*

Company directors

Prior to April 1975, generally only those company directors employed under a contract of service were in Class 1 employment. From April 1975, liability for Class 1 contributions extends to all company directors whose emoluments are chargeable to tax under Schedule E. Where such company directors receive their emoluments by way of a combination of salary, fees and share of profits, etc, it may not be clear which earnings period should be applied for calculating national insurance contributions. Any employer who is in doubt as to the earnings period to be applied should seek advice from the local social security office.

National Insurance contributions for self-employed persons

Class 2 contributions payable by self-employed earners are at a flat rate. The rates, which no longer include separate rates for those under 18, are set out below — and may be paid either by means of a stamped card or by direct debit of a bank or National Giro account.

Rates for 1976–7:   Men   £2.41
                           Women   £2.20

Those whose earnings from self-employment are less than £775 a year (rate current during 1976–7) may apply for exemption from liability to pay Class 2 contributions. Married women and certain widows who are self-employed may choose not to pay Class 2 contributions.

Class 4 contributions are payable (in addition to the flat-rate Class 2 contributions) by self-employed persons at the rate of 8 per cent of annual profits or gains between £1600 and £4900 (1976–7) which are assessable to tax under Case I or Case II of Schedule D. The contributions, which are generally collected along with Schedule D tax, do not attract benefit. A married woman's or widow's choice not to pay Class 2 contributions does not extend to Class 4 contributions.

People who have two or more jobs at the same time

A person who derives his earnings partly from employment and partly from self-employment is liable for both Class 1 and Class 2 (and, where appropriate, Class 4) contributions. Similarly, where a person has more than one employer, Class 1 contributions are due in respect of each employment in which the lower earnings limit is reached in any given pay period. If he pays more than a specified amount during a tax year, the excess will be refunded. Where he has a Class 1 contribution liability, he may apply to have any Class 2 and Class 4 liability deferred until after the end of the tax year so as to avoid any unnecessary refund action.

Payment of Class 3 contributions

Class 3 (voluntary) contributions are at the flat rate of £2.10 a week. They may be paid on a regular basis in a similar way to Class 2 contributions, by stamped card or direct debit. Or they may be paid by an employed or self-employed person who wishes to make up his record for entitlement to certain benefits, in which case payment may be by remittance after the end of the year.

The procedure for claiming is simple. When a man or woman is ill and cannot work, he or she obtains a medical certificate covering a period for which the doctor thinks incapacity will continue. The certificate incorporates a claim for benefit which the claimant completes and sends to the local social security office. On receipt of this certificate the local office have to obtain the claimant's contribution record, normally from the central records at Newcastle, to establish his entitlement to benefit. Benefit is usually paid weekly by Giro-cheque. The claimant should send in further medical certificates as each one expires. There are time-limits for claiming and benefit may be lost if certificates and claims are not sent in promptly. Benefit for dependants has to be claimed separately. Sickness benefit is not paid for the first three days in spells of sickness separated from each other or from spells of unemployment by more than thirteen weeks.

Unemployment benefit

For those who become unemployed and are capable of and available for further employment the Act makes provision by way of unemployment benefit. The contribution conditions are the same as those for sickness benefit except that only Class 1 contributions give cover for unemployment benefit. The rates of benefit, including those for children, are the same, but it is payable for a maximum of 312 days (a year excluding Sundays) only in any one spell or linked spells of unemployment. Claims for benefit should be made as soon as possible at the nearest unemployment benefit office (or careers office for anyone under 18 years old.

From 2 January 1977 title to unemployment benefit will depend amongst other things, upon the 'earnings factor' derived from contributions paid or credited in the previous tax year (ending on 5 April each year).

Earnings-related benefits

An earnings-related supplement is payable where a claimant satisfies the following conditions:

1 Is under minimum pension age (65 for a man, 60 for a woman)
2 Is entitled to flat-rate sickness benefit or unemployment benefit or maternity allowance; and
3 For periods of interruption of employment beginning on or after 2 January 1977, has an earnings factor (the amount of earnings on which Class 1 (employed earner's) contributions have been paid) in excess of fifty times the lower earnings limit for the relevant tax year.

Amount of supplement. For claims based on the 1975–6 tax year the earnings-related supplement is at the rate of one-third of 'reckonable weekly earnings' (see below) between £11 and £30 plus 15 per cent of so much of those earnings between £30 and £69. The maximum additional payment is thus £12.18 to the claimant with reckonable weekly earnings of £69 or more. It is paid in addition to flat rate sickness benefit, unemployment benefit or maternity allowance, including increases for dependants, subject to a maximum total benefit of 85 per cent of reckonable weekly earnings in the relevant tax year. Tables of the precise amounts of benefit payable are included in the leaflet NI155A applicable to the relevant tax year.

Period for which supplement is paid. Earnings-related supplement is payable from the thirteenth day of a period of interruption of employment and can continue for up to 156 days (26 weeks, excluding Sundays) in that period. Spells of incapacity and unemployment not separated by more than thirteen weeks are treated as parts of one and the same period of interruption of employment.

Reckonable weekly earnings. The Social Security Act 1975 provides for the rate of supplement to be based on reckonable weekly earnings for the relevant tax year. These are ascertained by dividing the claimant's earnings factor (as in item 3 above) by 50.

The relevant tax year is the last complete tax year (6 April to 5 April) preceding the earnings-related benefit year (beginning on the first Sunday in January each year) in which the period of interruption of employment begins.

Earnings factors for earnings-related supplement purposes are recorded on the Department's computer at Newcastle and will be supplied to local offices of the Department of Health and Social Security and Department of Employment on receipt of a claim to benefit.

Widow's earnings-related addition to flat rate widow's allowance is payable for the first twenty-six weeks of widowhood to a widow under 60 or a widow whose husband was not a retirement pensioner when he died. Entitlement to the addition is determined by reference to the late husband's reckonable weekly earnings and the amount payable is calculated in the same way as for earnings-related supplement of sickness or unemployment benefit except that the restriction of maximum total benefit to 85 per cent of the reckonable weekly earnings for the relevant tax year does not apply.

Retirement pension

If the contribution conditions are satisfied, a pension of £15.30 a week is payable from age 65 on retirement, or at age 70, whichever is the earlier (at age 60 or 65 for a woman). For a married couple, where the wife has not herself been paying standard-rate contributions, the pension is £24.50. The pension is subject to an earnings rule during the first five years following minimum pension age.

Extra pension. By deferring retirement after age 65 (60 for a woman) extra pension may be earned. This is an increase of $\frac{1}{8}$ per cent of the basic pension rate (ie basic rate without any increases except invalidity allowance) every six days (excluding Sundays) for which a person has not drawn his pension or another benefit), between the ages of 65 and 70 (60 and 65 for a woman).

Graduated pension. Every £7.50 £9 for a woman) that a man paid in graduated contributions up to 5 April 1975 when these contributions ceased, gives rise to a pension unit of 2½p a week graduated addition to pension. Any odd half unit or more in the final total counts as a whole unit.

BENEFITS

NATIONAL INSURANCE BENEFIT

Sickness benefit	£12.90 a week*
Invalidity benefit	
Invalidity pension	£15.30 a week
Invalidity allowance	
— under age 35 when illness began	£3.20 a week
— 35–40 when illness began	£2.00 a week
— 45–60 (55 for a woman) when	
illness began	£1.00 a week
Unemployment benefit	£12.90 a week*
Maternity benefit	
Maternity grant	£25.00
Maternity allowance	£12.90 a week* (18 weeks)
Widow's benefit	
Widow's allowance	£21.40 a week*
Widowed mother's allowance	£15.30 a week*
Widow's pension	£15.30 a week
Retirement pension	£15.30 a week*
Non contributory retirement pension	
for people over 80	£9.20 a week
Child's special allowance	£7.45 a week for 1st child
	£5.95 a week each other child
Death grant	£30 (adult)
Guardian's allowance	£7.45 a week

* Increases of benefit are payable in addition for dependants

Flat-rate sickness benefit

Flat-rate sickness benefit is paid for up to twenty-eight weeks to insured people who are incapable of work because of illness.

Men and single women normally receive £12.90 a week standard benefit (single person £12.90, wife or other adult dependant £8.00, married women (normal rate) £9.20 and £4.05 for the first or only dependent child under the age limits, £2.55 for the second and each other dependent child, in addition to any family allowances. For men over 65 and women over 60 (who have deferred or cancelled their retirement) the rate of benefit is payable at the same rate as their basic retirement pension would have been had they retired at 65 (60).

If the illness continues beyond twenty-eight weeks, sickness benefit is then replaced by invalidity benefit, which consists of an invalidity pension payable at the same rate as the basic retirement pension, increases for dependants on a par with those for retirement pensioners, and an invalidity allowance payable at one of three rates depending on the person's age when his illness began. Invalidity allowance is not payable to men whose illness began at age 60 or over, or 55 in the case of women).

Industrial injuries

Injury benefit	Adults £15.65 a week
(Payable during incapacity for work for up to 26 weeks from date of accident or development of	
prescribed disease)	Under 18 £11.10 a week
Disablement benefit	
(Payable at the end of the injury benefit period and depending on the degree of the disablement)	
Ranging from 100 per cent to	£25.00 a week
20 per cent	£4.36 a week
Gratuities of up to £1260 for 19 per cent are payable for assessments below 20 per cent	

Additional allowances are payable with disablement benefit where because of the accident or the prescribed disease the person is unable to follow his regular occupation, requires constant attendance, is exceptionally severely disabled, is unemployable or requires hospital treatment. Additions are payable for dependants with injury benefit, and certain of the additional allowances.

Widow's benefit (if contribution conditions are satisfied)

Widow's allowance. Usually paid during first twenty-six weeks £21.40 (a widow's earnings-related addition of up to £10.27 a week, based on the late husband's earnings, may also be payable for the same twenty-six weeks).

Thereafter:

Widowed mother's allowance — Widow with qualifying children £15.30.

Widow's pension — Widow over age fifty at date of husband's death or over age 50 when widowed mother's allowance ceases £15.30.

Widows aged 40–50 at that time are entitled to a pension scaled down according to their age.

Increases of widow's allowance and widowed mother's allowance are payable for dependent children.

SPECIAL DUTIES OF EMPLOYERS UNDER THE INDUSTRIAL INJURIES SCHEME

An employer is required to take reasonable steps to investigate any accident notified by or on behalf of an employee to him or his servant or agent as having arisen during the employment. If the employer is unable to reconcile the circumstances notified with those found by him, he should record the facts as found. The purpose of the requirement to investigate an accident is to ensure that the facts are confirmed by a responsible person while they are still fresh in the minds of any witnesses, so that, if a claim for benefit is made, the inquiry from the local social security office can be answered readily.

Accident book

Every owner or occupier (being an employer) of any mine or quarry or of any premises to which any of the provisions of the Factories Act 1961 applies and every employer by whom ten or more persons are normally employed at the same time on or about the same premises in connection with the employer's trade or business, is required to keep readily accessible an accident book in a form approved by the Secretary of State. Supplies of a suitable book (form BI510 or BI510A) can be obtained from the Stationery Office or through any bookseller.

All accident books must be preserved for three years from the date of the last entry.

The purpose of this arrangement is to facilitate the giving of notice of accidents by injured persons, and any entry in the book by an injured employee or by someone acting on his behalf is to be regarded as sufficient notice to the employer, of the accident, for the purposes of the Industrial Injuries (Claims and Payments) Regulations 1964.

Powers of inspectors

An inspector appointed by the Secretary of State under the Acts has power to enter at all reasonable times any premises (except a private dwelling house not used for a trade or business) where he has grounds for supposing that anyone is employed; and to make such examination and inquiry as may be necessary:

1   To ascertain whether the provisions of the Acts are being complied with
2   To investigate the circumstances of any industrial injury or disease giving rise to a claim for benefit

He may examine anyone found in the premises and call for the production of all documents required, to ascertain whether contributions are payable or have been payable or paid by or for any person, or whether benefit is or was payable to or for any person. He may also exercise such other powers as may be necessary for carrying the Acts into effect.

An inspector has a certificate of appointment which he must produce, if required to do so, on applying for admission to any premises. It is an offence under the Acts to wilfully delay or obstruct an inspector in the exercise of any of his powers or to refuse or neglect to answer any question, furnish any information or produce any document when required to do so.

The powers of inspectors, as broadly defined above, are retained by the Social Security Act 1975 which came into effect on 6 April 1975.

Sources of information

The administrative headquarters of the Department in London consists of a number of separate divisions each responsible for a particular section of the social security schemes and arrangements. On the social security side, the day-to-day administration of social security benefits is exercised through a network of about 900 local offices under the control of ten regional offices with central offices for Scotland and Wales.

Any employer who is in doubt about the social security provisions should consult the local social security office for advice. The address of the local office is obtainable from any post office or telephone directory.

The Department publishes a range of over 100 detailed leaflets and there are a number of posters designed for display on employers' notice boards.

EARNINGS-RELATED CONTRIBUTIONS CLASS 1 RATES (1975–6)

There are three categories of these contributions. The percentage of earnings due from the employee under category A is 5.75 per cent, under B, 2.0 per cent, and no contributions are due from the employee under category C. For all three categories, the employer's contribution stands at 8.75 per cent.

Calculating earnings-related contributions

The employee's and the employer's contribution is read off from the appropriate contribution table: category A, standard-rate basic contributions; category B, reduced rate basic contributions; or category C, employer's contributions only. Contributions are payable on all earnings, provided at least £13 a week is earned, up to £95. Equivalent amounts are calculated to find the threshold and ceiling of the monthly tables. If the exact gross pay figure is not shown on the tables, the next smaller figure should be used. (For information on earnings periods, etc, see leaflet NP15.)

It is the employer's responsibility to pay both his and the employee's contributions, but he may deduct the employee's contributions from his pay.

Precise calculations

Employers may calculate earnings-related contributions on the basis of exact percentages instead of using the tables. See Payment of earnings-related contributions, above. The appropriate earnings-related contribution tables are published in The Department of Health and Social Security's publication 'The Employers' Guide to National Insurance Contributions' (Leaflet number NP15).

Entry of the PAYE deduction card.   The final contribution must be rounded to the nearest penny (£0.01) ½p being rounded down, except where the employer, as he is entitled to do, has already rounded the separate elements before addition. If either method of rounding produces a figure greater than is specified in the appropriate contribution table, the figure shown in the table is the one payable.

How to use the tables

Find in the first column of the table, the gross pay figure for the income-tax week or month (as entered on the PAYE deduction card), or, if the exact gross pay figure is not shown in the table, the next smaller figure shown. Then read off from the table the corresponding contribution figures. The amount of the employee's contribution is to be entered in column 1(b) of the deduction card. The total of the employer's and the employee's contribution is also entered on the deduction card at column 1(a).

26

Administering Redundancy

Peter A Mumford

The Redundancy Payments Act 1965 defines redundancy as occurring when an employer ceases to carry on the business for which the employee was engaged in the place where he was employed, or has insufficient work of the type which the employee was engaged to do.

It is only when an actual redundancy situation has to be administered and precise decisions made about the treatment of individuals which will affect not only their own immediate future (and perhaps their long-term employment prospects), but also the success and profitability of the organization, that the many variations in interpretation and the implications of this apparently clear-cut definition become apparent.

Redundancy is an emotional situation bringing into play moral, social, financial and operational issues such as the right of a man to his job, the worth of one individual as opposed to another, the role of the employer and his responsibilities to his employees, the community, the owners and short-term expediency opposed to long-term needs.

In these circumstances, clear unbiased judgments become most difficult. Decisions taken under the emotional or moral pressures of a redundancy situation can adversely affect goodwill and long-term plans laboriously built up over considerable periods of time.

To the majority of organizations, the people employed are its most valuable asset. On purely financial grounds their recruitment, training and bank of experience represent a very considerable investment per head. Like any other asset, therefore, they should not be lightly disposed of or neglected. Furthermore, they are thinking, feeling, individual human beings.

REDUNDANCY POLICY

Need for a policy

The best way of dealing with redundancy is to avoid it, not by ostrich-like tactics hoping it will go away, but by drawing up a positive policy with specific plans for regulating and controlling the manpower of the organization to achieve the desired overall objectives.

There is no doubt that the greatest safeguard and security the employees can have is an efficient, profitable organization, in which forward thinking and planning are of prime importance, so that the necessary action can be taken quickly to take advantage of changing circumstances, rather than have circumstances manage the organization.

The most sophisticated forecasting techniques cannot, of course, cover every eventuality and, undoubtedly, there will be circumstances so outside the organization's control that rapid reductions in the manpower requirements are inevitable. Effective planning of resources may also mean that it will be necessary to change the manpower requirements to such an extent that redundancies are the best way of effecting these changes.

To meet these requirements, it is essential that an effective plan for dealing with redundancy is an integral part of the organization's manpower policies.

The right time to draw up a manpower strategy — which stems directly from the overall corporate plan — is now. The best time for formulating the redundancy provisions of the manpower plan is when the organization is recruiting hard; when the emotional issues are least likely to obscure judgment.

Content of a policy

In drawing up redundancy policies and plans, decisions will have to be taken on the following items:

1   The objectives of the policy
2   The different ways in which redundancy situations will be treated.
    The two broad categories are:
    (*a*) Those forced on the organization by reductions in business or other outside factors
    (*b*) Those designed to benefit the organization by, for instance, taking advantage of technological change
3   Methods of avoiding redundancy
4   Methods of reducing the impact of redundancy
5   Selection methods to be used
6   Consultation
7   Transfers and retraining
8   Voluntary retirements

9   Compensation
10 Pension rights
11 Re-engagement

In all these subjects, both the human aspect and the legal requirements have to be taken into account in order that positive plans and procedures can be agreed.

Social and company considerations

If the short-term efficiency of the labour force were the only consideration, it would probably be desirable to use a redundancy as an opportunity of getting rid of the unwanted, the troublemakers, the least able, the least adaptable and the least hard-working.

Human sympathy would, however, probably manifest itself in this situation and even those who had previously been a cause of discontent to their fellow workers, be made a source of friction and dissention if they appeared to have been singled out for adverse treatment.

It is at least arguable that if management had allowed any significant number of these categories to continue in employment until the need for redundancy occurred, their policies and practices would be such that getting rid of them at this late stage would be merely locking the stable door.

Equally, management must consider the social implications of their actions, both upon individuals and the community in general.

So far as individuals are concerned, the chief considerations must be the comparative degree of hardship they will suffer, which will be affected immediately by their commitments and family responsibilities and, in the longer term, their age, fitness and chances of finding alternative employment.

Sympathy for individuals must not be allowed to prevent management ensuring that the organization has a properly trained and balanced labour force to give it the best possible chance of meeting its objectives in the future.

In a community where there is a shortage of various categories of labour, the release of suitable staff by one organization would obviously be welcomed.

Where there is already unemployment and redundancy, where one organization is a major or sole employer then redundancies will have far-reaching consequences on the community and individuals.

Where the redundancy is foreseeable, as part of changes which will benefit the organization, consideration should be given to the possibility of timing, either by speeding up or delaying the dismissals to suit the circumstances in the community.

The prospect of substantial redundancies should be notified to the local community and area authorities. Especially in development areas, the Department of Trade should also be advised.

These notifications should take place as early as possible so that the authorities concerned have the maximum time in which to assist in finding suitable alternative employment. These notifications are in addition to the statutory notifications to the trade unions affected and to the Department of Employment required by the Employment Protection Act 1975.

Publicity

The way in which publicity is handled will have an important effect within the organization and the community at large. Adequately prepared information presented in good time, with perhaps an earliest release date stipulated, will have a better effect on public relations and the image of the organization than a hastily prepared justification of a leak, or embellishment of local gossip by a news-hungry reporter. It should cover the reasons for the dismissals, the action which is being taken to safeguard individuals, and future prospects for the organization in general.

Manpower policies and forecasting future requirements

Detailed forecasting and planning starts from the overall corporate plan which will show the long-term growth pattern, changes in methods and products which will affect the requirements for skills of different types, the grades and perhaps the ages of staff needed in the future.

In many organizations, this plan may exist only in a most rudimentary form so that the discussion with senior executives, in order to formulate their views, will be a valuable exercise in itself. Once this process has been started, it proves far less difficult to build up an overall picture than is usually imagined. Like all other techniques, forecasting improves the more it is practised.

A good starting point is to plot the age ranges of the senior and junior managers to determine what recruitment and development is needed to maintain the present organization. A similar plot can be made for the rest of the staff by departments, jobs or types of skill. By superimposing transparencies on the main graph, the effect of various changes can be estimated by projecting forward losses through normal wastage, the effect of changes in market demands, products, methods.

A critical factor in forecasting is the survival rate of existing staff, that is, the number of staff who will stay with the organization, and the length of time that various categories will stay.

These can be plotted by age, by occupation and by social factors, and will provide valuable information on which to base recruiting plans to give the required balanced labour force. Care is necessary to reduce the risk of offending the antidiscrimination bodies.

AVOIDING REDUNDANCY

In a period of economic recession for the organization, it is still possible to avoid or reduce the impact of redundancy if the forecasting methods are able to give sufficient advance warning.

Methods which can be used include:

1 Identifying and attempting to sell surplus capacity even at marginal cost in order to retain skilled staff
2 Bringing subcontracted work into the organization's own workshops
3 Stopping overtime so as to share out the work available: retraining of staff may be necessary
4 Restricting recruitment and filling vacancies by internal transfer and retraining wherever this is possible
5 Dismissing employees who have been allowed to work on past normal retirement age
6 Dismissing part-time workers — assuming there are full-time employees available with the required skills
7 Retraining staff to give greater flexibility, increased efficiency in future
8 Building up stocks against future needs to avoid losing markets to foreign competition

The Temporary Employment subsidy scheme may be useful in offsetting costs of both 7 and 8 above.

Fixed-term contracts. Where there is a need to recruit staff to maintain a job for a defined period, the possibility of fixed-term contracts should be investigated.

Recruitment and training

Given some idea of the future as well as immediate demand for staff, it is possible to be more precise in specifying the characteristics of the individual required.

If, for instance, it is estimated that the number of operatives will be reduced by the phasing-out of a product in two to three years, it would be wise to confine recruitment to those categories who are known to have a survival rate of about this time. Such selection could eliminate or, at least, considerably reduce the size of the redundancy which would otherwise be necessary.

When drawing up job specifications for recruitment purposes, the addition of a section specifying the career effects and the time the job is likely to last in its present form, will make it possible to include consideration of the development potential needed in the individual and the age range most likely to suit the future requirements. This will help to avoid building up a staff who, through age, lack of adaptability or potential, cannot be redeployed or developed and so will have to be dispensed with.

Equally, long-term training or retraining programmes allow staff to acquire the skills and knowledge needed for new jobs or processes, rather than be dismissed because they cannot be retrained quickly when the change occurs.

Modern training methods, such as the common skills approach and discovery learning, have shown that factors such as age that were thought of as barriers to learning can be overcome. People can be retrained to the experienced worker standards in new skills reasonably rapidly. Complementary programmes can encourage flexibility, adaptability and willingness to accept necessary changes.

Transfers

The numbers to be dismissed can often be reduced, or a valuable man retained in the organization, by transferring staff from one department to another or even to another company in a group.

Providing the work offered and the conditions are not significantly worse than the employee's present job and the work is within the employee's capacity, then he will not, in law, be considered to be redundant even if he refuses the transfer. He is, of course, able to appeal to an industrial tribunal if he feels the offer is unreasonable.

However, should another worker be dismissed as a result of the transfer, then he will be considered to have been made redundant and entitled to compensation.

The offer of alternative work or transfer should be made to the employee, before his notice expires, in writing, specifying the work and the conditions. Providing the transfer takes place within four weeks of the end of the original job, the employee's service will be considered to be continuous.

If the employee is offered a different type of work, he is entitled to a trial period of four weeks.

A longer period to cover necessary retraining may be agreed between employer and employee. Details of such an agreement must be written.

Where there may be differences in earnings due to the operation of bonus schemes or other factors, it is usual to allow a period of make-up pay until the employee has had an opportunity to adjust to the new conditions.

It would also be reasonable to give assistance with removal expenses if the transfer would involve moving house. In the case of experienced workers, the cost of this would probably be less than the total of compensation, plus recruitment and training costs of a new employee.

Voluntary retirement

This is a useful method of reducing the impact of redundancy which has the added attraction of relieving the employer of the need to make the choice between individuals.

It has been used extensively by large organizations to offset the effects of reorganization creating a surplus of senior staff who would otherwise clog the avenues of promotion for younger men who must be developed for the future.

It depends for its success on generous cash payments and subsidy of pension funds to ensure that the income available will be adequate. This is particularly important since the entitlement to unemployment benefit by people below the official retirement age has been limited to sixty working weeks.

There is no reason why the voluntary principle cannot be extended to earlier age groups. Many men will welcome the lump sum and the opportunity of an early start in looking for other work.

It must be remembered, however, that in order to claim rebate under the Redundancy Payments Act, it must be seen that work no longer exists for the people concerned. There can also be problems of retaining key workers.

SELECTION OF WORKERS TO BE MADE REDUNDANT

The most controversial aspect of any redundancy is the method for selecting those who are to be dismissed.

The simple solution is last-in first-out (LIFO), based purely on the length of service. This is favoured by many unions, is easy to operate, understandable and allows people to know fairly accurately where they stand.

The Redundancy Payments Act itself favours this method by making it more expensive to dismiss long-service employees.

If all employees were of equal worth and if all sections of the organization were equally affected, then this policy could satisfy most needs. In most redundancies, and particularly in those caused by technological or product changes, it is unlikely that all departments or all grade of staff will need to be reduced by the same amount, and even in those departments whose overall numbers have to be reduced, there will be certain key jobs for which skilled workers are in short supply and whom it would be quite wrong to dismiss.

Additionally, there will be problems created by hardship cases, the registered disabled, those under training for skills required in the future and, perhaps most important of all, the future age structure of the company.

The effect of a number of even small-scale redundancies can be to bias the age structure significantly upwards, which may in turn create difficulties in say, five years' time.

From the broader social point of view, there is also a danger of creating a category of worker who will always be first out and who, through no fault of their own, will never be able to build up any service to qualify them for redundancy payments.

These are the main difficulties which can arise from the LIFO policy.

An ideal selection method would strike the balance between the requirements of the organization and the social needs of individuals.

Factors which should be considered are:

Organization needs
(*a*) Now
(*b*) In the future
Worth of the individual:
Variety of skills
Quality of work
Quantity of work
Reliability
Potential
Cost of replacement

Individual needs
Commitments and family responsibilities
Difficulty in obtaining new work
Age
Length of service

Whatever selection methods are to be employed, it is essential that they are known and agreed beforehand.

Where LIFO is used, it is essential that jobs are categorized within departments so that selection can be made within a group of skills, rather than across the whole department which may include skills which are still required. Thus, in a general machine shop, there may be turning, drilling and milling skills. If the shortage of work is for turning only, it is important that the selection be made from those with turning skills only and is not applied to drillers and millers. Arrangements must also be made to ensure that key personnel, whose absence could affect the output of other sections, are not dismissed purely because of seniority considerations.

Trade union attitude to selection methods

Although most unions are committed to the principle of a man having a right to his job, which means no dismissal unless there is no alternative job available, full-time union officials are realists and accept that some redundancy is inevitable. They also accept that the LIFO principle must be applied only within the grades of jobs affected. Where it can be shown that there are substantial differences in the skill and worth of one individual over another, they will generally accept the organization's need in preference to rigid adherence to seniority.

CONSULTATION

Although management must obviously make the decision about the need for redundancy and the scale of it, the more employees are consulted about the way in which they are to be treated, the better.

Under the terms of the Employment Protection Act 1975, the union(s) concerned – the recognized trade union for the group of employees to which the affected personnel belong (whether or not they are individually trade union members) – must be consulted as early as possible to allow the trade union representative to suggest alternative action, retraining, etc.

If more than 10 employees are likely to be made redundant during one month, this consultation should start at least 60 days before the dismissals take place. If more than 100 people are to be made redundant over a period of 90 days, then the consultation has to start 90 days before the dismissal date. Trade union representatives have to be given the following information:

1 The reasons for the proposed redundancies
2 The numbers and description of affected
3 The total number of these descriptions employed at the establishment
4 The proposed selection method
5 The proposed methods and timing for the dismissals

Although union membership is likely to increase considerably in the future, there will remain large numbers of firms with no union representation. In these, staff committees or a system of representatives from appropriately sized departments or sections should be instituted. Such representation will have far wider uses than consultation on redundancy, and it is wise therefore to set them up so that they are recognized and working well in normal, as well as emergency circumstances.

NOTICE

The Contracts of Employment Act as amended by the Trade Union and Labour Relations Act 1974 and the Employment Protection Act 1975 stipulate the minimum periods of notice set out in Figure 26.1.

In cases where the change can be foreseen longer in advance, it would seem reasonable to give longer notice of intention. Should, however, such announcements precipitate a rush of key workers to secure first place in the queue for scarce jobs in other organizations, so putting the continuance of the existing methods in jeopardy, then little will have been accomplished.

Staff can, of course, be encouraged to work out their notice by a system of premium payments, and may lose their entitlement to redundancy payments under the Act if they do not obtain their employer's permission to leave before the expiry of their notice. Even so, a severe unemployment situation locally can make it more attractive for individuals to secure the long-term advantage of another job rather than a once-only cash payment.

Length of continuous service	Minimum period of notice
4 weeks	1 week
2 years	2 weeks
3 years	3 weeks
4 years	4 weeks
5 years	5 weeks
6 years	6 weeks
7 years	7 weeks
8 years	8 weeks
9 years	9 weeks
10 years	10 weeks
11 years	11 weeks
12 years	12 weeks

Where necessary payments may be given in lieu.

Figure 26.1   Formal notice required by statute

In spite of these risks, the best policy will be to restrict formal notice to the requirements set out above, but to give notice of intention to individuals as part of the normal consultation procedures, so as to maintain good faith with employees and prevent the spread of rumour and loss of confidence.

COMPENSATION

Under the Redundancy Payments Act, lump-sum payments are made to employees dismissed through redundancy on a scale according to age and length of service as shown in Figure 26.2.

Employee's Age	Payment for each complete year of service
18–22	½ week's pay
22–41	1 week's pay (max. 20 weeks)
41–64 (men) 41–59 (women)	1½ weeks' pay (max. 20 weeks)

Service under the age of 18 does not count for this purpose.
For men of 64–65 years, and women of 59–60, the entitlement is reduced by one-twelfth for every month over 64 or 59.
Full details are set out in leaflet RPL2.

Figure 26.2   Redundancy pay

Because a year is counted as 52 weeks, there are a number of cases where the odd extra days in a calendar year make it appropriate to round up service to the next highest year.

These cases occur when actual service is less than 14 days short of a whole number of years, or 31 days for service after 5 years, for example, 5 years 50 weeks. The service calendar RPL4 published annually by the Department of Employment must then be used.

The method of calculating a week's pay is set out in the Revised Guide to the Redundancy Payments Scheme.

These lump-sum payments to the employee are tax-free up to a maximum of £5000 and do not affect his entitlement to unemployment benefit or earnings-related supplements. The payments are made by the employer who then claims 50 per cent of the amount from the Redundancy Fund.

Where redundancy is due to insolvency and the employer is unable to make these payments, they are made direct to the employee by the Department of Employment.

Many employers consider that these payments represent a minimum and supplement them by scales of their own, usually related to length of service. A simple way of doing this is to add a fixed percentage to the statutory payment. Only the statutory scale of payment is eligible for rebate.

It is much easier to justify more generous treatment where the redundancy is due to circumstances from which the company will benefit and there is, therefore, merit in making additional payments in these circumstances only. Certainly in the extremes of redundancy where the organization is insolvent, only the redundancy scheme scale can be applicable.

An alternative method of supplementing payments is to make weekly and monthly payments – again on a scale according to service – until the employee has either used his entitlement or obtains alternative employment. To avoid reducing entitlement to unemployment benefit, these payments must be limited to one-third of normal earnings.

Pension rights

The Social Security Act 1973 requires that occupational pensions of redundant employees, aged 26 and over who have completed at least five years' service must be preserved. The possible methods include:

1 Benefits already earned may be preserved to normal retiring age
2 Transfer of benefits to another scheme
3 Payment of reduced benefit before normal retiring age
4 Payment of increased benefit after normal retiring age
5 Repayment of members' contributions made before 6 April 1975

Arrangements must also be made for early leavers to receive any increases in benefit for which the pension scheme provides.

A proportion of pension may be offset against redundancy payments, as outlined in leaflet RPL1.

Full details of possible pension arrangements are set out in memorandum 18 of the Occupational Pensions Board. This Board exists mainly to advise on preservation aspects of pensions.

RE-ENGAGEMENT

Should circumstances change more rapidly than anticipated, it may be possible to re-engage those dismissed; the fairest way being to re-engage in reverse order to dismissal.

Before re-engagement takes place, the question of service must be clarified. If payments under the redundancy payments scheme have been made, then clearly service under the re-engagement can count only from this date and similarly, if payments against pension rights have been made, then pensionable service must restart from the date of re-engagement.

Providing no payments have been made, it is usual to count service for pension purposes as continuous if the period between dismissal and re-engagement does not exceed one year. Thereafter, it is preferable to regard any re-engagement as a completely new period of service for all purposes.

WELFARE

Much can be done besides financial compensation to assist those selected for dismissal.

Finding new job

The first priority is a new job. The personnel department, through personal contact with other organizations, employment agencies, the trade unions and the Department of Employment, can help to find alternative jobs, and from its records is able to give strong recommendations to potential employers.

To avoid duplication of effort, the personnel department should act as the coordinators for all the various sources of information and assistance.

Time for interviews

Under the Employment Protection Act redundant employees with two or more years' service are entitled to reasonable time off with pay to look for another job or to arrange for training for a new job. 'Reasonable' is not defined since individual requirements may vary so much.

The TUC in their publication *Job Security* cite two full days as a common entitlement. Excessive demands from individuals are obviously to be discouraged.

Cases of hardship

Cases of special difficulty can be assisted by *ex gratia* payments or other more favourable consideration. To avoid charges of favouritism, a small committee of a senior executive, a staff or union representative, and the personnel manager or welfare officer can be formed for this purpose. The committee may be given a special budget, or terms of reference within which they make recommendations. It is essential that decisions are made rapidly.

Date of leaving

If a redundant worker finds another job he may be released before expiry of his notice (without affecting his entitlement to redundancy payments) providing he gives written notice, and this is accepted by the employer. Wherever possible, arrangements should be made to release the employee in time to take up his new employment.

LEGAL REQUIREMENTS

The principal legislation is contained in the Redundancy Payments Act 1965, which set up the Redundancy Fund and requires employers to make payments to redundant employees and makes provision for disputes to be resolved by industrial tribunals.

Contracts of Employment Act 1972 amended by the Trade Unions and Labour Relations Act 1974 and the Employment Protection Act 1975. This specifies:

1 The periods of formal notice to be given
2 The conditions of employment which must be stated in a contract
   of employment
3 How length of service is to be calculated
4 How earnings should be calculated

It also defines how length of service and earnings should be calculated.

If an employee has an individual contract of service which gives him more advantageous terms than are laid down in the Contracts of Employment Act, then the individual contract will have preference.

The Employment Protection Act 1975 contains regulations on unfair dismissal which are applicable to redundancy.

An employee declared redundant may appeal to an industrial tribunal if he considers he has been unfairly dismissed on the following grounds:

1   The dismissal is for reasons not covered by the definition of the Redundancy Payments Act
2   The means of selection are unfair because
   (*a*) They concern membership, or non-membership, of a trade union
   (*b*) The accepted or agreed selection procedures have been disregarded
   (*c*) The warning given was inadequate, or efforts have not been made to find alternative employment within the organization
   (*d*) Any other reason which the employee considers unfair

To avoid such claims, it is essential that shortage of suitable work, however caused, is the only reason for redundancy; selection procedures are agreed and followed, and that each employee is given written notice of dismissal.

This formal notice should state the reason, the period of notice and termination date, the appeals procedure. Copies of such notice may then be used in evidence at any subsequent tribunal appeal by the employee.

TRIBUNALS

Industrial tribunals are independent judicial bodies established by the Department of Employment which handle all disputes concerning redundancy. Industrial tribunals must first attempt conciliation between the two parties to the dispute and call on the Advisory, Conciliation and Arbitration Service for this purpose. Failing settlement, the tribunal will hear the case and is empowered to give a ruling on points such as:

1   Whether the dismissal counts as redundancy under the terms of the Act
2   The amount of payment due
3   The amount of rebate due to the employer from the Redundancy Fund
4   Offers of alternative work or transfer
5   Refusal to allow an employee to leave before expiry of notice

In the case of claims of unfair dismissal, the tribunal may make an order for reinstatement in the employee's old job, re-engagement in another job or payment of compensation. Compensation is limited to a maximum of two years' pay at a rate of up to £50 per week.

If an employer is considered not to have met the requirements of prior consultation, a tribunal may make an order to postpone the dismissals or make a protective award requiring payment of normal wages for a specified period. The maximum protective award may not exceed the period specified for consultation (28, 60 or 90 days as appropriate).

Approaches to an industrial tribunal are made, using:

Form IT1 for employees seeking decisions on their entitlement to compensation and the amount due

Form IT17 for employers seeking a decision on their entitlement to rebate against redundancy payments

Form IT18 for all other cases

for complaints arising in England or Wales to:

> The Secretary
> Central Office of Industrial Tribunals
> 93 Ebury Bridge Road
> London, SW1

or for those arising in Scotland:

> The Secretary
> Central Office of Industrial Tribunals (Scotland)
> St Andrew House
> 141 West Nile Street
> Glasgow

The proceedings of tribunals are held informally, but applicants and witnesses may be required to give evidence on oath. They may be represented by lawyers, trade union or employers' association officials.

Details of the procedures are given in leaflets:

> ITL1 for employees
> ITL2 for respondents
> ITL7 for employers appealing against failure to pay rebate

COSTS AND CLAIMS

The basic costs of making a man redundant are the payments due to him under the Redundancy Payments Act (maximum of 30 weeks at £80 per week = £2400) less the amount which can be claimed from the Redundancy Fund. This is normally 50 per cent of the payment made.

To this basic cost must be added any supplementary payments under an organization's own scheme, which are not eligible for rebate from the Redundancy Fund plus all the administration charges ranging from negotiation, consultation, selection, interview and documentation. To these must be added the intangibles: loss of goodwill and confidence, loss of morale.

Unless the reductions in staff are likely to last for a considerable time, it is worth while to consider the possibilities of retaining long-service employees in some capacity where they can make even a minor contribution to costs.

Claims for rebates must be made to the Department of Employment within six months of the payment to the employee. Rebate may be reduced by up to 10 per cent if the necessary notification is not given:

> 21 days if payments are to be made to more than 10 employees
> 14 days if 10 or less are affected

The notification is made on form RP1 which requires the following information for each employee: Name, sex, national insurance number, income-tax reference number, date of birth, date of engagement, expected date of dismissal, amount of a week's pay.

The weekly pay should be calculated in accordance with Appendix D of the revised guide to the Act.

It should be noted that the department may call for the production of records to check the claims or may ask permission for an officer to carry out the required checks on the employer's premises.

STANDARD PROCEDURES

Although every instance of redundancy is likely to be different in detail, drawing up a standard procedure will help to ensure that, if a redundancy becomes necessary, it can be dealt with rapidly and efficiently, so that administrative failures will not intensify an already emotional and critical situation.

Many of the procedures suggested have value and relevance to the organization in general, quite apart from their value in the avoidance and administration of redundancy. They should be included in a redundancy agreement to demonstrate to staff that all possible efforts are being made to protect their interests and secure the well-being of the organization.

Topics which should be covered in a redundancy procedure include:

1* Manpower planning as a positive part of the overall corporate plan
2* Consultation machinery
3* Categories of redundancy involving varying treatment

4*   Means of avoiding redundancy, such as not subcontracting work,
     restriction of recruitment, restriction of overtime working, volun-
     tary retirement, retiring staff over retirement age, laying off part-
     time workers
5*   Transfer arrangements
6*   Training
7*   Method of categorizing jobs and workers
8*   Selection procedures to be used
9*   Notification procedure – for staff and Department of Employ-
     ment
10* Formal notice including arrangement for amendments
11* Compensation
12* Welfare and assistance to dismissed employees
13* Assistance in finding new jobs
14* Pension arrangements
15* Terms for re-engagement
16* Publicity
17* Calculations of payments due and notification of amounts to
     staff concerned
18* Formal dismissal procedures
19   Claims for rebate from Department of Employment
20   Appeals:
     (a) By the organization
     (b) *By individuals
21   Records
22   Evaluation of procedures after redundancy has occurred in order
     to improve

Once the basic procedures have been drawn up, they should be discussed with
staff representatives through the normal consultation machinery.

Items marked * in this list or extracts from them, should then be used to
formulate an agreement with the staff. Details of the administrative procedures
are not necessary in such an agreement. In the case of item 1, for instance, it is
sufficient to give an undertaking that forward planning and forecasting of
manpower requirements will be carried out in order to constrain the availability
and supply of staff as near to the requirements as possible.

EMPLOYMENT SERVICES AND AGENCIES

The Department of Employment is responsible for administering the Redundancy Payments Act and, together with the Manpower Services Commission, the
Employment Services Agency and the Conciliation and Arbitration Service, is
responsible for providing a wide range of services to industry and individuals

including:

Advice on manpower planning and forecasting methods
Assistance and advice in documentation for redundancy
Guidance on alternative employment available for dismissed employees
Guidance on assistance and service available to help those dismissed
Advice on retraining facilities
Advice on appeals and industrial tribunals

All these services are available in a redundancy situation, the advance warning called for by the Act providing time for them to be alerted and brought into use.

Where large numbers of staff are to be dismissed, an employment office can be set up on the organization's premises.

Initial contact with the services should be made to the local employment exchange. The larger offices have specialist departments for dealing with all aspects of redundancy.

The following leaflets are available:

RPL1	Offsetting pensions against redundancy payments
RPL2	Ready reckoner for payments
RPL4	Service calendar
RPL5	Calculation of a week's pay for employees on shift and rota work

FURTHER READING

The Redundancy Payments Scheme, Tenth Revision (effective 1 June 1976), Department of Employment, HMSO, London.
Employment Protection Act:
1   *An Outline*
2   *Procedure for handling redundancies*
3   *Employees' rights on insolvency of employer*
4   *New rights for the expectant mother*
5   *Suspension on medical grounds*
6   *Facing redundancy? – time off for job hunting or to arrange training*
Department of Employment, HMSO, London.
The Contracts of Employment Act 1972; A guide to the Act incorporating changes made by the Employment Protection Act 1975, Department of Employment, HMSO, London.
Dismissal – Employees' Rights, Department of Employment, HMSO, London.

A Short Guide to the Preservation of Occupational Pension Benefits, Occupational Pensions Board, London.

W.W. Daniel, *Whatever Happened to the Workers at Woolwich?* Political and Economic Planning, London, 1972.

C.M. Smith, *Redundancy Policies*, British Institute of Management, London, 1974.

A. Hillier, *Contracts of Employment-Engagement, Termination and Redundancy*, Training for Business.

R.O'Brien, 'Points of Procedure', *Personnel Management*, August 1972, pp.23-5.

P.A. Mumford, *Redundancy and Security of Employment*, Gower Press, Epping, 1975.

27

Management-Union Relations

Derek Torrington

The subject of this chapter is what is popularly known as industrial relations, and we can define it as: the regulation of the working relationships between employers and groups of employees through the intermediary of managers and employee representatives.

It is a field of activity which has suffered close scrutiny in recent years, and it is the aspect of the world of work which is perhaps the best known and the least understood outside the close-knit society of the experts. The politician and the economist take an interest in it because they see the level of industrial disruption through strikes and similar causes as having a serious influence on the country's prosperity and growth. The social reformer takes an interest because he sees the world of the factory floor as being a place where social revolution might be achieved. The televiewer takes an interest because he sees raw emotion, intensity of feeling and incipient violence.

The growing interest by outsiders in industrial relations is demonstrated in the increasing amount of state intervention that has come in the last decade. Contracts of Employment Act, Redundancy Payments Act, Race Relations Act, Sex Discrimination Act and Equal Pay Act are all major pieces of legislation that have set legal fences round bits of industrial relations practice. More recently we have had attempts at comprehensive legislative intervention through the Industrial Relations Act 1971 and the Employment Protection legislation of the 1974 Labour Government.

The main precursor to the 1971 Act was the setting up of the Royal Commission on Trade Unions and Employers' Associations in 1965 under the chairmanship of Baron Donovan. Later came the Conservative Party policy document, 'Fair Deal at Work'; shortly after that came the report of the

Donovan Commission and then the Labour Government's proposals, 'In Place of Strife', which formed the basis of the Industrial Relations Bill in the spring of 1970. The change of government in the summer of 1970 led to the scrapping of the bill and the substitution of a Conservative bill, which became the Industrial Relations Act in August 1971. Following intense controversy and the relative ineffectiveness of the Act, it was largely repealed in the summer of 1974, repeal being followed by a different type of intervention by a different type of government. The new approach was not to attempt improvement by restraint of the bargaining process, but to seek to redress what was seen as an unsatisfactory balance of advantage in employment, favouring the employer rather than the employee. State intervention has come, as a result of managers and trade union officials appearing *to the observers* as being incapable of conducting their affairs in a way which provided adequate safeguards for those in the community outside the factory, shop and office.

This comes at a time when trade union membership is increasing. For decades trade unions were regarded as being the exclusive province of the 'working class', with their membership predominantly in manual grades of employment. Unions for clerical personnel were established only at the beginning of this century and began to make real headway in membership after the 1939–45 war, helped by the industrial relations policies of the nationalized industries, which encouraged trade union representation. During the 1960s we have seen a considerable increase in the number of supervisory, managerial and professional employees who are not only taking up trade union membership, but also conducting their affairs in a very determined and efficient way. When you have a situation in which a group of airline pilots—with all their glamour and prestige—take industrial action in support of a pay claim for £13 500 a year, then there has indeed been a great change since the 1950s. Membership of unions affiliated to the TUC exceeded ten million for the first time in 1971.

Against this background let us consider the processes and institutions that go to make up industrial relations and the place of the company administrator in regulating working relationships between the employer and groups of employees.

COLLECTIVE BARGAINING

To some extent, the process of regulating working relationships between employers and groups of employees is done by the imposition of rules from outside industry, as in the standards laid down for employees in the Factories Acts and in the Offices, Shops and Railway Premises Act. Here standards are decreed, and the employer must meet them.

Mainly, however, this regulation comes through the process of collective bargaining within industry. This is defined in the *Industrial Relations Handbook 1962* as:

...arrangements under which wages and conditions of employment are settled by a bargain, in the form of an agreement made between employers of associations of employers and workers' organizations.

Later the *Handbook* defines the scope of collective bargaining:

They [collective bargains] cover a great variety of matters including not only rates of wages, but also hours of work, overtime conditions, special allowances, piecework arrangements, holidays, allocation of work, employment of apprentices, redundancy, guaranteed week agreements, and working conditions generally.

National agreements

The established method of collective bargaining is through the national or industrywide agreement, where employers' representatives and union officials meet and conclude an agreement covering the employment rules to be followed in all organizations which are members of the particular employers' federation or association concerned in the negotiations. Many such sets of negotiations are carried out in joint industrial councils (JICs), either for a complete industry, like building or wallpaper-making or for a section of an industry with special characteristics.

Some national negotiations are carried out without a JIC framework, the main example being the engineering industry, for which agreements covering the working conditions of some three and a quarter million people are negotiated intermittently between the Engineering Employers' Federation and the Confederation of Shipbuilding and Engineering Unions.

In some industries there is a different system for national negotiation: a wages council, set up by the State to conduct the collective bargaining process because the employers and trade unions concerned in that industry are not well enough equipped to organize their own collective bargaining. In practice this means those areas of work in which unions are not well established, and particularly in industries employing a large proportion of women; hairdressing and catering being examples.

Wages council negotiations consist of an encounter between a group of employer and employee representatives in the presence of three independent members of the council, one of whom takes the chair. If the employers and employees cannot agree, then the three independent members can break a deadlock by voting with one side or the other. The decisions of a wages council are communicated to the Secretary of State for Employment, who embodies them in order, placing a statutory obligation upon the employers henceforth to meet the new conditions that have been agreed.

Wages councils are to be replaced by the statutory joint industrial councils, having power to issue their own wage orders without reference to the Secretary of State.

Workplace bargaining

In theory the national agreement establishes standard terms and conditions of employment to be observed by each employer in every part of the country. In practice there has been a wide discrepancy opening up over the last twenty years, and the actual amount of money earned in a plant is substantially more than the amount agreed in national negotiations in most cases. This is because of the growth of *ad hoc* bargaining in the workplace between individual managements and shop stewards.

The practice has become established of the stewards within a plant 'bidding up' the management in the plant, so that the local rate for the job is built up with strange accretions. Frequently these consist of variations of incentive payment to stimulate output—though the motivational effect of these is seriously questioned—but there are also sundry additional payments for conditions, such as dirt money, mask money, bad weather money. Overriding them all is the 'lieu bonus', which is a straight addition to the rate of pay to produce an earnings level which is acceptable for the work to be done. The negotiations for this type of additional payment have been carried on in a largely haphazard way, to produce a disorganized and thoroughly unsatisfactory situation in payment systems. The Donovan Commission, reporting in 1968, regarded the disorder in workplace bargaining and payment systems as being the central defect in British industrial relations.

Plant agreements

Donovan advocated the extension of company and factory agreements to be coupled with industrywide agreements in the future, so that collective bargaining should be be conducted at two levels. At industrial level there would be agreement on such matters as hours in the standard working week, minimum rates of pay for typical grades of job, and the amount of holiday to be taken during the year. At company or factory level this would be filled out by a local agreement between employer and employees on precise levels of pay, job evaluation practices and so forth.

The examples were already there to be seen when Donovan reported, as there were in existence a number of what were known as 'productivity agreements', which had attempted to clear up the muddle existing at shopfloor level by negotiating a comprehensive agreement containing new pay structures and conditions together with new arrangements about working practices leading to meaningful increases in productivity. This type of agreement was further endorsed by the National Board for Prices and Incomes, which saw this as a means of allowing wage increases within the framework of a prices and incomes policy. The practice is also advocated in the major recent legislation.

Collective bargaining has been practised at industry level and at shopfloor level. We are in the process of a gradual development, within the new legal framework, of collective bargaining at an in-between level: the plant. This will largely replace shopfloor haggling and will take away some of the importance of the industry-level agreement.

Substantive and procedural agreements

The agreements concluded are normally regarded as being of two types: those concerned with substance and those concerned with procedure. The distinction between the two is set out at some length in the Code of Industrial Relations Practice.

Briefly *substantive* agreements are made about rates of pay in all manner of different circumstances, and hours of work and leisure. *Procedure* agreements regulate the way in which these agreements may be challenged and updated. Predominantly this concerns the machinery for settling grievances and differences of interpretation, but it also determines the position of shop stewards, the scope of negotiating bodies and the procedure to be adopted at times of redundancy, dismissal or discipline. Agreements of both kinds may be made at industry or plant level. Also a single agreement may well cover both substantive and procedural matters.

THE INSTITUTIONS

What now are the institutions of the industrial relations scene? We will look here at a selection of the many institutions, choosing the main central body and the main employer and employee collectives.

Advisory Conciliation and Arbitration Service

The Advisory Conciliation and Arbitration Service was set up in 1974 and is responsible for providing various services to both government and industry. It is headed by a council of ten members with no direct reporting through the Civil Service to the Cabinet. This was an important element in its establishment, to ensure its independence.

The main service to mention is that of conciliation, which is available from the various regional offices. ACAS officials are empowered to take such steps as they can to settle a dispute. Seldom do they intervene of their own volition; usually it is at the request of one of the parties to the dispute—sometimes at the request of both parties. Their aim is to be available to give prompt assistance to managements or to unions who request it. They will attempt to break a deadlock which exists because management and union can not agree. They will do this as an independent, unbiased outsider with wide and usually local experience, so that they may well have encountered similar problems before and know of solutions that have been tried successfully elsewhere. Apart from actually proposing solutions in certain circumstances, the concilliation officer may sometimes act as a go-between where the relationship between union and management has become so acrimonious that they are not even prepared to speak to each other.

Employers' associations

If there is to be national-level collective bargaining, there needs to be a representative and authoritative body to speak on behalf of the employers—an employers' association. In the context of this chapter, this is the main purpose of such associations, although it should be noted that they perform many other functions and many employers depend on them for advice on such matters as technical information, advice on trade union matters, representation to government and similar bodies, advice on wage rates, training and so on.

Employers' associations do not appear to have developed authority over their members in the way that seemed likely in the twenties and thirties, and some major firms have withdrawn from their appropriate association because they feel limited in their activities by the conservative thinking of their fellow members. Nevertheless their influence in national collective bargaining is considerable. The Confederation of British Industry gave evidence to the Donovan Commission about the organizations affiliated to them through employers' associations and federations:

> Many federated companies employ 80 per cent or more of the labour force in an industry, and in few industries is the proportion below 50 per cent.

Employers' associations thus cover appreciably more of the country's labour force than do trade unions, who claim little more than 40 per cent of the labour force as members.

Employers' associations making national agreements with representative trade unions are concluding agreements which lay down certain standard aspects of employment within the industry, and certain minima. Mainly they regard the conditions negotiated for hours, holidays and shift or overtime premium payments as being *standard* conditions. If an individual employer member of the association tried to improve on the nationally negotiated conditions, such an improvement would be strongly resisted by the association in most cases, as these standard conditions are regarded as necessary to avoid complicating interfirm competition for employees.

Pay negotiations are different, as nearly all employers' associations regard the rates they negotiate as being the minima to be paid in the industry, so that basic rates are negotiated nationally, leaving local managements to agree to higher rates or supplementary payments.

In private enterprise, at least, there is not usually a national pay structure, but from time to time an industry agrees to add to its levels of pay for all grades of employee, over and above whatever may be being done in individual companies.

Trade unions

Across the national bargaining table from the members of the employers' association sit the representatives of the trade unions to speak on behalf of the employees in the industry: manual, clerical or managerial. Just as employers associate for reasons that go beyond the field of industrial relations, so trade unions have purposes that go beyond attempting to increase the rate of pay for their members, and the company administrator needs to remember this.

The trade union exists to advance the social as well as the economic interests of its members, and it also exists to provide a representative element within the framework of a political democracy. Providing an independent challenge to the authority of employer over employee is only part of their function, and the social and political objectives must not be forgotten.

Although there are some 400 trade unions in the country, less than 120 are affiliated to the Trades Union Congress, which accounts for the great majority of trade unionists with fractionally over ten million members. It is interesting to contrast this with the 1400 employers' associations in the country.

The three largest unions are the Transport and General Workers, the Amalgamated Union of Engineering Workers and the General and Municipal Workers' Union, with over 3 500 000 members between them.

For negotiating purposes there are some federations of trade unions, the main one being the Confederation of Shipbuilding and Engineering Unions. This type of federation is needed because of the large number of unions which may have substantial numbers of members within a particular industry. Some unions may be in more than one federation. Other unions are limited to one industry, perhaps one employer, so that negotiation is more straightforward. The main examples here are the National Union of Mineworkers which negotiates with the National Coal Board and the National Union of Railwaymen, which is one of three unions negotiating for different categories of employee in the railways.

There is no standard pattern of union government but a common pattern is for the union to have an elected conference of several hundred union members and a union executive of a few dozen members which administers union affairs in accordance with the constitution and policies decided by conference. Responsible for day-to-day affairs to the executive is a general secretary and full-time officers. In some unions there is also a full-time president. Thus Mr Jack Jones is general secretary of the Transport and General Workers' Union and

Mr Hugh Scanlon is president of the Amalgamated Union of Engineering Workers.

At local level there will be a regional or area secretary who is a full-time employee of the union. According to the number of members in the area, there may be other full-time officers in support. This is the union official with whom the company administrator may have to negotiate. He will certainly have to negotiate with the main representatives of his own employees, working full time in the organization. These are usually referred to as lay officials, as they are not salaried employees of the union. The generic description is shop steward, although some unions use different terminology, such as staff representative in the clerical unions and corresponding member in the draftsmen's union.

The shop steward is elected by the employees in the department or shop within which he is employed, and he is elected by them to act as their representative in all dealings with the management on matters of pay and working conditions, and in assisting members to process issues of personal grievance. For the purpose of speaking with a collective voice to the management there will usually be a shop stewards' committee, and they will elect one or more leaders to speak on their behalf.

General union business will be conducted in branch meetings away from company premises and out of working hours.

The CBI and the TUC

The main employers' and trade union representative bodies are the Confederation of British Industry and the Trades Union Congress. They do not, however, carry out a direct role in collective bargaining in that they do not negotiate with each other on wages and conditions or the general regulation of employment. Their purpose is to represent the general employer or trade union view to government and other bodies, such as the Bullock Committee on Industrial Democracy.

COMPANY INDUSTRIAL RELATIONS PRACTICE

Although the detail of industrial relations practice in organizations is both varied and complex, there are certain broad generalizations that can be offered to company administrators.

Code of Industrial Relations Practice

The Secretary of State is required to produce a Code of Industrial Relations Practice, designed to set standards to be followed. The first version of the Code is obtainable from the Stationery Office at 15p. It deals first with the responsibilities of management, trade unions, employers' associations and individual employees. The second paragraph is:

One of management's major objectives should be to develop effective industrial relations policies which command the confidence of employees. Managers at the highest level should give, and show that they give, just as much attention to industrial relations as to such functions as finance, marketing, production or administration.

In advocating clear and comprehensive employment policies, the Code goes on to recommend the adoption of certain policies which may be regarded as overambitious by some employers. Two examples are:

Where practicable, management should provide occupational pension and sick pay schemes.
Differences in the conditions of employment and status of different categories of employee and in the facilities available to them should be based on the requirements of the job. The aim should be progressively to reduce and ultimately to remove differences which are not so based.

While many organizations have pension and sick pay provisions for all employees, many more have such facilities for white collar employees only. Also relatively few employers have completely eliminated the status differentials between white collar and other employees. Implementation of these two proposals could be cripplingly expensive to many companies.

Later sections of the Code make suggestions about communication and consultation, collective bargaining, shop stewards, individual grievance procedures and disciplinary procedures.

The Code of Industrial Relations Practice is not enforceable at law: it is an attempt to set acceptable and proper standards and it remains to be seen how much pressure will be put upon management by trade unions and other agencies to bring practices up to these standards. Perhaps the most important immediate effect is to provide an authoritative yardstick which a shop steward can use to determine how satisfactory or unsatisfactory are the standards obtaining in the plant within which he is employed.

Workers' rights

Each employee has a legal right to belong to a trade union of his choice, as well as the right to take part in union activities and to hold office.

This provision has the effect of preventing an employer from rejecting a job applicant on the grounds of union membership.

So far as notice is concerned, the Contracts of Employment Act 1972 has been amended to increase the period of notice that must be given to an employee to terminate his employment, up to a maximum of twelve weeks' notice after twelve years' service. The employer also has to expand the amount of information given in the contract of employment, on holidays and holiday pay, and the procedure available to him if he has a grievance about his work.

Finally, under the heading of workers' rights are the legal provisions about unfair dismissal. Dismissal will only be fair if it can be shown that the employer acted reasonably and had dismissed the employee, for example, because of incapacity or lack of qualifications, misconduct or redundancy. Any complaint about unfair dismissal should be taken by the individual to an industrial tribunal, which will have the power to recommend reinstatement or to award compensation the limit of the compensation being £5200.

There are a number of exceptions to the provisions on unfair dismissal, the most significant being those who work less than sixteen hours a week, those employed in undertakings with less than four employees, and those with less than six months' continuous service.

Grievance procedures

Whether employees are unionized or not, there is need for a formal procedure for handling grievances in all but the smallest of companies. This was an essential recommendation of the Royal Commission mentioned earlier, which saw it as essential to reduce the degree of disorder in workplace relations. The same thinking has been present in both Conservative and Labour attempts at legislation since then, and the Code of Practice makes this comment:

> Management should establish, with employee representatives or trade unions concerned, arrangements under which individual employees can raise grievances and have them settled fairly and promptly. There should be a formal procedure, except in very small establishments where there is close personal contact between the employer and his employees.

The need for formality is not always accepted readily by managers, who sometimes express a preference for informal, friendly, man-to-man discussions when any difficulty arises. This is conventionally known as the 'open-door' approach, but has certain disadvantages. First it is susceptible to unfair manipulation—by either side—and there is the danger of prevarication in the case of a knotty problem. Secondly, there is the lack of clear precedent and the likelihood that employees will not understand clearly what to do if they have a complaint.

Company administrators are advised to use a procedure which is as simple as possible. There are usually three separate steps:

Preliminary. The complainant lodges his complaint with his immediate superior.

Hearing. If not satisfied by the action of his immediate superior, the complainant could then ask for a more senior manager to 'hear' the case.

Appeal. If not satisfied with the outcome of the hearing, the complainant could then take his complaint to the final stage of appeal, which might be a more senior manager still, or it might be to a joint body.

Disciplinary and dismissal procedures

Running alongside arrangements for employees to ventilate and seek satisfaction on feelings of dissatisfaction, there is the need for procedures to ensure that the management has the opportunity to correct aspects of employee behaviour which are coming into conflict with the objectives of the organization. The Code of Practice gives the following advice:

> Management should ensure that fair and effective arrangements exist for dealing with disciplinary matters. These should be agreed with employee representatives or trade unions concerned and should provide for speedy consideration by management of all the relevant facts. There should be a formal procedure except in very small establishments where there is close personal contact between the employer and his employees.

It can be helpful to view the operation of discipline as a series of activities surrounding the work done:

Organizational justice. A framework of organizational justice in the form of working rules and arrangements broadly acceptable to the employer and employees, thereby ensuring general compliance with the rules, which are seen as fair and worthy of moral support.

Management control. Managerial control of performance by individuals and small groups to ensure compliance with the agreed rules, and to take initiatives to correct any deviations.

Self-discipline. Individual control of own performance to meet both personal and organizational objectives.

We may regard these as being interrelated; management control not being possible unless there is an organizational-justice framework and self-discipline not being possible unless there is performance feedback and corrective assistance from management. It is also a desirable sequence, leading to a lessening of control of the individual by management without lessening effective performance. The emphasis in management control must, of course, be positive and constructive, rather than punitive. The procedural steps relate closely to those of grievance handling, and a common procedure is frequently used, the important extra consideration being to ensure that there is no possibility of an unfounded dismissal decision being taken at any time.

MANAGEMENT RESPONSIBILITY

Finally in this chapter we can consider the question of where managerial responsibility for industrial relations should lie.

The Code of Practice requires that it should be at board level and should rank equally with matters such as marketing and finance. The dilemma in practice is to decide how much of the responsibility is in the hands of the line manager and how much in the hands of the personnel manager. It is difficult to detach this particular aspect of managerial responsibility from the overall responsibility for running a plant or a company. On the other hand the personnel specialist is essential in industrial relations matters because of the great amount of extensive knowledge and skill that is required in the contemporary industrial relations situation.

Ideally the personnel role is an advisory one, but it is essential that the advice is followed and taken unless there are very strong reasons against. Without direct authority will the personnel manager be able to get his advice accepted? Without direct accountability will his advice be responsible?

The solution to this problem will depend on the organization and upon the executives concerned, but a common approach is to give the line manager the authority to decide what to offer and how far to go in negotiations, while giving the personnel manager the right to veto such a decision if he cannot persuade his line manager colleague to follow his advice. Then the decision would revert to the superior of the two executives—presumably the managing director—to resolve. Seldom would the personnel manager use the veto, but having it available as an ultimate sanction would lend additional weight to his counsel.

FURTHER READING

E.G.A. Armstrong, *Industrial Relations—An Introduction,* Harrap, London 1969.

H.A. Clegg, *The System of Industrial Relations in Great Britain,* Blackwell, Oxford, 1972.

The Role of Management in Industrial Relations, C.I.R. Report 34, HMSO, London, 1973.

Communications and Collective Bargaining, C.I.R. Report 39, HMSO, London, 1973.

In Working Order—A Study of Industrial Discipline, Manpower Paper No 6, Department of Employment, HMSO, London, 1973.

The Reform of Collective Bargaining at Company Level, Manpower Paper No 5, Department of Employment, HMSO, London, 1971.

W.E.J. McCarthy and N.D. Ellis, *Management by Agreement,* Hutchinson, London, 1973.

R. Naylor and D.P. Torrington, *Administration of Personnel Policies,* Gower Press, Epping, 1974.

Royal Commission on Trade Unions and Employers' Associations Report, HMSO, London, 1968.

D.P. Torrington, *Handbook of Industrial Relations,* Gower Press, London, 1972.

28

Labour Relations

F W Rose

The current law on industrial relations is embodied in the Trade Union and Labour Relations Acts 1974 and 1976 (TULRA), and the Employment Protection Act 1975 (EPA). The Industrial Relations Act 1971 (IRA) has been repealed, but some of its provisions have been re-enacted in the TULRA, notably the law on unfair dismissal. The main purpose of the new law is to strengthen the bargaining position of trade unions. Disputes arising under TULRA, except unfair dismissal claims are referred to the ordinary courts. Matters arising under the EPA and unfair dismissal claims are dealt with by tribunals (see Chapter 2).

CONCILIATION AND ARBITRATION (EPA)

The statutory conciliation and arbitration service provided by the Department of Employment is administered by a council of nine members appointed by the Secretary of State, three after consultation with organizations representing employers and three after consultations with organizations representing employees.

It is proposed that if a trade dispute either exists already, or is expected to arise, the Department's services may be made available at the request of one or more of the parties to the dispute.

Stable and effective procedures to regulate relations between an employer and a trade union representing a substantial number of workers carrying out the same type of job are essential to effective collective bargaining and industrial peace. Harmonious industrial relations may be jeopardized and strikes caused by:

1   Ineffective and piecemeal bargaining procedures
2   An employer's reluctance to recognize and negotiate with a trade
    union
3   Rivalry among different unions over the right to represent the same
    body of workers

Where voluntary negotiations on recognition break down, the issue may be
referred by an independent trade union to the Conciliation and Arbitration
Service for settlement.   A trade union is independent if it is not dominated,
controlled or financially supported by an employer or employers' association.
Where the union concerned is affiliated to the TUC, the procedures set out by
the TUC must be followed for resolving interunion disputes as to which of two
different unions shall be recognized as having the right to represent a particular
body of workers.   Where an employer refuses to recognize a trade union as
recommended by the Conciliation and Arbitration Service, the Central
Arbitration Committee may be asked to make an award granting improved terms
of employment to the workers whose union is seeking recognition.   The
employer is then forced to implement those improved terms since they become
an implied term of the individual worker's contract of employment.

TRADE UNIONS AND EMPLOYERS' ASSOCIATIONS (TULRA)

An employers' association is a permanent or temporary organization of
employers formed with the main objective of regulating relations between
themselves, workers and trade unions.

A trade union is a permanent or temporary organization of workers formed
with the main objective of regulating their relations with their employer. Since a
temporary organization falls within the scope of this definition, it covers bodies
such as committees of shop stewards setting themselves up as separate entities on
becoming disenchanted with the policies of their own union.

A number of statutory duties are imposed upon trade unions and employers'
associations, subject to a fine or failing to implement those obligations. There is
a duty to:

1   Maintain proper accounting records
2   Make an annual return before 1 June, in any given year, covering
    events in the preceding calendar year, including a revenue account
    specifying income and expenditure, a balance sheet, the auditor's
    report and details of any change in officers or the address of the
    main office

All bodies traditionally regarded as trade unions or employers' associations will be allowed to register as such, this being a function to be discharged by a certification officer. The legal significance of registration which was so vital under the IRA has been largely swept away, but registered bodies do enjoy tax concessions which may be vital to their continued existence and effectiveness.

The certification officer has power to certify that a trade union is independent and issue a certificate to that effect, subject to later withdrawal if the union ceases to be independent. The trade union concerned may appeal to the Employment Appeal Tribunal against refusal to issue or withdrawal of a certificate.

The advantages of being an independent trade union may be summarized as follows:

1   It is unfair to dismiss an employee for wishing to join such a body or for taking part in its activities, or for refusing to join a non-independent trade union (TULRA)

2   Ability to seek recognition from the employer as a negotiating body for workers on employment matters, through the medium of the 'Service' (EPA)

3   Disclosure by the employer of information concerning his business on such matters as profits and losses, orders for goods and planned expansion or reduction of the workforce. This enables unions to negotiate pay structures that are realistic and reasonable in the light of the employer's financial position. If there is a refusal to disclose, the Central Arbitration Committee may make an award granting improved terms of employment which would become an implied term of the individual worker's contract of employment (EPA)

4   Where a company makes a significant contribution to a particular section of the manufacturing industry, disclosure of its future plans may be required by the government to allow formulation and furtherance of national economic policy or enable consultations to take place between government, employers and employees. The information may be passed on to each relevant, independent trade union recognized by the employer as having negotiating rights, so that they may assume an informed role in considering planning agreements to be made. On failing to make a voluntary disclosure, the Minister may make an order requiring disclosure of information on a whole range of matters such as capital expenditure, output, productivity and export goods (Industry Act 1975). Failure to make these disclosures may lead to a fine

5   An employer must not take action against his employee such as suspension or stoppage of wages, or refusing to promote, in order to prevent or deter him from being a member of an independent

trade union, or from taking part in its activities at any appropriate time outside working hours, or within working hours where permitted by the employer, or compel him to become a member of a trade union which is not independent (EPA)

6   Members may claim time off work for union activities though not necessarily with pay, and they may seek interim relief if allegedly dismissed for their union activities (see section on Unfair Dismissal) (EPA)

7   Officials are entitled to time off work with pay to discharge their union duties or to be trained on industrial relations matters (EPA)

8   Representatives must be consulted on future redundancies (EPA)

TRADE DISPUTES (TULRA)

Acts otherwise wrongful, such as inducing a breach of contract, restraint of trade, and conspiracy, may not give rise to legal action if committed in contemplation or furtherance of a trade dispute, as where one worker induces another to go on strike and violate the express terms of his contract of employment. It is important to assess the extent and scope of the phrases 'trade dispute' and 'worker' for the purposes of the TULRA, so that it can be clearly appreciated when protection is given against acts normally regarded as legal wrongs.

A trade dispute is a dispute between either employers and workers, or workers and workers, connected with matters affecting working conditions such as pay, hours of work, redundancy, demarcation disputes, disciplinary matters, facilities for trade union officials, recognition of a trade union and negotiating procedures. If these matters occur outside Great Britain they still qualify as being a trade dispute, provided it is not a political dispute. It is immaterial whether workers in this country are directly affected. This means that car workers in Great Britain may strike in sympathy with car workers in other countries and still be covered by the various statutory protections.

Interunion rivalry is also a trade dispute, and acts done in contemplation or furtherance of that dispute will not be actionable. For example, workers employed as drivers usually join the Transport and General Workers Union. Amalgamated Iron Limited may concede recognition to another union to which the majority of drivers employed by that company belong. In retaliation the T & GWU, which was also seeking recognition by Amalgamated Iron Limited as the union able to negotiate on behalf of its drivers, may instruct its members working for other employers not to handle goods supplied to or sent out from Amalgamated Iron Limited, thereby halting production. Although a dispute does not exist between Amalgamated Iron Limited and its own workers concerning their conditions of employment, nonetheless the interunion dispute on recognition, attempting to force recognition of the T & GWU, is in law a trade dispute. It is not tortiously wrong for the T & GWU to induce its members to breach their contracts of employment by refusing to handle goods on behalf of Amalgamated Iron Limited.

A worker is a person who works or seeks work under:

1 A contract of employment or apprenticeship, or
2 A contract for the services of an independent contractor, excluding professional services, eg an accountant
3 A contract to provide some of the professional services under the national health scheme
4 Employment with a government department, excluding the police and the armed forces

The concept of a worker embraces a person who 'seeks work', for example unemployed persons organized into a group in order to secure work, or redundant workers taking industrial action after breaking away from their own union following what they consider to be an unsatisfactory handling of a redundancy situation with their former employer.

Inducing a breach of contract

A trade union or its officials may persuade an employer to give proper notice to a worker terminating his employment, where he refuses to join that union to which most of his fellow workers belong. Alternatively, a worker may be persuaded to give proper notice terminating his employment if the employer refuses to concede recognition rights to that trade union. It is not a tortious wrong to induce a person to terminate a contract of employment, provided there is no recourse to a wrongful act such as intimidation. It is legally actionable however to attempt, intentionally, to persuade a party to a contract of employment to refuse to carry out its terms as by going on strike, since here the requisite period of notice is not given, lawfully terminating the agreement. Such action is calculated to cause some loss to the employer as the other contracting party. Freedom of industrial action is secured however by the TULRA which, with amendments proposed, provides that acts inducing breach of contract and allied conduct such as interfering with performance of a contract, inducing interference with performance of a contract, threatening breach of a contract, or threatening to induce a breach of contract, will not be actionable in tort if they are in contemplation or furtherance of a trade dispute. The act in question must have been committed by a trade union official, worker in dispute with his employer, or other person taking action in support though not directly connected with the dispute, for example students engaged in militant acts in support of strikers. The worker successfully induced to breach his contract of employment in contemplation or furtherance of a trade dispute may be sued in damages by his employer or dismissed, although this is not usually done. There are special provisions on unfair dismissal of strikers (see page 548).

Commercial contracts as well as contracts of employment are within the scope of the protections now under discussion. For example, workers at Allied Metal Tools Limited may be on strike for higher pay. Their union officials may, in contemplation or furtherance of that dispute, induce drivers employed by various suppliers not to deliver raw materials to the strike-bound company, thereby inducing breach of a commercial contract of supply.

In all the situations discussed above, there is no immunity from tortious action if unlawful means, such as threats of violence, are used to induce the contracting parties to act in breach of an existing contract.

Conspiracy

Trade union members may go on strike in pursuance of their objectives at the suggestion of the union's executive committee. This action is both a restraint of trade and a criminal conspiracy. It is a restraint of trade to infringe a person's freedom to work or to employ workers as he wishes. It is a criminal conspiracy for two or more persons to act unlawfully, or do a lawful act by unlawful means, although no damage results and no crime would have been committed if each person had acted singly rather than together. There are express provisions however, providing that:

1   Agreements made by either a trade union or an employers' association in restraint of trade are not void, and
2   Members of a trade union or employers' association cannot be prosecuted for committing any crime, including conspiracy for acting in restraint of trade

It is a tortious conspiracy for two or more persons, such as union officials, to act together for the purpose of:

1   Committing an unlawful act, as by inducing workers to go on strike contrary to the term of their respective contracts of employment, or
2   Wilfully injuring another person, such as an employer, without using unlawful means, provided some damage results. Combining together to act in concert makes an otherwise innocent act a. tortious conspiracy

For example, a group of workers may agree with their employer to refuse to handle the goods from the Supply and General Services Company Limited, on the ground that workers there — who are members of the same union — are not paid the union's recommended rate for the job, as generally accepted by the majority of employers. As such, this is a wilful attempt to injure the Supply and General Services Company Limited in an unlawful manner causing financial loss to the company. It is provided that trade union activities by two or more persons acting together in contemplation or furtherance of a trade dispute are not actionable as tortious conspiracies, so long as the acts would not be wrongful if committed by one person acting alone.

IMMUNITY FOR TRADE UNIONS AND EMPLOYERS' ASSOCIATIONS (TULRA)

A tortious act is not actionable if committed by a trade union or employers' association and connected with regulation of relations between employers, workers and trade unions. Such acts as inducing a breach of contract, interfering with an employer's business or conspiracy are not tortious, whether or not they are committed in contemplation or furtherance of a trade dispute, and irrespective of whether the act is that of the organization itself, the trustees, officers or members. Nonetheless the following wrongs are actionable:

1 Breach of contract, thus a union member wrongfully expelled can sue for damages
2 Wrongful use of funds for an unlawful object
3 Misapplication of funds by trustees who must make good losses caused
4 Legal wrongs that cause personal injury, or breach of duty connected with ownership, control or use of property, unless committed in contemplation or furtherance of a trade dispute. This covers injury to a person employed by a trade union or employers' association during the course of his employment, caused by a failure to provide a safe place of work

COLLECTIVE AGREEMENTS (TULRA)

Wages and working conditions may be settled by negotiations between an employer, or group of employers, and one or more trade unions representing the workers involved, recognized by employers and workers as having the right to negotiate collectively in this manner. Collective agreements made before 1 December 1971, being the date when the Industrial Relations Act 1971 became effective on this issue, and after 16 September 1974 TULRA, are conclusively presumed not to be legally enforceable, but binding in honour only. This means that the agreed terms may be violated without any legal redress. An express statement in a collective agreement may make it wholly or partially enforceable in law to the extent so indicated. Trade unions are against legal enforceability especially if it inhibits strike action.

Some terms in a collective agreement, usually on matters such as wage rates and hours of work, may become part of the individual worker's contract of employment by virtue of a clause in that contract providing that certain terms governing working conditions will change automatically as each new collective agreement is negotiated. It is provided however that any term in a collective agreement, irrespective of when it was made, prohibiting or restricting a worker's right to strike or take other industrial action — such as a procedure for discussion and possible settlement of the dispute — to precede industrial action, does not form part of any worker's individual contract of employment and bind him in law, unless that collective agreement:

1   Is in writing
2   Embodies a clause expressly stating that the term in question may
     be incorporated into a worker's individual contract of employment
     as part of it
3   Is readily accessible at the place of work, for the worker to read
     and discuss
4   Is an agreement where each trade union which is a party thereto
     has the status of independent trade union

As an additional, fifth requirement the worker's individual contract of employment must expressly or impliedly permit incorporation into it of terms from the collective agreement.

PICKETING (TULRA)

A picket, acting in contemplation or furtherance of a trade dispute, may present himself at a worker's place of employment or other premises where he happens to be, excluding his residence, in order to:

1   Peacefully obtain or pass on information, as by handing out leaflets
     explaining why some workers are on strike, or persuading lorry
     drivers not to deliver or collect goods
2   Peacefully persuade persons, such as other workers, to join the
     strike or return to work

A picket acts unlawfully if he disobeys lawful instructions given by police, such as refusing to allow persons and vehicles to enter and leave work premises without harassment. In practice the police rarely bring charges of illegal picketing; instead they rely on allied offences such as threatening behaviour, assault, battery, nuisance, breach of the peace, obstruction of the highway or carrying offensive weapons.

INTERNAL MANAGEMENT OF TRADE UNION AFFAIRS

Trade unions have successfully demanded the right to regulate their own internal affairs free from legislative control. Some employers in conjunction with a particular trade union operate a closed shop, consequently on joining the work-force the new employee's membership of that union is a condition of continued employment. Refusal to allow an individual to join a particular union, or expulsion of an existing member, may affect that person's ability to earn a livelihood, thus fair and proper rules should exist governing the right to join, take part in the affairs of, and remain a member of a union.

The rules of a trade union must be strictly observed since they are a contract between that union and its members. The rules may state the description of workers who are entitled to join and also persons who are ineligible for member-ship. Clearly a union formed to protect the interests of mineworkers will wish to restrict membership to workers of that particular type.

The courts have in the past assumed the right to declare void any union rule that arbitrarily and unreasonably restricts membership as contravening public policy. The need to seek legal redress may be rendered unnecessary in most cases since the TUC has set up a non statutory Independent Review Committee of a legally qualified chairman and two trade unionists to determine an employee's appeal against refusal to admit or expulsion from a particular union where membership is a condition of employment. The committee is empowered to recommend admission or re-admission and the union is expected to accept and act upon any decision so made. Unions should settle these matters themselves as far as possible by setting up investigatory internal procedures. An appeal to the committee will only occur in cases of continued difficulty and disagreement.

Termination of membership (TULRA)

There is an implied term in every contract of membership of a trade union permitting a member to terminate membership on giving reasonable notice and complying with any reasonable conditions, such as paying arrears of subscrip-tions. A person may wish to resign from a union if he disagrees with its policies or does not wish to obey directions to go on strike. It appears that a member now has a legal remedy for breach of contract for wrongful termination of membership.

Exercise of disciplinary powers

Union rules governing internal discipline and exercise of the power to fine or expel a member must be followed to the letter, otherwise the decision may be challenged however slight the irregularity. The union's decision cannot be made final and binding. The aggrieved member may test any alleged irregularity in the procedure by appeal to the ordinary courts, even though union rules purport to exclude such an appeal. Further, a union cannot take any form of disciplinary action unless the necessary power has been expressly granted by union rules. In cases of alleged wrongful expulsion the aggrieved member may seek a court injunction restraining the union from so acting and award damages for any losses suffered, for example, loss of wages after being dismissed from a job where union membership is a condition of employment.

There are no statutory rules requiring trade unions to observe the principles of natural justice when disciplining members, nonetheless it is arguable that the common law rules are still applicable. This means that the member concerned must be notified of the charges against him, given an opportunity to prepare a reply and be allowed to attend a hearing to state his case before persons hitherto unconnected with the dispute.

UNFAIR DISMISSAL (TULRA)

The TULRA Schedule I empowers a worker who has worked for his employer continuously for twenty-six weeks or more to claim reinstatement, or compensation up to £11 760, if the individual can prove that he or she has been unfairly dismissed. Employers are advised to set up their own internal procedures to investigate proposed dismissals to ascertain whether they are fair so that the possibility of infringing the law on unfair dismissal will be reduced.

A worker will be regarded as having been dismissed if:

1   His contract of employment is terminated with or without notice
2   A fixed-term contract expires without renewal, excluding cases where the worker has voluntarily agreed in writing to forego his statutory protection in relation to a contract for a fixed term of two years or more
3   He terminates his employment, with or without notice, for some justifiable reason, eg improper behaviour by the employer, or refusal to pay wages at the agreed time

An employer is justified in dismissing any worker instantly without notice or payment of wages in lieu of notice, on grounds of dishonesty, incompetence, negligence, disobedience, misbehaviour or prolonged illness, provided that evidence can be adduced substantiating these allegations.

Statutory definition of unfair dismissal

A number of situations are specified in which dismissal will be regarded as unfair:

1   Where the worker was, or proposed to become, a member of an independent trade union, or to take part at the appropriate time in its activities, or refused to become or remain a member of a trade union which was not independent. Dismissal for any one of these reasons is deemed to be an 'inadmissible reason'. This concept is important in relation to the other grounds of dismissal discussed below. In this type of case it is unnecessary for the worker to show that he has been continuously employed for twenty-six weeks as a prerequisite to claiming protection

2   On grounds of redundancy, where other workers employed by the same employer have not been dismissed and the real reason for dismissal is an inadmissible reason, alternatively, where agreed redundancy procedures have been contravened without justification, as where a shop steward is allegedly made redundant, but the employer's true motive is to dismiss him for his union activities

3   If the reason, or principal reason for dismissal was, to institute or further a lock-out, or participation in a strike or other industrial action, where other 'relevant' employees of the same employer were not dismissed, or if dismissed were offered re-engagement. A 'relevant' employee is one directly interested in the trade dispute in contemplation or furtherance of which the lock-out occurred

Statutory definition of fair dismissal

Dismissal is fair in the following situations:

1   Related to the worker's capabilities or qualifications for carrying out his job

2   Related to his conduct, for example, inefficiency or misbehaviour

3   If continued employment would be illegal, as where a woman is dismissed because statute now requires her work to be carried out only by male workers on the ground that it is too dangerous or physically arduous for a woman

4   If caused by redundancy

5   If the worker dismissed was not a member of an independent trade union recognized by the employer where there is a union membership agreement requiring members of a workforce to join a particular union (closed shop) unless he objects on religious grounds

When determining the reason for a dismissal, no account must be taken of any pressure exercised on the employer to dismiss the worker by actual or threatened industrial action, including a strike. For example, where the employer has been induced to dismiss a worker who refuses to join a particular trade union to which his fellow workers belong.

The employer must show that the principal reason for dismissal was:

1   A substantial reason in relation to an employee holding the position in question, or one of the reasons specified by statute,
2   That in the circumstances, having regard to equity and the substantial merits of the case, he acted reasonably in regarding that reason as a sufficient reason for dismissal. For example, a chief inspector, dismissed for redundancy without prior warning, successfully claimed that he has been unfairly dismissed. It was held that a failure to consult an employee, contrary to paragraph 46 of the Code of Practice, about to be dismissed reasonably for redundancy, could render the dismissal unreasonable and unfair

Determination of disputes

Unfair-dismissal claims must be referred to an industrial tribunal by the worker concerned:

1   Within three months of termination of the employment, or
2   Such further period as the tribunal considers reasonable where it was not reasonably practicable to present the complaint within three months. For example, where a delay is caused by negotiations with the employer on reinstatement which would have been jeopardized by presentation of an unfair-dismissal claim by the worker

Complaints may be presented from the date when notice of dismissal is first given to the worker. This will increase the chances of reinstatement if dismissal is held to be unfair by the tribunal, by cutting the time that elapses between dismissal and re-engagement.

A worker is entitled after 26 weeks continuous employment to obtain from his employer within 14 days a written statement of the reasons for his dismissal, to be admissible as evidence if an unfair-dismissal claim is brought. A tribunal will be able to award two weeks' pay to a worker whose request for reasons is unreasonably refused by the employer, irrespective of whether or not the dismissal is ultimately held to be unfair.

A dismissed employee may be reinstated in his old job or re-engaged in comparable or suitable alternative employment. When making either of these orders the tribunal must consider the complainant's wishes, the practicability for the employer who may have appointed a permanent replacement if a reasonable period elapsed after dismissal before a claim for reinstatement or re-engagement was made, and whether it is just to do so if the complainant caused or contributed to his dismissal. The tribunal may award:

1 Arrears of pay for the period between termination of employment, and reinstatement or re-engagement, less wages paid in lieu of notice, *ex gratia* payments from the employer or remuneration from other employment

2 Restoration of employment rights, including seniority and pension rights

3 Improved terms and conditions of employment granted during the period of unfair dismissal to other employees in the same grade

A basic, compensatory and an additional award, up to a maximum of £11 760 may be claimed where reinstatement or re-engagement is not ordered by the tribunal, or where the employer completely or partially refuses to implement such an order, with a reduction if the complainant's conduct unreasonably prevented any order taking effect, or if he failed to mitigate his losses by finding other suitable work available. A basic award is calculated as follows, with a deduction for any redundancy payment made on dismissal:

1 For each year of continuous employment (maximum 20 years) between the ages of 41–64 (59 women) (inclusive) 1½ times a week's pay (maximum £80 a week)

2 For every year of continuous employment (maximum 20 years) between the ages of 22–40 (inclusive) 1 times a week's pay (maximum £80 a week)

3 For every year of continuous employment (maximum 20 years) between the ages of 18–21 (inclusive) ½ times a week's pay (maximum £80 a week)

A compensatory award is a just and equitable amount reflecting the dismissed employee's losses, such as, expenses reasonably incurred in finding a new job and loss of benefits reasonably expected but for dismissal, like pay increases. The maximum award under this head is £5200.

An additional award of between 13–26 weeks' pay (maximum £80 a week) is also payable, increased to between 26–32 weeks' pay (maximum £80 a week) where the reason for dismissal is membership of an independent trade union or taking part in its activities at any appropriate time, or refusing to join or remain a member of a non independent trade union, or objecting to joining an independent trade union in a closed shop situation, or an unlawful act of racial or sex discrimination.

An employee alleging unfair dismissal for being a member of an independent trade union or taking part in its activities at any appropriate time may claim interim relief until the tribunal decides his unfair dismissal claim. If the employee's allegations are substantiated after a preliminary consideration, the employer may be requested to reinstate or re-engage pending a full investigation. If the employer fails to attend the hearing, refuses to reinstate or re-engage, or if the employee reasonably refuses re-engagement in a different job, then continuation of the original contract of employment will be ordered, failure to comply leading to a compensatory award.

29

Industrial Training Requirements

Derek Torrington

Industrial training has become big business since the passing of the Industrial Training Act in 1964. Before that time, training activity on an organized basis was limited to larger companies and public undertakings. The Act was intervention by the government to coerce employers to meet what were seen as their community obligations to increase the quality and quantity of training undertaken and to spread its cost.

Despite the efforts by officials of training boards, the passing of the Industrial Training Act has caused some managers to look upon training as a question of meeting legal obligations and breaking even in the levy/grant tussle, rather than as an aspect of personnel management important for its intrinsic merits and capable of making a significant contribution to the long-term success or failure of the undertaking. Because of this widespread feeling, this chapter starts by considering some of the advantages of running effective programmes of industrial training.

THE CASE FOR TRAINING

The advantages range from considerations of the effective use of resources to considerations of the overall purpose of the enterprise. The following list is by no means exhaustive.

Resources

The people in an organization are its major resource. If they are not appropriately trained for the work they have to do they will not do it as efficiently as they could and operations will not be as profitable as they might be. Some degree of investment in training can make the human resources at the disposal of the management more productive and more profitable.

Fragmentation of work

Specialization is growing so that the work to be done within the undertaking is constantly being broken up into smaller parcels. New departments are set up to specialize in a particular aspect of the company's affairs, and each employs people who are to work in a specialized rather than general field. In the management ranks, this takes the form of the functional specialist, who can do one or two things superbly, replacing the gifted amateur who could do all manner of things with reasonable competence. This means that each employee needs a degree of training to undertake his duties, and this is likely to become greater with the development of specialization.

New skills and knowledge

A development of this factor of the skilled specialist is the problem of obsolescence in skills and knowledge. Many people in the financial and administrative field have forced themselves through the traumatic experience of accepting electronic data processing in the last decade. This acceptance has made it necessary for them to take some training so that they understand the monsters spewing forth information at such an alarming rate. The technological innovation of the computer has rendered obsolete some of the established skills of the company administrator and he has needed to learn new ones.

This effect of technological development is apparent in every part of commercial and industrial activity. Few if any people will still be practising at forty the skills they find imperative to learn at twenty. The new skills have to be taught.

It is a short-term, expensive and impractical solution merely to hire new people who happen to have picked up the new skills elsewhere. The challenge of retraining the adult has to be faced, both by the employer and by the individual himself.

With managerial staff especially, there is the even more demanding need constantly to develop new understanding of the situation in which the undertaking is functioning. Changes in law, economic situation and social forces in the community outside the organization have great influence on affairs within the organization, and knowledge of the environment is essential to managers

On-the-job training

Some people hear this sort of argument and reply by saying that training arrangements should be made outside the field of employment, and that the substantial proportion of the gross national product that is channelled into further education should take care of industrial training needs by training people in colleges and government training centres in the whole span of skills and areas of knowledge that are developing.

Those who make this point would usually be surprised by the extent of what is done in this way, but still the training that is done off the job cannot be completed off the job. Just as the person learning to drive has to sit in the driving seat and drive along the street during his training, so the apprentice engineer, the trainee typist, laboratory technician, supervisor, personnel officer, sales manager and other industrial trainees all have to get their academic training in practical perspective, which is best done in the working situation. Also much necessary training is in routines which are peculiar to one company, so that a supervisor may learn much of great value on a supervisors' course at the local college, but it will be equally important for him to learn how his own company disciplinary procedures are administered, and this can obviously come only from an agent of the employer.

Employee expectation

There is a standard of expectation which prospective employees have about what the company provides for its recruits. They will expect canteen facilities and locker rooms. Many will expect pension provision and sick pay. If these basic expectations are not met, they will not come and work for the company unless they have no choice, or unless they are likely to earn much more money than they would elsewhere. More and more employees are expecting to receive training for the job when they join a new company rather than having to sit next to Nellie until the penny drops. A well-run training scheme will be an aid to recruitment. Complete lack of training will be a disincentive to prospective recruits.

Social purpose

All company administrators and managers have a view to the purpose of their enterprise that goes beyond mere survival and profitability. Management has as one of its many objectives that the company should be a place worth working in, and that the people working there are there to some extent to achieve personal fulfilment as well as to carry out instructions for the achievement of profitability.

Assuming that a company has a personnel policy that recognizes its employees as people rather than simply human resources, then the requirements for industrial training are the requirements of the people employed as well as the requirements of the employer.

ADMINISTERING THE TRAINING FUNCTION

The passing of the Industrial Training Act led to many companies taking the concept of specialization too far, with a resultant setting up of training departments with managers reporting to the managing director or general manager and being quite independent of the personnel department.

The reason for this was usually the calibre of the incumbent personnel manager or the alarm of the managing director at the propsect of being 'fined' by his industrial training board for not meeting their training requirements. In the mid-1960s many personnel managers were limited in their thinking to aspects of employee welfare such as canteen, lavatories and record-keeping rather than to the fuller view of personnel which is common today. As a result this type of personnel manager was not considered the appropriate person to be responsible for training with its new levy sanction, and most of the bright, keen training officers who started emerging were not prepared to report to that type of company executive.

This produced a split in the personnel function, requiring the different specialisms to be coordinated by the managing director. Fortunately this practice is now less common except in the largest organizations, but it is important for company administrators to appreciate that personnel work is a three-legged stool, with the different legs defined by the Institute of Personnel Management as:

1   Employment and employee services
2   Industrial relations
3   Manpower development and training

Each of these interlocks with the other two and they have to be coordinated and administered under an overall personnel policy. If one of the legs is removed the stool falls down. Effective training depends on effective selection. Improved industrial relations often need new training programmes and training innovations frequently influence the industrial relations environment.

In considering how the training function is administered, it is therefore of first importance to see it as part of personnel work.

The personnel function should not usually report to a functional line manager. If the responsibility for any aspect of personnel comes under, say, the production manager, then managers in marketing, R & D and other areas will regard it as a specifically production function—as may the production manager. It must be seen to be available to, and necessary for, all company functions. Furthermore the responsibility of training specialist does not interfere with the line authority of the manager. The training officer provides a specialist service to all line managers in the organization. His specialist usefulness lies in his understanding of the requirement of the training board for the industry of which the company is a part, his acquired expertise in the skills and knowledge needed to administer a training programme, his awareness of how people learn, his knowledge of sources of supply of courses and visiting lecturers. He has a general responsibility for the quality of training provided in the organization, but the individual line manager remains responsible for the performance and competence of his own staff. The line manager needs to appreciate what the training function can do for him in developing that competence: he cannot wash his hands of the responsibility and 'leave it to personnel'. They can only provide him with some services that he has to appreciate and use.

Integration

Responsibility for the provision of specialist training services needs to be integrated with the whole of the personnel function, which must in turn be integrated with the overall management of the enterprise. Personnel and training are combined activities which have a job to do in ensuring that the organization meets its business objectives. This is not an agency of the Welfare State latched onto the outside in some parasitical, unwanted way.

Objectives

The company objectives need to be reappraised to consider the place of training within the total personnel activity. What is it there for? What are its objectives? How do these align with the existing business objectives? What targets have to be achieved?

Identification of training needs

The person responsible for training has to establish what the training needs within the organization are. He will look at two aspects of this. First he will look at the operational efficiency of the organization. Later he will look at the needs of individual people for training, and the need of the organization for people to be trained.

In looking at operational efficiency, he will seek to identify those jobs within the organization that appear to be holding back the achievement of proper levels of performance and where training may help to lift this level to one that is acceptable. He will look at the various indicators which personnel people use to 'take the temperature' of working groups. Absenteeism, labour turnover, punctuality, sickness, changes in output level, complaints and labour troubles are all indicators which can point to the state of morale in a department, and low morale may be caused by inadequate training methods. There may be data available from work study officers who feel that the work standards in a particular department are not satisfactory. Conversations with managers and supervisors will suggest other areas needing attention. The training officer's own experience and training will suggest others, as will the officers of the industrial training boards.

The training officer will therefore collect together a mass of information about the training needs that exist within the company, and he can then begin to draw up proposals about what training should be done and in what order, the priority usually being determined by the likely pay-off. He may suggest that the training of typists could be altered to enable newly recruited school-leavers to reach an acceptable level of proficiency in half the time now considered as necessary, at a saving of £x a year, followed by specially designed programmes of operator training in selected departments to reduce the level of labour turnover and to boost output. He might suggest middle managers attending courses at a business school, or supervisors having a series of discussions on the implications of recent legislation. Whatever the detail of his proposals, he will draw these up and require them to be endorsed by his management colleagues or superiors, so that he has a mandate to start work.

Implementation of training programme

When the training officer has received his mandate he will also be empowered to spend some money to implement his programme. This will be based on his prediction of how much he can produce in the way of operating economies.

The expenditure will come broadly under two headings. First there will be expenditure on hardware and fees, which are outgoings that would not be incurred if the training were not done. Hardware will range from boxes of chalk to overhead projectors, teaching machines and fully equipped, soundproof lecture theatres adjacent to luxurious offices for the training staff. Fees will be either the fees payable for employees to attend courses, or payable to outside experts to come and take part in internal courses. The training officer, like any other executive submitting a budget for approval, is likely to ask for more than he needs under this heading, as he expects those who have to sanction his budget to be Philistine and to cut it. Company administrators will be familiar with this tactic and will know how to deal with it. Also, it may be sensible for a newly established training function to start off with a minimum of equipment and to invest more heavily when experience has been gained. The reason for saying this is that most training programmes change fundamentally after a spell of running in and the benefits of experience. Heavy initial investment can result in an accumulation of expensive equipment that is unused, and a dearth of equipment that is needed but not available because the budget has been overspent.

The second broad heading of expenditure is salaries and wages of trainees, where the administrator perhaps needs to look at proposals with close scrutiny. Employees away from work on training courses are still being paid. In the case of most managerial personnel and supervisors this adds nothing to the cost of their duties being carried out. Someone else will pinch-hit for them in their absence, they will catch up with their work when they return, and that is that. In some other cases, however, there may be the expenditure of either increasing the establishment for a department so that people absent for training can be covered, or arrangements for colleagues to work expensive overtime to make up the shortfall. The training is necessary, but this type of consideration needs to be thought of before the training begins so that the implications are fully appreciated.

Apart from hardware, referred to above, the training officer will need some space to run his schemes in. Some training will be done on the job or in a training section of the normal job environment, such as the apprentice bench in an engineering shop. Some training will be done away from the premises altogether, as when a young manager goes to the nearby polytechnic to take a management course. But there will be a need for some of the training programme to be carried out away from the job and on company premises. Typists are often trained in a small school within the company, and a number of short courses will be run to give managers or others an appreciation of a subject or to give specific training in certain skills that are needed.

Evaluation of training effectiveness

Finally in setting up a training function, the company administrator will want some means of evaluating the training that is being run, and this is one of the most nebulous and unsatisfactory aspects of the training job. There is at least one guide to effectiveness that can be used, and that is the balance in the levy/grant equation. Most of the training boards make their own assessment of how adequate the training within a company is by comparison with the industry as a whole and this is reflected in the extent to which levy exceeds grant or grant exceeds levy.

This may not, however, be enough for the company because the criteria being applied are likely to be the criteria for the whole industry or the general community—not necessarily the needs of the individual company. The next step is to compare the results achieved with the original objectives and, where possible, to measure the degree of improvement. This can be done in such things as labour and material utilization, or the reduction in the number of dispatch errors being made in a warehouse. It can only be guessed in the more difficult areas such as the quality of supervision by a foreman before and after a training course. This often depends on a subjective assessment that can be influenced by the reactions of the trainee rather than on more objective factors.

Another possible means of evaluation is to measure the benefits that are set up as objectives at the beginning of the programme. It might be a drop in labour turnover and other measures of improved efficiency and employee morale. There may be lower levels of accidents or reduced overtime. It is also important to attempt some evaluation of the intangibles, such as atmosphere in industrial relations, satisfaction of customers, self-confidence among managers and so on. To some extent this can be done by the use of an outside adviser who can come along for a day to examine the situation relating to training within the organization and then report upon it; rather like an auditor. Clearly such a person needs to be expert in the field and with experience in other companies. An appropriate person may be a consultant or an academic specializing in the field of industrial training.

It is useful from a training point of view to carry out some form of performance appraisal regularly among employees. If this is done systematically and thoroughly over several years, the validity of training arrangements will be confirmed or made suspect.

TRAINING FOR PARTICULAR GROUPS OF EMPLOYEES

Operators

The largest single grouping in the employed population is the operator on the shop floor who has no craft skills: the general worker. His job may be one requiring such a small amount of skill and knowledge that he requires no training other than a short period of 'being shown how' by his supervisor. There are, however, very few jobs which genuinely come into this category. Most would be done better by more satisfied employees if they were preceded by a period of training, which covered general induction to the organization and the place of the job in the manufacturing process, as well as the mechanics of how it was done.

As operator jobs in manufacturing are usually specific to each employer, the training needs to be set up and run within the company, as there is no outside body either with the understanding of the job or any alternative source of supply of trainees. The work will be a job for the training officer to study the operations and to use a process of skills analysis to devise a programme of training, which is then followed by an instructor in instructing trainees. Seldom is the training load large enough to justify a full-time instructor, and it is usual for an experienced operator in each department to be trained in instruction so that he does all the instruction needed by new recruits. Another method is for the foreman to be trained so that he inducts and trains all those in his department. This may be the best method as long as the training job is not going to take up too much of his time.

Skills analysis can be learned at one of the many introductory courses for training officers run within the further education system. Alternatively there are short, crash courses available. Instructors can be trained by the Government Training Centres at Letchworth and Glasgow. The occasional instructor can attend a course available in most areas of the country from the Training Services Agency under the title of Training Within Industry (TWI) Job Instruction.

Clerical

Very little training is provided in clerical duties in most organizations, although the practice is now spreading and companies find that training pays big dividends in cost savings and employee satisfaction. The practice of clerical training is similar to that for operator training, although there are certain more general occupational skills involved, so that the further education system is more helpful. Widely available is a course in office skills which is taken by young people—usually girls—on leaving school. They attend technical college for one day a week and learn simple office skills and routines to fit in with the working experience they are beginning to acquire. There are also many courses in shorthand and typing, although the demand for shorthand is beginning to fade, and the school-leaver with reasonable GCE 'O' level achievement can take the Ordinary National Certificate in business studies on day release.

Craft

One of the first areas requiring attention is the training of craft apprentices, as this is a long and expensive business. Some of the training boards gave the largest amount of their attention to this area in the first few years of their operation.

Apprentices are recruited at the age of sixteen on leaving school, and serve a period of several years' apprenticeship before being accepted as craftsmen at the end of their training, usually in their twenty-first or twenty-second year. Most apprentices are young men, although young women do follow apprenticeships as well, but these are heavily concentrated in hairdressing. Many companies follow the customary practice of binding apprentices by indentures, under which the apprentice is obliged to stay with the employer until finishing his 'time' and the employer agrees to provide his training.

A major part of the apprentice's time is spent in further education at the local college, learning the theoretical background of his craft and some manual skills. While with the employer, he needs to practise the skills he is learning and to develop them by applying his knowledge and ability to a growing range of work. Traditionally this has been done by watching, helping and copying a craftsman at work. Gradually this method is being replaced by systematic and full-time training under an instructor in charge of a group of apprentices.

If an organization is not big enough to warrant the services of a full-time instructor, it is often possible to join a group training scheme, in which a number of small and medium-sized companies pool resources to employ a training officer who organizes the training of the apprentices in all the companies. In return, the individual company pays a relatively modest fee to the group scheme, which spreads the cost thinly. Also, the individual apprentice has a better training as he probably moves from one firm to another in the group.

Company administrators should remember that there are usually national agreements between employers and trade unions regarding the employment and training of apprentices.

Technician

A category in which the number of employees is growing is that of technician, who is one step up from a craftsman and is likely to be concerned more with design than with manufacture. In the field of engineering, the fitter is the craftsman and the draftsman is the technician, although there are many others classified as craftsmen and technicians respectively in that industry.

To some extent the training needs are common, as the basic technology is the same, but the technician's training needs go further. He is likely to have better educational qualifications at the outset and his further education will go to a higher theoretical level. His practical training will tend to lie in conventional white collar rather than manual operations. It is usually carried out in close conjunction with a qualified man.

Technologist

It is difficult to distinguish between technicians and technologists and in many · industries such a distinction cannot be drawn. A rough and ready identification would be the word 'professional'. Pursuing the engineering example, the technologist is the professional engineer who has achieved membership of one of the constituent bodies of the Council of Engineering Institutions. This requires a high level of academic qualification together with the appropriate working experience.

In this category will be the ex-technician who has plugged away through day release or evening courses to HNC/HND and endorsements, as well as the technical graduate who starts his working life in his early twenties. These are the men on whom the technical competence and progress of the organization will depend.

The man who comes up through the ranks will need facilities to pursue his academic studies, either by day release or by sandwich course. His practical expertise will be acquired almost incidentally as long as he has reasonable opportunities for varied working experience, rather than being classified as a trainee who cannot be given a proper job just yet because he has not finished his education.

The technical graduate who comes to industry in his early twenties with academic qualifications of a high order but no practical experience needs usually some form of graduate apprenticeship while he spends a number of months acquiring the practical experience that is needed to go with his theoretical grounding.

Management

Training managers is a very different matter from training other categories of workers in industry. This is largely because a smaller proportion of the manager's job content can be isolated and taught. To be effective a manager needs to learn management techniques, such as various methods for the quantification of data so that decisions may be soundly based. He also needs to extend his knowledge in such areas as the behavioural sciences so that he may more readily understand how employees may react in certain situations, and so that he may plan sensibly for the future. Beyond this, however, there is still a large area of training or development needed for the individual management trainee, so that he acquires the stature and confidence needed for the job of leadership, so that he develops judgment and determination, so that he develops good timing and a sensitive awareness in handling people.

Largely because of the difficulty and lack of definition of the task of management training, most large organizations separate out this particular aspect of the training function and give the responsibility to management development officers within the training function.

The body of knowledge and some of the skills can come from the educational system. In addition to the business schools, which cater for a small fraction of the total amount of management training, there are a number of polytechnics and universities with specialized management departments running courses with recognition from some professional body. The most widely recognized management qualification available in the field of further education is the Diploma in Management Studies, run under the auspices of the Department of Education and Science. It is operated at a limited number of centres and provides a broadly based management education for the well-qualified entrant with limited practical experience. There are also courses run under the aegis of, for instance, the Institute of Personnel Management and the Institution of Industrial Management which provide a broad management education with particular emphasis on the management specialism that the professional body represents.

In conjunction with further education, the trainee manager will need controlled working experience and career development so that he can apply his developing skills and knowledge. He may also need careful coaching to help him develop qualities such as judgment and timing. All managers need constantly to bring themselves up to date with new techniques or with new knowledge. Thus, professional bodies like the British Institute of Management and many firms of professional consultants conduct admirable short courses running for a few days or a few weeks to update the experienced manager. Typical of these have been the endless variety of courses and conferences to brief managers on the implications of EEC membership.

Supervisory

Training of first-line supervisors is generally unsatisfactory in the United Kingdom, and the foreman has more than once been referred to as the forgotten man of British industry. Much of the problem lies in the uncertainty about what the job really is. The only aspect of the supervisory job on which most managers can agree is that none of them would have it for all the tea in China! In the early years of this century the foreman was a man of considerable power and authority in a factory, with extensive discretion in decision-making, and was often a general manager in all but name. Since then we have seen the professionalization of management and the development of shop steward authority. The professionalization of management has spawned countless middle managers who have taken bits of the foreman's job away from him, like the production engineer and the training officer. The development of shop steward authority has largely done away with the foreman's role as representative of shopfloor feeling, and he is constantly bypassed as shop stewards go and negotiate with middle and senior managers at meetings he is not invited to attend.

As the position of first-line supervisor is so difficult to define, training for it has obvious problems, and the most useful approach is probably the in-company course which aims to inform foremen of the changes taking place around them and give them an understanding of company procedures together with an introduction to such vague but necessary subjects as leadership and human relations.

An attempt has been made to establish a course for foremen within the further education system, but this has not received widespread support.

Administrative

The term 'administrative' covers an amorphous group of people who are lumped together because they are not clerical, but neither are they managerial.

They are such people as cost accountants, computer programmers and systems analysts, salesmen and O & M staff.

For the cost accountant and his ilk, training will usually be on the job as a cost clerk while he makes his way through the further education courses for cost and works accountants, perhaps after starting with an Ordinary National Diploma in business studies while he is making up his mind about the area in which he wishes to specialize.

The training of computer personnel is embryonic at the moment and the only valid sources are either computer manufacturers' courses or other companies' staffs.

Salesmen are an interesting special case, as they have to know two things—first the product and ordering procedures; second how to sell. The first area of knowledge must obviously be acquired within the company, and the training officer needs to take in responsibility for this type of training. Training in selling is provided by certain firms of consultants who have attempted to identify a common body of knowledge and skill for all types of selling, and who run frequent and popular courses in salesmanship.

Shop stewards

The final category is shop steward. The Code of Industrial Relations Practice firmly states that it is the joint responsibility of management and trade unions to train shop stewards. The best courses for stewards are run by the trade unions, and an introductory course for newly elected shop stewards is run at many educational centres under the auspices of the TUC. It is difficult for many employers to run satisfactory courses of their own, as stewards are likely to be suspicious of being conned, but this field of training will no doubt develop.

INDUSTRIAL TRAINING ACT AND ITS IMPLICATIONS

The institutions

In 1964 the Industrial Training Act became law, with the declared intention of increasing the supply of skilled manpower in industry. Under the responsibility of the Secretary of State for Employment there is now the Central Training Council. This Council consists of representatives of employers, trade unions and nominees of the Department of Education and Science, together with a chairman. It has the duty of advising the Secretary of State on the implementation of training policy and is a body with some influence in the training field through the many subcommittees it has set up.

The operational teeth of the Act are the various industrial training boards which have been steadily set up to implement the Act within specified industry groupings, on the basis that the training needs of different industries vary considerably from each other. At the moment there are some thirty of these boards.

Levy/grant system

The boards were set up with a major sanction at their disposal to encourage employers to follow their advice on training matters. Each is empowered to impose a levy on every employer within their terms of reference according to information about the scale of operation of the company which the boards are also empowered to obtain. Having obtained the levy, the boards then make grants to individual employers according to the amount and quality of the training they provide for their employees. If the employer provides no training he pays his levy and obtains no grant. If he has excellent training arrangements he pays his levy and later receives a grant towards the cost of the training he undertakes, and the grant may exceed the levy. This is one means of spreading the cost of training between companies that train and those that do not.

The size of the levy varies from board to board. The Engineering Industry Training Board has persisted with a levy that represents 2.5 per cent of the annual level of wages and salaries paid to company employees, while the Electricity Supply Industry Industrial Training Board, with different objectives and different problems, has established a levy of 0.025 per cent of employee emoluments. Most of the levies are in the region of 1.0 per cent of emoluments.

Training services agency

In 1973 there were further government moves in relation to industrial training. The Training Services Agency was set up as part of the Manpower Services Commission. It is to coordinate the work of the various industrial training boards and to develop training in areas outside the scope of the boards.

FURTHER READING

J.P.J. Kenney and E. Donnelly, *Manpower Training and Development,* Institute of Personnel Management, Macmillan, London, 1972.

J. Morris and J.G. Burgoyne, *Developing Resourceful Managers*, Institute of Personnel Management, London, 1973.

R. Naylor and D.P. Torrington, *Administration of Personnel Policies,* Gower Press, Epping, 1974.

B.M. Bass and J.A. Vaughan, *Training in Industry,* Tavistock, London, 1968.

W. McGehee and P.W. Thayer, *Training in Business and Industry*, John Wiley, Chichester, 1961.

Training for Commerce and the Office, Central Training Council, HMSO, London 1966.

J.P. de C. Meade and F.W. Creig, *Supervisory Training–A New Approach for Management,* HMSO, London, 1966.

A. Mumford, *The Manager and Training,* Pitman, London, 1971.

M. & P. Berger, *Group Training Techniques,* Gower Press, Epping, 1972.

K. Oakley and W. Richmond, *Systematic Approach to Clerical and Commercial Training,* Pergamon, Oxford, 1970.

PART SIX

Management of Physical Assets

30

Occupation, Ownership and Administration of Property

ACL Grear & J Oxborough

Whatever the trade or purpose of a company, it will nearly always be involved in some way with property. For most companies, property forms the major part of its assets and for this reason, it is vital to ensure that property is properly managed and put to its maximum economic use.

Property will be dealt with in two chapters in this Handbook. Chapter 30 outlines the day-to-day administration arising from ownership or occupation: Chapter 31 deals with property transactions which are not a day-to-day occurrence, including such special events as sales, acquisitions, extensions and redevelopments and compulsory acquisition together with the consequent impact of taxation upon such transactions.

These chapters relate to 'Business' property only but include comments on transactions carried out by way of share deals.

PROPERTY REGISTER

An up-to-date register of the basic facts of all property owned or occupied by the company is a valuable aid to efficient administration. The format of a typical register is shown in Figure 30.1. The register should contain the following information:

1   Description of the property and its postal address
2   Physical data, including frontages, depths, site and floor areas, type of construction

3   Ownership and tenure
4   Details of rent payable
5   Details of repairs and other responsibilities under the lease
6   Details of rating assessments and address of rating authority
7   Insurances effected on the property and the amount of cover and premiums, with date of last cover revision and name of insurers
8   Details of existing planning uses, notes on how property is affected by local planning authority plans and the address of the planning authority
9   Details of Party Wall Awards, office development permits, industrial development certificates, restrictive covenants and other legal restrictions on the property

Property (Full postal address)		Ground rent property only		
Freeholder		Leaseholder:		
Description		Ground rent		Payable on:
Leaseholder or tenant		£	per annum	
Rental payable:		Payable in:advance/arrear		
Amount £	per annum Due	25 March 24 June 29 September 25 December		
		£	£ £ £	
Tenancy term Lease dated		Period commences		Lease expires
Term of years Whole of period	years	First rent period	years	Rent reviews at years
Rent Proportion of rent payable rent		% Proportion applicable on rent review		Yes/No
Service charges				
Repairs Landlord: Tenant:		Exterior every Interior every	year Last done year Last done	
Rating Address of rating authority:				
Assessment number	Gross value	Ratable value	Rate poundage	Date
Principal dimensions Frontage	Depth	Floor area: Number of floors:	Site area: Site depth:	

Figure 30.1   Typical property register

10   Important dates to remember, for example options and renewals of leases, often referred to as 'action' dates
12   Details of sublet property including name of tenant, terms of lease and division of liability including repairs, insurance and rates
13   Original acquisition price
14   Date of original acquisition, name of solicitor and other advisers, place at which deeds are held and information concerning registration of title

15   Value of property as at 6th April 1965 (if acquired before then)
16   Date and amount of the last professional valuation, by whom
     made and for what purpose

In many cases, additional optional sections will be necessary. Four typical sections covering repair clauses, planning permissions, insurance and sublet properties are shown in Figure 30.2.

The property register is a convenient record, not a legal requirement. It is for each individual company to draw up its own register to meet its own requirements.

PROPERTY VALUATION: THE LEGAL REQUIREMENTS

Paragraph 5 of the Eighth Schedule to the Companies Act 1948 defined the way fixed assets, including land and buildings should be valued in the statutory balance sheet (see also Chapter 5). Basically the value to be shown (called the *net book value*) is the difference between:

1   Their cost or, if they stand in the company's books at a valuation,
    the amount of the valuation and
2   The aggregate amount provided or written off since the date of
    acquisition or valuation for depreciation or diminution in value

The 1967 Companies Act amended this procedure which is now contained in paras 4 and 5 of Schedule 1 and in Schedule 2 of the Act. Paragraph 11(6A) now requires that when the amount of a fixed asset is arrived at by reference to a valuation, then the year of the valuation and the value (before provision for depreciation to arrive at the net book value) must be noted in the balance sheet. Further, if the valuation was made during the financial year to which the balance sheet refers, then the note must give the names of the valuers (and their qualifications) as well as the basis of their valuation.

Acquisitions, disposals or destroyed assets are to be stated in a company's balance sheet for the year in which the event happened. They are usually shown, for a large company, in a table of movements.

The Companies Act 1967 (s16(*a*)) requires that any significant changes in the fixed assets of a company, particularly land, shall be drawn to the attention of shareholders in the directors' report. The report must also draw the attention of shareholders to a significant difference between the actual value of fixed assets and their value as shown in the balance sheet. Assessment of what is 'significant' is left to the discretion of the directors.

Where mergers or takeovers are involved, special provisions and procedures are contained in 'The City Code on Takeovers and Mergers', with regard to information and valuations relating to property which are to be published in any prospectus or circular.

Lease covenants

Repairs (extracts of clauses from lease)	Date work due	Date work done
(eg External decorations, each 3rd year Internal decorations, each 7th year)		

Options, renewals, landlord and tenant notices and other important dates				
Event	Preparation of notice	Date notice served	Date of completion	Result

Town Planning					
Change of use as new building	Reference No.	Date consent granted	Conditions	ODP /IDC	*

*Planning consent implemented

Figure 30.2   Some typical optional sections

Insurance	Responsibility: Landlord/tenant			
Risks covered	Company	Policy number	Cover £	Date of the last valuation
Fire Buildings				
Landlord's fixtures				
Contents				
Storm and tempest Landlord's fixtures				
Contents				
Public liability Including fire and explosion				
Employer's liability				
Property owner's liability				
Theft				
Stock-in-trade				
Goods in trust				
Food poisoning				
Goods lifts, hoists, passenger lifts, etc				
Boilers				
Boilers (Excess)				
Inspection				
Other risks				

Figure 30.2   Some typical optional sections (continued)

Charges

By $s95(5)$ of the Companies Act 1948, details of charges on the company's land, in particular, mortgages, must be registered within 21 days of their creation. Registration is made on form 47B (England) or form 47C (Scotland) which must be accompanied by a certified copy of the instrument creating or evidencing the charge (Companies (Forms) Order, SI 1949/382, paragraph 4).

Registration is made with the Registrar of Companies; whether the company is public or private. There is a penalty of £50 per diem charged on the company and every officer of the company in default if not made within the 21 day period. A Register of Charges must be kept at the registered office of the company ($s104$ and $s195$ Companies Act 1948) and it should be available to any person on payment of a fee not exceeding 5p and no charge to members of the company or the company's creditors. Inspection should be allowed during reasonable business hours and fines of £5 and £2 a day can be imposed on the company and its officers respectively in default.

PROPERTY VALUATION: DIRECTORS' AND SHAREHOLDERS' REQUIREMENTS

In the Institute of Directors report, *Common Board Room Practice,* first published in 1961, the comment was made:

The disparity between market price and true value, which is the takeover bidder's opportunity, generally arises from one or both of two causes. The first is that directors have failed to utilise the assets of the business, whether in cash securities or property, to the best advantage. It may be that directors have failed to realise that in a period of rapid inflation properties have reached an intrinsic value greater than their value merely as working assets in the business, and have failed, whether by way of sale and leaseback, or by some other method, to take advantage of the situation for the benefit of the company. The other main cause of disparity between the market price and true value is the absence of proper and full information, whether as to profits and reserves or as to asset values. If these are properly made known the market is quick to readjust share prices accordingly.

The above comments apply mostly to public companies but the principles and standards which the Institute was trying to pinpoint are of equal application to the small business under family control. It is open to a shareholder in a public company to decide for himself when and how to dispose of his shares: the absence of a public quotation and therefore of public comment on performance still does not relieve the board of a private limited company of its responsibilities towards all the classes of shareholders who have shares in the company, whether members of the family or not. Small companies merge, amalgamate, buy and sell in much the same way as public quoted companies and the company should be aware of the intrinsic value of its assets and therefore of its shares.

Apart from safeguarding shareholders' interests, a company needs to know the true value of its property assets for a number of reasons:

Legal charges

A company needs to know the relationship between money borrowed against the security of its property and the realizable value of that asset. Recent experience has shown that property values can fall substantially and one of the root causes of recent company difficulties has been that property values have fallen below the outstanding secured loan which has had grave consequences on foreclosure for both borrower and lender.

Capital taxes

It is important for a company to know the true value of its property in relation to the effect of tax upon ownership and on contemplated transactions before company policy can be formulated.

Capital Gains Tax is chargeable, at the date of disposal, on all realized increases in the value of property which have accrued since 1965 or the date of acquisition, whichever is the later. Tax is chargeable at a true rate of 30%. Methods of calculation, and details of 'roll over' provisions are set out in more detail later.

Taxes on Development Value. Increases in the value of land which are attributable to development in accordance with the Town Planning Acts are taxed but at a higher rate than Capital Gains Tax. Under the present transitional arrangements:

1   Chargeable development gains realized on disposal (which includes a 'first letting') between 18 December 1973 and 1 August 1976 are taxed as income – currently at 53 per cent for companies – under Development Gains Tax.
2   Chargeable development gains realized on disposal (which includes the start of a development scheme) after 1 August 1976 are charged at rates from $66\frac{2}{3}$ to 80 per cent, rising by successive stages in future years to 100 per cent, under Development Land Tax.

These two taxes will eventually be phased out when the second appointed day under the Community Land Act 1975 is fixed – at some time in the next five to ten years. At that time, all development land will be acquired by local authorities at current use value and there will be no development value to be taxed.

The Capital Transfer Tax, as enacted in the Finance Act 1974, replaces and extends the principle of Estate Duty and is a tax on capital gifts and sales at less than market value. Whilst this tax does not directly affect companies, it vitally affects shares and it is, therefore, necessary for a company to know the true net value of its property assets and it may well affect a company's policy in relation to its property holding. For example, should a company buy or rent its own property?

Wealth Tax is a further stated government policy although only at the Green Paper stage. It is not expected that this will directly affect a company but it will seriously affect its shareholders and it may well influence company policy with regard to its property holding.

Further details of these taxes are set out in Chapter 31.

Efficient use of assets

Quite apart from the requirements of the law and the complexities of legislation and taxation in the society in which we live, there remains the basic need to know whether the asset is being properly used as a working asset in the business or whether it could be used or sold for a greater value than that which it has to the company. Many small companies are freehold minded and often forget that the return on the volume of their trading activities is probably greater than the return appropriate to property ownership as such.

Consideration under this heading may well lead a company to extend, adapt or otherwise alter its property holding to improve return on capital.

A source of capital

In moments of shortage of working capital and in conditions where a general restriction is placed on bank lending or where interest rates are high the sale and leaseback operation is one means of realizing fresh capital. In this type of transaction, a buyer purchases the freehold of a company's land and then leases it back to the company.

To take a sale and leaseback it is necessary to determine the rent that the property would command in the open market and the rent the company can afford to pay in relation to the profitability of its activities. These figures will determine not only two, possibly different, capital values, but also the ratio at which an 'equity' leaseback arrangement can be made, if the rental agreed to be paid and accepted is lower than that established by general market demand. The exercise is not only one which calls for examination of the return on capital locked up in property, but equally for an examination of the transaction in relation to the capital employed in the business as a whole. The effect of an equity lease is to leave over a long term (usually ninety-nine years) some part of the rental value in the hands of the original vendor and, as the years pass, this equity could well become an asset which requires to be taken into consideration in the determination of balance sheet information and values.

Similar principles apply to the question of leases which are held by companies for a term of years at something less than their rack rental value. (The *rack rent* of a property is the fair rent that a tenant will pay to a landlord in an arrangement where both parties are ordinarily attentive to their business interests.) Such a lease can be sold to pension funds and the like, and a new sub-lease taken by the company so that the company is in receipt of a capital or premium amount, although taking over the burden of a higher rent commitment. Again, this is an exercise which should be related to the use of the net capital realized from the transaction. The various combinations which can be devised in this sort of arrangement are quite diverse: sublease at a full rent, sublease at an equity rent or sublease at the existing rent subject to payment of a full premium.

Two words of warning about sales and leasebacks. Notwithstanding the fact that rent is payable on the gross capital realized, that capital will be subject to Capital Gains Tax. Any decision must consider the net proceeds from a sale and not the anticipated open market value when considering the rental which in effect is the investment cost of that capital.

In the case of sale and leasebacks of leases with less than 50 years to run, part only of the rent will be chargeable against profits: the remainder will be treated as a repayment of borrowed capital. It is not usually profitable to contemplate leasebacks where the term is less than 15 years duration. Property may also be used as a security against a loan or mortgage. Whilst interest rates at the present time make these methods more expensive than the sale and leaseback, it is nevertheless a method used by many companies as a last resort. Capital Gains Tax does not apply when a mortgage is taken out but the sum should be such that it is well secured against the net realizable value of the property because a foreclosure, in the event of failure to repay the mortgage, will be a disposal and therefore, subject to Gains Tax.

The essential fact to grasp on property, whether freehold or leasehold, is whether it is properly valued in terms of its existing use and, if not, what is that value and how does it affect the structure of the company and its policy.

STATUTORY CONTROLS ON BUILDING STRUCTURES

A wide range of legislation affects the construction and use of buildings, including:
1   Local Government Act 1933 *s*249 (public health and building
     by-laws made by local authorities).
2   Public Health Act and Public Health (London) Act 1936.
3   The London Building Acts 1939 (as amended).
4   Shops Act 1950.
5   Clean Air Act 1956.
6   Factories Act 1961.
7   Public Health Act 1961.

8   Offices, Shops and Railway Premises Act 1963.
9   The Fire Precautions Act 1971.
10   The Building Regulations 1972 (for all areas excluding London).
11   Local Government Act 1972.
12   The Health and Safety at Work Act 1974.

There are a large number of more detailed Acts and statutory orders and all these measures control the quality and methods of building design and construction. They are quite separate from town planning controls which relate to land uses: where work is 'development' within the provisions of Town Planning Acts, planning permission must first be obtained before construction starts (see p.595).

This legislation is intended to secure:

1   Safety of design and construction, and stability of buildings.
2   Suitability of materials including fire resistant qualities.
3   Cleanliness, adequate heating, lighting, ventilation and drainage of buildings.
4   Means of escape from buildings.
5   Adequate fire precautions in buildings.
6   Protection of plant installed as part of the buildings and machinery and stores used in connection with trades.
7   Protection of employees and occupants.

Details of the legislation as it affects personnel including welfare, health and restrictions on employment of women and young persons, will be found in Chapter 22.

General structural requirements

All new buildings, of whatever kind, and all extensions or major structural alterations to existing buildings, must comply with one or other of the statutory codes currently in force. These are as follows:

1   For Inner London (that part of Greater London within the area formerly administered by the London County Council) the requirements are those contained in the London Building Acts, 1930 to 1939 as amended.
2   For the rest of England and Wales, including those parts of Greater London which are outside the former London County Council area, the regulations are made under the Public Health Acts 1936 and 1961 and are contained in The Building Regulations 1972 (SI 1972/317) and the various amendments to them issued from time to time.
3   Similar provisions apply for Scotland.

The contents of these three codes vary in detail but cover the same general ground. Among the chief matters dealt with are the design and structural stability of buildings, structural fire precautions—including design and materials, thermal insulation and sound insulation, resistance to damp, ventilation, provision of open space outside windows, drainage and sewerage, sanitary conveniences, heating appliances, chimneys and flues, stairways and balustrades, and built-in means of refuse disposal.

If restrictive covenants under a lease prevent the occupier of a factory, office or shop from making alterations that are necessary in order to comply with the law an application may be made to the High Court (or, in Scotland, to the sheriff) asking for such restrictions to be set aside. The court can also apportion the cost of such alterations between the owner and the occupier if they have failed to agree between themselves.

Administration of these building controls is carried out by Local Authorities at district level, with some matters reserved for Government control.

Powers of local authorities

The purview of the local authority in public health matters as it affects the construction of buildings, is controlled by The Building Regulations and the London Building Acts and can be summarized as follows:

Sewers and drainage
1   Powers to inspect, test, control, and maintain drains, sewers, cesspools, septic tanks and so on in both public and private ownership
2   Powers to charge for connection to sewers and to disallow certain obnoxious fluids from being discharged into public sewers. (These powers also extend to River Conservancy Boards)
3   Control of sanitary conveniences in new buildings and within the scope of the Factories Acts in factories and in other places of work
4   Powers to serve notices on owners to remedy a nuisance—for example, an overflowing cesspool

Buildings
1   Supervision of forms of construction in both public and private buildings with regard to:
    (*a*) Drainage.
    (*b*) Ventilation.
    (*c*) Floor loading and general structure.
    (*d*) Suitability of design of structure in relation to subsoil.
    (*e*) Suitability of materials.
2   Powers to enforce reasonable means of access to and egress from public buildings, such as theatres, stores and shops, and to secure adequate provision for fire escapes

3   Removal of waste materials from cesspits, and so on, and provision for removal of dustbin waste and trade waste
4   Powers to disinfest storage and other buildings, of rats and other vermin.
5   Powers to regulate construction affecting party walls

Activities in the use of buildings

1   Powers, to prevent boilers and so on from causing smoke pollution, derived from the Clean Air Act, 1956
2   Powers to abate nuisance or noise. These are usually enforced by abatement notices, which require the person on whom they are served to desist, for example, from using his radio at a volume that causes a nuisance to the neighbours
3   Powers to control buildings where notifiable diseases have been prevalent
4   Powers of registration and inspection of 'common lodging houses'
5   Power to require the installation and proper maintenance of an adequate supply of fresh water
6   Powers of inspection in relation to structure, maintenance and so on of premises used for food preparation or manufacture, to ensure a proper standard of hygiene

This is merely a summary of some of the powers which a local authority may exercise. The detail is contained in the Building Regulations and, in the case of the County and City of London, in the London Building Acts. The high density of building in London requires numerous small facets of building construction and technique to be more stringently applied than in other areas.

Building Regulations are extremely important. Minimum standards required are set out in great detail and no work may be started without full details being submitted to the local authority, in accordance with the regulations, and the necessary approvals obtained. Following approval, the local authority has powers to check work as it proceeds to ensure minimum standards of construction. Authorities have some powers of control and enforcement in the event of non-compliance with the regulations: failure to comply with the Regulations is, upon conviction, a criminal offence and heavy penalties are imposed by the Courts.

PROPERTY OWNERSHIP AND THE LAW

There are two types of legal estate by which a company can own an interest in land:

1   A fee simple absolute—a freehold
2   A term of years absolute—a lease

The difference between the two legal estates is that a lease always has a definite end, following which full rights will revert to the landlord, but a freehold estate continues indefinitely. Both estates can be transferred to others on sale or on death and lesser interests, that is leases or subleases, may be created from them.

Equitable interests.   All other types of land•ownership are known as equitable interests. An equitable interest in effect separates legal ownership from the right to enjoy the use of land. The owner of a legal estate can defend his ownership against anyone, but the owner of an equitable interest cannot defend his interest against someone who purchases a legal estate in that land without having, at the time of purchase, given notice of the equitable interest. The purchaser of the legal estate may be required to take reasonable steps to discover the equitable interest by asking relevant questions or making appropriate searches in official registries where the interest should be recorded.

Rights of ownership

The rights of ownership which attach to legal estates in land, both freehold and leasehold, are described as proprietary rights and natural rights:

Proprietary rights give owners of land the free use and enjoyment of it without control or diminution, subject only to restrictions by statute law, for example town planning, public health. These rights are absolute provided that in the exercise of them an owner does not infringe upon the rights of others, for example, an adjoining owner.

Natural rights are based on the principle that an owner is entitled to enjoy his land to the full although these too are subject to some statutory restrictions. They comprise:

1   A right of natural support by neighbouring land
2   A right to secure that air passing from one property to another is unpolluted
3   A right to light and air vertically over the property
4   Rights to secure free passage of water in, over, and through land and against inundation by draining and against pollution in flow or percolation

Natural and proprietary rights are absolute and cannot be waived or set aside except by statute law. Where the right is extinguished, provision is often made for compensation to be paid.

These rights of ownership are normally investigated by a solicitor when property is acquired. Infringements arising during ownership should be referred to a solicitor in view of many unforeseen complexities than can arise.

LEASES

Where a lease is granted, the freeholder, or landlord, grants away limited use and occupation of the land in return for some consideration—rent. The tenant then stands in the landlord's shoes as far as enjoyment is concerned and has the benefits of both natural and proprietary rights, for the period.

In addition, both parties assume certain mutual responsibilities towards each other and these, together with the terms of the lease, are set out in the documents as 'covenants'. These may be divided into implied and express covenants.

1 *Implied covenants* are those which reason and justice will dictate and which the law presumes every man will undertake to perform. Such covenants are not necessarily written into a deed or formal lease document. A simple example of an implied covenant at law is when a tenant sells his leasehold interest, then the law implies that he covenants that the lease is valid and in full force, that he has paid the rent and has complied with the written covenants in the lease.

2 *Express covenants* are those which are written into the lease document and may be classified in the following ways:

Real covenants are those which are said to run with the land or be a part of the title so that an assignee is as much bound as was his predecessor in title.

Personal covenants are collateral to the thing demised. For example not to use other premises for a similar purpose or trade within a certain distance of the demised premises. This is binding on the tenant who makes the covenant and not on another who may afterwards acquire his interest.

Positive covenants are those which require certain specific things to be done, for example rebuilding after a fire.

Negative or restrictive covenants are those which forbid certain things to be done, for example not to erect on land property of less than a certain value. (These covenants may be modified or discharged on certain grounds as set out by *s*84 of the Law of Property Act 1925, as amended by *s*28 of the Law of Property Act 1969.)

Dependent covenants are those which do not arise until some prior covenant has been observed, for example when a landlord agrees to put the structure into repair for a tenant before the tenant enters and agrees to keep in repair after his entry.

Independent covenants are those obligations which are not dependent on the observance of another covenant.

It is preferable for a lease to be as specific as possible and an express covenant in a deed will, in general, supersede an implied covenant. Implied covenants are normally incorporated into a modern lease, but however defective, short or simple a lease document may be the law allows certain common ground for both parties and implied covenants as 'covenants in law' are just as actionable as would be an express covenant contained in a deed.

Covenants found in a lease

It is not proposed to go into very great detail concerning the various covenants which are to be found in modern leases, but when a lease is made it is sometimes stated that the lease shall be subject to or shall contain the 'usual' covenants. Various cases have occurred in the courts and in the list which follows those marked with an asterisk have been held to be 'usual'.

Typical tenants' covenants
1   *To pay the rent
2   *To pay rates and taxes
3   To repair and keep in repair
4   To paint, paper, whiten and so on at certain times
5   To insure and produce receipts therefor
6   *To permit the lessor, or his agents, workmen and so on to enter and view the premises
7   To use or not to use the premises for a particular purpose
8   Not to alter the structure
9   Not to assign (without consent, such consent not to be unreasonably withheld)
10   To pass on to the landlord notices received
11   *To surrender the premises at the end of the term
12   To keep and deliver up the premises in repair

Typical landlords' obligations
1   *To give quiet enjoyment
2   To give terms for renewal (in some cases)
3   To give an option to purchase
4   To repair and insure 'common parts'

A proviso for forfeiture is not 'usual' although it is almost invariably found in a lease. In this connection many leases contain clauses which provide for forfeiture in the event of bankruptcy, petitioning of creditors and liquidations other than voluntary liquidations or schemes of rearrangement.

It should be remembered that the various covenants in a lease are specific and the document in common with other contracts states what the relationship between the parties to the lease is intended to be.

IMPROVEMENTS MADE BY THE TENANT

The Landlord and Tenant Act 1927 gives to the tenant certain rights at the end of a lease to claim against the landlord for improvements made during the tenancy provided that statutory procedures are followed. The rights of both landlord and tenant are set out in the 1927 Act, as amended by the Landlord and Tenant Act 1954 and the Law of Property Act 1969 and may be summarized as follows:

1   A tenant who wishes to carry out improvements to the property during his tenancy must first obtain landlord's approval. The request must be made in a prescribed form and there are time limits during which the landlord must reply. Improvements which are not approved do not rank for compensation at the end of the lease. Town Planning and Building Regulations approvals are quite separate from landlord and tenant approvals

2   At the expiration of the lease, a tenant who proposes to vacate may claim compensation from his landlord for approved improvements. The tenant must make his claim in statutory form not earlier than 6 months nor later than 3 months before the end of the tenancy.
The basis of compensation is the higher of
(a) the current cost of carrying out the improvements or
(b) the increase in market value in the property created by those improvements
It is for the tenant to prove the amount of his claim.
In the event of those improvements being such that the value of the property is depreciated, then the landlord may claim damages from the tenant or alternatively the tenant may agree to reinstate the building if possible.
If a tenant is evicted during the term by notice to quit, then he must make his claim within three months of the date on which notice was given.

3   At the expiration of the lease, if the tenant wishes to take a new lease, then the new rent shall exclude any value attributable to the improvements for the period of the new lease subject to a maximum of 21 years.

4   It should be noted that improvements carried out by a tenant as part of an original bargain for a lease, eg in return for a reduced rent, may not form the subject of a claim. Neither may any works done to a building as part of the repairing covenants in a lease. A landlord may ignore improvements carried out during the last 3 months of a term.

5   Mesne (in between) landlords, if liable to pay compensation to a

tenant, shall be entitled to claim back that compensation from their superior landlords who ultimately receive the benefit of the improved premises.

It is, therefore, quite important for a company to record improvements made to its property whether as landlord or tenant and ensure that claims for compensation are made or answered in the prescribed time limits. The compensation or reduced rental will also be a factor for companies when deciding whether to vacate or continue to occupy premises.

CONTINUITY OF TENURE

A lease is a contract between landlord and tenant and one of the basic principles is that, at the expiration of the term, the tenant is obliged to give up possession. This can be hard on the tenant who has spent many years building up his business at the premises and who is naturally unwilling to abandon those premises at the end of his lease and go through the difficult and expensive process of re-establishment elsewhere. The law of contract has, therefore, been varied by legislation in the form of the Landlord and Tenant Act 1954 Part II, as amended by the Law of Property Act 1969, which now provides that:

1   A tenant is entitled to the grant of a new lease of his business premises, upon expiration of the old, on similar terms but with the exception of rent payable and the length of the lease. There are certain exceptional circumstances in which a new term can be refused by the landlord (see p. 586) in which case modest compensation for dispossession is payable.
2   The landlord is bound to grant a new lease to a tenant of business premises upon request but, so that he shall suffer no financial disadvantage, the rent for the new term is fixed at current market value, all other terms remaining the same. There are a number of special circumstances in which the landlord can reclaim possession, subject to the payment of modest compensation. (See p. 586).

Thus, the tenant now enjoys security of tenure whilst the landlord retains his investment and suffers little, if any, loss in normal circumstances.

It should be noted that only premises used for business enjoy protection under the 1954 Act. The words 'business' and 'premises' are not defined in the Act but virtually all property, with or without buildings, which is used in connection with either a trade or profession, with or without a profit motive, is protected including partnership interests.

Security of tenure for residential accommodation is dealt with quite separately under the Rent Acts. Where property is in dual use, then both sets of legislation must be applied side by side.

The 1954 Act lays down strict procedures for the timing and form of notices. Failure to comply can mean the loss of rights for either landlord or tenant. A word of warning: a substantial body of case law has been built up through the Courts since 1954, the details of which should not be ignored.

Procedure at expiration of tenancy

Both landlord and tenant have a right to terminate a tenancy or request a new tenancy (ss25 and 26, Landlord and Tenancy Act 1954). In each case, neither party may serve his request on the other more than twelve months, or less than six months, before the date of termination of the lease.

A landlord's notice on a tenant to terminate a lease under s25 must inform the tenant that, if he is unwilling to give up his tenancy, he must give notice within two months to that effect to the landlord (s25(5)).

A tenant's notice under s26 should also be in the prescribed form but cannot be served if the landlord has already served notice under s25. Landlords are required to give an answer to a tenant's request for a new lease within two months.

The Act is of a beneficial nature and is intended to encourage the parties to reach agreement. They may reach agreement between themselves but it is open to them to apply to the Court to determine the future tenancy. The Court will grant a new lease for a term and on such conditions as may appear reasonable in all the circumstances, although conditions generally will be similar to those contained in the old lease with the exception of the rent payable and sometimes the length of the new term (ss29, 33 and 35).

Where an application to the Court is made, but no decision is reached at the date of expiration, it is provided that the current tenancy shall continue in the interim. But the Court, in making its award, will have regard to this carry-over period. An interim rent increase may be payable (s24).

Grounds for opposition by the landlord

A landlord may oppose the grant of a new lease to a tenant on seven grounds, commonly known as 'the seven deadly sins' (s30). These are:

Failure to repair. That the tenant has failed to comply with the repairing covenants and in view of the state of the premises he ought not to be granted a new lease.

Delay in paying rent. That the tenant has been persistently overdue in his rent payments.

Breaches of obligations.   That the tenant has, during the tenancy, caused or permitted substantial breaches of covenant or has mismanaged the property.

Alternative accommodation.   That the landlord is willing to offer and provide reasonable alternative accommodation which will protect his tenant's goodwill and provides a suitable alternative to the existing facilities which a tenant enjoys.

Letting as a whole.   That if the tenant's occupancy is created by letting of a part of the whole and is such that the aggregate of the rents, of all the parts, on renewal, would be less than the rent obtainable for the whole, then the landlord may require possession of the *whole* and the tenant ought not to have a renewal lease on the let part.

Demolition or reconstruction.   That the landlord intends to demolish, reconstruct or carry out substantial works of construction which he could not reasonably do without obtaining possession. By *s*7 of the Law of Property Act 1969 a landlord cannot now oppose a tenant's application for a new tenancy of business premises if the tenant is prepared to accept a new tenancy of all or part of the premises and the landlord can demolish and reconstruct without interfering to a substantial extent or for a substantial time, with the tenant's business. The tenant is, however, obliged in these circumstances to give his landlord reasonable access.

Personal occupation by the landlord.   That the landlord intends, at the end of the current tenancy, to occupy, as a whole or in part, the premises for his own business or residential purposes. To avoid an unfair situation, the landlord cannot claim this ground for opposition if his interest was purchased, or created, less than five years before the termination of the tenancy.

In practice, where a particular hardship exists, the parties may apply to the court to determine a reasonable solution in the circumstances.

Compensation to the tenant

Where a landlord is successful in opposing a tenant's request for a new lease, the Law of Property Act 1969 gives the tenant compensation as a matter of entitlement but he is still obliged to pursue the 1954 Act notice procedures to establish his rights payable when the tenant quits the holding. If a new tenancy is granted by the Court but the tenant turns it down, for example because he cannot afford the rent, there is no right, on the tenant's part, to compensation.

The compensation payable may be a sum equal to one year's rateable value, if the tenant's period of occupancy is less than fourteen years. If the tenant and his immediate predecessors have occupied the premises in the same business for fourteen years or more, then a sum equal to twice the rateable value is payable (*s*37).

Terms of a new lease

Where a tenant is successful in his claim for a new lease:

1   The rent payable shall be the market rent
2   The conditions of the lease shall be consistent with those of the old lease, or as the court may direct
3   The term of the new lease shall be not more than fourteen years. Provision may be made by the court for a rent review during the term

It is important to realize the rules by which rent is determined by the courts. The courts are expected to regard the rent as the amount at which the holding might be reasonably expected to let in the open market by a willing landlord to an able tenant.

Such a rent will exclude the following factors:

1   Any effect on the rent due to the tenant's occupation of the holding or the prior occupation of the tenant's predecessors in title: the effects of a sitting tenant position on the value are excluded
2   Goodwill attached to the holding, by reason of the tenant having carried on a particular business or the predecessor's business thereat
3   The effect of any improvement made by the tenant or his predecessor otherwise than as part of an obligation to the immediate landlord (see p.584).
4   The effect of any additional value attributable to premises which are licensed if it appears to the court that the benefit of the licence belongs to the tenant

COVENANTS TO REPAIR

A tenant's covenant to repair and keep in repair is an express and not an implied covenant. There is nevertheless implied in any tenancy that the tenant will use the premises in a tenantlike manner and that he will deliver the premises up to the landlord at the end of the term in the same state of repair as at the beginning of the term, fair wear and tear excepted. This is based on the old established and much quoted case of Proudfoot *v* Hart (1890). An implied covenant to repair is a covenant in law and as such is just as actionable as would be an express covenant in a deed. The premises are therefore to be kept in repair at all times and if the tenant fails to perform the covenant, the landlord may recover the premises by forfeiture.

There are detailed restrictions and procedures which both landlord and tenant must observe and the detail of these should be studied in the Law of Property Act 1925, Landlord and Tenant Act 1927 s18(2), Leasehold Property (Repairs) Act 1938 s1 and Landlord and Tenant Act 1954 s51 as they may affect both parties. The effective dates for repairs, both internal and external should be inserted in that section of the property register which covers the important dates to watch.

The customary form of lease in many parts of the country is known as a 'full repairing and insuring' lease. Such a lease usually requires the tenant to do external work every three years and internal works every seven years, and both during the last year of the term granted. Failure to repair is often covered by a dilapidation clause in the lease, and, on any default, the landlord has the right to enter the premises, carry out the works in default and recover the costs from the tenant. Where repairs remain outstanding at the expiration of a lease, the landlord may carry out the repairs and recover the cost from the tenant. However, in cases where it would be wasteful to complete repairs, eg where a building is to be refurbished either by the landlord or an incoming tenant, then it is open to the landlord and tenant to negotiate a cash settlement taking into account all the circumstances. Dilapidation payments will be settled by the Court in the event of disagreement.

COOPERATION BETWEEN LANDLORD AND TENANT

In all landlord and tenant relationships, it is important that the tenant keeps in touch with the landlord on any matters which may affect the property, apart from the legal obligations as above.

This might include a compulsory purchase of the property or a party wall award or the effects of a road widening. In these cases, both parties, acting together, can often obtain a better result than separately and in some cases, may avoid action which would otherwise unwittingly damage the other's interest. It is for this reason that many leases carry a clause requiring the tenant to pass on all legal and other notices to the landlord.

RATING

Rating is a tax or levy on the occupation of real property. Rates are a part of the income of local authorities, water boards, river conservancy and sewage authorities. They may be classified as:

1   General rates
2   Water rates
3   Owner's drainage rates (in some areas)
4   River Board and sewage general service charges

The purposes of the rate charge are well known: they are to meet the costs of public services such as education, police, fire, lighting, public health and all other aspects of requirements of the community. The charge is made on the rateable value of the property and it is in the rateable value that every businessman has an interest. Rateable values broadly follow property values, so that occupants of more valuable property make a greater contribution to the cost of local services.

Basis of assessment

The basis of assessment is usually made by reference to gross value and rateable value, commonly known as GV and RV. *Gross value* is defined as the annual rent at which a property might be expected to let from year to year if the tenant undertook to pay all the usual rates and taxes and if the landlord undertook to bear the cost of repairs, insurance and other expenses, if any, necessary to maintain the property in a state to command that rent.

Rateable value is defined similarly with the exception that the onus to bear the costs of repairs and insurance is the responsibility of the tenant.

Gross value is now virtually a hypothetical definition as almost all business lettings put the onus for repairs and insurance on to the tenant. The allowance for repairs and insurance made between GV and RV is now a statutory deduction fixed on a sliding scale by the Government. Industrial properties are assessed direct to RV.

The basis of rating assessments is tied to a uniform date, at present 1973. It will be noted that, as revaluations only take place periodically, the relationship of RV to actual rents becomes distorted. However, the size of RV is not important in itself. Its purpose is to determine the share of rates which each property occupier shall pay to his Local Authority: the important point to determine is whether the RV of a property compares with those of similar properties in the district.

The rate demand

The basis of notification to a rated occupier of the amount of his indebtedness is the rate demand and rating authorities cannot recover rates without making a demand which follows the rules set out in the Statutory Rates Demands Rules.

Assessment procedure

Before a demand can be made the rating authorities must go through their own referencing and valuation procedure, the results of which are set out in the 'valuation list', a standard form of document applicable all over the country (with modifications for Scotland) so that the Inland Revenue follow common ground.

Rating documents and lists are open to inspection by any ratepayer at all reasonable times and where valuation courts are concerned the ratepayer is entitled to see minutes of the proceedings.

Altering the valuation list

The present valuation lists, which came into force in 1973, may be challenged at any time by either the Valuation Officer or the property occupier, by the submission of a proposal for alteration in prescribed form. The criteria upon which proposals may be made are based on 'a material change of circumstances' which may be:

1　A new structure, or one which has had the benefit of structural alterations

2　A structure which has been partially damaged by fire, or other hazard.

3　An event where a property may cease to be rated, for example, if it is vacated

4　Property which has been previously rated as a single property, but is now in a multiple tenancy and, therefore, liable to be rated in parts

5　Property which was formerly rated in parts but becomes the subject of sole occupation

6　Change of use from a dwelling house or private garage to some other use

7　Premises which are used to a greater or lesser degree for residential or private dwelling purposes

8　Development in a locality, adjoining or sufficiently near to, the property which may affect the rated property, either by increasing or decreasing its value, for example a town centre development, including new ring roads

Proposals may also be made for temporary alterations to the list where the material change of circumstances is of limited duration, for example a period of adjoining rebuilding works.

Proposals, after the publication and coming into force of the list, may be made by the Valuation Officer or by any person who is aggrieved, including the rating authority itself.

Proposals, may be made at any time, and should be made in the form prescribed in the Valuation List (Proposal for Alteration) Regulations 1963 (SI 1963/567) (General Rate Act 1967 *s*69).

Any proposal should be made in the statutory form and should state the grounds on which the alteration is sought. In general, the grounds may be related to:

1　The inclusion of the property in the list as such

2   Matters of values ascribed to or statements made, or omitted to be made, in connection with the property

3   The rating of the property as a single hereditament as opposed to a multiple rating

Where a valuation officer makes a proposal for alteration of the valuation list, he must serve copies on the occupier and the rating authority within seven days. If a proposal is made by a person other than the occupier, the valuation officer must serve copies of the proposal on the rating authority and on the occupier within twenty-eight days of service of the proposal on him.

Following receipt of the proposal, the owner, the rated occupier or rating authority, may object to the proposal within twenty-eight days of service of the notice. If there is no objection, or any objection is unconditionally withdrawn, the valuation officer will request the rating authority to amend the list to make the proposal effective.

Where a proposal is made, the list may be altered by agreement between the valuation officer and the maker of the proposal, subject to the concurrence of the rating authority, owner, rated occupier, or other party concerned. (The maker of a proposal can be any person, not necessarily the occupier or the owner.)

Appeals to local valuation and other courts

Where proposals are made to the valuation officer and these are not withdrawn, the valuation officer is obliged to submit to the clerk of the local valuation panel a copy of the proposal and the objection, within six months of the date of the proposal.

Where the valuation officer makes a proposal on the advent of a new list, he is allowed only four months in which to submit his documents to the local valuation panel.

Such submissions have the effect of an appeal to the local valuation court.

The valuation officer has powers to cause the list to be altered, without proposal, in the case of a clerical or arithmetical error.

Following direct and inconclusive negotiation with the valuation officer, a disputed proposal will be taken to the local valuation court (General Rate Act 1967 (ss88 and 91).

Local valuation courts have a limited jurisdiction. The court's jurisdiction is to hear whether the representations of one side or the other are well founded or justified. It has no power to reduce an assessment as such, but can, and must, give directions necessary to put the court's decision into effect. It is the valuation officer's province to direct the rating authority to amend the list. The rating authority is the only body able to determine the effective date of the proposal.

Further appeal from a local valuation court rests with the Lands Tribunal and, on a point of law only, to the Court of Appeal and, with leave, to the House of Lords.

Information required before an assessment is made

An alteration to the valuation list may be proposed at any time when the valuation officer has reason to believe that an alteration of the circumstances has occurred, or on the publication of a new list.

The valuation officer has powers under s82 of the 1967 Act to serve notices on the owner, occupier or lessee of any hereditament or premises in the rating area. The notice will ask for information which the valuation officer will need to know to compile his list. Such returns will ask questions about the ownership and occupation of the premises; the date of the lease and the date from which the rent started; the amount of the rent reserved; details of amounts paid by way of premium or on improvements.

Returns are to be completed within twenty-one days of date of service, subject to liability on failure to do so to a fine of £20 on a finding to this effect by a court of summary jurisdiction. Similar provisions are made in respect of reckless or false statements made in returns, the penalty being up to three months' imprisonment or a fine not in excess of £100 or both.

Factors in rating valuation

The methods of valuation adopted by rating valuers vary for different classes of property. The various factors which are brought into account are character and age of the property; its trading position if retail in a High Street or similar area; its internal floor areas; the lease rent passing; the levels of the floors and their suitability for the purpose of the function carried out; the means of access and vertical communication.

Other factors include such matters as lighting, car parking, facilities for staff and public health generally; whether the property is adapted for a purpose or purpose built to suit use; maintenance costs.

In industrial and similar properties, whether used for light or heavy industry, certain aspects of plant and machinery require to be rated as well as the property itself. The various items which are to be so rated are defined in the Plant and Machinery (Rating) Order of 1960 and this is set out in detail in Schedule 3 to the General Rate Act of 1967.

Rating of unoccupied premises

The General Rate Act 1967 empowers local authorities to charge 50 per cent of the full general rate to owners of unoccupied premises after three months of non-occupation.

The exercise of this rule is discretionary and few authorities adopted it. However, since the passing of the Local Government Act 1974, most authorities exercise their discretion and charge the full rates.

Water and drainage rates

Water rate differs from the general rate in that it is not a tax but a payment for the supply of a commodity. General rates are regarded as preferential debts in a winding up, but water rates are not.

Water rates are normally charged on the basis of powers granted to the various water undertakings and, on asking for a supply of water, the property owner would be prudent to ask for a copy of the regulations. Commercial properties do not usually have garden hoses, swimming baths and domestic baths and special facilities and rates exist for small users which should be looked at in detail.

Owner's drainage rates are payable in certain areas of reclamation such as Lincolnshire, Ely, Bedford and other areas in East Anglia and in those areas where large-scale engineering works have reclaimed land for agricultural use and are collected by rating authorities. These rates are assessed by a river conservancy board and continue to be levied on the owner whether the premises are occupied or not.

INSURANCE

The principles of insurance are discussed in Chapter 33 but insurance is an integral part of property management; indeed, most lease documents require either the landlord or tenant to insure the demised premises. A trader will obviously have regard to a wide variety of insurable risks—a typical selection of these is set out in the draft property register in Figure 30.2. From the property aspect certain specific points might be mentioned:

1   Insurance cover should be based on the cost of rebuilding a property. Costs should be sufficient to cover special forms of construction, for example where site conditions require special treatment such as piling and should allow for additional costs where adjoining buildings may have to be shored up during rebuilding.

    With continuing inflation and rising prices, a company will be wise to increase the amount of cover regularly in line with the increase in building costs.

2   In addition, policies should include cover for professional fees and loss of rent if alternative premises have to be occupied. By tradition the cost of preparation of a claim and its negotiation is never covered by an insurance policy.

3   Where buildings are of obsolete design and style or of an ornate character which would be disproportionately expensive to rebuild in their existing forms, it is common practice to insure for a sum sufficient to rebuild accommodation of a similar size and

standard as before but in a simpler and cheaper modern style. Where old buildings are deficient in services, for example, numbers of toilets, it should be noted that the replacement building will be constructed to comply with current Building Regulations and the accommodation may be better than the original.

Insurance cover, in this event, will provide for repairs to the existing building up to a point near the total cost of a new modern building. The decision whether to rebuild completely or repair will depend upon the extent of damage suffered.

4   It should be emphasized that insurance covers only the buildings and not the value of sites on which they stand.

It follows from this that insurance valuations have no connection with open market valuations and the two should not be confused.

TOWN PLANNING

In an ever changing community, company administrators will need to keep a watch on development in the neighbourhood and to follow the activities of the Local Authority in its role of 'Town Planning'. Information may be found either as advertisements or news in the local press or as other publicly distributed or advertised information. The importance of local knowledge is stressed as developments in a community can be carried out without official notification on an owner but to the disadvantage of that owner. Such proposals fall into two categories:

1   The use to which the subject property can be put or any proposals for acquisition which the Local Authority may have. In this case, notices are served upon owners and occupiers before any changes are made.

2   The effect of changes or developments on adjoining property or in the locality which may affect the subject property indirectly without touching it physically. The changes may also affect the trade or business carried out in those premises and, therefore, may be doubly important.

Before examining these in some detail, the structure of Town Planning control must first be considered.

The planning framework

The whole of the country is covered by a planning framework, laid down by the planning authority under statutory obligation, and known as a development plan or a structure plan. Development plans have existed since 1947; structure plans, together with local plans were introduced in 1968 and are replacing development plans throughout the country on a phased basis.

The purpose of these planning frameworks is to set out regional and local strategy, to define the use of each parcel of land, whether developed or not, to show what use can be made of land or buildings which are ripe for development and to indicate where the government or local authority propose to take action on behalf of the community, for example, in constructing new roads or building schools and hospitals.

The result is that all new development can be channelled to the most effective site and the planning authority may achieve its objective of controlling development in the best interests of health, safety, efficiency, economics, employment, transport, convenience, amenities, and welfare of the community.

Direct effect on property

The actual use to which property may be put, known as zoning, may be found by making inquiry of the local planning authority. Zoning usually follows existing uses, more particularly in post-1947 buildings. It may well be found that other uses are defined particularly if property is old. For example a factory may be zoned for residential purposes or included in a comprehensive development area and therefore, becomes a 'non-conforming' user. In these cases, no immediate action is necessary by the owner but the long-term use and particularly rebuilding or extension proposals will be barred and the use is thus limited to the existing life of the building. This, of course, affects values, security for loan purposes and long-term expenditure on improvements.

The property may also be defined for some other use which will require acquisition by a public authority, for example, a site for a road or a school. In these cases, a date for acquisition will be indicated and action will come from the authority in the long- or short-term. This means that the life of the building may be considerably shortened and, in view of the inevitability of purchase, possible alternative disposals will be frustrated or 'blighted.'

There are certain limited circumstances where a company may compel an authority to acquire blighted property where no sale at a proper price can be made. This is only possible for small properties and the effect normally is that a company must continue to hold property until it is acquired, even though several years may elapse during which the company may suffer in the intervening period without any remedy at law.

The basis of compensation where compulsory acquisition occurs is set out in Chapter 31.

It should be noted that where planning uses are already defined in the plan no opportunity for objection remains. Planning is a continuing process and new schemes and uses are being produced regularly. Proposals affecting property are advertised by the planning authority through the press and owners have rights of objection either through informal representations to the planning authority or at a public hearing when owners may submit their case for formal consideration. These rights are complex and advice should be taken immediately on the best course of action available.

However, public participation prior to the taking of a decision is now encouraged by Planning Authorities as part of their policy. Early informal discussions are well worth while and may well produce better schemes or remove the threat of compulsory acquisition.

The indirect effect on property

Although the property itself may not be directly affected, proposals affecting other land in the area may drastically affect the value or use of property. The most common example is a road proposal which diverts traffic and pedestrians from a shopping street but provides much better vehicular access to factories.

Proposals will again be publicized by the planning authority through the press and other media. Objections may be made either informally or at a public enquiry. Again with the emphasis on public participation, informal discussions with the planning authority can be most beneficial, particularly if proposals can be altered for the better in the early days rather than awaiting confirmation of a scheme and then pursuing the expensive and lengthy procedure of opposition at a planning enquiry.

In practically no case can compensation be claimed for loss arising from these changes and it is important to know the future plans for an area together with the prospects of alterations, in order to avoid basing future company policy and actions on false or misleading facts.

Community Land Act 1975

The provisions of this Act radically alter the planning processes in two ways:

1 It enables a local authority to initiate development to a far
   greater extent than before and thus play a more positive role
   in planning when a need is seen.
2 It gives local authorities an option to acquire development
   land — with the obligation to acquire *all* development land
   to follow in the next five to ten years, thus giving the
   'community' a planning and financial stake in development.

Further details, together with the financial provisions which enable a local authority to retain development value are set out in Chapter 31.

The Act will have far reaching effects on an owner's land and full information should be sought from the local authority before any transaction or planning application is put in hand if the land has an element of development value.

FURTHER READING

D. Heap, *Outline of Planning Law,* 6th edition, Sweet and Maxwell, London, 1973.

Walton and Essayan, *Adkins: Landlord and Tenant,* Estates Gazette, London, 1967.

P.R. Bean and A. Lockwood, *Rating Valuation Practice,* Stevens and Son, London, 1969.

R.H. Burn, *Cheshire's Modern Law of Real Property,* 11th edition, Butterworth. London, 1972.

K. Davies, *Law of Compulsory Purchase,* Butterworth, London, 1972.

31

Property Dealings

ACL Grear & J Oxborough

Chapter 30 dealt with administrative matters concerning the ownership and occupation of property and the problems which might arise in its daily use.

This chapter covers the wide use of what might be termed 'transactions' and relates to changes of ownership, including sales and purchases, the use of land including extensions and developments, and pinpoints the principal physical and legal problems which might be met and defines the incidence of capital taxation which is an important consideration.

SALES, PURCHASES AND LEASES

These are the most common transactions in property and can come about for a variety of reasons including the setting up, expansion or closure of a business, moving to bigger premises or different areas or having to move elsewhere in the face of redevelopment or compulsory acquisition. The list is endless but the principles are the same. Acquisitions and disposals of premises on a rental basis are also included.

Methods of acquisition and disposal

The two methods of disposal and acquisition of property at law are:

1   *Freehold.* The sale of a freehold interest which means that all
    legal rights of ownership are transferred outright from one person
    to another for a capital sum.

2   *Leasehold.*   The grant of a leasehold interest which means that rights of occupation, use and partial ownership are transferred from a freeholder (the landlord) to a tenant for a limited period of time in consideration of an annual rent payment.

A tenant who wishes to dispose of an unexpired term of a lease, has two methods open to him:

1   Assignment of a lease: which means that the unexpired term of years remaining is transferred from a 'vendor' tenant to a 'purchaser' tenant who stands in the shoes of the vendor tenant for the remainder of the term, taking over all the rights and obligations under the lease.

    If the market rental value exceeds the rent reserved in the lease, 'a profit rent' is said to exist for which a premium is paid.

2   The grant of an underlease: which means that a tenant may create an underlease on terms, similar to those which he enjoys, for an annual rental. The sub-tenant takes over all rights and obligations under the lease; an increased rent may be payable if market rental value exceeds the rent reserved in the lease.

Open market value

In each method outlined above, the consideration passing is known as 'open market value' and this is defined as 'the value of property in the open market as between a willing seller and an able buyer'.

Market value is normally the figure which a trader or businessman can afford to pay out of his earnings and it follows that the man who runs the most profitable business can afford to pay either the highest price or the highest rental value. It should be noted that special circumstances may exist in which a property might have a special advantage to one particular purchaser eg a next-door neighbour, who might then be prepared to pay more than market value.

Some properties, by reason of their construction and design, are capable of use by a wide variety of traders and therefore command higher prices than would be expected from 'special' types of property such as banks, garages and other purpose built structures. In all cases, a variety of factors affect the values, including size, condition, design, situation and location. Each facet has a bearing on the trader's profitability and therefore the resultant price.

Other assets   In all disposals or acquisitions other assets including fixtures and fittings, plant and machinery, stock and goodwill may be included in the transaction. The consideration passing will need to be apportioned for taxation purposes. Where the net realization is greater than the written down value of each asset in the company's accounts, a balancing charge ie the repayment of tax allowances previously received, will become payable.

Types of transaction

By private treaty   When two parties, often using agents, agree terms by private negotiation. This method is the most widely used; it is relatively simple and details are normally kept on a confidential basis.

By public auction   When a property is offered publicly at an appointed time and place, potential purchasers gather to make their best verbal offers and the property is sold to the highest bidder. The advantage of this method is that there is every chance of a definite conclusion being reached on a specified day. Acceptance of a bid is followed by signature, in the sale room, of a binding contract which is normally incorporated in the auction particulars. Serious bidders will therefore need to have consulted their solicitors prior to the auction.

Where bids are made which do not reach the reserve price and the property is withdrawn from sale, it is common practice for potential purchasers to negotiate privately with the vendor and, if terms are agreed, to sign the contract immediately after the sale, so that the interest arising from the wide publicity given to the auction is not lost.

A further advantage of public auction is that the best price obtainable can be seen to have been realized; a requirement, for example, where a trustee or a liquidator is selling on behalf of others. Auctions are commonly used where there is strong competition between purchasers; auctions are rarely suitable for the disposal of leases or where complex transactions are involved.

By tender   When potential purchasers are invited to submit their best written offers for a property on an appointed day to enable a vendor to decide which, if any, to accept. This method allows both vendor and purchaser time to consider their decisions away from the excitement of the auction room but again it has the advantages of wide publicity and every chance of a definite conclusion on a specified day. The secrecy of the sealed tender bid which has to be made without knowledge of competition and with no chance of a second attempt, normally ensures that the best price is obtained.

This method is useful where there is competition for property, but also, where complex factors other than price are involved; for example, the grant of a building lease which includes details of the design of the building, or financial arrangements, which may need time for consideration and possibly negotiation with the vendor prior to final acceptance.

Tender bids may vary in type, between mere offers which are subject to contract and actual signed contract documents which only need the addition of the vendor's signature to create a binding contract.

The role of the agent

Agents are commonly appointed by an owner to act as a form of broker in finding a purchaser able and willing to complete the purchase. It is a growing practice for prospective purchasers to 'retain an agent' to seek and acquire property.   The problems of a purchaser, after all, are no less than those of a vendor.

An agent normally works on a sliding scale commission based on the consideration passing for the property. A client may not require advice during a transaction but a range of services are available if required, at no extra cost, including advice on handling negotiation problems, taking up references and solving practical difficulties, planning and associated problems. Advice on other matters, including landlord and tenant matters, the incidence of capital taxation, raising finance, and structural surveys are charged as additional items where required and may be charged either on the consideration or on a time taken basis.

It might be noted that the person paying the fee obtains the service and other persons would be unwise to rely too heavily on advice given to third parties. Since the Misrepresentation Act 1967, however, the position has been somewhat improved. A client's rights under the law of fraud and negligence remain the same.

There is no law which restricts persons from acting as agents. The professional institutions have set up their own training curricula and the benefit of this to the public is that practitioners can and do offer comprehensive advisory services in land administration while at the same time adhering to a common code of conduct.

The role of the solicitor

A solicitor's function is basically to ensure that a purchase and a vendor obtain the bargain which was originally agreed between them. The work involved falls into two parts: the first is the signing of the contract and the second the actual conveyance. These may take some weeks as there are numerous necessary processes involved. The contract is a statement of the terms of the bargain set out in legal phraseology. Prior to its being drawn up, the various searches will have been carried out to confirm, amongst other things, that the property has planning permission for its existing use and that there is no likelihood of it being acquired by compulsory acquisition. The existence of rights of way, restrictive covenants, Party Wall Awards and many other possible legal restrictions which affect value will be investigated. Thus, offers made 'subject to contract' allow for details to be investigated and confirmed.

Between exchange of contracts and completion, that is conveyance, the vendor's solicitors must 'prove title'. This can be complex and lengthy but it is necessary to prove that the vendor is able and in a position to convey the legal interest which he has contracted to sell. Ownership only passes on completion and a purchaser has no prior rights, except by agreement, to enter the property.

A solicitor works for a scale fee but may charge on a 'work done' basis in certain circumstances. By law, only qualified solicitors may deal with conveyancing.

Points to consider

There are a large number of matters which can arise in dealings, any of which may affect the bargain and some of which will kill it. Some of these are as follows:

1 *Structure and condition.*   The nature of the structure and its condition together with the costs of any necessary expenditure on repairs, are normally taken into account in arriving at market value. Structural surveys are undertaken by the purchaser to establish what he is buying, the existence of any hidden defect, and the general condition of the building, and to give an approximate estimate of expenditure needed to put the building into good repair.

2 *Town planning situation*   To assess the value of a property, it is vital to know the use to which it may be put. Checks should always be made to ensure that the intended use is either approved or likely to be approved. Costs of works which may be necessary, such as the construction of car parks, will be taken into account. Offers and contracts may be made subject to planning permission where fresh applications are needed and time is pressing. Planning inquiries will also reveal whether any public authorities have earmarked the property for acquisition and public use in the future. If land has any potential for development, enquiry should be made of the local authority to establish whether it is likely to be taken into public ownership and then leased or sold back for actual development – a procedure which, if adopted, could well affect both values and the owner's proposals.

3 *Leases and covenants*   Covenant leases can be of many types and these have been discussed in Chapter 30. Generally, they cover details of the terms, set out repairing obligations and state the permitted use. These should all be examined closely to ensure that the property can be put to its full use, and therefore justify the price paid for it

There may be other covenants and restrictions running with the land, and these may come to light when the solicitor makes his investigations.

Finance

A number of sources of borrowing exist for companies which are unable to finance acquisitions from their own reserves. Sources of borrowing may include:

Banks   Either on a long-term loan against a security or a short-term overdraft

Merchant banks   Can often finance from private or public sources on long- or short-terms. Raising of cash by share issues of various types is also covered by these banks

Loan companies   Other private companies often have funds available although often at higher-than-usual interest rates

Insurance companies   Loans are arranged with cover secured by insurance on individuals lives, for example, that of a director of a company.

Mortgages   Many reputable companies offer these loans which are usually limited to 75 per cent of the mortgage valuation

Sales and leaseback transactions   Freeholds and substantial leaseholds can be sold away subject to a leaseback at an agreed rental. Cash can be realized by this method and a number of combinations exist to establish the appropriate cash/rental ratio. This is normally a last alternative when other sources fail or become too expensive.

Government and Local Authorities   Substantial sums may be made available from public resources particularly in support of policies to decentralize business from congested urban areas to encourage businesses to move to depressed areas. Government intervention through the National Enterprise Board and other legislation is beyond the scope of this chapter.

The choice of source will be governed by the overall state of the economy, prevailing Government policy and the state of the money market, all of which affect the amount of capital funds available at any one time and the prevailing rates of interest. A key to successful lending is the lender's understanding of the borrower's business, his need for capital and his capacity to repay interest and capital. Consequently, lenders often specialize in certain classes of trades or types of loan.

The borrower will find that the strength of his covenant and the size of the loan will affect both the availability and the cost of a loan. In more complex cases, in order to spread risk and achieve cash flow, loans may be an amalgam of short and long terms and may be of varying types and from different sources. It will be wise for prospective borrowers to consult their financial advisers at an early stage; the small businessman would do well to consider the Bolton Report

(HMSO Comd.4811) Chapter 12 in which various sources of finance open to a small trader are discussed at greater length.

Taxation is also a consideration in all matters of finance, both in deciding on treatment of capital and the interest on the loan and this can often influence the choice of a source. Capital Taxes are referred to later. Corporation Tax is dealt with in Chapter 7.

Decentralization and removal to the New Towns

A further aspect of buying and selling is the positive policy of Government and planning authorities in the direction of industry and commerce. The policy has two aims:

1 To remove residents of centrally congested areas to new and expanding towns. Naturally, work must go with them and towns are therefore designed for industry and commerce to grow together with the population. The methods are mostly persuasive and by agreement with companies and authorities. For this reason, incentives are given which include help with removal costs, attractive rental terms and capital incentives for the setting up of business.
2 To attract industry and commerce to 'depressed areas' where employment is poor and there is a large supply of labour, made available perhaps by the contraction of old industries. A number of incentives are offered to the companies, including removal help with key staff and provision of housing, attractive property terms, capital loans and grants.

It is open for businessmen to apply to move to new towns even if they are not first approached by one of the local authorities or the Departments of Trade and Industry. Companies may find themselves forced into removal. For example, where premises occupied have a 'non-conforming' industrial use. Such use may be thought harmful to the area. The local authority may therefore buy the land and premises and persuade the users to move.

Another example is where a company may wish to develop but may find itself restricted by planning policy or the lack of an office development permit or industrial development certificate, and will, therefore, need to seek other premises.

In both examples, in view of the availability of suitable property and Government and planning controls in the more heavily occupied areas, a complete removal to a new or expanding town or a depressed area may be most attractive, and will almost certainly be the cheapest, line of approach.

Matters under this heading are normally dealt with by local authorities, in association with the Departments of Trade and Industry. The Location of Offices Bureau also provides an advisory service.

Capital Taxation on disposals

In any disposal of property, which includes the sale of leases at a premium as well as disposals by way of share transactions, Capital Gains Tax will be chargeable, at the date of disposal, on all realized increases in the value of property which have accrued since 1965 or the date of acquisition, whichever is the later. Tax is chargeable at the rate of 30 per cent. Methods of calculation, the details of 'roll over' and other provisions are set out in more detail later.

In addition, any part of a realized capital sum which is attributable to 'development' in the context of the Town Planning Acts is charged to tax at a higher rate under either Development Gains Tax or Development Land Tax and, in the long term, might even be taken into public ownership at current use value, thus leaving no development value to be taxed.

The Capital Transfer Tax (Finance Act 1974) and the Government's proposed Wealth Tax do not directly affect acquisitions and disposals at market value. However, the impact of each will vitally affect a company's shareholders. Directors will need to take the provisions of these taxes into account when deciding on plans for acquisition or disposal or property eg should a company own a freehold or take a lease of a property.

Capital taxes are discussed in more detail later.

EXPANSIONS, IMPROVEMENTS AND REDEVELOPMENTS

During the course of a company's life, the point is reached where premises in their existing form are no longer adequate, perhaps because of size, design, or obsolescence, and the directors may decide that it is better to extend or rebuild their existing buildings rather than move elsewhere.

It is for the directors to consider in principle the need for and the nature of their future plans, in the light of their current and future trading patterns and profitability. The following comments are set out to indicate the principal steps which need to be taken in the planning and implementation of alterations and improvements. The chronological order will be different in every scheme. Each step interacts with others and, in practice, will need to be considered as part of one overall scheme. Similar principles apply where complete redevelopment is contemplated.

The buildings

The first step is to call in an architect who will advise on the practicality of the proposals and produce sketch schemes to show alternative ways in which the accommodation required by the directors can be provided. In drawing up his sketches, an architect will need to consider the following points:

Structure The most important factor to be determined is the size of floor space to be provided, including trading and working floor areas, staff and storage accommodation and service areas. The next consideration is the layout and design of accommodation to allow for the most effective and therefore most profitable use by the occupier concerned. This includes such matters as number of floor levels, minimum area of each floor together with minimum width of clear span between columns, frontages to street and access for customers, ceiling heights (to allow for mechanical and electrical services) and natural lighting.

Schemes of extension require special attention to ensure that the new accommodation fits in with the existing as near as possible to provide one overall unit.

The bulk, character, and elevations of the building must also be taken into account, including its relationship to nearby buildings, and the local environment as a whole.

Access and car parking Alterations to buildings often require improved access for loading, visitors or staff and additional parking facilities. These are important from the occupier's viewpoint and make the use of the whole building more efficient. The planning authority is also concerned with these aspects and will, in any event, lay down minimum requirements. Their policy is more likely to be concerned with the immediate adjoining area, including roads and parking spaces, rather than internal design.

Public health, staff and fire requirements Alterations must take these items into account; they will not directly affect trading space but will increase the cost of providing that space.

Strict minimum standards are laid down in the Building Regulations (for London, the London Building Acts). These are administered by Local Health and Fire Authorities and cover the structure of buildings, materials used, drainage, staff facilities, ventilation and natural light, fire precautions and means of escape.

It is for a company to decide whether the minimum requirements are to be exceeded; in many cases, better staff facilities or the provision of fire sprinkler systems can more than repay the extra capital outlay through cheaper or more efficient running costs.

Timetable In any extension or rebuilding, business must be carried on in the interim period, and a phased programme should be set down at an early stage. Ill-considered programmes cause delays in building contracts, increases in cost and cash flow problems; schemes of extension are often altered in order to allow for a smooth building programme.

Town planning

The Planning Authority's policy for an area in which the site is located will need to be considered to establish whether permission for a development or for a change of use would be given. For example, expenditure on an extension when a long term compulsory acquisition of property is threatened, is clearly unwise.

Planning consent will ultimately be required prior to commencing work and an architect will produce sketch schemes which are most likely to be accepted by planning standards. When substantial extensions or changes of use are planned, consideration must be given to whether an office development permit or an industrial development certificate would be granted. These are political as opposed to planning controls and take into account such matters as availability of staff for new premises. These restrictions now apply only where additional space exceeds:

For factories—5000ft^2 (464m^2) in London and the South East and parts of the Midlands and 10 000ft^2 (929mm^2) elsewhere (this figure includes ancillary offices)
For offices — 15,000 ft^2 (1393 m^2) in London and the South East
Restrictions are now removed for the rest of the country

Special considerations apply in depressed areas, congested urban areas and in New Towns.

The likelihood of the local authority taking the land into public ownership must also be investigated carefully to ensure that proposals are not frustrated.

Possession of site

Whilst the site available for an extension will normally limit the accommodation to be provided, it is common practice for owners to acquire additional land if it would be advantageous. Surplus sites can also be disposed of which will help the financial situation and reduce maintenance costs.

In cases where all or part of the site is occupied by a tenant, possession may be obtained by the landlord at the end of the lease, subject to payment of compensation. The Landlord and Tenant Act 1954 gives to a tenant several grounds for claiming renewal of a lease but proposals by a landlord to reconstruct or alter to form a more satisfactory trading unit provide sufficient grounds for recovery of possession. Compensation payable to a tenant in this event amounts to a sum equal to the rateable value of premises if the tenant or his predecessor in business have occupied the property for less than 14 years and a sum equal to twice the rateable value if occupation has been for 14 years or more. (See Chapter 30).

Negotiations for site sales and purchases and for the repossession of leased premises are normally carried out by a surveyor, with legal documentation completed by a solicitor.

Costs

When the architect has produced his preliminary sketches a quantity surveyor will be needed to advise on the likely overall cost which at this stage can only be approximate. In addition, a quantity surveyor, in his role as a cost consultant, can often suggest alterations to the design or structure of a building and the materials used which will enable similar accommodation to be provided but at a lower cost. Costs should also include for demolition of existing buildings, alterations to adjoining buildings and professional fees. It might be noted that extensions and alterations are often more costly than new buildings.

Finance

The availability of finance should be considered at an early stage, particularly if all or part of the total costs need to be borrowed from outside sources. Interest on borrowed capital should be taken into account as part of development costs. A cash flow programme should be produced to determine the extent and timing of cash availability, including stage payments to a contractor during construction.

In certain areas, government grants are available for new buildings.

The advice of an accountant will be needed to determine such matters as the effect of capital expenditure upon the capital structure of the company and the treatment of expenditure in relation to corporation tax.

It should be noted that, in addition to construction costs, there will be substantial costs for stock, fixtures and fittings or plant and machinery not normally included as part of a building.

Taxation

Tax impinges on extensions and developments in two ways: Capital taxation and Corporation Tax and its impact should be considered as part of the development process.

Capital taxation. The directors will need to know the effect of taxation on the net realizable value of the company's existing and proposed property assets for a number of reasons which include:

1 Where property is charged as a security against a loan or mortgage, it is the net value after tax which provides security. A mortgage is not a disposal but a subsequent foreclosure on the mortgage for non payment is a disposal and a borrower will be liable to Capital Gains Tax thereon.

2 Where a sale and leaseback is contemplated, Capital Gains Tax will be chargeable on the disposal and only the net realizable value will be available unless 'roll-over' provisions apply.

3 The impact of tax will affect the real value of a company's shares, either directly or indirectly. Although not strictly a company matter, share values are becoming increasingly important; sales of shares are subject to Capital Gains Tax, lifetime gifts and transfers on death are subject to the Capital Transfer Tax and a proposed 'Wealth Tax' is a stated part of future Government policy.

Capital taxation on disposal of property is currently chargeable in two parts:

1 Capital Gains Tax is chargeable at a true rate of 30 per cent on realized gains which have accrued since 6th April 1965 or the date of acquisition, whichever is the later.

2   In addition, that part of a realized capital gain which is attributable to development in the context of the Town and Country Planning Acts is chargeable at a higher rate than Capital Gains Tax as follows:

Development Gains Tax applies to all disposals between 18 December 1973 and 1 August 1976 and is charged at income rates, i.e. 53 per cent for companies. Disposals also include 'first lettings of new buildings'.

Development Land Tax applies to all disposals after 1 August 1976 and is charged at an initial rate betwen $66\frac{2}{3}$ and 80 per cent, rising in successive stages in the future to 100 per cent. Disposals also include the commencement of a development project.

In the long term, the Community Land Act 1975 will provide for local authorities to acquire all development land at current use value so that there will in effect be no development value to be taxed.

In view of the fundamental and complex nature of these current and proposed taxes, it is recommended that early attention is given as part of the consideration of development proposals.

Further details of these taxes are set out later.

Corporation Tax   This tax does not directly affect development schemes but will need to be taken into account as part of the financial appraisal in at least two ways:

Firstly, certain items of expenditure, for example on shop fronts and plant and machinery, will rank for depreciation in the company's accounts, thus affecting such matters as the amount and terms of capital to be borrowed.

Secondly, the choice of method of raising capital, which will give rise to such questions as whether to take a mortgage, long or short, or to sell a freehold and take a leaseback, will depend to some extent on Corporation Tax liability on existing and future profitability.

Careful attention to the impact of Corporation Tax is recommended at an early stage to ensure that the scheme chosen will in the long term produce the greatest net profits at the lowest capital cost.

Details relating to Corporation Tax can be found in Chapter 7.

Conclusions

When investigation into each of the above aspects has been completed, and a preliminary scheme, consisting of sketch plans and estimated costs has been produced, it is for the directors to decide whether the scheme provides the accommodation required and whether the estimated increase in profits or other benefits cover the estimated capital costs, before making a decision to put the work in hand.

In reaching their decision, the directors may wish to take the following points into account:

1 In assessing the profitability of a scheme, regard should be had not only to the profits arising from the new buildings but also to the increased profits which can be earned in the existing buildings. For example, where more efficient loading facilities have been provided, or where, with an increase of floor space, larger units of machinery can lead to economies of scale or more comprehensive ranges of goods can increase the attraction of a shop.

2 Care should be taken to ensure that capital expenditure on the new work will not be greater than the increase in open market value of the finished buildings when completed.

This might relate to a number of factors, for example, the quality of structure and materials used, the fact that the more specialized the building the less the number of potential traders to whom it will be of interest. For example, a shop with a small frontage in relation to an excessively large warehouse at the rear, and the possibility that, although a building might be excellent, its location in a town centre is such that insufficient trade can be done to justify its construction costs.

3 In assessing the market value of the new buildings, in relation to costs, account must also be taken of the existing buildings whose market value may well have been increased. For example, where more efficient access or loading facilities have been provided which, in themselves, would not otherwise be profitable.

In this context, it should be noted that increases in value realized by extensions and alterations will bring about an increase in rates payable, not only for the new buildings but also in respect of the latent value realized in the existing buildings.

In considering any preliminary scheme, it will often be found that the original ideas will have required substantial amendment in the light of the various physical, financial and legal and planning requirements outlined above.

When a decision is made, the chosen scheme will be carried out by the company's advisers, including Architect, Quantity Surveyor, Property Consultant, Accountant and Solicitor, working as a team. It is not within the scope of this book to set down the various steps of preparation of working drawings, obtaining planning consent and competitive tenders, as these matters are merely procedures necessary to put in hand the legal, practical and financial matters as discussed above.

Inevitably, unforeseen problems will arise and will have to be resolved as work proceeds, even at the expense of altering a scheme and increasing its cost. Careful thought and thorough investigation in the early stages will therefore pay dividends by ensuring that long term difficulties may be foreseen and true costs are known in good time so that any decisions necessary to alter or abandon a scheme may be taken before it is too late.

COMPULSORY ACQUISITION

From time to time, property is acquired compulsorily by a government department or local authority for public purposes. This procedure is only practised where it is judged that the need of the community for that property overrides the rights of the individual owner. Parliament has laid down strict safeguards and procedures but, whilst these are complex, some brief comments may be of help.

Compensation payable on acquisition

The principle which lies at the heart of compulsory acquisition, is that vendors, known as 'claimants', are to be put back into the same position as they were before the acquisition in so far as money will allow. Compensation falls under three main headings:

1 *Property values*   The full market value as between an able buyer and a willing seller is payable for freehold and leasehold interests.

All relevant factors including the design, condition and location of property together with its existing planning use and future development potential are taken into account.

Property with development potential is acquired by the local authority at open market value but net of the vendor's liability to Development Land Tax. After the second appointed day of the Community Land Act 1975, a local authority will be obliged to acquire all development land at current use value.

2 *Disturbance*   All other losses suffered by the claimant are included under this heading. Losses must be related to actual facts and figures and cover such items as: Stock, fixtures and plant—losses incurred on forced sale. That is, the difference between the value to the owner of these assets whem employed in the business and the net proceeds realized on disposal, whether by way of a closing down sale or on a breakup basis.

Goodwill. A sum equal to the price that could have been obtained in the open market and calculated by reference to the net annual trading profits.

Closing down expenses All costs and losses incurred including notification of customers, redundancy payments and costs of breaking trading agreements.

Removal to alternative premises Every claimant has an obligation to reduce his losses where reasonably possible and this includes the removal of a business if reasonable alternative premises are available. In this case, disturbance includes all removal costs, including advertising, and temporary losses of profits.

Professional fees A claimant's legal costs together with a contribution to his Surveyor's fees are also payable.

This list of items is by no means exhaustive. Any losses which flow directly from the compulsory acquisition may be claimed.

3 *Injurious affection* In cases where part only of a property is taken, compensation is assessed on similar principles but, in addition, where the remaining part of the property is reduced in value as a result of the severance, compensation known as 'injurious affection' is payable.

Compensation may not be claimed for personal loss or upset.

In each of the above cases, compensation is payable only where some property is acquired. Since the Land Compensation Act 1973, limited rights of compensation exist where the value of property is depreciated by nearby highways or public works. Only properties with RVs of less than £2250 are eligible.

There is a substantial body of case law built up through the Courts to complement Statutes.

Procedure for compulsory acquisition

The law regulates procedures by which Government Departments and Local Authorities may obtain powers of compulsory acquisition. Whilst not detailed here, it should be noted that most powers are obtained by way of a Compulsory Purchase Order (CPO). An Acquiring Authority has to obtain a Ministerial approval for its proposals but, prior to this, the proposals must be published, owners will be notified and they do have a right to object. If substantial objections are made, a public inquiry must first be held. It should be noted that objections at an inquiry may concern the principles relating to the proposals, but objections concerning the amount of compensation are excluded.

The procedure involved in obtaining powers, including a public inquiry can often take up to three years.

When an authority has obtained power, a 'notice to treat' is served, which, in effect, opens negotiations, allowing a claimant to submit a claim and to open discussions with the authority. Negotiations are normally carried out by the District Valuer on behalf of the government department concerned or by the District Valuer for a local authority unless it employs its own valuer.

In the event of disagreement on compensation, either party has the right to refer the matter to an independent body known as the Lands Tribunal which has powers to determine compensation payable. Rights of appeal on points of law only may be made to the Court of Appeal and the House of Lords.

In the event of possession being required before compensation is agreed and the sale is completed an acquiring authority has power to serve a notice of entry and following this to compel an occupier to give up possession, if necessary by force.

CAPITAL TAXATION

Introduction

There are four taxes which currently affect capital transactions, namely Capital Gains Tax, Development Gains Tax, Development Land Tax and Capital Transfer Tax. In addition, the Community Land Act 1975 has a long-term bearing on capital values where development potential is present and the Government has announced its intention of producing a Wealth Tax at some future date. The impact of these current and proposed taxes is fundamental to the ownership of and transactions in property and the consequences of these taxes should never be underestimated by directors when considering future company policy. For example, taxes can radically reduce any net proceeds of disposals, vitally affect the financing and cash flow positions in any redevelopment or extension scheme and exert a strong influence on a company's structure and shareholding and the ways in which it holds its property.

The following notes are intended to give an overall guide to the principles, application and impact of each tax. The legislation is long, complex and far reaching and there are many exemptions and pitfalls which may not be immediately apparent. It is, therefore, recommended that the early advice of an expert be taken in relation to both the Company's existing property assets and that any proposed transactions will ensure the principles adopted provide the maximum advantage to the Company and its shareholders within the framework of the existing and the proposed legislation.

Whilst this chapter is not concerned with the respective political motives behind each tax, the following notes are included as an aid to understanding the reasoning on which they are based.

Capital Gains Tax

Capital Gains Tax is chargeable on all gains realized from the disposal of assets which have accrued since 6th April 1965 or the date of acquisition whichever is the later. The tax covers a wide variety of assets but for the purposes of this book, comment is limited to transactions in property although similar principles in many cases apply to shares.

The relevant legislation is contained in the Finance Act 1965, as amended by each subsequent Finance Act.

The objective is to ensure that income made by way of a Capital Gain by either Companies or individuals is charged to tax in line with income received from trade or employment.
 Since December 1973, that part of the realized gain which arises from 'Development' is dealt with under separate rules. See Taxes on Department Value.

Chargeable assets include property, both leasehold, where a premium passes and freehold and shares in a Company. The only exemptions for property and shares are disposals up to a maximum of £1000 in any one year and an individual's main private residence.

A disposal includes sales of freehold property and leases where a premium is paid. Other payments including insurance monies in respect of property destroyed by fire, the sale of options and the surrender of rights in property are also classed as disposals. Gifts, or transactions at other than market value, are also disposals in that the donee has the right to dispose of his property as he pleases. Capital Transfer Tax will also be payable in these cases. See pp628-30.
 Assets passing upon death are disposal but exempt from Capital Gains Tax. See pp628-30.
 A disposal is deemed to have taken place upon the exchange of contracts or when an existing contract becomes unconditional.

Chargeable persons includes all persons and Companies able to own property or shares and normally liable to pay tax. Special rules apply for persons and Companies owning property in the UK but who are 'non-resident', for charitable bodies which are normally exempt from tax and for trusts who pay special rates of tax.

The chargeable gain on which tax is levied is the difference between the net realization from disposal and the value as at 6th April 1965 or the net acquisition cost if the property was acquired later. Gains which accrued prior to 6th April 1965 are not liable for tax.

The computation of a chargeable gain depends upon three things: the 'net realization' on disposal, the 'base value' ie the value as at 6th April 1965 and the money spent on 'enhancing' the property during the period during which the gain accrued.

1   The net realization is the sale price of the asset after allowance has been made for costs of sale which can include Solicitors', Accountants' and Estate Agents' fees and incidental costs such as advertising.

2   Base value can be calculated in two ways:

> Firstly, where an asset has been acquired since 6th April 1965, then base value is its acquisition cost, deemed to be open market value, less an allowance for costs of acquisition including structural surveys and fees.

> Secondly, where an asset was acquired before 6th April 1965, then the base value is taken as its open market value at that date.

Two methods of arriving at this 1965 value are available and it is for the vendor to choose the more advantageous. The first is to assess the open market value by reference to known market conditions and values of comparable property in the market at that time.

The second, known as the 'Time Apportionment' method, is computed by taking the original net acquisition cost, after deduction of expenses, making the assumption that the Capital Gain has accrued by equal annual instalments throughout the period between acquisition and disposal and then apportioning, on the straight line method, the gain that has accrued since 1965. In this case, the original date of acquisition is limited to 6th April 1945.

It should be noted that the Time Apportionment method will be used unless the taxpayer elects to use his option to substitute the 1965 open market value method. This election must be made before any discussions on value take place with the District Valuer. Once made, the election is irrevocable even if it leads in the long run to a larger tax liability.

The Time Apportionment method does not apply to gains which include the realization of development value.

Special rules apply to shares, both in respect of quoted and unquoted Companies.

3 'Enhancement' expenditure includes such items as improvement and modernizations to the property but excludes maintenance and repairs and any expenditure which has already been set against trading profits.

The chargeable gain is then determined by deducting base value and any enhancement expenditure from the net realization from the disposal.

Leases with less than 50 years unexpired at the date of disposal are classed as 'wasting' assets and special rules apply for the computation of gains. Premium values depreciate during the normal course of a lease and a special formula exists which reflects the fact that the rate of depreciation accelerates as the unexpired term nears its end. It might be noted that a Capital Gain only arises on a lease when an increase in an underlying factor occurs ie either an increase in rental value or in the rate percent tied to the 'profit rent'.

It is thus quite possible that a gain will arise even when the premium at the date of disposal is less than the base value premium ie but for the increase in an underlying factor, the disposal premium would have been lower than that actually realized.

Part disposals occur when either a part of a whole building is disposed of eg the sale of a flat in a block or where, for example, a lease is created out of a freehold. In this case, a special formula applies so that the base value for computation purposes is apportioned in the same ratio as that between the part of the property disposed of and the part retained. Enhancement expenditure is similarly apportioned.

The rate of tax levied on chargeable gain is 30% for individuals although this is subject to an alternative method of charge for small gains known as the 'half income' rule. For Companies, it is effectively 30% although actual tax paid is 'Corporation Tax (52%) on 15/26ths of the chargeable gain'.

Disposals which include the realization of development values attract higher rates of tax. Gains realized by trading companies which deal in land are charged to Corporation Tax.

Capital losses which are suffered as a result of a capital disposal may be set off against gains from other disposals in the same year and unused losses may be set against gains in future years.

Retirement relief is available on the first £20 000 of any gain to any businessman provided he has owned the business for ten years and is over 65 years of age.

For those retiring between 60 and 65, 'tapering' relief of £4000 for each year over the age of sixty is available.

'Roll-over' provisions give relief against tax otherwise chargeable on gains which arise from disposal of business assets provided those proceeds are reinvested in new assets in the same business within three years of the disposal. This 'Roll

Over' is only in the nature of a deferment and continues only as long as those assets or other future replacement assets are held.

Asset values are normally agreed by negotiation with the District Valuer who then reports agreed figures to the Revenue for assessment and collection in the normal way.

Disputes on matters either of value or of fact may be referred to the Lands Tribunal whose decision is final except on points of law which may be determined by the Court of Appeal.

Taxes on Development Value

The objective of taxing development values is to restore to the community a substantially greater share of increases in value attributable to development than would otherwise be received under Capital Gains Tax. The political justification is that it is the community which creates development value by its own need for development and by its extensive capital expenditure on public buildings and works.

'*Development value*' is, in broad principle, the difference between the value of land, including buildings, in its current use, and the value with the benefit of planning permission for an alternative and more valuable use.

Tax is levied on development values at the time of realization, ie at the date of disposal.

Present Position — At the time of writing, September 1976, the laws governing the calculation of tax are in a state of transition. A major change in the treatment of development values is taking place — from the days before 18 December 1973 when development value was treated as a capital gain and taxed at 30 per cent to the day in five to ten years time when it is envisaged that the tax on development values will have risen in successive stages to 100 per cent. At that time, the Community Land Act 1975 will finally bring in the permanent arrangements which provide that all development land will be acquired by local authorities at current use value, no development value will be realized by a vendor and, as a consequence, taxation on development will have ceased.

The following timetable sets out the tax to be levied on realized development values during the transitional stages:

Disposals before 18 December 1973   Development value is chargeable to Capital Gains Tax at 30 per cent.

Disposals between 18 December 1973 and 1 August 1976   Development value is chargeable to Development Gains Tax and is taxed as a trading profit under Case VI Schedule D. Under 'DGT', a disposal also includes the 'first letting' of a new building which is retained by the developer.

Disposals after 1 August 1976   Development value is chargeable to Development Land Tax which replaces Development Gains Tax and is calculated initially at 80 per cent rising to 100 per cent in successive stages at some future dates.   Under 'DLT', a disposal includes the commencement of a development project.

During this period, acquisitions by local authorities will be at market value but net of vendor's Development Land Tax liability.

Disposals after the 'Second Appointed Day' of the Community Land Act 1975   Once this day has been fixed – and it is expected in five to ten years' time – then all development land will be acquired by the local authority at current use value and taxes on development value will cease.

Although a major change in the law of the land will have been effected at this date, the development tax rate immediately beforehand will have been at 100 per cent and the difference in net proceeds realized by the vendor on disposal will therefore only be small.

It should be noted that Capital Gains Tax will continue to be levied on realized increases in the current use value of land and is not affected by the above changes.   No part of any realization will be taxed twice although tax paid on that realization may be charged under several different taxes.

The choice of the appropriate set of rules to be applied to any disposal and the amount of tax payable depends upon the dates of the original acquisition of the land and its subsequent disposal together with the dates of the town planning permission and commencement of development.

Some words of advice   There are a large number of detailed rules, exemptions and exceptions to be applied in the assessment of liability to tax and these differ between each of the taxes as outlined above.

In any event, it is recommended that any company which holds land with development potential, whether for occupation, investment or future development, should consider the implications of the above taxes very carefully.   For example, the impact of tax could affect substantially the realizable value of land used as security against a loan and will certainly affect cash flow calculations on any development to the point where the scheme may even be no longer viable. Finally, in view of the transitions in the law, a company may well find it advisable to delay or hasten on a project in order to minimize the burden of tax payable and to take the best advantage of the different exemptions available.

Taxes on development value are considered below in more detail.

Development Gains Tax

Development Gains Tax is, in broad principle, an extension of Capital Gains Tax in so far as any part of the realized capital gain which is attributable to 'development' shall be taxed as income or trading profits under Case VI of Schedule D.

In addition, where new property is let for the first time, Development Gains Tax shall be paid even though there is no actual disposal of the investment.

The relevant legislation is contained in the Finance Act 1974.

Development Gains Tax applies to all disposals of property on or after 18 December 1973 but before 1 August 1976 with an element of development value.

The development gain is broadly the difference between the development value of land, 'the net proceeds' and the current use value as defined below. The gain is taken as the lowest of three following formulae:

1   The net proceeds of disposal less 120 per cent of the allowable cost which includes expenses and enhancement expenditure.
2   The net proceeds of disposal less 110 per cent of the 'current use value' at the date of disposal.
3   The whole capital gain realized on disposal (including development gain) less the increase in 'current use value' since 6 April 1965 or the date of acquisition whichever is the later.

Current use value is the open market value of property in its existing use and on the assumption that no 'material development' within the context of the Town and Country Planning Acts can be carried out.

Development includes building works as well as changes to alternative uses for example from a house to an office. There are certain permitted minor developments which may be carried out, however, the principal of which are:

1   The rebuilding of existing buildings
2   Extensions to existing buildings up to a maximum of 10 per cent of the cubic content
3   Changes of use which fall within the same 'use classes' as summarized below:
    Class A   Use as a dwelling house or for any non profit making activity
    Class B   Use as an office or retail shop
    Class C   Use as an hotel, licensed premises etc.

Class D   Use for any profit making activity other than
those in Class B, C or E
Class E   Use for manufacturing or warehouse purposes
4   Development of a minor nature permitted under the General
Development Order under the Planning Acts

The above list is not exhaustive. It should be noted that many of these terms are
found in the Planning Acts but do not necessarily have precisely the same
meaning.

Roll-over relief is available in respect of 30 per cent of the Development Gain
realized on business assets provided the proceeds are re-employed in the same
business within three years of the disposal.

The Rate of Tax levied on development gains is as follows:

For individuals — income tax rates apply up to a maximum of
83 per cent but investment income surcharge does not apply.

For companies — Corporation Tax at 52 per cent applies
subject to the lower rate for small companies.

Special rules apply for close companies, trusts and pension
funds.

In certain circumstances, net proceeds from the disposal of
shares in close companies may incorporate an additional tax
on realized development gain inherent in the disposal.

Small disposals relief is available for individuals where net proceeds do not
exceed £10 000 in one year and further marginal relief is available for a further
£10 000 of net proceeds. Main private residences are exempt.
Similar relief is provided for companies whose net disposals in any one year
do not exceed £1000; marginal relief is provided for a further £1000.

Capital Gains Tax is payable on disposals where a development gain is realized.
In such cases, the total capital gain is calculated in the normal way as set out on
pp.610-612. The development gain is then deducted and Capital Gains Tax
rates are then applied to the balance.

First lettings of buildings after material development. The first letting of any
new building which takes place after 17 December 1973 and falls under Development Gains Tax is classed as a disposal for the purposes of Capital Gains Tax and

Development Gains Tax and tax becomes payable on the deemed gains even though the landlord retains the property as an investment.

Tax becomes payable as soon as more than 25 per cent of the building has been let. The notional net proceeds of this deemed disposal are based on the open market value of the building at the time of letting.

Tax may be paid over a period of up to 8 years but interest will be charged on the outstanding sum.

Buildings commanding a total rent of less than £5000 are exempt provided that rents do not exceed £5000 p.a. during the first 5 years of occupation.

Developing owners who occupy builders for their own use are exempt from First Lettings Tax although they will be subject to tax on disposal in the normal way.

Development Land Tax

Development Land Tax is again, in broad principle, an extension of Capital Gains Tax in so far as any part of a realized capital gain which is attributable to 'development' shall be taxed but at a higher rate as provided for in the legislation.

DLT replaces DGT as from 1 August 1976; the principal difference between the two is that DLT is levied at a flat rate — initially 80 per cent — and is not charged as profit. There are variations in detail and provision is made for DLT to be levied in conjunction with the Community Land Act 1975.

The relevant legislation is the Development Land Tax Act 1976.

Development Land Tax applies to all disposals of land, including buildings, on or after 1 August 1976 where an element of development value is realized.

A disposal occurs when the contract for the sale of development land is signed. The grant of a lease of development land is classed as a part disposal and gives rise to a tax liability on either the premium or the rent passing if these include development value.

For purposes of DLT, the start of building works on a development project is classed as a 'deemed disposal' and tax is payable as though the land had been sold at open market value and bought back again.

Disposals of land by way of a gift or on death or between companies in the same group are not classed as disposals for DLT purposes. The Act contains lengthy detailed provisions in relation to these three matters.

It should be noted that disposals after 1 August 1976 will not be subject to DLT if certain events have taken place before that date; for example, where planning consent has been granted or applied for before 12 September 1974 or where work on a development project had been commenced prior to 1 August 1976.

The realized development value on which DLT will be charged is:

1 The *net proceeds* from the disposal of the land, ie at open market value with the benefit of planning permission less incidental costs of sale

minus

2 *Base value*, which is the highest of the three following formulae, calculated by reference to either the original cost of acquisition of the land or its current use value as defined below:

Base A: the cost of the original acquisition of the land plus the increase in its current use value since the date of its acquisition. The original cost may be increased by a special addition dependent upon the date of acquisition but subject to a maximum addition of 60 per cent for land held at 12 September 1974 and 40 per cent for land acquired after 12 September 1974 and before 1 May 1977.

Base B: the current use value at the date of disposal plus 10 per cent.

Base C: the cost of the original acquisition plus 10 per cent. Allowance will be made for expenditure on improvements to the land during the period of ownership.

The calculation of realized development value follows the calculation of development gains under DGT (see above) in principle but there are substantial differences of detail.

Current use value is the open market value of land in its existing use and on the assumption that no 'material development' within the context of the Town and Country Planning Acts can be carried out.

Material development includes the construction and alteration of buildings as well as changes of use of existing buildings, for example, from a house to an office. There are certain permitted minor developments which may be carried out and which for the purposes of DLT are not classed as 'material developments' and do not therefore give rise to a tax liability. They are classed as 'exceptions', the principal of which are as follows:

1 The rebuilding of existing buildings
2 Extensions to existing buildings up to a maximum of 10 per cent of the cubic content

3   Changes of use which fall within certain permitted Use
     Classes and which, it should be noted, are similar to those
     for Development Gains Tax (see above) but differ in some
     detail from those set out in the Planning Acts
4   Minor works permitted under the General Development
     Order within the Planning Acts which are too small to
     require planning permission.

The above list is not exhaustive and the regulations covering 'material development' are similar to those laid down in the Town Planning Acts and in
Development Gains Tax but differ in points of detail from both.

Rate of tax.   Tax is charged initially at a flat rate of 80 per cent of the chargeable development value but it is to rise by successive stages at unspecified
dates over the next few years to 100 per cent.

Interim relief.   There is, however, an interim relief in that a lower rate of
$66\frac{2}{3}$ per cent will be charged in respect of the first £150 000 of chargeable
development value realized in any financial year up to the end of 31 March
1979.

General exemption.   The first £10,000 of chargeable development value realized
in each financial year is exempt.   There is no carry forward provision.

Deferments for industrialists.   A special relief is available to an industrialist who
may defer payment of DLT in a case where he carries out a project of 'material
development' on his own land and for use in connection with his business, until
such time as he disposes of the land or ceases to use it for his business. Where
an industrialist leases the land, the relief is not available to his landlord.

Losses suffered upon disposal of any development land may not be set off
against chargeable development values.

Acquisitions by local authorities.   A special situation applies where a local
authority acquires development land in that the open market price is paid but
is net of the vendor's liability to DLT. Whilst there is no difference in the net
sum received by the vendor, this provision means that the local authorities are
in many cases able to buy land for public use at much lower prices than hitherto.
     It should be noted that, in addition to buying by compulsory purchase or
by private agreement for public use, a local authority now has an option under
the Community Land Act 1975 to buy any development land at market value
but net of DLT so soon as planning permission for relevant development has
been granted to a landowner.

Community Land Act 1975

The objective of the Community Land Act 1975 is said to be firstly to enable the 'community' to control the development of land in accordance with its needs and secondly to restore to the 'community' the increase in value of land created by its efforts. In effect, local authorities will be able to initiate development projects where the need arises in a positive manner, and will also be able to buy land for public use more cheaply, thus retaining the development value on development in their area.

The relevant legislation is the Act itself but it should be noted that a large number of matters are to be determined by future Ministerial Order and that the Minister has reserved for himself substantial discretionary powers.

This Act is to be read in conjunction with the Development Land Tax Act 1976 in relation to interim tax measures.

The Act applies to all land and buildings with development potential which might be suitable for 'relevant development'.

The Act proposes to meet the above objectives by providing that local authorities acquire all land, with certain exceptions, on which relevant development is to take place at its current use value, ie excluding any value attributable to development. The local authority may acquire land whether the initiative to develop is taken by the landowner or by the authority itself.

Development land will then be disposed of by the authority, either by sale or by lease at market value to include development value or alternatively the authority may carry out the development itself.

This long-term position is expected to take five to ten years to achieve but, in the interim period measures are provided which give the local authority an option to acquire development land net of the vendor's liability to DLT where an authority does not exercise its option. DLT will be paid by the vendor in the usual way.

This far reaching legislation is considered from the viewpoint of the property owner for the purposes of this chapter.

Implementation The Act comes into effect in three stages and the situation at each stage may be summarized as follows:

Current situation. The first stage came into effect on 6 April 1976 and now provides that:

1 All local authorities will draw up a Land Acquisition and Management Scheme together with a five-year rolling programme of proposed acquisitions and disposals to include a land policy statement. There may also

include the making of 'Disposal Notification areas' where a comprehensive development is proposed. A landowner will be well advised to examine these documents as soon as they are available to establish what his local authority is proposing in his area, whether his land is affected and whether he must go through the Disposal Notification procedure if he wishes to sell.

2   During the first stage, development procedures, including planning permission and disposals of land, will continue but with two major differences:

Firstly, where development is initiated by an owner by the submission of a planning application, the local authority, which is also the planning authority, has the *duty to consider* whether it wishes to take that land into public ownership. If permission is granted and if the local authority does not exercise its option, then the owner is free to develop or dispose of his land but he will be liable to pay Development Land Tax. If the local authority exercises its option and decides to buy the land, then planning permission is *suspended* by up to 12 months whilst negotiations, by agreement or by compulsory acquisition if necessary, take place. The price paid in this case will be open market value less the Development Land Tax for which the vendor would otherwise be liable.

Following acquisition, a local authority will then decide whether to develop the land itself or dispose of it for the purpose to others. Commercial and industrial development land must be disposed of by way of a long lease but residential land may be sold freehold. In each case, full market value including development value will be charged. Thus, the local authority firstly obtains the development value and secondly retains the freehold ownership of commercial and industrial development land. As part of these arrangements, a local authority may enter into joint partnership arrangements with developers and thus by procedure might be suitable for major town centre development schemes.

If a Local Authority disposes of development land, then the vendor has a 'prior negotiating right' to acquire the development site at open market value but this is subject to satisfactory terms being agreed and to his satisfying the authority that he is able to carry out the scheme.

Secondly, the local authority, whilst continuing to use its existing powers of acquisition, may also initiate its own development if it foresees the need in accordance with its five-year rolling programme. Acquisition will be either by agreement or by compulsory purchase powers. It should be noted that a local authority and the Minister have sweeping powers of acquisition, that the authority does not have to disclose why it wants the land, that the Minister may dispense with a public enquiry and that a landowner has very restricted rights of objection. Any landowner contemplating development should examine these aspects very carefully at an early date.

Acquisitions by the local authority upon its own initiative are at a price net of Development Land Tax.

Second stage. This replaces the local authority's *duty to consider* the acquisition of land for which permission for relevant development has been sought with *an obligation to buy* that land. This obligation is brought into effect by a Duty Order made by the Minister. Orders will be on individual authorities as they are administratively and financially ready and will lead to a series of dates for individual areas throughout the country and for certain specified classes of development in those areas.

The methods of acquisition and subsequent disposal together with the tax implications will remain the same but no longer will a vendor be able to dispose of development land in the open market.

Third stage. This occurs upon the fixing of the Second Appointed Day which is expected to be in five to ten years' time when the Minister has made Duty Orders for the whole country.

After the Second Appointed Day, all development will take place on local authority land the basis of acquisition will change in that the purchase price will be assessed at current use value and not at market value less DLT. Thus, DLT will cease to operate after that date. From the vendor's point of view, there will be little difference in net realization as, by that time, the DLT rate is expected to have risen to 100 per cent.

Although it is the local authority which receives the benefit of development value, all the expense of the vendor, when that land is disposed of, is at full market value including development value. The cost of new development is therefore not reduced — there is simply a shift between landowner and community as to who obtains the benefit of development value.

'Relevant development'. The normal definition of development is as set out in the Town Planning Acts and includes all building and other works together with change of use of buildings and land. Relevant development is based on similar principles but with the *following exceptions* which in fact make for a much 'narrower definition':

1 Development for which planning permission was granted before 12 September 1974.
2 Residential or industrial development on land owned by builders or developers since 12 September 1974.
3 Industrial development on land owned by an industrialist since 12 September 1974.
4 Industrial buildings of not more than 16,146 ft^2 gross floor space (1500 m^2).
5 Non-industrial buildings of not more than 10,764 ft^2 gross floor space (1000 m^2).

6   The enlargement of an existing building by a maximum of one-tenth of its floor space.
7   Any changes of use which do not require any building works.

It should be noted that this definition differs substantially from that used in the Planning Acts and also from that used for DLT and DGT. This is partly to take account of the general aim that the Community Land Act is intended to deal with medium and large sized developments and not to be included in small projects.

There are also *exemptions* from relevant development of a minor nature, for example the addition to buildings of extensions of a small size.

Any landowner contemplating development of his land should enquire of the local authority whether its land policy or detailed acquisition proposals affect his property lest he finds that his planning application produces a response from the local authority which frustrates or radically alters his proposals. It is also recommended that land owners who are not contemplating development should make similar enquiries to establish the likelihood of compulsory acquisition on the initiative of the authority and to see how other proposed developments in the locality could affect their land.

Capital Transfer ('Gifts') Tax

Capital Transfer Tax ('CTT') is, in broad principle, the replacement and extension of Estate Duty so that tax is now to be levied on the cumulative total of transfers made during a person's lifetime as well as on his property passing on death.

Companies are not directly affected by CTT but comment is made here in view of the fundamental effect which it has on shareholders, the consequences of which will influence directors in making decisions about what property they own, the structure of companies and the methods of raising finance.

The relevant legislation is contained in the Finance Act 1975.

The tax is levied on all transfers of property, cumulatively and as they occur, which are made during a person's lifetime at other than full market value ie where there is a complete or partial element of gift, and on property passing at death. It applies to all gifts made after 26 March 1974 and all deaths since 13 March 1975.

The transfer to be taxed is assessed, in the case of a gift, as being the decrease in the value of a donor's total 'estate' and in the event of death, the value of the total estate.

For the purposes of calculation, property is to be taken at open market value at the date of gift or death. Where retained property is depreciated in value as a result of the transfer, then the total loss is found by valuing the estate before and after the transfer.

There are special rules for the valuation of shares, particularly where a controlling interest is concerned or where there is no general market.

The total loss to the donor must take into account CTT. In the case of death, the total value of the estate is calculated and CTT is deducted from that total so that the beneficiary receives a net inheritance. In the case of a gift, similar principles apply and the total loss to the donor's estate will include both the value of the gift and the CTT or alternatively the recipient will receive the gift out of which he must pay tax.

Neither expenses of transfer nor any liability to Capital Gains Tax are included as part of the total loss chargeable to CTT.

The rates of tax are based on two sliding scales, the scale for lifetime transfers being lower.

For transfers at death (including lifetime transfers within three years of death), the first £15 000 is exempt, thereafter a progressively increasing rate is applied dependent upon the total value of the estate. The following extracts from the statutory tables indicate the current rates:

Portion of Transfer Value			Rate %
Up to	£15 000		Nil
Between	£15 000	– £20 000	10
	£80 000	– £100 000	45
	£150 000	– £500 000	60
Over	£2 000 000		75

For lifetime transfers made more than three years before death, a similar table exists but, as a concession, the rate per cent is half of that charged at death for transfers up to £100 000 after which the rate per cent rises more steeply to coincide with the death transfer rate from £300 000 upwards.

Lifetime transfers will be aggregated throughout the life of the donor and the tax on each succeeding gift will be levied at the point on the scale which equates with the current accumulated total of his transfers.

In the event of death within three years of a lifetime transfer, the higher death transfer rate per cent will be charged retrospectively.

Limited exemptions exist of a minimum nature including a maximum gift to any one person of £100 in each year and arrangements within the families, and limited gifts to charities.

Relief is provided where a recipient dies within four years of the gift. Certain arrangements exist for the payment of tax by instalments.

Relief for business assets of a minor nature is provided in the form of a reduction of interest chargeable where tax is paid by instalments and applies only to business assets limited to the first £250 000 in value.

Tax planning, particularly for the smaller company is recommended in view of cash flow difficulties which could arise in the event of the transfer of shares within families either during a lifetime or at death. Such planning will also be beneficial to all owners of substantial property holdings or shares.

Proposed Wealth Tax

The Government has further stated that it intends to introduce a Wealth Tax as part of its policy to achieve the redistribution of wealth as well as income. Current proposals suggest that the tax will be in the form of an annual levy, on a sliding scale basis, on the total assets held by an individual. At present, proposals are in the form of a Green Paper prepared for public discussion and a Select Committee is considering public reaction and the overall implications of this proposed tax in relation to existing capital taxes. It is likely that the introduction of this tax will have a far reaching effect on the private ownership of wealth and will no doubt require substantial alteration to existing capital taxes.

FURTHER READING

A.S. Silke and W.I. Sinclair, *Hambro's Tax Guide 1976–7,* Robert Yeatman, London, 1976.

K. Munkman, *Capital Transfer Tax,* Jordan and Sons, Bristol, 1975.

K.R. Tingley and P.R. Hughes, *Key to Capital Gains Tax,* Taxation Publishing Company, London, 1975.

Dobry, Stewart-Smith and Barnes, *Development Gains Tax,* Butterworth, London, 1975.

C. Joseph, *Development Land Tax,* Oyez Publishing, London 1976.

V. Moore, *Community Land – the new Act,* Sweet and Maxwell, London, 1976.

32

Building Management and Maintenance

Frank Bex

Ideally the design, management and maintenance of buildings should be conceived and carried out with a clear purpose and as a single process. Where buildings are erected for leasing or adapted to new uses, the present occupant may find the original design and his own needs in conflict. The skill of building management has to be applied in a variety of situations, seldom approaching the ideal and all too often struggling with unsuitable buildings or a lack of purpose.

OBJECTIVES OF BUILDING MANAGEMENT

The prime objective of the building management team should be to enable the occupants of the building to function successfully. This means providing the right environment and services at a reasonable cost. The rightness and reasonableness will vary according to circumstances, but must involve looking beyond statutory or leasehold requirements and the minimum expectations of those involved in the enterprise.

Secondary objectives should include protection of the asset value of the buildings and their plant or contents (or performing the requirements of a lease in these respects). While important, however, this has too often been made the prime purpose—creating a suspicion among the occupants that people are thought to matter less than things. An important secondary objective must of course be to look after the security, safety and well-being of the people in, or likely to visit, the building.

RESPONSIBILITY FOR BUILDING MANAGEMENT

Involvement of senior management

As in every successful enterprise, good thinking and balanced judgment are required in building management, as well as specialized knowledge and full information. The definition of needs—in terms of environment and services—is a job for top management, which must also control the resources employed and see that value is obtained. This is a mainstream activity too often seen as a sideline,' resulting in frustration and missed opportunities. Whatever the size of the organization, top management needs not only to take continual care of the 'hygiene factors' so that its staff is able to work well but also to make sure that its future plans and operations can be developed without building constraints. This must therefore be the responsibility of one of the top team and he must be able to devote a sufficient share of his attention to it, and ensure that he knows what is going on.

Execution of building management policy

Before policy can be executed effectively, it must be clearly expressed and understood, and correctly interpreted. This implies a degree of foresight, planning and expertise whatever the size of the undertaking—the activity must therefore be managed and not just left to the caretaker or odd-job man. Having assisted top management to define its objectives, the building manager should set out to review the situation and draft a plan and budget which strikes a balance between cost and efficiency. In practice, this balance will need adjusting and he should therefore keep adequate records of what is intended, what is done and how much it costs.

DRAFTING THE PLAN

Specification of requirements

These will fall into three categories, each of which must be researched in some detail:

Personal requirements, eg Heating/cooling, Lighting, Sanitation, Safety and security.

Work requirements, eg Communications and porterage, Plant/equipment, Main services and drainage.

Building requirements, eg Structural condition, Condition of services, fixtures and fittings, Leasehold, by-law and planning conditions

The list of items under each heading may be extensive. Certain parts of the organization may have particular needs or environmental problems which must be explored. The identification of building requirements may involve the employment of a professional specialist. Certainly, the next stage cannot be carried through without such knowledge or help.

Analysis of requirements

Having established the outline of what is required, it is necessary to review the building facilities available, the space and its arrangement, the services provided or obtainable and to see how good a match can be achieved and at what cost. For this purpose, the building manager must have adequate estate records, including drawings showing the layout and area of the building, its services, plant and other facilities.

Building records

The information available should be kept in a systematic and readily accessible way, whatever the size and resources of the estate. An up-to-date set of master drawings and a card index of significant data may be sufficient. Suitable forms are suggested in the Ministry of Works and Public Buildings R & D Bulletin, *Practice in Property Maintenance Management* (HMSO). These can be adapted to circumstances.

BUDGETING

Classifying expenditure

For recording and reporting purposes, a convenient framework is provided in the standard form of accounts recommended by the Building Maintenance Cost Information Service, of 85/7 Clarence Street, Kingston, Surrey. This has now been running for some years and can also provide useful cost yardsticks, since it publishes historical costs relating to various types of buildings owned by subscribers to the service. For budgeting purposes, it is more useful to think in terms of 'fixed' or basic costs which are not particularly amenable to management action and 'flexible' or variable costs which can, at least to some extent, be managed.

Fixed costs

Include items such as rent, rates, insurance and depreciation; other expenses such as the cost of meeting leasehold or statutory requirements may also be considered in this category.

Flexible costs

Depend on the scale of operations required to meet the objectives of management. They include maintenance expenditure and the running costs of services, which are unavoidable but to some extent manageable from year to year, and may also include the cost of alterations, which are clearly optional but also in the long run probably unavoidable if the organization is to be free to perform efficiently.

Long-term assessment of costs

In order to make sensible budget decisions from year to year, management must have sufficient knowledge of the cost of its long-term objectives, including the cost of maintaining its property to the standard required, and a plan for achieving them. The implications of varying, which usually means postponing, planned maintenance operations can then be realistically assessed. The maintenance manager should be able to plan work sufficiently far ahead to stabilize the workload of his own staff and of his contractors and thus obtain good and timely performance. Therefore the ability to manage 'flexible' costs should not be abused, otherwise waste will occur and the management will lose interest in future planning ahead.

Conflict of requirements

Having assessed the 'fixed' costs and the desirable level of 'flexible' costs, management must usually reconcile its objectives with its resources. However, forward planning and estimating will have enabled the building manager to state the alternatives, and it is then up to top management to judge the priorities.

Budgetary control

The approved budget must of course be regarded as a provisional programme which is to be adjusted according to the organization's cash flow, the progress under each item and the occurrence of unanticipated events or of changes in circumstance. Regular reporting and updating of forecasts, preferably on a monthly basis, will allow problems and deviations to be quickly identified and corrective action to be applied in time.

THE BUILDING MANAGEMENT ORGANIZATION

General principles of organization

The building manager, responsible to a senior executive, holds a key position and can have a considerable effect on the organization as a whole and on the morale of its staff. He should be chosen therefore for his administrative ability and sensitivity to other people's problems, as well as for his technical skill. He should employ no more staff than required for the normal level of activities in his department and should consider the use of contract labour for jobs that 'peak' or are occasional or highly specialized. He should be allowed adequate cover for all regular work, and whether this is done by contract or direct labour it must be adequately planned and supervised. His cover should therefore have sufficient management and supervisory strength.

Contractor or direct labour

The question of employing contractors or direct labour to provide the building services required is not for prejudgment. Some work will almost certainly have to be done by specialist contractors. They often have difficulty in obtaining staff capable of giving a good standard of service. Much will depend on local conditions, the sort and size of organization involved and the in-house management resources available. Contract work often fails to provide a satisfactory service if the employer is unable to specify and supervise adequately.

Other considerations

Some servicing can be done on a regular basis, eg external and interior decoration. But a large proportion of maintenance requires inspection and the exercise of skilled or semiskilled judgment as to the appropriate preventive or remedial measures. The first question therefore is how much of this can be done by in-house staff. If professional advice is required and is not available within the organization, the cost of an independent survey has to be considered as an alternative to going straight to a contractor.

Again it is not possible to lay down firm rules, but the advice of a contractor who values your custom may be no less worth while than that of a consultant. If outside advice would otherwise be necessary over a broad range of service questions, the employment of an in-house specialist capable also of planning and supervising 'good housekeeping' is worth considering. Safety should be a major consideration, and the specialist should at least know how to avoid exposing others to danger and when to call for qualified help in matters outside his own field.

Framework of a building management department

The functions involved can be listed as follows:

Management and supervision
Recording and ordering
Other regular operations
Inspection
Occasional services

and of these, the first three must involve the direct employment of staff—even in the smallest organization. There must be someone on the premises to replace a washer or a fluorescent tube, to deal with a flood or an intruder. At the other end of the scale, the department may have sufficient plant in its care to justify setting up a full engineering team of fitters, electricians and so on. The economic mean has to be determined by trial and error. Generally, a rough estimate of minimum staff requirements could be based on the labour hours involved in operational services, eg Sanitation, Plant attendance, Security, Porterage, Breakdown maintenance.

In addition, it may well be economic to undertake with direct labour those 'good housekeeping' operations which are within the capacity of the sort of staff employed for the operational services, eg Daily and periodic cleaning, Minor repairs and oiling, Painting and decoration.

However, much of this sort of housekeeping work—and many other types of maintenance work also—needs to be carried out at weekends or outside normal hours on weekdays. This can give rise to problems of supervision and recruitment of labour, and it may therefore be preferable to have this work done by a competent contractor. If it is undertaken by direct labour, the service department may be faced with the need for relay work or a six day week.

Reaction time

An important factor governing the standard of service and in determining staffing requirements is the reaction time considered necessary or desirable. An early response to all service calls may be desirable, but it presupposes a reserve of labour and therefore the acceptance of extra costs. The establishment of a system of agreed priorities and service intervals will help to avoid friction.

Work planning

The filtering of service requests—and good progress-chasing—are essential. When work is obtained as a favour or by buttonholing a serviceman in the corridor, the management has abdicated and should be due for replacement. Service staff must be trained to operate within an overall work plan and of course be provided with the right tools, materials and equipment and with clear instructions. The work plan should allocate adequate resources to operational services and regular maintenance, and the management should not allow these resources to be diverted, for example to building alterations or fetching private shopping, except by conscious decision. Perhaps the best safeguard against favouritism and frustration is the maintenance of good customer communications and relations at management level, so that services can be modified and updated, and complaints dealt with before they fester.

OPERATIONAL SERVICES

Safety

Observing the spirit as well as the letter of the many regulations controlling the use of buildings is good policy. There will be regular inspections by officials of the fire brigade, and the district surveyor's and public health departments. These are occasions for obtaining advice. Strict control of unpacking, storage and waste collection is essential so that fire risk is minimized.

Fire precautions

The local fire prevention officer will help to devise a thorough system of precautions. Fire stewards must be trained. It is no good hoping that all will be well, unless there has been forethought and practice. The whole staff must be informed and occasionally involved in training exercises. A post-mortem should be held after each exercise, so that slipshod methods do not become a habit.

Other operational services

Security is covered in Chapter 35. In most buildings, some arrangements for porterage are essential. Other services will depend on the nature and extent of the operations of the occupants. As a general principle, it may be economic to provide centralized services of various kinds but this should not be allowed to divert staff from their proper jobs—it is often more pleasant to be beguiled into activities 'on the side' than to keep at the routine of everyday work. Services should be initiated or continued by conscious decision that the workload can be absorbed and will provide value.

Furnishing and decor

This is too large a subject to be covered adequately here. These are not primarily matters of taste or fashion, though good taste must obviously be involved. Furnishings should be durable, easily maintained and functional: this should not mean that they need to be any the less good-looking, but they must be chosen with clear requirements in mind. A good source of information are the handbooks in the Architects' and Specifiers' Guide series (A4 Publications Limited, Press House, 25 High Street, Edenbridge, Kent). Lighting requirements to a great extent control the use of decor, and useful advice on this subject is contained in the Illuminating Engineering Society's handbook *IES Code for Interior Lighting*, from the Society, York House, 199 Westminster Bridge Road, London SE1.

Alterations

Few organizations are static and the need for alterations of layout and services is likely to arise occasionally or regularly. If the need is regular, a small planning section and a formal arrangement with a contractor may be advantageous. Alternatively, work can be programmed for action by direct labour or put out to tender. In any case, alterations should not be allowed to interfere with the execution of important maintenance work. There is often a tendency for this to happen, and if alterations are frequent, maintenance gets sadly neglected.

MAINTENANCE SERVICES

Cleaning

Whether executed by contractor or direct labour, there should be a detailed specification of daily and periodic cleaning opeerations, and skilled supervision. Getting the right quality of work is difficult, as most labour is still part-time and poorly paid. An efficient contractor will ensure that supervision is adequate but the building management should check that value is received. Too often the contractor submits his invoice on a regular monthly basis whether he has been able to keep a full staff and complete the work required or not. The number of staff to be employed should therefore be agreed in advance and booked in and out.

Cleaning specification and supervision

The British Institute of Cleaning Science will give advice. There are courses in cleaning at some polytechnics, which can lead to a City and Guilds or equivalent diploma for supervisors.

Redecoration

A regular cycle of redecoration is required internally and externally. Advice can be obtained from a reputable paint manufacturer regarding the right materials and their application. Modern paint finishes can stand up to severe conditions for several years, provided that cleaning is done carefully and with a good-quality detergent. The standard of appearance required will therefore determine whether internal redecoration is carried out every three or four years or at longer intervals, but painting carried out at longer intervals involves more preparation and probably an extra coat. It may be more convenient therefore to adopt a short cycle. Painted surfaces should be matt in work areas, to avoid glare.

Other periodic maintenance

Floors and floor coverings, ironmongery, lifts and many items of plant require regular servicing or lubrication. The advice of suppliers or manufacturers should be sought as to the frequency and extent of regular maintenance work. It is essential not to overdo this—frequencies should be adjusted by experience according to need. Shampooing a carpet itself creates wear, so does taking apart a machine.

Periodic inspections

The building staff should of course be encouraged to be on the look-out for faults, dirt and wear and to report them immediately. In addition, periodic inspection is necessary for building fabric, plant, fittings and contents. Some inspections—on lifts and boilers, for instance—will be carried out as a condition of insurance and are legal requirements. Others will be made by the local authority. The building manager should be present or well-represented on such occasions and consider it a failure on his part if a serious defect is discovered. The in-house inspections need to be programmed so that the work arising can be planned and budgeted if major repairs are involved. Minor repairs can be carried out by direct labour, on the spot if convenient. Electrical inspections, including the testing of circuits and earth continuity, are of particular importance since so many accidents and fires are caused by neglect of aged wiring and switchgear. The use of the correct pattern and rating of fuses must also be periodically checked—hasty or 'do it yourself' repairs involving the use of silver paper, paper-clips and the like occur in even the best-ordered establishments.

Unplanned maintenance and breakdowns

There is likely to be an occasional breakdown, and the attempt to obviate this by preventive maintenance can lead to uneconomic levels of servicing without achieving success. The need to attend to faults and emergencies should be covered in maintenance planning. Staff should not be overloaded therefore with routine or programmed work. On the other hand, a close watch should be kept on the level of unplanned work. Adjustment of maintenance periods or interception of overfussy service requests may be required. Where action is needed, it should be timely and positive: prompt attention breeds confidence, neglect breeds complaints, reminders and unreasonable demands which clog the system and waste management time.

Maintenance records

Periodic work and inspections should be programmed, and a reminder system may be useful. This can be combined with a maintenance log, since it is important to build up a history of each maintenance item. Memory can be very misleading and impressions different from facts. A card index and job-sheet system which enables the manager to review what has been done and identify where his resources are being applied is likely to pay off. Material stock cards, with details of reordering, should also be kept to control waste and obtain a smooth flow of stores.

Cost control

The accounting system should permit the building manager to keep costs under review, and within budget. Costing of individual job sheets may not be practical or economic but some analysis of labour utilization should be considered. Obviously, the major budget items may offer the best prospect of significant savings. Building management budgets tend, however, to be made up of a small number of major 'fixed' costs and a larger number of 'flexible' costs spread over a multitude of smaller items. His staff will need therefore to be kept on their toes, looking for the many ways and means of saving. The manager's job is to take a longer-term view, to be conscious of the design defects and opportunities affecting his building and to consider what alterations and replacements should be budgeted.

Cost savings

The building management operations are labour-intensive. Savings can therefore be made mainly in two ways:

1 Reducing work by automation, eg improving access and goods-handling equipment, mail delivery by pneumatic tube, remote control of entrances, plant items, etc

2 Obviating work, eg using low-maintenance materials, keeping dirt out by

efficient dust control especially at entrances, reducing the number of dust traps, avoiding damage by fitting buffers to trolleys.

Many of these possibilities can be covered without incurring much, if any, extra cost when replacements are due or layout alterations are required. Additional capital expenditure, whether on a new building or an existing one, often pays good dividends however. Without investment, the relative cost of building operations is bound to increase, since the days of cheap service labour are over. Building designers will have to be prompted to respond.

LEGAL REQUIREMENTS

Minimum standards

The organization which merely adopts the minimum standards permitted by law is unlikely to be efficient and will certainly have staff difficulties. However, many employers have low standards, and the system of legislation and by-laws governing working conditions is being revised. This is covered in Chapter 22. The building manager must of course familiarize himself with with existing legislation, as listed in Schedule I of the Health and Safety at Work Act 1974. He will also need to be aware of local by-laws and regulations in force for the time being. Local authority staff will advise him about these. There are also regulations made under the various Acts, and there will be uniform regulations under the Health and Safety at Work Act to replace many of the local by-laws, which show remarkable differences from district to district.

Building regulations

New buildings, and additions or alterations to existing buildings, are controlled by stringent building regulations. The local Building Inspector should therefore be called in at an early stage of planning, unless a professional adviser is employed, when he will be responsible for making all necessary contacts with the authorities. It is as well to check that he has done so, and copies of the planning and by-law consents obtained should be filed with copies of the plans deposited for approval. The local authority keeps copies of all such plans and will refer back to them when further alterations are proposed. Existing regulations will be replaced in due course by uniform regulations under the Health and Safety at Work Act 1974.

Town and Country Planning Act 1971

New buildings require planning permission. Alterations may also involve it, unless the existing envelope is retained and additions to floor space do not exceed certain limits. The local Planning Officer should be consulted in case of doubt.

FURTHER READING

BRE Digests: *Services and Environmental Engineering; Building Materials,* Medical and Technical Publishing Company, Lancaster.

Other BRE Digests (published monthly), HMSO, London.

Costs in Use, Department of Environment, Property Services Agency, HMSO, London, 1972.

Modern Offices: A User Survey, National Building Studies No 41, HMSO, London, 1966.

Fire Prevention, Fire Protection Association, London.

Building Maintenance, Turret Press, Watford.

Cleaning and Maintenance, Turret Press, Watford.

33

Insurance of Company Assets

R W Rooke

To the optimist, the establishment of a new company brings visions of steady employment, expanding wealth, increasing power and strength. To the pessimist, a new company means uncertainty, worry and possible financial disaster. Whatever the natural inclination, however, there must be somebody whose responsibility it is to face squarely the possible catastrophes to which the company is exposed, and devise economical means of preventing them or containing their cost.

RISK BEARING

Some risks are endemic to business. Even assuming that a company knows its trade, performs it well and markets its products intelligently, certain hazards of trade remain. The company may manufacture products for which there is no demand. A change in fashion may destroy an existing demand. These and similar risks, often called 'dynamic' risks, cannot be transferred to somebody else's shoulders, for they are the inevitable consequences of venturing into trade.

Other risks may arise from natural phenomena or human weakness, affecting a company's fortunes with unexpected suddenness. A fire may engulf an important building, a ship exporting its wares may sink, the carelessness of an employee may cause injury to a member of the public and cause that person to sue the company. Risks of this kind, often called 'static' or 'pure' risks, can be just as crippling in their effects. A company may decide to chance its arm, meeting such risks when or if they arise, or it may take the precaution of setting capital aside in advance. On the other hand, it would be more prudent to try to avoid both the vicissitudes of fortune and the tying-up of capital which can more profitably be used in the actual business. This can often be done by transferring the risk, that is, paying a premium to an outside party (an insurer) in return for his accepting financial responsibility for any loss. The terms of the transfer are subject to free negotiation, and defined in a legal document (the insurance policy)

A list of such insurable risks would be quite formidable, and to pay for protection against every single one (even if it were possible) would be so costly as to leave the company unable to compete against rivals. It is essential to be selective, using the concept of catastrophic loss as a criterion. Protection is mainly required against catastrophic losses which can imperil the business at one go, rather than against the small losses which occur with more frequency but even collectively could never endanger the solvency of the firm. The latter are more in the nature of overheads, and can well be costed and included as a trading expense.

Potential catastrophe is, however, relative to the size and spread of the business. Breakage of the plate-glass window could be a severe blow to a small shopkeeper, whereas a multiple store expects to have a certain number of windows broken every year and prepares for this in its budget.

In all cases, methods of preventing or avoiding losses should be fully explored first, and insurance should be reserved for those areas where the possibility of serious loss still remains. A factory may be entirely dependent upon one boiler for its production, and failure of the boiler would cause serious dislocation. Rather than seek insurance protection against such an eventuality, it might be preferable to purchase a standby boiler.

THEORY OF INSURANCE

The decision having been taken to ask an insurer to assume a certain risk of catastrophic loss, what is the theory underlying the practice of insurance? This is admirably expressed (albeit in quaint terms) in the preamble to an Act of Parliament in 1601:

> Whereas it hath been time out of mind an usage amongst merchants, both of this realm and of foreign nations when they make any great adventure (especially into remote parts), to give some consideration of money to other persons (which commonly are in no small number) to have from them assurance made of their goods, merchandises, ships and things adventured, or some part thereof, at such rates and in such sort as the parties assurers and the parties assured can agree, which course of dealing is commonly called a policy of assurance; by means of which policies of assurance it cometh to pass, upon the loss or perishing of any ship, there followeth not the undoing of any man, but the

> loss lighteth rather easily upon many than heavily upon few, and
> rather upon them that adventure not than those that do
> adventure, whereby all merchants, especially the younger sort, are
> allured to adventure more willingly and more freely.

Insurance is essentially a pooling of financial resources by a large number of
individuals exposed to a certain risk, so that the unfortunate few who suffer loss
may be reimbursed. Premiums collected by the guardian of the pool, the insurer,
are stored against the evil day suffered by the one or two. The insurer calculates
the probability and cost of expected losses and fixes the premium accordingly,
with due allowance for cost of administration and profit. The insured is spared
anxiety and left free to engage more fully in his chosen trade.

THE INSURANCE MARKET

A wide diversity of organizations has emerged to cater for this need for
insurance, much of this diversity being accounted for by history. Moreover, a
wide range of different types of insurance has also arisen. Many insurance
organizations try to cater for a majority of these different forms of cover,
whereas others specialize in a chosen few.

Composite offices

The 'composite' offices are prepared to underwrite all the major forms of
insurance that have evolved, although it is acknowledged that an office which is
a leader in certain fields may be less competitive in others. It is possible for a
company to place all its insurance needs with one particular office, and for a
small firm this may be convenient. Composite offices will no doubt have
branches in most large towns, providing ready access and local service where
required. The majority can be approached direct, without need of an
intermediary. In structure, they are mainly limited companies.

Lloyd's

As an insurance market, Lloyd's evolved from the practice of underwriters in
London at the end of the seventeenth century of meeting for business at a
coffee-house managed by one Edward Lloyd. Today, the Lloyd's building ('the
Room') houses a large number of insurance syndicates, individually open to
business offered to them on behalf of clients by specially appointed Lloyd's
brokers. Each syndicate is composed of individuals of a certain financial
standing, pledging their capital as surety in unlimited liability. The syndicate is
represented by an underwriting agent sitting at a special 'box' in the Room,
transacting insurance business on its behalf.

Mutual offices

In certain fields, mutual offices have arisen whereby those insuring (sometimes restricted by the articles of association) also share the profits accruing from the operation, usually in the form of a dividend calculated according to the total premium originally contributed. The majority may be approached direct and have a network of local branch offices.

Tariff offices

For certain types of business (mainly fire), insurers have banded together to produce minimum premium rates and standard Policy wordings, so as to impart stability and reliability into their operation. These insurers (known as 'Tariff Offices') also cooperate with each other by collating statistics of experience in those types of insurance, and discussing together any unusual requests for cover. Competition to tariff offices is, however, provided by Lloyd's underwriters and other insurers (non-Tariff Offices) who prefer their own independent line.

Reinsurance offices

Reinsurance offices have arisen from the need for ordinary direct insurers to spread the load of business, particularly where a catastrophic loss might otherwise place a severe financial strain upon the pool. Business is obtained solely from the direct insurers, and there is no official contact between the original insured and the reinsurance office.

Co-insurance

It is quite possible for an insurance (for example, a multimillion-pound factory complex) to be too big for any one insurer to assume single-handed. The normal practice in such cases is for the business to be offered first to a large insurer (the 'leading office'), to formulate the terms and conditions of the insurance and agree to bear a percentage of the total insurance. Other offices (co-insurers) are then approached with a view to their accepting other percentages on the same terms and conditions until complete cover is obtained. Each office may, of course, have its own domestic arrangements for reinsuring some of its potential liability. By such co-insurance it is possible for a large insurance to be spread over the whole market, not only at home but also abroad, and thus the risk of catastrophic loss could be shared world-wide.

It must be stressed that in co-insurance, the various insurers stand parallel to each other and are liable for meeting only their own percentage of any loss. In particular, the leading office has no responsibility for any of the insurers which follow the lead given.

PRINCIPLES OF INSURANCE CONTRACTS

For any insurance contract, whether it be with a composite office, Lloyd's or a mutual office, there are certain basic, unwritten principles which must be observed.

Insurable interest

The potential insured must, first, have an 'insurable interest', that is, he must stand to gain by the preservation of the object insured and suffer loss by its damage or destruction. Correspondingly, where he is insuring a legal liability, he must stand to gain by absence of the liability, and lose by incurring the liability.

Utmost good faith

The contract of insurance is based on the principle of *uberrimae fidei*, the 'utmost good faith'. Whereas other commercial contracts follow the common law principle of *caveat emptor*, 'let the buyer beware', and the seller is only bound not to tell lies or practise fraud, contracts of insurance greatly exceed this minimum stipulation. It is accepted that the potential insured knows all the relevant facts concerning the transaction, and is in duty bound to disclose them. These 'relevant facts' are deemed to be any features which would affect an insurer's judgment whether in the first place to offer insurance cover, and secondly on what terms. Similarly, the insurer is bound by the utmost good faith to disclose all relevant features of the cover offered before the potential insured accepts the proposition, or agrees to its renewal.

Indemnity

Most forms of insurance are, thirdly, based on the principle of indemnity. Thus, in the event of a claim upon a Policy, compensation should place the insured in the same position after the loss as he was before it. The insured must not make a profit out of his misfortune, neither should he be out-of-pocket if the degree of insurance was satisfactory. The principle of indemnity does not, however, apply in the case of a person insuring his own life or limb, for it is held that he has an unlimited interest in his own well-being.

Two important corollaries apply in the field of indemnity, namely contribution and subrogation.

Contribution. If the same risk is insured twice, whether inadvertently or deliberately, it would transgress the principle of indemnity for an insured to be able to claim for the same loss twice, and in fact it would encourage 'manufactured' losses. Where double insurance has occurred, over-compensation is avoided either by each insurer contributing only a proportion of the whole loss, or by one insurer (where a clause in the Policy allows this) being excused payment.

Subrogation.   Similarly, the insured may, in the event of a loss, be able to claim not only against the insurer, but against another party causing the loss. Once again, it would be invidious to allow the insured both claims, for success in both cases would provide a handsome profit out of the loss. It is therefore accepted that if the insurers meet the loss, they are 'subrogated' to any rights of recovery which the insured may have elsewhere, that is the benefit of such rights passes from the insured to the insurer.

As the principle of indemnity does not operate in the insurance of life or limb, then the corollaries of contribution and subrogation do not operate either.

AVERAGE

Many Policies contain a clause relating to 'average' being applied in the case of partial losses. It is the responsibility of the insured to make certain that the amount of cover is adequate if a total loss should occur. This particularly applies where values increase by virtue of inflation. Often this duty is neglected and under-insurance occurs. If a total loss should arise in such circumstances, only the sum insured under the Policy would be paid and the neglectful insured would have to bear the difference between this amount and the full cost of his loss. By the principle of average, this process would apply to partial losses also and only a proportion of the cost would be borne by the insurers. This proportion would be calculated by dividing the sum insured (as per the policy) by the true value, and multiplying the amount of the loss by this fraction. Thus for an £80 000 building insured for only £60 000 but suffering £20 000 damage, the insurers would pay only

$$\frac{£60\ 000}{£80\ 000} \quad x \quad £20\ 000 = £15\ 000$$

and the insured would have to find the remaining £5000 from his own resources.

PORTFOLIO OF INSURANCE

With all this background information in hand, how does the responsible official set about protecting his company against catastrophic loss? It is possible to regard an insurer as a supermarket and choose from the merchandise on sale what are considered to be the 'best buys'. In this, he receives advice and assistance from a representative of the insurer. Recognizing the competition for business that exists between insurers, a better method might be to obtain quotations from a number of insurers to see which office offers the best terms, both in extent of cover and size of premium. Negotiation with the most competitive office could well bring even further improvement in the terms. But how can he be sure of recognizing what his company's real needs are and satisfying them? May there not be some vital risk he has not spotted?

Another method is to consult an expert in the field, and after agreeing upon a programme, instruct him to obtain the necessary cover on the best terms available. In other words, the official would use the services of a reputable insurance broker.

Whichever approach is made, either directly to insurers or indirectly through a broker, the official must be well-informed upon the risks to which his business is exposed and the insurances which may be required. This may appear at first sight a formidable task, the concept of 'risk' being somewhat nebulous. It becomes manageable by dividing the subject into more tangible parts as follows:

1   Property protection
2   Loss of income
3   Legal liabilities
4   Personnel

The extent to which these different parts apply will vary from one company to another.

Property protection

Every commercial undertaking will amass property of various kinds, whether buildings, machinery, stock, furniture, cars. Some of these it will own outright, some it will lease but nevertheless be responsible for under the terms of the lease. The continued safety of these physical assets may well be crucial for the well-being of the company.

The first line of defence is to prevent this loss or destruction, for even if full compensation is received after a catastrophe, there has still been the disruption to the business and strain upon its executives which cannot be expressed in financial terms.

Attention should be given to defence against fire by consultation with the local fire safety officer, with companies specializing in fire detection and prevention, and with fire insurance surveyors. This should be done during the planning stage for new buildings, and also during any major transformations or extensions of a plant. Similarly, advice on burglary protection could be obtained from specialist companies and burglary insurance surveyors. In certain cases, attention might be given to possible water damage, particularly where vulnerable materials are being stored.

It is then necessary to consider the perils to which the property is exposed.

Some property may be very important to the company and expensive to replace, yet prone to damage of many kinds. For this it is expedient, even if the insurers do not demand it, that all reasonable precautions be taken to prevent, or at least minimize, loss. The fullest available insurance is advisable upon this property. Such insurance is known as All Risks (rather incorrectly, seeing that there are various exclusions), and may be recommended for items such as computers. This cover is frequently provided for goods in transit, ships and their cargo, aircraft.

In other cases, it is possible to select the more likely perils and insure against these only (for example, fire, explosion, burglary or water damage), remembering that less obvious perils can be equally important. This requires an appraisal of the types of property owned and the nature of the particular perils to which they are exposed.

Yet again there may be property which it is decided should not be insured, either because there are no catastrophic perils to which it is open, or because the cost of its replacement would not impose undue financial strain.

Loss of income

If a physical asset is destroyed, there can still be other loss to the company stemming from this, namely loss of profit and increase in cost of working during the period of reconstruction. If important stock is destroyed by fire (whether in the company's premises or those of a vital supplier), or a vital piece of machinery is put out of action for a long time, there can well be loss of business and therefore profits if customers turn elsewhere for their supplies. Buying from a competitor in order to keep a customer stocked can be an expensive way of retaining his business. Moreover, certain expenses (for example local rates) continue, even if a factory is out of action for a while.

It may therefore be just as important to insure against these lost profits and increased costs as to insure against the underlying loss or destruction of the asset. This type of insurance is called Consequential Loss, or Loss of Profit, but is superimposed upon the underlying property damage (for example fire or engineering breakdown), and applies only to the consequences arising from it.

Further loss of income may arise from bad debts, or loss of rent from a tenant through fire damage to the premises. Insurance protection is available against these risks also.

Legal liabilities

The business activities of any company may cause injury to employees or outside parties, or damage to their property, arising from negligence of some kind in its activities, including the negligence of employees. There may be an unsafe method of work, or impurities in goods supplied which should have been noticed during manufacturing. An individual or corporate body taking the company to court might succeed in obtaining heavy damages from the company.

Since the passing of the Employer's Liability (Compulsory Insurance Act) 1969, all employers apart from a few exceptions are obliged to insure against their legal liability for injuries to employees arising out of and in the course of their employment. Insurance must be arranged with an insurer satisfying certain requirements, for a limit of liability not less than £2m. Certificates to this effect are supplied by the insurer and these must be displayed in suitably prominent places (eg works or office notice-boards).

Similarly, responsibility for injury or damage may devolve upon the company as a result of committing a breach of statute. Particular attention is drawn to the various Factories Acts, which impose many statutory duties upon employers arising out of occupation of premises, processes of manufacture, use of machinery and other activities incidental to an industry. Similar obligations are placed on employers under the Offices, Shops and Railway Premises Act 1963 as regards employees in those types of premises.

Since the possible causes of liability are legion, there is much sense in insuring against them. The main forms of cover available are Employer's Liability, Public (or Third Party) Liability, and Products Liability.

Personnel

The most important asset which any company has is its personnel, for the entire success of the enterprise basically rests on them. While it is possible to think only of the financial effect on the company of loss of personnel and in certain respects insure against it, most companies exhibit a more humanitarian approach and provide insurance protection for the employees themselves against certain eventualities. In the long run, it is to the company's advantage that its staff shall be spared anxieties about financial hardship, whether by accident during working life or the advent of old age.

In this respect, consideration should be given to pension schemes, group life assurance and personal accident cover.

Although the various aspects (property protection, loss of income, legal liabilities, personnel) have been differentiated for convenience, certain types of insurance to be considered in a company context stretch over two or more aspects. Thus private car and commercial vehicle insurance combine all aspects but loss of income.

Policies of insurance upon steam boilers, lifts, lifting gear and certain other types of equipment or installation will embrace inspection by a qualified person as prescribed by statute, public liability cover, and possibly also cover against material damage (both to the property insured and also to surrounding equipment).

Summary of portfolio

The exact contents of the insurance portfolio will depend on many factors, but principally the nature of the business and the extent to which the company management decide to bear risks uninsured.

The following types of insurance are suggested as a nucleus which would be appropriate for most companies:

1   *Property protection*
     (*a*) fire and explosion insurance (and selected perils if appropriate) upon buildings, machinery, contents, stock and office equipment
     (*b*) money insurance, covering losses in premises or in transit
     (*c*) all risks insurance upon expensive, vulnerable items and goods in transit
2   *Loss of income*
     loss of profits insurance, to meet loss of profit and increased cost of working following loss or damage by fire
3   *Legal liabilities*
     (*a*) employer's liability insurance, to cover legal liability for injury to employees
     (*b*) public liability insurance, to cover legal liability for injury to third parties or damage to their property arising out of business activities (including products liability insurance if engaged in manufacture or distribution of goods)
4   *Personnel*
     (*a*) pension scheme, to provide adequate retirement pensions to employees
     (*b*) personal accident insurance, for employees injured during business activities
5   *Combined*
     (*a*) vehicles owned by the company
     (*b*) engineering insurance upon steam boilers, lifts, lifting gear, etc.

This list is by no means exhaustive, but will serve as a guide to those forms of insurance which might prudently be obtained.

SELF-INSURANCE

Whether consciously or not, all companies practise forms of self-insurance (or sometimes, more correctly, non-insurance), that is, accept the possibility of loss arising from certain directions without financial recovery from an insurer. A non-catastrophic hazard may be so remote as not to warrant special provision for it, or so regular as to be rather an overhead cost.

In this context, can 'catastrophic loss' be assessed in financial terms, bearing in mind that this must be relative to the size and spread of the business? Where no fixed criteria are used, the process becomes entirely subjective, and the limits beyond which potential losses are insured are chosen on 'psychological' rather than financial/economic grounds. It merely 'feels right' to have a certain level of insurance for safety's sake.

If, on the other hand, a more objective approach is required, there are certain bases within the company's financial operations which can be used, namely:

1   Assets
2   Return on capital employed
3   Profits
4   Cash flow

While there can be no hard and fast rules for calculating the degree of financial loss which would be tolerable in any one year, it is suggested that the maximum degree of self-insurance is such that the annual potential cost of uninsured losses would not:

1   Reduce the value of the total net assets attributable to the ordinary share capital by more than 2 per cent
2   Reduce the return on capital employed by more than about ½ per cent when subtracted from the previous year's before-tax profit
3   Reduce the value of the profit by more than 5 per cent when subtracted from the previous year's before-tax profit
4   Exceed 10 per cent of the previous year's after-tax profit plus depreciation less distributions

Where application of these criteria produce different limits, it would be prudent to choose the lowest figure as the tolerable degree of self-insurance.

To assist the mechanics of self-insurance, it might be decided to set up a fund within the company in readiness for meeting any losses which may arise. This fund may be built up by regular contributions from participating sections of the business over a period, and maintained at an adequate level thereafter. This is, after all, how an insurer operates. On the other hand, it must be borne in mind that although premiums to outside insurers rank as an expense for taxation purposes, contributions to an internal fund do not, and taxation of the internal fund can have a serious effect on the economics of the operation.

Moreover, for an accurate assessment of the financial provision required against such risks, it is essential that full statistics of losses be kept and that the company's operations be large enough to give a reliable guide to the incidence of such losses.

Part insurance

Excess.   A further method of self-insurance is to insure only part of the risk and bear the remainder internally. This can be effected by accepting a large 'excess' or 'deductible', that is, meeting any loss internally up to an agreed amount and claiming from the insurers whatever balance there may be.

Co-insurance.   A second form is co-insurance, where the company accepts an agreed percentage of any loss, however great or small.

First loss.   A third form is known as 'first loss' insurance, applicable in situations where a complete loss is unimaginable (for example, theft of a company's entire stock of large machinery). In this case, a maximum loss is estimated and insurance for that amount arranged, but in the remote chance of a loss exceeding the estimate, the company bears the remaining cost.

Aggregate deductible.   A fourth method is by means of an 'aggregate deductible', under which the company bears all losses of a particular kind until an agreed total is reached, whereupon the insurer accepts all further losses beyond that point.

Captive insurer.   The company may consider that its operations are sufficiently large and well-spread that the premium otherwise payable to outside insurers would provide sufficient income for promoting an insurance company subsidiary, or 'captive insurer'. Suitable reinsurance would protect the 'captive' against an unacceptable level of potential loss.

   Whether or not self-insurance in one or more of its forms is a practical proposition may depend upon the financial structure of the company, and on its costing procedures. Many giant corporations which might appear to have abundant funds for the operation are in fact split into a large number of independent profit centres, and neither central funds nor possibly even central administration are available to make the most of the overall strength.

COST OF INSURANCE

To a large extent, the total cost of insurance will vary according to the size of the company. Expansion of business will mean expansion of premium outlay. It is difficult to give guidelines upon the degree of cost that must be expected, for so much will depend upon the size and nature of the business, the prevalence of losses, and many other factors which vary from one industry to another, or between different companies in the same industry.

   Furthermore, it is difficult to establish a reliable standard of comparison. Should the cost of insurance be calculated as a percentage of turnover, capital employed, assets? Whichever basis is used, there will be anomalies, but in the few cases where research has been undertaken, there has been a tendency to use turnover as the standard of comparison.

As such, premium expenditure can generally be expected to reach up to one per cent of turnover, although higher percentages are not unusual in certain occupations. Much will depend on the degree of self-insurance assumed by the company. With the steady increase in fire losses, motor accidents, and crime in recent years, the cost of most forms of insurance has tended to increase, and this may be expected to continue for the time being.

ADMINISTRATION OF INSURANCE

The number of staff required to handle insurance will depend on the size of the company. In a small undertaking, it may only be necessary for one individual to spend an occasional hour on insurance matters. In a larger company, there will come a stage at which an insurance specialist will need to be appointed in a full-time capacity. In a giant concern, there may well be an entire insurance department.

As in many other spheres, size and overall buying power count for a great deal in obtaining insurance, and it would seem obvious that centralization is essential for the most effective administration of insurance in the larger companies. Concentration of premium expenditure gives negotiating strength vis-à-vis insurers, the cost of administration is less for each party, and thus there will be scope for cutting premium rates which will benefit the entire company. Furthermore, it is more economic to recruit specialist insurance knowledge, for it will be used to the fullest advantage in a central function.

On the other hand, many giant companies favour a decentralized structure so that responsibility for profitability is more widely shared. Administration of insurance is then divided accordingly, and seeing that the fortunes of the smaller unit then have a much more direct bearing on the level of its insurance costs, it is argued that this gives greater incentive to the containment of premium expenditure.

Certain large companies have evolved a combination of these two viewpoints in their insurance administration. Wherever possible, group policies are effected so as to take fullest advantage of 'purchasing power' both as regards premium outlay and also extent of insurance cover. Within these group policies, apportionment of premium expenditure is made between separate units according to the normal underwriting factors such as claims experience, size of operation, etc. In addition, the separate units are able to effect their own particular insurance covers as dictated by their own special needs and circumstances. Thus it is possible to combine the advantages of centralization with the greater freedom of manoeuvre provided by decentralization.

REPORTING CHANGES IN RISK

Whichever philosophy is adopted, it is imperative that there be strong lines of communication so that all matters affecting insurance, whether new losses occurring or new risks arising, are reported for the necessary action to be taken. In this respect it is surprising how much within a company's activities can have a bearing upon insurance. New liabilities may arise from entry into different fields of industry or commerce, from new contracts and agreements or new legislation, and these must be considered in relation to the company's liability insurances. Before new buildings are erected it is advisable to notify the fire insurers so that suitable protection is incorporated against the risk of fire outbreak. Financial statistics of various kinds must be supplied to insurers, and convenient methods of collation must be evolved. These are but a sample of the ways in which communication of knowledge is vital for the most effective administration of insurance.

Liaison must be built up with a large cross-section of senior staff—works managers, accountants, transport managers, solicitors, personnel managers, sales managers, research staff— to ensure a two-way transmission of information. In this way, a clear watch may be kept to make certain that insurance provision is geared to the ever-changing face of company operations, and that specialist insurance advice is available in the right places at the right time. There will be continual need for education of all appropriate staff with regard to insurance, both formally by dissemination of written instructions and informally by social contact.

ADMINISTERING CLAIMS

Well-defined procedures are required for administration of claims. These may arise from any sector of the business, and it is vital that staff should have a judicious appreciation of what accidents or losses may be the subject of insurance claims. With some (for example, motor accidents) it is quite obvious that they must be reported, but others (for example, damage to outside property by a faulty product) may not so obviously prompt thoughts of an insurance claim.

At the very least, certain key staff such as works managers, transport and personnel officials should be trained to report incidents for insurance purposes. Agreed reporting procedures should be in force, possibly in the shape of questionnaires or insurers' report forms for submission at the earliest opportunity. Where a company's operations are scattered over a wide area, it may be appropriate for certain types of insurance claim (for example motor accidents) to be negotiated direct between the local official responsible and the district branch of the particular insurer.

In the case of major claims, consideration should be given to an early visit to the scene of operations. This will permit evidence to be taken whilst still fresh, and a detailed approach made to rectification and ultimate presentation of the claim upon the insurers. This visit may well be undertaken in company with a representative from the insurers, or with an independent assessor appointed by the insurer to handle the claim.

It is possible that in such claims, assistance or advice may be necessary from a miscellany of company officials.

INSURANCE OF OVERSEAS COMPANIES

Communication may also be of prime importance where a company has operations overseas. Even if there are no bases abroad, there may be products or services exported which must figure in insurance provision. Directors and sales representatives may travel abroad, and for them personal insurances will be necessary. It is essential that information be made available upon these overseas activities so that the implications for insurance may be considered.

Companies having only a few subsidiary offices or works abroad may control them fully from head offices and allow little local autonomy. This form of administration may affect the provision of insurance, in that as far as possible, the relevant cover may be provided within the head office Policies, and only where local convenience is of prime importance will insurance be arranged locally. In some cases, overseas legislation will dictate where insurance cover is to be obtained.

Overseas subsidiary companies may well have a great deal of independence from head office control, and among other freedoms, may have the right to arrange their own insurances. In such cases there will still be wisdom in participating in the major group, world-wide Policies. These must, of course, have the greatest flexibility and interpretation of cover for such world-wide application. Premiums are no doubt paid by the parent company to the main offices of the insurers, but there should be arrangements for claims to be negotiated and settled locally. Where insurance is deliberately obtained locally, care should be taken in deciding whether foreign insurers or overseas offices of British-based companies are to be used.

RENEWAL DATES

Although the cost of insurance has already been seen as a relatively modest percentage of a company's turnover, modern methods of costing and budgetary control take full note of the effect which such an item can have upon profitability. The incidence of renewal dates can have a distinct bearing upon this.

The eventual premiums for certain types of insurance (for example employer's liability, third party, money) depend on certain statistics applicable to the year of insurance, which can only be known when the year is completed. Where these statistics are primarily financial (for example, salaries paid or volume of money carried), it is sensible for the year of insurance to coincide with the company's accounting year. This makes the collation of statistics easier, in that only one year's accounts are involved. The cost of the insurance is equated with the past year of accounts, and correspondingly the forecast cost of insurance for budget purposes is more reliable.

Whether all company insurances should coincide with the accounting year is a matter of opinion. This is undoubtedly very helpful in preparing annual accounts, for premiums do not have to be apportioned between different accounting years. On the other hand, negotiation of all Policies in one concentrated period can mean that there is insufficient time for judicious thought to be given to each Policy. Where renewal dates are spread over a whole calendar year, deeper investigation of the cover is possible and the workload is more evenly distributed.

RECORDS

Although statistics of various kinds can be obtained from other agencies (for example, from insurers or brokers or other departments), it is advisable for certain domestic records to be kept. Renewal negotiations frequently hinge upon 'claims experience', that is, the proportion of premium expenditure swallowed up by claims payments, and it is of great benefit to have one's own facts and figures. (It is always possible for the insurers' figures to be wrong.)

Details of premiums and claims for several years of insurance are vital when considering any change from insurance to self-insurance.

These details are also useful for internal administration, such as forecast budgets. The actual method of recording is open to personal choice, but it is recommended that, at the very least, details be kept of premiums and claims paid according to insurance years.

USE OF BROKERS

For many companies, the purchase of insurance is identical with purchase of any other goods and service. Approach is made to the supplier direct and the transaction is finally effected to the satisfaction of both parties. Insurance departments of many large companies are administered in the same way. All insurance is negotiated direct with insurers (except Lloyd's), and either the commission earned pays the cost of operating the department or the net premium cost is relayed to the division which generates the cover, and their overheads are correspondingly reduced. Insurance at Lloyd's can only be placed through a specially appointed Lloyd's broker, for the syndicates do not transact business direct with the general public (including industrial and commercial clients).

Many other companies, however, employ insurance brokers as intermediaries in negotiations with insurers. This is particularly the case where the responsibility lies with one official in the company, often not an insurance specialist. The main services and advantages to be obtained through the use of brokers are:

1 Availability of expert knowledge of the varying strengths of differing insurers, and their representation in different parts of the world. It is hardly possible for one person to hold and keep up to date such a fund of knowledge

2 Access to Lloyd's is only possible through the agency of Lloyd's brokers

3 By constant intercourse with insurers of all kinds, brokers can be expected to have a knowledge of how a company's insurance needs can best be met at an economic cost

4 The very size of many brokers enables them to exert independent pressure upon insurers in the interest of their client

5 For large-scale Policies involving many co-insurers, insurance brokers collate the various part-premiums and present one total debit note for the client, thus simplifying accounting procedure

6 Various ancillary services are provided at no additional cost, for example, discussion of contract conditions relating to insurance, surveys of premises

The argument for use of insurance brokers is that such services can be provided at a more economic cost than is possible for a company providing a similar level of expertise.

It is possible to combine these approaches, by making direct contact with insurers wherever it is warranted but negotiating through brokers where their services are of particular value.

Payment of brokers

Remuneration is made by the insurer in the form of percentage commission based on the gross premium paid. The percentage varies according to types of cover and the size of the brokers. This method has the merit of simplicity of accounting, in that the broker merely deducts the percentage when remitting to the insurers premiums paid by his client.

There are, however, various objections to this time-honoured method:

1 By being indirect, it may be difficult for a company to know exactly how much commission is earned over a year by the

broker and thus to assess whether the cost of his services is economic

2   The volume of work required of a broker is not necessarily proportional to the premium. The commission earned on a large Policy may greatly exceed the cost of servicing it. Conversely, many brokers are finding the cost of administering small Policies out of proportion to the commission earned

3   More fundamentally, perhaps, the implied principle of 'no premium, no pay' must inevitably place a strain upon the integrity of insurance brokers, for it is in their financial interest to urge clients to have as much insurance as possible, yet the interests of the clients may be towards a greater degree of self-insurance (upon which no commission would be earned)

To a small extent, the practice of paying brokers a fee (either annually or per assignment), is gaining favour as satisfying these objections. Thus a company uses the full services of a broker in negotiations, pays premiums net to the insurer, and pays a separate fee to the broker. Negotiation of the fee is based on the cost of the work undertaken by the broker, irrespective of the amount of insurance arranged.

RISK PREVENTION

Real catastrophe apart, the cost of insurance is ultimately decided by the cost of the losses sustained. In recent years, losses by fire, theft and other insurable risks have been increasing at a steady if not an alarming rate, and the price of insurance has risen accordingly. Measures which can halt or reverse this process are of benefit to all parties and to the community at large.

Insurers have always emphasized the importance of preventing losses if at all possible, on the basis that prevention is better than cure. As part of their service, they insist upon inspecting premises for fire insurance, safes and other devices for burglary insurance, accounting procedures for fidelity guarantee insurance (eg against dishonesty on the part of the insured's staff). No extra charge is made for these services, but their importance is such that insurance will not be offered unless they are undertaken and any protective recommendations put into force. It is urged, for example, that plans for a new building should be vetted by fire insurers so that measures to reduce the risk of fire may be incorporated at the outset. The offer of reduced premiums is a powerful inducement to effect such protection.

Many insurers apply similar reasoning to the reduction of accidents, and the services of qualified surveyors are made available to investigate potential causes of accident and make recommendations for reducing or eliminating them.

These specialist services do not, of course, detract from the importance of domestic attention to all potential sources of injury or loss.

UP-TO-DATE KNOWLEDGE

The whole subject of risk-bearing is one that is constantly changing, for it is moulded by so many factors that are themselves constantly changing. New legislation is continually being promulgated, not only in this country but also abroad, and some will have an influence upon insurance to greater or lesser degree. Changes taking place within the company will frequently necessitate review of the insurance portfolio, by increasing some hazards and reducing others. The insurance market itself has been subjected to radical change in recent years through mergers and takeovers, and it is likely that this place of change will continue.

There will never be a time when the entire subject will have been completely mastered. On the contrary, there will always be a need to increase further knowledge and keep abreast of current developments in many fields.

FURTHER READING

A.I.M.I.C. (ed), *Company Insurance Handbook,* Gower Press, Epping, 1973.

W.L. Catchpole, *Business Guide to Insurance,* Heinemann, London, 1974.

H.A.L. Cockerell, *Insurance,* English Universities Press, Teach Yourself Books, London, 1957.

R.L. Carter and N.A. Doherty, *Handbook of Risk Management,* Kluwer-Harrap, London, 1974.

N. Curer-Briggs, P. Hamilton and A.R.D. Norman, *Handbook of Security,* Kluwer-Harrap, London, 1974.

34

Managing Transport Services

Frank H Woodward

There are two basic activities which are the responsibility of a transport services function:

1   Movement of goods and material necessary for the business
2   Movement of personnel

In both of the above activities, the objective is to achieve a cost-effective operation in order to reduce the impact of the additional cost burden on product price.

The transport function is called upon to provide a service to every single function within industry. It is hard to name a function which at some time will not require goods, services or personnel to be moved. Because of this broad responsibility to give a service, those engaged in the management of the transport function come into direct contact with all other departments within a company and will incur costs on behalf of those departments. With this licence to accept costs, comes the added responsibility of ensuring that value is received for costs incurred, and to constantly check costs and performance of all activities within the function against alternative services available.

ORGANIZATION STRUCTURE

The person responsible at board level for the control of transport operations can vary from the sales director to the company secretary, from the production director to the chief executive. With increased activity in the distribution of goods and escalation of costs in all areas of transport operations, the arguments over the rightful place of the transport function in a company organization have become more intense. Despite the strength of many proposals, it has become increasingly obvious that there is no answer which would be suitable or acceptable as a general rule for all types of industry.

A company whose activity is centred around the packaging, warehousing and distribution of goods to retail outlets would find that 'transport', a word used in the broadest sense, is responsible for anything up to 40 per cent of annual turnover and would justify direct representation on the board of directors to ensure that a full account of this expenditure is presented at the highest level in the organization. A company whose transport requirement is only a few cars, and whose budget was a very small part of total company expenditure would not need such total executive responsibility. Unless a company 'sells' transport as a means of adding directly to the profit of the company, in other words, a company engaged in road haulage, then transport is a service function in exactly the same way as the catering activity of a company. The value of this service to the profitability of the company will determine its correct place in the organization structure.

Line or staff. Line management is that which is responsible for achieving the main objectives of the business. Staff functions are those which assist line management to achieve those objectives. Transport is primarily a line function,

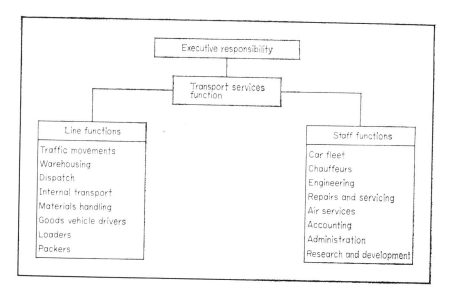

Figure 34.1   Line and staff functions within the transport services activity

especially when applied to the movement of a company product. To manufacture goods and to leave them at the end of the production line is not 'achieving the objectives of the business'. They must be placed before a customer, and to achieve this implies movement or transportation of the product.

The management organization of a road haulage operation would be of line responsibility, in that the main objective of the business is to achieve profit by selling transport services. In the manufacturing industry, it all depends on who gives the instructions about the movements. If the manufacturing or sales function state where, when and how the goods are to be moved, then the transport function has no line responsibility and merely provides the service requested without question. On the other hand, if the transport function takes over the final stage of customer satisfaction, and is able to decide the method of movement after having been given instructions on where and when, then it is in a position of line responsibility, accountable for its own decisions. Figure 34.1 shows the distinction between line and staff functions in the transport services activity.

Developing the organization structure

Figures 34.2 to 34.4 show different types of organization structure suitable for the transport services function of a manufacturing company. The transport services requirement is of a general nature and is not confined to a major warehousing or retailing operation. It is intended that the types of organization illustrated will assist readers in developing their own organization structure after taking into consideration their own special needs.

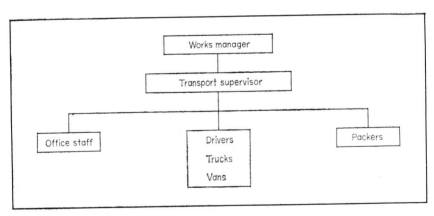

Figure 34.2   A simple organization for a small company

A typical organization for the transport services function of a single factory location of a small company with only a few cars and light vans and one heavy truck used on local deliveries is shown in Fig. 34.2. Dispatches are by local carrier and rail. All vehicle maintenance is carried out at local garages. A dispatch section is established which is responsible for packaging and loading goods on to vehicles.

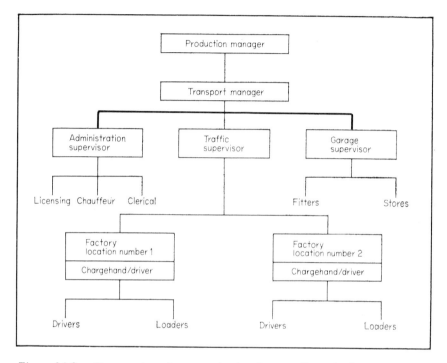

Figure 34.3   Transport services organization for a medium-sized company

Organization for the transport services function of a medium-sized company with two factory locations is shown in Figure 34.3.There are twenty cars for management and sales staff use, a number of light vans for customer after-sales service, four trucks for goods delivery to customers and a personnel carrier for personnel movements between factories. Distribution is by company transport and local carrier as well as by rail services. A company garage is available to service and repair the majority of company-owned vehicles.

Figure 34.4 shows the organization for the transport services function of a large group of companies with many factory locations spread across the United Kingdom. A mixed vehicle fleet of over 2000 has to be controlled and administered, consisting of executive and management cars, a large sales fleet of cars and light vans, and a truck fleet exceeding 200 vehicles. A full distribution service from all factory locations to customers is carried out using company vehicles. Local carriers are used to meet peak demands. Extensive use is made of all rail facilities. Company garages are established in each transport location. The whole of the transport function is based on a regional organization with line

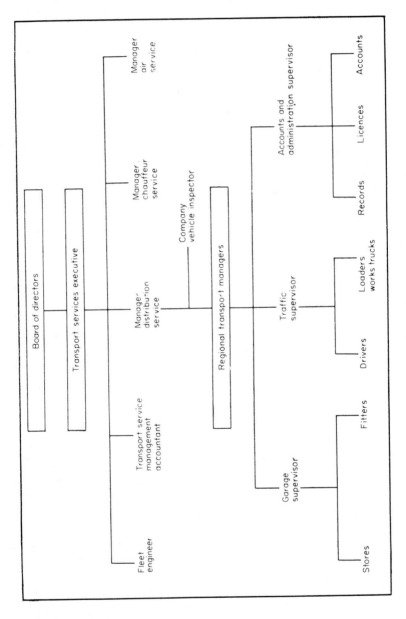

Figure 34.4   Transport services organization for a large group of companies

responsibility for the movement of company products. A company air service is the responsibility of the transport services function.

TRANSPORT PLANNING

Before starting to develop any vehicle plan, a number of questions need to be asked:

1   Does the distribution of the product, or movement of personnel need vehicles? Liquids and gases can be distributed by pipeline, personnel can communicate by telephone or closed-circuit television
2   If vehicles are needed, must they be road vehicles? Will railways or aircraft give a more efficient and economic service?
3   If road vehicles are needed, are the services of a haulier or hire car operator more efficient than a company operating its own fleet?
4   If road vehicles are to be operated by the company, should they be leased, on contract hire, or owned?
5   If it is finally decided to have company-owned vehicles, how many are required, what types are needed, and where are they to be based?

These are vital questions and will affect all future transport planning. The answers must be based on sound commercial reasoning, not only taking into account basic costs, but looking at real costs, which includes service to the customer and the total value of the whole operation to the overall profitability of the company.

VEHICLE MANAGEMENT AND VEHICLE STANDARDS

The object of setting vehicle operating standards is to obtain the most efficient utilization of a fleet of vehicles. This is the key to a minimum-cost operation. Standing costs can account for over half the total operating costs of a vehicle and it follows that the higher the utilization, the cheaper the cost per mile. Figure 34.5 shows the standing costs and running costs of various types of vehicle.

There are four main areas of vehicle operation where an attack on utilization can be made, and which can provide a basis for comparison of planned performance against actual performance.

Vehicle preparation.   Includes checking of the vehicle before a day's work, driver administration and documentation. Work study techniques can be applied to this area of work, and standard times are easy to establish.

Vehicle loading and unloading.   One way of achieving higher productivity is to keep loading and unloading time to a minimum. The use of 'swop bodies', containers and trailers are all ways of preloading vehicles while the motive unit is delivering another load. The size of a pallet, side loading, double-deck loading are all areas where a work study investigation may be applied with advantage. Standard forms of labels and consignment notes, colour coding identification of depots, factories, warehouses or customer delivery areas are all ways of speeding up the loading procedure.

	13 ton GVW rigid	24 ton GVW articulated	32 ton GVW articulated	2500cc private car–chauffeur driven
Standing costs per year	£	£	£	£
Licences	200	416	720	40
Wages (55 hours)	2750	2900	3100	2800
Insurance	400	765	1085	206
Depreciation	1026	1770	2700	1300
Total	4376	5851	7605	4346
Running costs per year (based on 36 000 miles)				
Fuel	1500	2250	2900	1371
Lubricants	85	90	90	50
Tyres	486	800	972	85
Maintenance	2210	2300	2900	610
Total	4281	5440	6862	2116

Figure 34.5   Standing costs and running costs of various types of vehicle

Vehicle running time.   The running time of a vehicle between two points is governed by the speed limit of the road over which that vehicle has to travel. Figure 34.6 shows the present speed limits in the UK and the generally accepted vehicle speeds used in transport operations as a basis for calculating time taken over road routes.

The working day of a delivery vehicle can be divided into three sections:

1   Proceeding to actual delivery area
2   Delivering the goods in the delivery area
3   Returning to base

The speed-limit factor will only affect the first and last sections as the main controlling factor in the delivery area is the number of delivery points and the number of units to be delivered at each point.

Delivering the goods. This is an area of uncertainty when trying to calculate standard times of performance and the approach to the problem will differ with each company and product. Calculations can be based on:

1   Number of delivery drops
2   A basic time allowance for each delivery point
3   Standard times for handling each parcel delivered
4   An average speed for the vehicle when delivering in towns

Type of road	Type of vehicle	Legal road maximum speed	Acceptable average speed for route calculations
Restricted to 30 mph (built-up areas)	All types of vehicle	30 mph	20 mph
De-restricted roads	(a) Goods vehicles not exceeding 30 cwt ULW not drawing a trailer	50 mph	32 mph
	(b) Goods vehicles exceeding 30 cwt ULW including articulated vehicles	40 mph	28 mph
	(c) Dual-purpose vehicles not drawing a trailer (Dual carriage-way)	60mph	36mph
	(d) Goods vehicles with draw bar trailer with four or more wheels	30 mph	20 mph
Motorways	(a) Goods vehicles including articulated vehicles, exceeding 3 tons ULW	60 mph	36 mph
	(b) All other goods vehicles not drawing a trailer	70 mph	36 mph
	(c) Goods vehicles with draw bar trailer with four or more wheels	60 mph	36 mph

Figure 34.6   Speed limits for goods-registered vehicles in the UK

The setting of vehicle and operating standards in a transport operation is called 'load assessment' and there are many ways of applying these techniques. The object in every case is to establish a standard against which the performance of a driver can be measured.

VEHICLE SELECTION AND DESIGN

Vehicle design is an essential part of the responsibility of transport services management. Vehicles are available in standard designs, but very few such vehicles will be as efficient as one which has been specifically designed for an intended task. As the product structure of a company changes, vehicles designed specifically to carry that product may become obsolete. Long-term planning is essential and a degree of flexibility should be built into the design features of any industrial fleet.

Once it has been decided that a custom-built vehicle is needed, the following main points must be considered:

Type of chassis.   Length, possible chassis extension, additional shock absorbers, extra springing, automatic lubrication points, access to chassis for servicing.

Size of body.   Are pallets to be carried, if so, what size and will they be two or four-way entry? What is the maximum height of the product carried? Are there any low entrances in the factory or warehouse area?

Body design.   Box or flat? Size of door openings, rear or side entrances. Roller shutter or hinged doors? Fixed body or demountable? Strength of floor and bulkhead.

Choice of material.   Wood, metal, or fibreglass panels? Steel, alloy, or wood framing? Translucent roof?

Interior fitments.   Lighting requirements, handling aids, tie rails, security alarm systems, double-deck fitments, suspended loans.

Loading aids.   Vehicle-mounted crane, tail gates, tilts, tipping gear.

Special requirements.   TIR facility, sleeper cab, two-way VHF radio, cab ergonomics.

The choice of vehicles for the movement of goods varies from a 6 cwt van to a 32 ton gross train weight drawbar trailer outfit. The design of vehicles within this range is just as varied. Today the increasing use of unit loads has seen the development of demountable bodies in almost every type of transport operation.

The development of the container concept has also affected the design of modern trucks. In selecting the body for a particular task, transport management should look to reduce the handling of the product and keep to a minimum the time a vehicle is required to stand idle for loading and unloading to take place.

ACQUIRING VEHICLES

Owning, leasing, hire-purchase or contract hire are the alternative ways of acquiring a fleet of vehicles. The first thing to understand is that an operator of a single goods vehicle receives exactly the same tax benefits and allowances per vehicle as would an operator or contract-hire company owning over a thousand vehicles. The only direct cost advantage to a large fleet operator is in the terms of purchase when bigger discounts can be negotiated. An operator who decides to obtain vehicles by lease or contract hire is only buying money, for which he has to pay interest. Once this is understood, it will be much easier to make a correct decision regarding the method of acquiring a vehicle.

Purchasing

To buy a vehicle an operator needs cash and this can be obtained by:

1   Reducing his own cash balances
2   Increasing his own bank overdraft
3   Borrowing the money from a finance company, normally through hire-purchase

All the above methods cost the purchaser a price. Reducing cash balances means that interest is foregone, increasing an overdraft entails additional interest charges, and a hire-purchase agreement will include interest charges on the repayments. Buying for cash will also have an additional advantage of being able to negotiate a discount from the dealer, and the larger the fleet and purchasing power, the larger the discounts available.

4   Goods vehicles are subjected to value added tax based on the *invoice* price of the vehicle. Therefore, higher discounts mean less VAT payable.

Hire-purchase

Trucks do not come under the control of hiring orders, and deposits and repayment periods vary with different finance companies. Under a hire-purchase agreement, all tax benefits and allowances may be claimed by the purchaser.

Under a leasing or contract-hire agreement, all tax benefits and capital allowances are claimed by the finance company.

Leasing

The usual method is for the finance company to purchase a vehicle in its own name, and then the capital cost and interest charges plus usual profit margins are spread over the period of lease in either monthly or quarterly fixed amounts. The operator will be responsible for the servicing and maintenance costs during the period of the lease. At the end of the stated period, the operator has the choice of continuing the lease for a nominal monthly or quarterly payment or the leasing company will sell the vehicle, crediting the operator with up to 95 per cent of the proceeds.

Contract hire

As in a leasing agreement, vehicles obtained under contract-hire arrangements remain the property of the contract-hire company during the period of the contract. The main differences are:

1   At the end of the contract, the total proceeds of the disposal are
    retained by the contract-hire company
2   The contract-hire company is responsible for all costs of servicing,
    maintenance, licensing and, in some instances, a relief vehicle
3   A mileage charge may also be included, either by an excess charge
    over an agreed maximum per year, or a charge for each mile run

Effect of taxation on purchase, leasing and contract hire

An argument used in favour of leasing and contract hire is that the payments are wholly allowable for tax purposes. This is quite true, but the fact is that tax is neutral. No matter by which method a vehicle is acquired, the payments, either revenue or capital, will qualify for tax relief in their own peculiar way. The only real difference is in the pace at which relief is given.

Tax allowances on purchase of vehicles.   Capital allowances given by the Finance Act 1972, and still current are:

1   A first-year allowance of up to 100 per cent of the expenditure
    incurred. This is called free depreciation
2   A continuing allowance in the second and subsequent years of 25
    per cent calculated on any balance not claimed in the first year

The object of granting capital allowances is to enable a company to spread the reduction in value of the asset over a period of years. Vehicles bought and sold within a period of a company's financial year need not be subject to a claim for annual capital allowance. The total loss on resale would be set against taxable profits for that year. For assets retained for more than one year, a system of 'pooling' applies.

Cars. Free depreciation does not apply to vehicles used as private vehicles, and this includes dual-purpose vehicles which can be adapted for the carriage of goods and people, such as estate cars. In the case of this type of vehicle a straight 25 per cent capital depreciation allowance is given each year based on a reducing balance. An exception to this rule applies to those companies who provide vehicles wholly or mainly for hire to, or for the carriage of, members of the public in the ordinary course of trade.

Tax allowances and hire-purchase. The 1971 Finance Act now provides that if a person incurs capital expenditure (including vehicles) under a contract whereby he becomes the owner (for example, hire-purchase), then capital allowances may be taken on the total cost of the asset purchased at the time of making the contract. This makes hire-purchase arrangements attractive in that, even though only part of the repayments have been made, the full 100 per cent first-year allowance can be claimed. The cash flow will benefit because, in some cases, the benefit will exceed the actual hire-purchase payments.

Tax allowances on contract hire and leasing. Because the ownership of the asset does not pass to the user under a contract hire or leasing agreement, no capital allowances are allowed to the user of the asset. All contract-hire and leasing rentals are treated as revenue expenditure and as such the total payments in any one year are allowed against taxable profits.

Comparison of costs of methods of acquisition

A decision on the best way to obtain a vehicle can be taken by an operator only after taking into account the present cash situation of his company and the terms of purchase, lease or contract hire offered. It is also important that any calculations are subjected to discounted cash-flow analysis so that all calculations are reduced to net present value. This is the only way to achieve an accurate comparison of real costs. Figure 34.7 is an example of how to lay out a comparison of each method of acquiring a vehicle, to assist an operator in arriving at a decision. The figures are not based on any quotation or operation, but do take into account tax benefits, and the running costs are based on those give in the *Table of Operating Costs of Goods Vehicles* published by the Technical Press. The following should be noted:

1   *Outright purchase.* No account is taken of interest charges on
    bank loans, or the reduction of interest on bank deposits if these

have been reduced as a result of a purchase

2   *Hire-purchase.* No account has been taken of any interest charges on an initial deposit

3   *Drivers' wages.* These are common to all calculations and have been excluded

4   *Contract hire.* A charge of 6p is made for each mile run

5   *Cash flow.* To obtain a truer evaluation based on present values a discounted cash-flow analysis must be carried out.

Vehicle 6 ton GVW flat truck. Initial cost £3500. Estimated life 5 years
Estimated annual mileage 40 000. Residual value £250.

	Outright purchase	Hire purchase	Leasing	Contract hire
Standing costs	£	£	£	£
Depreciation	700	700	–	–
Licence/Insurance	350	350	350	200
Administration/Overheads	300	300	300	300
HP charges (average)	–	250	–	–
Leasing costs	–	–	900	–
Contract-hire costs	–	–	–	1650
Total	1350	1600	1550	2150
Running costs				
Fuel/Oil	0.033	0.033	0.033	0.033
Maintenance/Repair	0.043	0.043	0.043	0.060
Tyres	0.009	0.009	0.009	per mile*
Cost per mile	0.085	0.085	0.085	0.093
Cost per annum	3400	3400	3400	3720
Total (excluding wages)	4750	5000	4950	5870
Total cost over 5 years	23 750	25 000	24 750	29 350
Less residual value	250	250	nil	nil
Total (net)	23 500	24 750	24 750	29 350
Tax allowances (5 years)				
Capital allowances (cost less resale)	3250	3250	nil	nil
Revenue costs	20 250	21 500	24 750	29 350
Total allowances	23 500	24 750	24 750	29 350
Tax relief at 52% (Corporation tax)	12 220	12 870	12 870	15 262
Actual cost	11 280	11 880	11 880	14 088

*as agreed in contract.

Figure 34.7   Comparison of the costs of methods of acquiring a vehicle

MAINTENANCE POLICIES

Good vehicle maintenance and well-planned servicing schedules are essential if a transport operator is to be allowed to continue using a fleet of vehicles to carry his company product. The Department of the Environment have stated the following guidelines around which operators should formulate a policy for vehicle maintenance:

1   A positive check should be made at predetermined intervals of time or mileage on items which affect the safety of the vehicle. These are listed in the *Goods Vehicle Tester Manual* (HMSO)

2   Staff carrying out the servicing and repair of vehicles must be aware of the significance of defects

3   Any vehicle inspector or other staff whose duty it is to inspect vehicles must have the authority to have any defects rectified and to take unsafe vehicles off the road

4   Written records must be kept showing when and by whom inspections were carried out, the results of those inspections, when and by whom any remedial work was done and details of that work

5   Under-vehicle inspection facilities should be available, with adequate lighting in order that a full and detailed inspection of individual components can be carried out

6   A system whereby drivers can report defects must be provided, and this should be in writing. The clearance of a defect should be recorded on the same defect report

7   The mechanical condition of vehicles hired, including trailers, is the direct responsibility of the user. The user is defined as the employer of the driver

Planned maintenance and inspection

A number of ready-made planned maintenance and inspection schemes are available to operators, all of which have been designed to ensure compliance with the legal requirements. Basically, each contains the following documents enabling a complete history of a vehicle's maintenance and inspection to be recorded and preserved:

1   Driver's defect report
2   Vehicle inspection check sheet
3   Servicing sheet for predetermined intervals of time or mileage
4   Stores requisition form
5   Work order sheet or job card
6   Servicing, planning and record chart
7   Vehicle history folder

No matter what method of planned maintenance and inspection a company adopts, whether it be in company premises by company employees, or by contracting out the entire task of maintenance, inspection and documentation, the onus of responsibility for the roadworthiness of the vehicle is always with the vehicle operator. He is still responsible in law even though an outside contractor providing the service and maintenance facilities has been neglectful.

FINANCIAL CONTROL OF THE TRANSPORT FUNCTION

The only way to ensure a cost-effective operation is to establish a system of budgetary control and accounting responsibility which ensures that any overspending is immediately highlighted at the point where the cost was incurred.

In my opinion, the best way to impose effective financial control on the transport services function is to make it an independent profit and cost centre. This principle puts an own-account transport operation on a par with the haulier.

A rate schedule for the carriage of goods within the company and to customers should be produced in exactly the same way as one would expect to see from a haulier. Similar rate schedules can also be prepared for the use of other services such as chauffeur-driven cars, pool cars, and even for the repair and maintenance of vehicles in company garages. These rate schedules should be fixed for the period of a company financial year and published to all departments to be used by the production and marketing functions as a basis for determining the transport and distribution costs borne by the product. By adopting such a system, the transport function receives regular revenue for its services against which it incurs costs.

To be cost effective two requirements must be met:

1   Actual expenditure should be within the budgeted expenditure
2   Recoveries should equate actual expenditure

It is to be noted that recoveries should equate expenditure—excess recoveries only add an unnecessary price burden on the product, and an under-recovery will indicate a loss due to an insufficient charge being made for distribution costs.

To establish financial disciplines, it is necessary to keep adequate costing information for each vehicle and also to have a system of budgetary control in order that over the whole of a financial period regular checks can be made on areas of excessive expenditure and corrective action can be taken by management.

COSTING THE OPERATION

There are two main components of vehicle costs:

1   *Standing costs.*   These generally include:
     (*a*) Depreciation cost of the vehicle, together with a charge
     equivalent to the interest which the capital invested in the vehicle
     can earn
     (b) Licences, including vehicle licence and operator's licence
     (c) Insurance, for both vehicle and goods in transit
     (d) Wages of the driver
2   *Running costs.*   These are the result of operating the vehicle on
     the road and include:
     (*a*) Fuel and oil
     (*b*) Repair and maintenance
     (*c*) Tyres
     (*d*) Driver's expenses

The most informative costs of own-account transport operation are the running
costs of a vehicle.

Monthly cost record

The vehicle monthly costings record (Figure 34.8) ignores all costs other than
those directly associated with day-to-day operation. These are:

1   *Fuel.* Issues   from   company   bulk   installations   are   shown
     separately from the fuel picked up from garages by means of
     agency cards or cash. This helps to control the amount of fuel
     picked up from outside sources and to maximize the greater
     discounts available from having bulk stocks
2   *Lubricants.*   Only issues to a vehicle during normal running are
     recorded. Oil changes will be recovered on maintenance job cards
3   *Tyres.* Expenditure on new tyres is recorded from invoices
     received. Sale of old casings will be entered as credits
4   *Repairs.* A distinction is made between repairs and maintenance
     carried out in company garages and repairs by outside agents
5   *Miles run.* This is recorded daily from driver log sheets and gives a
     simple but clear picture of vehicle utilization

This vehicle costings record also shows registration number or fleet number,
make, vehicle group and operating base. Dividing a fleet into groups of similar
vehicles, eg vehicles under 3½ ton GVW, vehicles 3½ ton GVW to 7½ ton GVW,
etc allows the costings to be arranged in groups and this will highlight any
variance within a group so that action can be taken to investigate the reasons for
the variance.

Vehicle costing record		Speedometer reading	
Registration number	XYZ 456 L	Finish	29 155
Make	BEDFORD	Start	22 108
Depot	WATFORD	Miles	7047
Vehicle group	3\3\8		
Month	MARCH '73		

Date	Fuel issues				Lubricant		Tyres	Repairs		Miles
	Bulk		Agency					Workshop	Agency	
	Gallons	£ p	Gallons	£ p	Pints	£ p	£ p	£ p	£ p	
1	16	3.80								22 121
2	32	9.60			4	0.32		6.10		22 471
3			10	3.60						
4	14	4.20								23 372
5	18	5.40								23 763
6	26	7.80			2	0.16			2.40	24 191
7										24 597
8										
26	8	2.40					34.50	16.20		
27	24	7.20								26 923
28			6	2.00	2	0.30				
29	22	6.60						1.40		28 058
30	10	3.00			4	0.32				28 508
31	16	3.80								28 732
Totals	293	37.90	28	9.25	16	1.40	34.50	35.30	2.40	

Gallons	Cost
328	£97.15

Figure 34.8   Layout of simple monthly vehicle costing record

Note — The above is an example of layout only and costs shown are not indicative of current levels.

Vehicle operating cost sheet

A layout for a vehicle operating cost sheet is shown in Figure 34.9. All costs recorded refer to the direct operation of the vehicle. Overheads, rent, rates and wages are excluded as these would tend to reduce the value of the costings as a means of comparing the costs of operating different types of vehicle. The following vehicle data is shown:

VEHICLE OPERATING COST SHEET

VEHICLE DATA

Registration number	XYZ 456 L
Make	BEDFORD KFSC
Cost group	3/3/8
Date purchased	SEPTEMBER 1972
Invoice cost (less tyres)	£2450
Estimated life	300 000 MILES
Gross vehicle weight	10.4 TON
Unladen weight	4.1 TON

STANDING COSTS

Interest	306
Licence	148.60
Insurance	120
Operator's licence	4
Total per year	578.60
	= £48.21 PER MONTH

TYRES

Size	8.25 x 20 (12PR)
Number per set	6
Cost per set	£175
Estimated life	40 000 MILES

ESTIMATED COST PER MILE

Tyres	£0.00437
Depreciation	£0.00816

Month	Mileage	Fuel gallons	Fuel Cost (1)	mpg	Oil gallons	Oil Cost (2)	Tyres Estimated cost (3)	Tyres Actual	Workshop	Agents	Total (4)	Depreciation (5)	Total running costs (1–5)	Running costs per mile	Standing costs	Total operational costs	Operational costs per mile
1972 October	4284	211	72	20.3	7/8	0.75	18.72	–	21.20	0.80	22.00	34.95	148.42	0.034	48.21	196.63	0.046
November	4291	214	71	20.0	3/4	0.80	18.73	–	16.80	1.20	18.00	34.96	133.49	0.031	48.21	181.70	0.042
December	4838	236	80	20.5	3/4	0.40	21.14	–	21.21	2.90	24.11	39.48	165.13	0.032	48.21	213.34	0.044
1973 January	6083	297	89	20.5	1 3/4	1.15	26.58	–	41.10	5.60	46.70	49.64	213.07	0.035	48.21	261.28	0.043
February	2612	124	39	21.0	7/8	0.65	11.41	–	14.60	1.80	16.40	21.31	87.77	0.037	48.21	135.98	0.052
March	7047	328	97	21.0	2	1.40	30.80	34.50	35.30	2.40	37.70	57.50	224.40	0.032	48.21	272.61	0.039
April																	

Figure 34.9 Example of a vehicle operating cost record sheet

Note — The above is an example of layout only and costs shown are not indicative of current levels

1   Registration or fleet number
2   Make, group type, gross vehicle weight, unladen weight (3/3/B indicates the HGV driving licence class, the size of the vehicle in that class and 'B' denotes a box van)
3   The invoice cost of the vehicle, reduced by the value of a set of tyres and the expected life of the vehicle in miles
4   Details of tyre size and cost of complete set. The estimated tyre life is used as a basis for costing
5   Standing costs will include interest on capital invested, licences and insurance
6   Depreciation is calculated in terms of cost per mile, based on the actual cost and the estimated life of the vehicle in miles (2450 ÷ 300 000 = £0.008 16 per mile)
7   Tyre costs per mile (175 ÷ 40 000 = £0.00437)

The details of running costs are taken from the monthly vehicle costing record and over the life of the vehicle a permanent record is built up. The following points are to be noted:

Fuel.   Calculating mpg is suspect unless the tanks on the vehicle are full at the start and end of a monthly accounting period.

Oil.   Calculating mpg or miles per pint serves no useful purpose. Excessive oil use can be seen quite easily from total usage each month.

Tyres.   Calculations are based on the tyre wear. Actual purchases are shown and if the estimated mileages are correct, then actual expenditure on tyres should balance the estimated costs over the agreed mileage.

Depreciation: Obtained by multiplying monthly mileage by estimated cost per mile.

Running costs.   Total cost of fuel, oil, estimated tyre wear, repairs and depreciation, divided by miles run. This figure can be compared with the performance figures of other vehicles in the fleet within the same vehicle group, with its own performance figures over previous months and with cost tables published by the transport journals.

Standing costs.   These are now added to the total running costs to give the total monthly operating costs. The total operating cost per mile is of little use as this entirely depends upon the mileage recorded for the period. It will be seen from the example that total operating cost per mile varied between 4p (£0.039) per mile to cover 5p (£0.052) per mile where the performance figure of running cost was reasonably stable.

MOVEMENT OF PERSONNEL

The transport services function should be responsible for personnel movement in order to minimize the problems involved and to increase the overall efficiency of the company by reducing the fatigue associated with people moving.

Sales and service function

The responsibility for the mobility of the sales force of a company comes within the function of transport services in that the provision of small vans and cars and the maintenance and servicing of such a fleet is the direct responsibility of the transport department of a company. The transport services function will need to advise on the choice of vehicle allocated to personnel of the sales and service force, and will need to know the difference of law and taxation in the use of vans, estate cars, and saloon cars.

Law on small goods vehicles

Before the Transport Act 1968, the law on the use of small goods vehicles (including goods registered estate cars) was the same as that for heavy trucks. Today different legal requirements exist both for vehicle and driver. A small goods vehicle is defined in s60(4) of the Transport Act 1968 as:

One which does not form part of a vehicle combination and has a relevant plated weight not exceeding 3½ tons, or if not having a plated weight, has an unladen weight not exceeding 30 cwt

The law for the small goods vehicle and its driver can be summarized as follows:

Operator's licences. Exempt.
Vehicle testing. An annual test for roadworthiness when three years old or more.
Speed limits

1   On derestricted roads, not drawing a trailer: 50 mph
2   On derestricted roads, when drawing a trailer up to 5 cwt ULW: 40 mph
3   On derestricted road, when drawing a trailer exceeding 5 cwt ULW: 30 mph
4   Dual-purpose vehicles (estate cars goods-registered): 60mph
5   Dual-purpose vehicles drawing a trailer: 40 mph
6   *Motorways*—not drawing a trailer: 70 mph
7   *Motorways*—when drawing a trailer: 40 mph
8   *Trailers*—subject to the weight of the vehicle not being less than the weight of the trailer being towed, the speed limit on derestricted roads and motorways is 50 mph. A 50 mph disc must be displayed on the rear of the trailer, and the kerb weight of the vehicle and the maximum permitted unladen weight of the trailer

must be shown on each

Driving licences. Ordinary driving licences Group 'A' or Group 'B' if restricted to automatic transmission vehicles.

Drivers' hours. Section 96 Transport Act 1968 applies to drivers of all goods vehicles, including light vans and estate cars. There are, however, a number of exemptions which apply to drivers of small goods vehicles and these are:

1   *Part-time drivers.*   A driver who on *no* day of the working week drives for more than four hours is exempt from all the hours rules for the whole of that week.

2   Drivers of small goods-registered vehicles engaged solely in certain professional activities and persons using their vehicles to assist any service of inspection, cleaning, maintenance, repair, installation or fitting, are exempt from all drivers' hours rules except the ten-hour driving day regulation. This exemption would cover most of the duties carried out by a sales or service engineer.

3   There is a complete exemption from all drivers' hours regulations when extra hours need to be worked for the purpose of saving life or prevention of damage to property or to deal with serious interruptions to public services.

Drivers' records (log books). Completely exempt.

Servicing and maintenance of sales and service vehicles

Although this class of vehicle is normally exempt from the requirements of operator licensing, it is important to understand that any convictions against a company or a vehicle user for contravention of the Construction and Use Regulations, 1973 or for instances of using, or causing to be used, vehicles which

```
          DRIVER'S REPORT OF VEHICLE DEFECTS

  Date_____

  This form to be used only to report defects and must be handed to the Transport Office
  IMMEDIATELY on your return. No verbal reports please

  Depot_____

  Registration number_____      Make _____

  NATURE OF DEFECT. Faults must be reported at once, even if only of a minor nature



  Speedometer reading_____      If anything is wrong, don't be afraid to say so

  Driver's signature _____

  Date rectified_____      By_____
```

Figure 34.10   Form for reporting vehicle defects

are found to be unroadworthy, may be taken into consideration when application is made for the renewal of, or the initial granting of an 'O' licence. A system of reporting defects by the driver of the vehicle is recommended and a suitable form is illustrated in Figure 34.10. Drivers should also be asked to send in weekly reports stating any work done on the vehicle by outside garages.

The company car

Mobility of personnel costs money. Just as the cost-effectiveness of a goods distribution service is judged on its contribution to the total profitability of a company by giving an efficient customer service, the value of a fleet of company cars should also be assessed on its contribution to the efficient mobility of management and executives, as well as the part it plays in recruiting the right calibre of person to fulfil the needs of the company. There are many different approaches to determining a policy for the supply and allocation of cars to company employees. Each company will decide its own policy based on its own needs. For a medium-sized fleet, there are several ways of obtaining cars:

1   Outright purchase, negotiating for the highest discount
2   Leasing, generally without maintenance but sometimes with the
     cost of the vehicle licence included
3   Contract hire, with maintenance costs included in the hire charges

Each of the above methods has advantages and disadvantages and, as stated in the section dealing with the purchase of trucks, it all depends on the financial position of a company, and how it views its cash flow. There is no doubt that provided the cash-flow situation of a company will permit, outright purchase at the highest discount, followed by a direct disposal policy to trade outlets is the most cost-effective way of obtaining cars. As long as the price of new vehicles tends to increase annually, then the operator has the advantage of minimizing the difference between invoice price and disposal price.

Replacement policies

Any replacement policy will again depend upon the cash-flow situation of a company, and any policy should be flexible in order to take advantage of changes in secondhand market values, or impending price increases of new cars. It is possible to negotiate guaranteed buy-back prices for cars when they are purchased, but this type of arrangement tends to become less flexible and arguments will arise over delays and damage when vehicles are returned to the dealers. A well-tested policy which has an in-built flexibility is as follows:

1   Outright purchase of all cars after negotiating for highest fleet
     discounts

2   Replacement policy:
     (*a*) Cars 1600 cc and under, replaced after 1 year
     (*b*) Other cars replaced after 40 000 miles or 3 years whichever
     comes first
3   Disposal policy. Sell to the trade (not to the dealer who sold the
     original vehicle) or through car auctions where special fleet terms
     are available

With the above policy, the transport services function will be carrying out a
responsible task and obtaining every possible cost benefit for the company. The
policy is flexible in that no firm contracts are entered into and the purchase and
disposal dates can be delayed or brought forward for reasons of cash flow, to
avoid heavy repair bills and to take advantage of minimizing the impact of
balancing charges at the end of a financial year.

Chauffeur services

One of the neglected areas in a transport function is that of the provision of an
efficient and well-managed chauffeur operation. Even the smallest company will
have a driver, whose duties will include meeting visitors at airports and stations,
and driving customers between company locations. Larger companies have
chauffeurs allocated to directors and executives, whose duties may include tasks
other than driving a company car. A chauffeur should be trained to keep himself
and his car in immaculate condition, so as to portray an image of an efficient
organization. Very often a chauffeur is the first contact a visitor will have with a
company, and the initial impression can be of vital importance.

Company air services

The company aircraft, owned and operated by a company for use by company
personnel is now firmly established in the United Kingdom. The need for a
company air service and its justification on financial grounds are very difficult to
assess, and indeed any cost exercise based solely on financial justification must
fail. The task of the transport services function is to operate a service based on
the highest standards of safety and also to minimize the additional costs which
accompany the operating of a company aircraft. Safety, comfort, punctuality
and reliability are the most important features of an efficient company air
service. Safety means operating to a high standard and strict compliance with the
current Air Navigation Orders. Comfort of passengers means a reasonably
comfortable cabin layout, quietness, facilities for reading and writing,
temperature control and, above all, commonsense thinking of the crew to find a
comfortable flying altitude for that particular journey. Punctuality and
reliability are the two features which will test the efficiency of the service. Crews
must ensure that the aircraft is always waiting for the passengers. Timings are

important, not only must the passengers know the take-off time, they must also know at what time they will be at their destination.

Obtaining an aircraft. As with vehicles, there are a number of ways to obtain an aircraft.

Charter from a company which specializes in this type of operation. They will supply the aircraft, crew, and carry out all maintenance, route-planning and management.

Lease. This is similar to contract hire of a car. It will include all maintenance and management. The company leasing employs the crew.

Purchase the aircraft and contract out all maintenance and management and also the provision of crews to an aircraft operating company.

Purchase the aircraft and employ your own crews as well as providing the necessary management and maintenance controls.

Operating the aircraft. Owning your aircraft does not give you the right to operate outside the public category, and if the crew is supplied by a charter company and not employed directly by your company (that is, on the company payroll), then the operation will be subject to all the restrictions placed by the Department of Trade on a public-category operation. By employing your own crew to fly the aircraft, it is possible to operate in the private category and be free from a number of regulations which are mainly designed for the control of schedule airlines carrying fare-paying passengers.

Choosing the aircraft and costing the operation. A wide variety of aircraft are available which are suitable for company operation. They range from the single engine helicopter which flies 'point to point' at speeds of up to 150mph to the twin fan-jet aircraft capable of speeds approaching 600mph. The cost of operating helicopters and fixed wing aircraft range from:

Helicopters	Single engine (turbine) £95-£130 per hour
	Twin engine (turbine) £160-£250 per hour
Fixed wing	Twin engine (piston) £65-£90 per hour
	Twin engine (turbine) pressurized £120-£240 per hour
	Twin engine (jet) £300-£400 per hour

FURTHER READING

P.R. Attwood, *Planning Distribution Systems,* Gower Press, Epping, 1971.

D. Lowe, *Transport and Delivery to EEC Customers,* Kogan Page, London, 1974.

D. Lowe, *Transport Managers Handbook,* Kogan Page, London, 1976.

R.E. Sussams, *Efficient Road Transport Scheduling,* Gower Press, Epping, 1971.

B.A. Thompson, *Croner's Road Transport Operation,* Croner Publications, London, 1967. (By subscription and kept up to date monthly).

B.A. Thompson, *Professional Driver's Guide,* Croner Publications, London, 1975.

C.C. Toyne, *Motor Vehicle Technical Regulations,* Liffon Engineering Services, London, 1972.

Tables of Operating Costs, 1976; *Commercial Motor,* IPC Business Publications, London.

Felix Wentworth, *Handbook of Physical Distribution Management,* Second Edition, Gower Press, Epping, 1976.

F.H. Woodward, *Managing the Transport Services Function,* Gower Press, Epping, 1972.

What a Haulier Needs to Know; Commercial Motor, IPC Business Publications, London.

Yearbook, The Freight Transport Association, Tunbridge Wells, 1976.

Peter C. Cooke, *The Company Car,* Gower Press, Epping, 1975.

35

Security Policy
and Administration

Eric Oliver and John Wilson

A number of books, documents, records and other papers, mandatory by law or required for the efficient administration of a company, have been referred to in this book which are usually in the care of the company secretary. These include the company seal, statutory books, for example, the register of members, share certificates and transfers; the general register, where applicable and required under the Factories Act 1961; contracts of service and other agreements, titles to land and property, accounts of debtors, private ledgers, signature blocks, senior management salary records, cable code, valuable silver possibly for use in the board room and inventory records with identifying numbers of office equipment. Many have little intrinsic value to make them attractive to a thief, but their loss could have serious consequences, and absorb time and money in replacement.

DOCUMENTARY LOSS

The most likely cause of massive loss is fire, therefore the storage of such original documents must be in properly constructed fireproof cabinets. Specialist advice should be taken when buying these; occasionally old safes may be suitable for the purpose.

Another cause of damage can be water, so when siting the repositories, regard must be given to the possibility of flooding—particularly on lower floors—through breakage of water pipes or tanks on or adjacent to the premises. Consideration should be given to having some important records photographed for daily use and storing the originals in a safe deposit elsewhere.

THEFT OF INFORMATION

The theft of books, records and documents has been said to be unlikely, but there are other forms of record which, if not of value in themselves, contain valuable information to unauthorized but interested parties. The minutes of board meetings or of committees where policies and decisions of importance are recorded are examples.

The contents of these in the wrong hands could have disastrous results beyond the immediate company.

Minutes: limitation of copies

Such minutes are usually typed for duplication and distribution to a limited-circulation list. Both typing and copying must be by trusted permanent employees and not by temporary staff who conceivably might later work for a competitor. If a matrix is used in the preparation, it must be destroyed, as must spoilt or surplus copies, shorthand notes taken of the proceedings and any readable carbon papers used. 'Once only' plastic typewriter ribbons are a particular source of information because what has been typed may be read directly from them; burning is the simplest form of destruction.

These observations although directed especially towards records of important meetings apply also to documents originated by the company secretary that are of a confidential nature.

Restriction of circulation of information

A clear system of marking documents to indicate degrees of restriction should be laid down and insistence made on adherence to it. If this is done, specific instructions can be used about the safekeeping of such material and action taken if these are disregarded. The terminologies should be restricted in number as much as possible and there is no sense in using these indiscriminately. One system with merit utilizes 'personal' on a sealed envelope to denote restriction, the contents then being marked 'personal/private' or 'personal/secret'; the former contains matters affecting the addressee only and he can therefore disclose as he wishes, but further circulation of the latter is allowed only in accordance with prearrangement or special permission. One of the points for early agreement in connection with special projects should be a distribution list showing the limits to which papers and records relating to them are to be confined. Institution and enforcement of such measures are likely to come within the company secretary's province.

Storage of information

The storage of all confidential information is important; locks of cabinets used for the purpose should be non-standard and not bear an identifying number through which key duplicates can be obtained. No keys of cabinets or drawers should ever be hidden in other drawers, albeit locked—this is a fault of many otherwise first-class secretaries and must be guarded against. Such keys should be taken away and their duplicates kept in a place of safety from which they can be withdrawn by an authorized person in emergency. Where a safe is used solely by one person, he should retain the key in his personal possession and deposit any duplicates in the company's bank with arrangements for withdrawal on a written request signed by two of a list of signatories previously supplied. Where a combination lock is fitted, the code should be committed to memory but a copy placed in the bank. Codes should be changed at frequent intervals remembering to change the copy at the bank. This should always be done when responsibility for the safe and contents changes, as may happen with promotions, dismissals and holidays.

Thefts of safes

The possibility of having a safe containing vital documents stolen should be guarded against. In a thief's eyes a safe means money and he is not to know otherwise. Those weighing more than a ton are unlikely to be removed, but smaller ones, particularly on ground floors, are apt to be taken elsewhere to be forced open in comfort. To prevent this it is recommended that they be fixed to the floor. If the floor is concrete, this should be done by using substantial rag bolts sunk and grouted in to match corresponding holes drilled in the base of the safe which is then set over the threaded ends of the bolts. Mild-steel locking plates, linking each pair of bolts, are fitted before the nuts are put on. Similar means, though less satisfactory, can be used to attach the safe to walls by the side or back instead of the base. Wooden floors need special measures and it is advisable to consult a specialist safe manufacturer and utilize his experience and advice.

SECURITY POLICY

So far, what has been described are some of the potential areas of risk which have to be appreciated and the necessary preventive measures to be taken to minimize the possibility of loss.

What also has to be anticipated is theft of company property by an employee or an outsider. What is to be the policy of the company in those circumstances? Are police to be called in every instance? Who is to investigate the circumstances and implement that policy?

Who is responsible for security?

In companies where no professionally equipped person is employed to be responsible for security in the capacity of security manager or chief security officer, this often falls to the company secretary.

Policy must be universally known

When a policy has been decided it must be made known to all employees through notice boards, or, where issued, in an employees' handbook. No distinction must be made between grades of employees. If the policy is to take a firm line with employees found stealing company property, a suggested wording is:

> In all cases of theft of the company's property or from a fellow employee, the offender will be dismissed from the company's employment immediately and may render himself liable to prosecution.

This still leaves an ultimate discretion whether or not to prosecute and room to manoeuvre in cases where there are mitigating circumstances. It is important that two similar instances should not be dealt with in entirely different ways. Consistency and fairness must be observed.

When to report to police

The question of what should be reported to police is worth considering. It is not mandatory. The firm's interests are paramount. If the police are called in they are likely to be unfamiliar with procedures, persons and places all of which might have to be explained. Their presence automatically attracts attention from workers who may have to be taken from production jobs to be questioned. The loss in production may be out of all proportion to the effect of the offence which is being investigated.

When not to prosecute

There are other circumstances which can militate against instigating a prosecution which might be merited by the nature of the offence:

1   Will the company receive adverse publicity by:
    (*a*) A lax system which has thrust temptation in the way of the offender
    (*b*) Having entrusted a low-paid man with too much responsibility
    (*c*) The ventilation of grievances in open court which might show

the company in a bad light

(*d*) The compulsory exposure of matters in court which would be against the company's interest

2   Will weaknesses in the company security be spotlighted and possibly exploited by others?

3   Will the end-product of the prosecution be worth the time consumed and the inconvenience?

4   Should the age, length of service and previous good repute of an employee be taken into consideration, and the hardship he might suffer through dismissal for a minor offence?

Intruders

If, however, intruders are involved in an offence of any consequence, the police should be informed. Where identifiable property has been stolen from the company by unknown persons, police assistance is the only means of recovery, and it should immediately be sought. The factors that may be attached to employees do not apply to outsiders and they should always be prosecuted as a deterrent to others.

Right of search

No private person has a right to search anyone without consent. A company may include a 'search clause' in its conditions of employment but, though refusal may involve dismissal for non-compliance, it does not justify search without consent nor does it constitute sufficient grounds of suspicion of theft to detain, and notify the police.

DISMISSAL, SUSPENSION AND PROSECUTION

Dismissal

An alternative or addition to prosecution is dismissal of an employee concerned. If management is reluctant to lay down a positive ruling that dishonesty incurs dismissal, there are several aspects it ought to consider before agreeing to the retention of the offender.

1   Will the leniency extended encourage others to emulate, with the impression that the firm does not regard theft of its property as being of particular importance?

2   When a precedent of leniency has been established, how will the management be able to vary the procedure and then explain their actions if challenged?

3   Should an offender fall from grace again, who will accept the
      onus of explaining to a board of directors why someone who has
      previously shown a lack of honesty has been given the
      opportunity to defraud the firm again?
4   Is an offender, knowing that those around him are aware of his
      dishonesty, likely to be able to work to his full capacity; (there
      will be inevitable suspicion on him when anything goes astray).
5   Is his continued presence fair to his colleagues?
6   What is the atmosphere in a department likely to be if a fellow
      employee's property has been involved?

While a 'black and white' attitude to offenders has its difficulties, reluctant
management should have these considerations in mind when arriving at a
decision less than dismissal. Above all, even trivial thefts should not be condoned
by taking no action. This gives an invitation to others to steal and may create
a most undesirable precedent to be quoted in subsequent appeals against
dismissal.

Suspension without pay

On the principle that a person is not guilty until proved so, a firm's action in an
incident where an employee denies the facts alleged against him is worthy of
prior thought.

   Where he admits the theft in circumstances which put his guilt beyond doubt,
the issue is straightforward; theft is regarded as one of the extreme forms of
industrial misconduct and the firm, if it so desires, can dispense with his services
forthwith. Where prosecution is not intended it is advisable to obtain written
admission. Where he denies the theft and the police—as an independent third
party judging the circumstances—think the issue so self-evident that they are
prepared to arrest and charge the man at the time, irrespective of the denial on
his part, the firm could feel justified in suspending him from work without pay
until the hearing; this is a very sensitive area in current industrial relations and
great care should be exercised. Should disciplinary charges meriting dismissal be
involved, consider dealing with them at once—prejudice could be alleged if they
followed acquittal on the criminal charge. (NB: right to suspend without pay
should be incorporated in Conditions of Employment.)

   If the management consider they have adequate proof of dishonesty and
intend to dismiss the man in the face of strenuous denial of responsibility, they
should think several times before doing so without referring to the police,
otherwise lengthy complications may ensue, culminating possibly in an award of
compensation against the company.

Suspension with pay

It is more difficult when the facts are not self-evident and the police wish to consider explanations, or obtain further evidence, before commencing a legal action. If a firm continues actively to employ an individual it is virtually condoning the offence and gives a defending counsel a formidable red herring, in that it enables him to imply doubts on the part of the employer about the guilt of his client. There is an alternative: suspend the individual from work and pay him a union-agreed wage until the hearing. This is an important matter: in the present congestion of courts, it may be many week before a case is tried: a firm can find itself having paid a large sum in wages for no return of work to a person subsequently convicted of having stolen from it. Good industrial relations make it essential that any action resulting in limitation or withdrawal of pay should be reasonable and acceptable to union officials.

Prosecution

The actual mechanics of instigating and carrying out a criminal prosecution are best left entirely to the police whose professional business it is. The law in England does not preclude any person or body from instituting or carrying out criminal proceedings in which police will assist, but unless there are very good reasons, there is little point in acting as a private prosecutor. (In Scotland there is no such thing as a private prosecution in criminal matters, all of which have to be referred to the police and then presented by the Procurator Fiscal's department.) Once notified, the police will ensure that all necessary statements are taken, the case is prepared and witnesses are warned of the time, date and place of hearing. Their representative will present the evidence and there can be no suggestion of bias in the conduct of the whole affair. In other words, a minimum of inconvenience and cost is incurred by the firm.

Bargaining with an offender

Until 1967, to strike a bargain with a thief under which he would not be prosecuted if he returned the property he had stolen, was to 'compound a felony', with a punishment of up to two years' imprisonment. The Criminal Law Act 1967 provides (s5(1)), that an offender can agree to make good to the owner the loss or injury or give reasonable compensation in lieu, to avoid prosecution—if the owner is so inclined. This is not to be construed as meaning that the loser can impose any demand upon the thief in excess of his actual loss. It is clear from this that Parliament recognizes that prosecution is within the discretion of the owner of stolen property.

POLICE PROCEDURE

It might be as well here, to give a brief description of the action of police when they are called upon to take action against anyone whom the company wishes to be prosecuted. The officer attending will ask to be told, in the presence and hearing of the person detained, the evidence that he has committed an offence. The identification of property alleged stolen and its value is required by the officer from a competent witness.

The officer then cautions the suspect and asks him whether, having heard what has been said, he wishes to say anything. Anything he says the officer will then record in writing. If the evidence shows a *prima facie* case against the suspect, the officer will then arrest him and will take him to the police station. He may ask the witnesses to accompany them.

At the police station, the evidence will be outlined to the officer in charge who must then decide whether it is adequate and sufficiently credible for a formal charge to be laid against the accused. If so, he will make out a 'charge sheet' showing, among other detail, the offence in simple but precise language; practice is not uniform but the prosecutor may be asked to sign this sheet. A written notice beginning with a caution and describing the offence is also prepared and given to the accused so that neither he, nor any legal representative he may instruct, will be in any doubt about the subject of the allegations.

Statements and attendance of witnesses

Until the passing of the Criminal Justice Act 1967, it was the unfortunate experience of many witnesses in criminal cases that much valuable time was taken up by repeated attendances at court. Through the provisions of that Act, this has been largely obviated. Statements of witnesses taken under prescribed conditions may now, with the agreement of the accused or his legal representative, be read in court in lieu of the personal attendance of the witness. The accused, however, has the right to require such attendance should he wish to question a witness; the court itself may also require such attendance.

Retention and restitution of property recovered

Property recovered by the police in connection with a criminal offence may be retained by them until the final disposal of proceedings; then, if the accused has pleaded or has been found guilty, it will be returned to the loser. This is not, however, automatic. A convicting court *may* order it but is unlikely to do so if there is the slightest legal dispute over ownership—as could arise if the property has changed hands again after the theft. In straightforward circumstances the police will probably return it without seeking formal permission from the court. It is advisable if there is an indication of a counterclaim to obtain legal representation at an early stage.

Where an accused is found not guilty, the accused may be prepared to sign a disclaimer waiving his rights. Legal action may be necessary otherwise and may be at the instigation of the police themselves whereby they apply to a court to make an order restoring the property to the person appearing to be the owner (Police (Property) Act 1897). In the event of an appeal against conviction, the police will retain possession until it has been dealt with and will also do so during the period in which an appeal can be lodged.

Where stolen goods have been converted into other goods or cash, an order may be made that these other goods can be given to the loser on application and recompense can be awarded from any monies found in the thief's possession at the time of his arrest.

Compensation

Where loss has occurred from theft or damage, and a person is convicted of that offence, under the provisions of the Powers of Criminal Courts Act 1973, the convicting court *may* order compensation to be paid to the sufferer. The relevant section is self-explanatory and reads:

1   (1) Subject to the provisions of this Part of this Act, a court by or before which a person is convicted of an offence, in addition to dealing with him in any other way, may, on application or otherwise, make an order (in this Act referred to as 'a compensation order') requiring him to pay compensation for any personal injury, loss or damage resulting from that offence or any other offence which is taken into consideration by the court in determining sentence.

'Offence' can be widely interpreted, the main exclusions are offences under the Road Traffic Act, and compensation to dependants of a dead person. The power is extended to instances where property has been recovered in a damaged condition—including motor vehicles. The amount which can be awarded in respect of an individual charge is limited to £400, but there is no restriction, other than commonsense and the feelings of the courts, on the number of charges which may be laid. To facilitate proceedings, it is conventional to allow offenders to have offences taken 'into account' without the preferring of charges and adducing of evidence; there is now power to make compensation awards in respect of these likewise, but the gross amount permitted is limited by the factor of £400 and the number actually charged, ie five offences maximum compensation £2000 irrespective of number 't.i.c.' A substantial loser should definitely ask that his offence be the subject of a specific charge—if evidence to prove it is adequate.

The Act specifies that the order *may* be made 'on application or otherwise'; there is no doubt that a court is much more likely to direct its attention to the issue of compensation if it has before it the loser's written notification of a desire for it; this can most easily be done by incorporating the intention in any written statement given to the police. This is an award made by a criminal court immediately after conviction, and in passing sentence; of course civil action can also be taken but any award then made would take into account that of the criminal court. An itemized account of the loss or damage sustained should be available including the cost of making good, not just cost of materials. Where large amounts are concerned, the court may desire that documents should be at hand to prove the claim.

In the past, companies have appeared to think it *infra dig*, too much trouble or pointless to pursue these claims, but there is a substantial detrimental effect upon prospective predators in doing so, especially those among their own employees. The operative word however remains 'may'—it can be expected that, if there is a contentious issue of any kind involved, the wrangling will be left to civil action.

COMPANY SECURITY STAFF

Where circumstances justify the employment of security officers it is essential that they should be good calibre, and properly trained and utilized. It is a total waste of money to follow the outdated practice of internal recruitment from redundant or ageing employees—worse, this gives an impression that security surveillance exists whereas the resultant inefficiency causes the reverse to be true.

Authority

Morale is increasingly important and an efficient security staff must be capable of earning the support and respect of the whole working community, while at the same time producing an image of authority which effectively deters dishonesty or non-cooperation on the part of the minority. This is a demanding role and one in which prevention is of greater importance than cure.

Duties

The duties required of the staff must be committed to writing in the form of 'Standing Orders'. Training in security duties is available from the Industrial Police and Security Association, which holds courses at different levels in various parts of the United Kingdom. Fire-fighting and first aid are customary inclusions among responsibilities, but every firm will have others where continual presence of responsible men on premises can be utilized. The contribution that security staff can make in accident prevention is very relevant. It would be unrealistic to suggest that security staff should be given special training in this subject, except in very exceptional circumstances where recurrent risks may arise. Nevertheless, there are a number of things which may be temporarily overlooked by personnel intent on production where commonsense observation by a patrolling officer may be used to advantage.

Instructions should be given to deal with these matters tactfully to avoid intrusion into the disciplinary authority of line management, bearing in mind also that a procedure that appears unsafe to the uninitiated may be one which has been considered and found acceptable.

If unsafe practices are seen, security staff should draw them to the notice of the supervisor and not approach the worker himself.

Responsibility for security

Every commercial and industrial concern should have a member of senior management who has fixed responsibility for the security of its property and the safety of its employees and their belongings while they are engaged at work. The status of that person will depend on the size and importance of the concern and this can range from a member of the board of directors downwards in the operating structure. For instance, at a factory engaged on government classified contracts it is likely a director will be responsible. In other circumstances it could be the senior man on the site such as factory general manager, or equivalent in responsibility with a different title.

The amount of attention a person given the responsibility for security should devote to that job will depend on a number of factors which will also determine the degree of expertise in security practices and techniques which he should acquire. These factors will include, apart from the size of the organization, the known losses and unexplained deficiencies, the value of materials at risk, insurance requirements, the location and type of premises, and the calibre of employees. It could well be that security is included among other responsibilities. If so, and the incumbent has neither training nor aptitude for it, the attention he will give may be far less than he gives to his other duties. Security is not the most popular job if incorrectly handled. If the factors creating the need for a security function are cogent, the time has then arrived to consider the appointment of a qualified individual whose overriding responsibility will be that of security, bearing in mind there are other administrative spheres in which his presence can be utilized.

The title given to the holder of the position can be Security Manager, Security Officer, or Chief Security Officer if he is responsible for personnel engaged on security duties. The status to be given must reflect the importance the management attaches to his position and responsibilities. He normally would be a member of the management structure which would assist him in dealing with managers in general. He would wear civilian clothes or protective clothing in the same manner as other managers.

Before making the appointment, it is advisable to seek the opinion of those departmental heads with whom he is likely to come in contact during the course of his duties and ascertain the type of man they would find most acceptable.

They could also indicate the fields of activity which they would like him to employ his services in. What is required before the appointment is a decision as to whom he will be responsible to, where he fits in in the organizational structure of the concern, and a list of his duties—in other words a job description.

Job description

It should specify his responsibility for establishing and maintaining security standards, the extent of discretion permitted to him and any limitations placed on his authority over employees.

So that all members of management are aware of the responsibilities, they should see the job description. It must be made clear that no alterations or additions to the documents will be allowed except by agreement of the person responsible for its compilation.

Reporting responsibility

The person to whom the security head is to be answerable is very important. The principle held very strongly by those experienced in professional security duties is that this should be the senior member of management in whose area his main responsibility falls. What is clearly undesirable is that the person in charge of security should be required to go through an ascending series of subordinates. Such an arrangement would inhibit the making of decisions, allow too many personal idiosyncrasies to affect policy and disseminate confidential information too widely. It would also reduce the respect in which the security function was held by other employees.

Attachment to the company secretariat in many ways is the ideal one; this provides a departmental head divorced from considerations of production, industrial relations and personnel discipline, but with immediate access to the senior personnel in each of these fields. The familiar attachment to the personnel manager has features that militate against it—he could find himself in some respects in the combined roles of prosecutor, judge, juryman and conciliator, and the responsibilities might obviously affect the regard in which he is held in his other spheres of welfare and industrial relations. Perhaps the best impartial alternative to the line via the company secretary is that of the accountancy branch.

HIRING THE SERVICES OF A SECURITY COMPANY

Some of the services which can be obtained are:

1   The transporting of cash to and from banks and in other

circumstances where intermittent security protection is advisable; making up and paying out wage packets

2   Transporting computer tapes, data, etc
3   Security attention to premises, with or without guard dogs
    (a) Continuously over twenty-four hours, seven days a week
    (b) For specified shorter periods
    (c) For visits at irregular intervals
4   To act as key holders of premises to reduce the inconvenience of having to attend them at all hours in consequence of some incident which requires attention
5   To protect especially valuable property on display at, for example, exhibitions
6   To survey premises and to recommend security measures
7   To provide a store detective service in retail premises and make check purchases
8   In some instances a facility to carry out internal investigations; in others to give a debt collection service

Transporting cash

When a contract is arranged for this service, it must specify with some detail the place at which the delivery is to be made. It is not sufficient to give just the address: the precise location of the transfer of the money must be given, for example, the cashier's office on the second floor. Regrettably attacks during the act of delivering money occur frequently, so the precise liability on the carriers at the time of the theft is important where an insurance claim is to be made.

The nationally known cash-in-transit companies have adequate cover spread over several insurers, but positive written confirmation of that cover should be available and the wording of contracts carefully studied; if a small local company appears to satisfy requirements and is being seriously considered, these precautions become the more important. Those with current national coverage are Securicor, Group 4 and Security Express, but other internationally known—and equally reputable ones—also operate in the larger cities.

A wage-packeting service is offered in many areas; there is very little difference between charges for this; it is quite likely that, if internal expenses of make-up are costed against that of the service, the latter would be found the more economical.

Competitive quotes should be obtained—the police crime prevention department will not hesitate to give the names of reputable carriers in the area. The tenders of these may vary considerably; there may be a necessity to integrate the run into other commitments which may involve an extra vehicle or trip.

Very firm arrangements must be made with the carriers, and with the bank authorities, to agree procedures for cheque submission, cash collection and delivery, with adequate means of identification of both signatures and persons, to preclude any possibility of fraudulent attack.

If an unknown person purporting to be from the security company attends premises to collect cash or anything valuable, his identity documents must be inspected and his employers telephoned to confirm his instructions—his documents might have been stolen or forged.

Containers of cash

Where money is being collected for deposit at the bank, the container in which it is carried should be sealed and locked if possible. No keys to the lock should be carried in transit. The serial number of the seal must be written on the receipt by the customer's representative before the security officer conveying to the bank signs it. At the bank the respective numbers must be compared before the consignment is opened with a key which has been previously supplied.

Money collected from a bank can be delivered either in an unlocked container, when it will have to be counted on delivery, or in a locked and sealed container. Before the seal is broken, the numbers should be compared with those on the copy of the receipt given to the bank. These checks are specially necessary as instances have happened of money being extracted from sealed containers in transit, and different seals substituted in circumstances where the approved security procedures have not been carried out in full.

Cash-in-transit—own personnel

If it is intended that wages or, for that matter, any large sums of money, should be carried in circumstances where they are exposed to attack, the insurers *must* be consulted. They are not enthusiastic about sums in excess of £2000 being carried without extra precautions by way of guards and vehicles which probably will outcost the expense of a professional carrier. This of course is a reasonable ploy by the insurer since it transfers the period of greatest risk to someone else's insurance.

If, however, the amounts are relatively small, or a decision (unwisely) is taken to accept the risk, again the advice of the police crime prevention department should be sought, and their recommendations strictly followed as to how the job should best be done. Special waistcoats, alarmed bags and others that deface the contents, or throw out clouds of smoke, are commercially available.

Cash-in-transit: security checklist

A suitable list appears in Eric Oliver and John Wilson's *Practical Security in Commerce and Industry* (Gower Press, 1974).

SECURITY OF CASH IN OFFICES

Money in any form is just about the most attractive target for theft; it is normally non-identifiable, does not need the intervention of a receiver, and there is no delay in benefiting. Insurance against loss can be obtained either in transit or on premises; the cost is progressively rising, and premiums will be heavily loaded if claims are sustained—the first £50 or more will probably be excluded in any case.

The weight of claims has caused insurance companies to insist on rigorous security precautions, without compliance to which they will not offer cover. Even so, failure to observe elementary precautions may cause the refusal of a claim, such as has happened with an unguarded till in retail premises and failures to set alarms or to lock doors on delivery vehicles.

Cash on premises should be the minimum for needs; if it accrues to a greater than desirable amount, transfer arrangements to the bank should be made. Key holding for cash boxes and safes must be kept to an absolute minimum, and keys retained in personal possession so that the field of those who may be responsible for losses is restricted.

Procedures are apt to become slack after periods without incidents; it is advisable therefore to review the situation periodically and repeat previous instructions if necessary.

Companies are apt to regard safes as continuing to fulfil their purpose long after they have become antiquated. It must be anticipated that if an insurance company insists on an examination prior to renewal of policies, many such safes will be condemned as unfit for the storage of cash, and insurance cover will not be extended to them. The surveyors have a classification which includes all types of safes in manufacture and equates them with the maximum amount of money the insurers are prepared to accept that they should hold. Before buying new safes, it is therefore essential to obtain confirmation that they will meet the insurers' requirements.

It does not follow that old safes should automatically be discarded. Most may still be serviceable for fire protection purposes and can be used to house confidential matter and documents of interest to prying eyes but not to thieves.

Petty cash and floats must not be left in locked drawers overnight but should be returned to safes and withdrawn again the following morning. Special care should be taken of cheque books, and the absolute minimum of presigned cheques be retained at any time. If possible, these should be restricted to the possession of a single person. It is preferable that, so far as possible, cheques should be signed as required. This is a function which may well come within the purview of the company secretary.

Cash in private possession

The company secretary will no doubt be involved in the drafting of policy instructions of various kinds, one of which may well relate to the keeping of money arising from football pools, clubs and collections of all kinds. It should be clearly spelt out to employees that the company will not accept responsibility for such monies kept on the premises, unless they are handed over to a responsible managerial person who is prepared to accept them and lodge them in suitable safe keeping. Any cases coming to notice where such monies are left in drawers should be the subject of verbal reprimand and, if a theft does occur, the opportunity should be taken to stress to everyone the importance of compliance.

Paying-out stations

Increasingly, attacks are being made on offices where money is in the process of being paid out. Shotguns and pickaxe handles are frequently used – and there should be no heroics in the face of a gun. It is strongly recommended that consideration is given to providing personal attack alarms (button or foot operated) in cashiers' offices and at pay points. Thieves are under strain and may be 'trigger-happy', so there should be an audible alarm at the scene but an indication at a safe point from which police assistance can be sought.

Where new positions are being constructed to act as pay points, thought must be given, and if necessary professional advice obtained, as to protection from violence, including the threat of firearms, for those paying out. The point must also be so devised as to prevent casual theft of wage packets through an aperture. Complete armoured glass window and shelf units are available from specialist suppliers. It is also good practice to exhibit at each paying-out point a notice that clearly indicates that the recipient is responsible for his own wage packet after collection. Where control of the pay packets and pay points changes during a wage issue, proper checking and handing over should take place between the clerks concerned. The paying-out system itself should be such that the possibility of an employee being able to draw another's pay packet fraudulently is minimized. This can be done by issuing the payslips which authorize collection twenty-four hours before the pay-out.

Cash on premises: security checklist

A suitable list appears in Eric Oliver and John Wilson's *Practical Security in Commerce and Industry* (Gower Press, 1974).

OCCUPIER LIABILITY FOR DAMAGE OR INJURY TO TRESPASSERS

Since the case of British Railways Board *v* Herrington (1972 A.C. 877), this question of liability has become of increased importance to all occupiers of land and especially building sites, where there are potentially more sources of danger, than in established areas such as factory sites.

The facts are that a boy aged 9 received severe burns when crossing an electrified rail line at a point where the protective fencing was, and had been for some time, in a delapidated condition. The Board were held negligent at all stages of appeal to the House of Lords. Lord Denning subsequently interpreted this ruling, saying that among the circumstances to be taken into account were the gravity and probability of injury, the character of the trespasser ('you may expect a child when you may not expect a burglar'), the nature of the place where the trespass occurred and the knowledge the defendant ought to have had of the likelihood of trespassers being present.

There have been a number of subsequent similar cases and indeed a Law Commission has sought to consider revision of the relevant Occupier's Liability Act 1957—this is apt to be long deferred but, if you have a known danger point and know that you will have trespassers, especially children, steps must be taken to keep the two apart, or you are in danger of being held negligent if injury is caused.

BUILDINGS

A company secretary will inevitably be closely concerned with purchase of property and new buildings. He is therefore in a unique position to ensure that security considerations are borne in mind at all stages.

Old property, though satisfactory in every respect of location, floor space and amenities, may be totally unsuitable for high-risk commodities. If this is suddenly realized after acquisition, considerable unbudgeted expenditure may be needed to rectify the condition and this will reflect on the foresight of those conducting the negotiations.

New construction does not offer the same difficulties, provided that—from the draft-plan stage—civil engineers, architects, planners and builders have in mind what is at risk and the steps that can be taken to minimize it, without jeopardizing the essential functions of the building. If no company specialist is employed, the police crime prevention officers will be delighted to give their views and advice—they regard this stage as the best time to utilize their services. Simple adjustments to plans can easily cut out avenues for walk-in theft, or such invitations to a thief as obscured windows or doors which may be forced at leisure.

A few basic essentials: endeavour to keep all parking facilities outside the premises proper: provide maximum lighting on perimeters: restrict the number of entrances to a building or site to the absolute minimum (it is much harder to do so when employees have become accustomed to using them): ensure that persons using any entrance can be seen, either by a receptionist, or by occupants of adjoining offices: restrict keys to an absolute minimum and prohibit the making of duplicates. Do not overlook the possibilities of close-circuit television which can survey several entrances from a central point and be coupled with remote control of locks by electronic means.

Alarm systems

The electronic alarm industry has grown to major proportions and several firms have nationwide coverage. Their equipment can be extremely sophisticated; its cost therefore should be in relation to the risk. Whole areas or selected danger points can be covered; warning can be by immediate bells, '999' connection to the police, or by direct line to the police (which is currently being stopped in some areas—there is no uniformity) or to a central station operated by the alarm company. Delayed bells can be fitted so that the message can be transmitted to the police but loss restricted if for some reason their arrival is delayed. Reliance on bells alone is a dubious proposition—little attention is paid by the public. Facilities offered include ordinary door contacts, rays, pressure pads, tautened wiring, radar and sonic detectors; new conceptions are continually being developed. When costing such an installation, it is advisable to consult and seek estimates from at least three unconnected companies. They may vary considerably and, knowing that others are in competition, none will recommend an unnecessarily expensive system which might exclude their quotation. The names and means whereby they can be approached will be given by the police crime prevention officer who may be willing also to indicate those that have the local servicing facilities that are essential to eliminate waste of time. He cannot be expected to recommend any particular one.

A certain number of false alarms must be anticipated in the early teething stages of an installation but should clear within two or three weeks. The police will look with a jaundiced eye if false alarms continue thereafter since they implement a prearranged plan to cover the premises on each occasion as a priority to other duties; they also require key holders to be nominated who are conversant with the contents of the building, have means of transport, and preferably are available by telephone. The National Supervisory Council for Security Alarm Systems has now been established to ensure that new installations conform to British Standards and that complaints are investigated.

Locks and keys

A lock is just as good as its price, and a key as good as the precautions taken to restrict the holders and the opportunity to copy it. For security purposes, a five-lever lock is the minimum insurance requirement and again the insurers' advice can be obtained in cases of doubt; for privacy the 'Yale-type' lock will suffice. The locking of internal doors can frequently result in excessive damage by intruders and it is a waste of time and money putting a first-class lock on a poor door. The same is applicable to padlocks—the best are close shackled and of hardened steel. An average price for one acceptable for security risks would be about £8. Both padlocks and ordinary door locks of all kinds can be 'master-suited', which implies that the keying is such that, for example: an executive will be able to open all doors within his jurisdiction with the one key he holds: his departmental managers will have access to the offices in their departments only; and individuals will only be able to enter their own offices. This type of system must be used where work of a highly confidential nature is being carried on so as to restrict access to it.

Duplicated locks on doors are not desirable, even with cheap locks, but the main danger in this field is that of desk locks where it is not unusual to find a single key will open almost all the desks in an office. If the desk contains matters demanding privacy, the lock itself should be unique in its environment. To obtain a desk or filing cabinet which will resist forcing, even with limited violence, is wellnigh impossible—fire-resistant cabinets are the nearest available type and even the smaller substantial ones may reach £150 in price; old safes are preferable. Keys to safes should never be left in desk drawers.

Use of dogs

Trained dogs can be a valuable aid for patrolling or guarding premises, particularly on dispersed sites. They afford protection and give confidence to those using them and their very presence is a formidable disincentive to potential intruders.

Liability for injury caused by them is governed by the Animals Act 1971, which lays down that a keeper is not liable for damage if (a) it is wholly due to the fault of the sufferer, (b) the sufferer has voluntarily accepted the risk (an employee is not regarded as a 'volunteer'), or (c) it is caused to a trespasser by an animal kept on premises and it is proved that either it was not kept there for protective purposes or if so used, it was not unreasonable to do so.

Section 1 of the Guard Dogs Act came into force on 1st February 1976. This lays down that a guard dog shall not be used on any premises unless:
1 There is a warning notice of its presence at each entrance.
2 It is in the charge of a capable handler at all times, except 'while it is so secured so that it is not at liberty to go freely about the premises'.
Other sections dealing with guard dog kennels and licensing thereof have not yet been implemented (July, 1976) — these do not apply to instances where the dogs are used at premises belonging to their owners. 'Liberty to go freely about the premises' has not yet been interpreted by the courts, but the obvious implication is that any dog, not directly under the control of a handler, must be adequately tethered and restricted in its scope of movement.

Closed-circuit television

Closed-circuit TV is increasingly being found of value particularly in retail concerns for observation of purchasers and employees. It is possible to create permanent records for later scrutiny by means of video-tape recording. A further use, which could result in substantial manpower economies, is that of remote control of doors and gates by coupling TV observation with microphones for 'speak through' and electronic control of the locks.

It is advisable to point out reasons for installing a system to employees before doing so. To avoid employee opposition, it may be necessary to agree not to take any action if purely disciplinary matters are seen.

FIRE AND SAFETY

A company secretary may not have direct responsibility for the implementation of fire precautions and safety measures but he will, almost certainly, be the recipient of any summons issued against his firm for non-compliance with regulations. He will also be concerned with common law claims in respect of injury and insurance after fire damage. It behoves him therefore to establish that there is a clear onus placed upon a specified person of managerial status to ensure that legal obligations are carried out, especially in connection with the new Health and Safety at Work legislation which is to be detailed to discuss here.

The creation of an immediate avenue of notification to the company secretary of happenings that might result in claims or proceedings is important. A fire assessor wants to know of damage as soon as possible after it has occurred so that he can survey it to ascertain extent and causation. Any delay in checking the details of an accident can result in essentials being missed and possible failure to inform the Factory Inspectorate of one notifiable gravity. A standardized and comprehensive system of reporting should be instituted, especially in connection with accidents.

Fire prevention officers

Full use should be made of the services of the local fire prevention officer. Under the Fire Services Act 1947, the fire authority must maintain efficient arrangements for giving, on request, advice to firms in its area on fire prevention, means of escape, and the restriction of the spread of fires. Consultation with the fire prevention officer should always take place when building alterations or new buildings are contemplated, to avoid unnecessary work and later recriminations. Advice will also be given on the provision and siting of extinguishers and other means of putting out fires. Fire drills should be carried out at regular intervals—it is too late to do so after a tragedy. Very explicit instructions should be given so that all staff know exactly what to do in emergency, and appropriate notices should be displayed. The appointment of fire wardens to be given proper training to combat fire is well worth while, and again the fire prevention officer will be glad to cooperate.

Fire: security checklist

A suitable list appears in Eric Oliver and John Wilson's *Practical Security in*

Commerce and Industry (Gower Press, 1974).

First aid

First aid requirements are also laid down in health and safety in industry legislation; they refer to the equipment that should be provided and the trained first aid staff that should be available on premises. This latter requirement should always be treated as one for security staff to cover where these are available. This obviates difficulties during shift working of ensuring that first aiders are always present.

Delegation in all three aspects of fire, safety, and first aid is advisable for the company secretary, in light of the extent of the legislation applicable.

PRECAUTIONS AGAINST TERRORIST ACTION

Regrettably, it has now become necessary for all firms to consider precautions against apparently indiscriminate and senseless acts of violence designed to achieve political ends. These are not entirely confined to the IRA or to the anti-Israeli organizations; others are being tempted to emulate, and terrorism—coupled perhaps with kidnapping—may increase before final containment.

Apart from productivity considerations, the safety of employees is involved; the topic is of board level importance and the company secretary, at least in smaller companies, may be required to advise on policy, to draft instructions and perhaps initiate action. Not least, he should keep an eye on insurance implications.

The threats can take several forms, ranging from malicious telephone calls to explosive and incendiary devices, and letter bombs. The first steps that need to be taken are those of formulating and agreeing policies to deal with particular contingencies—these will be identifiable from the experience of other firms.

Bomb-threat calls

These may be by direct call, anonymous letter, or via a third party, ie the police or newspaper office; the IRA have used a code to the police to confirm the presence of a bomb but this is by no means an accurate yardstick of veracity. If sufficiently prevalent, and treated as needing automatic evacuation, these calls can disrupt a firm's activity almost as effectively as a device itself can. The decision is not easy and any individual, whatever his convictions about the validity of a message, will have at the back of his mind the consequences of ignoring a genuine call; this decision therefore must rest with the senior person available, who should be influenced by preconsidered guidelines.

Bomb-threat policy

Fundamentally, there are three basic possible alternatives:

1   To evacuate and search before re-entry
2   To search without evacuation
3   To ignore the message

Amongst points to be considered are:

1   Nature of the call—apparent age of the caller, speech, attitude, general approach, etc
2   Recent history of such threats, genuine or otherwise, locally and nationally
3   Prevailing conditions of industrial tension, strikes and political unrest in the neighbourhood and at the recipient's premises particularly
4   Any trading relationships between the company and countries whose opponents have used bombs
5   The implications and dangers of an evacuation

In all instances, police and fire authorities should be informed immediately, whether an evacuation is to be ordered or not. As a neighbourly gesture, adjourning firms should be told what is happening.

It must be anticipated that the police will be reluctant to take the initiative in advising on evacuation or otherwise—unless they have positive information.

Signal your supervisor and conform to prearranged drill for nuisance calls: tick through applicable word below, insert where necessary.

TIME ....   *DATE* ....

| *Origin* | S.T.D. | | Coin box | | Internal | |
| *Caller* | Male | | Female | | Adult | Juvenile |

Voice	*Speech*	*Language*	*Accent*	*Manner*	*Background*
Loud	Fast	Obscene	Local	Calm	Noises
Soft	Slow	Coarse	Regional	Rational	Factory
Rough	Distinct	Normal	Foreign	Irrational	Road traffic
Educated	Blurred	Educated		Coherent	Music
High pitch	Stutter			Incoherent	Office
Deep				Deliberate	Party atmosphere
Disguised				Hysterical	Quiet
				Aggrieved	Voices
				Humorous	Other
				Drunken	

Text of conversation

Figure 35.1   Bomb-threat checklist (Note that 99 per cent are hoaxes)

Telephone operators

As first recipients of a message, it is most important that operators have clear instructions on what to do so that there is a minimum of alarm and subsequent confusion about the content of the message. In addition to the instructions suggested below, a stereotyped form of the type shown in Figure 35.1 could be provided to the operators, and its mere availability could relieve natural tension.

Guidelines to telephonists

1   Let the caller finish his message without interruption
2   Get the message exactly—bearing in mind the points shown
3   If it is possible to tie the supervisor or another operator into the conversation, do so
4   Ensure that senior management or a predesignated person are told exactly the contents of the call as soon as possible
5   If the caller is apparently prepared to carry on a conversation, encourage him to do so and try to get answers to the following:

   (*a*) Where has the bomb been put?
   (*b*) What time will it go off?
   (*c*) Why has it been done?
   (*d*) When and how was it done?

In general, if the caller is prepared to continue, try to get him to talk about possible grievances as they affect the firm, and anything which bears upon the truthfulness of the message and the identity of the caller.

It is essential that senior management should be told as soon as possible so that there is no delay in implementing policies and procedures.

Evacuation

Communications should be such that the general warning to evacuate is given simultaneously in all parts affected; otherwise there will be confusion, with people coming and going, difficulty in checking that everyone is out, and garbled messages being passed. If time permits the warning to be given verbally through a managerial chain, it should be on the lines 'At 2pm instruct your staff to begin evacuation, ensure that it is complete not later than 2 15pm.'

Based on experience in the USA, a clear radius of 100 yards should be allowed from the threatened area, 200 yards if a car bomb is suspected. Assembly points for evacuation will not of necessity coincide with those used for fire drills. Car parks are definitely not acceptable, for obvious reasons, and there are advantages in housing evacuated staff in substantial buildings if of suitable size and outside the prescribed distance, ie there must be facilities for checking employees to ensure complete evacuation, the passing of messages and for expediting the return to work.

In case of evacuation

1 Persons who are instructed to get out must, if time permits, collect and take their personal parcels, bags and other belongings to avoid complications during searching (particularly important in cloakroom areas and office blocks generally)
2 If the time-limit given by the warning permits, there should be a quick search by supervisory staff and/or designated employees before the premises are vacated. A system should be devised to ensure that everyone is out. (Special provisions may be needed for disabled employees.)
3 After the time-limit of the threat has elapsed, a reasonable margin should be allowed before a search by security/supervisory personnel, and employees are allowed to re-enter. (Searching of course is a voluntary matter but, in general, supervisors will cooperate.)

No evacuation

A search should be made by security/supervisory personnel of likely 'planting' areas, ie entrances to buildings, cloakrooms and toilets, and the perimeter of buildings—with special attention to parked cars. Police and fire brigade should nevertheless be informed.

Search

1 Responsibility for search of premises lies with the occupiers. The police cannot be expected to accept this though they may assist, since they will be unfamiliar with buildings and likely contents
2 Bearing in mind the multiplicity of forms that a bomb may take, it is the unusual object—not normal in the particular environment—which is suspect. Again the occupants are best qualified to identify
3 Any search made must be methodical with areas designated to individuals to ensure that the whole is covered, and with a coordinator to make certain that this is done
4 Unaccountable or suspect objects should not be interfered with. If such are, found the police should be advised and they will then instigate any necessary action.

Recognition of explosive/incendiary devices

These can be encountered in almost any form. In retail premises, small incendiary packets put in pockets of clothing left in cloakrooms or among inflammable textiles may be one of the reasons why the arson rate has trebled over the past three years. From the terrorist point of view, they have the virtue of completely eliminating any sign of their existence.

Explosive types have been planted in parcels, suitcases, dustbins, postboxes, biscuit tins, or where large bulk has been used, lodged in hijacked cars; on casual inspection, they may not be recognizable for what they are and it is not unusual for the obvious device to have been booby-trapped as a means of attacking anti-bomb personnel. A relatively new type is clearly identifiable and potentially very lethal to those nearby—a conventional bomb is placed with polystyrene padding between two cans of petrol and then lowered into premises where inflammable matter is contained, via a hole cut in the roof.

It follows that anything of a foreign nature—rough parcels, plastic shopping bags left in odd corners or near entrances, dustbins out of place, etc should be regarded as suspect. In effect, there is no easy way for a layman without special equipment to identify or otherwise a potential bomb.

In the near vicinity of a suspect bomb, the military advise that personal or other types of radio intercommunication be switched off as a precaution against activating a sophisticated device.

GENERAL PRECAUTIONS

A general tightening of precautions in or around plant and offices can reduce the opportunity for incidents and at the same time have the added benefit of minimizing other sources of loss. For example,

1   If not already in existence, inaugurate a registration system for immediate identification of cars and motor cycles used by employees
2   Control entrance of visitors, suppliers and contractors to the site. Visitor and vehicular passes can be used to provide a record, and to check that the person or vehicle leaves
3   Do not allow visitors to enter on any pretext without prior confirmation that they are expected/welcome. Arrange collection from reception point in cases of doubt. Always check identity of purported public officials—gas, electricity repairmen etc—who will be in possession of the necessary cards
4   Review physical protection of buildings, ie adequacy of fencing, external lighting, doors, groundfloor windows, fire escapes, alarms, etc
5   Ensure that the standard of housekeeping around buildings is such

that unfamiliar objects will at once become noticeable.

6   Restrict parking outside particularly important facilities such as computer installations, gas terminals and power substations

7   Establish a central control point which will not be evacuated unless there is a substantiated positive danger to it. This should have means of communication with outside authorities should the firm's switchboard be obliged to close down, and it should be easily accessible to incoming police and fire services.

8   In the event of a bomb warning, small rough parcels and plastic-type shopping bags left in odd corners or near entrances should be at once suspect, likewise unfamiliar cars parked haphazardly, especially those with Irish registration plates.

Letter bombs

There is of course no warning given in respect of these; reasons can usually be thought of as to why a particular target has been selected but the senders are irrational, and immunity for lack of causation should not be assumed. It has been suggested in one instance of injury that the employers may be liable in that no guidance, appropriate to present circumstances, had been given to the person opening the mail.

Letters or parcel bombs mainly take the form of substantial envelopes not less than 3/16 inches thick or of parcels containing paperbacked books delivered through normal postal channels. The weight in letter form is unlikely to exceed 4oz.

General features

1   Letter bombs are made to withstand the handling that any normal letter or parcel would sustain during delivery; they are to all intents and purposes safe until steps are taken to open them, and can be handled normally until then

2   So far as is known, no letter/parcel bomb has been received which has borne a franking mark on the envelope or wrapping, but a franked stuck-on address label has been used on letter bombs originating on the continent

3   Spraying with an aerosol of the Boots pain-killing type as used for sporting purposes or Holts 'Cold Start' (the first is the better) may make a manilla envelope or wrapping sufficiently transparent for contents to be identified enough to alleviate suspicion if not to establish dangerous nature

4   Conventional components include detonators, connecting wire and minute batteries; no device yet used has been known to have been activated when tested with a low-power metal detector or X-ray (a

wide variety of hand-held metal detectors are commercially available). The military advise that if X-ray equipment is used, it should be operated by remote control

5 The police have already dealt with innumerable suspect but innocuous letters/parcels and may be able to give immediate clearance if provided with pertinent details, ie town of origin, size and shape, franking or other distinctive stamping

Points which may make unfamiliar material received suspect

1 The postmark, if foreign and unfamiliar
2 The writing, which may have an 'un-English' appearance, lack literacy, or be crudely printed
3 Name and address of sender (if shown), if address differs from area of postmark
4 'Personal'/'Only to be opened by' or 'Private' letters addressed to senior management under the job title, eg Managing director
5 Weight, if excessive for size and apparent contents. Thickness: 3/16 inch or more
6 Weight distribution, if uneven may indicate batteries inside
7 Grease marks showing on the exterior of the wrapping and emanating from inside may indicate 'sweating' explosive
8 Smell—some explosives smell of marzipan or almonds
9 Abnormal fastening—sealing excessive for the type of package. If such an outer contains a similar inner wrapping, this may be a form of booby trap
10 Damaged envelopes which give sight of wire, batteries or fluid-filled plastic sachets should be left strictly alone; those that rattle or feel springy should be treated with caution; and naturally, any ticking noise should be treated as a 'red' alert. Pinholes in the outer wrapping may indicate where devices for the safety of the bomb-maker have been removed. Where conventional paperback books have been used, the resultant parcel bomb may be discernibly softer in the centre that at the edges

If suspicions cannot be alleviated

1 Do not try to open the letter/parcel or tamper with it
2 Do not put it in water or put anything on top of it
3 Isolate it where it can do no harm with minimum handling, ie enclose it in a nest of sandbags but ensure that it is in a position for easy visual inspection
4 Open any windows and doors in the vicinity. Keep people away from it

5   Inform the police and seek their guidance: give them full details of
     the letter/parcel, its markings and peculiarities which have led to
     suspicion

KIDNAPPING

In Great Britain, this has not materialized other than in infrequent instances.
In the Americas, it is sufficiently widespread for the term 'executive kidnapping'
to be applied to a practice which is being used for both financial gain and
political advantage. Some American security firms do tender advice on the
precautions that should be taken, and insurance can be obtained against it
from Lloyds. If the company secretary is called upon to arrange an itinerary
for a senior director in an area where instances have occurred, there is nothing
to be lost by inquiring to the appropriate government department for guidelines to be followed. This advice is now available but the essential ingredients
are — maintain low profile and minimum publicity, accept that there is a risk
however unattractive a target you consider yourself, and use commonsense
precautions in your behaviour and movements accordingly. The countries of
current highest risk are the Argentine and Italy, but publicity of success elsewhere could easily create new trouble points.

MISCELLANEOUS

The Rehabilitation of Offenders Act 1974 is often misunderstood. Essentially,
it is intended to prevent the stigma of criminal conviction attaching itself indefinitely to an individual; according to the severity of the sentence, after a
specified period of time elapses from the date of conviction, he shall be treated
for all purposes in law as a person of previous good character. For example, in
applying for jobs he need not give true answers to questions indicating he has
'lapsed convictions' and cannot subsequently be dismissed for lying about
them; it also penalises unauthorized disclosure of such by any person. Briefly,
sentences of over 30 months are excluded and never lapse; 6 — 30 months
persist for 10 years; not exceeding 6 months — 7 years; Borstal Training likewise; fines — 5 years. Penalties on younger offenders have reduced periods.
It should be noted that one of the objectives of the Act is 'to amend the law
of defamation' and indiscreet wording of references should be guarded against.

FURTHER READING

Oliver and Wilson, *Practical Security in Commerce and Industry,* Second Revised Edition, Gower Press, Epping, 1975.

Oliver and Wilson, *Security Manual,* Gower Press, Epping, second edition, 1974.

Walsh and Healey, *Protection of Assets Manual*, Merritt Co. (USA)

Walsh and Healey, *Industrial Security Management: A cost effective approach,* Merritt, (USA).

K.G. Wright, *Cost Effective Security,* McGraw-Hill, Maidenhead, 1973.

Handbook of Security, Kluwer-Harrap Handbooks, London, 1974.

R. Post and A. Kingsbury, *Security Administration,* Charles C. Thomas, Springfield, Ill. second edition, 1973.

Index